LAW OF INTERNATIONAL ON-LINE BUSINESS
A Global Perspective

AUSTRALIA
LBC Information Services
Sydney

CANADA and USA
Carswell
Toronto

NEW ZEALAND
Brooker's
Auckland

SINGAPORE and MALAYSIA
Thomson Information (S.E. Asia)
Singapore

LAW OF INTERNATIONAL ON-LINE BUSINESS
A Global Perspective

PUBLISHED UNDER THE AUSPICES
OF THE CENTER FOR INTERNATIONAL LEGAL STUDIES

General Editor

Dennis Campbell

Director, Center for International Legal Studies
Salzburg, Austria

Editor

Christian Campbell

Sweet & Maxwell
London
1998

Published in 1998 by
Sweet & Maxwell Limited
of 100 Avenue Road
London NW3 3PF, England

Published under the auspices of
the Center for International Legal Studies
Salzburg, Austria

Typeset in Sabon by
the Center for International Legal Studies

Printed and bound in Great Britain
by MPG Books Ltd, Bodmin

No natural forests were destroyed to make
this product only farmed timber
was used and re-planted.

ISBN 0421 58930 2

*A CIP catalogue record for this book is
available from the British Library*

List of Contributors

Susana Albuquerque, A. M. Pereira, Sáragga Leal, Oliveira Martins, Júdice e Associados, Lisbon, Portugal — Portugal (Chapter 15).

Yann Baden, Etude Georges Baden, Luxembourg — Luxembourg (Chapter 12).

Paul Barnett, Chapman Tripp Sheffield Young, Wellington, New Zealand — New Zealand (Chapter 14).

Matteo Bascelli, Studio Legale Fondato da F. Carnelutti, Milan, Italy — Italy (Chapter 11).

Peter Bräutigam, Nörr, Stiefenhofer & Lutz, Munich, Germany — Germany (Chapter 10).

Giovanni Carcaterra, Studio Legale Fondato da F. Carnelutti, Milan, Italy — Italy (Chapter 11).

Philippe Coen, Panthéon-Sorbonne University, Paris, France — France (Chapter 9).

Javier Cremades, López, Lozano, Cremades & Sánchez Pintado, Madrid, Spain — Spain (Chapter 16).

Michael Erdle, Deeth Williams Wall, Toronto, Ontario, Canada — Canada (Chapter 5).

Ilya Fisher, Freehill Hollingdale & Page, Melbourne, Australia — Australia (Chapter 3).

Hugh Flemington, Bevan Ashford, Exeter, England — England (Chapter 7).

Tristan Forrester, Freehill Hollingdale & Page, Melbourne, Australia — Australia (Chapter 3).

Alan M. Gahtan, Borden & Elliot, Toronto, Ontario, Canada — Introduction (Chapter 1).

Mark Krenzer, Freehill Hollingdale & Page, Melbourne, Australia — Australia (Chapter 3).

Andreas Leupold, Nörr, Stiefenhofer & Lutz, Munich, Germany — Germany (Chapter 10).

Alexander Liegl, Nörr, Stiefenhofer & Lutz, Munich, Germany — Germany (Chapter 10).

Ieuan G. Mahony, Sherburne, Powers & Needham, P.C., Boston, Massachusetts, United States — United States (Chapter 17).

J. Fraser Mann, Borden & Elliot, Toronto, Ontario, Canada — Introduction (Chapter 1).

Paulo Marques, A. M. Pereira, Sáragga Leal, Oliveira Martins, Júdice e Associados, Lisbon, Portugal — Portugal (Chapter 15).

Corinne Mertens, Cabinet C.M. Mertens, Brussels, Belgium — Belgium (Chapter 4).

Kelvin Ng, Freehill Hollingdale & Page, Melbourne, Australia — Australia (Chapter 3).

Cassie Nicholson, Chapman Tripp Sheffield Young, Wellington, New Zealand — New Zealand (Chapter 14).

Melanie Noble, Chapman Tripp Sheffield Young, Wellington, New Zealand — New Zealand (Chapter 14).

Greg Noonan, Freehill Hollingdale & Page, Melbourne, Australia — Australia (Chapter 3).

Lau Normann Jørgensen, Kromann & Münter, Copenhagen, Denmark — Denmark (Chapter 6).

Dayan Quinn, Freehill Hollingdale & Page, Melbourne, Australia — Australia (Chapter 3).

Pekka Raatikainen, Ahola & Sokka, Helsinki, Finland — Finland (Chapter 8).

Alan Smithee, Center for International Legal Studies, Salzburg, Austria — European Union and International Aspects (Chapter 2).

Rob van Esch, Rabobank, Utrecht, The Netherlands — The Netherlands (Chapter 13).

Contents

Table of Cases

Table of National Legislation

Table of International Treaties and Conventions

Table of E.C. Legislation

REGULATIONS

RECOMMENDATIONS

CHAPTER 1

Overview of the Legal Framework for Electronic Commerce

J. Fraser Mann and Alan M. Gahtan
Borden & Elliot
Toronto, Ontario, Canada

INTRODUCTION

This chapter provides an overview of the main legal issues that arise from **1-1** on-line commerce transactions. Country-specific chapters that examine the national laws that are applicable to individual countries follow it.

Many types of on-line commerce initiatives will involve transactions that span multiple jurisdictions and may be regulated by the laws of more than one country. As will become more evident in the section that follows on jurisdictional issues, a better understanding of the basic issues and their general treatment in other jurisdictions should be of relevance to any business about to embark on an on-line commerce initiative.

We begin this chapter by surveying how the Internet is actually being used to facilitate electronic commerce. The next section contains an overview of the major regulatory regimes that may apply to the Internet and to electronic commerce. This is followed by a brief discussion of payment mechanisms and a section on jurisdictional issues, together with a look at intellectual property issues and an exploration of service provider liability. In the final section, we consider issues relating to the formation of enforceable on-line contracts.

FACILITATING ELECTRONIC COMMERCE

On-line Marketing

One of the most common commercial applications of the Internet is the **1-2** use of the World Wide Web to display advertising and promotional material about the originating entity. For example, many business entities now include in their Web sites copies of corporate brochures, press releases, product catalogues, investor relations information[1] and e-mail address directories. Some computer companies are also using their Web site to provide access to beta or time-limited demonstration versions of software programs, as well as for purposes of product support. Many companies, especially high-tech firms, are also incorporating a recruitment section on their corporate Web site.

On-line Retailing

On-line Ordering of Products and Services

1-3   Some business entities are making use of the Internet to provide order-processing services. A potential customer can be provided with an interactive product demonstration. The potential customer can then request additional information or in some cases make an on-line purchase.

Where the product consists of information or software that can be delivered electronically, then the entire transaction can be initiated and completed across the Internet (for example, a subscription to an electronic edition of a newspaper such as the *Wall Street Journal*). In other cases, the Internet is used to complete the sale transaction but physical delivery of the product is made by mail or courier service.

The Internet is also being used to facilitate order processing for services, including travel-related services such as hotel accommodations, car rentals and airline reservations. These services can be offered to end-users directly by suppliers, potentially eliminating the need for intermediaries such as travel agents.

Financial Services

1-4   The Internet is also being used to provide electronic access to different types of financial services such as banking and trading in securities. A number of major banks now provide various levels of access for their account holders using the Internet as the communication vehicle. Many banks are also offering a wider range of services (such as approval of loan transactions) through so-called "virtual branches" which are meant to replace the more traditional and expensive brick and mortar equivalents.

Major brokerage firms now also increasingly provide on-line trading facilities. The advantages to the customer include lower commission rates and round-the-clock access (although trades can only be executed while exchanges are open for business). In most cases, a representative of the broker must still confirm transactions submitted electronically before being released to the

---

1 For example, Microsoft provides investors with on-line access to its annual report, 10-K, earning releases, proxy and other securities filings. In Microsoft's case, this not only provides access to current financial information about the company but also demonstrates the capabilities of some of its products.

exchange. Subject to regulatory controls, expert systems in the future may allow many transactions to be completed without any human intervention.

Publishing

One of the more prominent uses of the Internet is for electronic publishing. Many publishers of print publications such as newsletters, magazines and newspapers now provide Web sites which include varying amounts of information from the print editions. These on-line publishing initiatives may be either supported by advertising,[2] or in more limited cases made available only to paid subscribers.[3]

1-5

In 1996, the market for banner ads was approximately U.S. $110-million with 63 per cent going to the top ten Web sites. The market is expected to grow to over U.S. $400-million by the end of 1997.[4]

The advertising-supported sites can be directed to a targeted audience with common characteristics. On-line advertising provides the opportunity for immediate interaction with consumers, an advantage not offered by traditional media. In some cases the advertisers can leverage off the brand name of the sponsor's site.

Alternative to Private Network

The Internet is increasingly being utilised for the exchange of electronic messages and documents that in the past required the use of a private network. These services include EDI,[5] remote employee access, electronic filings and the establishment of wide area corporate networks to connect branches and subsidiaries within a corporate group. These applications are made possible due to the growing number of resources connected to the Internet as well as the use of sophisticated encryption and authentication systems that can create a secure virtual private network across the Internet.

1-6

Many early EDI applications utilised the services of a value-added network (VAN) for message exchange. These VANs performed a number of services including storage, logging, translation and interconnection with other VANs. Many EDI trading partners are now evaluating or experimenting with the use of the Internet instead of the much more expensive services of VANs.

---

2 Banner ads, small rectangular images, are displayed along with the relevant content. Advertisers pay a fee based on either the number of "impressions" (people who see the ad) or on the number of "click-throughs" (people who actually click on the ad and go on to visit the advertiser's site). An example is Time Warner's Pathfinder site, which provides access to many leading print publications including *Time, Fortune, Life, Money Magazine, and Sports Illustrated.*

3 For example, the *Wall Street Journal* charges a subscription fee for access to its electronic edition.

4 *Internet Magazine*, February 97, at p. 119.

5 Electronic Data Interchange, or EDI, is the exchange of business data in a structured format from one computer to another.

REGULATION OF THE INTERNET

Introduction

1-7   The Internet is often described as unregulated. However, this is not correct since many existing laws apply both to the deployment and use of the infrastructure of the Internet, and to the transmission of content on the Internet. In fact, communications sent by means of the Internet may pass through many jurisdictions, and accordingly may be subject to a greater number of laws than would apply to other forms of communication. The real difficulty, however, typically lies in the enforcement of the applicable laws.

A number of jurisdictions have undertaken reviews of the application of existing laws to the Internet and of the changes that may be desirable. For example, the United States Intellectual Property Rights Working Group (Task Force) issued a report entitled "Intellectual Property and the National Information Infrastructure" (the "White Paper") in September 1995.[6] The White Paper explains the application of laws in cyberspace and recommends certain changes in the intellectual property laws to accommodate the digital age.

Many business entities already operate in highly regulated sectors. Their activities on the Internet would generally come within the scope of any legislation that already governs their conduct.

Customary rules and self-regulation may also restrict the activities of Internet users. For example, the Usenet service on the Internet has a type of self-regulation called netiquette.[7] A breach of these rules can result in sanctions by other users and other detrimental consequences.

In considering the appropriate means for regulating conduct on the Internet, it is important to recognise that international law is founded on the premise that physical space is divided into geographical units called states, each of which is sovereign and can exercise control over persons and things within its physical territory. A strong argument may be made that because the Internet transcends physical and political space, it should be recognised as a separate community with its own definition of jurisdiction.[8] If the Internet is found to constitute a new form of community, the interests of its users may not be best served through the collective exercise of individual state action. Actions taken, or not taken, in one jurisdiction can have a dramatic effect on activities and users located in another jurisdiction.

---

6   A copy is located at http://www.uspto.gov/web/ipnii/ipnii.pdf.

7   These are informal rules of behaviour which include a tolerance for free speech and an intolerance for commercial advertising.

8   This argument was made by the Electronic Frontier Foundation (EFF) in their *amicus curie* brief filed in the *United States* v. *Thomas* appeal (1996 U.S. App. LEXIS 1069, 1996 Fed. App. 032P (6 Cir.)). The EFF is a non-profit civil liberties organisation that attempts to protect privacy, free expression and access to public information and resources on-line (www.eff.com).

One possible means of co-ordinating the regulation of the Internet would be through an international treaty. However, there appears to be little movement in this direction. Presently, neither the United States, the birth place of the Internet and the country which currently contains the bulk of the world's Internet users and services, nor its major trading partners, appear to perceive a need for co-ordinated international regulation of the Internet.

An important consideration for anyone contemplating Internet-based activities is the extent to which that entity's activities may be governed by domestic legislation in other countries, and particularly in countries where that entity may have assets. For example, an American motion picture studio with a subsidiary in the United Kingdom will wish to ensure that the contents of its United States-based Web site do not run afoul of United Kingdom regulations, especially if the content is directed at users located in multiple jurisdictions, including the United Kingdom.

Telecommunications and Broadcasting Regulation

A strong trend in the communications industry is the convergence between   **1-8** cable television and telephone services. Cable operators would like to upgrade their facilities to provide two-way communications with a view to providing telephone services for their subscribers. Similarly, telephone carriers are seeking to increase the bandwidth of their system, using technology such as Asymmetrical Digital Subscriber Line (ADSL), to provide the capacity for delivery of video and multimedia services. Both industry groups have been petitioning regulators to permit them to enter each other's territories. However, each group's initiatives will require substantial investments and are not likely to be completed for some time.

Substantial progress has been made to allow the delivery of real-time video programming through the Internet. Recently developed "streaming" technology permits users to commence playing an audio or combined audio/visual program in real time within a few seconds after the material is requested. In addition to providing playback of pre-recorded content, many streaming media products allow live broadcasts to be sent through the Internet.

The distinction between computer networks, on the one hand, and broadcasting and cable undertakings, on the other hand, is becoming increasingly blurred. As the transmission quality arising from the use of streaming technology over the Internet continues to improve, and as traditional broadcasters begin retransmitting or simulcasting their off-the-air broadcasts through the Internet, broadcast regulators will likely turn their attention to this new communications channel.

A government commission or agency responsible for enforcement of broadcasting regulations may view the unregulated distribution of Internet-based broadcasting as a threat to its mandate. Indeed, widespread distribution of such programming may undermine the broadcasting regulatory framework within a jurisdiction because video servers located in a foreign country could provide programming in competition with domestically regulated entities.

The definition of "broadcasting" for the purpose of broadcasting legislation may be broad enough to encompass multimedia programming sent through the Internet. Broadcasting legislation may even apply to pre-recorded video files accessible from Web pages or downloadable from FTP sites.[9]

Providers of video and multimedia services that utilise telecommunications media, including the Internet, may therefore be subject to the licensing and regulatory requirements of broadcasting legislation. However, a number of possible exemptions may be available and some may be applicable to Internet-based broadcasting services.

Another challenge for regulators has been the recent growth of Internet telephony. Over a dozen vendors are marketing software products that allow Internet users to place local or long distance voice telephone calls. As a growing number of Internet Service Providers (ISPs) offer flat-rate Internet access, there may be virtually no incremental cost of placing phone calls through the Internet.

Privacy

Introduction

1-9   Information privacy, which may be regarded as one aspect of the right of privacy, has been defined as "the claim of individuals, groups or institutions to determine for themselves when, how and to what extent information about them is communicated to others".[10] In *R v. Duarte*,[11] privacy was defined as the "right of the individual to determine for himself when, how, and to what extent he will release personal information about himself". More simply, privacy has been defined as "the right to be left alone by other people".[12]

The growth of computer databases in the public and private sectors, and the potential for cross-linking of such databases, raise important issues as to the rights of privacy and the measures that can be taken to protect personal information. At the same time, the interconnection of these databases to the Internet and ability of transmitting or accessing large amounts of information world-wide raises issues as to political sovereignty and economic decision-making which may have a major impact on the lives of citizens within any country.

---

9 For example, many motion picture studios now commonly provide short previews of new movies that can be downloaded through the Internet.
10 Westin, *Privacy and Freedom* (Atheneum, 1967).
11 (1990), 53 C.C.C. (3d) 1, 65 D.L.R. (4) 240, [1990] 1 S.C.R. 30, 24 C.R. (3d) 281, subnom *R v. Sanelli*.
12 *Katz v. United States* (1967), 389 U.S. 347 (U.S.S.C.); quoted by Dickson J in *Hunter* v. *Southam Inc.* [1984] 2 S.C.R. 145, 11 D.L.R. (4) 641, at p. 652, 14 C.C.C. (3d) 97, 2 C.P.R. (3d) 1.

At least two privacy interests may be the subjects of regulation. The first is the expectation of privacy in messages sent by users through an employer's or third party's computer system or local area network (LAN). Although corporate LAN administrators and Internet Access Providers (IAPs) have a legitimate interest in ensuring that their systems are not used for unlawful or improper purposes, the interception of messages may be in violation of users' rights of privacy. The second privacy interest that is commonly the subject of regulation is the collection, use, and disclosure of personal information by certain kinds of institutions and corporate entities.

Privacy rights may be protected by various means, such as by criminal legislation, Common Law causes of action, privacy legislation affecting the public or private sector and self-regulation.

Criminal Legislation

In certain countries, the interception of private communications may be a **1-10** violation of criminal legislation. For instance, in Canada section 184 (1) of the Criminal Code[13] (the "Criminal Code") makes it an offence for any person to use a device to wilfully intercept a private communication. Any wilful use or further disclosure of an unauthorised interception may also constitute a separate offence.

However, criminal prohibitions against unauthorised interception of private communication may not apply to all types of interception of communications. For example, transmission logs captured by the system may be distinguished from the contents of messages and may not constitute "communications" for the purposes of criminal legislation. Accordingly, the monitoring or logging by an IAP of sites visited by its users, or the logging of certain routing information concerning e-mail messages, whether for the IAP's marketing purposes or for purposes of assisting a law enforcement agency with a warrantless search, may not attract criminal liability.

Common Law Torts

In some countries, including the United States, a number of privacy-related **1-11** torts are recognised and, under appropriate circumstances, one or more of these might be relevant to the use and disclosure of information on the Internet. These torts include:

- public disclosure of private facts;
- misappropriation of personality;
- wrongful intrusion on another's seclusion or solitude, or into his or her own private affairs; and
- unauthorised disclosure of trade secrets.

---

13 R.S.C. 1985, c. C-46, as amended.

1-12   The use or disclosure of either the contents of messages sent by users on a network or information generated by the network (*i.e.*, the identity of the sender and recipient of messages) could constitute an unjustified invasion of privacy giving rise to civil damages. In determining whether there is an invasion of privacy, a court will examine all of the circumstances of the use or disclosure, and consider the damages suffered by the user. The risk of liability of a network operator would be substantially increased if messages were intercepted for purposes unrelated to the exercise of control over the use and operation of the network.

Some of the above-mentioned causes of action may apply even if there is no disclosure or publication to others. Unauthorised access by a system operator or other person to a user's private e-mail or data files may be sufficient.

Although various causes of action at Common Law may be relied on to protect rights to privacy, the protection granted may be limited in scope. For example, in the case of an action for defamation, it must be shown not only that the information that is disseminated is untrue, but also that damage has been caused to an individual's reputation as a result.[14] In general, such a cause of action does not enable an individual to prevent the collection or the widespread dissemination of information which is accurate, nor does it enable the individual to control the uses that may be made of such information.

Privacy Legislation Affecting the Public Sector

1-13   Some jurisdictions have enacted privacy legislation specifically applicable to public sector entities. For instance, in the Province of Ontario, Canada, government "institutions", such as provincial and municipal ministries, boards, commissions and agencies, are subject to the provisions of the Freedom of Information and Protection of Privacy Act[15] or the Municipal Freedom of Information and Protection of Privacy Act[16] (collectively referred to as the "Privacy Acts"). The Privacy Acts govern the collection, use and disclosure of information by such institutions and may apply to a wide variety of computer systems and networks that may be operated by such institutions, ranging from the bulletin boards operated by school boards to the systems used to store motor vehicle registration information.

Privacy Legislation Affecting the Private Sector

1-14   Some jurisdictions have enacted legislation creating a statutory tort for one person to violate the privacy of another. For instance, certain Canadian provinces including British Columbia, Manitoba, Newfoundland and Saskatchewan have enacted legislation making it a tort for a person, wilfully

---

14 Special damages may be assumed with certain types of defamation, such as libel or slander *per se.*
15 R.S.O. 1990, c. F.31.
16 R.S.O. 1990, c. M.56.

and without a claim of right, to violate the privacy of another. The interception of messages or the disclosure of the contents of messages sent by means of a computer network may be a violation of such legislation, even if such conduct may not be a violation of any criminal legislation.[17]

Some jurisdictions have also adopted legislation to provide specific protection for personal information in the private sector. For example, the 1995 European Community Directive on the Protection of Individuals in Regard to the Processing of Personal Data and the Free Movement of Such Data (the "Privacy Directive"),[18] imposes certain obligations on entities collecting, retaining, using and communicating information that concerns a natural person. The Privacy Directive also provides for the establishment of a regulatory framework for the protection of personal data by prohibiting transfers of such data to non-Member States unless they are deemed to provide "an adequate level of protection" of that data.

In Canada, the Province of Quebec has also adopted an Act respecting the protection of personal information in the private sector.[19] This Act sets out detailed rules governing the purposes for which any private enterprise may collect personal information, the uses to be made of such information, and the purposes for which the information may be communicated to third persons. The Act also sets out the rights of any person about whom personal information is collected to obtain access to that information and to exercise certain recourses arising from any inaccuracies in the information or any improper use of the information.

Certain industries such as insurance companies may be subject to industry-specific statutory requirements with respect to the retention of records. For example, the Alberta Financial Consumers Act[20] provides that personal financial information provided by a consumer for the purpose of obtaining advice about or investing in certain financial products may be used only for the purpose for which it was given, unless the consumer otherwise consents.

Some of the laws governing the protection of personal information also include rules governing the manner in which the information may be collected. For example, under the United Kingdom Data Protection Act (1984),[21] persons asked to provide personal information must be informed of the identity of the entity collecting the data, the purpose of the collection

---

17 In *Ferguson v. McBee Technographics Inc.*, [1989] 2 WWR 499, it was held that listening to and recording a telephone conversation with the knowledge of only one of the participants was a *prima facie* violation of the Manitoba Privacy Act (S.M. 1987, c. P125, C.C.S.M. c. P125). This was the case notwithstanding that section 184 of the Canadian Criminal Code provides that it is not an offence to record a conversation where the consent of only one of the parties to the communication is obtained.

18 Directive 95/46/E.C. of the European Parliament and of the Council of October 24, 1995.

19 S.Q. 1993, c. 17.

20 S.A. 1990, c. F-9.S.

21 1984, c. 35.

and the persons to whom the data may be disclosed. Such notice must be provided before the information is collected. This requirement means that it may be a violation for an entity operating a Web site to require visitors to register before obtaining full access to the Web site even if such registration only involved providing name and address information. Instead, the operator should provide certain information[22] to such persons before information from them is collected.

Self Regulation

1-15   In response to the growing use of computer systems and electronic networks, model codes have been developed. For example, the Canadian Standards Association (C.S.A.) has issued a Model Code on the Protection of Personal Information (the "Model Code"). The Model Code is intended as a voluntary standard that may be adopted by any organisation concerned about the protection of personal information. Once the Model Code is adopted, the provisions containing prescriptive language become requirements. An organisation may tailor the Model Code to meet its particular circumstances, such as by developing an organisation-specific code and by providing organisation-specific examples.

The Model Code addresses the manner in which personal information is collected, used, protected and disclosed, and the rights of individuals to obtain access to that information and where necessary, to have it corrected. The Code is based on the Guidelines on the Protection of Privacy and Transborder Data Flows, as adopted by the Organisation for Economic Cooperation and Development (O.E.C.D.), of which Canada is a signatory.

Privacy is on the mind of many Internet users. A distrust of Web sites leads many users to avoid sites that require registration. It also leads many users to provide false information. A voluntary privacy code specific to the Internet has also been developed. eTrust, launched in January 1997, labels participating Web sites with seals of approval or "marks". To participate, the owner of a site must agree to abide by a stringent set of privacy guidelines developed by eTrust. The guidelines require Web sites to set out their information-gathering practices, what personal identifiable data they collect, the purposes for which the information is used, and the persons with whom it will be shared. Users must be allowed to correct, update, and delete personal identifiable information. Monitoring of personal communications between users is also prohibited.

A number of other self-imposed regulations or guidelines may also be applicable to the collection or use of personal information. Many trade associations and industry groups (for instance, the Canadian Bankers

---

22 This information would include the name of the entity collecting the information and the purpose for which and the persons to whom the information may be disclosed.

Association) have established voluntary codes of compliance and, in some cases, companies have established company-specific privacy policies and guidelines.[23]

Export Controls

Most countries have enacted legislation governing the import or export of certain goods. Such restrictions may extend to computer hardware and software, including infrastructure components of the Internet, and may extend to any product that utilises encryption technology. For example, in Canada, the Export and Import Permits Act[24] authorises the Governor in Council to establish a list (called the Export Control List) of articles, the export of which is controlled for any one of several purposes.

1-16

Encryption Technology

The full potential of the Internet for electronic commerce will not be achieved until consumers and users are confident of the security of transmitted information. Encryption is used to protect private messages transmitted across the Internet. However, the import, export, or use of encryption is regulated in a number of countries. The original rationale for the regulation of encryption, the Cold War, has long ended but restrictions on encryption have continued. Since most schemes being developed for the use of digital cash[25] or secure payment systems depend on the use of strong encryption, these legal restrictions pose a threat to the continued commercial development of the Internet.

1-17

The United States has enacted laws to restrict the export of certain types of encryption technology.[26] Products which utilise weak forms of encryption,

---

23 For example, the Bank of Montreal, a Canadian chartered bank, has a booklet entitled "Your Privacy", which sets out the Bank's commitment to protect the privacy and confidentiality of certain types of personal information collected from customers. The Bank also has an internal Confidentiality of Information Policy (the "Policy"). All directors and personnel are required to be aware of the Policy and designated personnel are also required to acknowledge their understanding of the Policy in writing.

24 R.S.C. 1985, c. E-17, as amended.

25 For instance, DigiCash from DigiCash Corp and CyberCash from CyberCash Inc.

26 United States export restrictions on encryption technology are based on the Arms Control Export Act (A.C.E.A.), 22 U.S.C., section 2778, which allows the President to designate certain items as defence articles or defence services. These items make up the United States Munitions List. The import and export of items on the United States Munitions List is controlled by regulations adopted under the A.C.E.A., entitled "International Traffic in Arms Regulations" (I.T.A.R.), 22 C.F.R., sections 120–130 (1994). Section 121.1 Category XIII (b) (1) covers "components or software with the capability of maintaining secrecy or confidentiality of information or information systems" and therefore encompasses cryptographic software.

(*i.e.*, with a key length of 40 bits or less) can be exported.[27] Products that utilise more powerful encryption cannot be exported without a permit. However, a 40-bit key length is not commercially secure. On January 30, 1997, a graduate student at the University of California at Berkeley used a network linking about 250 workstations to crack a 40-bit algorithm in less than four hours. The use of algorithms with a longer key length increases the time required to crack an encrypted message exponentially. It woulds take about 22 years to break a 56-bit algorithm using the same resources. The constitutionality of United States export restrictions on encryption products has been challenged.[28]

Canada, like the United States, also imposes export controls on certain goods, including encryption products. Most types of goods, including encryption products, can be freely exported to Canada from the United States subject to a bilateral agreement whereby Canada has agreed to restrict the further export of such United States origin goods. However, unlike the United States, Canada characterises encryption technology as an information security product rather than as a munition.

United States regulations provide a number of exemptions to permit the export of devices not capable of encrypting user-supplied data, devices used to unscramble video or audio signals for a restricted consumer type audience, and cryptographic equipment specially designed and limited for use in machines for banking or money transactions.

United States and Canadian restrictions on the export of encryption technology do not affect its internal use. It is therefore legal to use encryption technology within these jurisdictions and even to transmit an encrypted message internationally, as long as the encryption program itself is not transmitted.

The European Union has not yet adopted a uniform set of rules governing the use or export of encryption technology. Some Member States, such as France, restrict the distribution, use or export of encryption without a government permit, while other countries are also considering such legislation.

A further issue relating to the use of encryption technology across the Internet is that because the Internet involves use of packet switching technology, a user typically has little control over which of many possible routes is selected to transmit a message to the destination. This means that an encrypted message may start and end its journey from countries that do not prohibit

---

27 The strength of an encryption process depends on the integrity of the encryption algorithm used (*i.e.*, that it does not contain any "back doors" which could be used as opposed to a "brute force" attack) and the length of the encryption key (*i.e.*, password) used to encrypt and decrypt the messages. The size of an encryption key is measured by the number of "bits" or the number of digits. The strength of the encryption increases exponentially as the key length is increased.

28 *Bernstein* v. *United States Department of State*, number C95-C.V.-582 (N.D. Cal. February 21/95); decision filed December 9, 1996, and released December 16, 1996. The court held that certain provisions of I.T.A.R. are unconstitutional.

the use of encryption (even if the export of the technology is prohibited), but may be transmitted through a country which does restrict the use of encryption and may therefore violate the law of the intermediate country.[29]

Transborder Data Flow (TBDF)

In some jurisdictions, no laws of general application have been enacted to regulate the transfer or transmission of computerised data outside the jurisdiction. However, certain laws of this nature may apply to specific industries, such as consumer reporting agencies and banks.[30]   **1-18**

As noted above, some jurisdictions, including the Province of Quebec and many European Union Member States,[31] have enacted legislation governing the use of personal information. Such legislation may restrict the export of personal information to countries that do not have an adequate level of protection for such data.

An interesting issue is whether the transmission of personal information through the Internet to another country with the requisite level of protection may nevertheless constitute a violation of such legislation if the information is routed through other jurisdictions without adequate protection before reaching the destination. This can be a problem because even data exchanged between two users in the same jurisdiction using the Internet may pass through another jurisdiction.[32]

Contests, Games of Chance, Gambling

Contests and sweepstakes on the Internet may be subject to a variety of legislation in different jurisdictions.[33] Many jurisdictions require extensive disclosure.[34] In some jurisdictions, sweepstakes must be registered   **1-19**

---

29 Even if the encryption technology itself does not pass through this country.
30 For example, the Canadian Bank Act provides that subject to certain exceptions, all registers and records required or authorised to be kept by any bank must be prepared and maintained in Canada, and information or data relating to the preparation and maintenance of such records must be both maintained and processed in Canada.
31 For example, the United Kingdom. The Data Protection Act (1984) regulates the use of computerised data relating to a living person who can be identified from the data, sets out registration formalities and regulates the categories of people to whom the information may be disclosed.
32 For example, the path between two users attached to different IAPs may need to cross into another jurisdiction before finding a common route between the two IAPs. Also, one or both users may be using the facilities of a foreign IAP or on-line service. For example, many Canadian residents utilise America Online, CompuServe or other United States-based on-line services or IAPs to gain access to the Internet. Any communications between two Canadian users may be routed through the service provider located in the United States.
33 In Canada, the Criminal Code sets out the structure and nature of promotional contests and prohibits certain actions. The Competition Act addresses the need for adequate and fair disclosure.
34 The information required to be disclosed may include the anticipated number of participants, the approximate value of prizes, the full cost of the chance to win each prize and any other fact known to the promoter that may materially affect the chances of winning.

and a bond posted to cover the value of the prizes. In addition, the overall impression conveyed may not be misleading.

Different rules may apply to games of chance, such as lotteries or sweepstakes, as opposed to games of skill, such as contests. In some jurisdictions, it may be lawful to require an entrant to provide consideration[35] as a condition of participating in a game of skill, but the imposition of the same requirement as a condition of entering a game of chance may result in the activity being characterised as an illegal lottery. It is therefore important to provide an alternative method for a consumer to enter a sweepstakes other than through the purchase of a product or service.[36] Where both chance and skill are involved, courts may consider which element predominates. In some jurisdictions, additional restrictions may be applicable to certain types of promotions or industries.[37]

Securities Legislation

1-20   In many jurisdictions, activities related to investments, trading and related advisory services are highly regulated. Some jurisdictions, including the United States, assume jurisdiction over securities transactions on the basis of United States citizenship. Other jurisdictions, including Canadian provinces, assume jurisdiction on the basis of residency.

A growing number of electronic newsletters and Web sites related to investments are available on the Internet. The providers of such information may be characterised as investment advisors and therefore may be required to register under the securities legislation of jurisdictions where the information is received.

Concerns also arise with respect to the dissemination of information that might be construed as solicitations to purchase securities. Any offering of, or solicitation regarding, securities using the Internet would likely be subject to the same regulatory regime as may be applicable to offerings or solicitations made through other forms of communications. Securities regulators may assert jurisdiction over a foreign-based advisor who sends out electronic newsletters or other information to residents of the securities regulator's local jurisdiction. The issue that must be determined is whether the activities in question constitute either the solicitation of the public or an offering of securities, or the provision of investment advice, for which there must be compliance with the applicable securities legislation.

---

35 Consideration may, but need not, be a cash payment. Any detriment by the contestant, such as trying out a software program, or enrolling as a trial member in an on-line service, may constitute consideration.

36 For example, a Prodigy Internet "Make it Yours" sweepstakes which had permitted contestants to install the Prodigy software and enrol in Prodigy Internet prior to December 31, 1996, also provided an alternative "write-in" method of enrolment. Presumably, this was done to not characterise the sweepstakes as requiring consideration and therefore constituting an illegal lottery.

37 For example, telemarketing, gasoline promotions, and the use of 900 numbers.

Securities regulators are also exploring the use of the Web to help locate persons who may have violated applicable legislation or regulations. In October 1996, for example, United States regulators with the Commodity Futures Trading Commission set up a "wanted" page to seek out a pool operator alleged to have embezzled U.S. $3-million from investors involved in an unregistered commodity pool. The same regulators also initiated enforcement actions against two unregistered trading advisers who operated over the Internet.

Taxation of Internet Services and Transactions

Uncertainty exists as to the manner in which sales, value added, or similar   1-21
taxes apply to transactions in the Internet and on-line services industry.

Generally, IAPs must purchase underlying transmission capacity from telecommunications carriers and pay sales taxes on such purchases. IAPs then resell their bandwidth to customers and typically such transactions are also subject to taxation. However, some IAPs may provide national or international dialup access and may not otherwise be doing business in a particular customer's jurisdiction. The taxation rules applicable to the access charges paid by such a customer may not be certain.

Another difficult and increasingly significant question is the taxation applicable to sales of products and services that are effected through the Internet.[38] In some cases, the product being sold consists of information and services that are delivered electronically via the Internet (*e.g.,* an on-line newsletter or downloadable software program). In other cases, the product is tangible personal property where the sales transaction occurs through the Internet but where the physical product is delivered to the purchaser through the mail or a courier service. In still other cases, the product acquired through the Internet is in fact a service and not a "good".

In some countries, including the United States, sales taxes are levied at the state or provincial rather than the federal level, and the taxing authority of the states or provinces may extend to out-of-state/province sellers of tangible personal property only if sellers have a sufficient presence, or nexus, with the taxing jurisdiction. In many cases where a seller and purchaser are not located in the same jurisdiction, and goods are shipped from one jurisdiction to another, no sales tax is paid either to the seller's home jurisdiction or the purchaser's jurisdiction. This problem has arisen in the context of phone and mail-order sales even before the Internet became a popular medium for

---

38 Although the estimated revenues from Internet and on-line services, as well as from sales of products made through such services, are still relatively small, they are expected to grow rapidly in the coming years. Subscription and advertising revenues from Internet access and consumer on-line services are projected to range from U.S. $7-billion to U.S. $14-billion by the year 2000, while on-line sales of consumer products are projected to reach more than U.S. $6-billion (although the latter would still represent less than four per cent of mail-order sales).

electronic commerce. When the entire transaction (including delivery of the product or service) is made electronically, the seller's lack of any presence with the purchaser's jurisdiction may insulate the seller from that jurisdiction's taxing authority.

In the case of countries that impose a value-added or sales tax at the federal level (for example, the Canadian Goods and Services Tax or G.S.T.), such tax would presumably apply to all sales made within the country. If goods are ordered from a foreign supplier then existing customs procedures may capture the G.S.T. applicable on the transaction. However, when a foreign supplier delivers the "goods" by electronic means, such as in the case of software, then there is a potential loss of tax revenue.[39]

Any government attempting to impose a tax that must be collected by the seller will be faced with a formidable enforcement challenge because the nature of the Internet makes the location of a particular party irrelevant and difficult to determine. The only type of tax that a government may be in a position to implement is a transaction tax that is imposed on the purchaser. Developments, including the increasing availability of electronic cash, can be expected to produce even more challenging tax collection issues.

Criminal Legislation

Fraud

1-22   The Internet is increasingly being used as a tool to carry out fraudulent activities, such as pyramid schemes and stock manipulations. In the United States, the S.E.C. has begun investigating stock touting services that use the Internet to recommend the purchase of certain stocks. In many cases, these services are conducted in such a manner that potential purchasers are lead to believe that the recommendations are based on independent research when, in fact, the studies are paid for by the companies whose stocks are recommended.

As of 1997, the United States Federal Trade Commission had issued warnings to approximately 500 Web sites regarding operation of potentially illegal pyramid schemes and filed 15 lawsuits alleging on-line scams. The United States Food and Drug Administration, in conjunction with approximately 40 state attorney generals, are evaluating the policing of fraudulent medical claims on the Internet.[40]

Unlawful Materials

1-23   **Pornography and Obscenity** The laws of many jurisdictions contain prohibitions on the transmission or distribution of obscene materials. In some

---

39 This loss may occur although the foreign supplier may technically be required to collect the tax.

40 *PC Magazine*, February 18/97, Volume 16, number 4, at p. 28.

cases, these laws deal specifically with on-line behaviour. For example, the United States Communications Decency Act of 1996[41] imposes criminal liability on those persons who knowingly and intentionally use or permit their telecommunications systems to be used for the creation and transmission of obscene, indecent or patently offensive materials to minors.

Even where legislation regulating the transmission or distribution of obscene materials does not deal specifically with electronic transmissions, such legislation can likely be applied to prosecute an individual who engages in the prohibited activity using the Internet as a transmission medium. Such legislation would be applicable to electronic commerce applications to the extent that the product sought to be supplied falls within the prohibited content. Such laws are also of concern to ISPs and on-line service providers who in some cases may be held liable for the actions of their users or subscribers. This issue is discussed further below.

Hate Literature A number of jurisdictions have legislation that prohibits   1-24
activities that lead to the incitement of hatred. For example, in Canada, subsection 319 (1) of the Criminal Code provides that every one who, by communicating statements in any public place, incites hatred against any identifiable group that is likely to lead to a breach of the peace is guilty of an offence. The Criminal Code also provides that every one who, by communicating statements, other than in private conversation, wilfully promotes hatred against any identifiable group is guilty of an offence.[42]

Publication Bans

Some countries impose legal controls on the publication or dissemination of   1-25
certain types of information in specified circumstances. These controls may be for the purpose of ensuring that an accused obtains a fair trial in a criminal matter. For example, a Canadian court prohibited the publication of information from a murder trial to protect the rights of the accused person's spouse who was charged with the same offence and whose trial was to be held at a subsequent date. Information relating to the initial proceeding became available on a number of the newsgroups carried through the Internet in violation of the publication ban.

---

41 The Communications Decency Act of 1996 (C.D.A.), 47 U.S.C. section 223, part of the Telecommunications Act of 1996, signed into law February 8, 1996, Pub. L. Number 104–104, codified, as amended, at 47 U.S.C. section 151 (1996). The American Civil Liberties Union (A.C.L.U.) challenged certain sections of the CDA as infringing on First Amendment rights (*A.C.L.U.* v. *Reno*). On June 12, 1996, the A.C.L.U. succeeded in obtaining a preliminary injunction. On July 1, 1996, the Justice Department filed a direct appeal to the United States Supreme Court in the A.C.L.U. case. On July 29, 1997, in a related lawsuit, *Shea* v. *Reno*, 924 F.Supp. 824 (E.D. Pennsylvania, June 12, 1996). On June 26, 1997, the United States Supreme Court affirmed and held that 47 U.S.C.A. 223(a) and 223(d) violated the First Amendment due to their vagueness and overbreadth.
42 Criminal Code, subsection 319 (2).

In other cases, certain points of view or speakers may be the subject of the ban. For example, the United Kingdom imposed a broadcasting ban on the transmission of the views of any official representative of the Sinn Fein political party due to its alleged involvement with terrorism.

Advertising and Sales

Advertising Standards and Codes

1-26   Most jurisdictions do not specifically regulate advertising on the Internet but have adopted rules concerning the advertising of certain regulated products and services. Regulated products may include tobacco, drugs, and alcohol. Other rules may govern the advertising of services, such as financial services or legal services. These regulations must be complied with when the Internet is being used as the advertising medium.

In many jurisdictions, codes or standards have been adopted that govern advertising appearing in most types of media, which may or may not include the Internet. Some codes have been modified to apply specifically to Internet-related advertising. For example, the British Codes of Advertising and Sales Promotion, which are administered by the Advertising Standards Authority (A.S.A.), were modified in 1995 to extend to non-broadcast electronic media, including the Internet. The requirements for such media are now consistent with those for press, poster and cinema advertising, i.e., that the advertising be legal, decent, honest, and truthful. Such codes are typically voluntary codes of compliance; however, non-compliance can result in adverse publicity, peer pressure, or possibly difficulties in running advertising in other media. In some cases, legal recourses may be available to deal with persistent or deliberate offenders.

Laws Governing Sale of Goods or Services and Misleading Advertising

1-27   Many jurisdictions have enacted legislation that provides for certain representations, warranties, and conditions to be incorporated into contracts for the sale of goods and, in some cases, for the supply of services. For example, the sale of goods may be subject to certain implied warranties or conditions such as that the seller will convey good title to the goods, that the goods are of "merchantable quality", and that they are fit for a particular purpose. The legislation may permit the parties to exclude the statutory warranties and conditions by express agreement, but such exclusion may not be permitted in some circumstances, such as in the case of consumer sales. Legislation for the protection of consumers is discussed below.

Some jurisdictions also prohibit any misrepresentations or false statements being made in the course of the sale of any goods or services. Where they occur, the customer may have a right of rescission, and possibly damages. It may also be an offence to use a false trade description for goods offered for sale in the course of a business.

Consumer Protection Legislation

Many jurisdictions have enacted legislation to deal specifically with trans-   1-28
actions directed to consumers. The legislation may provide for statutory
warranties and conditions governing the sale of goods or services that may
not be disclaimed by agreement of the parties. The legislation may provide
for a cooling off period for certain types of transactions, during which time
the consumer may rescind the transaction. Consumer protection legislation
may also restrict a supplier from limiting liability, may require contracts to
be drafted in plain language, and it may prevent the imposition of "unfair"
or unconscionable terms.

Some jurisdictions have also enacted legislation dealing specifically with
mail-order transactions. This legislation may require those persons engaged
in this type of trade to provide the name and address of the person carrying
on the business. Such legislation may be applicable to on-line sales trans-
acted through the Internet.

The European Union is also considering the adoption of a common
directive in respect of distance contracts.[43] The current form of the directive
would cover most forms of direct marketing and should encompass Internet-
based marketing using the Web or e-mail. Some of the important provisions
of the proposed Directive are that:

- consumers must be given certain minimum information both at the
  time that the contract is solicited and at or near the time of delivery;
- subject to certain exceptions, consumers must be given a "cooling off"
  period; and
- solicitations may not be made through telephone, fax or e-mail unless
  the consumer has provided his or her consent.

PAYMENT MECHANISMS FOR ELECTRONIC COMMERCE

Many transactions for the supply of products and services are now con-   1-29
ducted by means of electronic data interchange between trading partners as
an alternative to the exchange of purchase orders and invoices in paper
form. Business transactions are also increasingly being conducted electronically. New forms of payment mechanisms are required to support on-line
transactions between parties that do not have established trading partner
agreements.

---

43 Common Position (European Community) 19/95 of the European Parliament and of the
   Council on the Protection of Consumers in Respect of Distance Contracts, 1995 O.J. (C.
   288/1).

Alternative Payment Schemes

On-line and Off-line Transmission of Payment Information

1-30   There is currently no single payment mechanism in use for transactions conducted through the Internet. The most frequently used method is the transmission of credit card information either through an encrypted electronic channel using the Internet, or through an off-line alternative such as through a voice telephone call or a fax transmission. In the latter case, most of the information concerning the transaction is exchanged on-line, and the information provided off-line to effect payment must be matched to the on-line transaction.

In the above-mentioned payment mechanisms, the credit card information is sent to the merchant for processing like a mail order or phone order transaction. An alternative model for electronic payment is for the bank or credit card organisation to participate in the transaction in a manner that precludes the need for providing the credit card number to the merchant. Instead, the information is transmitted either directly or by means of an encrypted envelope sent via the merchant's system to the bank or credit card company which then issues a confirmation code to the merchant.

Electronic Money

1-31   Several mechanisms for implementing electronic money have been conceived. Although electronic money systems can provide a cost-effective mechanism for micro transactions or small denomination purchases on the Internet, they are still in the relatively early stages of development. Issues that must be addressed to ensure future growth include interoperability, privacy, authentication, and verification. While many of these issues will be solved, the growth of electronic money systems may still be slower than expected by some proponents.

Electronic money is based on public key encryption technology that creates a block of digital data that can represent money and be used for payment. In general, there are two distinct forms of electronic money: identified electronic money and anonymous electronic money. Identified electronic money contains information that can reveal the identity of the person who was issued the money from the bank. Some forms of identified electronic money also allow the issuing bank to track the electronic money as it moves from one person to another. In contrast, anonymous electronic money cannot be tracked by the issuing bank and can be spent or transferred without leaving a transaction trail.

Some electronic money schemes permit person-to-person transfer, like real cash, while others require that a consumer transfer the money directly to a merchant as payment for an on-line transaction. Some electronic money schemes also require access to an on-line network connection when the money is transferred, while others permit transactions to occur off-line without the involvement of the bank. The most complex form of electronic money is anonymous electronic money that can be transferred off-line because some sort of mechanism is required to prevent double-spending.[44]

With some forms of electronic money, specifically a tokenised system where the real electronic money is transmitted electronically, a loss of the digital representation of the money can result in a real loss to the owner. With other systems, the electronic money is simply a notational system or record rather than the money itself. In the latter case, the money can be returned to the consumer on the bank being notified of its loss or destruction.

Trade in drugs and the taking of profits from organised crime as well as other types of criminal activities generate money that must be integrated into the financial systems for criminals to make use of the money. Law enforcement agencies have historically relied on the intermediation of banks and other financial institutions to provide choke points through which funds must pass. Therefore, a major concern regarding the use of electronic money, especially anonymous electronic money, is the potential that it will be utilised for money laundering purposes. However, some of the anonymous electronic money schemes allow at least one of the parties to be identified so that the resulting tender does not become a useful tool for criminals.

Security for Electronic Commerce

In order for electronic commerce across the Internet to reach its full poten-   1-32
tial, the infrastructure must first be capable of providing the same levels of trust found in traditional business exchanges. This will occur only if the parties involved in Internet commerce can be assured of the confidentiality, security, and integrity of the messages transmitted via the Internet.

Confidentiality and Integrity of Transaction

Encryption is a process for protecting information by scrambling the con-   1-33
tents to make it difficult and time consuming for an unauthorised recipient to unscramble and view the information. The use of encryption can provide assurances regarding the confidentiality of a communication, *i.e.,* to ensure that the message remains private. Encryption can also serve to protect the integrity of a transaction, *i.e.,* to ensure that the communication is not modified in the course of transmission. The protection of message integrity may also involve the utilisation of a time-stamping function to provide a means of verifying the time of transmission of a message.

---

44 Anonymous money can be structured to accumulate information as it travels from person to person. The system can be structured so that the transaction trail will only be revealed if the electronic money is spent on more than one occasion. If the money is not double-spent then the bank will not have sufficient information to determine the identity of the original spender or reconstruct the path taken as the electronic money moves from one person to another.

It may be desirable or even necessary to utilise encryption for communications other than those involving electronic commerce. Various data protection laws may require those entities maintaining personal information on systems accessible through the Internet to exercise reasonable forms of technological protection to safeguard the confidentiality of such data, including its confidentiality in the course of transmission. For example, the United Kingdom Data Registrar has recommended that prior to being asked to provide personal data, Internet users should first be warned that the Internet is not a secure medium absent the use of strong encryption, and be provided with an opportunity to cancel the transaction.

The more familiar system of encryption, technically referred to as symmetrical cryptography, is based on using a single key (*i.e.*, the same password) for both encryption and decryption. However, even if a very secure encryption algorithm is used, symmetrical encryption systems have a number of inherent weaknesses.

The first problem is that both parties to a communication must share knowledge of the secret encryption key or password. This means that each party must trust the other party not to disclose the secret key.

The parties must also trust the method used to distribute secret key information. Key distribution is not a problem if the sender and recipient can meet in person to exchange information about the key or if they both have access to a secure channel for transmission of the secret key. However, key distribution can be a problem where the parties cannot exchange keys in private or where other parties may be involved.

Finally, since both parties know the private key, it is difficult to implement a non-repudiation function as the sender of a message can always claim that the recipient forged the message.

An asymmetric or "public key" encryption cryptosystem (PKE) solves these problems. PKE is based on the use of two mathematically related keys where a message encoded using one key requires the second key for decoding. Each user possesses a pair of keys, one that is kept secret and one that is made public. While the keys are mathematically related, it is not feasible to determine the private key from knowledge of the public key. A certification authority may also be utilised to assure that the public key really does belong to the person who purports to have published it.

The use of PKE is now prevalent in many Internet-related products. Most popular Web browsers now incorporate PKE functions that can automatically set up encrypted communication sessions when used to access a Web server that supports the use of encrypted communications.[45] It can therefore be used to allow a consumer to send personal information or a credit card number securely to a merchant's Web server.

---

45 Early versions of Netscape's Navigator Web browser were subjected to a number of attacks and a few flaws were discovered and rectified. However, these flaws were due to the implementation of PKE rather than holes in the underlying algorithms.

While no system of cryptography can be guaranteed to be completely secure, public key cryptography is based on widely used mathematical algorithms, which have been tested to such an extent that their integrity is universally accepted. The real hindrance to the availability of true security for electronic commerce has been the unwillingness of certain governments, such as that of the United States, to permit the export of cryptographic systems that cannot be easily broken.

Authentication of Counter-Party and Non-Repudiation

The convergence of computer and communications technologies has made it   1-34
possible for many transactions to be carried out without reliance on original signed agreements or indeed any paper instrument. Printed forms of many standard business documents, such as purchase orders, quotations, invoices and acknowledgements, have been replaced by electronic data interchange systems. Electronic funds transfer systems permit payment instructions to be communicated electronically without the issuance of cheques or other bills of exchange. Documents produced by an organisation's word processing system may be transferred directly to another company's computer system without the production of a paper document by either the originator or the recipient. Business transactions may be conducted by facsimile transmissions of correspondence and agreements rather than the delivery of the original signed documents.

The use of an electronic communication system to effect a legal transaction gives rise to several evidentiary issues where no physical document is created, or no original signed document is exchanged between the parties. One such issue is the need to authenticate that an electronic message originated with the person by whom it purports to have been sent; in other words, in the absence of an original signed document, the courts must be satisfied as to the genuineness of an "electronic signature".

The need to authenticate the source of an electronic message may be satisfied by the use of identifiers to confirm the identity of the originator. Among the techniques that could be built into any system to establish the genuineness of the originator's identity are the following: the use of confidential passwords, access codes or personal identification numbers assigned to individual users of the system; the use of smart cards or other physical cards to be used to obtain access to the system; and personal identification techniques involving some personal traits of the person sending the message.

In many cases the use of simple passwords is no longer enough. A more reliable scheme is required to identify the sender of a transmission. Attention is turning to the use of a digital certificate based on public key cryptography and certification techniques, to authenticate the identities of parties to a transaction conducted electronically. Such a mechanism not only would verify the identity of the sender but also could provide for non-repudiation of the transaction.

Each of the parties involved in a communication or transaction will wish to ensure that the other party may not repudiate that party's actions. The recipient of a message will want to ensure that the sender cannot later deny that he or she had sent a particular message. As well, the sender will want to ensure that the recipient will not at a later date be able to deny receipt of the communication.

The PKE cryptosystems referred to above, in which a private encryption key is known only to its owner, can be used to create a digital signature. A message that can be decrypted using a person's public key must have been encrypted using that person's private key as such key is known only to such person. This means that the encryption of a message by a person using his or her secret key can serve the function of a manual signature in the electronic world. This topic is discussed below under "Formation of an Enforceable On-line Contract".

JURISDICTIONAL ISSUES

Introduction

1-35   The growing importance of computer networks, the development of new communications systems, and the increasing internationalisation of business mean that most uses of computers often involve multi-country activity. In a number of reported computer crime cases, the activities involved in the commission of the offence have taken place in more than one country. Such cases raise the question of whether the courts of one country have jurisdiction to try an offence where some of the activity necessary to constitute the offence occurs in another country. This question must be resolved according to the principles of law in effect in the jurisdiction where the charges are laid. In general, jurisdiction refers to the power of the courts to commit persons for trial and to enforce judgments against them.

In a civil dispute, multi-jurisdictional activities will typically include a determination of which jurisdiction's law should govern the resolution of the dispute, which jurisdiction's court should hear the dispute and how a successful plaintiff can have the judgment enforced against a defendant located in a different jurisdiction.

The rules applicable to the assumption of jurisdiction may be different for criminal or regulatory offences as compared to civil actions. In countries that share a heritage with English Common Law, criminal jurisdiction is generally based on physical presence within the jurisdiction. Under this principle, the courts of one country do not have jurisdiction to try matters that relate to activities performed outside the jurisdiction. The rationale underlying the territorial principle is first that a country has generally little direct concern for the actions of malefactors abroad; and second that other states may legitimately take umbrage if a country attempts to regulate matters taking place wholly or substantially within their territory.[46]

---

46 *Libman* v. *The Queen* (1985), 21 C.C.C. (3d) 206 (S.C.C.), at p. 228.

A court following such a principle will assume jurisdiction to try a case only where the offence in question has been "committed" in that jurisdiction. There are several alternative interpretations as to when an act may be deemed committed in a particular jurisdiction. For example, it may be necessary to show that:

- the act is carried out in totality in that jurisdiction;
- the act is "commenced" in that jurisdiction (reflecting what is commonly referred to as the subjective territorial principle);
- the act is completed in that jurisdiction, *i.e.,* the last constituent element occurs in this country (reflecting what is referred to as the objective territorial principle); or
- the act has an effect in that jurisdiction.

International comity, however, does not prevent a particular country from **1-36** exercising jurisdiction with respect to criminal acts in that country that have consequences abroad, nor does it give immunity to any person for conduct carried out abroad that has harmful consequences in that country. Furthermore, the rules of international comity are not static and modern nations are no longer as sensitive about exclusive jurisdiction over crime as they may have been formerly, a court declaring:

"In a shrinking world, we are all our brothers' keepers. In the criminal arena, this is underlined by the international co-operative schemes that have been developed among national law enforcement bodies."[47]

If electronic commerce on the Internet is to realise its full potential, the parties doing business must know what rules will be applied to their activities. The principles governing jurisdiction are still under development and in many cases will depend on the laws in force in the country in which the question is raised. In addition, there may be conflicting policy objectives. On the one hand, any rule that requires a retailer engaged in commerce on the Internet to identify and conform to the laws of each country in which consumers may be located would hamper the ability to use the Internet as a way to expand beyond the local market. On the other hand, consumers should not need to give up the protection of their laws when they venture into Cyberspace, especially if a particular retailer is actively targeting them.

Enforceability of Foreign Judgments and Extra-Territorial Application of Law

Even if a court from outside a defendant's jurisdiction of residency assumes **1-37** jurisdiction to hear a dispute, there is still an issue of whether that court's

47 *Libman* v. *The Queen* (1985), 21 C.C.C. (3d) 206 (S.C.C.), at p. 233.

judgment will be enforceable in the defendant's jurisdiction. A number of countries have enacted legislation for the recognition of foreign judgments. In other countries, the courts may look for a certain level of connection between the defendant and the foreign jurisdiction where the action was heard.

The laws of some countries provide that even if the laws of a foreign country govern a consumer contract, the consumer may still receive the protection of the laws of the country in which he or she is resident. This would likely mean that the domestic court in the jurisdiction where the consumer is located may refuse to enforce a judgment obtained in a foreign court if the consumer would have had a defence had the action been prosecuted in the domestic jurisdiction.

Courts may also refuse to enforce a foreign judgment if the foreign jurisdiction does not provide for the same protection of constitutional rights as may be recognised by a domestic court. For example, United States courts have shown a reluctance to recognise British libel judgments, as repugnant to public policy, because British defamation laws lack First Amendment protections.[48]

Implications of Server Location to Determine Jurisdiction

1-38   The transparent nature and broad reach of the Internet means that any entity desiring to set up a Web site may do so from any one of many physical locations. This decision is made based on a number of considerations such as cost and bandwidth issues.

The very existence of a Web site in a particular jurisdiction may in certain cases constitute the carrying on of business within that jurisdiction. For example, a Web site that supports electronic commerce activities or performs other retailing functions may be programmed to "accept" orders from visitors to the Web site. A court may construe such pre-programmed order-taking activity as the carrying on of business within that jurisdiction.

Activities Relating to Trades in Securities

1-39   In many jurisdictions, activities related to investments, including trading and related advisory services, are highly regulated. As discussed above, some jurisdictions, including the United States, assume jurisdiction over securities transactions on the basis of United States citizenship. Other jurisdictions, including provincial regulators in Canada, focus their investor protection activities on the basis of residency.

There are a growing number of electronic newsletters and Web sites on the Internet related to investments. The supply of such information may

---

48 *Matusevitch* v. *Telnikoff*, 877 F.Supp. 1 (D.D.C. 1995); *Bachchan* v. *India Abroad Publications Inc.*, 585 N.Y.S. 2d 661 (N.Y. Sup. Ct. 1992).

result in the providers being characterised as investment advisors and thereby being required to register under the securities legislation of the jurisdictions where the information is received. Where such activities are regulated and the information provider and the recipient are both residents of the jurisdiction, the provider of the newsletter would likely be required to be registered as an investment advisor. The same result would apply to information that might be construed as a solicitation to purchase a security. Securities regulators may also seek to exercise jurisdiction over a foreign person who sends out electronic newsletters to, or who solicits purchases from, persons who reside in the securities regulator's local jurisdiction. Similar concerns may also apply to information provided on a Web site, although the concerns may be alleviated if the information is not directly targeted to persons residing in the securities regulator's jurisdiction.

The Securities and Investment Board in the United Kingdom has taken the position that the Financial Services Act 1986 could apply to an entity located outside the United Kingdom that runs a Web site which includes an "investment advertisement". This is the case notwithstanding that the advertisement is published outside the United Kingdom. Two factors to be considered are whether the offer is directed, as a matter of fact, to potential investors in the United Kingdom, and the degree to which technical steps are taken to restrict the material from being accessible by residents of the United Kingdom.

In Canada, the recently retired Chairman of the Ontario Securities Commission, Edward Waitzer, has suggested a new approach to policing the Internet. Specifically, he suggested that regulatory authorities should focus more on transactions rather than attempt to regulate the information that is posted from their own geographic area.

The inclusion of a disclaimer at the Web site indicating that the contents are not directed to residents of a particular jurisdiction may not be sufficient. In certain cases, the use of a registration process may be necessary to limit access to the site.

INTELLECTUAL PROPERTY

Copyright Protection for Contents

Copyright law provides a relatively inexpensive and easily enforced bundle of rights for protecting information on the Internet. Some of the rights granted to copyright holders which are useful for protecting works on the Internet include the exclusive right to reproduce the work, either in whole or in substantial part, and the right to communicate the work by telecommunication. Copyright legislation in many jurisdictions also grants certain moral rights to the creators of works. 1-40

Copyright law will protect only the expression of an idea rather than the idea itself. Registration is usually not required for copyright to subsist in a work; however, certain presumptions useful to litigation may arise on registration of a work. Under the copyright regimes of many jurisdictions, authors are the first owners of copyright in their works. A few exceptions may exist (for instance, authors who write articles in the course of their employment but not freelancers). Until recently, the relationship between freelance writers and their publishers was often informal. It has been common industry practice for the authors to retain copyright to their articles, including the right to use the same for other publications, and to grant the publisher only a right of first use or publication.

In recent years, the value of providing electronic access to printed information has become increasingly evident and major publishers have either commenced their own on-line services or have negotiated agreements with third-party on-line database services to provide electronic access to their publications. In either case, articles that were originally submitted for and published in print publications are now being "recycled" in a new medium and additional royalty or licensing payments are flowing to the publisher. Authors have taken an interest and commenced litigation in a number of jurisdictions seeking compensation for such additional uses of their works.[49]

A dispute between authors and publishers may arise in a number of ways. The first is where a publisher relies on old contracts for print and broadcast media without taking into consideration the unique issues raised by new technologies. If articles were originally obtained for a single use only in North America, the re-publication or electronic distribution of the articles may be an infringement of the author's copyright.

Major publishers have generally revised their freelance agreements to acquire a broad range of rights without being required to pay additional compensation. New contracts seek a grant of electronic rights in all forms "now in existence or hereinafter invented". Some contracts may also require freelancers to waive their "moral rights". However, industry associations representing authors and journalists are recommending to their members that they retain full electronic rights or, where this is not possible, to provide for a strictly limited grant of electronic rights.

Disputes may arise where authors refuse to accept provisions granting electronic rights to publishers or, more commonly, when publishers attempt to create on-line works from older editions of their publications for which the contributors did not agree to transfer the electronic rights to the publishers.

---

49 For example, a suit by 10 freelance writers and the National Writers Union against the *New York Times*, Time Warner and an on-line database operator in the United States. Canada also witnessed a launch of a C. $100-million class action suit by Heather Robertson, a prize-winning, non-fiction author, against Thompson Corp. for its part in placing freelance materials in electronic databases without authorisation or the payment of additional compensation.

Protection of Databases

Any examination of intellectual property protection for works accessible on the Internet must also involve a consideration of the protection available for databases. In some jurisdictions, such as the United States, a minimum level of originality or creativity in the selection and arrangement of facts may be necessary to obtain copyright protection for databases (*Feist* v. *Rural Telephone*).[50] Courts in European Union Member States have also denied copyright protection to databases unless a high degree of originality is present. In other jurisdictions, such as the United Kingdom and Canada, copyright protection may be available based on the so-called "sweat of the brow" test.

1-41

A proposed Database Directive of the European Union would reduce the scope of copyright protection for databases by requiring that the selection or arrangement of the contents constitutes the author's own intellectual creation. If the compilation or collection does not meet the originality requirements for copyright protection, then a *sui generis* protection right is to be provided. This new "unauthorised extraction" right permits the maker of a database to restrict the unauthorised extraction or re-utilisation of its contents, "in whole or in substantial part", for commercial purposes for a period of only 15 years.

An interesting question is how the new *sui generis* right may be applied to certain Internet infrastructure components such as router tables and domain name service (DNS) databases. Because these are typically computer-generated databases, they may not be protectable under copyright law. However, if the *sui generis* extraction right under the European Union Database Directive becoming applicable, it may necessitate the use of cross-licensing agreements between Internet network operators.

The copyright status of databases within a particular country may also be subject to bilateral agreements. For instance, the North American Free Trade Agreement[51] requires each party to protect compilations of data which by reason of the selection or arrangement of their contents constitutes intellectual creations. The agreement provides further that such protection shall not extend to the data or material itself, or prejudice any copyright subsisting in that data or material.

Intellectual Property Infringement

Some of the information available on the Internet may be in the public domain, while most material is likely to be protected by copyright. The material may have been placed on the Internet by a third party that did not have legitimate rights to do so. Sometimes, it can be very difficult to

1-42

---

50 *Feist Publications, Inc.* v. *Rural Telephone Service Co.*, 499 U.S. 340, 1111 S. Ct. 1282 (1991).
51 North American Free Trade Agreement, section 1 of article 1705: Copyright.

determine whether the material was placed on the Internet with or without authorisation. For example, in *World Library* v. *Pacific Hitech*,[52] an unidentified third party had taken over 800 works from a CD-ROM published by World, removed the copyright notices and uploaded the material onto the Internet. Pacific, assuming the information was in the public domain, downloaded a copy and published it on its own CD-ROM.

An issue may also arise where a business entity may have acquired a license to use certain information or content for a particular purpose, such as internal print publication or for distribution to its clients or customers. However, the right to distribute the work electronically or to the general public may have been retained by the original owner or may have been licensed to another party.

It is not uncommon for rights in a work to be granted to different persons in respect of different jurisdictions. A related problem is that a work may be made available on a Web site located in a jurisdiction where the person placing the work holds the copyright to the work but may be accessed by a user residing in a different jurisdiction where copyright to the work has been granted to another party. Similarly, a work may be in the public domain in one country but still protectable by copyright in other countries.

Another problem with respect to the application of copyright law to the Internet is the availability of exemptions or defences provided in the copyright legislation of many jurisdictions.[53] A copyright work may also be hosted on a computer system located in a country which may provide that copyright does not subsist in certain types of works or that does not provide for effective enforcement measures. The material may nevertheless be accessible world-wide through the Internet. Examples include databases which may be subject to different levels of protection in various jurisdictions, and legislative or judicial material which some governments treat as "public domain" or freely reproducible.

A party that publishes an infringing copy of another person's work may be liable for infringement of such copyright in the same manner as if the work were published by means other than the Internet. A further issue is whether an ISP may be liable for secondary infringement due to its role in the distribution of the infringing copies. An important element of liability for secondary infringement will typically be some level of knowledge or imputed knowledge that infringement is taking place. This issue, known as contributory infringement in some countries, or authorisation of infringement in other countries, is discussed further under the heading "Service Provider Liability".

Potential liability for trade mark infringement may also arise where a trade mark is utilised on a Web site that is accessible from a foreign jurisdiction and where another party has rights in that foreign jurisdiction to an identical trade mark. However, prosecution may be difficult unless the

---

52 (N.D. Cal. 1993) [unreported]. See Coleman, "Copycats on the Superhighway", (July 1995) A.B.A. J. 68.
53 For example, the United States "fair use" defence or the Canadian "fair dealing" defence.

infringing party is specifically targeting the audience in that foreign jurisdiction or has assets in that foreign jurisdiction.

Protecting Intellectual Property on the Internet

Use of Technical Devices to Protect Intellectual Property Rights

A number of vendors are developing technology that can be used to protect   1-43
digital information on the Internet. One such technology that is specific to protecting pictures is PictureMarc from Digimarc Corp. PictureMarc works by inserting a digital watermark into an image without a noticeable effect on the image itself. The digital code is hidden within the random variation normally found in an image. According to Digimarc, the watermark is detectable even if the image is cropped, colour corrected or otherwise edited.

When a watermarked picture is opened with a compatible graphics program, PictureMarc alerts the viewer to the image's copyright status. The watermark can be used to identify the author, the copyright owner and even specific permissions.

IBM is another vendor with technology solutions to protect digital information. Under IBM's solution, electronic information can be sealed in "cryptolupe" containers. Once secured, the package can only be opened with a matching cryptographic key. Cryptolupe containers can protect copyrighted material against unauthorised access and provide a mechanism for owners of intellectual property to be reimbursed for the use of their content, which can include text, audio, visual information, and other rights-protected digital data.

Legal protection against tampering with devices intended to protect copyrighted works may soon be available. Article 11 of the WIPO Copyright Treaty adopted by the Diplomatic Conference in Geneva on December 20, 1996 requires "Contracting Parties" to provide adequate legal protection and effective legal remedies against the circumvention of effective technological measures that are used by authors in connection with the exercise of their rights under that treaty or the Berne Convention and that restrict acts in respect of their works, which are not authorised by the authors concerned or permitted by law.

Use of Licensing to Protect Intellectual Property Rights

License agreements may also be used to supplement protection provided by   1-44
copyright. In *ProCD* v. *Zeidenberg*,[54] the defendant purchased and mounted a copy of ProCD's "yellow pages" CD-ROM directory on the Internet. Relying on the United States Supreme Court decision in *Feist*,[55] the defendant claimed that the data contained on the CD-ROM was not protected by

---

54 908 F.Supp. 640 (W.D. Wis. 1996).
55 *Feist Publications, Inc. v. Rural Telephone Service Co.*, 499 U.S. 340, 1111 S. Ct. 1282 (1991).

copyright. The defendant also wrote his own search program to avoid use of ProCD's search program that was protectable by copyright.

The Supreme Court agreed with the defendant on the copyright issue and found that the ProCD listings did not show the necessary originality in their selection and arrangement to qualify for protection. However, the court held that the ProCD product was protected from unauthorised reproduction by reason of a shrink-wrap license agreement that accompanied the product.[56] This decision illustrates that the content transmitted on the Internet may be protected by the use of "click through" on-line license agreements.

Protection of Trade Marks

1-45   Trade mark law protection can also be used to protect material from unauthorised distribution on the Internet. Trade mark laws might also be relied on to deal with a growing number of "unofficial" sites appearing on the Internet. In many cases, these sites trade on the trade mark owner's reputation to re-direct users who would otherwise visit the trade mark owner's own Web site.

A growing number of Web sites criticise or parody entertainment studios and product offerings from corporations. Often, these sites misappropriate text material, logos, graphics, and even video clips from the official Web site and therefore infringe on copyright and trade mark rights.

Deviations in how trade marks are used and presented may result in the marks losing their distinctiveness which, in turn, may lead to their invalidity. Accordingly, trade marks must be used properly both by the trade mark owner and any authorised users. A trade mark owner wishing to ensure optimum protection for its trade marks should conduct periodic searches to determine where there is any unauthorised use of its marks by other parties on the Internet.

Domain Names and Trade Marks

1-46   Each computer connected to the Internet is assigned a unique numeric address, called an Internet Protocol (IP) address. A numeric address is difficult to use, and a domain name, which is a mnemonic associated with a particular IP address, makes Internet resources much easier to access.

A domain name that consists of a business entity's trade mark or trade name, or that is related to its mark or name, can make it easier for customers and other persons to locate that entity on the Internet. The use of such a related domain name can also be a means of enhancing the goodwill associated with a particular business entity or product.

---

56 The Supreme Court made this finding even though the product's exterior packaging lacked notice of the terms of the shrink-wrap license agreement.

Domain names are generally registered on a "first come, first served" basis. However, disputes may arise when the owner of a trade mark is denied use of that mark as a domain name because another party has already obtained a domain name registration for the mark. The potential for conflict is exacerbated by the fact that trade mark law allows the same mark to be used by sellers of different goods and services as long as there is no confusion in the marketplace regarding the origin of such goods and services. By contrast, Internet technology allows only one entity to utilise a particular domain name.

In the United States, the authority to assign domain names is exercised by Network Solutions Inc. (NSI). NSI has issued a domain name resolution policy, which has been amended on several occasions, to deal with domain name disputes. This policy has been used to resolve various disputes related to unauthorised use of a trade mark as a domain name. In the future, however, it is likely that disputes will increasingly be settled according to traditional trade mark doctrines and processes.

In the United States, for example, it is becoming generally accepted that trade mark law applies to the use of domain names on the Internet.[57] In *MTV Network v. Curry*,[58] an early domain name dispute, the Court analogised domain names to telephone number mnemonics. Such numbers may be recognised as trade marks if they are used to indicate the source of goods or services. However, the use of a domain name outside the context of providing goods and services to others may not result in the creation of any rights under trade mark law.

Other trade mark requirements, such as that of distinctiveness, may also be applicable to domain names. Descriptive domain names may need to acquire secondary meaning before they are entitled to trade mark protection, and generic domain names may never be entitled to trade mark protection.

In the United States, the enactment of the Federal Trademark Dilution Act of 1995[59] should also assist trade mark owners who are concerned about protecting their marks from being used as Internet addresses by other persons. In *Hasbro, Inc. v. Internet Entertainment Group, Ltd.*,[60] the Court granted a preliminary injunction against the defendants for diluting the value of the "Candy Land" mark, which was used by Hasbro to identify its board game for children. The defendants used a "Candyland.com" domain name to identify their Web site containing pornographic content.

While trade mark law may be relied on to protect trade mark owners against "domain name pirates", such laws provide little assistance in resolving

57 See *The Comp Examiner Agency v. Juris Inc.*, (CD. Cal. April 25, 1996); See also the United States Patent and Trademark Office, Registration of Domain Names in the Trademark Office, at http://www.uspto.gov/web/uspto/info/domain.html.
58 867 F.Supp. 202 (S.D.N.Y. 1994).
59 109 Stat. 985 (1996), codified as amended at 15 U.S.C. sections 1125 and 1127.
60 1996 U.S. Dist. LEXIS 11626 (February 9, 1996).

disputes between owners of the identical marks used in conjunction with different products or services. In this regard, the technical nature of the Internet makes it difficult or impossible for multiple users of the same mark to distinguish their own use of the mark. While some companies use capitalisation, mixed irregular capitalisation, special fonts, or designs to distinguish their marks, such distinctions are technically precluded as a means of distinguishing different domain names.

The problem of competing interests of multiple legitimate trade mark owners is also compounded by the technical limitation of 24 characters for the length of domain names. In most cases, the practical limit is even less as shorter domain names are easier to remember.

The "many mark owner, one domain name" problem, however, is slightly less serious in countries which utilise top-level domain hierarchy based on a two-letter country code. In some jurisdictions, such as Canada, domain names are qualified down to a provincial or local level depending on where the entity has operations. Therefore, while a corporation such as the Canadian Broadcasting Corporation that operates nationally may obtain a domain name such as "cbc.ca", a company called XYZ that only has operations in Ontario would be issued a domain name of "xyz.on.ca". Another company by the same name that operates in the Province of British Columbia would be issued a domain name of "xyz.bc.ca".

SERVICE PROVIDER LIABILITY

1-47   Aside from simply providing network access to the Internet, many ISPs provide users with access to upload materials to a shared Web server that may then be accessed by other users. Many ISPs also operate a Usenet news server that can be used to post or read messages. Some also set up e-mail distribution lists (or list servers) that may be managed by a particular user for an additional fee.

Internet users may use these facilities to upload unlawful, defamatory or infringing materials. Examples of unlawful material include hate propaganda, materials that are subject to a publication ban, pornography and obscene material. Infringing materials may include works that infringe copyright, trade mark or privacy laws.

In almost all cases, users can upload content directly to the ISP's storage devices without such material being reviewed by the ISP. In the case of a Usenet news server, messages are received from other sites in addition to those that may be posted by local users.

In considering potential liability for materials distributed on the Internet, it is important to distinguish between an operator of a Web site, where material is created and stored, and a service provider, such as an IAP or a telecommunications carrier that is simply providing a communications channel.

In some jurisdictions, attempts are being made to clarify the liability of ISPs for materials carried on their system. For instance, reforms proposed by the Copyright Subcommittee of the Canadian Information Highway Advisory Council in its Final Report of the Copyright Subcommittee[61] (the "Report") included a recommendation that operators of bulletin board systems (BBSs), presumably ISPs, should be liable for materials carried on their systems as they are not common carriers. However, the operators would have a defence if they do not have actual or constructive knowledge of the infringing material and acted reasonably to limit abuses.

An ISP may also be prosecuted under the criminal law for aiding and abetting in the commission of an offence, such as the distribution of pornography or publication of hate literature. However, liability would arise for "aiding" in the commission of an offence only if the ISP was aware that the network was being used to commit an offence and performed some act for the purpose of aiding the offence. Similarly, a person would normally be guilty of "abetting" the commission of an offence only if the person encouraged its commission; this generally would require prior knowledge that the offence was being committed. If an ISP was aware that the network was being used for the commission of an offence and, having the means to do so, did not act to prevent its continu- ation, the ISP may be liable for having encouraged the commission of the offence.

Libel and Defamation

The potential of third-party liability for defamation is a serious concern of 1-48 ISPs, IAPs, and on-line service operators. Many operate facilities, such as Web hosting, e-mail discussion lists and Usenet newsgroup servers that can be used by subscribers to publish defamatory statements to third parties.

In two Internet-related defamation actions, United States courts appeared to establish a proportional relationship between a service provider's liability for libellous statements posted by their subscribers and the amount of editorial control the service provider sought to exercise over such on-line content.[62] However, legal developments in this direction can discourage service providers from taking any steps to regulate content.

---

61 See Information Highway Advisory Council, Copyright and the Information Highway: Final Report of the Copyright Subcommittee (Ottawa: Information Highway Advisory Council Secretariat, 1995).

62 In *Cubby, Inc.* v. *CompuServe, Inc.*, 776 F. Supp. 135 (S.D.N.Y. 1991), the court accepted CompuServe's argument that it was acting as a distributor rather than a publisher and should not be held responsible for libellous statements posted by one of its subscribers. However, in a later case, *Stratton Oakmont, Inc.* v. *Prodigy Services Co.*, 1995 N.Y. Misc. LEXIS 229, 23 Media L. Rep. 1794, where a service provider attempted to exercise some editorial control over content posted to its system, the service provider, Prodigy, was held liable as a publisher. Prodigy had assumed a duty to screen offensive messages from its service and was liable as a publisher based on its use of content guidelines, use of forum leaders who were responsible for enforcing the guidelines, and use of software which pre-screened messages for certain obscenities.

Some jurisdictions have responded by amending their defamation legislation to provide a defence for a party that is not primarily responsible for the publication of the defamatory statement, who has taken reasonable care and who had no reason to suspect that his or her assistance was assisting the publication of the defamatory statement. For example, the United Kingdom's Defamation Act (1996) may have reduced the liability of ISPs for defamatory materials placed on their system where a person over whom they had no effective control did the posting. However, such ISPs must still take precautionary steps, such as publishing and enforcing "use policies", to rely on the statutory defence.

Even in the United States, Prodigy may have been effectively overruled by the "Good Samaritan" provisions of the Telecommunications Act of 1996,[63] which provides a defence against civil liability for a service provider or user of an interactive service in respect of any action taken in good faith to restrict access to or availability of material that the service provider or user considers to be obscene, lewd, lascivious, filthy, excessively violent, harassing or otherwise objectionable.

The Telecommunications Act also contains a provision to the effect that "no provider or user of an interactive computer service shall be treated as the publisher or speaker of any information provided by another information content provider". If interpreted broadly, this provision may effectively establish the distributor-type knowledge requirement for the imposition of liability for IAPs, ISPs and on-line service providers where the defamatory information originates on the Internet or another service provider's system and is only passing through.

One interesting issue that is being increasingly discussed is the extent to which a different standard should apply to defamatory statements made on the Internet in circumstances where the defamed person may have the same ability to communicate with a large audience as the person making the defamatory statement and therefore has an ability to rebut another's statement or correct an error. Recourse to the courts is arguably not as necessary when defamed individuals have the capability themselves to set straight the public record and therefore avoid or substantially reduce the potential damage to their reputation.

Liability for Infringement of Third Party Rights

1-49   An ISP may be liable for its role in allowing a subscriber or user to utilise its facilities to infringe the right of another. For example, under Canada's Copyright Act, any person who "authorises" any act which is an infringement of copyright is deemed to be a party to such infringement. The concept

---

63 The Good Samaritan provisions are codified at 47 U.S.C., section 230 (c) (1)–(2).

of "authorisation" has been defined judicially to include such acts as the countenance, sanctioning, or encouragement of infringing activities by other persons.

Recent case law in the United States also suggests that operators and owners of on-line systems or networks may be liable for infringement of copyright by other parties in certain circumstances. For example, the operation of computer bulletin boards which are used to upload or download unauthorised copies of video games[64] or photographs[65] may constitute copyright infringement. In some cases the courts have stated that it was inconsequential to copyright infringement whether or not the defendant had knowledge of the specific unauthorised copying nor did it matter that the systems operator himself did not copy the infringing material. An ISP that facilitates or encourages the use of its system to exchange infringing copies may be liable for contributory copyright infringement.

Even when the facts do not support a finding that an ISP is liable for direct infringement, the ISP may nevertheless be liable for contributory infringement. Generally, liability for contributory infringement can be established if a person with knowledge of the infringing activity of another person, induces, materially contributes to, or causes such activity. An ISP may be deemed to have sufficient knowledge so as to be liable for contributory infringement if it receives notice that a user is infringing the copyright of another person and it takes no action to prevent the continuation of such infringing activities. However, an ISP may not be liable for infringement in respect of incidental copies automatically made on their system as part of a process initiated by a third party, if the ISP did not take any action to facilitate the unauthorised copying other than installing and maintaining the system. This may be the case, for example, where a Usenet news server exchanges messages with other similar services.[66]

It can be argued that an ISP cannot reasonably be expected to be aware of the contents of the vast amounts of information which may be uploaded to, downloaded from, and accessed through its system, or to know whether, in any particular case, the owner of the copyright has consented to the copying or distribution of any work by means of its system. However, it would be reasonable to expect an ISP to establish rules governing the use of its system, which may include prohibitions against the distribution of material that infringes the rights of third parties. It is also reasonable to expect an ISP to take appropriate steps to remove any infringing material on learning that such material is stored on its system. Finally, the ISP may also have an

64 *Sega Enterprises Ltd.* v. *MAPHIA*, 857 F. Supp. 679 (N.D. Ca. 1994).
65 *Playboy Enterprises, Inc.* v. *Frena*, 839 F. Supp. 1552 (M.D. Fla. 1993), where the BBS operator was held liable for direct infringement and infringement of Playboy's display rights for allowing its users to download infringing copies of *Playboy* photographs.
66 *Religious Technology Center* v. *Netcom On-Line Communications Services, Inc.*, 907 F. Supp. 1361 (N.D. Cal. 1995). In this case, a critic of the Church of Scientology had posted portions of its texts to the Internet "alt.religion.scientology" Usenet newsgroup.

obligation to take reasonable steps to restrict access to a particular user who, to the knowledge of the ISP, is obtaining access to infringing materials stored on an interconnected network.

Liability for Hosting of Unlawful Materials

1-50   Unlawful material may include hate messages, information that is the subject of a publication ban, pornography, and other types of information might also be unlawful and could expose the operator of a computer network to liability.

Hate Messages

1-51   Under Canadian legislation dealing with hate material, an ISP could be liable for "communicating statements in any public place" if hate messages were transmitted on its system. Liability will depend on the scope of access to the system, which will determine, in turn, whether the system could be considered a public place for the purposes of this legislation. While the ISP is providing a medium through which others can communicate statements, the question of whether or not the ISP has any responsibility for the contents of such statements will depend on the control that the ISP can exercise over the contents of the statements. The ISP could be found liable for "communicating statements" where their representatives are aware of the contents of messages being transmitted through their system and they have the capability of deleting such messages.

Publication Bans

1-52   Where there is a prohibition against the "publication" of certain information, an ISP could be in violation of the ban, if it permits the distribution on its system of restricted information of which it is aware. This follows from the wide definition of the term "publish" to include acts such as to cause to be seen or read. The making available of a news group containing a large body of unrelated information which includes a small portion of information covered by a publication ban should not constitute an act of publication if the ISP is not specifically aware of the prohibited material. Conversely, selecting out information covered by the ban and calling attention to its availability or making available a news group, the focus of which is a discussion of banned information, may constitute a publication in violation of the ban.[67]

---

67 For example, the name of a newsgroup may provide sufficient notice that it may contain discussions or content that is subject to a publication ban.

Pornographic or Obscene Material

Another growing concern for ISPs is liability for pornographic or obscene ma-   1-53
terials placed on their systems.[68] In some jurisdictions, ignorance of the nature
or presence of the obscene material may be a defence if the accused made an
honest and reasonable mistake of fact. However, a mistake of law, which causes
the accused to believe that material is not obscene, where the person knows the
nature or presence of such material, may not be a defence. Unfortunately, there
is usually not a simple test for determining whether any given material is
obscene within the meaning of relevant legislation governing such conduct.

For the reasons noted above with respect to banned information, an ISP
may be liable for having published, distributed or circulated pornographic
material where the ISP knows such material is available on its system and
the ISP has the capability of deleting or restricting access to such material
but fails to do so. It will be a question of fact in each case as to whether the
ISP has sufficient knowledge and involvement to be a party to the publication, distribution, or circulation of the information. The risk of liability
would be greater where the ISP (or another person involved in its operation,
such as the moderator of a news group) takes an active role in reviewing the
material prior to its distribution on the system. An ISP would not likely face
liability in respect of materials which are available through the Internet but
which are not stored on its system and where the ISP is not aware of their
contents. The ISP in this case should not be deemed either to have published
or to have "possession" of such materials.

In some cases a specific exemption may be available to an IAP, an ISP or
on-line service provider. For example, the C.D.A. contains a "provider exception" which exempts from liability an entity that merely provides access to
connection to a system, facility or network not under its control, including the
transmission, download, storage or other activities incidental to the provision
of access that do not include the creation of the content. The C.D.A. also
provides a defence for an entity that has undertaken good faith reasonable
measures to prevent access by minors to prohibited materials. The focus of
liability under the C.D.A. is on those who create and assist in the distribution
of prohibited content. IAPs and on-line service providers are therefore not
made liable for indecent material accessed by means of their services.

As noted above, the constitutionality of certain provisions of the C.D.A.
are currently being reviewed by the Supreme Court of the United States.
However, IAPs, ISPs and on-line service providers should consider taking the
steps necessary to avail themselves of the defences and exceptions available
under the C.D.A.

---

68 Even if an ISP has the resources and desire to screen its system for pornographic materials,
   this may not always be possible. Unlike images in paper form, electronic images must be
   viewed through software that can reconstruct the visual image. There are currently more
   than a dozen commonly used formats for representing images digitally and countless
   proprietary formats.

FORMATION OF AN ENFORCEABLE ON-LINE CONTRACT

1-54   The ability to form enforceable contracts on-line is a fundamental requirement to the growth of electronic commerce on the Internet. Generally, an
enforceable contract can be formed by oral or written agreement and may
be implied from the conduct of the parties. Key requirements for the
formation of an enforceable contract include the communication of an offer
and the communication back of an acceptance of that offer. An offer and
acceptance can be communicated orally, by written documents or by electronic communications such as e-mail. Many of the legal issues that arise
with respect to contract formation are no different than those encountered
with other electronic means of communications such as telephones, fax and
telex machines.

Making Offers On-line

1-55   An offer can be communicated orally or in writing. An offer may also be
published or transmitted electronically through the Internet. For example,
an offer may be published on a Web site, posted to a Usenet newsgroup
or an electronic mailing list (or listserv) or sent by e-mail to a specific
recipient.

   In many cases, a merchant will want to invite offers from potential
customers rather than actually making an offer. Advertisements placed in
traditional media are generally regarded as an "invitation to treat" rather
than an offer. This results in the communication from the potential buyer
being treated as the offer, which can then be accepted or rejected by the
merchant.

   The characterisation of a party's communication as an offer or an
acceptance can affect which party assumes certain risks. It may also determine where the contract is deemed to have been made when the parties are
located in different jurisdictions and, therefore, what laws will apply and
which courts will have jurisdiction. Thus, a merchant will usually want to
ensure that any promotional material placed on the Web is not capable of
being construed as an offer. The operator of a Web site may want to make
an exception to this rule for purposes of ensuring that any use of the site is
subject to certain terms and conditions, as further discussed below.

Acceptance in On-line Transactions

Electronic Acceptance

1-56   As a rule, to accept an offer, the offeree must communicate his or her
acceptance back to the offeror or someone authorised by the offeror to
receive it. An offer can generally be accepted by the same mode of communications used to make the offer or a more reliable mode. In the United
States, an offer may be accepted "in any manner and by any medium

reasonable in the circumstances".[69]   Therefore, an offer received by e-mail may also be accepted by e-mail unless the offer specifies some other mode of acceptance. A more difficult issue will be whether an offer received by another mode of communication such as by post or fax may be accepted using e-mail communications.

Web-wrap or Click-through Agreements

An acceptance leading to an enforceable contract can generally be mani-   1-57
fested by conduct as well as by verbal or written agreement. It may be possible, therefore, to display the terms of an agreement to a user who is asked to signify acceptance by clicking on a particular button (*i.e.*, marked ACCEPT) or hypertext link, or by entering a particular symbol or code in a box on a Web form. The acceptance of a contract through such conduct is analogous to the acceptance of a shrink-wrap software license agreement by opening the cellophane wrapping surrounding the package or envelope containing the diskettes.

The enforceability of such a procedure can be enhanced if a user is required to scroll through the actual terms before being presented with the mechanism to accept. However, in practice, this is not always done. Many Web sites are using forms where an offeree is given the opportunity to view the terms by clicking on a hypertext link from a highlighted word such as "rules" or "terms and conditions", but such terms are not actually presented unless the offeree takes such further action.

It is also suggested that the offeree be given a clear method to accept or decline and that the offeree's actions be logged as part of a business process. As well, any unusual or onerous provisions not normally found in the type of contract contemplated should be emphasised or otherwise brought to the user's attention.

Some Web sites purport to impose terms and condition on visitors by including a legal notice page on the Web site and stating on that page that use of the Web site will constitute acceptance of the terms and conditions listed on that page. However, in such cases there is an issue of whether the terms and conditions are actually brought to the attention of the offeree. Moreover, any action taken by the offeree without contractual intent, such as continued viewing of the content on the Web site, might not constitute acceptance of the offeror's terms.

Timing of Acceptance

General rules of contract formation should be applicable to Internet-based   1-58
commerce. One such rule is that a contract is formed when the acceptance is communicated to the offeror.[70] However, an exception to this rule has

---

69 U.C.C., section 2-206 (1) (a).
70 However, this rule may not be applicable to international transactions.

developed in the case of contracts made through the mail. Under the "mail box" rule, acceptance is effective when mailed even if it never reaches the offeror. The timing of acceptance is important because an offer can generally be revoked until it is accepted.

It is not clear whether or not the mail box rule will be held applicable to the types of electronic communications used on the Internet. In the United States, the Restatement of Contracts (Second) provides that acceptances given by telephone or other medium of substantially instantaneous two-way communication are governed by principles applicable where the parties are in each other's presence. The rationale for this rule is that in such a case, the offeree can accept without being in doubt as to whether the offeror has attempted to revoke before receiving the acceptance. Proposed draft revisions to the U.C.C. would reject the mail box rule for electronic communications.

However, the logic supporting the rejection of the mail box rule for instantaneous communications does not appear applicable where a message is being sent by a one-way form of electronic communications. Parties communicating electronically using the Internet are not usually engaged in real-time conversations such that the sender knows immediately if the message has reached the recipient. In a real-time two-way communication, both parties usually make a statement at the same time to signify the end of the conversation. This is not the case with many types of Internet-based communications.

An offeror, wishing to avoid assuming the risk of becoming bound to a contract without knowledge of the acceptance, may impose as a term of the offer that the contract will only be formed when the offeror has received the communication containing the acceptance.

Identity of the Other Party and Role of Digital Signatures

1-59   Electronic communications, and the Internet in particular, present opportunities for an impostor to assume the identity of another person or to assume a fictional identity. Therefore, before entering into an electronic agreement with another party, and commencing performance, a party will be well advised to verify or authenticate the identity of the other party.

This issue should also be of concern to parties who may potentially be subject to legal claims because of electronic communications engaged in by other persons. Under some circumstances, an impostor (such as an employee, former employee or hacker) may gain access to confidential passwords or other means of authenticating messages, and may thereby seek to bind the impersonated party or subject the impersonated party to a claim in negligence.

It is likely that digital signatures will be increasingly used to authenticate transactions conducted over an electronic communication medium such as the Internet. A digital signature may be defined as an electronic identifier, created by computer, and intended by the party using it to have the same force and effect as a manual signature.[71] It is anticipated that the growth of electronic commerce will lead to an increasing use of such digital signatures to replace traditional paper-based signatures.

Digital signatures can be given legal effect through legislation, judicial determinations and through contracts between the parties acknowledging the validity of the subsequent use of digital signatures between them. Digital signature legislation has been enacted in some jurisdictions and is being considered in others. For example, the Utah Digital Signature Act[72] authorises the use of digital signatures in commercial transactions. In Utah, a digitally signed document is recognised as valid as if it had been written on paper. Other jurisdictions, such as California, have taken a more incremental approach and only provide recognition to digital signatures used in communications with a public entity.

The American Bar Association Committee on Science and Technology has issued draft Digital Signature Guidelines (October 5, 1995) and the United Nations Commission on International Trade Law has proposed guidelines to expand the recognition of digital signatures as valid signatures.

Writing and Signing Requirements

While many types of contracts may be formed through the exchange of electronic communications across the Internet, many jurisdictions require certain types of contracts or consents to be "in writing" and in some instances to be "signed". Compliance with this requirement may mean that a customer must print out, sign and mail in a copy of an agreement or consent form, even if certain elements of the transaction may be completed on-line.   **1-60**

"Statute of Frauds" legislation in many jurisdictions requires that certain contracts be in writing and signed by the person against whom enforcement is sought. In the United States, for example, the Uniform Commercial Code (U.C.C.) requires a "signed writing" for contracts involving the sale of goods valued at over U.S. $500 and those not capable of being performed within one year.[73]

Writing Requirement

In some cases, an electronic message may be found to comply with a writing requirement. Some jurisdictions have also recognised that an unsigned fax transmission may satisfy a writing requirement.   **1-61**

In some cases, the writing requirement will be met if the message can be reduced to a tangible form. For example, with respect to the sale of goods

---

71 California Gov. Code, section 16.5.
72 Utah Code Ann., section 3-46-101.
73 U.C.C., section 2-201. Note, however, that draft revisions to the U.C.C. may eliminate the writing and signature requirements set out in this provision.

in the United States, the U.C.C. definition of a writing includes printing, typewriting or any other intentional reduction to a tangible form. Certain types of messages, such as those exchanged on an Internet Relay Chat (IRC) facility or on-line chat facility, will not likely have sufficient permanence to constitute a writing.

Any requirement that the message be in a tangible form may be met if either the sender or the recipient reduces the message to tangible form. Therefore, a party engaging in electronic commerce who wishes to comply with a requirement that the electronic messages be in writing should ensure that the messages are printed out or otherwise archived in some sort of tangible or permanent form.

Signature Requirements

1-62   A requirement for a signature does not necessarily mean that only a hand-written signature will be sufficient. For example, a signature is defined by the U.C.C. as "any symbol executed or adopted by a party with present intention to authenticate a writing".[74] Similarly, the United States Restatement (Second) of Contracts, in section 134, provides that a signature may be "any symbol made or adopted with intention, actual or apparent, to authenticate the writing as that of the signor". A commentary to this provision provides that a signature may include "an arbitrary code sign".

A digital signature may meet a requirement that a writing be "signed". However, the legal effect of digital signatures has not been judicially addressed in most jurisdictions. Also, most consumers do not currently have digital signatures and generally are not technically sophisticated enough to understand the use of digital signatures.

Many business entities interested in pursuing electronic commerce transactions in spite of any legal uncertainty are looking for alternatives. Some financial institutions, for example, allow customers or potential customers to apply for a loan over the Internet. The loan transaction is approved in principle by electronic means, but a signed agreement may still be required before the loan transaction is finalised.

The writing requirement has also lead some merchants to use the Internet to provide a copy of an agreement which must then be downloaded, printed, signed and mailed in by an applicant. However, there is a risk that an applicant may modify the contents of the agreement prior to printing, and the merchant may not detect the modification.

Competency or Authority to Enter into a Transaction

1-63   A prerequisite to the formation of an enforceable agreement is that both parties must be legally competent to enter an agreement for a particular

---

74 U.C.C., section 1-201 (39).

transaction. For example, for certain types of contracts, such as those for the purchase of non-necessities, defences to the enforcement of the contract may be available to minors and individuals suffering from mental disability. Although minority or mental disability is not always ascertainable even in face-to-face transactions, it becomes even less apparent when transactions are conducted electronically.

Another issue related to the formation of electronic agreements is whether a party acting as a representative or agent of a third party has actual authority to bind that third party. The authority must be verified using the same mechanisms as those used with non-electronic agreements. However, in some cases, these can reduce the benefits otherwise available from the use of electronic commerce.

Computer-Generated Offers and Acceptances

In some cases, an offer or acceptance or both may be generated as a pre-programmed response by a computer system. For example, in an EDI transaction, a purchaser's computer system may respond once the inventory level of a particular item is below a specified threshold, and automatically send an EDI message containing an order to a supplier's computer system. The supplier's computer system may then send an acknowledgement back confirming acceptance of the order. A similar process may occur in a consumer transaction or in a transaction between entities that do not have any prior dealings. For example, a new customer may visit a supplier's web site, scroll through an on-line catalogue, and then place an order. The order may then be acknowledged (*i.e.*, accepted) and processed automatically by the supplier's computer system.

In some circumstances, it is likely that such computer-generated communications will be held to create a binding contract. Pending draft revisions to the U.C.C. would give legal recognition to computer-generated offers.[75]

1-64

---

75 U.C.C., section 2-208 (October 1/95 draft).

Chapter 2

European Union and International Aspects

Alan Smithee
Center for International Legal Studies
Salzburg, Austria

Introduction

International Treaties and Conventions

A number of international and supranational or regional instruments affect 2-1
on-line transactions. This chapter will introduce some of the most important
international instruments and European Union (E.U.) instruments in this field.

The United Nations Commission on International Trade Law (UNCI-
TRAL) has produced a draft Model Law on Legal Aspects of Electronic Data
Interchange and Related Means of Communication,[1] together with a draft
Guide to Enactment[2] published on 24 April 1996.

The Model Law applies to any kind of information in the form of a data
message used in the context of commercial activities, whether contractual or
not.[3] It is based on the recognition that current legal requirements prescrib-
ing the use of traditional paper-based documentation constitute the main
obstacle to the development of modern means of communication. The Model
Law does not attempt to define a computer-based equivalent to any kind of
paper document. Instead, it singles out basic functions of paper-based form
requirements with a view to providing criteria that, once they are met by data
messages, enable such data messages to enjoy the same level of legal recognition
as corresponding paper documents performing the same function.

Three articles in the Model Law deal with the problems of statutory
requirements for writing, signature and originals. First, the Model Law suggests
that "where a rule of law requires information to be in writing, or presented in
writing, or provides for certain consequences if it is not, a data message satisfies

---

1 Annex II to Document A/50/17.
2 A/CN.9/426.
3 UNCITRAL Model Law, article 1.

that rule if the information contained therein is accessible so as to be usable for subsequent reference";[4] secondly, the requirement for a signature will be satisfied in relation to a data message if a reliable method is used to identify the originator and to indicate the originator's approval of the information in the message;[5] thirdly, a data message will satisfy a rule that information be presented or retained in its original form if a method of authentication based on the following elements is established: (a) a simple criterion as to "integrity" of the data; (b) a description of the elements to be taken into account in assessing the integrity; and (c) an element of flexibility (*i.e.*, a reference to circumstances).[6]

The Model Law establishes the admissibility of data messages as evidence in legal proceedings, and their evidential value according to the reliability of the manner in which the data message was generated, stored or communicated; the reliability of the manner in which the integrity of the information was maintained; and the manner in which the originator was identified, together with any other relevant factor.[7]

On the question of attribution of data messages and the problem of an unauthorised person sending a message, the Model Law establishes a presumption that, under certain circumstances, a data message is considered that of the originator if it is communicated by the originator, or by a person with authority to act on behalf of the originator in respect of that data message. The addressee is entitled to regard a data message as being that of the originator if he applies an agreed procedure to verify it, or a procedure that is reasonable in the circumstances. The position is the same if the data message results from the actions of a person whose relationship with the originator, or any agent of the originator, enables that person to gain access to a method used by the originator to identify data messages as its own.[8]

However, the presumption that the data message emanates from the originator does not apply beyond the time when the addressee receives notice from the originator that the data message is not that of the originator, or at any time when the addressee knows or should have known, based on previously agreed procedures or a reasonable procedure in the circumstances, that the data message is not that of the originator.[9] In this way, the risk placed on the purported originator is balanced by the heavy burden of proof placed on the addressee who would have to prove what checking procedure was "reasonable in the circumstances".

The Model Law allows for the time of dispatch of a data message to be the time when it enters an information system outside the control of the

---

4 UNCITRAL Model Law, article 5.
5 UNCITRAL Model Law, article 6.
6 UNCITRAL Model Law, article 7.
7 UNCITRAL Model Law, article 8.
8 UNCITRAL Model Law, article 11.
9 UNCITRAL Model Law, article 11.

originator (*i.e.,* becomes available for processing). It may be an information system of an intermediary or of the addressee. If the addressee has designated an information system for the purposes of receiving such data messages, receipt occurs at the time when the data message enters the designated information system, but if the data message is sent to an information system of an addressee that is not the designated information system, receipt occurs when the data message is retrieved by the addressee.[10]

The Model Law stipulates that the place of dispatch and receipt of the data message should be the place of business of the originator and addressee, respectively. Where either party has more than one place of business, it is the place most closely related to the transaction or, where there is no transaction, the principal place of business.[11]

European Community Law

On-line services are subject to the provisions of the European Community   2-2 (E.C.) Treaty. Articles 52 and 59 of the Treaty are particularly relevant.

Article 59 lays down the principle of the freedom to provide services. A member state cannot restrict the provision of services originating in another member state. Article 59 provides that a service must comply with the law, and is subject to the control, of the member state in which the service provider is established. This country of origin rule leads to a system of mutual recognition which ensures that on-line service providers do not have to comply with the different regulatory regimes of the member states, irrespective of the destination of their services.

The provisions of article 52 guarantee the right of establishment and protect service providers from obvious or disguised discriminatory restrictions or, in certain cases, unreasonable non-discriminatory restrictions.

Certain secondary legislation also governs on-line services, although within a wider context. The Directives of particular relevance are listed under individual subject headings below. In addition, there are many E.C. consultation documents and legislative proposals. As might be expected, possible future measures far outnumber adopted E.C. legislation.

The Commission produced its first overall plan in its Action Plan, Europe's Way to the Information Society.[12] The Action Plan covers four areas: the regulatory and legal framework; networks, basic services, applications and content; social, societal, and cultural aspects; and the promotion of the information society.

Where the regulatory and legal framework is concerned, the Action Plan lists different priorities in three annexes: pending measures, new measures under consideration, and possible partnerships.

---

10 UNCITRAL Model Law, article 14.
11 UNCITRAL Model Law, article 14.
12 COM (94) 347 final.

Many of these measures, such as standardisation of technologies, introducing competition into telecommunications, questions of media ownership, and research and development programmes, fall outside the scope of this chapter.

The Commission now considers it time to review the original Action Plan in order to give the information society a new political impetus. It has published a Communication entitled "The Implications of Information Society on European Union Policies — Preparing the Next Steps",[13] accompanied by the following three Communications:

- "Living and Working in the Information Society: People First"[14] — A number of actions for the benefit of people will be based on this document;
- "Standardisation and the Global Information Society"[15] — The document analyses Europe's position in the standardisation of electronic commerce, identifies technical barriers to electronic transactions, and submits proposals on the dissemination of standards, particularly for SMEs; and
- "Regulatory Transparency in the Internal Market for Information Society Services".[16]

2-3   The Communication "Regulatory Transparency in the Internal Market for Information Society Services" is accompanied by a proposed Directive amending for the third time Directive 83/189/E.E.C. Laying Down a Procedure for the Provision of Information in the Field of Technical Standards and Regulations.[17]

A Commission Communication entitled "Europe at the Forefront of the Global Information Society: Rolling Action Plan",[18] adopted in 1996, updates "Europe's Way to the Information Society: An Action Plan"[19] and identifies four new priority areas:

- Improving the business environment through liberalised telecommunications and the thorough application of internal market principles; promoting the introduction of new technologies into daily business activities and ensuring that the necessary conditions are met for the introduction of electronic commerce (*e.g.*, copyright, data protection, digital signatures.) On the latter, the Commission envisages launching a new strategic initiative to identify and remove the barriers to the development and take-up of electronic commerce.

---

13 COM (96) 395 final.
14 COM (96) 389 final.
15 COM (96) 359 final.
16 COM (96) 392 final.
17 COM (96) 392 final.
18 COM (96) 607 final.
19 COM (94) 347.

- Investing in the future information society through education and research. Implementing the initiative "Learning in the Information Society"[20] will assist education; research priorities was to be set out in the Fifth Framework Programme to be presented in March 1997.
- Establishing a number of actions based on the Green Paper "Living and Working in the Information Society: People First". The actions will address the development of new jobs and working patterns; co-operation between public administrations; review of regulation; and harnessing the Structural Funds.
- Setting global rules on market access, intellectual property rights, privacy and data protection, harmful and illegal on-line content, tax issues, information security, frequencies, interoperability and standards.

The Rolling Action Plan includes forthcoming actions, out of which the following have been selected as being of particular relevance to on-line transactions: 2-4

- Communication and Draft Directive on Secure Transactions including Digital Signatures in Electronic Commerce — These initiatives will set the necessary framework for commercial transactions via the networks; they were planned for the first quarter of 1997.
- Communication on an Internal Market Framework for New Online Commercial Communications Based on Home Country Control and Mutual Recognition — This Communication will be a follow-up to the consultations held in the framework of the Green Paper on commercial communications.[21] It may be issued in late 1997.
- Draft Directive on the Harmonisation of Certain Author's Rights and Related Rights — This instrument proposes to further harmonise a number of copyright and related rights aspects where necessary for the proper functioning of the internal market in the information society and the need to protect and stimulate creativity and innovation. Its adoption is expected in late 1997.
- Draft Directive on the Legal Protection of Encrypted Services — The directive will establish a common framework for the legal protection of encrypted services. Its adoption is expected in late 1997.
- Green Paper on the Implications of the Regulatory Framework for Telecommunications, Audio-Visual, and Publishing — This consultation document will examine the regulatory implications of the increasing convergence of the telecommunications, audio-visual and publishing industries and will make appropriate proposals. It was planned for the end of 1997.

20 COM (96) 471.
21 COM (96) 192.

- Communication on an Action Plan to Combat Illegal and Harmful Content on the Internet and Similar Networks[22] — A range of measures to carry out policy options adopted by the Commission in late 1996 will include addressing the question of liability for access or service providers.
- Directive concerning the Processing of Personal Data and Privacy in the Context of Digital Telecommunications[23] — Progress is being made on this Directive, which is expected to be adopted in 1997. It provides a specific set of safeguards, based on Directive 95/46/E.C. on the Protection of Individuals with regard to the Processing of Personal Data and on the Free Movement of Such Data,[24] but adapted to the telecommunications sector.

Co-ordinating the Measures of National Legislatures

2-5   In the field of Online services, the Commission predicts a surge of regulatory activity in the member states that will threaten to re-fragment the single market if it is not co-ordinated. It has therefore drafted a proposed Directive Amending for the Third Time Directive 83/189/E.E.C. Laying Down a Procedure for the Provision of Information in the Field of Technical Standards and Regulations.[25] It will provide for notification by member states of any proposed national rules on "Information Society Services" — defined as any service provided at a distance, by electronic means and on the individual request of a service receiver (*i.e.*, interactive services).

The purpose of the notification procedure will be for the Commission and other member states to examine proposed national regulations to ensure their consistency with other national measures in the single market. It will prevent isolated and uncoordinated national regulatory activity.

The Commission intends to use the well-tried procedure established by Directive 83/189/E.E.C. Laying Down a Procedure for the Provision of Information in the Field of Technical Standards and Regulations[26] which has ensured consistency in standards relating to manufactured goods. Several member states have expressed doubt about whether a procedure created for simple goods can be adapted to the realm of information services.

The draft-amending Directive, which provides only for an administrative co-operation procedure and not for any harmonisation of substantive rules, will amend Directive 83/189/E.E.C. by including information society services within its scope. "Service" is defined as "any service provided at a distance, by electronic means and on the individual request of a service receiver".[27]

---

22 COM (96) 487, O.J .C 1996/12, at p. 2.
23 Amended proposal COM (94) 128 final.
24 1996 O.J. L281/31.
25 1996 O.J.C307/11.
26 1983 O.J. L109/8.
27 Directive 83/189/E.E.C., article 1.

Member states will have to communicate to the Commission any draft technical regulation at a stage in its preparation at which substantial amendments can still be made.[28] The Commission will circulate the information among the member states. A three-month standstill period will enable the Commission and the other member states to examine the draft measures and make their reaction known. Four possible courses of events will follow:

- No comments from the member states and/or the Commission — the Member State concerned may adopt the draft rule upon the expiry of the three-month standstill period.
- Comments by the Commission or a member state on the possible consequences of the proposed measure were they to be adopted and applied to goods from other member states, and requests for amendment.[29] The member state concerned will be required to consider the comments as far as possible. Such comments often result in a mutual recognition clause.
- Detailed opinion issued by the Commission or a member state where they consider that, were it to be applied to goods from other member states, the measure would contravene the Community rules on the free movement of goods.[30] The issue of a detailed opinion will extend the standstill period to six months (or four months in the case of voluntary agreements) to allow for the matter to be re-examined.
- Declaration that the Commission is going to propose, or has proposed, Community measures in the area in question.[31] The announcement will extend the standstill period to 12 months, or to 18 months if the Council adopts, before the end of the period, a common position on the Community proposal.

In the proposed amending Directive[32] member states may be authorised to adopt a technical rule for urgent reasons, such as rules relating to public order, without having to observe the standstill period.[33]   **2-6**

The Commission Communication on the non-respect of certain provisions of the Council Directive 83/189/E.E.C.[34] states that unnotified technical rules will not have legal effect against third parties.

The anticipated date for the proposed amending Directive to become law in the member states is currently 31 December 1997. It will only apply in areas of regulatory activity which are not specifically covered by other E.C. Directives.

---

28 Directive 83/189/E.E.C., article 8(1).
29 Directive 83/189/E.E.C., article 8(2).
30 Directive 83/189/E.E.C., article 9(2).
31 Directive 83/189/E.E.C., article 9(3) and (4).
32 1996 O.J. C307/11.
33 Proposed amended Directive 83/189/E.E.C., article 9(7).
34 1986 O.J. C245/4.

SPECIFIC AREAS

Advertising

2-7 A Green Paper from the Commission entitled Commercial Communications in the Internal Market[35] was issued in May 1996. It consulted on the effect of differing national regulations on cross-border "commercial communications" (the term covers all forms of advertising, direct marketing, sponsorship, sales promotions, and public relations promoting products and services).

Included in the Green Paper is consideration of the implications of the new digital communication infrastructures. It observes that cross-border commercial communications are greatly facilitated by the speed of transmission and targeting made possible by the new technology. It also observes how commercial communication services can be integrated with distance retailing, allowing interactive distance shopping to take place practically instantaneously.

In relation to electronic communication, the Green Paper acknowledges that the existing regulatory approach is increasingly ineffective for consumers, and provides insufficient security for users. Unless regulatory measures are introduced, the full benefits to be derived from the information society will not materialise for businesses, consumers, and the European Union economy as a whole.

The Green Paper goes on to consider the differing regulatory measures of national legislatures, which it groups into three categories, and follows with suggested criteria by which national measures affecting the single market might be assessed. The European Commission also considers how it could ensure coherence with national legislation, and proportionality in its own proposals.

Consultation will be completed at the end of March 1997.

The proposed Directive amending 84/450/E.E.C. concerning Misleading Advertising so as to Include Comparative Advertising[36] is concerned to protect firms which may be exposed to forms of advertising developed by competitors to which they cannot reply in equal measure owing to differences in national laws. It defines the conditions under which comparative advertising will be permitted. However, the proposal allows member states to retain national provisions ensuring, for example, more extensive consumer protection and banning the advertising of certain goods and services.

The proposed amending Directive does not make specific mention of advertising by means of electronic digital interchange. When it is formally adopted, it must enter into force 30 months after its publication in the *Official Journal* at the latest.

---

35 COM (96) 192 final.
36 O.J. C1997/32/ E.E.C., at p. 9, and 1984 O.J. L250/17.

The proposed Directive on Television Broadcasting Activities,[37] amending Directive 89/552 of the same name,[38] has experienced an extended legislative battle.

It contains provisions on "teleshopping" which it defines as "direct offers broadcast to the public with a view to the supply of goods or services, including immovable property, rights and obligations, in return for payment".[39]

Teleshopping must be readily recognisable as such and kept separate from other parts of the programme service by optical and/or acoustic means.[40] It should not use subliminal techniques[41] nor be surreptitious.[42] The directive lays down rules on the insertion of teleshopping spots between programmes, or parts of programmes.[43]

The selling of tobacco products is prohibited.[44] So too are medicinal products that require marketing authorisation, and medicinal treatment.[45] Minors must not be exhorted to contract for the sale or rental of goods and services.[46]

The transmission time of teleshopping spots and advertising are defined as percentages of daily transmission time[47] and the maximum number of windows devoted to teleshopping broadcast by a channel not exclusively devoted to teleshopping, shall be a minimum uninterrupted duration of 15 minutes.[48] The maximum number of windows per day shall be eight. Their overall duration shall not exceed three hours per day.[49] Advertising on channels exclusively devoted to teleshopping is limited to 15 per cent of the daily transmission time.[50]

Banking and Financial Law

Commission Recommendation 88/590/E.E.C., concerning Payment Systems 2-8 and in Particular the Relationship between Cardholder and Card Issuer,[51] may be selected for updating when the Commission announces a general initiative on the legal aspects of electronic payment products such as prepaid cards. It offers a Code of Practice on the terms and conditions covering payment cards. The Recommendation includes provisions on: the consumer's

---

37 1995 O.J. C185/4 and 1996 O.J. C264/52.
38 1989 O.J. L298/23.
39 Proposed Directive on Television Broadcasting Activities, article 1 (f).
40 Proposed Directive on Television Broadcasting Activities, article 10.1.
41 Proposed Directive on Television Broadcasting Activities, article 10.3.
42 Proposed Directive on Television Broadcasting Activities, article 10.4.
43 Proposed Directive on Television Broadcasting Activities, article 11.
44 Proposed Directive on Television Broadcasting Activities, article 13.
45 Proposed Directive on Television Broadcasting Activities, article 14.2.
46 Proposed Directive on Television Broadcasting Activities, article 16.2.
47 Proposed Directive on Television Broadcasting Activities, article 18.
48 Proposed Directive on Television Broadcasting Activities, article 18a (1).
49 Proposed Directive on Television Broadcasting Activities, article 18a (2).
50 Proposed Directive on Television Broadcasting Activities, article 19.
51 1988 O.J. L317/55.

liability before notification of loss or misuse of a payment card; liability for failures to carry out a transaction; the burden of proof in a disputed transaction; the sending of unsolicited cards; and alteration of terms.

The Directive 91/308/E.E.C. on Prevention of the Use of the Financial System for the Purpose of Money Laundering[52] has implications for on-line banking. It requires evidence of identity when opening accounts and the monitoring of transactions to detect possible money laundering. The reporting of suspicious activities to the proper authorities is also mandatory. The directive has now been implemented in the member states.

The Directive 93/13/E.E.C. on unfair terms in Consumer Contracts,[53] which has been implemented in the member states, is applicable to bank contracts.

When it is implemented, Directive 95/46/E.C. on the Protection of Individuals with Regard to Processing of Personal Data and on the Free Movement of Such Data[54] will be relevant to electronic banking.

The Directive on Cross-border Credit Transfers[55] acknowledges the likelihood of on-line transactions. It includes the provision that information indicating the timing of the transfer, fees and charges, complaint procedures available and exchange rates used should be provided in writing, including where appropriate by electronic means.[56] A similar reference to electronic communication is contained in the provision that governs information to be supplied subsequent to the transfer.[57] The Directive must enter into force in the member states within 30 months after its formal adoption.

Conflict of Laws

2-9   The freedom to provide services enshrined in article 59 of the Treaty is explained in the Commission Interpretative Communication concerning the Free Movement of Services across Frontiers.[58] The Communication refers to the case law of the European Court of Justice, summarising and consolidating its judgments that prevent a member state from restricting the freedom to provide services originating in another member state. The law applicable to a service provider is the law of the member state in which it is established. A system of mutual recognition of Member States' regulatory provisions flows from this country of origin control system.

The Rome Convention contains rules about applicable law in relation to a contract for the supply of goods or services to a person for a purpose that is regarded as being outside his trade or profession ("consumer").[59] Irrespective

52 1991 O.J. L166/77.
53 1993 O.J. L95/29.
54 1996 O.J. L281/31.
55 1997/5/E.C.
56 Directive 1997/5/E.C., article 3.
57 Directive 1997/5/E.C., article 4.
58 1993 O.J. C334/3.
59 Rome Convention, article 5.

of the choice of applicable law, the consumer has the benefit of any mandatory terms under the national law of the consumer's country of residence[60] provided any one of three conditions are met:

- That in the country of the consumer's habitual residence, the conclusion of the contract was preceded by a specific invitation or by advertising and the consumer had taken all the steps necessary for concluding the contract in that country;
- That the seller or his agent received the order in the country where the consumer is habitually resident; and
- The third condition relates to border-crossing excursion selling and is not relevant to on-line transactions.

If the contract includes no provision as to the applicable law, the applicable law will be that of the country where the consumer is resident.[61]   **2-10**

At the time of writing, all E.U. member states except Austria, Finland and Sweden had ratified the *rome convention*.

Jurisdiction and Enforcement

The Brussels, San Sebastian and Lugano Conventions regulate jurisdiction and enforcement of judgments in the member states of the E.U. and of the European Free Trade Area. The conventions are nearly identical. They cover "civil and commercial matters", but not matters of legal capacity, status, matrimonial property rights, wills, succession, bankruptcy, insolvency, etc., social security and arbitration.[62] They establish the defendant's domicile as the general jurisdictional basis[63] and exclude the application of certain extraordinary bases in national law against domiciliaries of other State parties to the conventions.[64]   **2-11**

They provide several special jurisdictional bases that allow a defendant to be sued outside the State of its domicile.[65] Special provisions deal with jurisdiction for matters involving consumer contracts,[66] with exclusive jurisdiction involving matters of real property rights, the existence of companies, entries in public registers, intellectual property and the enforcement of judgments,[67] and with choice of jurisdiction.[68]

---

60 Rome Convention, article 5(2).
61 Rome Convention, article 4.
62 Brussels, San Sebastian and Lugano Conventions, article 1; see also *Bavaria Fluggesellschaft Schwabe & Co. KG & Another.* v. *Eurocontrol* [1977] E.C.R. 1517, *LTU Lufttransportunternehmen GmbH & Co KG* v. *Eurocontrol* [1976] E.C.R. 1541.
63 Brussels, San Sebastian and Lugano Conventions, article 2.
64 Brussels, San Sebastian and Lugano Conventions, article 3 in conjunction with article 2 second sentence, and article 4.
65 Brussels Convention, articles 5–12a.
66 Brussels Convention, articles 13–15.
67 Brussels Convention, article 16.
68 Brussels Convention, article 17.

The conventions' regulation of the enforcement of judgments establishes a uniform framework for the obligatory recognition of judgments emanating from a state party by the courts of the other state parties.[69] They specify, *inter alia*, the exceptions to obligatory recognition,[70] the appropriate courts for recognition and enforcement, and for appeal against such decisions.

The conventions' provisions on consumer contracts may have the greatest impact on Internet commerce. A party concluding a contract for a purpose that may be deemed outside that person's trade or profession is a consumer. A consumer may elect to sue the other contracting party either before the courts of the latter's domicile or those of the consumer's domicile if the contract involves the sale of goods on credit or the supply of goods or services where the supplier advertised in the state of the consumer's domicile and the consumer concluded the contract there. Where the other party maintains a branch or agency in a state, a consumer may treat that party as domiciled there. On-line transaction will frequently be caught in the consumer contract net and persons offering goods on the Internet should be aware of this.

Consumer Law and Sale of Goods

European Union

2-12   The Commission Green Paper, Commercial Communications in the Internal Market,[71] invites comment on the effect of different national regulatory regimes on advertising, sponsorship, direct marketing, sales promotions and public relations in the internal market. It draws attention to the advent of the information society on the role of commercial communications, concluding that it needs to take action to ensure coherence in this field. The consultation period ended on October 30, 1996.

Commission Recommendation 92/295/E.E.C.[72] on the establishment of codes of practice for the protection of consumers in respect of contracts negotiated at a distance recommends that trade associations of suppliers should adopt codes of practice concerning sales methods, information provision, reimbursement of payments, and the consumer's right of withdrawal from a contract. This Recommendation was adopted shortly after the Commission presented its first draft of the proposed Directive for the protection of consumers in respect of distance contracts.[73]

The Directive for the protection of consumers in respect of distance contracts[74] specifically responds to the new information technologies enabling

---

69 Brussels Convention, articles 26 *et seq*.
70 Brussels Convention, articles 27 and 28.
71 COM (96) 192 final.
72 1992 O.J. L156/21.
73 Amended proposal, COM (96) 36 final.
74 Amended proposal, COM (96) 36 final.

consumers to place orders electronically. The proposal covers transactions for products and services that involve no face-to-face contact, for example e-mail, videophone, videotext, teleshopping, mail order, telesales, and fax sales.

In view of the consumer's inability to actually see the product or experience the service provided before concluding a contract, the Directive gives the consumer a right to withdraw during a cooling-off period of seven working days from the date of the contract. There are further provisions prohibiting the charging of supplementary costs in case of withdrawal, and concerning reimbursement where advance payment has been made. Certain exceptions to the right to withdraw include the sale of tourist services and of books.

Confirmation of information provided to the consumer will have to be supplied in a "durable" medium. This term is employed by the directive in order to eliminate the ambiguity between "written" and "paper medium". If confirmation can be stored on a computer hard disk, this may satisfy the requirement.

Financial services are excluded from the effect of the above proposed directive but the Commission Green Paper, Financial Services: Meeting Consumers' Expectations[75] was concerned with creating a regulatory framework to encourage the cross-border purchase of financial services by the private consumer. It included requests for comment on the question of whether new technologies and new marketing techniques call for additional consumer protection. The consultation period ended on October 15, 1996. In February 1997, the Commission announced that it would soon be presenting a proposal for a Directive on distance sales of financial services based on the provisions of the Directive for the Protection of Consumers in Respect of Distance Contracts, but taking account of the specific nature of financial services.

The Directive 93/13/E.E.C. on Unfair Terms in Consumer Contracts[76] was intended to be implemented into member states' laws by 31 December 1994. The directive covers contracts made between businesses and consumers, but not those that are purely between businesses. It is concerned to safeguard consumers' essential rights and to eliminate disparities between member states' laws. It defines the "consumer" as a natural person who is acting for purposes that are outside his business.[77]

Under the Directive, a contractual term that has not been individually negotiated is unfair if, contrary to the requirement of good faith, it causes a significant imbalance in the rights and obligations of the parties, to the detriment of the consumer.[78] The annex to the Directive contains an indicative and non-exhaustive list of the terms that may be regarded as unfair.

75 COM 96/209 final.
76 1995 O.J. L95/29.
77 Directive 93/13/E.E.C., article 2.
78 Directive 93/13/E.E.C., article 3.

A term will always be regarded as not individually negotiated where it has been drafted in advance and the consumer has not been able to influence the substance of the term, particularly in the context of a pre-formulated contract.[79] If one specific term, or part of a term, has been individually negotiated and an assessment of the rest of the contract indicates that overall it is nevertheless a pre-formulated standard contract, the Directive still applies to the pre-formulated part of the contract.[80] The burden of proof that a term has been individually negotiated rests on the business party to the contract.[81]

In assessing good faith, the Directive states that particular regard shall be had to the strength of the bargaining positions of the parties, whether the consumer had an inducement to agree the term, and whether the goods or services were sold or supplied to the special order of the consumer.[82]

Questions as to the quality of the main subject matter of the contract and its price cannot be included in an assessment of unfair terms, although the quality and price may be taken into account where they have a bearing on the fairness, or otherwise, of other terms in the contract.[83]

If certain terms are found unfair, the contract may continue to bind the parties if it is capable of continuing in existence without the unfair terms.[84]

Written contracts must be drafted in plain, intelligible language and the consumer must be given the opportunity to examine all the terms. Where there is doubt about the meaning of a term, the interpretation most favourable to the consumer is to be applied.[85]

If the contract has a close connection with the territory of a member state, choice of law of a non-member country must not be used so as to deprive the consumer of the protection of the Directive.[86]

International

2-13   The Vienna International Sale of Goods Convention of 1980 applies to contracts for the sale of goods between parties whose places of business are in different states that are both contracting states[87] or their places of business are in different states — of which at least one is not a contracting state, but the forum's private international law rules indicate the law of a contracting state.[88] Some contracting states have excluded this second avenue of the

---

79 Directive 93/13/E.E.C., article 3.
80 Directive 93/13/E.E.C., article 3(2).
81 Directive 93/13/E.E.C., article 3(2).
82 Directive 93/13/E.E.C., recital 16.
83 Directive 93/13/E.E.C., article 4(2).
84 Directive 93/13/E.E.C., article 6(1).
85 Directive 93/13/E.E.C., article 5.
86 Directive 93/13/E.E.C., article 6(2).
87 Vienna International Sale of Goods Convention, article 1 (1) (a).
88 Vienna International Sale of Goods Convention, article 1 (1) (b).

Vienna Convention's application by reservation.[89] On-line transactions could frequently fall under the Vienna Convention's regime although it applies only to transactions between merchants and not to those with consumers. Article 11 of the Vienna Convention provides that no written form is required, but article 12 in connection with article 96 allows each contracting State to make a reservation as to requiring a particular form for the formation of a sales Contract.[90] Where such reservations apply, it may be unclear whether an on-line communication's fulfilment of the "writing" requirement would be assessed according to the law of the forum, the law of the reserving State, or "autonomously" under the Vienna Convention.

In most cases, merchants will wish to record their transactions by some means. Electronic records will probably raise similar questions and answers as telexes. It is likely that the many merchant sales conducted on-line will be EDI transactions and fall under that regime.

Contracts

The European Commission recommends that operators and organisations con-   **2-14**
ducting their trading activities via EDI use the European Model EDI Agreement, which forms annex 1 to Commission Recommendation 94/820/E.C.[91] Commentary is provided by annex 2 to the Recommendation.

The model agreement contains legal provisions that may be modified by the parties, according to national law. It should be supplemented by a technical annex, drawn up by the parties, defining technical specifications, and time limits to meet their specific needs. The agreement should be signed in writing. The provisions of the model agreement cover:

- Validity and formation of the contract;[92]
- Admissibility in evidence of EDI messages;[93]
- Processing and acknowledgement of receipt of EDI messages;[94]
- Security of EDI messages;[95]
- Confidentiality and protection of personal data;[96]

---

89 For example, the United States. The German declaration points out an interesting anomaly in this context where the forum's private international law indicates the law of a contracting state that has excluded appliction of article 1 (1) (b).
90 For example, Argentina, Belarus, Chile, China, Estonia, Hungary, Lithuania, Russia, Ukraine.
91 1994 O.J. L338/98.
92 European Model EDI Agreement, article 3.
93 European Model EDI Agreement, article 4.
94 European Model EDI Agreement, article 5.
95 European Model EDI Agreement, article 6.
96 European Model EDI Agreement, article 7.

- Recording and storage of EDI messages;[97]
- Operational requirements for EDI;[98]
- Liability;[99]
- Dispute resolution;[100]
- Applicable law;[101] and
- Effect, modifications and severability.[102]

2-15   Note that alternative provisions are provided for dispute resolution.[103]

Data Protection and Privacy

European Union

2-16   Directive 95/46/E.C. on the protection of individuals with regard to the processing of personal data and on the free movement of such data[104] is currently awaiting implementation in the member states; the deadline is November 1998. The Directive obliges member states to protect the rights and freedoms of natural persons, and in particular their right to privacy.[105] The effect of the Directive extends to all processing of personal data by any person whose activities are governed by E.C. law.[106]

"Personal data" is defined as "any information relating to an identified or identifiable individual".[107] Data in the form of sound and images are included.[108]

The definition of "controller" allows both individuals and organisations to be controllers under article 2(d). When messages are sent by telecommunications or electronic mail, the controller will normally be considered to be the person from whom the message originates, rather than the person offering the transmission services.[109]

The law of the member state in which the controller is established will be the law applicable to the data processing.[110] The meaning of "established" is explained as being the territory where "the effective and real exercise of activity through stable arrangements" takes place. The legal form of such an establishment is not the determining factor. Where a single controller is

---

97 European Model EDI Agreement, article 8.
98 European Model EDI Agreement, article 9.
99 European Model EDI Agreement, article 11.
100 European Model EDI Agreement, article 12.
101 European Model EDI Agreement, article 13.
102 European Model EDI Agreement, article 14.
103 European Model EDI Agreement, article 12.
104 1996 O.J. L281/31.
105 Directive 95/46/E.C., article 1.
106 Directive 95/46/E.C., article 3.
107 Directive 95/46/E.C., article 2(a).
108 Directive 95/46/E.C., recital 14.
109 Directive 95/46/E.C., recital 47.
110 Directive 95/46/E.C., article 4.

established in several member states, he must ensure that each of the establishments fulfils the obligations imposed by the national law applicable to its activities.[111]

Although processing in one member state may be subject to the national laws of another member state, the supervisory authority in the member state where the processing of data takes place may take appropriate enforcement measures.[112]

When processing of data is carried out by a person established in a non-member state, it is governed by the national law of the member state in which the equipment used for processing is located (*e.g.*, a computer).[113]

Six criteria justify processing. At least one of them must be satisfied. The first criterion is that the data subject has unambiguously given his or her consent.[114] Consent is required to be "freely given, specific and informed",[115] although later in the Directive "explicit consent" is referred to in relation to the processing of sensitive data as defined in article 8.1.

A very high proportion of processing operations will fall within the other five criteria which justify processing, thus avoiding the need for consent. They are processing:

- Which relates to contracts;[116]
- Where there is a legal obligation on the controller;[117]
- Which is necessary to protect the vital interests of the data subject;[118]
- Which is necessary for a task carried out "in the public interest or in the exercise of official authority";[119]
- Which is necessary for the legitimate interests of the controller.[120]

However, this must be balanced against the fundamental rights and freedoms of the data subject. Member states may determine the circumstances in which personal data may be used or disclosed to third parties for legitimate, ordinary business activities or for the purposes of marketing.[121]   **2-17**

Article 7 (e) and (f) are subject to the provision in article 14 (a) allowing the data subject to object on compelling legitimate grounds to the processing of data, and for that data to be excluded from processing where the objection is justified.[122]

---

111 Directive 95/46/E.C., recital 19.
112 Directive 95/46/E.C., article 28.6.
113 Directive 95/46/E.C., recital 20.
114 Directive 95/46/E.C., article 7(a).
115 Directive 95/46/E.C., article 2(h).
116 Directive 95/46/E.C., article 7(b).
117 Directive 95/46/E.C., article 7 (c).
118 Directive 95/46/E.C., article 7(d). see also recital 31.
119 Directive 95/46/E.C., article 7(e).
120 Directive 95/46/E.C., article 7(c).
121 Directive 95/46/E.C., recital 30.
122 Directive 95/46/E.C., article 14 (a).

The Directive requires certain information to be given to the data subject either where they are collected directly from the data subject[123] or from some other source.[124] In all cases, the information must reveal the identity of the controller (and any representative), and the purposes of the processing. Both articles 10 and 11 require certain other information to be provided, but only where necessary to guarantee fair processing.

The data subject has a right of access to the data about him or her.[125] Furthermore, the data subject must be able to learn from the controller whether the personal data are being processed, and to gain information about the purposes of the processing, the categories of data concerned, the recipients of the data and available information about the source of the data as well as a knowledge of the logic involved in automatic processing.[126] The right to be informed about logic "must not adversely affect trade secrets or intellectual property and in particular the copyright protecting software" providing that data subjects are not deprived of all information.[127] The data subject's rights extend to the rectification, erasure or blocking of data which does not comply with the Directive,[128] including a right to notification of such actions to third parties to whom the data have been disclosed.[129]

Under the Directive, member states are permitted to make exemptions[130] to certain provisions, including the data protection principles,[131] the requirement to provide information to data subjects,[132] and the data subject access provisions.[133]

Provisions on confidentiality and security of processing are included in the Directive.[134] In addition, there are particular rules concerning the processing of data revealing racial or ethnic origin, political opinions, religious or philosophical beliefs, trade-union membership, and data concerning health or sex life.[135] Member states are permitted to provide exemptions from certain provisions of the Directive to allow for freedom of expression for journalistic purposes or artistic or literary expression but such provisions must be reconciled with the data subjects' right to privacy.[136]

Member states have a choice of how to legislate for a data subject to object to data processing for direct marketing purposes. They may either provide a

---

123 Directive 95/46/E.C., article 10.
124 Directive 95/46/E.C., article 11.
125 Directive 95/46/E.C., article 12.
126 Directive 95/46/E.C., article 12(a).
127 Directive 95/46/E.C., recital 41.
128 Directive 95/46/E.C., article 12 (c).
129 Directive 95/46/E.C., article 12(c).
130 Directive 95/46/E.C., article 13.1.
131 Directive 95/46/E.C., article 6.1.
132 Directive 95/46/E.C., articles 10 and 11.1.
133 Directive 95/46/E.C., article 12.
134 Directive 95/46/E.C., articles 16 and 17.
135 Directive 95/46/E.C., article 8.
136 Directive 95/46/E.C., article 9.

right for a data subject to ask the controller not to process their data for these purposes, or the right to be informed, and to be offered the right to object in two sets of circumstances: (a) before the personal data is disclosed for the first time to third parties for direct marketing purposes; and (b) before the personal data are used on behalf of third parties for marketing purposes.[137]

Controllers must notify the national supervisory authority before they process personal data when processing is an automatic operation.[138] However, member states may specify exemptions to, or simplify, the registration rules where categories of processing operation "are unlikely, taking account of the data to be processed, to affect adversely the rights and freedoms of data subjects". Additionally, national provisions allowing the appointment of in-house personal data protection officials, acting independently, would also allow member states to simplify or exempt data processing operations from notification to a supervisory authority.[139]

No restrictions are to be placed on data flows across borders within the E.C., but trans-border flows to third countries may only take place if those countries provide adequate protection for personal data.[140]

The proposed Directive on the Protection of Personal Data and Privacy in the Context of Digital Telecommunications Networks[141] (proposed privacy Directive) is to be applied in conjunction with Directive 95/46/E.C. The proposed directive describes the successful cross-border development of services delivered by the new digital technologies, such as video-on-demand and interactive television, as partly dependent on the confidence of users that their privacy will not be at risk.[142] Protecting the fundamental rights of individuals and legal persons in the automated storage and processing of data relating to subscribers and users is another concern.[143] The proposed Directive contains provisions on:

- security of services and networks;
- confidentiality of communications;
- erasure of personal data when retention is unnecessary;
- itemised billing;
- calling line identification;
- call forwarding;
- personal data to be included in directories; and
- unsolicited marketing calls.

Once adopted, the Directive must be implemented in the member states by October 24, 1998.

---

137 Directive 95/46/E.C., article 14 (b).
138 Directive 95/46/E.C., article 18.1.
139 Directive 95/46/E.C., article 18.2.
140 Directive 95/46/E.C., article 25.
141 O.J. 1996 C315/30.
142 Proposed Privacy Directive, recital 2.
143 Proposed Privacy Directive, recital 6.

In the telecommunications sector, the provisions of Directive 95/46/E.C. cover data protection matters that are not specifically covered by the amended proposal.[144]

International

2-18   The Council of Europe has produced a model contract to ensure equivalent data protection in the context of trans-border flow.[145]

Intellectual Property

European Union

2-19   Several Directives, although not exclusively concerned with on-line services, will play a key role in protecting the intellectual property rights linked to works (*e.g.*, performances, books, films) transmitted via on-line services. The following have already been implemented into the national laws of the member states:

- Directive 91/250/E.E.C. on the Legal Protection of Computer Programmes,[146] which grants computer programs the same protection as literary works;
- Directive 92/100/E.E.C. on Rental Right and on Lending Right and on Certain Rights related to Copyright in the Field of Intellectual Property;[147]
- Directive 93/83/E.E.C. on the co-ordination of certain rules concerning Copyright and Rights Related to Copyright Applicable to Satellite Broadcasting and Cable Retransmission,[148] which clarifies from whom satellite broadcasters and cable operators must obtain permission in order to transmit programmes within the Community; and
- Directive 93/98/E.E.C. Harmonising the Term of Copyright and Certain Related Rights,[149] which defines the period of protection for works and performances.

2-20   Directive 96/9/E.C. on the Legal Protection of Databases[150] is due to be implemented into member states' national laws by 1 January 1998. It will provide two kinds of protection for databases:

- Copyright protection for the database as a whole (*i.e.*, the compilation itself) provided it required creativity in its selection or arrangement; and

---

144 Proposed Privacy Directive, recital 9.
145 14 September 1992, T-PD (92) 7.
146 1991 O.J. L122/42.
147 1992 O.J. L346/61.
148 1993 O.J. L248/15.
149 1993 O.J. L290/9.
150 1996 O.J. L77/20.

- A new *sui generis* right providing protection for the contents of the database from unauthorised extraction and/or re-use of the database contents.

In 1995, the Commission carried out a consultation exercise based on their   2-21
Green Paper, *Copyright and Related Rights in the Information Society*.[151] By contrast to the wide area covered by the directives listed above, this initiative was wholly concerned with on-line services. The Green Paper surveys the technological, economic and legal framework for the information society and then directs questions to interested parties followed by an examination of the following specific rights: reproduction right; "communication to the public"; digital dissemination or transmission right; digital broadcasting right; and moral rights. On the question of the exploitation of rights, the Green Paper has two sections:

- acquisition and management of rights; and
- technical systems of identification and protection.

The consultation exercise ended on October 31, 1995, and the Commission   2-22
is currently analysing the submissions.

The Community Trade Mark System came into force on 1 April 1996 with the implementation of Directive 89/109 on Trade Mark Harmonisation[152] accompanied by Regulation 40/94 on the Community Trade Mark.[153] The Community Trade Mark Office (formally known as the Office for Harmonisation of the Internal Market) administers it in Alicante, Spain.

The Community Trade Mark registration system enables trademark owners to submit a single application for registration covering all countries of the E.U.. Any identifier that can be represented in graphical form can be registered. This includes letters and numeral combinations, logo trade marks and business names, designs, and colour arrangements.

A domain name can be registered as a Community Trade Mark, even if not being used as a trade mark on goods or services. However, it would be in a weaker position to withstand a challenge.

On July 26, 1996, the European Commission presented to the Council two proposals to link the Community Trade Mark System with the international trade mark registration system of the World Intellectual Property Organisation (W.I.P.O.): the proposed Decision Approving the Accession of the E.C. to the Protocol relating to the Madrid Agreement concerning the International Registration of Marks;[154] and a second proposal which contains provisions to amend Council Regulation 40/94 on the Community Trade Mark in order to give effect to the accession.

151 COM (95) 382 final.
152 1989 O.J. L40/1.
153 1994 O.J. L11/1.
154 1996 O.J. C293/11.

International

2-23   The Agreement on Trade-Related Aspects of Intellectual Property Rights (TRIPs) was one section of the Final Act of the Uruguay Round (G.A.T.T. 1994). Covering all World Trade Organisation members, TRIPs embrace a wider number of states than many other intellectual property conventions. Fundamentally, TRIPs seeks assure national standard and most-favoured-nation treatment with respect to intellectual property. While referring to existing conventions (*e.g.,* the Paris and Berne Conventions) for some of its substantive provisions it also extended protection, for example, by making clear that computer programs would be covered as literary works. It also states that data compilations that constitute "intellectual creations" will be protected. Significantly, TRIPs is the first international agreement dealing with undisclosed information such as trade secrets and know-how. Its article 39 protects secret information of commercial value where reasonable steps to maintain secrecy have been taken. It is protected from disclosure by way of breach of contract, breach of confidence, and inducement to breach. Article 39 would make parties liable that were negligent in not knowing that such practices were involved in the acquisition of information. Most European states' laws already meet or surpass the TRIPs standards.

The Berne Convention for the Protection of Literary and Artistic Works and the Universal Copyright Convention 1952 both aim to enable each signatory State to respect the claims of nationales of each other signatory state arising within the former State's territory. Both published and unpublished works of nationals of the "Union" created by the Berne Convention are protected in that Union. The works of persons not nationals of Union states are protected if first (or simultaneously) published in a Union state.[155] This protection is that enjoyed by nationals of the respective Union states in their home states and those specifically granted by the Convention.[156] The new Protocol extends coverage to computer programs, databases, and introduces a new exclusive rental right that is compulsory for computer programs, data collections, other machine-readable materials and phonogram-borne musical works.

The Universal Copyright Convention 1952 attempts to achieve some degree of protection between the Berne Union States and those signatory the Pan American Convention that have not signed the Berne Convention. The more restrictive protection that it affords, based on the distinction between published and unpublished works, indicates that the concerns of the United States, with its copyright registration system, had to be accommodated.

The Madrid Agreement 1891 sought to create an international registration system for trade marks. Registrations in all party states could be obtained by a single filing. It sets out rules for the scope of protection, examination by the International Bureau, refusal of protection, effect of registrations,

---

155 Berne Convention, article 3 (1).
156 Berne Convention, article 5 (1).

duration of protection, central attacks on registrations and changes to registrations. The non-adherence of countries such as the United States, the United Kingdom and Japan led to the adoption of the Madrid Protocol, which is open to any party to the Paris Convention. Unlike the Agreement, the Protocol does not require registration in the country of origin; application for registration suffices. Where long pre-registration examination and opposition procedures are possible, this difference can be significant. Protocol applications can also be made in English and registrations may become less vulnerable to central attack. The accession of the E.U. to the Protocol coupled with the Community trade mark will provide persons developing and using trade marks several options.

Security

European Union

The European Commission has published a Green Paper on the Legal   2-24
Protection of Encrypted Services in the Internal Market.[157] It examines problems raised both by the absence of specific legislation on encrypted services in some member states and regulatory differences in others. In the Commission's view, establishing an equivalent level of protection amongst all member states could prove necessary for the proper working of the single market.

The document raises questions on: whether harmonisation is desirable; the form of any harmonisation instrument (i.e., whether a Directive or a Regulation); and its content — in particular the scope of any proposal, whether to include the possession by private individuals of unauthorised decoding devices, and claims for damages. The consultation period ended May 31, 1996.

International

The Council of Europe has adopted a Recommendation on the Legal   2-25
Protection of Encrypted Television Services.[158] It sets out a range of unlawful activities concerning the manufacture, importation, distribution, promotion, and possession of decoding equipment. The Recommendation urges member states to provide for criminal or administrative sanctions and civil remedies but does not provide for rights of action by intellectual property rights holders.

The Council's view is that, if illicit access occurs, the damage is indirect and rights holders can require the broadcaster to take legal action. The Recommendation has provided the basis of regulation in those member

---

157 COM (96) 76 final.
158 Recommendation (95) 1) in 1991. It was amended in 1995 by a Recommendation on Measures against Sound and Audiovisual Piracy (Recommendation (95) 1).

states where it has been transposed into national laws. However, there are many regulatory variations between member states.

Taxation

2-26   The problems for national administrations in the taxation of cross-border Online transactions include defining where the transaction took place, which party is responsible for payment of the tax, and jurisdictional questions. When agents are involved, the complexity may be compounded. Where value-added tax is concerned, the international element of value-added tax may arise from a cross-border transaction within the E.U., or from a transaction involving jurisdictions outside the E.U..

European Union

2-27   In March 1997, the European Commission started to examine pre-legislative proposals put forward by a group of experts for taxing transactions made over the Internet. The proposals favour an electronic transmission tax levied by on-line access providers on the basis of the amount of digital data down-loaded.

Apart from this pre-legislative activity specific to the Internet, the taxation of Online transactions is not yet treated separately from the taxation of more traditional forms of transaction and it is therefore necessary to construe existing legislation as being applicable where appropriate.

The Sixth Value-Added Tax Directive 77/388[159] is the basis of E.C. legislation on value-added tax. Although it has been extensively amended since its original adoption, it requires further adaptation to deal with Online transactions. The rate of value-added tax varies from one Member State to another. It is intended that value-added tax will eventually be harmonised throughout the European Union. The Sixth Value-Added Tax Directive applies differing criteria to define the "place of taxable transactions" for goods and services.

Supply of Goods

2-28   The place of supply is the place where the goods are located at the time when dispatch or transport to the person to whom they are supplied begins.[160] Distance selling rules will apply to on-line transactions provided that other criteria for distance selling are met. Therefore, when a supplier in one member state supplies goods to a non-value-added tax registered customer in another member state, and is responsible for their delivery, the place of supply will be the supplier's member state.

---

159 1977 O.J. L145/1.
160 Directive 77/388, article 8.

Each member state may opt to apply a distance selling threshold of either 35,000 ECU (approximately £24,000) or 100,000 ECU (approximately £70,000) per calendar year. As soon as the value of sales to the customer's member state exceeds the relevant distance selling threshold, the supplier will be obliged to register for value-added tax in that member state which will become the place of supply. As such, the value-added tax treatment of goods supplied to individuals through on-line transactions does not differ substantially from such treatment in cases where more traditional arrangements for transactions are used.

Supply of Services

The basic rule of supply is contained in article 9.1 of the Sixth Value-Added   2-29
Tax directive. Under the rule, the place where a service is supplied is defined as the supplier's place of business or fixed establishment, or his permanent address or where he usually resides. Where a supplier has a business or other fixed establishment in more than one country, the supplier is regarded as occurring in the country in which the establishment most directly concerned with each individual supply of services is situated. The carrying on of a business through a branch or agency creates a business establishment in the country where the branch or agency is situated.[161] In reality, it may be impossible to trace the physical location of a company or person offering services via electronic means. Article 9.2 of the Sixth Value-Added Tax Directive provides a number of variations to the basic rule of supply. The variations were drafted before the advent of on-line transactions was foreseeable, but it is possible for it[162] to be applied to some categories of supplies of services via on-line systems.

For example, consultancy services (including the provision of bespoke software), data processing, the provision of information, transfer and assignment of copyright, licences and similar rights. Services that fall within the provisions of article 9.2 are treated as supplied in the member state where the recipient is located. Likewise, where the recipient is outside the European Union, the services are treated as supplied in the State to which the recipient is attributed. The precise nature of the supply of services in question is critical to determining whether they fall under the basic place of supply rule contained in article 9.1, or within the variations allowed for in article 9.2. Exports of goods from one member state to business users in another member state are exempted from value-added tax in the country of export[163] but become liable in the country of import.[164] Exports from the E.U. to countries outside the E.U. are exempted from value-added tax.[165]

161 Directive 77/388, article 9.1.
162 Directive 77/388, article 9.2.
163 Directive 77/388, article 28C.
164 Directive 77/388, article 28D.
165 Directive 77/388, article 15.

Direct Taxes

International

2-30   Taxing the income derived from Online transactions again raises jurisdictional questions — specifically, the location of the provider of goods or services. The Organisation for Economic Co-operation and Development (O.E.C.D.) Model Treaty is accompanied by commentary on the "fixed place of business" which is linked to a permanent physical presence of persons or equipment. The O.E.C.D. also stated in its 1992 Report on Software that under most circumstances payments for software should be treated as sales of products. If the purchaser will use the software personally, the licence — even if there are restrictions on the software's use — should be considered a sale. Where the payments permit the user to exploit the software commercially, they should be classified as royalties. How national tax authorities follow these recommendations will impact on the tax treatment of software acquired over the Internet. The revision of double tax treaties may be necessitated by the commercial changes that on-line trading will create.

Customs

2-31   The European Union Common Customs Tariff governs the rate of customs duties on all imports to the European Union. Customs duties are leviable on goods but not services. The duties are collected at the point of entry into the E.U.. Problems may arise where it would be arguable that a service constituted goods, for example, the provision of software via a computer network.

Telecommunications

2-32   The measures described below are those that have relevance to on-line transactions although often within the context of a wider purpose. The proposed Decision on a Series of Guidelines for Trans-European Telecommunications Networks[166] includes the objective of creating an electronic tendering network for public procurement between public administrations and suppliers in Europe.

When adopted, the Decision will be binding upon the member states. The proposed Directive on the Protection of Personal Data and Privacy in the Context of Digital Telecommunications Networks[167] is described in the Data Protection and Privacy section, above.

---

166   1996 O.J. C175/4.
167   Amended proposal COM (94) 128 final.

CHAPTER 3

Australia

Ilya Fisher, Tristan Forrester, Mark Krenzer, Dayan Quinn
Kelvin Ng, Greg Noonan
Freehill Hollingdale & Page
Melbourne, Australia

INTRODUCTION

One of the most oft quoted benefits of the Common Law is its supposed   3-1
flexibility in the face of changing circumstances, allowing for change which
is evolutionary, rather than revolutionary.

Recent developments in information technology certainly appear, however, to have a revolutionary quality. The rapid expansion in access to and
the use of the Internet for all kinds of activities, including business, is only
one indicator. Governments across Australia and the world are realising the
possible benefits of electronic communications for both internal efficiencies
and service delivery to their citizens. The Federal Department of Administrative Services recently contracted Telstra Corporation Limited, Australia's
largest telecommunications carrier, to develop the Commonwealth Electronic Commerce System (C.E.C.S.). Through this facility, government agencies
will be able to the advertise tendering opportunities, communicate with
suppliers and provide information on doing business with government.
Telstra is developing C.E.C.S. as part of a wider system, however, to be called
Transigo, which will also allow private sector businesses to carry out secure
transactions with other businesses and consumers.[1]

To date, however, the volume of on-line sales in Australia is disappoint-
ingly low. As in any commercial system, confidence and certainty are essential
to growth. Consumers must have the confidence of effective consumer
protection and privacy laws before they will be enticed to participate in
electronic commerce. Vendors require secure and enforceable transactions, and
a certain regime for the conclusion of electronic contracts, and associated
services such as on-line banking. In turn, service providers and similar

---

1 Transigo was due to be launched in mid-1997. Access and information is available through
  the Transigo web site at http://www.transigo.com.au/.

facilitators of electronic commerce need to know the scope of their liability for the actions of users under defamation, censorship, and copyright laws. It remains to be seen, however, whether in Australia the legal regime relevant to electronic commerce will adapt quickly enough to allow on-line commerce to flourish.

Achieving Information Security

3-2 Fundamental to a system of electronic commerce is user confidence. System security is essential to ensure confidentiality of electronic messages, particularly where the message contains commercially sensitive or personal information. For example, a consumer applying for life insurance over the Internet may be required to provide a comprehensive medical history.

The provision of information by consumers to vendors is not new to electronic commerce; however, there is a risk that information sent electronically, for example, over the Internet, will be read by parties other than the recipient. Confidentiality of messages can be achieved on a number of levels.

Privacy Protection

3-3 At present, information related to consumer transactions is not protected by Australia's main privacy legislation, the Privacy Act 1988. The Privacy Act 1988 is confined to government departments, credit-reporting agencies and credit providers. In September 1996, the Federal Attorney-General's Department released for public comment a discussion paper that outlined a scheme for private sector privacy protection.

The Internet Industry Association of Australia has also prepared a draft Internet Industry Code of Practice that contains provisions limiting collection, use, and disclosure of personal data by Internet industry participants. The Code is not regarded as enforceable by any law.

Public Key Cryptography

3-4 Cryptographic techniques are likely to play an important role in electronic commerce. Generally, cryptographic techniques rely on an algorithm and a key. The key is a piece of data that is used in conjunction with the algorithm to encrypt and decrypt data. If a person does not know the key, then they are prevented from deciphering an intercepted message.

Public key cryptography provides for the creation of a pair of keys, consisting of a public key and a private key. If, say, a buyer wishes to communicate with a seller, the buyer can obtain the seller's public key either from a register of public keys or from the seller itself, and use it to encrypt the communication. Only the seller will be able to decipher the message, because only the seller will have the corresponding private key. Encryption is therefore an important technique in ensuring that the intended recipient only reads information exchanged in the course of commercial activity.

Obligations of Confidentiality

The courts in Australia have adopted a flexible approach to the type of 3-5
information that can be protected by an action for breach of confidence. The
types of information that have been protected include "personal" information as well as know-how or trade secrets.

Fullagar J., in *Deta Nominees Pty Ltd.* v. *Viscount Plastic Products Pty
Ltd.*,[2] stated that cases dealing with breach of confidence fall into two
classes: the first is where the obligation of confidence arises in a contractual
context, and the second is where equity intervenes to prevent misuse or
disclosure of information. It is possible therefore that a party to an electronic
communication may have an action for breach of confidence available to it
in circumstances where confidential information is disclosed by the other
party, and perhaps also where the other party has permitted unauthorised
access to the information.

Legal Effect of Electronic Signatures

The traditional function performed by a hand-written signature is to identify 3-6
a person, provide certainty as to the personal involvement of that person in
the act of signing and to associate the person with the content of the
document. A handwritten signature might also operate to evidence the intent
of a person to be bound by the contents of the document. In relation to
electronic communications, the original of a message is indistinguishable
from a copy, there is no handwritten signature and, of course, the message
is not in printed form.

To reduce the scope for fraud, an electronic signature can perform the
functions of a handwritten signature. At its simplest, an electronic signature
can simply be a digitised signature, or a computerised image of a written
signature, which may be appended to a word-processing document as an
image of the original written signature. Digital signatures based on public
key cryptography are gaining greater exposure for confidentiality purposes.
Standards Australia has defined a digital signature as:

> "a technique or procedure which creates a unique and unforgeable (*sic*)
> identifier of the owner of the distinguished name. This may in turn be
> checked by the receiver to verify authenticity and integrity and provide
> non-repudiation."[3]

In simplified form, the digital signature is generated using the author's 3-7
private key. The recipient of the message can use the author's public key to
decrypt the signature and hence verify the originator of the message and

---

2 [1979] V.R., 167.
3 Standards Australia, *Strategies for the Implementation of a Public Key Authentication
Framework (PKAF) in Australia*, 1996, at p. 16.

ensure the authenticity and integrity of the message. The digital signature therefore plays a role in electronic communications similar to the role of a handwritten signature for printed documents, in the sense that:

- The recipient of the communication can verify the communication originated from the author and the communication was not altered since it was signed; and
- The author cannot deny the communication or the fact that it was sent.

3-8   Unlike handwritten signatures, however, the digital signature cannot be forged (unless the integrity of the cryptographic system is compromised).

At present, no legal framework in place in Australia gives the same legal effect to a digital signature on an electronic communication as a pen and ink signature on a printed document. Standards Australia has recommended that a legislative structure be established to provide that where a digital signature is attached to an electronic document, the recipient is entitled to accept the signature as if it had been placed on a hard copy document, provided:

- The signature was issued in accordance with the rules of a recognised digital signature scheme;
- A valid certificate containing the public key of the signer exists;
- The recipient could be reasonably expected to have access to it; and
- The recipient could reasonably be expected to have the capability to verify it.[4]

3-9   The use of a digital signature may arise out of an established contractual relationship between the parties. For example, clause 3.1 of the Model EDI Trading Agreement prepared by the EDI Council of Australia provides that any digital signature "affixed to or contained in any Message shall be sufficient to verify such party as the Sender and to authenticate the related Message as valid". Further, clause 3.3 deems any message to which is affixed a digital signature to be "written" or "in writing", to have been "signed" and to constitute an "original" when printed from electronic files or records.[5]

These clauses may not achieve their intended effect in the event of a dispute arising between the trading partners having regard to the requirements of the laws of evidence generally and as varied by legislation in each of the States and Territories of Australia, and any legislative requirements as to the need for "writing" and the need for a document to be "signed" or "executed".

---

4 Standards Australia, *Strategies for the Implementation of a Public Key Authentication Framework (PKAF) in Australia*, 1996, at p. 78.
5 Version 1, October 1990.

At present, it would appear that the Australian position is that, if a person receives an electronic communication to which a digital signature is attached, it is up to that party to decide whether to act on the signature and for the courts to determine the legal status of the signature in the particular case.

ELECTRONIC TRANSACTIONS IN AUSTRALIA

Creation of Contracts Electronically

This section discusses some of the legal issues arising out of contracts created 3-10 in Australia using modern technology without an exchange of paper. These issues are addressed against the background of general considerations, such as:

- The subject matter of the contract — Computer-based contracts may deal with subject matter which is external to the relevant computer systems, for example, the purchase of certain products, or may deal with subject matter that falls within the bounds of the relevant computer systems, for example, access to information stored in the computer system;
- The extent to which humans are involved in the transaction; and
- Whether the contractual arrangement is occurring in a closed network between a limited number of participants, in which case there is likely to be a master contract in existence, for example, a "trading partner" agreement to govern electronic data interchange (EDI)— EDI refers to a "technology and method that enables one party to transfer information and legally relevant "documents" electronically to another for direct processing in the other party's information systems".[6] Most EDI relationships occur between two large organisations with a strong trading history, and generally in the context of a supply contract over a period of time. Generally, the agreement between the parties relating to EDI will deal with the terms and conditions relating to the EDI system.

Offer and Acceptance On-line

One of the fundamental requirements for a valid, enforceable contract to 3-11 arise is offer and acceptance. To create a contract in Australia, an offer by one party to another must be accepted by the other party without qualification. An offer consists of a willingness to enter a contract in sufficiently certain terms. If there is any qualification to the original offer, then the response is likely to be regarded as a counter-offer. This fundamental requirement has essentially

---

6 Nimmer, "Electronic Contracting: Legal Issues", *John Marshall Journal of Computer and Information Law*, 1996, at p. 5.

evolved on the basis of decisions being directly made by humans, for example, a buyer accepts an offer to purchase goods from a supplier at a certain price.

The introduction of technology into business practice has implications for the traditional offer and acceptance requirement. A computer may make decisions and issue responses without direct human involvement. A number of issues therefore arise in the context of electronic contracting:

3-12   **Communication of Offer and Acceptance** With certain exceptions, for example, sale of shares in a public company, there is no requirement at law that an offer must be communicated in writing or in any particular form.

The manner in which the acceptance is to be made generally must be in the form specified by the offeror. Therefore, in a trading agreement context, the terms of any EDI agreement may be relevant. In some circumstances, however, where an alternative method of acceptance is as timely as, and no less disadvantageous to the offeror that method of acceptance will suffice. For example, in respect of an offer requesting a reply "by return of post", a reply by telegram, or some other means that would be received no later than the letter by post, would be effective.[7]

If no particular manner of acceptance is prescribed, the courts will have regard to all of the circumstances of the case to determine whether an acceptance is effective. For example, it has been held that an acceptance sent by ordinary post was ineffective where the offer was made by telegram as the fact that the offer was made by telegram was an indication that a prompt reply was expected.[8]

It is likely, therefore, that Australian courts will adopt the approach that where an offer is made by the offeror by means of a computer system, for example, over the Internet, and no form of acceptance is specified, communication of acceptance must generally be by electronic means.

In the context of a trading partner arrangement, the issue also arises as to whether automated acceptance constitutes an effective acceptance at law. Traditional contract law presumes that an effective acceptance will only arise where the acceptance was communicated with knowledge of the offer and intent to accept the offer. Although the requirement of intent arguably requires some form of human involvement in the acceptance process, in the absence of any specific term in the EDI agreement governing automated acceptance, Australian courts will likely take the view that the requisite intention will be inferred from the acts of the computer under the control of the person to whom the offer was made in accepting the offer, particularly if the automated acceptance has been relied on by the other party. In any electronic communication responding to an offer, however, there must be

---

7 *Tinn v. Hoffman & Co.* (1873) 29 L.T. 271.
8 *Quenerduaine v. Cole* (1883) 32 W.R. 185.

some indication that the response is an acceptance of the offer and not merely an acknowledgement of receipt of the offer.

Timing A further question arises in relation to electronic contract formation   **3-13** as to when a contract is formed. This question has particular relevance to the ability of a party to revoke the offer or acceptance and to when the parties' respective obligations are to commence.

An acceptance of an offer is generally effective on communication to the offeror, that is, receipt of the acceptance of the offer by the offeror (the "face to face" rule). The main exception to this general rule is the operation of the "postal acceptance" rule. The postal acceptance rule operates to deem acceptance to have occurred immediately a properly pre-paid and addressed letter is posted. This rule, which had its origins in England, has been adopted in Australia; however, the courts "in more recent times and in the light of modern means of communication have shown no disposition to extend the postal acceptance rule".[9] In this respect, in the case of instantaneous electronic communications, Australian courts will most probably apply the general rule that acceptance is effective on communication to the offeror.

In the context of an electronic contract, communications breakdowns or message backlogs pose problems to the application of the "face to face" rule. Guidance in these circumstances could be derived from the following passage of Lord Wilberforce in discussing the situation where a telex message may not reach the intended recipient due to prevailing circumstances:

"No universal rule can cover all such cases: they must be resolved by reference to the intentions of the parties, by sound business practice and in some cases by a judgment where the risks should lie."[10]

Clearly, timing issues should be addressed in any EDI trading agreement. The Model EDI Trading Agreement prepared by the EDI Council of Australia provides that a message will be deemed to have been received when an "acknowledgement has been transmitted to the Sender".[11] The Model EDI Agreement does not endeavour to deal with the point at which contracts between trading partners are formed.

Enforceability Problems of proof arise where a party seeks to establish the   **3-14** terms of an electronic contract. Generally, a party seeking to prove a breach of contract will need to prove that a contract was in fact formed and also the terms of the contract, in particular the term or terms that were allegedly breached. All evidence relied on by a party to establish either or both of these grounds tendered before a court in Australia must be admissible according to established rules of evidence.

9 *Bressan* v. *Squires* [1974] 2 N.S.W.L.R. 460 at p. 462, per Bowen C.J..
10 *Brinkibon Ltd.* v. *Stahag Stahl GmbH* [1983] 2 A.C. 34, at p. 42.
11 Clause 4.1 (3).

Traditionally, Australian courts have been reluctant to admit computer records as evidence due to the risk of the original record having been modified or tampered with.

On April 18, 1995, the Commonwealth Evidence Act 1995 ("the Commonwealth Act") came into effect and made a number of changes which are of significance in the context of electronic commerce. The Commonwealth Act applies to all proceedings in the Federal Court of Australia and the courts of the Australian Capital Territory. Substantially identical legislation came into force in the State of New South Wales on September 1, 1995, and it is expected that the other States and Territories of Australia will each soon introduce uniform legislation.

The Commonwealth Act makes admissible any computer-generated or computer-sourced document. Specifically, section 69 of the Commonwealth Act makes admissible a document which "forms part of the records kept by an organisation for the purposes of the business". "Document" is defined as:

". . . any record of information, and includes:

(a) anything on which there is writing;

(b) anything on which there are marks, figures, symbols or perforations having a meaning to persons qualified to interpret them; or

(c) anything from which sounds, images or writings can be reproduced with or without anything else; or

(d) a map, plan, drawing or photograph."

3-15   The provisions of the existing Australian State and Territory Evidence Acts provide for certain prerequisites to be met in order for computer records to be admissible. These provisions generally vary from State to State, however, in each case they generally reflect a concern as to the reliability of the computer records as evidence.

Some contracts are required to be in writing due to the operation of the Statute of Frauds. Contracts for the sale of land and for the assignment of debts fall within that category. Documentation relating to bills of lading and documentary credits are also required under Australian law to be in writing. The operation of the various Commonwealth and State Evidence Acts does not alter this requirement.

In respect of EDI trading agreements, evidentiary issues relating to the messages sent by the parties may be addressed in the terms of the agreement. For example, clause 3.3 (3) of the Model EDI Trading Agreement deems a hard copy of each message to be an original. Further, clause 3.4 provides for the parties to agree not to contest the validity or enforceability of a message in any legal proceedings between them relating to a transaction and to expressly waive any right to raise any defence or waiver of liability based on the absence of a memorandum in writing or failure of execution except to the extent that messages can be shown to have been corrupted as a result of third party failure.[12]

Terms and Conditions If a legally enforceable contract is established, the   3-16
terms and conditions of that contract may be derived from the following sources:

- The terms actually negotiated and agreed between the parties in relation to the transaction under consideration (including orally agreed terms);
- The terms of any "umbrella" agreement, such as an EDI trading agreement, if the electronic contract is made pursuant to that agreement;
- Terms that may be implied by fact or law (on the basis of what the parties would have agreed if they had turned their minds to the question); and
- Terms implied by statute, for example, in relation to contracts for the supply of goods or services, under state sale of goods legislation and the Commonwealth Trade Practices Act 1974, terms may be implied relating to title, correspondence with description, fitness for purpose and merchantable quality.

Mistakes in On-line Contracts

Before considering mistakes in on-line contracts, it is appropriate to classify   3-17
the types of mistakes that may effect contractual obligations:

- The first type of mistake is a "common mistake", that is, where the mistake is shared by both parties. An example of such a mistake is where the parties contracted in respect of certain goods where, in fact, the goods did not in fact exist.
- The second type of mistake is a "mutual mistake". With mistakes of this kind, the parties mean different things, for example, the contract is in respect of land known as Blackacre in a certain street and there are in fact two blocks of land in the street known as Blackacre and the buyer is referring to one and the seller to the other.
- The third type of mistake is a mistake by one party, the other not being mistaken at all, otherwise known as "unilateral mistake".

The concept of "unilateral mistake" may arise in the context of electronic   3-18
commerce where the mistakes or encoding errors may occur in a message. The fact that one party is mistaken is not, in the absence of additional factors, a reason for finding that the contract is void or that a right of rescission is available. The High Court of Australia was required to consider

---

12 Version 1, October 1990.

the circumstances in which a party under a mistake as to the terms or subject matter of a contract would be entitled to an order rescinding the contract in *Taylor* v. *Johnson*.[13] Mason A.C.J., Murphy, and Deane J.J. stated:

> "The particular proposition of law which we see as appropriate and adequate for disposing of the present appeal may be narrowly stated. It is that a party who has entered into a written contract under a serious mistake about its contents in relation to a fundamental term will be entitled in equity to an order rescinding the contract if the other party is aware that circumstances exist which indicate that the first party is entering the contract under some serious mistake or misapprehension about either the content or subject matter of that term and deliberately sets out to ensure that the first party does not become aware of the existence of his mistake or misapprehension."[14]

3-19   In the context of a unilateral mistake caused by an encoding error in a message, it is therefore likely that the mistaken party will not be entitled to a remedy unless the sender was aware of the error and the recipient was acting under a misapprehension.

A unilateral mistake may also arise where a third party without authority obtains a sender's private key. In the absence of any contractual terms apportioning liability between the parties for such mistakes, it is likely that Australian courts will apply the Common Law principles relating to unilateral mistake in disputes arising out of electronic contracts. In this latter scenario, the recipient, who holds the public key corresponding to the sender's private key, may mistakenly believe it is dealing with the sender. There have been few Australian cases on mistake as to identity, however, it is likely that Australian courts will follow the English authorities[15] in finding that no acceptance of the offer by the offeree has occurred, and so no contract exists.

In an EDI trading arrangement, the parties may agree on when a mistake will be "operative" and what effect the mistake has. The Model EDI Trading Agreement states that the sender is responsible for the completeness and accuracy of any message transmitted that is authenticated with a digital signature. This responsibility is qualified by the proviso that the sender will not be liable for an incorrect or incomplete message if the incorrectness or incompleteness should in all the circumstances have been reasonably obvious to the recipient.[16] The recipient is also under an obligation to promptly notify the sender if the recipient is unable to fully decipher and understand the message (unless the recipient is unable to identify the sender).[17]

---

13 (1983) 151 C.L.R. 422.
14 *Taylor* v. *Johnson* (1983) 151 C.L.R. 422 at p. 432.
15 *E.g., Boulton* v. *Jones* (1857) 157 E.R. 232.
16 Clause 4.5.
17 Clauses 4.2 to 4.4.

Impact of Impostors or Persons without Authority

The issue of liability for unauthorised electronic transactions has not been   3-20
resolved at any government policy level. At present, in Australia, the
allocation of responsibility for unauthorised transactions is generally left to
be resolved by the parties to an agreement. Some examples of the early
direction taken on this issue are set out below. Under the Model EDI Trading
Agreement, clause 7.2 provides:

> "Each party shall be responsible to the other to prevent unauthorised
> access or transmissions and shall be liable for any costs or consequences
> which flow therefrom."

Therefore, in the case of forged digital signatures, responsibility for any   3-21
transaction resulting from the use of the forged signature would rest with
the owner of the signature.

Standards Australia has recommended that certification authorities (entities that verify the identity of users) should not be liable for any loss arising
out of the use of forged signatures, unless the forgery resulted from the
documented policies and procedures of the Public Key Authentication
Framework not being followed, or could be shown to permit the forgery.[18]

Consequences of and Responsibility for Unauthorised Access The legal   3-22
consequences of unauthorised access will ultimately depend on where that
unauthorised access occurs within the relevant network. This is something
that may be difficult to determine. Information can theoretically be intercepted at any stage during its passage between users.

A security breach within a party's technology and communication systems could permit unauthorised access. This could happen by a person
gaining access to those systems through the Internet or by modem and
reading or manipulating account information. It could also occur by physical access to a party's computer equipment. One critical aspect of a party's
defences is encryption. If the encryption software used by the party fails to
encrypt information properly, this failure could significantly compromise
system security. It may also be very difficult to detect such a fault. The
importance of encryption technology has been recognised by the Australian
government, where in its Australia on-line policy statement it said:

> "Encryption technology is essential to electronic commerce. Transactions will
> not be initiated unless people are confident that personal and financial
> information is protected from unauthorised interception. Heavy-handed
> attempts to ban strong encryption techniques will compromise commercial

---

18 Standards Australia, *Strategies for the Implementation of a Public Key Authentication Framework (PKAF) in Australia*, 1996, at p. 43.

security, discouraging on-line service industries (particularly in the financial sector) from adopting Australia as a domicile."

Unauthorised access to a communication can also occur while the message is being transmitted. This is a particular danger for messages sent in plain text. Further, there could be complex jurisdictional issues involved because the interception may occur outside Australia. Difficulties may also be faced in trying to trace the interception. An unauthorised access may give rise to a number of criminal sanctions. Some of these are set out below:

- There have been a series of cases in Australia which have held that obtaining unauthorised funds using cards to operate the bank's automatic teller machine amounts to theft or obtaining financial advantage by deception.[19] Obtaining funds or information from a computer system using a forged digital signature (or another person's card) could amount to theft or obtaining financial advantage by deception. Arguably, however, the unauthorised extraction of information from a computer system is not theft because there is no intention to permanently deprive the owner of property, and arguably no property is involved. In *Oxford* v. *Moss*,[20] it was held that a university student who dishonestly obtained a proof of an examination paper, read it and returned it, was not guilty of theft.
- Arguably, the unauthorised access of a computer system using a forged signature amounts to forgery on the basis that it involves the creation of a "false instrument". This argument, however, proved unsuccessful in the English case of *R* v. *Gold*,[21] which involved a prosecution under the Forgery and Counterfeiting Act 1981.
- In some circumstances, the interference of data stored on a computer system may amount to malicious damage to property.
- In respect of unauthorised access to government data banks containing personal information about individuals, a contravention of the Privacy Act 1988 (Commonwealth) may also occur.

3-23   If the unauthorised access amounts to an interception then this may in certain circumstances also constitute criminal activity under several different pieces of legislation. Three examples of such legislation are:

- Telecommunications Interception Act 1979 (Commonwealth);
- Telecommunications Act 1997 (Commonwealth; and
- Crimes Act 1914 (Commonwealth).

---

19 *Kennison* v. *Daire* (1986) 60 A.L.J.R. 249; *R* v. *Evenett* [1987] 2 Qd.R.753; *R. v. Baxter* [1988] 1 Qd.R 537.
20 (1979) 68 Cr. App. R. 183.
21 [1988] 2 W.L.R. 984.

The Telecommunications Interception Act 1979 prohibits the interception   3-24
of a communication passing over a telecommunication system. There are
exceptions for interceptions by mistake or under warrants. "Interception"
consists of listening to or recording, by any means, a communication in its
passage over a telecommunication system, without the knowledge of the
person making the communication. For these purposes, a telecommunication system is defined as the system or combination of physical facilities
through or over which services can be provided. This legislation provides a
remedy for improper access to line-based telecommunication systems,
PABXs, and voicemail boxes. It would not apply to communications carried
by means of radio communications.

The Telecommunications Act 1997 imposes a number of prohibitions on
carrier employees and service providers disclosing or using contents of
communications.[22] The Crimes Act 1914 creates a number of offences
relating to telecommunication services. It is an offence under the Act to
knowingly or recklessly:

". . . cause a communication in the course of telecommunications carriage
to be received by a person or telecommunications service other than the
person or service to whom it is directed (section 852D); or

"tamper or interfere with a facility belonging to a carrier."[23]

Other provisions of the Crimes Act 1914 relate to equipment used for   3-25
unlawful purposes (in particular, unauthorised call switching and interception devices) and the connection of such equipment to a telecommunications
network with the intention of committing an offence.[24] The Act also prohibits the manufacture, sale, or possession of devices of this kind.[25]

The Crimes Act 1914 also prohibits any unauthorised access to a
computer system, where the access is facilitated by means of a service
provided by the Commonwealth or any carrier. If the unlawful access to data
was obtained with the intent to defraud any person, or the access related to
particularly sensitive data, the penalty increases. It is also an offence to use
a telecommunications facility operated or provided by the Commonwealth
or by a carrier, to intentionally interfere with data, to unlawfully use a
computer or to impede access to or impair the usefulness or the effectiveness
of data stored in a computer.

---

22 Telecommunications Act 1997, sections 276–278 and 296.
23 Here it is sufficient to prove that there has been a use of the carrier's facilities for an irregular
   purpose; Crimes Act 1914, section 852J.
24 Crimes Act 1914, section 852KD.
25 Crimes Act 1914, sections 852KA and 852KB.

In addition, state legislation attempts to deal with unauthorised access to computer systems. This legislation varies from State to State. By way of example, section 9A of the State of Victoria's Summary Offences Act 1966 provides that:

"A person must not gain access to, or enter, a computer system or part of a computer system without lawful authority to do so."

Another possibility is that unauthorised access is obtained through a security breach in the machine of a service provider. As between a service provider and the service provider's client, whether such a breach would be the responsibility of the service provider could depend on the contractual arrangement in place between the service provider and its client, but such a contractual relationship will not necessarily exist between a party and those service providers who may be involved in the transmission of a communication. To minimise the risk of one party being directly liable to the other party for unauthorised access, the party may seek to exclude liability by providing a written acknowledgement to the other party, stating that electronic transactions, particularly when sent without encryption, are inherently insecure.

In addition to possible contractual remedies, there may be a number of other civil causes of action where the security of an electronic transaction is breached. These might include any one or more of the following:

- Negligence;
- Trespass;
- Breach of intellectual property entitlements (such as copyright and trade secrets); and
- An action based on misrepresentation.

3-26   Each of these causes of action may provide a potential remedy against the person who either gains access to the system or communication or the person who allows such access or breach of security to occur.

It is also possible that the software used by participants in an electronic communication for effecting that communication may contain a weakness that also allows unauthorised access. Where a third party provides this software, then the third party may bear some responsibility for defects in the software, depending on the terms on which the software was licensed.

Finally, the unauthorised access could occur because the user fails to protect secret information (such as their private key) or gives improper access to his or her software. Responsibility for these types of security breaches should clearly rest with the user. This has been the approach taken, by way of example, in the Model EDI Trading Agreement prepared by the

EDI Council of Australia. Clause seven of that agreement imposes four main obligations on the parties to the agreement:

- Each party must develop security procedures sufficient to ensure that all transmissions are authorised;
- Each party must be responsible to the other to prevent unauthorised access of transmissions;
- Each party must be responsible for the confidentiality of signatures; and
- Each party must, on becoming aware of a breach of security, immediately advise the other and take appropriate steps to investigate such breach.

In addition to contractual liability, a user responsible for a security breach   3-27
may also be subject to liability in negligence. All of these considerations rely on being able to identify the point in the transaction chain at which the security breach occurred. However, actually establishing who is at fault will obviously be difficult, given the number of parties involved and the potential for such parties to be dispersed throughout the world.

On-line Payments in Australia

The two most prevalent forms of retail electronic banking systems currently   3-28
in use in Australia are Automatic Teller Machines (ATMs) and Electronic Funds Transfer at Point of Sale (EFTPOS).

The growth in the use of these two systems has been dramatic. In 1980, there were 25 ATMs and no EFTPOS terminals operating in Australia. In 1996, there were more than 7,000 ATMs and 107,000 EFTPOS terminals.[26]

Other forms of electronic payments are also developing. Advance Bank (a subsidiary of St. George Bank) has been providing Internet services to customers for the transfer of funds between existing accounts since April 1996, and Commonwealth Bank of Australia introduced a similar service in March 1997. Credit Unions in Australia are also planning to allow their members to access their accounts and conduct financial transactions over the Internet, with one credit union launching its Internet product on July 31, 1997.[27] Further, Advance Bank began issuing digital coins on the Internet in June 1997.[28] These digital coins are denominated in Australian dollars using Digicash's e-cash software.

While payments by credit cards over the telephone are relatively common in Australia, Australian banks still discourage merchants from accepting credit card payments over the Internet.[29] This may change once the bank-endorsed Internet security protocol developed by Visa and Mastercard (Secured Electronic Transaction standard, or SET) is introduced.

---

26 *Weekend Australian*, November 30, 1996, at p. 19.
27 *Weekend Australian*, July 26, 1997, at p. 9.
28 *Australian Financial Review*, June 11, 1997.
29 *Australian Financial Review*, June 5, 1997.

This section will examine the legal environment in Australia surrounding the operation of the various forms of electronic payments referred to above. Issues unique to stored value cards (SVCs) will not be discussed, as they are beyond the scope of this section. However, many of the issues examined below will have relevance to SVCs, such as privacy and currency issues.

ATMS and EFTPOS

3-29   Both ATMs and EFTPOS facilities are operated by the combination of a plastic card and a personal identification number (PIN). The rights and obligations of a cardholder and the financial institution that issued the card are governed by the following:

- The contract between the cardholder and the financial institution;
- The non-excludable terms implied by statutes such as the Trade Practices Act 1974 (Commonwealth);
- The duties of a financial institution to its customers at general law; and
- The Electronic Funds Transfer Code of Conduct (EFT Code).

3-30   In addition, issues relating to the admissibility of electronic records as evidence apply equally to ATMs and EFTPOS.

Electronic Funds Transfer Code of Conduct

3-31   The EFT Code was introduced in late 1989. It is a form of "guided" industry self-regulation in the sense that its content was negotiated by financial institutions, consumer groups, and government regulators against a background of threat of legislation if its content was not acceptable to government. Its provisions are legally enforceable as they are incorporated by the financial institution into the contract with each cardholder and also because the financial institution warrants in those contracts that the institution will comply with the terms of the EFT Code. The Australian Payments System Council annually monitors and reports on financial institutions' compliance with the EFT Code.[30]

The EFT Code is not technology neutral. Under section 1.1 of the EFT Code it only applies to transactions intended to be initiated by an individual through an electronic terminal by the combined use of an EFT plastic card and a personal identification number (PIN). Hence, in general, the EFT Code will not apply to on line banking or digital cash. It may apply to SVCs where the SVCs are required to be accessed through a PIN. However, many SVCs will not have this requirement.

---

30 Sneddon, "A Review of the Electronic Funds Transfer Code of Conduct", 1995, *Journal of Banking and Finance Law and Practice*, at p. 29.

Currently, there are suggestions that the EFT Code be amended so that certain of its provisions are extended to apply to other forms of electronic payments systems (including SVCs). The more important provisions of the EFT Code include the following:

- Card issuers are to issue clear and unambiguous terms and conditions of use;
- Changes to the terms and conditions of use must be notified to cardholders in advance;
- Periodic statements must be issued;
- The cardholder's liability for unauthorised transactions is limited;[31]
- Card issuers are to be guided by certain privacy principles in respect of all EFT services they offer, including the obligation to treat customer records in the strictest confidence; and
- Card issuers must establish complaint investigation and resolution procedures.

It is of interest to examine in greater detail the way in which the EFT Code   **3-32** deals with liability for unauthorised transactions. Section 5.2 (i) of the EFT Code provides that the cardholder is not liable for losses which are caused by the fraudulent or negligent conduct of employees or agents of the card issuer, companies involved in networking arrangements or merchants who are linked to the EFT system. The cardholder is also not liable where it is clear that he or she has not contributed to any loss resulting from an unauthorised transaction.[32]

Where it is unclear whether or not the cardholder has contributed to loss resulting from an unauthorised transaction, the cardholder's liability is not to exceed the lesser of:

- A.$50;
- The balance of the cardholder's account (including any unused credit); or
- The actual loss at the time the card issuer is notified of the loss or theft of the card.[33]

However, the cardholder is liable for greater amounts if he or she has   **3-33** contributed to a loss in the manner set out in sections 5.6 and 5.7. Section 5.6 provides that where a cardholder has contributed to a loss resulting from an unauthorised transaction by "voluntarily disclosing the PIN, indicating the PIN on the card, or keeping a record of the PIN (without making any reasonable attempt to disguise the PIN) with any article carried with the card or liable to loss or theft simultaneously with the card", the cardholder is

---

31 This is considered in more detail below.
32 Electronic Funds Transfer Code of Conduct, Code, section 5.4.
33 Electronic Funds Transfer Code of Conduct, Code, section 5.5.

liable for the actual loss which occurs before the card issuer is notified that
the card has been misused, lost or stolen (with such liability being capped at
the amount of the balance on the cardholder's account or the relevant
transaction limit applicable to the account).

Section 5.7 provides where the cardholder has contributed to a loss
resulting from unauthorised transactions by "unreasonably delaying notification of the misuse, loss or theft of the card, or that the PIN has become
known to someone else, the cardholder is liable for the actual losses which
occur between when the cardholder became aware (or should reasonably
have become aware in the case of a lost or stolen card) and when the card
issuer was actually notified", with a cap similar to that in section 5.6 being
applied to the amount for which the cardholder is liable.

There are a number of problems with sections 5.6 and 5.7. In relation to
section 5.6, financial institutions are likely to infer from a successful transaction by a card and correct PIN that the customer has contributed to the
loss by being negligent with the PIN. On the other hand, the customer is
likely to maintain that the PIN was never disclosed or recorded or not
recorded in a manner to make it susceptible to a loss or theft of the card.
The EFT Code is unhelpful in resolving such disputes, as it does not assign
a burden of proof to one party, nor does it give any guidance as to how to
weigh the customer's assertion or the financial institution's inference from
the evidence of a successful account access.

Further, there is uncertainty with the meaning of the phrases "without
making any reasonable attempt to disguise the PIN" and "liable to loss or
theft simultaneously with the card" in section 5.6.

In relation to section 5.7, the meaning of the phrase "(or should reasonably have become aware in the case of a lost or stolen card)" is also
uncertain.[34]

Credit Card Payments On-line and Digital Cash and Cheques

3-34   It is reasonably clear what on-line credit card payments involve — simply
transmitting the credit card details of a cardholder through a telecommunications medium (*e.g.,* the Internet) to the merchant for payment of purchases. However, it may be useful to examine briefly the nature of digital
cash and digital cheques.

Digital cash is electronic token money issued by an electronic bank
issuer in exchange for actual money and is able to be transmitted by a
purchaser to a seller and banked by the seller at an electronic bank. A digital
coin is a packet of digitised data, electronically signed by the issuer (using
encryption) certifying that it is worth, and is redeemable for, a certain

---

34 For a more detailed discussion of these problems with the Electronic Funds Transfer Code
of Conduct, see Sneddon, "A Review of the Electronic Funds Transfer Code of Conduct",
1995, *Journal of Banking and Finance Law and Practice* at p. 29.

amount of real money. The coin may be sent over the Internet from hard disk to hard disk and redeemed at the issuer.[35]

A digital cheque is a packet of digitised data, electronically signed by the customer (using encryption) which acts as electronic authorisation from the customer to an electronic bank to transfer electronic value (previously purchased with real money) from the issuer's account to the payee's account. The electronic cheque is sent directly to the payee who will present it for collection directly or through the payee's financial institution.[36]

A digital cheque is not a cheque within the meaning of the Cheques and Payment Orders Act 1986 (Commonwealth). A cheque requires a signature. Currently, no legislation in Australia provides that an electronic signature is a signature within the meaning of that Act.

There is at present no digital cheque system operating in Australia, but Advance Bank has begun to issue digital coins. The following issues are common to on-line credit card payments, digital cash, and digital cheques.

Privacy Issues relating to privacy in Australia may be impacted directly by   3-35
domestic legislation and indirectly by foreign laws with extra-territorial effects.

Australian Legislation   Currently, the law in Australia relating to privacy   3-36
comprises the following:

- General duties of confidentiality imposed by law on financial institutions;
- Industry codes of conduct governing banks, building societies, and credit unions;[37]
- Various state-based privacy legislation, including the Credit Reporting Act 1978 (Victoria), the Fair Trading Act 1987 (South Australia), the Privacy Committee Act 1975 (New South Wales) and the Invasion of Privacy Act 1971 (Queensland). These mainly regulate credit reporting, although the New South Wales legislation only provides for the establishment of a Privacy Committee with investigatory and reporting powers regarding alleged violations of privacy; and
- Privacy Act 1988 (Commonwealth).

---

35 Sneddon, "Cyberbanking and Payment Products: Legal and Regulatory Issues", at p. 10, presented at the 14th Annual Banking Law and Practice Conference, Sydney, Australia, May 22, 1997.
36 Sneddon, "Cyberbanking and Payment Products: Legal and Regulatory Issues", at p. 10, presented at the 14th Annual Banking Law and Practice Conference, Sydney, Australia, May 22, 1997.
37 A duty of confidentiality is imposed for banking facilities provided wholly and exclusively for a customer's personal or domestic use.

3-37   The Privacy Act 1988 (Commonwealth) imposes restrictions on the collection, maintenance and use of data by government departments, credit-reporting agencies and credit providers. For these purposes, the definition of credit provider is sufficiently wide to capture almost any party which provides goods and services on credit or which is a financial institution.

The restrictions involve prohibiting the disclosure or use of "personal information" unless the particular disclosure or use is specifically permitted by one of the exceptions in the Act. It is always possible to disclose or to use personal information if the informed consent of a customer is obtained. "Personal Information" is almost any information that has a bearing on the credit worthiness of an individual.

The existing Australian legislation and codes of conduct will provide only incidental privacy protection in relation to on-line electronic payments, as they are mainly directed towards government departments, credit-reporting agencies and credit providers. For example, when information is passed to a financier on the Internet, the Internet service provider will obtain access to customer information. That provider could compile customer lists containing personal information and sell them to other parties. There is no existing legislation dealing with these issues.

In early 1997, there were suggestions that the Federal Government would extend the existing Privacy Act 1988 (Commonwealth) to the private sector generally to ensure the security, privacy and accuracy of personal information held by companies.[38] One impetus for this was the European Union Data Protection Directive discussed below. However, Australia's Prime Minister, Mr. John Howard, announced on March 21, 1997 that the Federal Government no longer intends to extend the Privacy Act 1988 (Commonwealth) to the private sector.[39] The reason cited was the need to reduce regulatory burden on business. The Prime Minister asked the States not to introduce their own privacy legislation, to avoid a patchwork of different legislation in each State and Territory. As an alternative, the Prime Minister suggested that the private sector may develop voluntary codes of conduct in consultation with the Federal Privacy Commissioner.

Queensland and the Northern Territory have agreed to the Prime Minister's request not to introduce their own privacy legislation. However, at this stage, New South Wales and Victoria are still likely to push ahead with legislative reform.[40]

3-38   *European Union Data Protection Directive*   The European Union Data Protection Directive was issued in 1995, and must be implemented by its member states by October 1998. That Directive forbids the transfer of personal information from a member state unless the destination country

---

38 *Australian Financial Review*, January 13, 1997, at p. 12.
39 *Australian Financial Review*, March 24, 1997, at p. 10.
40 *Australian Financial Review*, March 27, 1997, at p. 5.

has an adequate level of privacy protection. A number of commentators have suggested that, in the absence of legislative reform, Australia is likely to be considered a country with an inadequate level of protection in some or all areas. However, in relation to the banking sector in Australia, it is possible that it already has an adequate level of privacy protection. This is because Australian banks are subject to certain implied duties of confidentiality under general law and are also governed by the Code of Banking Practice, which imposes obligations in relation to privacy.

Security   Some existing legislation is directly relevant to the security of   3-39
on-line banking networks. At this stage, it is not particularly extensive.

Cryptography One method of achieving security for communications over   3-40
the Internet (and of overcoming the problems caused by not knowing the identity of the party one is dealing with) is through the use of public key cryptography. Encryption and decryption of messages using this technology involves the use of a public key and a private key. Users encode messages using the public key and decode messages using the private key. The public and private keys are unique-matched pairs and the private key is not computable from the public key.

Public key systems can therefore be used to provide digital signatures — a user can create a signature for a message by encoding it with the private key, and anyone can check the authenticity of signature by seeing whether it can be deciphered to the message using the sender's pubic key. This system envisages the public key being certified by a reliable body as the public key of a particular person or entity.

Certification Authority   Australia Post (the Australian postal service, an   3-41
agency of the Federal Government) has announced its plans to become such a certification authority in Australia. Under that arrangement, users will provide Australia Post with satisfactory evidence of identity and Australia Post will then issue the user with a public and private key pair. The public key could be disseminated broadly and would be used by anyone who wants to verify that he is dealing with the nominated individual. The user would retain the private key.

Export of Encryption Technology   In the past, Australia prohibited the   3-42
export of encryption software under the Customs (Prohibited Exports) Regulations. However, on December 12, 1996, those Regulations were amended and the prohibition has been removed.

Finance Industry Codes of Practice   There are three Codes of Practice, each   3-43
governing a different type of financial institution in Australia, *i.e.*, banks, credit unions and building societies. Each of these Codes regulates customers acquiring "banking facilities" exclusively for private, domestic or household purposes.

The provision of ordinary banking services electronically (for example, by the Internet), the issuing of SVCs and the issuing of digital cash are likely to constitute the provision of "banking facilities". Accordingly, the Codes of Practice will apply to the relevant financial institutions for the provision of electronic banking services. Some of the main requirements of the Codes of Practice include:

- Providing written terms and conditions at the time or before the contract for the banking facility is made (except where it is impracticable to do so, in which case it will be provided as soon as practicable after the provision of the service);
- Making certain information available to customers, including fees and charges;
- Providing of notice to customers regarding variations to terms and conditions;
- Imposing a duty on the financial institution to keep information concerning customers private and confidential; and
- Putting in place dispute resolution procedures.

3-44   **Implied Warranties: Trades Practices Act 1974 (Commonwealth)** Section 74 of the Trade Practices Act imposes certain implied warranties in every contract for the supply of services to a consumer by a corporation in the course of a business.[41]

Section 4B of the Trade Practices Act defines a consumer to be a person who acquires goods or services where the price does not exceed A.$40,000 or where the goods or services are of a kind ordinarily acquired for personal, domestic or household use or consumption. The implied warranties include the following:

- The services will be rendered with due care and skill;
- The material supplied in connection with the services will be reasonably fit for the purpose for which they are supplied; and
- If the consumer makes known any particular purpose for which the services are required, the services and the materials supplied will be reasonably fit for that purpose (unless the consumer does not rely, or it is unreasonable for him or her to rely, on the corporation's skill and judgment).

3-45   In the context of the supply of electronic banking services to customers, section 74 may impose on financial institutions and other providers of such services an obligation, having regard to domestic and international industry and technological standards, to provide a reasonable level of:

- Availability and access;

---

41 Equivalent provisions exist in the fair trading legislation in Western Australia and the Northern Territory.

- Maintenance of equipment;
- Security of transactions; and
- Successful completion of transactions.[42]

A corporation may not contract out of its obligations under section 74, as **3-46** any term of a contract that has the effect of excluding, restricting or modifying rights or liability under implied warranties is void.[43]

Electronic Records — Admissibility as Evidence The admissibility of elec- **3-47** tronic records is critical to on-line banking. For example, if a customer disputes that a request was made to purchase digital coins, or that his or her credit card details have been made available over the Internet, the financial institution and other parties involved in the transaction must rely on electronic evidence of the transaction to counter the customer's verbal evidence.[44]

Issues Relevant to Digital Cash
This section will examine those issues that are specific to digital cash. **3-48**

Licensing and Prudential Requirements The stored value on digital coins **3-49** (and on SVCs) represents a liability of the issuer in favour of the recipient. Hence, for such electronic payment systems to operate successfully, there must be public confidence that the liability will be met by the issuer and that certain safeguards are in place to protect the public.

In Australia, banks are subject to licensing requirements under the Banking Act 1959 (Commonwealth). The Reserve Bank of Australia (Australia's central bank) also applies very strict prudential rules. Certain other types of financial institutions such as credit unions and building societies are not subject to these regulations, but are subject to prudential standards developed by the Australian Financial Institutions Commission established by uniform State-based legislation (the Australian Financial Institutions Commission Code 1992).

An issuer of digital coins that does not possess a banking licence under the Banking Act and is not otherwise exempt from the licensing provisions of that Act (for example, credit unions and building societies) may need to apply to the Treasurer of Australia for an exemption[45] from the licensing requirements of that Act. This is because the taking of deposits is considered to be a part of the business of banking, and the issue of digital coins in

---

42 Sneddon, "Cyberbanking and Payment Products: Legal and Regulatory Issues", at p. 6, presented at the 14th Annual Banking Law and Practice Conference, Sydney, Australia, May 22, 1997.
43 Trade Practices Act, section 68.
44 The admissibility of electronic records and the Evidence Acts is discussed above in paragraph numbers 1–14 and 1–15.
45 Banking Act 1959, section 11.

exchange for currency may be characterised as the taking of deposits. However, whether this is the case has not been authoritatively determined.

The Federal Government recently commissioned an inquiry into the operation of the financial system in Australia (commonly known as the Wallis Inquiry, named after the Chairman of the Inquiry) and the report was handed down on March 18, 1997. One of the recommendations of the report was that all issuers of stores of value be subject to prudential regulation.

3-50   **Insolvency of Issuer** In Australia, government does not guarantee bank deposits and there is no insurance scheme to protect depositors in the event of bank failure. However, in the event of a bank becoming unable to meet its obligations, the Australian assets of the bank must be applied first to meet that bank's deposit liabilities in Australia.[46] Depositors at Australian banks in Australia are therefore entitled to preferential treatment in case of insolvency.

Clearly, a customer's holding of digital coins is not subject to this protection if the issuer is not a bank. Further, even if the issuer is a bank, liability represented by digital coins may not be a deposit liability, and therefore the customer may not be entitled to the benefit of the preference provision in the Banking Act.

Apart from the preference provision referred to above, ordinary insolvency laws apply to the allocation of losses if a digital cash issuer becomes insolvent. The holder of the digital cash would simply be an ordinary unsecured creditor, and would not receive any preferential treatment. The creditor would be paid out only after all secured creditors are satisfied.

3-51   **Currency Issues** In Australia, banking and currency legislation provides that only the Reserve Bank of Australia may mint money for circulation in Australia.

3-52   *Reserve Bank Act 1959 (Commonwealth)* Section 44(1) of the Reserve Bank Act 1959 provides that "a person shall not issue a bill or note for the payment of money payable to bearer on demand and intended for circulation".

Whether an issuer of digital cash will infringe this provision depends on whether a digital coin is a "bill" or a "note" and whether the digital coins are intended for circulation. A "note" is usually given the meaning in section 89 of the Bills of Exchange Act 1909 (Commonwealth), which states that:

"A promissory note is an unconditional promise in writing made by one person to another, signed by the maker, engaging to pay, on demand or at a fixed or determinable future time, a sum certain in money, to or to the order of a specified person, or to bearer."

---

46 Banking Act 1959 (Commonwealth), section 16.

In order for a digital coin to have legal effect, the issuer must be treated as having promised to guarantee payment.[47] In effect, the issuer promises to anyone who takes a valid coin in good faith and for value that the coin will be met. Digital cash will therefore fall within the definition of a "note" subject to the requirement that it be "in writing" and "signed by the maker". In the Acts Interpretation Act 1901 (Commonwealth), "writing" is defined to include "any mode of representing or reproducing words, figures, drawings or symbols in a visible form". It is arguable that digital cash is not "in writing", as the electronic message is not in a visible form. Further, it is unlikely to be construed as being signed, as presently no legislation in Australia provides that an electronic "signature" is a signature for the purposes of Commonwealth legislation.

More importantly, an issuer of a digital coin is unlikely to breach section 44(1) of the Reserve Bank Act as, generally, digital coins do not "circulate". Coins issued by e-cash issuers are generally cancelled or replaced by new coins with new serial numbers each time they are used (*i.e.*, presented by a merchant to the issuing bank for redemption). Digital coins issued by Advance Bank in Australia under its e-cash system do not "circulate".[48]

Currency Act 1965 (Commonwealth)   Another issue that arises is whether   **3-53** issuers of digital coins would infringe section 22 of the Currency Act 1965. This section provides:

> "A person shall not make or issue a piece of gold, silver, copper, nickel, bronze or of any other material, whether metal or otherwise, of any value, other than a coin made or issued under this Act, as a token for money or as purporting that the holder is entitled to demand any value denoted on it."

An issuer of digital coins purports that the holder of the coins is entitled to   **3-54** demand any value denoted on it. The main issue then becomes whether the issuer of digital cash has issued "any other material of any value".[49] In the context of section 22, the word "material" is likely to refer to physical material and not packets of digitised data. Hence, it is unlikely that an issuer of digital coins would breach section 22 of the Currency Act 1965.

---

47 Tyree, "Virtual Cash — Part II", 1996, 7 *Journal of Banking and Finance Law and Practice*, 139, at p. 140.
48 For a more detailed discussion of these issues under the Reserve Bank Act, see Klimt, "Applying Consumer Protection Laws to Retail Electronic Banking and Payment Products", at pp. 6–8, presented at an IIR Seminar on Legal and Regulatory Aspects of Electronic Banking in Sydney on December 2, 1996, and in Melbourne on December 9, 1996.
49 Klimt, "Applying Consumer Protection Laws to Retail Electronic Banking and Payment Products", at p. 8, presented at an IIR Seminar on Legal and Regulatory Aspects of Electronic Banking in Sydney on December 2, 1996, and in Melbourne on December 9, 1996.

3-55   **Prospectus Requirements** Section 1018 (1) of the Corporations Law (the legislation regulating corporations in Australia) provides that a person shall not offer for subscription, or issue invitations to subscribe for, securities of a corporation unless a prospectus in relation to the securities has been lodged with the Australian Securities Commission and the prospectus complies with the requirements of the Corporations Law. This provision is designed to protect investors, as the prospectus is required to contain all information that investors would reasonably expect to find for the purposes of making an informed assessment of the financial position of the corporation and the rights attaching to the securities.[50]

"Securities" is defined to include "debentures", and a debenture, in relation to a body, is defined as follows (subject to a number of exceptions):

> ". . . a document issued by the body that evidences or acknowledges indebtedness of the body in respect of money that is or may be deposited with or lent to the body."[51]

3-56   The question therefore arises as to whether an issuer of digital coins would be offering for subscription debentures of that issuer with the result that the prospectus requirements need to be satisfied.

A digital coin represents the indebtedness of the issuer to the holder of the coin for the face value of the coin. Hence, the question becomes whether the money that is used to purchase the coin can be described as "deposited or lent" to the issuer, and whether the digital coin constitutes a "document".

In relation to the first question, the purchase of digital coins involves the exchange of real money for a contractual right of the customer against the issuer such that the issuer is obliged to redeem those coins for real money on presentation. This contractual obligation of the issuer is not dissimilar to the contractual obligation of a deposit-taking financial institution to repay monies on withdrawal of amounts from a deposit account. Hence, it is arguable that the customer has "deposited or lent" to the issuer money in purchasing the digital coins. As to the second question, "document" is defined in section 9 to include the following:

> "(a) any paper or other material on which there is writing or printing."

> "(c) a disc, tape or other article, or any material, from which sounds, images, writings or messages are capable of being reproduced with or without the aid of any other article or device."

---

50 Corporations Law, section 1022.
51 A document issued by an Australian bank in the ordinary course of its banking business that evidences or acknowledges indebtedness of the bank is excluded from the definition of "debentures".

Given that a digital coin is a packet of digitised data, it is unlikely to fall within 3-57 either (a) or (c). However, this issue should still be kept in mind, especially in drafting the terms and conditions for the supply of e-cash from the issuer and the customer, so that the contract itself does not constitute a debenture.

Future Developments

As can be seen from the previous discussion, legislation in Australia needs 3-58 to be reviewed and updated to accommodate emerging electronic payments systems. The areas which require review include those which deal with privacy, electronic signatures, admissibility of evidence and regulation of issuers of stores of value. Further developments of industry codes of conduct may also be required.

In this regard, the Wallis Inquiry recommended that digital money and SVCs be subject to regulation to ensure the integrity of the payments system.[52] It also proposed that appropriate laws be enacted, and amendments made to existing laws, to accommodate electronic commerce. The relevant areas include:

- Digital signatures;
- Netting rules;
- Electronic provision of documents and notices;
- Adoption of public key authentication standards; and
- Uniform laws to provide for evidentiary issues for the electronic delivery of financial services.[53]

Finally, the Wallis Inquiry recommended that Australia adopt international 3-59 standards for electronic commerce.[54]

ELECTRONIC INFORMATION RIGHTS

Copyright

Requirements for Copyright Protection

Australia is a member of the Berne Convention. The copyright regime in 3-60 Australia is governed by the Copyright Act 1968 (Commonwealth), which provides for the protection of certain categories of works. The most relevant category for electronic commerce is the category of literary works, which specifically includes tables and compilations and computer programs.[55]

---

52 Recommendation 72.
53 Recommendation 91.
54 Recommendation 92.
55 Copyright Act 1968, section 10(1).

The requirement for copyright protection of a work in Australia are:

- Originality, in the sense that the work must not be copied from some other source, and is the result of the knowledge, judgment, skill or labour of the author; and
- The author of the work must be a "qualified person" within the meaning of section 32(4) of the Copyright Act 1968 at the time that the work is created or first published, *i.e.*, the author is a citizen, national or resident of Australia or of a country which is a member of the Berne Convention, Universal Copyright Convention or the World Trade Organisation.

3-61   Unlike the United States, there is no registration required for copyright. No specific protection is granted to computer databases under Australian copyright law. However, such databases may be protected as a compilation if sufficient originality is found in the contents of the database. Copyright protection generally commences when the work is created and ceases 50 years after the end of the calendar year in which the author dies.

Relevance of Copyright to On-line Communications

3-62   Copyright only protects original expression rather than information per se. Whether any particular work contains sufficient originality to justify copyright protection is a question of fact in every case. However, Australian courts have generally placed the threshold for copyright protection at quite a low level.

A literary work is created when it is reduced to a material form. The High Court has held that a literary work which is stored electronically satisfies this requirement.[56] A "computer program" is specifically included in the definition of "literary work". The definition of "computer program" appears in section 10(1) of the Copyright Act 1968, as follows:

". . . an expression, in any language, code or notation, of a set of instructions (whether with or without related information) intended, either directly or after either or both of the following:

"(a) conversion to another language, code or notation;

"(b) reproduction in a different material form,"

"to cause a device having digital information processing capabilities to perform a particular function."

---

56 *Computer Edge Pty Ltd.* v. *Apple Computer Inc* (1986) 161 C.L.R. 171.

The function performed by the computer is not itself protected — any author **3-63**
is free to create another computer program which carries out the same
function. In the context of electronic commerce, the above definition could
be applied to any protocol or set of instructions used in the conduct of a
transaction.

For example, a WWW page offering electronic commerce facilities would
arguably fall within the above definition of a computer program, as it is "a
set of instructions" (the HTML source for the page) "intended . . . to cause
a device" (the browsing computer) "to perform a particular function"
(display text and/or images in a certain way). A WWW page is even more
likely to be protectable as a computer program if it contains an embedded script
(in the Java language, for example).

Acquiring Copyright

The initial owner of a copyright work is the author of that work unless **3-64**
there is an agreement in writing to the contrary. An exemption is made
where the work is created pursuant to a contract of employment, in which
case the employer is the author. Copyright is personal property, and may
be assigned, in whole or in part. A partial assignment of copyright may be
limited as to time, territory, the exclusive rights assigned, or the use which
the assignee may make of the copyright work.

An assignment of copyright must be in writing and must be signed by or
on behalf of the owner of that copyright.[57] Where an assignment is made
without the required legal formalities, equitable ownership of the copyright
may be established.[58]

Licensing of Copyright

A copyright owner can grant a licence to do any of the acts which are the **3-65**
exclusive right of the copyright owner. An exclusive licence gives to the licensee
the right to do any act to the exclusion of all other persons, including the
copyright owner.[59]

As with assignments, an exclusive licence must be in writing and signed
by or on behalf of the copyright owner. One advantage of obtaining an
exclusive licence is that this allows the licensee to sue for infringement of
copyright in its own right.[60] There is no requirement for a non-exclusive
licence to be in writing – the licence may be written, oral or implied.

---

57 Copyright Act 1968, section 196(3).
58 *Acorn Computers Ltd.* v. *MCS Microcomputer Systems Pty. Ltd.* (1984) 6 F.C.R. 277.
59 Copyright Act 1968, section 10(1).
60 Although the copyright owner may need to be joined as a plaintiff; Copyright Act 1968,
  sections 117–119.

Ownership and Licensing of Copyright to Material Placed On-line

3-66   An owner of material who allows it to be placed on the Internet does not relinquish the copyright in that work. The ability of others to copy that work will depend on the licence (if any) that is included with the work. If there is no express licence to use or copy the work, then an implied licence may exist. This will depend on the purpose for which the work was distributed and the manner in which the work is made available.

A good example of these principles is the recent case of *Trumpet* v. *OzEmail*.[61] Trumpet distributed software as shareware, with one of its major methods of distribution being through the Internet. OzEmail copied the Trumpet software package off the Internet, changed part of the package and distributed free copies of the software to entice users to its own Internet connection service.

The court held that OzEmail had infringed copyright in the Trumpet software. The court there held that the following terms can be implied into a shareware licence:

- That the software package will be distributed without modification; and
- That the package will be distributed in its entirety.

3-67   The court also held that certain other terms need not be implied into a shareware licence:

- That shareware must not be distributed for a profit; and
- That shareware software must not be distributed together with other software.

3-68   Where works other than software are placed on the Internet, the principles applied should be similar — if there is no express licence included with the work, then it would be a question of which terms may be implied. At the very least, the implied licence would extend so far as to authorise other users to copy the work into the Random Access Memory of their computer, because this is the only way that the work could be perceived. From this minimal position, it is possible that broader implied licence terms may exist. In decreasing order of restrictiveness, these may include:

- A right to save the work to the hard drive of the recipient's computer;
- A right to make one reproduction of the work on another medium (*e.g.,* paper and tape);
- A right to redistribute the work in its entirety for a non-profit making purpose;

---

61 *Trumpet Software Pty. Ltd. and Another* v. *OzEmail Pty. Ltd. and Others* (1996) 34 I.P.R. 481.

- A right to reproduce all or a part of the work for a non-profit making purpose;
- A right to redistribute the work in its entirety for any purpose; and
- A right to reproduce all or a part of the work for any purpose (which would be similar to placing the work in the public domain).

Infringement of Copyright and Authorisation

Australian courts' approach to the issue of infringement, particularly with   3-69
respect to computer programs, is generally slanted towards the rights of the copyright owner. For example, in the leading case of *Autodesk v. Dyason*,[62] the court held that a 128-bit sequence used as part of a security device on a commercial software package was a substantial part of that package.

A direct infringement of copyright is the doing of any act comprised in the copyright without the permission of the copyright owner. The Copyright Act also contains several "indirect" infringement provisions, two of which are particularly relevant:

- Importation – the bringing into Australia for the purpose of trade articles, the making of which would be an infringement of copyright;[63] and
- Authorisation – authorising another person to commit an infringement of copyright is itself an infringement.

The latter aspect is particularly relevant in the on-line context because access   3-70
to on-line services would usually occur through an Internet Service Provider (ISP). Therefore, an ISP may find itself liable for authorising copyright infringement. An Internet Service Provider facilitates access to the Internet by the public by providing the technical facilities to:

- "Browse" the Internet, *i.e.,* to retrieve information from the Internet;
- Set up Internet sites, *i.e.,* to publish information on to the Internet.

Of course, both types of conduct may involve copyright infringement.   3-71
Internet Service Providers would see themselves as providing nothing more than a route to the Internet, without any responsibility for content. However, there has been no case in Australia to test this proposition. According to the High Court in the leading case on authorisation, *University of NSW v. Moorhouse*,[64] authorisation has three elements:

- Knowledge;
- Power to prevent the infringement;
- The infringement is allowed by express or implied conduct.

---

62 *Autodesk v. Dyason* (1992) 173 C.L.R. 330.
63 Copyright Act, sections 37 and 102.
64 *University of NSW v. Moorhouse* (1975) 133 C.L.R. 1.

3-72   **When Does an ISP Have Knowledge of Infringement?** Internet Service Providers can be expected to know that the equipment they provide may be used for the purpose of downloading or publishing infringing material. However, they would not normally know which material is infringing and the sheer volume of information on an ISP's system usually makes it practically impossible to monitor all data. Usually, an ISP would only become aware of an infringement when informed by the copyright owner.

3-73   **Does an ISP Have Power to Prevent Infringement?** An ISP has the technical power to prevent infringement by withdrawing access to its own users. However, whether it is entitled to do this depends on the terms of the agreement between the ISP and the end-user. This can be a difficult issue for an ISP. The ISP would normally want to have the power to withdraw access and to delete computer files stored on the ISP's system.

This may often be the quickest way of settling any allegation of copyright infringement by a user, as well as of infringement of trade mark, censorship and defamation laws. On the other hand, this would make it more likely that the second stage of the *Moorhouse* test would be satisfied. The current practice seems to be that ISPs reserve the right to terminate access and delete information.

3-74   **Does the ISP Allow Infringement Expressly or Impliedly by Conduct?** This is a more difficult issue because it is not clear what degree of complicity is required to satisfy this criterion. Again, it could be argued that once an ISP is aware that infringing material is present on the system, the ISP is allowing infringement by not terminating a user's account.

Although there is no Australian law on point, the most likely legal analysis is that an ISP can be liable for authorising infringement where the ISP is informed about the infringing material and takes no steps to stop the infringement. Practically speaking, ISPs, particularly smaller companies, would not have the resources to evaluate the merits of every infringement claim. Their only alternative in such a situation would be to remove the infringing material and to terminate a user's account if necessary.

Rights of Users – Defences to Infringement

3-75   The Copyright Act provides several defences to actions for infringement. The widest defence available is that of "fair dealing". "Fair dealing" is only available as a defence if the fair dealing is for one of the purposes prescribed in sections 40–43 of the Copyright Act 1968. These purposes are:

- Research or study;
- Criticism or review;
- The reporting of news; and
- Giving of professional advice by a legal practitioner or patent attorney.

Generally, these defences have not been given a broad interpretation by the   3-76
courts. For example, in the Federal Court case of *De Garis* v. *Neville Jeffress
Pidler Pty. Ltd.*,[65] a commercial news clipping service was found not to be
engaged in "research or study" because its activities were directed towards
a commercial purpose.

The "fair dealing" defences may prove useful in the case of infringement of works stored electronically, particularly where a work which has
been made electronically has been reproduced in part for the purpose of
criticism.

Trade Secrets

Correspondence passing between parties may contain highly sensitive infor-   3-77
mation that is plainly intended by both parties to be kept in the strictest
confidence. Any inadvertent disclosure of such information to a third party
may be not only a breach of contractual and equitable obligations of
confidence, but also, depending on the circumstances of the disclosure and
the nature of the information disclosed, could constitute:

- Negligence; and
- A breach of the party's implied obligations to exercise reasonable care
  and skill in acting on instructions and to observe confidentiality.

Any such disclosure may therefore give rise to substantial liability to the   3-78
party if damage flows from that disclosure.

Nature of the Equitable Obligation

In Australia, the leading authority on the elements required for an action for   3-79
breach of confidence where no contract exists is the English case of *Coco* v.
AN Clark (Engineers) Ltd.[66] Megarry J. held that three main elements are
required, as follows:

- That the information must have the necessary quality of confidence
  about it. It must not be something that is "public property and public
  knowledge";[67]

---

65 *De Garis* v. *Neville Jeffress Pidler Pty. Ltd.* (1990) 37 F.C.R. 99.
66 [1969] R.P.C. 41.
67 *Saltman Engineering Co. Ltd.* v. *Campbell Engineering Co. Ltd.* (1948) 65 R.P.C. 203 per
   Lord Greene MR. The courts have been flexible as to the types of information that can be
   protected. There is no accepted definition of the term "trade secret". The principal feature
   of what has become known to be a trade secret is that it is confidential information in a
   commercial context.

- That the information must have been imparted in circumstances importing an obligation of confidence; and[68]
- There must be an unauthorised use or disclosure of that information to the detriment of the party communicating it.

Impact of Electronic Communications on the Equitable Obligation of Confidence

3-80   Two important issues arise with respect to confidential information transmitted electronically.

3-81   **Unauthorised Access or Interception and Breach of Confidence**   If a plaintiff has established that it has imparted confidential information in circumstances imposing an obligation of confidence, then it is clear that accidental (or subconscious) "misuse" of the information by the recipient may amount to a breach of confidence.[69] These authorities suggest that an intention to disclose is not required. Arguably, therefore, although the circumstances have not been considered by an Australian court, the recipient of a confidential message that has been "disclosed" to a third party through the third party's unauthorised access to equipment may be liable for breach of confidence (the recipient may also be liable in negligence if adequate security measures have not been maintained). If the third party has contravened legislation relating to unauthorised access or interception to obtain the confidential information, then this may be a decisive factor in determining that the recipient is not in breach of confidence.

The responsibility for security/confidentiality of electronic communications may, of course, be dealt with in a contract between the sender and recipient. For example, the Model EDI Trading Agreement prepared by the EDI Council of Australia provides that "each party shall be responsible to the other to prevent unauthorised access or transmissions and shall be liable for any costs or consequences which flow therefrom".[70]

3-82   **Information Obtained through Unauthorised Access**   The second issue which arises in the context of electronic communications is whether a party who obtains information of a confidential nature through unauthorised access or by accident should be obliged to maintain its confidentiality even if that person has had no personal contact with the owner of the information.

---

68 *Smith Kline&French Laboratories (Australia) Ltd.* v. *Secretary, Department of Community Services and Health* (1990) 17 I.P.R. 545; *Fractionated Cane Technology Ltd.* v. *Ruiz-Avila* (1987) 8 I.P.R. 502; (1988) 13 I.P.R. 609. The Australian authorities in this area hold that in determining whether an obligation of confidence has been imposed a court must consider all relevant circumstances surrounding the disclosure.
69 *Seager* v. *Copydex* [1967] R.P.C. 349, *Talbot* v. *General Television Corporation Pty. Ltd.* [1980] VR 224.
70 Clause 7.2, Version 1, October 1990.

The judgment of Megarry J., in *Coco* v. *AN Clark (Engineers) Ltd.,*[71] suggests that the information must be "imparted" in confidence by the plaintiff to the defendant. However, in *Attorney General* v. *Guardian Newspapers (No. 2),*[72] Lord Goff indicated that the obligation may apply more broadly to any situation where "confidential information comes to the knowledge of a person in circumstances where he has notice, or is held to have agreed that the information is confidential". Lord Goff suggested that the obligation should extend to information accidentally obtained, such as a private diary dropped in a public place and picked up by a passer-by, as well as information surreptitiously or improperly obtained.[73]

In the Australian case of *Franklin* v. *Giddins,*[74] the defendant improperly obtained a budwood used to propagate a variety of nectarine known as "Franklin Early White". In an action for breach of confidence against the defendant, the court held in favour of the plaintiff, stating that it would be unconscionable for the defendant to obtain a benefit from the theft of a trade secret from the plaintiff.

The principle in *Franklin* v. *Giddins* could therefore be available to owners of confidential information in Australia against persons who have gained improper access to that information by intercepting an electronic communication.

Trade Marks and Domain Names

There is at present no reported decision by an Australian court in relation   3-83
to misuse of trade marks on the Internet, either as a domain name or as a trade mark for goods or services offered over the Internet.

Although the Internet has been accessible in Australia for many years, Australian traders have only recently realised the potential markets made available by the Internet, and increasing numbers of Australian consumers are being connected to the Internet.

Domain Names

The Australian Domain Administrator   The principal administrator of   3-84
the ".au" domain in Australia is Mr. Robert Elz, who is a computer systems administrator at the University of Melbourne.[75] In October 1996, Mr. Elz delegated to Melbourne Information Technologies Australia Pty. Ltd.

---

71 [1969] R.P.C. 41.
72 [1990] 1 A.C. 109.
73 As suggested by Eadey L.J. in *Lord Ashburton* v. *Pape* [1913] 2 Ch. 469.
74 [1978] Qd.R. 72.
75 Details of the policies applicable and procedures necessary for registering a domain name, other than a domain name in the ".com.au" domain, are available at http://www.aunic.net/.

(Melbourne IT) the responsibility for assigning and administering domain names in the ".com.au" domain.[76]

Melbourne IT is a "proprietary limited" company, which is a wholly owned subsidiary of Unimelb Limited, the commercial arm of the University of Melbourne. This has implications if Melbourne IT is found liable for trade mark infringement as a result of its activities in granting "licences" for domain names which are the registered trade marks of third parties. In particular, "wronged" trade mark owners may regard the University as a person with deep pockets and may choose to take action against it in preference to the licensee of an "infringing" domain name[77] who may only be a nominal party to the transaction.

There are presently a dozen second-level domain names under the ".au" top level country domain name, the most popular of which are ".com" (for commercial organisations), ".net" (for network service providers and the like), ".gov" (for government bodies and organisations) and ".edu" (for educational institutions). Given that the most popular second-level domain in Australia is by far and way the ".com" domain, the following discussion is limited to the ".com" domain.

3-85   **Domain Name Registration** Melbourne IT at its web site sets out the policy it applies to applications and existing registrations for domain names in the ".com" domain. This policy has been evolving over time and will probably continue to do so, with the latest version[78] as at the time of writing being a significant modification of the previous policies applied by Melbourne IT. These modifications may be partially as a result of industry discussion and a legal proceeding commenced against Melbourne IT in relation to its ".com.au" policy in 1997 which has, however, been settled by the parties. Melbourne IT's policy in relation to domain name applications includes the following elements:

- The domain name must be "unique"[79] within the ".com.au" domain, so that by implication domain names are allocated on a "first-in, first-served" basis, without Melbourne IT conducting any form of availability search other than to determine whether a domain name is identical to another already in the ".com.au" domain;
- The domain name must be at least two characters long;

---

76 The site to apply for registration of domain names in the ".com.au" domain and the policies applied to such ".com.au" domain name applications (and subsequent registrations arising as a result of such applications) is http://www.melbourneit.com.au.

77 The question of whether use of trade mark as a domain name by a "cybersquatter" is contrary to Australian law is considered further below.

78 Updated on July 3, 1997.

79 Although there is no explanation in the domain name policy, it seems that "unique" is likely to be interpreted as "no identical names" rather than as "no identical or substantially identical or deceptively similar names".

- The domain name must be directly derived from the characters in the full legal name of the applicant, in the order in which they appear in the name;
- The domain name cannot be a generic word describing products, industries or organisations, although a generic phrase of two or more generic words is permitted; and
- The domain name may not be an unqualified Australian place name.

The most interesting aspect of the domain name policy, for present purposes, is that the applicant must "ensure that use of the domain name does not contravene any third party's rights to use the name". This is to be compared with Melbourne IT's previous policy, which required a domain name applicant to warrant that the information provided in the application was true and correct, with Melbourne IT being said to rely on the information and warranties provided. In addition, the applicant was required to indemnify Melbourne IT against all claims and demands by third parties regarding registration and continued use of the domain name, but this aspect of the policy is also no longer included in the present form of the Melbourne IT policy.   **3-86**

The previous version of Melbourne IT's domain name registration policy expressed each registered domain name issued by Melbourne IT to merely be a "licence to use" the domain name for a given period, with such licence being renewed by Melbourne IT on the payment of the appropriate fee. The licence was expressed to not be transferable to another organisation.[80] The licence to use was revocable in circumstances that included:

- Breach of a warranty provided by the applicant;
- Where a court of competent authority determined that the domain name should not be allotted to the applicant or should be allotted to another party; and
- Under instruction by the applicant.

However, under the present version of Melbourne IT's policy there is no express provision to the effect that Melbourne IT merely grants a licence to the domain name and that Melbourne IT can revoke that licence in certain specified circumstances. However, the fees payable for registration of a domain name are expressed to be a "licence and maintenance fee", which indicates that Melbourne IT at least still regards itself as merely granting a licence to use the domain name. The question then is under what conditions   **3-87**

---

80 As a practical matter, *de facto* transfer of a domain name could still have been effected by the existing owner of the domain name requesting the domain name to be deregistered and for the other party to then immediately apply for the same domain name (although there was a one-month period during which the initial owner could reactivate the registration).

Melbourne IT has an implied right to revoke the licence, in the absence of any express circumstances for revocation.

It is arguable that a breach of the domain name rules would be a basis for revocation of the licence. Therefore, Melbourne IT may be able to revoke the licence granted in respect of a domain name if it believes that use of the domain name contravenes a third party's rights to use of the name, for example, because the domain name is the registered trade mark of a third party. The initial granting of the licence by Melbourne IT also has implications in those circumstances in relation to the accessorial liability of Melbourne IT for any trade mark infringement.

The potential ability for Melbourne IT to revoke a licence to a domain name is interesting, given that the legal proceeding against Melbourne IT referred to above in part related to the policy whereby Melbourne IT was able to revoke a licence for a domain name in circumstances other than with the consent of the domain name licensee. Although the domain name policy no longer has any express provision to that effect, it seems that as a matter of fact Melbourne IT may still retain such a power of revocation even where the licensee does not consent to the revocation.

3-88   **Disputes Policy of the Administrator** The dispute resolution process that Melbourne IT has adopted does not, at least at present, appear to allow for a rapid resolution of matters. Rather, it sets out a detailed process that the parties to the dispute must follow.

The dispute resolution policy requires the disputants to submit to and agree to be bound by a dispute resolution process providing for "mediation and resolution by an industry-accepted arbitration process". The policy then states that the dispute resolution process is as follows:

- The originator of the dispute must notify Melbourne IT that there is a dispute;
- The originator of the dispute, Melbourne IT and any third party must attempt to settle the dispute "by negotiation and conciliation"; and
- If the dispute is not otherwise settled, a disputant may refer the dispute for resolution to the Australian Commercial Disputes Centre, with the parties agreeing to be bound by any ruling of the "arbiter".[81]

3-89   The main problem with the dispute resolution process is that (as a matter of contract) it will only be binding on Melbourne IT and any applicant

---

[81] The Melbourne IT dispute policy therefore refers to four different kinds of dispute resolution techniques. It is not made clear which of these is in fact to operate in relation to a dispute. However, the policy will probably be applied by first requiring negotiation and/or mediation and, failing that, arbitration. The dispute resolution policy fails to make any rules for how the arbitration process is to proceed and who is to bear the cost of this often expensive process.

for/licensee of a domain name — there is no reason why a person who claims to have a better right to a registered domain name should be bound to follow the specified process. Presumably, Melbourne IT will attempt to persuade any disputant that the specified process is preferable to engaging in litigation, but there is no apparent reason why a trade mark owner who feels its rights to a trade mark have been infringed should follow this process.

The main omission from the Melbourne IT dispute resolution process is that the disputed domain name is not placed "on hold" while the parties seek to resolve the dispute.[82] Accordingly, a party claiming to have a better right[83] to an already registered domain name must commence a legal proceeding before a court to ensure that it obtains an interim injunction to prevent the continued use of the domain name until the conclusion of the alternative dispute resolution procedure. If the trade mark owner needs to take this step in any event, he or she may decide to simply bypass the prescribed alternative dispute resolution procedure completely. However, having obtained such an interim injunction, the trade mark owner may consent to the determination of the matter being referred to arbitration.

Causes of Action For "Misuse" of a Trade Mark

There are two main situations where a trade mark may be misused on the Internet by a third party. The following section will consider whether either or both of those uses may infringe the rights of the owner of the trade mark, regardless of whether the trader is the owner of the trade mark in Australia by reason of having registered the trade mark in Australia or by reason of the trader having goodwill in the trade mark by reason of using it in Australia or otherwise. The Federal Court held in *Conagra Inc.* v. *McCain Food Aust Pty. Ltd*.[84] that to establish reputation in respect of a trade mark in Australia sufficient to support a cause of action for "passing off" and/or breach of section 52 of the Trade Practices Act 1974 (Commonwealth) a trader need not have a place of business in Australia nor even to have traded in Australia, provided the trader has otherwise gained a reputation in this country with respect to that trade mark. 3-90

Domain Names Where a trade mark is registered and used in Australia as a third-level domain name for an Internet site, a number of causes of action may be available to the owner of the trade mark. 3-91

Actions under Trade Marks Act 1995 The Trade Marks Act 1995 (Commonwealth) deals in section 120 with trade mark infringement. Section 120(1) provides that a trade mark registered under that legislation (which includes any 3-92

---

82 This is to be compared to the dispute resolution process adopted by the United States of America Internet domain name registration authority, Internic.

83 Such as prior registration or use of the trade mark which is registered as a domain name.

84 (1992) 23 I.P.R. 193.

trade mark registered under its predecessor legislation) is infringed if a "substantially identical or deceptively similar" trade mark is used as a trade mark in respect of the goods for which the trade mark is registered.

Under section 120(2), a registered trade mark is also infringed if a "substantially identical or deceptively similar" trade mark is used as a trade mark in respect of "goods of the same description" or "related services" to the goods for which it is registered, and vice versa. This second form of infringement, however, is subject to a defence that there will be no trade mark infringement if the defendant can show that use of the trade mark is not likely to cause deception or confusion.

There is also a third situation of trade mark infringement, which is specified under section 120(3). This provides for infringement of "well-known" trade marks. A well-known trade mark is infringed even if it is used by the alleged infringer in respect of goods and/or services for which it is not registered by the owner (although the trade mark must be registered in Australia in respect of at least some goods or services). The trade mark will only be infringed, however, if, because the trade mark is well known, use of the trade mark by the infringer would be likely to be taken as indicating a connection between the goods or services of the alleged infringer and the owner of the well-known trade mark. Further, this connection must cause the interests of the trade mark owner to be adversely affected. A trade mark is to be taken as well known in Australia based on the following factors:

- The extent to which a trade mark is known within the relevant sector of the public;
- Whether it has become well-known as a result of promotion of the trade mark; and
- Whether it has become well-known for any other reasons.

3-93   Each of the three causes of action for trade mark infringement under the Trade Marks Act 1995 requires "use of a trade mark as a trade mark". A trade mark is defined under the legislation as a sign used or intended to be used to distinguish goods or services dealt with or provided in the course of trade mark by a person from the goods or services dealt with or provided by any other person. For a domain name to fall foul of any of the provisions of section 120, it is therefore necessary to establish that the domain name is "used in the course of trade" and that it is "used as a trade mark". In the case of a trade mark that is being used as a domain name, the requirement for "use in the course of trade" is unlikely to be satisfied unless commercial activity (in some form) takes place or is likely to take place at the site. Thus, use of a trade mark as the domain name for a personal home page which gives the details of a person's life would be unlikely to constitute "use in the course of trade".

However, if a soft drink manufacturer's trade mark was used as a domain name for a site that advertised a range of drinking glasses, this would more clearly be "use as a trade mark". Sites that are not used for commercial purposes but merely as a site from which to send and receive messages and provide information via the Internet, with the domain name therefore merely acting as a personal digital address for those purposes, are referred to as "pseudodomains".[85] Australian courts have in the past been willing to find that the offering of goods or services or the "encouragement of enquiries from prospective customers" constitutes use in the course of trade. Thus, if the site relates to goods in respect of which the trade mark is registered, with such goods being advertised or offered for sale at the site together with facilities to effect their supply in Australia, this is likely to satisfy the requirement of "use in the course of trade". There is also likely to be "use in the course of trade" where the site contains an advertisement (in whatever form) for the goods or services even though the goods or services are not directly available in Australia.

For the requirement that the trade mark must be used as a trade mark to be satisfied, the domain name must be used and regarded by people in Australia as indicating the origin or quality of the goods or services at the site. In particular, the question is whether the trade mark, when used in a domain name for a site, is regarded by visitors to that site as an invitation to purchase the product at that site. This paraphrases the test of Gummow J. in *Johnson & Johnson* v. *Sterling Pharmaceuticals*.[86] Other factors a court is likely to consider in determining whether there is use as a trade mark include:

- Whether the name, word or trade mark is a "coined phrase";
- Whether the name, word, or trade mark in question has acquired a secondary meaning in Australia; and
- The strength of any secondary meaning which the trade mark must members of the public in Australia.

Section 7 of the Trade Marks Act 1995 defines use of a trade mark as use of   **3-94** the trade mark on or in physical or other relation to goods and services, so that it is not necessary that the trade mark is applied directly to the goods. However, the use of a different trade mark on goods offered at the site may, in the context, mean that the domain name is not being "used as a trade mark" in relation to those goods. Even if the use of a domain name satisfies the above requirements, further questions to be considered include:

- Whether the Universal Resource Locater address (URL) for the site (which is, after all, the manner in which the domain name is usually used to access the site) is "substantially identical or deceptively similar" to the registered trade mark because it contains the third-level domain name; and

---

85 See Marcowitz, "ronald@mcdonalds.com — 'Owning a Bitchin' Corporate Trademark as an Internet Address — Infringement", 17 *Cardozo Law Review* 85.
86 1991, 101 ALR 200.

• Whether the domain name which is used in respect of a site for "goods of the same description or closely related services" to the goods for which the trade mark is registered or in respect of a site for "services of the same description or closely related goods" to the services for which the trade mark is registered will not be an infringement where the site prominently contains disclaimers that the licensee of the domain name does not own the trade mark in Australia (so as to take advantage of the defence under section 120(2)).

3-95   *Actions under Trade Practices Act 1974 (Commonwealth)*   The second principal alternative for stopping use of a domain name is on the basis of section 52 and/or section 53 of the Trade Practices Act 1974 (Commonwealth).[87] Section 52 prohibits a corporation in trade or commerce from engaging in conduct that is misleading or deceptive or likely to mislead or deceive.[88] One implication is that a personal or non-business Internet site could use a trade mark as a domain name and it may not be possible to successfully invoke the aid of the Trade Practice Act 1974 to stop this conduct. However, in the past "trade or commerce" has been fairly liberally interpreted, with even "one-off" transactions being capable of satisfying this requirement. Section 53 prohibits the making of a variety of misrepresentations, such as a false representation that a corporation has a sponsorship, approval, or affiliation that it does not have.[89]

These causes of action are directed to the protection of consumers, although Australian courts have in many situations applied the principles applicable to passing off to determine the effect of the conduct/representations. As a matter of practice, the Australian courts have held that the consumer protection provisions of the Trade Practices Act 1974 can be used by traders against other traders, although the courts will focus on what effect the conduct had on consumers and not the effect on the trader's goodwill in its trade mark.

The principal problem with the causes of action under the Trade Practices Act 1974 is that, to establish that the provisions have been breached, it is necessary to provide evidence that the plaintiff has established a reputation in the trade mark in Australia. This reputation is necessary as an

---

87 There are equivalent provisions in the fair trading legislation of each State and Territory of Australia, and these provisions apply to individuals.

88 The requirement that conduct be "in trade or commerce" is one of the major preconditions for the operation of the Trade Practices Act 1974 and the State and Territory fair trading legislation equivalents. Fair Trading Act 1992 (A.C.T.); Consumer Affairs and Fair Trading Act 1990 (N.T.); Fair Trading Act 1987 (N.S.W.); Fair Trading Act 1989 (Queensland); Fair Trading Act 1987 (South Australia); Fair Trading Act 1990 (Tasmania); Fair Trading Act 1985 (Victoria); Fair Trading Act 1987 (West Australia).

89 Such a false representation may be present where a corporation uses a trade mark that the public associates with another trader, such that the public is led to believe that there is an association between the entities that has resulted in the first being allowed to use the trade mark, name or domain name of the second.

evidentiary matter to establish that the public, when seeing the name or trade mark being used by a third party, would believe the goods or services under or by reference to the trade mark are connected with the person who has a reputation in respect of the name or trade mark. For the purposes of such an action, the trade mark need not be registered in Australia, provided that the trader has a reputation in Australia under or by reference to the trade mark so that consumers would be misled or deceived by use of the trade mark by a third party as a domain name — even potentially if the trade mark is used in relation to goods or services that are different to those in respect of which the first trader has an established reputation.[90]

It is also necessary to show that, by reason of another party using the trade mark as a domain name, the public (or the relevant sector of the public, at least) is likely to be misled or deceived as to the source or origin of (in the case of a domain name) the particular site or to be deceived as to any connection or association that it has with the trade mark or its owner.

If a site contains a disclaimer to the effect that the trade mark contained in the URL does not belong to the proprietor of the site in all countries from which the site can be accessed, this may prevent any action for breach of section 52 or 53 and/or passing off from succeeding.[91] The reason for this is that the effect of such a disclaimer is that this should prevent a consumer from necessarily being misled or deceived as to the source or origin of the site and the goods or services offered for sale at the site.[92]

Passing off The law of passing off also applies in Australia and provides   3-96
another means for seeking to prevent use of an unregistered trade mark as a domain name in Australia. Australian courts, in applying the law of passing off to situations of misuse of an unregistered trade mark, have generally followed the English courts as to matters such as the elements of the cause of action. The principal exception to this is that the English courts

90 As a matter of practice, however, it will generally only be possible to establish that consumers are misled or deceived or likely to be misled or deceived if the second trader uses the trade mark in respect of the goods or services in respect of which the first trader has developed a reputation, or closely related goods and services. If consumers are merely confused or caused to wonder about the origin of the goods or services bearing or under or by reference to the trade mark, for example, because they are different to the goods or services in respect of which they are familiar with the trade mark, the Australian courts have previously stated that the cause of action will not be established.

91 However, to be effective the disclaimer would in all likelihood need to be sufficiently prominent, it would have to be present at each page on the site at which the trade mark is mentioned and it would be desirable for the disclaimer to state that Australia is one of the countries in which the trade mark is not owned by the site's proprietor.

92 Such confusion may be further eliminated if the goods at the site bear a trade mark which is different to the trade mark contained in the URL. However, it has previously been questioned whether, for the purposes of an action under section 52, it is necessary for the misleading or deceptive conduct to continue to the point of sale, and therefore any misleading or deception that arises before the site is accessed and the disclaimer viewed may still give rise to a cause of action.

on balance still appear to prefer an approach whereby a trader seeking to bring an action for passing off must have goodwill in the jurisdiction that has arisen by reason of having a place of business and conducting business in the jurisdiction. However, it is now fairly well established that all that is required in Australia for the cause of action is that the trader has a reputation in Australia in respect of the trade mark, even if the trader has not actually traded in Australia under or by reference to the trade mark.

The application of the law of passing off in Australia to prevent use of a trade mark as a domain name will not be considered further here, however, because section 52 and section 53 of the Trade Practices Act 1974 are so broad that they have effectively superseded the Common Law action. For one thing, the statutory actions have the advantage that it is not necessary to establish that damage has been suffered.

3-97   **Trade Mark Infringement** Breaches of section 52 and section 53 of the Trade Practices Act 1974, passing off, and trade mark infringement are causes of action that are also available where a trade mark is used on the Internet, not as a domain name, but as a trade mark for goods or services offered for sale or advertised at a site.

When a trade mark is used in this context, it will be more straightforward to establish the necessary elements of "use in the course of trade" and "use as a trade mark" for a conventional action for trade mark infringement under the Trade Marks Act 1995. "Use in the course of trade" will be present either where goods or services are advertised at the site or where the goods are offered for sale at the Internet site and there is a facility for their distribution to Australia.[93] If the trade mark is applied to or in relation to goods or services offered at the site, then this will generally satisfy the "use as a trade mark" requirement. Effectively, the Internet in these circumstances is merely another means for promoting products and using the trade mark, the same as a radio or television advertisement or offering goods for sale in a store. The interesting issue, of course, becomes one of jurisdiction.

Once the element of "use in the course of trade" for trade mark infringement purposes is present, the "trade or commerce" precondition for an action under sections 52 and 53 of the Trade Practices Act 1974 should also be satisfied. Indeed, an action for breach of the Trade Practices Act 1974 is wider than an action for trade mark infringement insofar as there is with the former action no need to show that there is "use as a trade mark". Further, a court may be more willing to find that consumers are misled or deceived when a name or trade mark which they associate with a particular entity is

---

93 An example would be where a site based in the United Kingdom offers goods bearing an Australian registered trade mark which is owned in Australia by a third party; there is a facility that can be used by a person in Australia to pay for the goods; and the site offers a method by which the goods can be shipped to Australia. This is a fairly clear case of use of the Australian trade mark in Australia.

used in respect of goods or services advertised or offered for sale at an Internet site by an unrelated third party, as compared to where the trade mark is merely incorporated in a domain name.[94]

Jurisdiction In relation to the question of jurisdiction under the Trade Marks Act 1995, this depends on the scope of operation of the Act. Section 20 gives the registered owner of the trade mark the exclusive rights to use the trade mark and to authorise other persons to use the trade mark, without any geographic limitation being placed on the exclusive rights granted by the section. However, as a matter of sovereignty and international comity, there must be an implied limitation that the exclusive rights only extend within Australia. Thus, it must be shown that the trade mark is being used in Australia for the jurisdiction of the Federal Court of Australia in relation to an action for breach of a registered trade mark to be attracted when a trade mark:

3-98

- Is used in relation to goods or services which are shown (whether in the form of an advertisement or an offer to sell the goods or services or otherwise) at the Internet site;[95] or
- Is used as a domain name.

On one view, a trade mark is not used in Australia unless the Internet site is directed at Australia and Australian users. However, Australian courts have previously accepted[96] that use of a trade mark in an international magazine that is available in Australia will be use of the trade mark in Australia. On that basis, it is likely that an Internet site that is accessible from Australia can infringe the exclusive rights granted by section 20. However, even if a trade mark is regarded as being used in Australia, a court may conclude that Australia is a *forum non-conveniens* if the proprietor of the site is located overseas, particularly if it is in a country with which Australia does not have a treaty for reciprocal enforcement and registration of judgments.

3-99

Patents

The grant of patents in Australia is governed by the Patents Act 1990 and is a field reserved by the Australian Constitution[97] for the federal jurisdiction. The

3-100

---

94 The reason for this is that there is an argument that a domain name is merely an address by which users locate a site on the Internet, rather than needing to memorise the string of numbers which constitute the site's IP address. A brief discussion of this point is to be found in the article by Corneau, "A Practical Look at Internet Domain Name Issues", *Trademark World*, August 1996, 27 at p. 30, where the author discusses a case where a Canadian court held that a domain name was effectively a "telephone number" that was the same as a third party's name.

95 However, even if the court's jurisdiction was attracted and an Order obtained, enforcement of the Order in a foreign jurisdiction may prove problematical.

96 *Estex Clothing Manufacturers Pty. Ltd.* v. *Ellis & Goldstein* (1967) 116 C.L.R. 254.

97 Patents Act 1990, section 51(xviii).

responsible examining and issuing authority is the Australian Industrial Property Organisation (A.I.P.O.), which operates the Australian Patent Office, among other bodies. Although an infringement or revocation proceeding can be instituted in the Federal Court or in a State or Territory Supreme Court, the court of appeal is the Federal Court.[98] Further appeal to the High Court in patent matters requires specific leave of the High Court.[99] Appeals on matters of law from A.I.P.O. decisions are exclusively to the Federal Court.[100] For these reasons, the Federal Court has over recent years consolidated its position as the supervising court in patent matters.

There are two kinds of patents.[101] A "standard" patent has a 20-year term and is what is usually meant by the term "patent". A "petty" patent has a six-year term. There are no differences as to permissible subject matter between the two kinds of patents. In practice, the proportion of petty patents granted is very small, notwithstanding the seeming attraction of a procedurally simpler six-year term patent in rapidly changing technologies.

Australia is a member of the Paris Convention for the Protection of Industrial Property, and of the Patent Co-operation Treaty. Patent rights applied for in other member countries of the respective treaties may be extended to Australia in the manner provided for under those treaties and by the usual deadlines (one year under the Paris Convention, 21 or 31 months from the earliest priority date under the Patent Co-operation Treaty).

Patentability of Procedures and Software for Transacting On-line Commerce

3-101   Unlike the position in some other jurisdictions, no statutory or other legislative bar in Australia precludes the grant of patents for computer programs or software.[102]

Until the early 1990's, there were significant impediments to obtaining Australian patents where the invention resided in software or computational aspects. However, two decisions by the Federal Court[103] upheld the inherent patentability of the subject matter of, respectively, a set of computer steps for providing a graphics display of a curve, and a method for inputting Chinese characters into word-processing systems. As a result, A.I.P.O. in 1994 published revised practice guidelines[104] for determining the inherent patentability of software-related inventions. There, the essential

---

98 Patents Act 1990, sections 120, 138, 154–158, schedule 1.
99 Patents Act 1990, section 158(2) and (3).
100 Patents Act 1990, section 154(2).
101 Patents Act 1990, Schedule 1, sections 67, 68.
102 Patents Act 1990, section 18.
103 *IBM* v. *Commissioner of Patents* (1991) 22 I.P.R. 417, appealed to the Full Federal Court, but appeal withdrawn by the Commissioner and *CCOM Pty. Ltd.* v. *Jiejing* (1994) 28 I.P.R. 481, adverse finding overturned by Full Federal Court.
104 Australian Patent Office Manual of Practice and Procedure — National, section 8.1.18.

test to be applied is stated to be "Does the invention claimed involve the production of some commercially useful effect?".[105]

In practice, A.I.P.O. examiners do not object to a claim of a patent application that effectively sets out a sequence of steps implemented in software. Whether the courts will draw any boundary lines remains to be seen.

To be viewed as patentable, inventions implemented in software or involving an algorithm or computational procedures must meet the core requirements for patentability, *i.e.*, they must be novel and entail an inventive step.[106] The base for determining novelty is the body of all documents worldwide and public "acts" within Australia. The term "document" is defined in modern terms in other Australian federal legislation, as follows:[107]

"(a) . . . any paper or other material on which there is writing;

"(b) any paper or other material on which there are marks, figures, symbols or perforations having a meaning for persons qualified to interpret them; and

"(c) any article or material from which sounds, images or writings are capable of being reproduced with or without the aid of any other article or device."

A corollary of the requirement for novelty is that there can have been no **3-102** public disclosure of an invention in a document or act before the original date of the application for a patent in Australia or a foreign country. Unlike the position in the United States, there is no period of grace.

The "inventive height" required of Australian patents is considered to be lower than that established for non-obviousness in, *e.g.*, the United States, and under the practice of the European Patent Office. Simple combination of documents is not permitted. The base is common general knowledge in Australia at the original date of application for the invention — in Australia or elsewhere — plus at most one document or act, or multiple documents or acts if a person skilled in the relevant art in Australia would treat them as a single source.[108] The document or act in this context must have been one which the skilled person in the relevant art could be "reasonably expected to have ascertained, understood and regarded as relevant to work in the relevant art" in Australia.[109]

Drawing these threads together, software which implements or facilitates on-line commerce is patentable in Australia provided the application for a patent is originally lodged in Australia or another country before the invention is in the public domain, and provided it is novel and entails an

---

105 Australian Patent Office Manual of Practice and Procedure — National, paragraph 8.1.18.1.
106 Patents Act 1990, section 18(2).
107 Acts Interpretation Act 1901, section 25.
108 Patents Act 1990, section 7(2) and (3).
109 Patents Act 1990, section 7(3).

inventive step. The patent is not limited to the particular implementation but, if appropriately written, extends to the broad inventive concept involved. Protection may be obtained, by appropriate claim definition in the patent, for the set of steps as a "method", and for a computer when performing the "method".

On-line Trading in End-User Software

3-103   Of practical importance is whether the scope of an Australian patent can include (i) "a set of machine readable instructions" (stored, *e.g.*, on magnetic disk or CD ROM as object code), or (ii) the transmission of the object code on-line. End-user software which may be important in on-line transactions may be patentable as a set of method steps but this will be of limited value if the only parties able to be sued for infringement are end-users.

A claim in which the invention is defined only in terms of the method steps covers, in view of the definition of "exploit" in schedule one to the Patents Act 1990, only the use of the method or exploitation of the product of the method. To extend the patent scope to (i) above, the patent must contain a claim effectively to the object code, for example:

". . . a set of machine readable instructions which when installed in a computer with a suitable operating system allows the computer to perform a method of (x) comprising the following steps:"

"A storage medium containing a set of machine readable instructions which when installed in a computer, with a suitable operating system allows the computer to perform a method of (x) comprising the following steps:."

3-104   The traditional view[110] is that patents can properly be refused for lack of novelty in any case in which the only material product is a printed sheet, ticket, coupon — or punched card, pianola roll or magnetic tape— and the only alleged invention is an arrangement of "words or the like" on such sheet. However, if the "words" serve a mechanical purpose, or interact with the external environs, novelty can be established and a patent granted.[111] Under the aforementioned new guidelines for computer-related inventions,[112] there is still an insistence that:

A claim to a computer containing — but not using — a mathematical algorithm is not novel.[113]

---

110 Stated succinctly in the Australian Patent Office Manual of Practice and Procedure — National, section 8.1.10.
111 Australian Patent Office Manual of Practice and Procedure — National, paragraph 8.1.10.1; Moore Business Forms Application, 1979 AOJP 2521.
112 Australian Patent Office Manual of Practice and Procedure — National, section 8.1.18.
113 Australian Patent Office Manual of Practice and Procedure — National, paragraph 8.1.18.6.

The writer is of the strong view that these traditional authorities can in part be relied on and in part distinguished to achieve approval by the courts of the claims proposed at (i) and (ii) above.

The Federal Court is yet to consider a claim in this form. One would hope it will continue the liberal and pragmatic approach evident in the *IBM* and *CCOM* cases.[114]

Enforcing Patent Rights

Australian patents may be infringed by independent activity without knowl- **3-105** edge of the patented invention, *i.e.*, copying is not required as an element of infringement. However, a defence of innocent infringement[115] may be invoked to avoid damages or on account of profits — though not the grant of a restraining injunction. For these reasons, it is important that patentees give proper notice of the existence of patent protection. Such notice or marking is not compulsory in Australia. The exclusive right of exploitation of a patented product is defined in schedule 1, of the Patents Act 1990 in the following terms:

"'. . . exploit', in relation to an invention, includes:

"(a) where the invention is a product — make, hire, sell or otherwise dispose of the product, offer to make, sell, hire or otherwise dispose of it, use or import it, or keep it for the purpose of doing any of those things; or

"(b) where the invention is a method or process — use the method or process or do any act mentioned in paragraph [a] in respect of a product resulting from such use."

If a claim as envisaged above to a "set of machine readable instructions" is **3-106** upheld, then the claim could be infringed by (a) hire, sale or disposal on-line, (b) an offer, for example, at an Internet home page or website — to do so, (c) importing the software on-line to a user or reseller site, or (d) keeping the software at a website server for such purposes.

Australian patent applications are published 19 months after the earliest priority date — the original application date in Australia or a foreign country.[116] From that date, the applicant enjoys the rights of a patentee save that infringement proceedings cannot be instituted until after the grant of the patent.[117]

---

114 *IBM* v. *Commissioner of Patents* (1991) 22 I.P.R. 417, and *CCOM Pty. Ltd.* v. *Jiejing* (1994) 28 I.P.R. 481.
115 Patents Act 1990, section 123.
116 Patents Act 1990, section 54.
117 Patents Act 1990, section 57.

In particular, damages or an account of profits can accrue from the date of publication, provided the infringed claim of the application is a valid claim.[118]

In general, a patentee can obtain relief in proceedings by way of an injunction or, at the option of the patentee, either damages or an account of profits.[119] If the patent is confined in its coverage to a sequence of steps or algorithms implemented only in the end-users' personal computers, the patentee may still be able to pursue unauthorised distributors of the relevant software — whether on-line or by way of hard media — as a contributory infringement under section 117 of the Patents Act 1990. This provision reads as follows:

"(1) If the use of a product by a person would infringe a patent, the supply of that product by one person to another is an infringement of the patent by the supplier unless the supplier is the patentee or licensee of the patent.

"(2) A reference in subsection (1) to the use of a product by a person is a reference to:

"(a) if the product is capable of only one reasonable use, having regard to its nature or design — that use; or

"(b) if the product is not a staple commercial product — any use of the product, if the supplier had reason to believe that the person would put it to that use; or

"(c) in any case — the use of the product in accordance with any instructions for the use of the product, or any inducement to use the product, given to the person by the supplier or contained in an advertisement published by or with the authority of the supplier."

3-107   Australia does not have a strong tradition of contributory infringement, *i.e.*, infringement by the supply of components or materials required to infringe a patent, especially with instructions to infringe. Perhaps in consequence, the correct meaning and interpretation of section 117 has been debated since its enactment in 1990, and at least one decision has produced a rather individual view of its application.[120] The text of section 117 is under review. The writer is not aware of any attempt to invoke section 117 in the context presently discussed.

---

118 Patents Act 1990, section 57(4).
119 Patents Act 1990, section 122.
120 *Rescare Ltd.* v. *Anaesthetic Supplies Pty. Ltd.* (1993) 25 I.P.R. 119.

REGULATION OF ON-LINE CONDUCT

On-line conduct is regulated in Australia by a variety of laws. Many are laws   3-108
of general application that are especially significant in the context of on-line
communication, such as consumer protection legislation. Others, such as
recent legislation regulating the content of on-line communications, are
specifically targeted at the emerging on-line environment.

This section addresses four areas of regulation in Australia of on-line
conduct:

* The classification, censorship, and regulation of the content of on-line
  services;
* The application of consumer protection law to on-line services;
* Privacy aspects of on-line communications; and
* The application of anti-discrimination, vilification, and defamation
  laws to on-line communications and service providers.

On-line Content Regulation, Classification and Censorship

Legislation which now exists in the jurisdictions of Western Australia,[121] the   3-109
Northern Territory,[122] and Victoria[123] creates penalties for the transmission
and reception through on-line services of certain controlled material.

The major criticism of these legislative moves is that while they provide
exemptions for service providers who do not knowingly transmit objectionable material, they define on-line services or computer services very broadly,
so that the offences would almost certainly apply to cover private communications between individuals and that enforcing the legislation will be
practically very difficult.[124]

Western Australia and the Northern Territory

As the Northern Territory legislation was based on a draft of the Western   3-110
Australian bill, and the final Acts are identical where they deal with com-
puter services,[125] the possible liability of on-line service providers under these
Acts will be considered together.

---

121 Censorship Act 1996 (W.A.).
122 Classification of Publication and Films Amendment Act 1995 (NT).
123 Classification (Publications, Films and Computer Games) (Enforcement) Act 1995
   (Victoria).
124 Greenleaf, "Law in Cyberspace" 70 A.L.J. 33, at pp. 33–34.
125 Censorship Act 1996 (W.A.), Part 7, Division 6; Classification of Publication and Films
   Amendment Act 1995 (N.T.) Part VII.

These Acts classify "computer service" broadly, and include any transmission of any form of data between computers, or from a computer to a terminal device and vice versa.[126] The Acts create two categories of controlled materials:

- "Objectionable material", which broadly covers material that is prohibited in Australia;[127] and
- "Restricted material", which covers material that a reasonable adult would regard as unsuitable for a minor to see, read or hear.[128]

3-111   Offences Relating to Objectionable Material With respect to objectionable material the Acts prohibit a person from using a computer service to transmit, obtain possession of or demonstrate an article knowing it to be objectionable material.[129] Knowledge that the particular article being transmitted, or requested, or demonstrated actually contains objectionable material is a condition precedent to liability under these prohibitions. It is not clear from the Acts to what extent these prohibitions will apply to service providers. Clearly, they will where the service provider knowingly obtains objectionable material, or is directly involved in knowingly transmitting objectionable material to subscribers to their service.

Where the service provider is merely providing private e-mail accounts, or some similar service where the provider is a mere conduit, then even if the service provider has actual knowledge that the information being passed via its service is objectionable, the service provider may still not be considered to be the person transmitting the objectionable material. Until such a favourable interpretation is approved by the courts, however, service providers would be prudent to prevent transmission of material being passed through its system, and remove any material residing on its system, as soon as a service provider has actual knowledge that material is objectionable.

Subsections (1) (d) and (e) of the relevant sections[130] of the Acts prohibit, respectively, advertising that objectionable material is available for transmission, and requesting the transmission of objectionable material. Service providers will only be in breach of these prohibitions if they advertise the availability of objectionable material on their sites, or if they request

---

126 Censorship Act 1996 (W.A.), section 99, "computer service"; Classification of Publication and Films Amendment Act 1995 (N.T.), section 50X "computer service".
127 Censorship Act 1996 (W.A.), section 99, "objectionable material"; Classification of Publication and Films Amendment Act 1995 (N.T.), section 50X, "objectionable material".
128 Censorship Act 1996 (W.A.), section 99, "restricted material"; Classification of Publication and Films Amendment Act 1995 (NT), section 50X, "restricted material".
129 Censorship Act 1996 (W.A.), section 101(1) (a)–(c); Classification of Publication and Films Amendment Act 1995 (N.T.), section 50Z (1) (a)–(c).
130 Censorship Act 1996 (W.A.), section 101; Classification of Publication and Films Amendment Act 1995 (N.T.), section 50Z.

objectionable material to be transmitted to them (for example, a notice on a site requesting objectionable material to be e-mailed to a particular address for inclusion on the site). It is important to note here that the offence is constituted by a request or advertising of objectionable material, not articles which actually contain objectionable material. Given the requirements of actual knowledge in the other offences, these two offences are unlikely to be interpreted as imposing a higher standard.

There are no elements of constructive knowledge in the offences relating to objectionable material, and the undertaking of an editorial role by a service provider for material on the provider's system brings no greater risk of liability as actual knowledge must still be established. In addition, the burden of proof for establishing that a person who transmitted objectionable material knew it was objectionable lies with the prosecution. The Acts also provide defences if the offending articles are *bona fide* medical, or recognised literary, artistic or scientific articles.[131]

Offences Relating to Restricted Material With respect to restricted material, **3-112** the Acts prohibit a person from using a computer service to transmit or make restricted material available to a minor.[132] It is a defence under the Acts to have taken all reasonable steps in the circumstances to avoid transmission or availability of the restricted material to minors.[133] It is further a defence if the defendant believed, on reasonable grounds, that the restricted material would not be available to minors.[134]

To avoid liability under these prohibitions, service providers should, if there could be material that is available via their service that may be restricted material, develop procedures for either ensuring that users are a particular age, or for identifying and removing restricted material available from their services. Although the standard of reasonableness in these defences is an inherently ambiguous one, given the highly anonymous nature of on-line services (and particularly without any judgments on these provisions), the expectation would be that this standard would be relatively low. Taking on an active editorial role that included the searching for, and removal of, restricted material could well satisfy this standard. An alternative, such as only allowing subscriptions by persons with credit cards, would presumably also suffice.

---

131 Censorship Act 1996 (W.A.), section 101(2); Classification of Publication and Films Amendment Act 1995 (N.T.), section 50Z (2).
132 Censorship Act 1996 (W.A.), sections 102(1), (2); Classification of Publication and Films Amendment Act 1995 (N.T.), 1995 sections 50ZA (1), (2).
133 Censorship Act 1996 (W.A.), section 102(3) (b); Classification of Publication and Films Amendment Act 1995 (N.T.), section 50ZA (3) (b).
134 Censorship Act 1996 (W.A.), section 102(3) (c) (ii); Classification of Publication and Films Amendment Act 1995 (N.T.), section 50ZA (3) (c) (ii).

Victoria

3-113   The Victorian Act has a similar division of offences relating to:

- "Objectionable material", which is effectively the same definition as in the Western Australian and Northern Territory Acts;[135]
- "Material unsuitable for minors of any age", which mean objectionable material, and publications and films classified "R" under the Classification (Publications, Films and Computer Games) Act 1995 (Commonwealth); and
- "Material unsuitable for minors under 15" which means a film or computer game that is classified MA under the Classification (Publications, Films and Computer Games) Act 1995.

3-114   **Offences Relating to Objectionable Material**   Section 57(1) prohibits a person from using an on-line information service to publish, transmit, or make available for transmission, objectionable material.[136] This is much wider than under the Western Australian and Northern Territory Acts, as knowledge that the material is objectionable is not required, and the Victorian offence will therefore be easier to establish. It is a defence that the defendant believed on reasonable grounds that the material was not objectionable material.[137] Most importantly, however, section 57(3) provides an exemption from section 57(1) for providers of an on-line information service or a telecommunications service unless the service provider "creates or knowingly downloads or copies objectionable material".

A service provider's position is therefore substantially the same under the Victorian Act as it is under the Western Australian and Northern Territory Acts: to avoid liability a service provider must prevent transmission of material via the service, and remove any material available from the service, as soon as the service provider has actual knowledge that the material is objectionable. Again, it is actual, and not constructive knowledge that is required, and so there will be no increased risk of liability as a result of a service provider taking an active editorial or monitoring role in the provision of a service, so long as when objectionable material is discovered the necessary remedial measures are taken.

3-115   **Offences Relating to Transmission to Minors**   Section 58(1) prohibits the use of an on-line information service to publish or transmit, or make available for transmission, to a minor material unsuitable for minors.

---

135 Classification (Publications, Films and Computer Games) (Enforcement) Act 1995 (Victoria), section 56, "objectionable material".
136 Classification (Publications, Films and Computer Games) (Enforcement) Act 1995 (Victoria), section 57(1).
137 Classification (Publications, Films and Computer Games) (Enforcement) Act 1995 (Victoria), section 57(2).

Subsection (4) prohibits the use of an on-line service to publish or transmit, or make available for transmission, to a minor under 15 years of age material unsuitable for minors under 15 years of age. Most relevant for service providers is that it is a defence to show the defendant did not know, and could not reasonably have known, that the person to whom the material was being transmitted was a minor.[138] Unless the service provider keeps these details of subscribers to its service, this defence would probably apply. There is also a further defence, substantially the same as that which appears in the Western Australian and Northern Territory Acts, where a defendant has taken reasonable steps to avoid publishing or transmitting, or making available for transmission, the material to a minor.[139] The comments made above regarding the action that might be considered "reasonable" in the on-line service context are also applicable here.

The Victorian Act goes further than the Western Australian and Northern Territory Acts, however, in the protection from liability afforded to service providers. Under subsections (3) and (6), the offence prohibitions relating to transmissions to minors do not apply to providers of on-line information services or telecommunications services unless the service provider knowingly published, transmitted or made available for transmission to minors material unsuitable for minors. Actual knowledge is therefore required. Again, unless the service provider actually knows that minors are able to access material that the provider actually knows is unsuitable for minors, or knows that such material is being transmitted to persons the provider actually knows are minors, no offence will have been committed.

Future Regulation of On-line Content

On July 24, 1995, the Federal Minister for Communications and the Arts   **3-116**
directed the Australian Broadcasting Authority (A.B.A.) to investigate the content of on-line information and entertainment broadcasting services. The A.B.A. was chosen because of that body's long experience with content regulation in the television and radio broadcasting industries. On June 30, 1996, the A.B.A. presented its report. Recognising the effects heavy regulation of on-line content would have on the proliferation of these extremely useful services, and the controversy over proposed New South Wales legislation that was similar in its approach to legislation already in force in other States, the A.B.A. recommended the implementation of an industry-based self-regulation scheme incorporating registered codes of practice, perhaps to

---

138 Classification (Publications, Films and Computer Games) (Enforcement) Act 1995 (Victoria), sections 58 (2) (a) (i), (5) (b) (i).
139 Classification (Publications, Films and Computer Games) (Enforcement) Act 1995 (Victoria), sections 58 (2) (a) (ii), (5) (b) (ii).

be administered by the A.B.A.[140] The A.B.A. also recommended that access to content be regulated through a purpose-built on-line labelling scheme, to be managed by a combined government and industry task force.[141] The other important recommendation made was that a complaints handling regime be established under which complainants would go first to the service provider and then, if the matter was not resolved, to the A.B.A.[142] This self-regulatory approach implicitly rejects the approach of the State legislative measures, which adopt a regime of criminal penalties to deal specifically with on-line content issues. It also reflects very strongly the A.B.A.'s current role in the regulation of content in the television and radio broadcasting industries.

The Minister, Senator Richard Alston, has responded favourably to the A.B.A. report, stating that any regulatory framework "will be based on industry developed codes of practice which will be supported by relevant amendments to the Broadcasting Services Act".[143] The Senator also explicitly rejected the use of criminal sanctions in the regulation of on-line content, and indicated that the government believed a national regulator in the form of the A.B.A. was appropriate to create a uniform approach. The decision to nominate the A.B.A. was based on its experience with self-regulatory frameworks built on codes of conduct, rather than any identification of on-line services as involving broadcasting.

While the Senator regarded a uniform approach at both the State and Federal levels as desirable, the future of the legislation already enacted in Western Australia, Victoria and the Northern Territory must be in some doubt. The Commonwealth has the power to legislate for on-line services,[144] but whether the State legislation will be inconsistent with (and therefore invalidated by) any Commonwealth legislation obviously depends on the precise form of that Commonwealth legislation. If, however, the Government is to fulfil its aim of creating a single national content regulator in the

---

140 Australian Broadcasting Authority, "Investigation into the Content of on-line Services", June 30, 1996, Chapter 6. The A.B.A. also noted the overturning of the American Communications Decency Act, which was similar in approach to the Australian State legislation, in *American Civil Liberties Union* v. *Janet Reno, Attorney General of the United States; American Library Association Inc.* v. *United States Department of Justice* (1996) 6 CCH Computer Cases 47-431, but did not draw any significant conclusions from the case: Australian Broadcasting Authority, "Investigation into the Content of on-line Services", June 30, 1996, p. 52.

141 Australian Broadcasting Authority, "Investigation into the Content of on-line Services", June 30, 1996, Chapter 5.

142 Australian Broadcasting Authority, "Investigation into the Content of on-line Services", June 30, 1996, Chapter 8.

143 Senator Richard Alston, "Address to the Internet Industry Association of Australia", July 5, 1996.

144 Commonwealth Constitution section 51(v), gives legislative power over "postal, telegraphic, telephonic and other like service". This power covers all communication services: *R* v. *Brislan; Ex Parte Williams* (1935) 54 C.L.R. 262, at p. 280.

form of the A.B.A., it would seem that it would be necessary to exclude the operation of current state legislation in any proposed Commonwealth Act.

Consumer Protection

Consumer protection law in Australia is a combination of substantially   **3-117**
similar Federal and state Acts. The Commonwealth Government's power to legislate is limited to those areas that fall under one of the heads of power enumerated in the Commonwealth Constitution. The main constitutional basis for the Trade Practices Act 1974 (Commonwealth) is the corporations power.[145]

However, the Trade Practices Act 1974 has been extended using other heads of power in the Constitution to apply to individuals engaging in interstate trade or commerce and individuals who aid, abet, counsel or procure a breach of the Trade Practices Act 1974 by a corporation. However, the Trade Practices Act 1974 does not, for constitutional reasons, apply to the actions of an individual as distinct from a corporation, providing the actions are confined within a State border and do not come within the Trade Practices Act 1974 on any other basis. All States have, however, passed Fair Trading Acts,[146] which overcomes the constitutional gap in relation to consumer protection. For brevity, only the provisions of the Trade Practices Act 1974 will be referred to here.

While it is clear that these provisions, being laws of general application, will apply to on-line transactions conducted wholly within Australia, the position in relation to international transactions will differ from transaction to transaction.

Domestic On-line Transactions

Parts IVA and V of the Trade Practices Act 1974 are the parts of the Act   **3-118**
dealing with, respectively, unconscionable conduct and consumer protection. They contain, *inter alia*:

- Prohibitions against misleading or deceptive or unconscionable conduct; and
- Provisions that imply into all consumer contracts particular non-excludable statutory warranties.

---

145 Commonwealth Constitution, section 50(20).
146 Fair Trading Act 1992 (A.C.T.); Consumer Affairs and Fair Trading Act 1990 (N.T.); Fair Trading Act 1987 (N.S.W.); Fair Trading Act 1989 (Queensland); Fair Trading Act 1987 (South Australia); Fair Trading Act 1990 (Tasmania); Fair Trading Act 1985 (Victoria); Fair Trading Act 1987 (West Australia).

3-119   Part V also contains provisions prohibiting certain types of "schemes" which present particular dangers to consumers, such as pyramid selling,[147] bait advertising,[148] and referral selling.[149]

3-120   **Misleading and Deceptive Conduct**   Section 52(1) provides that a corporation shall not, in trade or commerce, engage in conduct that is misleading or deceptive or is likely to mislead or deceive.

In proceedings under section 52 (and section 53), the intent of the defendant corporation is not relevant. All that is relevant is whether the conduct was in fact misleading or deceptive, or was likely to mislead or deceive. Therefore, a representative of a corporation may act honestly and with reasonable care, yet may nevertheless render the corporation liable to be restrained by injunction or to pay damages (attributable to the corporation) if statements made are in fact misleading or deceptive or are likely to mislead or deceive.[150]

Silence can constitute misleading or deceptive conduct for the purposes of section 52 if the circumstances warrant it.[151] For example, an omission to mention a qualification, in the absence of which some absolute statement made is rendered misleading, is conduct that should be regarded as misleading. So, too, is an omission to mention a subsequent change that has occurred after the making of some statement that was correct at the time it was made, so that the original statement is now incorrect and misleading.

3-121   **Representations Relating to Future Matters**   This section provides that representations relating to a future matter made by a corporation that does not have reasonable grounds for making a representation will be taken to be misleading. It is clear that promises or predictions that do not come to pass are not for the reason alone to be characterised as misleading or deceptive even if the representee has relied on them and altered his position on the face of them.[152] In order not to fall within the ambit of section 51A, the corporation must prove that it had reasonable grounds for making the representation.

Predictions and forecasts may, however, breach section 52 without reference to section 51A. A statement relating to the future may contain an implied statement as to a present or past fact. It may impliedly represent that the maker has the means to make good the promise. In such cases, the

---

147 Trade Practices Act 1974, section 61.
148 Trade Practices Act 1974, section 56.
149 Trade Practices Act 1974, section 57.
150 *Parkdale Custom Built Furniture Pty. Limited* v. *Puxu Pty. Limited* (1982) 149 C.L.R. 191, at p. 197.
151 *Rhone-Poulec Agrochimie S.A.* v. *UIM Chemical Services Pty. Ltd.* (1986) 12 F.C.R. 477.
152 *Bill Acceptance Corporation Ltd.* v. *GWA Ltd.* (1983) 78 F.L.R. 171.

misrepresentation can arise from the representor's "failure to qualify the statement or disclose the risk of non-fulfilment" of the prediction.[153]

Further, statements involving the state of mind of the maker (promises, predictions and opinions) ordinarily convey the meaning that the maker had a particular state of mind when the statement was made and that there was a basis for that state of mind. If these implied representations are not true, there will be a contravention of section 52.[154]

Section 53: False Representations   Section 53 prohibits certain false repre-   **3-122** sentations relating to the supply of goods or services, including false representations as to the standard or quality of services or as to the identity of persons who have agreed to acquire goods or services. In this provision the term "false" can be equated to "contrary to fact" and therefore requires no knowledge on the part of the person making the representation.[155] Section 53 has been held to apply to (among other things) false representations:

- About the price of goods;[156]
- Of the origin of goods;[157] and
- That goods are new.[158]

Representations within this section may be active or passive and may arise   **3-123** as a result of statements made or by implication from conduct. Hence, in the *Given* case[159] the court held that the displaying of a motor vehicle with a wound-back odometer amounted to a false representation within section 53(a).

Unconscionable Conduct   Part IVA introduces a general duty to trade fairly   **3-124** in relation to consumers by proscribing unconscionable conduct in the supply of domestic consumer goods or services.

The term "unconscionable" is not defined in the Trade Practices Act 1974. In general terms, conduct will be regarded as unconscionable where, in accordance with the ordinary concepts of humanity it is seen to be so against conscience that the court should intervene.[160] The Trade Practices Act 1974 leaves this issue to the courts to be determined on the facts of each particular case, but section 51AB (2) does contain a list of considerations to which the court may have regard in determining the issue. Those matters are:

- The relative bargaining strengths of the parties;
- Whether the consumer was able to understand the documentation;

153 *Wheeler Grace Pierucci Pty. Ltd.* v. Wright (1989) A.T.P.R. 40-940 at p. 50, 251.
154 *James* v. *ANZ Banking Group Limited* (1986) 64 A.L.R. 347.
155 *Given* v. *C.V. Holland Holdings Pty. Ltd.* (1977) 29 F.L.R. 212 at p. 217.
156 *A.C.C.C.* v. *Nationwise New Pty. Ltd.* (1966) A.T.P.R. 41-519.
157 *Siddons Pty. Ltd.* v. *Stanley Works Pty. Ltd.* (1990) A.T.P.R. 41-044.
158 *Annand & Thompson Pty. Ltd.* v. *Trade Practices Commission* (1979) 40 F.L.R. 165.
159 *Given* v. *C.V. Holland Holdings Pty. Ltd.* (1977) 29 F.L.R. 212 at p.217.
160 *Zoneff* v. *Elcom Credit Union Ltd.* (1990) 80 A.T.P.R. 41-009.

- Whether undue influence or pressure was exerted or unfair tactics used;
- Whether the consumer was required to comply with conditions which were not reasonably necessary for the protection of the legitimate interests of the supplier; and
- The amount to which and circumstances under which the consumer would have acquired equivalent goods or services from another party.

3-125   The above considerations are not, however, exhaustive. The court is entitled to take into account such other considerations as it sees fit in accordance with section 51AB (2).

The type of situations in which a court will grant relief on grounds of unconscionable conduct varies greatly. The special disadvantage of the other party may spring from factors which include poverty or need of any kind, sickness, infirmity of body or mind, drunkenness, illiteracy or lack of education, or lack of assistance or explanation where such is necessary. Relief is granted because "unconscientious advantage is taken of an innocent party whose will is overborne so that it is not independent and voluntary".[161]

For example, in *George T Collings Aust Pty. Ltd.* v. *HF Stevenson Aust Pty. Ltd.*,[162] the court held that the Standard Real Estate and Stock Institute of Victoria sales listing form was unconscionable because it failed to draw to the attention of the seller the liability to pay commission on sales made after the expiration of the sole agency period.

The relief available to a party taken advantage of in this manner is normally rescission of any contract concluded as a result of the unconscionable conduct and may also include re-adjustment of the position of the parties to their original position.

3-126   **Merchantable Quality and Fitness for Purpose** Where a corporation supplies (otherwise than by way of sale by auction) goods to a consumer there is an implied condition that the goods supplied are of merchantable quality. However, there is no such condition by virtue of section 71:

- As regards defects specifically drawn to the consumer's attention before the contract is made; or
- If the consumer examines the goods before the contract is made, as regards defects that that examination ought to reveal.

3-127   This section also provides that where a consumer makes it known to the corporation (or a person with whom negotiations are conducted) any particular purpose for which the goods are being acquired, there is the implied condition that the goods supplied are reasonably fit for that purpose,

---

161 *Commercial Bank of Australia Ltd.* v. *Amadio* (1983) 151 C.L.R. 447 at p. 461, per Mason J.
162 (1991) A.T.P.R. 41-104.

whether or not that is the purpose for which such goods are commonly supplied. The exception to this rule is where the circumstances show that the consumer does not rely, or that it is unreasonable for him to rely, on the skill or judgment of a corporation or that person.

Supply by Sample In contracts where it is expressly provided or implicit that 3-128 the goods are supplied by reference to a sample (for example, in the supply of software after providing a demonstration or scaled-down version), section 72 establishes:

- An implied condition that the bulk will correspond with the sample in quality;
- An implied condition that the consumer will have a reasonable opportunity to compare the bulk with the sample; and
- An implied condition that the goods will be free from any defect, rendering them unmerchantable, that would not be apparent on reasonable examination of the sample.

International On-line Transactions

It is far less certain that the Australian consumer protection regime will 3-129 apply to on-line transactions conducted between Australian consumers and foreign suppliers. Typically, on-line vendors will be offering products for sale from a single jurisdiction to multiple jurisdictions. The basic question in such transactions will be whether it is Australian law, or the law of the foreign jurisdiction that is the "proper law".

Where the parties expressly agree on a particular law, then generally that choice will be respected by Australian courts.[163] Where no express choice is made, a choice may be implied from the language and the form of the contract.[164] Where neither an express or implied intention can be discovered, the courts must determine the proper law by considering the legal system to which the contract has the "closest and most real connection".[165] Important indicia of the proper law in such cases are the currency of payment, where payment is made and where the main obligations under the contract are performed.[166] Where a vendor is supplying to many jurisdictions it would be likely, therefore, that it would be the law of the jurisdiction where the vendor is located that would have the most real connection, and would therefore be the proper law of the contract.

Practically, of course, there is little to gain from a favourable judgment from an Australian court against a foreign vendor if that vendor has no assets in Australia. Although it is possible to apply to have Australian

---

163 *Vita Foods Products* v. *Unus Shipping* [1939] A.C. 277.
164 *John Kaldor Fabricmaker Pty. Ltd.* v. *Mitchell Cotts Freight (Aust) Pty. Ltd.* (1989) 90 A.L.R. 244.
165 *Bonython* v. *Commonwealth of Australia* (1950) 81 C.L.R. 486.
166 *Mendelsohn-Zeller Co. Inc.* v. *T & C Providores Pty. Ltd.* [1981] N.S.W.L.R. 366.

judgments enforced in many foreign jurisdictions, there is always the risk that a foreign court will decide the question of which law is the proper law of the contract differently from the Australian court. This raises the possibility that a buyer could obtain a judgment from an Australian court only to find when attempting to enforce it in the foreign jurisdiction that the foreign court believes the proper law was the foreign jurisdiction, requiring the buyer to re-litigate the issue in the foreign court. In practice, therefore, the choice of jurisdiction for litigation will often depend on where the assets of the proposed defendant lie.

Future Regulation of On-line Transactions for Consumer Protection

3-130   While the current position regarding consumer protection in the on-line environment may be somewhat unclear at present, particularly in respect of international transactions, the issue has received some attention at the Federal level in the past year.

The Australian Competition and Consumer Commission (A.C.C.C.), which is responsible for, among other things, the administration and enforcement of the Trade Practices Act 1974, released a draft Distance Selling Code of Practice in December 1996.[167] The A.C.C.C. developed the code in response to a request of the Ministerial Council of Consumer Affairs, which had been alerted to the potential dangers to consumers from telemarketing fraud by studies conducted in the United States.[168] While the Code was focused on telemarketing and mail order sales, the difficulties for consumers with on-line selling were specifically addressed by the A.C.C.C.. For example, distance sellers are required to provide, prior to the formation of any contract of sale, "clear, unambiguous and easily accessible information covering the name of the relevant distance seller and a street address at which it can be contacted". The Code specifically notes that electronic mail addresses are not sufficient for this purpose.[169] While these information provision rules are additional obligations to those that presently exist under law, for the most part the Code simply reinforces the legal position of the Trade Practices Act 1974 and the State and Territory Fair Trading Acts with respect to consumer protection. One area of contention in the Code, however, is the proposed new right of a consumer to cancel a distance selling contract within a seven-day "cooling off" period.

The Federal Bureau of consumer Affairs (F.B.C.A.) has also voiced support for regulation of on-line transactions through the development of industry codes of practice, although its preference was for a code

---

167 A copy of the draft code is at http://www.accc.gov.au/docs/draft/discpap.htm.
168 United States Department of Justice, Federal Bureau of Investigation, "Telemarketing Fraud", undated.
169 Australian Competition and Consumer Commission, "Draft Distance Selling Code of Practice", December 1996, clause 12.

directed specifically to Internet business.[170] The F.B.C.A. believed that the major advantages of industry self-regulation in Internet commerce were that:

- The Internet business community itself has a strong incentive to provide consumers with an acceptable environment in which they can confidently do business, to promote on-line commerce;
- Industry codes are well adapted to providing detailed, flexible guidelines for specific businesses with specialised needs and problems; and
- Industry self-regulated codes may be able to avoid the jurisdictional problems associated with "strong" regulation that is based on national laws.[171]

The Internet Industry Association of Australia (Intiaa) has drafted an **3-131** Internet Industry Code of Conduct[172] aimed at a range of businesses involved in Internet commerce, including vendors and Internet access providers. Businesses that register to the Code may display a Code Compliance Symbol, but may be deregistered where they then fail to comply with the Code. This Code presently addresses:

- Mediation of disputes between the consumer and the vendor;
- Privacy;
- Provision of information about the identity and location of a vendor or service provider;
- Provision of information relevant to a sale including refund policy;
- Laws applying to the sale; and
- Delivery costs and time.

Both the F.B.C.A.[173] and the Deputy Chairman of the A.C.C.C.[174] have noted **3-132** this Intiaa initiative with approval. The limitations, however, of applying industry based regulation to international transactions was clear to both the F.B.C.A. and the A.C.C.C. Specifically, the F.B.C.A. noted that:[175]

- In practice, industry codes tend to operate within national boundaries and be administered by industry associations at a national level;

---

170 Federal Bureau of Consumer Affairs, "Untangling the Web: Electronic Commerce and the Consumer", April 3, 1997; see http://www.dist.gov.au/consumer/publicat/untangle/index.html.
171 Federal Bureau of Consumer Affairs, *Untangling the Web: Electronic Commerce and the Consumer*, April 3, 1997, at p. 5.
172 A copy of the draft code is at http://www.intiaa.asn.au/codeV2.htm.
173 Federal Bureau of Consumer Affairs, *Untangling the Web: Electronic Commerce and the Consumer*, April 3, 1997, at p. 7.
174 Asher, *International Perspective: Access to Justice for Consumers in the Global Electronic Marketplace*, March 17, 1997.
175 Federal Bureau of Consumer Affairs, *Untangling the Web: Electronic Commerce and the Consumer*, April 3, 1997, at p. 6.

- Gaining wide adherence to a code dealing with Internet commerce poses problems where Internet selling involves participants in a very broad range of business sectors making internal industry organisation difficult; and
- To be effective, a code would need a strong basis for achieving compliance, especially if it sought to provide a mechanism for resolving disputes between vendors and consumers.

3-133   Recognising these inherent difficulties in regulating international transactions, both the A.C.C.C. Deputy Commissioner[176] and the F.B.C.A. perceived the need for a parallel internationalisation of industry groups with global codes of practice. Recognition of, and contribution to, foreign industry codes of practice could, the F.B.C.A. has suggested,[177] be a way of progressing international self-regulation of the Internet business community. An Australian code that was geared to assisting overseas as well as Australian consumers in their dealings with Australian Internet vendors might also be useful in this regard.

Privacy Law

Privacy Act 1988

3-134   The Common Law in Australia does not recognise any right to privacy. However, the federal Privacy Act 1988 does provide some protection for personal information held by federal government agencies and some parts of the private sector. For some time, it has been suggested that the Commonwealth Government would extend the operation of the Act to the private sector, however, any concrete proposals appear unlikely in the short term.

The Privacy Act is based in part on the information privacy principles adopted by the Organisation for Economic Co-operation and Development (O.E.C.D.) in 1980. These 11 principles under the Act are set out in section 14 of the Act, but some of the more important principles are set out below. The principles relate to "personal information" which is defined as:

". . . information or an opinion (including information or an opinion forming part of a database), whether true or not, and whether recorded in a material form or not, about an individual whose identity is apparent, or can reasonably be ascertained, from the information or opinion."[178]

---

176 Asher, *International Perspective: Access to Justice for Consumers in the Global Electronic Marketplace*, March 17, 1997, at pp. 8–9.
177 Federal Bureau of Consumer Affairs, *Untangling the Web: Electronic Commerce and the Consumer*, April 3, 1997, at p. 7.
178 Privacy Act 1988, section 6.

Some of the more important principles are set out below:

- Collected personal information must be used for the purpose for which it was collected;[179]
- Individuals are entitled to know the purpose for which personal information has been collected;
- The collector of the information should keep the information accurate and up-to-date;
- The information should be kept secure, *i.e.*, free from unauthorised access by people outside the organisation, or of improper use within the organisation;
- Individuals are entitled to access information concerning themselves, and to correct errors in that information;
- Information should not be used if it was collected for a different purpose, without that person's informed consent; and
- Individuals can object to, and prevent, their information from being used for a different purpose.

Application of the Privacy Act

The Privacy Act applies to government agencies, credit-reporting agencies   **3-135**
and to credit providers. A "credit-reporting agency" is defined as a corporation that prepares or maintains records containing personal information for providing a credit history or credit details. A "credit provider" includes a bank or other financial institution and some corporations whose business involves the provision of loans.[180]

Obligations of Credit Providers

A credit provider may collect and use any personal information obtained   **3-136**
directly from an individual for its own internal purposes. However, the credit provider is restricted in its ability to provide information to a credit- reporting agency without obtaining an individual's informed consent.

Credit providers are also required to provide information to credit-reporting agencies to ensure that the information stored by the credit-reporting agency is up to date. Where credit providers refuse to provide credit on the basis of a credit report, they must provide a copy of that report to the individual.

Obligations of Credit Reporting Agencies

Credit-reporting agencies are required to only receive and keep certain credit   **3-137**
information. Credit-reporting agencies are also required to ensure that such information is kept secure and is only released in accordance with the Act.

---

179 As a corollary, the information held must not be excessive, when compared with the purpose for which the information is being collected.
180 Currently, any organisation which provides goods or services and allows the consumer more than seven days to pay is considered a credit provider.

State Developments

3-138   Several states have considered introducing their own privacy legislation, but no legislation has yet been passed. In 1996, the New South Wales government introduced the Privacy and Data Protection Bill, which would introduce non-binding obligations on the private sector.

To date, there has not been a concrete legislative proposal for the introduction of binding privacy provisions with respect to the private sector in any Australian jurisdiction.

Discrimination, Harassment, and Defamation

Prohibitions against Discrimination and Vilification

3-139   The Australian Broadcasting Authority noted in its report on on-line services some concern about "the potential to use the on-line environment to promote racial vilification and harassment".[181] Such "hate-speech", as it is usually referred to by Internet users, may be subject to the comprehensive regime of Australian anti-discrimination law.

Both Federal and State legislation exists which prohibits discrimination on the basis of race, religion, gender, disability, sexual preference or some other basis. This legislation has general application and, therefore, applies to the content of on-line services and the conduct of persons using those services. The major anti-discrimination and vilification legislation includes:

- The Racial Discrimination Act 1975 (Commonwealth);
- The Racial Hatred Act 1995 (Commonwealth), which incorporates prohibitions against racial vilification into the Racial Discrimination Act 1975 and against inciting racial hatred into the Crimes Act 1914 (Commonwealth);
- The Sex Discrimination Act 1984 (Commonwealth);
- The Disability Discrimination Act 1992 (Commonwealth);
- The Anti-Discrimination Act 1977 (N.S.W.);
- The Discrimination Act 1991 (A.C.T.); and
- Sections 76–78 of chapter XI of the Criminal Code (Western Australia).

3-140   Of these Acts, those with the broadest provisions are the Commonwealth and New South Wales Acts. The Racial Discrimination Act 1975 contains a very broad provision prohibiting:[182]

"... any act involving a distinction, exclusion, restriction or preference based on race, colour, descent or national or ethnic origin which has the

---

181 Australian Broadcasting Authority, *Investigation into the Content of On-line Services*, June 30, 1996, at pp. 50–51.
182 Racial Discrimination Act 1975, section 9.

purpose or effect of nullifying or impairing the recognition, enjoyment or exercise, on an equal footing, of any human right or fundamental freedom in the political, economic, social, cultural or any other field of public life."

The Racial Hatred Act 1995 amendments are more specific, prohibiting incitement of racial hatred, which is defined as any act done "otherwise than in private" with "the intention of inciting racial hatred against another person or a group of people" which is: "reasonably likely, in all the circumstances, to incite racial hatred against the other person or group of people; and is done because of the race, colour or national or ethnic origin of the other person or some or all of the people in the group."[183]   **3-141**

Racial vilification is defined along similar lines, as any behaviour prompted by the race, colour or nation or ethnic origin of a person that is "reasonably likely to . . . offend, insult, humiliate or intimidate another person or group of people".[184]

Section 18D of the Racial Discrimination Act, however, contains exceptions to this general prohibition, where anything act is said or done reasonably and in good faith:

"(a) in the performance, exhibition or distribution of an artistic work; or

(b) in the course of any statement, publication, discussion or debate made or held for any genuine academic, artistic or scientific purpose in the public interest; or

(c) in making or publishing:

(i) a fair and accurate report of any event or matter of public interest; or

(ii) a fair comment on any event or matter of public interest if the comment is an expression of genuine belief held by the person making the comment."

The New South Wales Anti-Discrimination Act 1977 has the most wide-ranging provisions of any anti-vilification legislation. It prohibits any public act that incites hatred towards, serious contempt for, or serious ridicule of, a person or group on the grounds of that person or group's race, sexual preference, or because that person or group is suffering from AIDS or is infected with HIV. Complaints made to the NSW Equal Opportunity Tribunal may, however, be dismissed where the complaint is frivolous, vexatious, misconceived or lacking in substance.[185]   **3-142**

---

183 Crimes Act 1914 (Commonwealth), section 60(1).
184 Racial Discrimination Act 1975, section 18C.
185 Anti-Discrimination Act 1977 (N.S.W.), section 20C.

The Sex Discrimination Act 1984 and the Disability Discrimination Act 1992 prohibits any person from treating another person less favourably than, in circumstances that are the same, they would treat a person, respectively, of the opposite sex, or without a disability. Division three of the Sex Discrimination Act 1984 also prohibits sexual harassment, under which a person will be engaging in sexual harassment if:[186]

- The person makes an unwelcome sexual advance, or an unwelcome request for sexual favours, to the person harassed; or
- Engages in other unwelcome conduct of a sexual nature in relation to the person harassed; and
- In circumstances in which a reasonable person, having regard to all the circumstances, would have anticipated that the person harassed would be offended, humiliated or intimidated.

3-143   Here, "conduct of a sexual nature" includes making a statement of a sexual nature to a person in writing,[187] which includes any visible text in e-mail and on bulletin boards and other on-line services.[188]

Defamation

3-144   Defamation cases involving the Internet and other widely accessible networks are only a recent addition to legal precedent in Common Law countries. In 1994, the West Australian Supreme Court awarded A.$40,000 in damages to the plaintiff in *Rhindos* v. *Hardwick*.[189] In that case, the defendant had made numerous defamatory claims regarding the professional competency of the plaintiff, and suggested that he was involved in sexual misconduct with a local boy known as "Puppy". The defendant had published these statements on a bulletin board that resided on a server owned by the University of Western Australia that was connected to the Internet. The court specifically took into account the wide international publication of the statements in determining the award of damages in this case.

While it is clearly correct to apply the ordinary rules of defamation to the authors of such defamatory statements, the nature of the Internet (and, indeed, any publicly accessible network) presents some difficulties. On-line access providers, whether Internet Service Providers (ISPs) or providers of any public networks, are potentially liable for another's defamatory statements as the publishers of those statements.[190]

Service providers may be attractive targets for litigation in such cases, for several reasons. First, the identity of the author of the statement may not be

---

186 Sex Discrimination Act 1984, section 28A(1).
187 Sex Discrimination Act 1984, section 28A(2).
188 Acts Interpretation Act 1901, section 25.
189 Unreported, WA Supreme Court, Ipp J., March 31, 1994.
190 *Webb* v. *Bloch* (1928) 41 C.L.R. 331.

known and may difficult, if not impossible, to discover. Second, the author may reside in a different jurisdiction from that of the target of the defamation. Last, the service provider may simply be the only defendant with the money to pay any judgment and is therefore the only party worth suing. Additionally, as *Rhindos* v. *Hardwick* shows, the widely accessible nature of the Internet means that the potential damages (and therefore the risk to on-line service providers) rises exponentially with every statement published on a network.

On-line services are, of course, fundamentally different from traditional mediums such as newspapers, and the real control service providers have over the material published on their networks is often very limited. It may therefore be possible for service providers to sustain the defence of innocent publication (also known as innocent dissemination). Although all persons involved in a publication are liable for a defamation, a person in the publication chain has this defence available if he can prove that:

- He was unaware of the defamation; and
- His arrangements regarding the publication involved reasonable care (that is that ignorance was not due to his or her negligence).

This defence is available, for example, to publication distributors and **3-145** retailers, and to libraries. It is not available, however, to "original" publishers of defamatory statements. The position of on-line service providers is somewhat unclear, however, as television stations broadcasting network feeds are still taken to be original publishers.[191]

McPherson v. *Hickie*[192] suggests that changing technologies may expand the scope of the defence. The plaintiff in those proceedings had claimed against the printer of a book containing a defamation, who in turn argued innocent publication as a defence. The defendant argued that precedents suggesting that a printer is always an original publisher of a defamation arose from an antiquated understanding that a printer must necessarily be aware of the contents of what they print. Modern printing technology meant, however, that printers often have no knowledge of what they print.

The New South Wales Court of Appeal upheld the defendant's appeal, stating that the defence of innocent publication may indeed have been available to the defendant. A finding against the defendant would have required the trial judge to inquire whether the defendant's printing process meant that he must have been aware of the defamatory nature of the publication, or that his ignorance was the result of his own negligence, rather than simply dismissing the defence as unavailable to the defendant.

As on-line service providers (in particular, bulletin board and discussion group organisers) would often have even less knowledge of the contents of

---

191 *Thompson* v. *Australian Capital Television Pty Ltd* (1994) 127 A.L.R. 317.
192 (1995) Australian Torts Reports 81-348.

publications on their services than printers, this case suggests the defence of innocent publication could be available to them. The requirement that the innocent publisher's ignorance may not be the result of his or her own negligence, however, suggests that on-line service providers might need to take some action to limit defamatory publications on their services, such as monitoring material (where possible) or removing defamatory material as soon as being notified of its existence.

CHAPTER 4

Belgium

Corinne Mertens
Cabinet C.M. Mertens
Brussels, Belgium

INTRODUCTION

Achieving Information Security

Multiple transactions on open networks such as Internet and the World 4-1
Wide Web (WWW) are highly risky because nobody controls them. Achieving the information society raises many essential questions. The major issues relating to transmitted data focus on the importance of access and security procedures. These procedures must meet three criteria, namely:

- Confidentiality — to ensure that electronic transactions can be read only by the parties involved;
- Integrity — to ensure that the content of the message sent is identical to the message received with no alteration; and
- Authentication and certification — to ensure that the message originates from the right person, that the signature is authentic and that the transaction is legal are essential between trading partners.

To ensure adherence to legal requirements, an audit of the system may be 4-2
employed. It should address:

- General risks, which are inherent in the introduction of open networks;
- Internal risks, which occur within the organisation and may arise as a result of inadequate internal control procedures;
- External risks, such as messages that are lost, altered, or transferred to the wrong recipient or are delayed;
- General controls (the existence of a formal agreement);
- Internal controls, which relate to access and security (encryption and PIN), with information on rejections being transmitted at the same time that the acknowledgement is sent;
- External controls, involving reliance on an external party (service provider) and existence of an agreement; and
- Conflict of interests, disputes and liabilities.

4-3   The legal requirements of data security reveal three aspects, namely:

- The legal obligation to implement data security procedures (*e.g.*, data protection);[1]
- Legal recognition of the use of certain security techniques (*e.g.*, trust services); and
- Legal restrictions on the use of certain security mechanisms (*e.g.*, encryption).

Legal Regime for Electronic Communication

4-4   Belgium's national telecommunications operator is BELGACOM, which was created by the Law of March 21, 1991. Article 64 of the Law refers to BELGACOM's liability for damages to users in case of the telecommunication infrastructure's malfunction or breach where providing "reserved services". BELGACOM limits its liability for damages because of:

- Death or personal injury;
- An error made by its staff; and[2]
- An error in managing data from users of "reserved services".

4-5   According to articles 4 and 5 of the Royal Decree of August 19, 1992,[3] to ensure the reliability of its services, BELGACOM commits itself to secure interzonal and international networks. BELGACOM undertakes to develop the capacity of digital networks to be able to transport all the digital links (*e.g.*, the mobile telephony)[4] and to improve the leased lines. It also undertakes to improve the accessibility of ISDN (90 per cent in 1995).

In article 6, Annex 2, the contract stipulates that BELGACOM shall manage its commuted data services so as to respect confidentiality of communications and personal data protection.

The security and confidentiality of voice telephony is outlined in *Le livre vert sur la sécurité des systèmes d'information*, Version 4.0, October 18, 1993. Article 8 of the European Convention of Human Rights recognises the right for every person to have the respect of his privacy and correspondence. Both the European Court of Justice and the Belgian Supreme Court of Appeal (*Cour de Cassation*) have decided that voice telephony is a part of privacy and correspondence and that any unauthorised person may not access it. The police can have access to other parties' voice telephony in certain conditions to identify the person who is calling.[5]

---

1 Law of December 8, 1992.
2 Law of March 21, 1991, articles 111 and 112.
3 *Arrêté Royal du 19 août 1992 portant approbation du premier contrat de gestion de* BELGACOM (RTT) *et fixant des mesures en vue du classement de cette régie parmi les entreprises publiques autonomes.*
4 Law of March 21, 1991, article 7.
5 Penal Code (introduced by Law of February 11, 1991).

The government may — whenever public security or defence of the Kingdom requires it — forbid for a determined period the use or the ownership of telecommunications means.[6]

The relationship between the user and the Internet service provider is contractual. Generally, the provider will limit its liability to the minimum, but both parties can agree on an "acceptable use policy".[7] Also, extra-contractual liability may arise for damage due to viruses or violation of privacy (data protection).

Confidentiality

Every person has the right to the respect of his privacy and correspondence[8]   4-6
and data transmitted electronically should be protected by reasonable security safeguards against risks such as loss or unauthorised access, destruction, use, modification or disclosure of data. Security procedures must meet three criteria, namely:

- Confidentiality, *i.e.*, safety measures against illegal disclosure;
- Integrity, *i.e.*, safety measures against unauthorised modifications or alterations; and
- Availability, *i.e.*, safety measures against abusive holding back of information or resources.

The confidentiality and security measures taken are encryption (double   4-7
encryption in the near future), compression, and PIN. No active function (stop and forward/mailbox) addresses security; the message enters and leaves the network without the latter being aware of its content.

The contracts between the end-user and the service provider determine the liabilities. Meanwhile, to give more efficiency and security, all companies and organisations are reinforcing their security procedures. A general audit is the best way to ensure that system integrity is maintained and that the effective flow of information is facilitated.

There are several main concerns. Suitable access control ensures that data are properly safeguarded thus protecting the rights of users in their levels of access to information (password and PIN). The legal questions of admissibility of electronic transactions as evidence and their authenticity when they lack an authorising signature need to be resolved. An important question is the legal authorisation of the use of cryptography.

Many governments want to access electronically transferred information because they are aware of the possibility of misusing electronic transfer for

---

6 Law of March 21, 1991, article 70.

7 Hance (ed.), *Business et Droit d'Internet*, MacGraw Hill, at p. 212.

8 European Convention of Human Rights, article 8, and Belgian Constitution, articles 22 and 29.

illegal information about drugs, money laundering, sexual crime and pedophilia, crimes against public safety, they information. In Belgium, the Law of Data Protection[9] and its implementing decrees provide for a duty to give a copy of the private key to a special institute called IBPT (*Institut Belge des Postes et Telecommunications*).

Legal Effect of Electronic Signatures

4-8   Signatures are unique. They comprise personalised signs that contribute to identifying a person. In 1988, an author gave another definition of a written document: ". . . characters reproducing a message, characters which can be decoded with an appropriate process in an understandable and readable language for man".[10]

Signature functions both to identify the signatory, as evidence that a signer exists and is physically present when the act is signed, and to demonstrate the signer's will to adopt the contents of the act signed, the so-called *animus signandi*.[11]

Conditions of Validity

4-9   For a signature to be valid, it must contain the name of the signer, that is, the reproduction in writing of a pronounceable word dedicated to the signer. The form of the signature must be in writing according to article 970 of the Civil Code (relating to inheritance matters) with evidencing the signer's presence and will as described above. Furthermore, the Law excludes any intermediary between the signature and its author, such as a typewriting machine or a stamp.

A signature's validity is restricted to the document on which it is placed. Generally, a signature at the end of a document certifies its validity.

Objectives of Signature

4-10   Some acts require writing to evidence their existence, for example, insurance agreements[12] or compromises.[13] Other acts require writing to establish the validity of their existence, for example, the establishment of a company, instruments drawn up by a notary, bills of exchange, or cheques. Some acts

---

9 Law on Data Protection of December 8, 1992.
10 Larrieu, "Les nouveaux moyens de preuve: pour ou contre l'identification des documents informatiques à des écrits sous seing privé?", *Cahiers Droit Informatique*, 1988, at pp. 11 and 12.
11 Fontaine, "La preuve des actes juridiques et les techniques nouvelles", *La Preuve Actes du colloque organisé à LLN les 12 & 13 mars 1987*, at p. 15; Van Quickenborne, "Quelques réflexions sur la signature des actes sous seing privé, note sous Cassation 28 juin 1982", R.C.J.B., 1985, at p. 69.
12 Law of June 11, 1874, article 25.
13 Civil Code, article 2044 (2).

must be in writing to protect third parties. This includes sales or gifts of property, mortgages, and leases for more than nine years.

Legal Constraints

There are certain legal constraints requiring writing. Article 1341 (1) of the **4-11** Civil Code requires that legal acts involving more than BEF 15,000 (£300) be in writing for civil matters. Article 1341 (2) of the Civil Code refers to commercial matters where "evidence is free", which means that such transactions can be proved by all legal means such as testimony and invoices Article 1347 of the Civil Code speaks of a "beginning" of evidence in writing. It refers to any document in writing that originates with the defendant — registers, personal documents — and that substantiate the fact pleaded. Article 1348 refers to the impossibility of producing written evidence — according to the circumstances, for instance, in case of fire or wreck or where the relationships between persons make it difficult.

Common usage makes it possible for electronic data transfer to serve as evidence. Agreements about admissibility of evidence, such as presumptions for log-in in the bank records in case of electronic transfer, are valid, but the law can limit them. The Law of July 14, 1991 on Trade Practices restrains freedom of contract if the agreement does not respect public interest, creates an irrebuttable presumption, detracts from the authority of the judiciary or the public registrar, or lends a means of evidence an "absolute constraining power" undermining the ability to act before a court. For example, for electronic fund transfers, banks cannot ask the user to be responsible for technical risks.[14]

Conclusive Evidence

Conclusive evidence is a concept whereby a means of evidence is legally **4-12** dispositive of an issue of fact. Instruments drawn up by a notary are conclusive. A judge can also evaluate the probative value of a means of evidence. Invoices are treated this way.

Electronic Identification and Authentication

There are technical and secure means to identify the parties who conduct **4-13** electronic commerce and to verify the correct transmission of the message.

The sender's identity can be checked by authentication techniques, such as PIN, special codes, cards, electronic signature with double key, and cryptography. The recipient's identity can be checked by cryptography. The content of the message only enjoys a high level of security

---

14 Mireille, "Le droit de la preuve face aux nouvelles technologies de l'information", *Cahiers du C.R.I.D.* n.7, 1992, at p. 51.

through electronic signature and encryption. These ensure that the document has not been altered and is error free.

Security Criteria

4-14   To be valid according to the law, an electronic document must meet several conditions. It cannot be altered by the parties or by a third party; it must be kept with its form and its content. Authentication techniques will ensure its integrity. Storage must be safe. The document must always be readable by a human. The document must be identified in time (date of transmission, receipt) and location (name and address of parties). The document always includes a part that is confidential and a part that is not (address).

The signature must be unique and allow identification of the signer. It can only come from the sender of the document and cannot be altered or counterfeited. The signature is a part of the document and it must be attached to the document in a permanent manner during the transport of the document.

The signature must be built in the document and be in conformity with the content of the document in that no delay is acceptable between transmission of the signature and the contents of the message. Secrecy of the signature is absolute and must be maintained by security measures. The signature must be checked and certified by a third party.[15]

Electronic transactions

Formation of Contracts Electronically

4-15   There is no specific legislation in Belgium on contracts concluded electronically. Nothing prevents the transmission of a contractual document by electronic means. Electronic contracts' validity and enforceability are a major legal issue. Record-keeping and evidential issues, the legal implications of redesigning business processes (*e.g.*, self-invoicing), the appropriateness of contractual mechanisms to establish legal security, and possibilities for statutory reform to embrace electronic commerce are major issues.

Consent is essential for the formation of a contract. The parties' consents must coincide. Mistake or wilful misrepresentation (advertising promising advantages that do not exist simply to induce a person to make a contract to buy something) will void the contract, and the innocent party may seek damages.

---

15 Mireille, "Le droit de la preuve face aux nouvelles technologies de l'information", *Cahiers du C.R.I.D.* 1992, at pp. 64–68.

The consenting party must have legal capacity. An employee who is not authorised cannot validly sign a contract for his or her company, but Belgian law recognises "the theory of ostensible authority".

The object of the contract must be clearly determined, lawful (according to the national law) and not offend morality.

Offer and Acceptance On-line

Article 1134 of the Civil Code states that "Legally formed, agreements have   **4-16** the binding force of law on those who have made them".

There are different theories as to the time and place of the contract's conclusion. An electronic contract is generally considered a distance contract between two parties not present. A manifest consensus of wills is necessary. According to the expedition theory, the contract is formed when the offeree manifests his intention to accept the offer. Due to evidentiary difficulties, this theory has been severely criticised. According to the information theory, the contract is formed when the expressed intentions actually meet, that is, when each party is made aware of the other's assent. This also presents an evidentiary problem. According to the theory of "qualified" reception, the contract is formed when and where the acceptance of the offeree becomes known (received) or must reasonably have become known to the offeror.[16]

Formation of contract by parties not in each other's presence is a question of fact to be determined by the judge. He can say that the moment of acceptance by the offeror is when the message is received in the electronic letterbox. Parties can by a prior agreement fix the place and time of formation of each electronic transaction.[17]

Revocation of Offer

As long as the offeree has not accepted the offer, the offeror can revoke it.   **4-17** Agreement can only exist if there are two wills. However, if the offeror has given a term for acceptance, he cannot revoke it before the end of the term.

Terms of Reference

To be valid, the supplier's terms of reference must be known and accepted   **4-18** by the buyer before the transaction is concluded. The best solution is if this is by paper, but by exchange of e-mail is also imaginable. The terms can also be on the Web server. In this case, it is an offer that must be accepted to have effect.

---

16 Belgian *Cour de Cassation* (Supreme Court of Appeal), May 25, 1990, *R.W.* 1990–1991, at pp. 149–151.

17 F. 't Kint, "Négociation et conclusion des contrats" in *Les obligations contractuelles*, Editions du Jeune Barreau 1984, at p. 35; Van Ommeslaghe, *Droit des obligations*, Presses universitaires de Bruxelles, 1985, at p. 175.

Another interesting theory developed in EDI is "the interchange profile". This means that it is a part of a message that refers to "terms of reference" kept by a TTP (Trusted Third Party).

International Sales

4-19   A sale can be national or international. A national sale is between two persons in the same country and national law will be applicable. In the case of international sales, international conventions may apply. The Internet is made for "business-to-business" and "business-to-consumer" relationships. sPayment is made for acquiring services or goods and the transactions are very often international.

In consumer transactions, the consumer is protected by the law and has seven days to change his mind.

Mistakes in On-line Contracts

4-20   Generally, the user will be liable for his mistakes on-line. If it is a technical mistake, the server or the service provider can be responsible.

Impact of Impostors or Persons without Authority

4-21   Legal capacity is one of the vulnerable factors of validity of electronic contracts. For legal security in commercial matters, the theory of appearance will apply unless there is a fraud, which is a matter of evidence.

On-line Payments

4-22   The purpose of a payment is to give money to a creditor in exchange for delivery of goods or services. Payment also extinguishes a legal obligation. Parties can agree that payment will be made offline for security or cost reasons.

Electronic Fund Transfers

4-23   Telecommunications has made electronic fund transfer (EFT) easy.

SWIFT (Society for World-wide Interbank Financial Telecommunication), a company incorporated under Belgian law, has developed its own EDI system in a close network only accessible to banks for worldwide EFT. It operates its own clearance room.

Electronic banking allows the conduct of all electronic banking transactions with a telephone line, a computer, a modem and special software provided by the bank. As every bank had its own software, the Interbank Standards Association Belgium (ISABEL) was set up by seven banks. ISABEL provides services to companies and enterprises with Internet access with standardised software to allow users to access different member banks.

Under this system security procedures are reinforced with PIN, passwords and signature, authentication. A system is secure when it respects data integrity, protects data against unauthorised access (confidentiality) and transmits data within a reasonable time, reducing the consequences of failure or accidental interruption.[18]

Two means of payment are mainly used. These are credit card and electronic fund transfer. E-Money will offer a third possibility.

Credit Card Payments On-line

Normally, when a client wants to pay with his credit card, he gives it to the 4-24
merchant who takes a print of the credit card, makes the holder sign it, and checks the signature. The merchant may also call the credit card issuer to receive a special code number.

If there is no signature or if the signature is roughly forged, case law says that the merchant alone will assume the consequences of the transaction[19] unless the credit card owner has declared the loss or the theft of the card.

Electronically, the client will give his name, credit card number, and the card's expiry date but he cannot sign the counterfoil. This means that fraud and misuse are easier. Practically, the first time a client uses the service, he will give his name and card number, possibly offline. He will receive a virtual code to use every time he has access to the service.

Following article 1315 of the Civil Code, the operation is called "imperfect delegation" where there is a relationship between client, bank (Visa, American express), and vendor and where the bank must prove the existence of debit.[20]

Use of Electronic Checks

Another means of payment is called E-money (Electronic Money). A soft- 4-25
ware company called DigiCash developed it. The bank[21] converts U.S. \$1 into one cyberdollar or cyberbuck. The cyberbucks are transferred to the client's hard disk. When the client wants to buy something, he simply transfers the cyberbucks electronically and the merchant can either download them to its hard disk or transfer them into its account Mark Twain Bank.

Security procedures (such as blind signatures) guarantee that each virtual buck is only used once like banknotes.[22]

---

18 Thunis, *Responsabilité des banquiers et automatisation des paiements*, Presses universitaires de Namur, 1996, at p. 159.
19 Corbisier "Les instruments de paiement et de crédit", *Journal des Tribunaux*, 1990; p. 441, n 81; *contra*: Civil Bruxelles, December 11, 1986, R.D.C. 1988, at p. 219.
20 Buyle, "Internet: quelques aspects juridiques", *Droit de l'Informatique et des Télécoms*, 1996/2, at p. 13.
21 The Mark Twain Bank in the United States was the first bank to propose it on October 23, 1995.
22 Hance, *Business et droit d'Internet*, 1996, at p. 162.

The major issue of such a payment is the evidence of the moment of payment and of the reality of content. The legal nature of this kind of payment can be analysed in three ways:

- Real payment — According to Belgian law, a payment is valid only if it is made with legal tender.
- Donation in payment *(dation en paiement)* — Both client and vendor are members of DigiCash and payment is made in cyberbucks. Dation en paiement imposes three conditions, namely, that the remitted item is different from the due item, that the item is remitted and that the obligation is extinguished.
- Means of payment — The vendor considers DigiCash a mean of payment. The payment will be effective only the day the vendor receives the payment in legal tender.

ELECTRONIC INFORMATION RIGHTS

Property Rights in Electronic Information

Copyright

4-26   The question arises why specific rules for authors' rights for on-line services are necessary. Case law about radio and cable television broadcasting is widely known, as are European Directives for cable television and satellite transmission. There was a need to harmonise legislation so that it could be determined where author royalties should be paid. For satellite broadcasts, it is the place where the signals are sent to an ascending station.

Similar problems are encountered with authors' rights applied to on-line technologies. Once information is available on the Internet, a worldwide audience can have access to it.

Currently, there is no specific legislation relating to on-line application of authors' rights. A major study is in progress as to adaptation of the law to the new technologies, but the first draft of the new legislation is not expected until mid-1997. For now, the existing legislation on protection of intellectual property will apply to these technologies. Article 1 (1) of the Law of June 30, 1994, on Authors' Rights and Related Rights says:

"The author of a literary or artistic work is the only one entitled to reproduce or to authorise to reproduce it in any manner or in any form."

"This right implies the exclusive right to authorise adaptation or the translation."

"This right also includes the exclusive right to authorise its loan."

"The author of a literary or artistic work is the only one entitled to communicate it to the public by any means."[23]

Although the law does not say "on-line communication", the provision is written in such general terms that it implies reproduction or communication of the work by any means. The Belgian system of protection of authors' rights is indeed an open system.[24] In general terms, the Law on Authors' Rights and Related Rights of June 30, 1994, can apply to any new technologies, even those which do not yet exist.   **4-27**

Information Protected on-line services are multimedia and allow transmission of any type of work (sound, image, video, and text). It is important to define precisely the required conditions for an on-line creation to be protected by authors' rights. For an item to be protected under Belgian law, it is a sufficient condition that the item be original and expressed in a certain form. The criterion of originality is appreciated very widely: pictures, a dictionary, hairstyle, anthology, or an advertising slogan can be protected if they are not common.   **4-28**

Traditionally, defined as the print of its author's personality, the criterion of originality has evolved toward a notion of creative effort of his author. As far as computer programs are concerned, the Law of June 30, 1994 gives more precision to this criterion: "an intellectual creation proper to its author".[25]

Putting the Idea into a Form For an item to be protected, it needs to be put into a form, which means that it must have been expressed by its author. An idea alone is not protected; it needs to be expressed in a certain form. Using a code that is only machine readable, *e.g.*, coding a work before disseminating it on-line is sufficient. The technique used to put an idea into a form is not a barrier to the application of authors' rights.   **4-29**

Ideas alone are not protected. The protection of intellectual property will be more difficult to apply to on-line communication modes. The question is whether an element is an idea alone or is a work that can be protected by the law.

Olivier Hance is convincing when he says that any kind of communication, even by electronic means, is sufficient for protection. For the condition of putting an idea into a form, the important issue is the content and not the supporting means; a creative idea spread by e-mail will be protected if the structure of the work is expressed in this e-mail. For instance, texts, musicals, and audio-visual works, images, software and databases will be protected.

---

23 Translation from French by the author.
24 Strowel, *Droit d'auteur et copyright*, Brussels Bruylant 1993, at pp. 144 *et seq.*
25 Law of June 30, 1994, article 2, matches word-for-word article 1, line 3, of the Directive of May 14, 1996, on Software Protection.

As far as software is concerned, the Law of May 14, 1991 states that programs are protected as literary works: This is an application of the Council Directive of May 14, 1991 on Protection of Computer Programs.

4-30   **Acquiring Authors' Rights** Contrary to the copyright system, no prior registration is required for a work to be protected. The author's right is applicable as soon as a work is created. The fundamental issue is to prove the quality of authorship and the precedence of the creation.

As messages are spread electronically, it is wise to add the copyright symbol to achieve the widest possible protection. This is not a condition of Belgian law. The purpose of this precaution is to help with respect to the Universal Convention of Geneva of September 6, 1952, and the Berne Convention.

4-31   **Ownership of Copyright** In principle, only the creator of a protected item owns the author's right. There are also related rights, such as producers' rights, radio, and television rights, and artists' and performers' rights. For one work, there can be several owners of distinct rights. For example, an audio-CD with the song "My Way" can be protected for the composer (Claude François — author's right), for the performer (Frank Sinatra — neighbouring rights) and for the producer.

When a work is created under an employment contract, in principle, it will be the author who will own the author's rights and not the employer. There are certain exceptions:

- The employer of a person who creates computer programs will be supposed to be the owner of the computer programs created by the employee;[26] and
- The film producer is the owner of the different author's rights (*e.g.*, director, adapter, screenwriter).

4-32   In the copyright system, the producer owns the intellectual property of the film from the beginning.

4-33   **Rights of Copyright Owner** The owner of authors' rights enjoys moral and patrimonial rights.

4-34   *Moral Rights* Moral rights were originally only known in Civil Law systems. They were only recently introduced in the United Kingdom.

Moral rights cover divulgence, authorship, and integrity of the work. According to the divulgence right, only the author can choose to communicate his work to the public, or not to communicate, and when to communicate his

---

26 Law of May 14, 1991, article 3.

work. According to the authorship right, only the author can decide whether his work will be signed, anonymous or if he will use a pseudonym. According to the right to integrity, the author can oppose any modification or deformation of his work.

Unlike patrimonial rights, these moral rights are personal to the author and are inalienable.

Patrimonial Rights The reproduction right means that the author is the only person who can authorise or forbid the reproduction of his work. Registration of an item in the ROM (read-only memory) of a computer or its saving is considered reproduction. If the work is in the RAM (random access memory) of a computer, it is not considered reproduction (necessary for consultation). 4-35

The public communication right means that only the author may authorise or forbid dissemination of his work by radio, cable, satellite, or any instrument transmitting signals or images.

Transformation rights mean that only the author can authorise translation, adaptation, arrangement, or any transformation of his work.

Applied to on-line technologies, this means the author only can authorise or forbid on-line communication or transformation of his work. Digitising an image to spread it on Internet violates two authors' rights, namely, those of transformation and reproduction.

For on-line exploitation of a work , it is important to know whether an author has transferred his rights and authorised exploitation.

Article 3(1) of the Law of June 30, 1994, states clearly, "patrimonial rights are movable, transferable, totally or partially, according to the Civil Code. They can be alienated or licensed exclusively or not". Significantly, it requires that all contracts must be proved in writing and that contractual clauses on authors' rights and their means of exploitation must be strictly interpreted. It also demands that for each means of exploitation, the author's remuneration and the duration of transfer must be expressly determined.

In Belgian law, the right to disseminate a work on-line must have been expressly transferred. The requirement of a document in writing is not a condition of validity but a mandatory means of evidence. An invoice, a letter, an order can be considered written evidence of the transfer.[27]

An issue is whether authors' rights may be transferred on-line. The most commonly used on-line transfers of authors' rights are shareware licences. The law contains no terms that these must be "in writing" or requiring "signature". The interpretation of these notions must be as wide as possible.[28]

---

27 Berenboom, *Le Nouveau Droit d'auteur*, Brussels, Larcier 1995, at pp. 158 *et seq.*
28 Thunis, "Responsabilité du banquier et automatisation des instruments de paiement", *Droit de l'informatique: enjeux et responsabilités*, Ed. Jeune barreau de Bruxelles, 1993.

Testimony and presumptions are allowed as means to evidence an electronic message and to prove the existence and the limits of the contract transferring the author's rights.

An electronic message (file or e-mail) should be considered an initial element of written evidence. A telex has already been considered as such,[29] and case law will extend this notion. The initial element of written evidence must originate from the person against whom something needs to be proven and must be considered plausible.[30] An electronic message can be considered an initial element of written evidence only against its author, who must be clearly identified. Unlike the traditional written document, an electronic message, even with all security and integrity guarantees, will never be a better means of evidence than testimony or legal presumption. There are no specific rules for electronic evidence and no guarantees of authenticity.

The conclusion is that an e-mail or the terms of a shareware licence downloaded and packed with the software, or a WEB page, can be invoked against the author of the work to prove the transfer of authors' rights. The rights that can be transferred must be clearly defined.

4-36   **Rights of Copyright User** The limits of author's rights and the authorised uses without the author's consent are important issues. Official speeches and acts of public authority can be reproduced and communicated to the public without restriction.[31] Short quotations for critical, polemical or educational purposes may be used subject to professional codes of conduct and justified for legitimate use without violating authors' rights. The name of the author must be mentioned.[32]

Once a work is published, an author can no longer forbid "reproduction and communication for information purposes of short fragments of works or plastic arts in full with reports of current events; reproduction and communication to the public of works of art in an area open to the public when the purpose of reproduction or communication to the public is not the work itself; communication free of charge and private in the family circle; fragmental or full reproduction of plastic arts on graphic support, when this reproduction is made for strictly private use or educational use and does not affect publication of the original work of art; reproduction of sound or audio-visual works only for private use in the family circle; caricature, parody or pastiche, according to codes of conduct . . . ."[33]

Neither case law nor Belgian legislation have answered to the question whether communication of a protected work by e-mail (point to point — not in a discussion group) violates authors' rights or is it a classical exception of authors' rights.

---

29 Civ. Turnhout, May 21, 1987, R.G.D.C. 1989, at p. 171.
30 Verheyden-Jeanmart, *Doit de la preuve*, Bruxelles, Ed. Larcier, 1991.
31 Law on Authors' Rights, article 8.
32 A selection of works in an anthology is not a quotation and authors' rights are applicable.
33 Law on Authors' Rights, article 22 (1).

Specific Problems On-line communication is anonymous. The major chal-   4-37
lenge of authors' rights in on-line communication is not exclusively legal but
mainly practical. How can an author identify a plagiarist who uses and alters
his work without his consent on an Internet site and how can he be sure that
penalties will apply?

Two Particular Issues Which national law should apply and what is the   4-38
competent jurisdiction are typical legal issues in this context.

An obvious risk for violation of authors' rights is where infringement
originates from a country that has no legislation protecting authors' rights.
This arose with regard to spreading a publication by Internet, *Le Grand
Secret*, about French President Mitterand's life and health.

Practically, to detect an infringement to authors' rights on the Internet
should not be complicated. Accessibility means that inspectors can surf to
ensure application of law and to find infringements. It will be more difficult
to identify the natural or the legal person to prosecute.[34]

As far as the applicable law is concerned about an on-line violation of
authors' rights, one should ask two questions:

Belgian courts are competent according to the Brussels Convention of
September 27, 1968 when someone who violates authors' rights can be
sued in the contracting State where the defendant has his legal domicile[35]
or before the court of the country where the damaging fact has occurred.[36]

If the defendant — *e.g.*, author of an on-line infringement — is domiciled
in Belgium, competence of Belgian courts is clear and the decision
rendered will be recognised by other states of the European Union. Jurisdiction based on localisation of damaging fact poses more problems; a work
spread on Internet can be seen worldwide. For radio and satellite television
broadcasting, a similar question has been solved by Council Directive
93/83/EEC of September 27, 1993, and implemented by Belgian Law of
June 30, 1994, article 49,[37] which says that communication is deemed to
occur where "signals are introduced in an uninterrupted chain of communication leading to satellite and coming back on earth". Such a rule can be
applied to on-line communications, limited to radio and television broadcasting. The Directive is not applicable to graphic arts or literary works
spread on the Internet.

Because a reasonable link is necessary between infringement and the
State with competent jurisdiction, it is preferable to base territorial competence on the defendant's domicile.

---

34 In Belgium, only a natural person can be criminally prosecuted.
35 Brussels Convention, article 2.
36 Brussels Convention, article 5(3).
37 *Moniteur Belge,* July 27, 1994.

The law that will be applicable depends on the private international law of the jurisdiction where the matter is tried. The applicable law for the protection of the work will be determined by the author's nationality or by his domicile.

If the author is domiciled in a country signatory of the Treaty of Berne Union, he will benefit from the same protection as a Belgian. Belgian law will be applicable, even if the author's national law is less protective.

When the author is not domiciled in a country signatory of the Treaty of Berne Union, or subscriber to the Universal Convention of Geneva of 1952, his rights will be limited by reciprocity. He will only enjoy the same rights that Belgians enjoy in the state of his nationality and for the same duration.[38] The growing number of signatories to the Treaty of Berne Union means that Belgian Law will apply to more and more matters referred to Belgian jurisdiction.

Trade Secrets

4-39   **General** Intellectual property rights do not protect business or trade secrets or know-how; there is no specific legislation. As there is no specific legislation to protect transfer of know-how, the rules for protection will be based on unfair competition law and on contract law. Know-how is a range of intangible elements that allow a company an advantage over its competitors. There are many definitions of know-how.[39] Some definitions insist on the content of know-how, while other focus on its characteristics. As to content, it has been said,

> "Know-how, that is to say factual knowledge, not capable of precise, separate description, but which, when used in an accumulated form, after being acquired as the result of trial and error, gives the one acquiring it an ability to produce something which he otherwise would not have known to produce with the same accuracy of precision found necessary for commercial success."[40]

4-40   This definition emphasises the following aspect of know-how: a wide range of elements of knowledge which help the owner to be more competitive.

---

38 Law on Authors' Rights and Related Rights of June 30, 1994, articles 79 *et seq.*
39 Azéma, "Fifth Meeting About Intellectual Property", *Le Know-How*, Ed. Librairies techniques, Montpellier 1975, at pp. 13 *et seq.*; Magnin, *Know-how et propriété industrielle*, Ed. Librairies techniques 1974, at pp. 21–124, Deleuze, *Le contrat de transfert de processus technologique — Know-How*, Ed. Masson, Paris 1976, at pp. 18–19.
40 Court of Maryland — *Mycalex Corporation of America v. Pemco Corporation*, 68 U.S.P.Q. 317 DC. Maryland 1946; see Deleuze, *Le contrat de transfert de processus technologique — Know-How*, Ed. Masson, Paris 1976, at p. 19, and Magnin, "Know-how et propriété industrielle", Ed. Librairies techniques 1974, at p. 36, note 18. See also reference in Dessemontet, *The legal protection of know-how in the United States of America*, Ed. Rothman, South Hackensack, New Jersey 1976, at p. 461.

The (legal) characteristics distinguishing know-how have been described as follows:

"As long as an invention is not patented, it can only be considered know-how, which is not an obstacle to a future request for patent . . .".[41]

Often a company chooses not to patent an invention but to use it and to keep it secret.[42] This strategy has several advantages over patenting. A patent application means disclosing an invention in exchange for a legal protection of this invention. This protection can only be given if the invention is new, inventive, and susceptible of industrial application.[43] However, computer programs are excluded.[44] An inventor can request a patent from the Industrial Property Department of the Ministry of Economic Affairs. If an invention is patentable, the patent is given by ministerial decree and the inventor must pay a special tax. A description of invention is published in the Book of Patents. The owner's patent monopoly of exploitation, and for claiming counterfeiting, is legally insecure. Someone else may seek to invalidate the patent before a court if invention does not meet conditions of patentability.[45] By choosing to exploit an invention in secret, the company avoids the risk of cancellation of the patent after the invention is disclosed.[46]

4-41

Know-how includes also negative know-how, knowledge of mistakes not to be made. Know-how includes technical expertise. This must be distinguished from technical ability. A company can transfer technical expertise to another company without necessarily transferring technicians. Technical expertise could be transferred with technical assistance to another company. It is not only the professional skill of technicians. It can be described in written documents.

---

41 Economic Commission for Europe, Document TRADE/222/Rev. I, Publication of the United Nations, New York, 1970; see Magnin, "Know-how et propriété industrielle", Ed. Librairies techniques 1974, Annexe VII, at p. 415.

42 Walschot, "Bescherming van Technologie. Enkele beschouwingen", X *Le juriste dans l'entreprise*, at pp. 486 *et seq*.

43 Law of February 28, 1984 on Invention Patents, M.B. March 9, 1985, article 2; Braun "Chronique de jurisprudence, droits intellectuels (1987–1991)", J.T., 1992 at p. 505 N2; Tilleman "De nieuwe Belgische octrooiwetgeving", Jura Falconis 1984–1985, at pp. 255–257; De Visscher "La nouvelle loi belge sur les Brevets d'invention", J.T. 1985, at pp. 382 *et seq*., N 11 *et seq*.; Verschaeve "Naar een nieuw octrooirecht", R.W. 1984–1985, at col. 2245 et sections; Van Hecke and Gotzen "Overzicht van Rechtspraak, industriële eigendom, auteursrecht 1975–1990", T.P.R. 1990, at pp. 1781 *et seq*.

44 Law of March 28, 1984, M.B. March 9, 1985, article 3.

45 Van Bunnen "Chronique de jurisprudence, Les brevets d'invention, 1983–1990", R.C.J.B. 1992, at p. 162 N11.

46 See also: Azéma, "Fifth Meeting About Intellectual Property", *Le Know-How*, Ed. Librairies techniques, Montpellier 1975, at pp. 20–21; Demin *Le contrat de Know-how*, Bruxelles, Bruylant, 1968, at p. 16; Deleuze, *Le contrat de transfert de processus technologique — Know-How*, Ed. Masson, Paris 1976, at p. 17.

"Know-how in fact is what we can call technical ability, professional skill and what case law has defined as a technical expertise of execution depending on care and ability of executant."

Technical ability does not amount to true know-how because it is not transferable.[47]

Protection of know-how is mainly based on secrecy. Inventions could be protected by know-how instead of patent. To avoid the risk of a patent's cancellation and open information, people prefer to keep a process or a technique secret and use it exclusively. This secrecy is protected by the Law on the Commercial Code of Conduct,[48] which forbids acts of unfair competition by merchants. This protection can be reinforced by certain contractual techniques. The Law of July 3, 1978 on employment contracts forbids employees from disclosing any business or manufacturing secret and any business secret with a personal or confidential character that the employee may know from his or her professional activity. Confidentiality is an obligation for the worker both during the employment contract and afterwards.

Article 17(3) of the Law of July 3, 1978, on Employment Contracts provides, ". . . a worker must refrain doing any act of unfair competition as well during the execution of the contract than after the termination of the contract." Consequently, an employer can forbid employees — under certain conditions and for a limited time — to refrain from competing activities. This protection can be reinforced by a non-competition clause, which forbids any kind of competition in the employment contract.

4-42   **Acquiring Trade Secret Rights** There are no specific rules for transferring or licensing know-how. The parties enjoy a wide freedom of contract. Generally, the contract will describe the obligations of both parties, such as a limitation of the use of know-how once it is transferred, a commitment to use it only for a specific application, a commitment to use it only for a limited period of time and a prohibition of communication of know-how transferred to third parties.

Trade Mark

4-43   In Belgium, the following instruments regulate trade marks: the Uniform Benelux Law of March 19, 1963; the Madrid Convention of April 14, 1991, and European Community Council Regulation 40/94 of December 20, 1993, on the Community Trade Mark. The trade mark regulation has been harmonised in the Benelux and in the European Union. Any verbal or

---

47 Azéma, "Fifth Meeting About Intellectual Property", *Le Know-How*, Ed. Librairies techniques, Montpellier 1975, at pp. 22–23; Magnin, *Know-how et propriété industrielle*, Ed. Librairies techniques 1974, at pp. 43–44.
48 Law of July 14, 1991.

figurative trade mark can be chosen. The only criterion is the distinctive, legal and available character of trade marks. The Benelux Trade marks Office does not allow on-line registration.

Trade marks are protected court claims against counterfeiting. Article 8 of the Law of April 1, 1879, on Trade Marks provides for punishment by imprisonment of eight days to six months or by a fine of BEF 26 to BEF 2,000. The following persons are punished: those who have counterfeited a trade mark or those who have used illegally a counterfeited trade mark; those who have illegally attached, added, deleted or altered a trade mark being the ownership of someone else on their own commercial products or objects; and those who have sold or offered for sale products with a counterfeited trade mark.

Article 14 of the Law requires that the prosecution initiated by the complaint of the penal claim can only be initiated by the injured party. Article 11 of the Uniform Benelux Law makes the transfer *inter vivos* not stated in writing and the transfer not available for Benelux territory void.

A transfer or licence will be effective *vis-à-vis* third parties only after registration of the trade mark and after payment of taxes fixed by the rules. An abstract of the title stating the right or a declaration by the interested parties must be provided.

A written transfer document is required for evidentiary purpose. The courts have not yet held that initial elements of written evidence could satisfy the need for writing.

Domain Names

General   Each server has an Internet Protocol (IP) address, which is digital   **4-44** and difficult to memorise. To allow users to find a server easily, a domain name is associated to this IP address. A domain name is chosen by the server to be identified. In common language, this is an Internet address.

Domain names are attributed as follows. The registration process creates a database that matches the names to the IP addresses used for Internet routing. Within each country, a local registration office ensures that new names are inserted in this database. In Belgium, this registration office is the Department of Computer Science of the Catholic University Leuven (http://www.dns.be).

An advisory board is set up to overview the operations of the registration office. Members of this board are representatives of the Internet service. The board takes decisions in case of conflicts about names between the organisation requesting a name and the registration office.

Protection of a Domain Name Server (DNS) importatnt. A DNS is an identification on the Internet and helps a company to be found easily. Many domain names actually are literal retranscription of a server's owner.

Commercial names are usually known and protected locally. Two merchants can share the same trade name for the same kind of activity if they are far enough from each other to avoid any confusion. The effect of on-line communication is to cancel any distance leading to a risk of conflict between users who wish to use the same domain name. Using the same domain name is also a risk of confusion between two servers, possibly resulting in commercial prejudice.

4-45 **Rules**   In Belgian law, at the present, there is no specific legislation about domain names. The rules applicable are the practice of the DNS-BE Registration Office and, generally speaking, the rules of commercial conduct, protection of trade names and trade marks.

The registration terms and conditions of DNS-BE state that DNS-BE is responsible for the registration of second level Internet domain names in the BE top level domain, and that DNS-BE registers these domain names on a "first come, first serve" basis.

DNS-BE has neither the resources nor the legal obligation to screen requested domain names to determine if the use of a domain name by an applicant may infringe up on the rights of a third party. Consequently, as an express condition and material inducement of the grant of an applicant's request to register a domain name, the applicant must represent and warrant the truth of the applicant's statements in the application and its right to use the domain name as requested in the application; that the applicant has a *bona fide* intention to use the domain name on a regular basis on the Internet; that the use or registration of the domain name by the applicant, to the best of the applicant's knowledge, does not interfere with or infringe the right of any third party in any jurisdiction with respect to trade mark, service mark, trade name, company name or any other intellectual property right; and that the applicant is not seeking to use the domain name for any unlawful purpose, including without limitation, tortious interference with contract or prospective business advantage, unfair competition, injuring the reputation of another, or for the purpose of confusing or misleading a person, whether natural or incorporated.

The liability for respect of trade names, trade marks, and company names is left entirely to the person who asks to register his own domain name.

Under article 4 of the registration terms and conditions, the applicant agrees that DNS-BE may withdraw a domain name from use and registration on the Internet on 30 days' prior written notice (or earlier if ordered by the court) should DNS-BE receive a properly authenticated order by a Belgian court or arbitration panel chosen by the parties (if the order is from an arbitration panel, it should include written evidence that all parties which will be bound by the decision, submitted the dispute for binding arbitration to such panel) that the domain name in dispute rightfully belongs to a third party.

The applicant must also connect effectively a server to the registered domain name within the 90 days of registry. When a registered domain name is not used, it becomes available again for registration and use by another party.

It is also important to note that a payment (BEF5,000 plus value-added-tax) is due for registration and a rental fee. When the owner of the domain ceases to pay the rental fee, the domain name is put on a "hold" status for 30 days. After these 30 days, the domain name may be assigned to someone else.

Because there is no specific legislation for domain names in Belgium, general commercial legislation will be applicable: protection of trade name, trade marks and commercial code of conduct, besides contractual rules decreed by DNS-BE Registration Office.

Although the case has not been submitted to Belgian jurisdictions yet, it seems that only the owner of a registered trade mark can reproduce and use it as a domain name.

As far as merchants are concerned, registering a domain name creating confusion with the trade name of another merchant can be considered an unfair practice according to articles 93 and 94 of the Law of July 14, 1991 on commercial code of conduct.

Even after a domain name is acquired, registered and attributed according to the rule "first come, first served", the same domain name can be registered in another Top Level Domain or a sub-domain. For instance, www.bosmans.be, www.bosmans.com, and www.bosmans.ping.be can all be registered. Risk of confusion is obvious.

Problems may occur if the owner of "bosmans.be" wants to create a site "bosmans.lu" and if this domain name is already used abroad. A person may seek to enforce his right to the trade mark against anybody within the territorial limits of protection of the trade mark. The trade mark right allows its owner to forbid:

- Any use which, in the conduct of business, could be made of the trade mark for similar products for which there is already a registered trade mark;
- Any use which, in the conduct of business, could be made of the trade mark or a sign that looks like the trade mark for products (or similar products) for which there is already a registered trade mark when there could be in people's mind a risk of association between the sign and trade mark;
- Any use which, in the conduct of business and without a legitimate reason, could be made of the trade mark that has a reputation in Benelux or a sign that looks like the trade mark for products non similar to those with the registered trade mark when the person who uses this sign could benefit unduly from the distinctive character or the reputation of the trade mark or could cause prejudice; and
- Any use which, in the conduct of business and without a legitimate reason, could be made of the trade mark or a sign that looks like the trade mark for a purpose other than to distinguish products when the person who uses this sign could benefit unduly from the distinctive character or the fame of the trade mark or could cause a prejudice.[49]

---

49 Uniform Benelux Law on Trade Marks, article 13.

4-46   This form of protection has limits. The trade mark owner can forbid any use of the trade mark in the conduct of business. It is essential — for the purposes of forbidding the use of a trade mark for other products — that the trade mark is famous and that the offending person benefits unduly from the trade mark. The following cannot be prohibited:

- A domain name corresponding to a trade mark that has not already been registered;[50] and
- On-line communication not within the conduct of business life territory. protection of a trade mark, even a famous one, could be ineffective against registration of a domain name literally similar to the existing trade mark for non-commercial purposes.

4-47   The rule for domain names is largely "first come, first served". The DNS-BE Registration Office only deletes a domain name if there is a decision from a court.

Patents and Patentability

4-48   In Belgium, patents are regulated by the Law of March 28, 1984. This Law is based on the Munich Convention of October 5, 1973 on European Patents.

For an invention to be protected by patent, it must exhibit innovation, inventive step and the possibility of industrial application. An invention is innovative when it is not part of the current technical knowledge. Belgian law requires absolute innovation.

For the criterion of inventive activity, article 6 of the Law says, "An invention is supposed to imply an inventive activity if, for a professional, it is not an obvious consequence of the current state of technology". Article 7 of the Law says, "An invention is susceptible of industrial application if its object can be manufactured or used in any kind of industry, even agriculture."

Software End Users, Developers, and Distributors

4-49   In the past, scholars debated giving the patent protection to software. Today, the European Directive on Computer Programs has solved the question, which was implemeted in Belgian law by the Law of 1994. This Law accorded the same protection as enjoyed by literary works. As a result, software cannot be protected by patent.

---

50 A third party may register a domain name corresponding to a trade mark with no fame for a non-commercial purpose or to sell totally different products and may deprive the trade mark owner of the possibility to register a domain name which is the literal transcription of his trade mark.

Licensing The rights related to patent can be transferred, partially or totally. 4-50
Article 44 of the Law of 1984 provides that any transfer, whether total or
partial, of patent rights or of an application for patent must be notified
to the registration authority (Industrial Property Office). It requires that
transfers *inter vivos* of patent must be made in writing; otherwise, they
will be void. Notification according to the registration authority must be
accompanied by either a certified true copy of title of transfer/official
document stating transfer of rights, or a certified abstract of this title or
document stating transfer and proof of payment of tax.

Unlike in the case of transfers of authors' rights, a written document is
not only a means of evidence against the author, but also an essential
condition of validity. Notification to the Industrial Property Office must be
made in writing with a revenue stamp of BEF 500, together with a certified
true copy of the title. Until now, on-line registration of transfer or licence of
patents is impossible.[51]

ON-LINE CONDUCT

Many authorities, some of which have already been mentioned in this article, 4-51
regulate electronic communication. For data protection, a special authority
named "Commission for Privacy and Data Protection" has been created. For
telecommunication, several laws apply. The Belgian Institute for Post and
Telecommunication (IBPT) is responsible for cryptography matters. For
domain names, the NIC is the University of Leuven.

Territorial Limits of Jurisdiction

Global electronic commerce creates difficulties for establishing the relevant 4-52
applicable law for a particular electronic transaction.

The time and place a contract concluded by electronic means is considered to have been formed will determine the applicable law and court with
jurisdiction to adjudicate any dispute arising in relation to the contractual
relations.[52]

If the transaction is made "business-to-business" or "consumer-to-
consumer", the parties can choose the applicable law. Otherwise, the law
where the characteristic performance is rendered governs the contract. In an
ordinary sale, usually admitted the applicable law will be that of the vendor's
domicile. If the transaction involves real estate (*e.g.*, sale or lease), the
location of the real estate will determine the applicable law.[53]

---

51 Van Reepinghen and De Branbanter, *Les brevets d'invention*, Bruxelles, Ed. Larcier 1987,
   at pp. 138 *et seq.*
52 Lodomez, "The legal position of the Member States with respect to EDI", T.E.D.I.S., at p. 76.
53 Law of July 14, 1987, implementing the Rome Convention of June 19, 1980.

If the transaction is "business-to-consumer", the consumer is protected by the Law of July 14, 1991, on the Commercial Code of Conduct and Protection of Consumers and the Law of June 12, 1991, on Consumer Credit. The parties in "business-to-consumer" transactions can choose the applicable law, but if they do not, the law of the country where the consumer lives will apply.

If litigation involves transborder transactions in Europe, the Brussels Convention of September 27, 1968, on Jurisdiction will apply.

Data Protection

4-53   Data protection is an important issue in electronic commerce. In the 1980s, many databases were created making their content available for commercial purposes. There is little control over these, and data can be false or used for illegal purposes. The users of these databases are often not identified. Some servers can be queried anonymously. Information is delocalised.

From the security point of view, control is difficult. It requires organising a prior control with the good will and the honesty of users. The Law on Data Protection was enacted in Belgium on December 8, 1992. This legislation only protects individuals, not companies, and it deals with personal data, not commercial data.

Data subjects can have access to their private data and have the right to change or correct this data. The Law requires that there must be a person responsible for the file in Belgium. Even if a foreign company or person processes the data, there must be a representative in Belgium. The responsible person must communicate the finality of data processing and allow access to data subjects.

For transborder data flows, according to the E.E.C. Directive of October 15, 1992, the Belgian law says that data can only be transmitted in other countries with the same level of data protection.

Sensitive data — religious or philosophical beliefs, political opinions or activities, health, sexual life, trade union membership, social security bodies membership, racial or ethnic origins — can only be collected, processed and transmitted with the personal and express consent of each data subject except in case of emergency. (e.g., in case of accident for medical purposes).

The authorities, such as the police, can collect and transmit information without the data subject's consent in criminal activities or for state or public safety.

The Law created a special control authority, the Commission for Privacy Protection. In the case of transborder data flow through the Internet, for instance, the Commission can exercise a prior control before the information is spread.

Belgian authorities might through the Commission create filters for transborder data flow to non-protective countries.

To allow freedom in crossborder data flow, the new European Directive on Data Protection foresees that the "controller of the file" who wants to spread information in the European Union on the Internet will be responsible according to his national law. If the controller spreads the information from overseas, he must designate a person responsible on European Union territory.

Liability

In terms of liability, the major issue is to identify the user or the author of   4-54
information transmitted on the network. Article 299 of the Penal Code obliges the author or the editor of a publication or a distributor of printed matter to make known his real name and address. Of course, this article is only valid in Belgium. Belgian television and radio are subject to prior authorisation for broadcasting. This is also only valid on Belgian territory.

The victim of untrue or illegally published information or information transmitted by television or radio can act against the person responsible for the damaging act. Difficulties arise where the information is spread through a network. It is unclear who is responsible: the server, the access provider, the telecommunications operator, or the author of the message?

Article 25 of the Belgian Constitution establishes a hierarchical chain of responsibility (cascade responsibility) for newspapers. Some judgments have transposed this to audio-visual information.[54] Some authors[55] suggest making the author, by default the editor, by default the access provider and finally the telecommunication operator responsible. This system has four advantages, namely:

- Victims are sure to find a person responsible;
- An automatic hierarchical chain facilitates the work of the judge and shortens the proceedings;
- Standardisation of control is applicable to information on any kind of support (newspapers, audio-visual, digital networks); and
- There is a rebuttable presumption, which means that burden of proof can be reversed or transferred by the person who is implicated.[56]

Some prefer to retain the classical regime of responsibility based on article 1382   4-55
of Civil Code.[57] Article 1382 requires a fault, damage, and a link between

---

54 Brussels, May 25, 1993, *Journal des Tribunaux*, 1994, at p. 104, observations, Jongen; Brussels June 7, 1991, *Revue de droit pénal*, 1992, at p. 131.
55 Olivier and Barby "Des réseaux aux autoroutes de l'information. Révolution technique? Révolution juridique?, Du contenu informationnel sur les réseaux", JCP, G, 1996, I, 3928, p 185, n43.
56 Based on the remarks of Prof. Montero of the University of Namur, Seminar "Internet and the law", held in November 1996.
57 The view of Professor Montero at Seminar "Internet and the Law", held in November 1996.

the fault and the damage for an author to be responsible. Cascade responsibility moves the author of a damaging act to go to another territory with more favourable legislation. The Brussels Convention 1968 foresees in article 5(3) that the court of the location where a damaging fact occurs will be competent. A victim, a user of the Internet, can issue a writ against a person responsible of a damaging act in the country where he received the altered information or in the country from which the information has been issued. Generally, the law applicable is that of the country where the fault has been committed. The judge must apply the law of the country from which the information has been delivered.[58]

Impact of Penal Law

4-56   Belgium lacks specific legislation on computer misuse, such as the "Computer Misuse Act" in United Kingdom or *Loi Godfrain* in France. In Belgium, the basic principle is *nulla poena sine lege*. An act can only be considered infringement of law if the law already exists. There are different types of illegal and harmful content and conduct on the Internet. These include information security, unauthorised access, computer misuse, passwords and virus traffic. National security (*e.g.,* combating drug trafficking, and terrorist activities, etc.,) protection of minors (from violence, pornography, and pedophilia) privacy (issues relating to manipulation of data and transmission) and intellectual property right (unauthorised distribution of copyrighted works) are major concerns.

Different legal regimes and instruments cover these concerns. For example, with regard to pornography, covered by article 380 (15) and article 383 *bis* of the Penal Code, the Law of March 27, 1995, added "by a telecommunication means". The Law of December 8, 1992 regulates personal data protection. Depending on the offences, the penalties in Belgium can range from imprisonment between three months and two years and fines between BEF 100 and BEF 100,000. The Law of 1991 on Telecommunications forbids misappropriating fraudulently transmitted information. In 1994, a law was adopted to regulate the use of eavesdropping and wire-tapping devices.

---

58 Buyle and Poelmans, "Internet, quelques aspects juridiques", D.I.T., 96/2, at p. 15.

CHAPTER 5

Canada

Michael Erdle
Deeth Williams Wall
Toronto, Ontario, Canada

INTRODUCTION

Legal Regime Relative to Electronic Commerce

Canada is a federal state. Responsibility for matters relevant to commerce generally, and electronic commerce in particular, is divided between the federal and provincial governments. The federal government has jurisdiction over matters such as currency and coinage, banking, and the regulation of trade and commerce. It also has jurisdiction over intellectual property law.[1] The provinces have jurisdiction over property and civil rights and all matters of "a merely local or private nature".[2] This has been interpreted over the years to include matters relating to contracts, leaving the federal government responsible only for inter-provincial and international trade and commerce.[3]

5-1

There are also many areas of concurrent jurisdiction. Examples include the laws of evidence[4] and laws and regulations governing financial institutions. Federally chartered banks and insurance companies are regulated federally by the Bank Act[5] and provincially chartered trust companies and credit unions provincially by the Loans and Trust Companies Act.[6]

Federal laws and regulations governing banking and insurance, income tax, copyright, and trade marks are all relevant to electronic commerce. Provincial laws relating to the sale of goods, consumer protection, securities regulation, and the regulation of local financial institutions all have a potential effect on electronic commerce. In addition, Canada has both Common Law

---

1 Constitution Act, 1867 (United Kingdom), 30 and 31 Vict., c. 3.
2 Constitution Act, 1867 (United Kingdom), 30 and 31 Vict., c. 3.
3 Hogg, *Constitutional Law in Canada* (3rd ed., 1992).
4 Federal: Canada Evidence Act, R.S.C. 1985, c. C-5; Provincial: Ontario Evidence Act, R.S.O. 1990, c. E.23; Civil Code of Québec (C.C.Q.).
5 S.C. 1991, c. 46.
6 R.S.O. 1990, chapter L.25.

and Civil Law systems. In the Province of Québec, laws relating to contracts and other matters within the province's jurisdiction relating to electronic commerce are governed by the *Code Civil* of Québec. Common law applies federally and in all other provinces and territories.

Federal Government Initiatives

Information Highway Advisory Council

5-2   The government of Canada has recognised the importance of information technology and electronic commerce to the national economy. To that end, it established an Information Highway Advisory Council (I.H.A.C.) to advise it on business, cultural and other policy issues in relation to Canada's information infrastructure. The I.H.A.C. submitted its first report to the federal government in September 1995.[7] Since that time, it has undertaken more detailed analysis of many of the key issues and is expected to submit a further report in mid-1997. The I.H.A.C. has identified a number of legal issues that relate to electronic commerce. It recommended that:

> "The federal, provincial and territorial governments should work together in addressing the principal legal, trade-control and other security-related issues that may be impeding the use of electronic commerce in the government, private sector and international trade. This should include the potential upgrading of federal legislation, such as the Canada Evidence Act and the Interpretation Act, to reflect the important role that electronic transactions and digital signatures will play in conducting electronic commerce on the Information Highway, and continued efforts to achieve greater legislative uniformity across Canadian jurisdictions and with Canada's major trading partners."[8]

The Council also recognised the need for privacy, confidentiality, authentication, integrity, and non-repudiation in electronic commerce. It concluded that a government-sponsored public key infrastructure was an important step in achieving those goals and recommended that:

> "Government, private sector service providers, users, privacy advocates and other Information Highway stakeholders should work together to develop and implement the policies and framework for a security infrastructure to support Canada's Information Highway. By furthering

---

7 *The Challenge of the Information Highway, Final Report of the Information Highway Advisory Council*, Industry Canada, 1995.
8 Recommendation 10.11, Final Report of the Information Highway Advisory Council, Ottawa: Industry Canada, 1995.

comprehensive privacy, confidentiality, and electronic commerce support measures, Canada can gain a competitive edge in the global information technology market."[9]

In Phase II of the I.H.A.C. study, begun in 1996, the Council has continued to focus on electronic commerce as a vehicle of economic growth and job creation. Committee reports tabled early in 1997 recommend that the federal and provincial governments put in place a legal, policy and regulatory framework for electronic commerce, to identify and remove impediments and barriers to electronic commerce and to clarify the ground rules for specific types of transactions. The Council recommends strengthening the role of the Internet as a platform for electronic commerce. The Council recognises the need to clarify existing federal and provincial laws relevant to Internet activities and to apply and enforce rules regarding privacy, copyright and consumer protection. It also sees a need to remove specific legal, policy, and regulatory impediments, although those are not identified in the recommendations of the Council.[10]

Internet Content-Related Liability Study

The federal government has also taken the initiative in commissioning a   5-3
report by leading legal experts on the current state of the law in Canada as it applies to Internet service providers and bulletin board operators. The report, published in March 1997,[11] rejects the often-heard claim that "cyberspace" is a lawless territory and describes how existing civil and criminal laws can be applied to the electronic frontier.

The study's specific findings on electronic commerce issues are described later in this chapter.

Information Technology Security Strategy Committee

Industry Canada is the federal government department charged with pro-   5-4
moting and implementing the information infrastructure necessary for the government to participate in electronic delivery of services, as well as electronic procurement of goods and services. An Information Technology Security Framework has been developed to provide government-wide support services needed to conduct electronic business in a manner that ensures

---

9 Recommendation 10.13, Final Report of the Information Highway Advisory Council.
10 "Building the Information Society: Recommendations of the Information Highway Advisory Council, Phase II", Presentation by Richard Simpson, Executive Director, Information Highway Advisory Council, to the Information Technology Association of Canada, March 20, 1997.
11 Racicot et al, Internet Content-Related Liability Study, Ottawa: Industry Canada, 1997.

the "security" (integrity, authenticity, authorisation, non-repudiation, and confidentiality) of electronic transactions and communications,[12] declaring that:

> "Electronic Data Interchange (EDI) will provide the standards-based approach for inter-enterprise information exchange with trading partners. The Internet will likely evolve to become the ubiquitous data communications vehicle of choice . . . The Internet, and other network services, will be used increasingly by individual citizens and corporations to communicate with the government for the purposes of submitting statutory information and receiving government services . . . . Electronic commerce systems will be completely integrated with revamped departmental financial information systems, which themselves will incorporate private sector concepts . . . ."[13]

5-5   The Final Report of the Information Technology Security Strategy (I.T.S.S.) Steering Committee identified legal issues as one of the key elements of the government of Canada's Information Technology Security Framework. The Legal Issues Working Group reported that there are areas where the law is not clear. However, the working group concluded that there are no legal impediments to the federal government implementing a Public Key Infrastructure and using digital signatures and confidentiality encryption for internal government activities.

In its Report to the Steering Committee, the Legal Issues Working Group recommended that a comprehensive review and amendment of all federal legislation be undertaken to remove any impediments to electronic commerce. According to the Working Group:

> "Omnibus legislation, such as amendments to the Canada Interpretation Act and the Canada Evidence Act, is desirable to provide greater certainty and consistency in the area of electronic commerce and record-keeping generally, and the area of digital signature specifically. A comprehensive review at the departmental level of all federal legislation is also desirable, to amend statutes that do not expressly contemplate electronic commerce and record keeping, the digital signature or a public key infrastructure, where applicable."[14]

---

12 Final Report of the Information Technology Security Strategy Steering Committee, Government of Canada Council for Administrative Renewal, February 8, 1996.
13 Final Report of the Information Technology Security Strategy Steering Committee, section 3.0.3.
14 Final Report of the Legal Issues Working Group of the Information Technology Security Strategy Steering Committee, chapter 10: Digital Signature, Confidentiality Encryption and Public Key Infrastructure, Ottawa: Industry Canada, 1996.

The Public Key Infrastructure (P.K.I.) program is a central component of the government's electronic information infrastructure. Implementation of the P.K.I. began in early 1996. Using public key encryption techniques, it will provide users with the private keys that can be used to electronically sign documents, messages, transactions and information processed and stored by the government. The P.K.I. will facilitate electronic commerce within government departments and, eventually, with other public and private sector organisations. According to the I.T.S.S. Steering Committee report, Canada is the first national government to invest in a P.K.I. that will provide public key encryption and digital signature services for electronic commerce transactions. The P.K.I. may also be used to secure sensitive information held by the government about individuals, organisations and corporations, including financial, commercial, medical, legal and other forms of personal or corporate information.[15]

ELECTRONIC TRANSACTIONS

Creation of Contracts Electronically

Contract Formation

There are no formal requirements under Canadian contract law for the formation of a contract. Contracts may be formed by oral or written agreement or by the conduct of the parties. However, some statutes and regulations impose specific writing or signature requirements for the contract to be enforceable in a court of law.   5-6

Electronic commerce presents new challenges to existing contract principles in several areas. Issues such as offer and acceptance, the location of the contract, and implied terms and conditions offer new scope for disputes between contracting parties. As yet, there is little or no case law in Canada with respect to electronic contracts, and it is impossible to know how the courts will resolve these issues. One may make some educated guesses on the strength of past responses to new technology such as the public postal service, telegraph, telex, and facsimiles.

In Canada, a contract is formed through the exchange between the parties to the contract of an offer and an acceptance of that offer.[16] In electronic transactions, it may not always be apparent which party is making an offer, in the contract sense, and which is accepting. For example, an advertisement is generally not viewed as an offer to sell but as an "invitation

---

15 Final Report of the Information Technology Security Strategy Steering Committee, section 3.2.
16 Waddams, *The Law of Contracts* (3rd ed., 1993).

to treat" or a willingness to consider offers to purchase. The prospective buyer makes the offer when he or she offers to buy the advertised goods or services. This may be done in person, for example, in a retail store, or remotely, when a person fills in the order form in a mail-order catalogue. Or it may be made when someone enters his or her name in an electronic order form on a computer network.

In each of those instances, acceptance of the offer occurs when the retail merchant, mail-order house, or on-line service provider receives the offer and processes the order. If the customer is offering to pay with a credit card, for example, the seller must await the credit card company's authorisation before accepting the offer.

The contract is completed when confirmation of acceptance is communicated to the offeror. Until that time, the offer may be withdrawn. In face-to-face transactions, acceptance may be communicated instantly by receiving payment and handing over the goods.

Various forms of communication have given rise to problems determining when and where acceptance has been communicated to the offering party. The rules governing communication of acceptance, first adopted in the United Kingdom, have been widely followed in Canada over the years. The general rule is that the contract is not complete until the acceptance has been received by the offeror. The principle exception to the rule arises in the postal acceptance or "mailbox" cases, in which acceptance has been held to be complete on posting a letter or dispatching a telegram, even if the letter or telegram is delayed or lost.[17] The courts have held that with modern forms of instantaneous communication, the rationale behind the "mailbox rule" does not apply. Acceptance by telephone, telex, and facsimile is effective only when it is received.[18]

According to one view, the mailbox rule is a limited exception, based on the practical limitations and delays inherent in conducting commercial transactions by mail. It was introduced to accommodate the new postal and telegraph technologies of the 19th century and should not be extended further than necessary. The view has also been expressed that the general rule requiring actual receipt of notice of acceptance should apply where the means of communication is instantaneous and bi-directional (*e.g.*, by telephone), but that the postal exception should apply where communication is time-delayed and unidirectional (*e.g.*, facsimile and telex, as well as mail and telegram).[19]

---

17 In the United Kingdom, this rule goes back at least as far as *Adams* v. *Lindsell* (1818) 1 B. & Ald. 681; it has been followed in Canada and its scope enlarged to include courier companies in *R.* v. *Commercial Credit Corp.* (1983), 4 D.L.R. (4) 314 (N.S.C.A.).

18 *Entores* v. *Miles Far East Corporation* [1955] 2 Q.B. 327 (C.A.); *Brinkibon* v. *Stahag Stahl and Stahlwarenhandelswgesellschaft m.b.H* [1983] 2 A.C. 34 (H.L.); *Entores* has been followed in Canada in *Re Viscount Supply* Co. (1963) 40 D.L.R. (2d) 501 (Ont. S.C.).

19 Waddams, The Law of Contracts (3rd ed., 1993), at pp. 73 and 74; see also, Macchione, "Overview of the Law of Commercial Transactions and Information Exchanges in Cyberspace — Canadian Common Law and Civil Law Perspectives", (1996) 13 *C.I.P.R.* 129, at pp. 133 and 134.

If this understanding of the rule's rationale is correct, Canadian courts may apply the general rule to situations where acceptance is communicated instantaneously, such as Internet transactions, but adopt the mailbox rule, perhaps in some modified form to adapt it to the new technology, where acceptance is communicated by electronic mail or via a third-party EDI network.

Issues may also arise when use of electronic commerce results in situations where acceptance is communicated and received by a computer, rather than a person. When the exchange of messages making up the offer and acceptance have been made entirely automatically, have the parties really agreed? Who bears the risk of communication errors? These questions have not yet been answered in Canada.

Perhaps a recent United States case will serve as a guide. In *Corinthian Pharmaceutical Systems Inc.* v. *Lederle Laboratories*,[20] an "order tracking number" issued by an automated telephone ordering system was found to be merely an acknowledgement of the order, rather than an acceptance which formed a binding contract. Applying the same reasoning to common electronic commerce practices, this could mean that a computer-generated message acknowledging receipt of an electronic order might not be sufficient to create a binding contract. The purpose of the message may be solely to confirm receipt of the order. It does not necessarily signify acceptance.

In some circumstances, the requirement for communication of acceptance may be waived, expressly or by implication. For example, conduct, such as delivery of goods or services or payment of money, has been held to constitute acceptance. Similarly, a course of dealing between the parties over time may lead one party to reasonably expect that an order has been accepted unless it is expressly rejected. Electronic trading partner agreements typically contain provisions that sending a specific message — or the failure to send a specific message within a stated period of time — constitutes acceptance of the proposed contract.

Location of the Contract

Offer and acceptance is important, not only to determine when a contract   5-7
has been completed, but also to determine where it is made. In the absence of an agreement to the contrary, the law of the jurisdiction where the contract is concluded (the location of the accepting party) will govern the contract. In an electronic commerce environment, where a seller may be dealing with potential buyers from around the world, it may be advantageous for the seller to control the jurisdiction of the contract. By selecting a favourable jurisdiction, the seller may be able to exclude or limit implied warranties and his liability.

---

20 (1989) 724 F.Supp. 605 (S.D. Ind.).

When the transaction takes place over an international computer network, neither party may know where the other is located. The potential for legal uncertainty increases when one considers that either or both of the contracting parties may be using an independent service provider to deliver and process the electronic message.

Civil Code of Québec

5-8   Article 1387 of the Civil Code of Québec provides, "a contract is formed when and where acceptance is received by the offeror, regardless of the method of communication used, and even though the parties have agreed to reserve agreement as to secondary terms". There is no "mailbox" rule under the Civil Code.

The Civil Code of Québec provides, "acceptance which does not correspond substantially to the offer or which is received by the offeror after the offer has lapsed does not constitute acceptance. It may, however, constitute a new offer".[21] This article is consistent with the Common Law in the rest of Canada.

The Civil Code also provides that where there is an offer of a reward made to a person who performs a particular act, the offer is deemed to be accepted and becomes binding when the act is performed.[22] This is analogous to, but somewhat narrower than, the Common Law doctrine of acceptance by performance.

Writing Requirements

5-9   The word "writing" appears more than 4,000 times in the federal statutes and regulations of Canada. The word "record" appears almost 2,800 times; "document" appears almost 3,000 times.[23] In Ontario statutes and regulations, the word "writing" appears almost 4,000 times; "record" appears over 2,700 times; and "document" appears more than 2,000 times.[24] These words are similarly used in numerous statutes and regulations in other provinces. It is a monumental task simply to determine when writing is required, and what the writing requirement really means.

Writing is defined in a number of federal and provincial statutes. The federal Interpretation Act states that: "'writing', or any term of like import, includes words printed, typewritten, painted, engraved, lithographed, photographed or represented or reproduced by any mode of representing or reproducing words in visible form".[25] In the Ontario Interpretation Act,[26]

---

21 Civil Code of Québec, article 1393.
22 Civil Code, article 1395.
23 Computer search by author of the Canada Citator Service, CD-ROM, Toronto: Canada Law Books, 1997.
24 Computer search by author of the Ontario Citator Service, CD-ROM, Toronto: Canada Law Books, 1997.
25 R.S.C. 1985, c. I-21, section 35(1).
26 R.S.O. 1990, c. I-11, section 29(1).

"writing", "written", or any term of like import, includes words printed, painted, engraved, lithographed, photographed, or represented or reproduced by any other mode in a visible form. The wording is slightly different from the federal Act, but the effect is the same. Neither statute defines the terms "document", "record", "signed" or "signature".

Both statutes refer to "words" but not to numbers or other recorded symbols. The federal Act expressly includes typewriting, but the Ontario Act does not. Neither Act makes express reference to data recorded digitally or electronically.

The federal Criminal Code defines writing to include "a document of any kind and any mode in which . . . words or figures . . . are written, printed or otherwise expressed".[27] The Criminal Code defines document as anything capable of being read or understood by a person, computer system or other device.[28]

A "record" is defined in the Canada Evidence Act as any part of a document or other thing on or in which information is written, recorded, stored, or reproduced.[29] The courts have interpreted this to include information stored on and reproduced by computer. The Access to Information Act definition of record expressly includes "any machine readable record, and any other documentary material, regardless of physical form or characteristics, and any copy thereof".[30] Article 2837 of the Civil Code of Québec states that:

> "Where the data respecting a juridical act are entered on a computer system, the document reproducing them makes proof of the content of the act if it is intelligible and if the reliability is sufficiently guaranteed. To assess the quality of the document, the court shall take into account the circumstances under which the data were entered and the document was reproduced".

The Civil Code, therefore, makes it clear that it is the reliability of the writing, and not its physical character, which makes the writing legally effective.

Nevertheless, there are numerous federal and provincial statutes which have very specific writing and signature requirements and which may be considered to act as an impediment to electronic commerce to a greater or lesser degree. Governments have begun to update these statutes on an *ad hoc* basis. To date, however, no government in Canada has completed a systematic review and amendment of all of the relevant statutes. There is room in this chapter to review only a few representative statutes that have given rise to concern.

---

27 R.S.C. 1985, c. C-46, section 2.
28 R.S.C. 1985, c. C-46, section 321.
29 Canada Evidence Act, c. C-5, section 30(12).
30 Access to Information Act, R.S.C. 1985, c. A-1, section 3.

Statute of Frauds

5-10   The Statute of Frauds provides that certain kinds of contracts are not enforceable, unless there is a written note or memorandum of the agreement. The Statute does not render the contract void or invalid; it provides only that the contract may not be enforced in court.

Legislation or judicial decision in most provinces has adopted the Statute of Frauds.[31] It requires a written note or memorandum of any contract relating to land, any contract of guarantee, and any contract that is not fully performed within one year.

The requirement of the Statute of Frauds relating to contracts that are not fully performed within a year has been repealed in Ontario,[32] but remains in force in other provinces. Its effect has been constrained by case law which has established that, if no fixed time for performance is specified in the contract, the Statute will not apply unless the contract, by its own terms, is incapable of being performed within a year. If all of the obligations of one of the parties may possibly be performed within the year, the Statute does not apply.[33]

The Statute of Frauds does not specify the form of writing required to make a contract enforceable. Over the years, courts have concluded that the note or memorandum need not be made contemporaneously with the formation of the contract, as long as it exists prior to the commencement of the legal action to enforce the bargain. It has also been held that the writing need not be any particular form to satisfy the Statute.[34]

Nevertheless, there remains a great deal of conflicting judicial opinion on the question of whether the Statute of Frauds applies to various types of contracts and what formal requirements must be met to satisfy the Statute. Courts are often reluctant to apply the Statute, particularly if a party seeking to escape an unfavourable bargain invokes it. On the other hand, the courts do not seem willing to ignore the Statute completely, so participants in electronic commerce transactions must keep it in mind.

Sale of Goods Act

5-11   Most provinces have legislation governing the sale of goods. In Ontario, the Sale of Goods Act[35] provides that a contract of sale may be made in writing, either with or without seal, or by word of mouth, or partly in writing and partly by word of mouth, or may be implied from the conduct of the parties. Until recently, the Act also provided that no contract for the sale of goods

---

31 R.S.O. 1990, c. S-19; the statute is also in force in New Brunswick, Nova Scotia and Prince Edward Island; equivalent Common Law rules have been adopted by the courts in Alberta and British Columbia.

32 Bill 175, An Act to Amend the Statutes of Ontario, S.O. 1994, section 55.

33 *Van Snellenberg* v. *Cemco Electrical Manufacturing Co.* [1946] 1 D.L.R. 105 (B.C.C.A.), affirmed [1947] S.C.R. 121.

34 *Moore* v. *Hart* (1683), 1 Vern. III 201 (Ch.), although it is doubtful whether the judges in the 17th century had electronic commerce in mind.

35 R.S.O. 1990, c. S.1.

valued at C. $50 or more, including contracts for the future delivery of goods, was enforceable unless the buyer: actually received and accepted part of the goods; gave a deposit to bind the contract or makes part payment; or unless some note or memorandum in writing was made and signed by the party to be charged with the contract.[36]

This section was repealed in Ontario in 1995, however, similar provisions remain in force in most other provinces.[37] The explanatory notes to the amending legislation in Ontario state that the change "will reduce the uncertainty of contracts made by electronic data interchange and will allow the public and private sectors to dispense with costly paper backup of these contracts".[38]

In jurisdictions where the writing requirement still applies, issues may arise as to its applicability to electronic commerce. Courts have struggled with the problem of determining whether a contract is for the sale of goods or for the provision of services. Where goods are ordered "off the shelf", this is generally not a problem. However, when the goods must be customised to meet the buyer's requirements or when the contract involves a combination of goods and services, the issue becomes more difficult to resolve. Although courts are inclined to decide each case on its own particular facts, the general rule is that if the substance of the contract is the provision of skill and labour, and the materials are simply an ancillary part of the services, the Sale of Goods Act will not apply.[39]

Consumer Protection Laws

The Ontario Consumer Protection Act[40] requires that all "executory contracts"   5-12
contain specified information and be in writing. An executory contract is defined as "a contract between a buyer and a seller for the purchase and sale of goods or services in respect of which delivery of the goods or services or payment in full of the consideration is not made at the time the contract is entered into".[41] This would include many electronic commerce transactions. Section 19 of the Ontario Consumer Protection Act provides that:

"(1) Every executory contract, . . . shall be in writing and shall contain,

(a) the name and address of the seller and the buyer;

(b) a description of the goods or services sufficient to identify them with certainty;

---

36 Sale of Goods Act, R.S.O. 1990, c. S.1, section 5.
37 See, for example, Alberta Sale of Goods Act, S.A. 1991, c. S-2, section 7.
38 Bill 175, An Act to Amend the Statutes of Ontario, section 54.
39 See, for example, *Robinson* v. *Graves* [1935] 1 K.B. 579 (C.A.), followed in Canada in *Casden* v. *Cooper Enterprises Ltd.*, [1993] F.C.J. Number 124 (F.C.A.); *Borek* v. *Hooper* (1994), 18 O.R. (3d) 470.
40 R.S.O. 1990, c. C.31.
41 Consumer Protection Act, R.S.O. 1990, c. C.31, section 1.

(c) the itemised price of the goods or services and a detailed statement of the terms of payment;

(d) where credit is extended, a statement of any security for payment under the contract, including the particulars of any negotiable instrument, conditional sale agreement, chattel mortgage or any other security;

(e) where credit is extended, the statement required to be furnished by section 24;

(f) any warranty or guarantee applying to the goods or services and, where there is no warranty or guarantee, a statement to this effect; and

(g) any other matter required by the regulations.

(2) An executory contract is not binding on the buyer unless the contract is made in accordance with this Part and the regulations and is signed by the parties, and a duplicate original copy thereof is in the possession of each of the parties thereto."

5-13   The Consumer Protection Act also provides rights for individuals when contracts are signed outside the seller's usual place of business and where unsolicited goods or credit are provided. Section 21 provides:

"Where a seller solicits, negotiates or arranges for the signing by a buyer of an executory contract at a place other than the seller's permanent place of business, the buyer may rescind the contract by delivering a notice of rescission in writing to the seller within two days after the duplicate original copy of the contract first comes into the possession of the buyer, and the buyer is not liable for any damages in respect of such rescission."[42]

5-14   Section 36 governs the delivery of unsolicited goods or granting of unsolicited credit. It provides:

"(2) No action shall be brought by which to charge any person upon any arrangement for the extension of credit evidenced by a credit card unless the person to whom credit is to be extended requested or accepted the credit arrangement and card in writing, and the obtaining of credit by the person named in the credit card shall be deemed to constitute such written acceptance by the person.

(3) No action shall be brought by which to charge any person for payment in respect of unsolicited goods notwithstanding their use, misuse, loss, damage or theft.

42 Consumer Protection Act, R.S.O. 1990, c. C.31, section 21.

(4) Except as provided in this section, the recipient of unsolicited goods or of a credit card that has not been requested or accepted in accordance with subsection (2) has no legal obligation in respect of their use or disposal."[43]

Under the Act, "unsolicited goods" means personal property furnished to a   5-15
person who did not request it. The Act further provides that a request shall not be inferred from inaction or the passage of time. However, an exception is made where the property is supplied under a contract in writing to which the recipient is a party, including a contract that provides for the periodic supply of property to the recipient without further solicitation.[44]

None of these provisions of the Consumer Protection Act is affected by the repeal of the provisions of the Sale of Goods Act and the Statute of Frauds referred to above. Accordingly, most electronic transactions involving consumers will be subject to the Consumer Protection Act, and to similar statutes in other provinces, unless the products or services involved are delivered immediately and they are fully paid for when the contract is made.

Financial Administration Act

The Financial Administration Act[45] governs the finances and business prac-   5-16
tices of the government of Canada. Similar statutes apply to the various provincial governments. Section 33(1) of the Act states, "no charge shall be made against an appropriation except on the requisition of the appropriate Minister . . . or of a person authorised in writing by that Minister". This gives rise to two possible issues.

First, it is unclear what form the "requisition" must take. Second, it is unclear what form of writing is needed to give government employees the authority to enter into binding contracts. Government lawyers have concluded that the requirements of the Financial Administration Act do not preclude electronic contracting by the government, however, they have recommended legislative amendments to remove any uncertainty as to whether the government's internal systems of electronic communication are effective to create the required evidence of proper delegation of contracting authority.[46]

Signature Requirements

In addition to the requirement of written documents, a number of statutes   5-17
require that the document be signed to be enforceable. For example, the

---

43 Consumer Protection Act, R.S.O. 1990, c. C.31, section 36.
44 Consumer Protection Act, R.S.O. 1990, c. C.31, subsection 36(1).
45 R.S.C. 1985, c. F.11.
46 Report of the I.T.S.S. Legal Issues Working Group, chapter 9, Electronic Records and Evidence, September 1996.

Statute of Frauds provides that, in those cases where a note or memorandum of agreement is required, it must be "signed by the party to be charged therewith or some other person thereunto by him lawfully authorised".[47] Similarly, the Sale of Goods Act requires that where writing is required, it must be signed.[48] The Ontario Consumer Protection Act provides that:

> "An executory contract is not binding on the buyer unless the contract is made in accordance with this Part and the regulations and is signed by the parties, and a duplicate original copy thereof is in the possession of each of the parties thereto."[49]

5-18   The Civil Code of Québec is the only Canadian statute which defines "signature". It explicitly states, in article 2827, "a signature is the affixing by a person, on a writing, of his name or the distinctive mark which he regularly uses to signify his intention".

Unfortunately, none of the Common Law jurisdictions define what is meant by a signature. In most cases it is assumed that what is intended is an autograph, a hand-written rendition of the name of the contracting party or, in the case of a business entity, the name of an authorised representative or signing officer. This is not necessarily the case. The courts have found that any mark or symbol which shows that the party intended to be bound to the contract can be sufficient. In the days before widespread literacy, a person could signify that intent by making a mark on the paper. The use of seals was also an accepted method of signifying the intention to make a legal contract. According to *Black's Law Dictionary*, "a signature may be written by hand, printed, stamped, typewritten, engraved, photographed, or cut from one instrument and attached to another".[50]

Canadian case law has followed the precedents in the United Kingdom and United States in holding that a signature need not be a person's entire name, fully written out. Any mark or notation is acceptable, if it identifies the party and authenticates the document. A printed or typewritten name or initials may be sufficient to constitute a signature in some cases.[51]

---

47 Ontario Statute of Frauds, R.S.O. 1990, c. S.19, section 4; similar provisions are found in the equivalent statutes in other provinces.
48 Alberta Sale of Goods Act, S.A. 1991, c. S-2, section 7; similar provisions are found in the equivalent statutes in other provinces; as noted above, this provision has been repealed in the Ontario Sale of Goods Act.
49 R.S.O. 1990, c. C. 31, section 19(2).
50 *Black's Law Dictionary* (6th ed., 1979), at p. 1553.
51 See, for example, *R. v. Kapoor*, [1989] O.J. 1887 (Ont. H.C.); see also *A&G Construction Co. v. Reid Bros. Logging Co.* 547 P. 2d 1207 (Alaska 1976); *Hillstrom v. Gosnay*, 614 P. 2d 446 (1980), cited by Leighton Reid, Senior Counsel, Canadian Imperial Bank of Commerce, in "Legal and Operational Concerns in Electronic Banking", *Insight Conference*, June 1, 1995.

In the United Kingdom, a signature has been held by the courts to include a rubber stamp with a facsimile signature, a thumb print and, more simply, initials.[52]

Canadian courts have also held that a reproduction of a signature sent by facsimile satisfied the requirement of a signed document under corporation law.[53] However, all of the case law to date has focused on the meaning of various marks on paper. No Canadian court has yet considered the legal effect of an electronic or digital signature.

Digital Signature

The use of encryption technology to create "digital signatures" makes it **5-19** possible to verify that persons exchanging documents electronically are who they say they are, that the messages exchanged between them have not been altered, that the parties cannot deny having sent them, and that no one else can read them. Encryption, and in particular "public key" encryption, therefore, provides electronic communication with authentication, integrity, non-repudiation, and confidentiality. Certification of public keys by a third party provides an additional level of reliability.

As far as the author has been able to determine, the validity of documents with digital signatures has never been challenged in court in Canada. Therefore, their legal status is not certain. However, one Canadian federal government lawyer has argued, "a Common Law court in Canada would not accept a digital signature as fulfilling the requirements of a "signed writing". The essence of a signature is the written name attached to a document".[54] He based this conclusion on the view that electronic communications lack the forensic qualities inherent in paper-based signatures which are needed to link the signature to the individual.[55]

Other writers have taken the opposite position, arguing that any symbol, including a string of electronic impulses, is adequate to constitute a signature, if it satisfies the requirements of authenticating the message and identifying the maker.[56]

According to the Final Report of the Legal Issues Working Group of the government of Canada's Information Technology Security Strategy Steering Committee:

---

52 Edwards, Savage and Walden, *Information Technology and the Law* (2d ed., 1990), at p. 240, cited by Final Report of the I.T.S.S. Legal Issues Working Group, September 18, 1996, chapter 10.
53 *Beatty v. First Explor. Fund 1987 & Co.* (1988), 25 B.C.L.R. (2d) 377 (B.C.S.C.).
54 Walker, Legal Counsel, Industry Canada, "Some Legal Aspects of Electronic Data Interchange Security in the Government of Canada", Paper presented to the Fifth Annual Canadian Computer Security Symposium, May 1993, at p.10.
55 Baum, "EDI and the Law", 2 *EDI Forum* (1989), at p.78.
56 Wright, *The Law of Electronic Commerce: EDI, Fax and E-Mail: Technology Proof and Liability* (1991), at p. 292.

"In the absence of legislation, Canadian courts will probably accept the digital signature as evidence, provided the party introducing the digital signature into evidence can give "foundation evidence" as to the integrity and accuracy of the digital signature system and record-keeping procedures."[57]

5-20   The Legal Issues Working Group has stated that the use of a digital signature algorithm and public key infrastructure which complies with an industry or national or international standard will likely be an important factor in the acceptance of digital signatures by the Canadian courts. Evidence of proper security and audit procedures and the use of a certification authority which is a trusted entity will also be relevant factors.

According to a senior Canadian bank lawyer, the Personal Identification number (PIN), used with debit and bank machine (ATM) cards, may be considered a form of electronic signature, because it achieves the principal purposes of a signature: identification and authentication.[58]

Canadian lawmakers have been involved in a number of international digital signature initiatives. Canada was represented on the EDI Working Group of the United Nations Commission on International Trade Law which, in 1994, approved a draft model electronic signature law. The United Nations model law states that electronic communications and contracts are to be as legally effective, valid and enforceable as written documents and signatures. However, laws for the protection of consumers are expressly excluded from the model law.

Public Key Infrastructure

5-21   The government of Canada in 1994 began considering the implementation of a public key infrastructure to support electronic communication, both within government and with members of the public. The government has concluded that both digital signatures and confidentiality encryption can be supported by a public key infrastructure.

The government has also identified a number of legal issues associated with the implementation of a public key infrastructure, including the lack of express statutory authority for digital signatures. Some recent federal and provincial legislation now specifically provides for the use of an electronic signature.[59] These have all been enacted on an *ad hoc* basis to address specific legal issues relating to electronic commerce or communication.

---

57 Final Report of the Legal Issues Working Group to the Information Technology Security Strategy Steering Committee, chapter 10: Digital Signature, Confidentiality Encryption and Public Key Infrastructure, Ottawa: Industry Canada, 1996.

58 Leighton Reid, Senior Counsel, Canadian Imperial Bank of Commerce, in "Legal and Operational Concerns in Electronic Banking", *Insight Conference*, June 1, 1995, at p. 20.

59 See, for example, Canadian Environmental Protection Act, c. 16 (4th Supp.); Ontario Business Regulation Reform Act, 1994, S.O. 1994, c. 32; Ontario Business Corporations Act R.S.O. 1990, chapter B.16.

There has, to date, been no attempt at ensuring that all such enactments are consistent. There is also Canadian case law supporting the use of electronic communication technology (such as faxes, e-mail, and computerised records), the formal requirements for which are governed by statutes or Common Law which do not specifically provide for such technology. No federal or provincial legislation of general application (such as the Canada Evidence Act or Interpretation Act) specifically permits the use of a digital signature to replace a hand-written one.

It is likely that a court would find a digital signature to meet the requirements that something be "signed" or "in writing". It is less certain whether the courts will conclude that a digital signature meets statutory requirements that documents be "certified", "commissioned", "notarised" or "in prescribed form", as required by a large number of federal and provincial statutes.[60]

The Public Key Infrastructure proposed by the federal government's Information Technology Security Strategy Steering Committee would:

- Manage encryption keys used for confidentiality;
- Manage encryption keys used for digital signatures;
- Certify that a public key matches a private key;
- Publish a secure directory of public keys;
- Provide keys to end users and manage use of the keys;
- Manage personal tokens such as smart cards, to identify the user with unique personal identification information or generate an individual's private keys;
- Provide non-repudiation services through message verification;
- Check end users' identification and provide related services; and
- Provide time-stamping services:

Certification Authorities

The proposed P.K.I. will comprise the following hierarchy of authorities. A 5-22 policy-making authority will establish the policies for the government's P.K.I.

A top-level root authority will be responsible for certifying the technology and practices of all parties authorised to issue public-private key pairs. By its nature, there is only one "root" authority. It has been proposed that the federal Communications Security Establishment (COS.) will implement the P.K.I. and will be the root authority. The Root Authority would not have the technical ability to retain or recreate private (confidential) keys.

A number of certification authorities would certify that each public key matches a person's private key. The certification authority provides this

60 Final Report of the Legal Issues Working Group of the Government of Canada's Information Technology Security Strategy Steering Committee, Ottawa: Industry Canada, 1996.

certificate electronically, by issuing a certificate encrypted with its own private key, which anyone else can decrypt, using the certification authority's public key. The certification authority's certificate acts as a form of guarantee to the world at large about the reliability of each private-public key pair. Certification authorities may include large government departments and private sector service providers. The certification authority can be established in a hierarchical structure, where some certification authorities do nothing more than certify other certification authorities, who provide services more directly to users. Certification authorities at the same level in the hierarchy may also cross-certify each other.

Local registration authorities will be established under the Certification Authority to take requests from users for public key/private key pairs and check identities of potential users. Notaries have been considered as likely candidates for Local Registration Authorities in Québec, where their attestations are given special recognition under the Civil Code and in several federal statutes. In 1996, the *Chambre des notaires du Québec* began a pilot project to computerise some real estate transactions. In the rest of the country, not all notaries have the qualifications or training to make them candidates for Local Registration Authorities.

Identification of Key Holders

5-23   When a Certification Authority certifies a user's public key, it must make that party's public key known to the world. To do this, each user must have a unique name. Individual names are governed by statute, such as the Ontario Vital Statistics Act,[61] and Change of Name Act,[62] and by the Common Law. No law prohibits two individuals having the same name. Therefore, some other unique identifier must be used for individuals. Social Insurance numbers could be used to identify individuals, however, the Income Tax Act makes it an offence to use a Social Insurance number for any purpose other than that for which it was provided and federal government policy requires any use of a Social Insurance number to be authorised by statute or regulation.

Corporate names are governed by corporate legislation. Both federal and provincial corporate statutes allow the use of number names, which are simply assigned in order, and are therefore guaranteed to be unique. All other names must be cleared through a name search process. The name must not be the same as the name of a known corporation, trust, association, partnership, sole proprietorship or individual, or similar to the name under which any of them carries on business or identifies itself, if the use of the name would be likely to deceive.[63] The use of confusingly similar names is also prohibited by trade mark law[64] and by the laws relating to passing off.

---

61   R.S.O. 1990, c. V.4.
62   R.S.O. 1990, c. C.7.
63   Ontario Business Corporations Act, R.S.O. 1990, chapter B.16, section 90.
64   Trade Marks Act, R.S.C., c. T-13, section 20.

Both the Ontario Business Corporations Act and the Canada Business Corporations Act require, "a corporation shall set out its name in legible characters in all contracts, invoices . . . and orders for goods or services issued or made by or on behalf of the corporation . . .".[65] Corporations engaged in electronic transactions must ensure that this requirement is complied with.

Contract Terms

When an electronic contract is formed, issues may arise with respect to the   5-24
precise terms and conditions of the agreement. In typical paper-based commercial transactions, standard terms are printed on the contract documents — quotations, purchase orders, invoices, shipping notices and the like. When these documents are replaced with electronic orders, there is a natural tendency to do away with "unnecessary boilerplate". In addition, electronic communications are by necessity rigidly structured, so that they can be received and processed automatically. Any attempt to deviate from the required form will likely result in an unsuccessful exchange of messages. The resulting lack of detail on many standard contract terms will normally not invalidate a contract, but it may result in the imposition of terms which neither party contemplated.

In most provinces, the Sale of Goods Act provides implied warranties that goods are of merchantable quality and that they are fit for their intended purpose.[66] It also imposes an implied condition that goods sold by description will correspond to the description.[67] These implied warranties may be disclaimed, but to be effective the disclaimer must be expressly set out in the agreement between the parties.

In consumer transactions, consumer protection laws in most provinces may impose further implied terms in certain types of contracts.[68] In most cases, consumer protection provisions cannot be waived.

The EDI Council of Canada Model Trading Partner Agreement attempts to overcome the legal impediments to contracting through EDI by means of agreement by the parties concerning security, allocation of liability for breaches of security, confidentiality, authenticity, integrity and non-repudiation. It does not contemplate the use of digital signature, but requires confidentiality of information and obliges the parties to exact similar undertakings from personnel.

Authorisation is achieved by placing the onus on each party to establish proper security and access controls, and by a warranty by the sender that

---

65 C.B.C.A., R.S.C. 1985, c. C-44, section 10; O.B.C.A., R.S.O. 1990, c. B.16, section 10.
66 Sale of Goods Act, R.S.O. 1990, c. S.1, as amended, section 15. See also Alberta Sale of Goods Act, S.A. 1991, c. S-2.
67 Sale of Goods Act, R.S.O. 1990, c. S.1, section 16.
68 Consumer Protection Act, R.S.O. 1990, c. C.31.

the document is duly authorised and is binding on it. Liability for unauthorised transactions is allocated by agreement between the parties. The sender has the ability to control access, and thus bears the risk of unauthorised access. The receiver is entitled to rely on the transmission as having been authorised.

The trading partner agreement establishes the legal relationship between the parties and the intent by parties to be bound by the electronic messages. The agreement normally establishes an obligation to keep transaction logs for evidentiary purposes. It may determine where the contract is made, *i.e.*, at the buyer's location, the seller's location, or neither. The agreement may allocate risk of non-performance or non-delivery of the goods and services and establish legal remedies. Trading partner agreements normally also include dispute resolution mechanisms and other miscellaneous contractual details. Trading partners agreements can be as brief as two pages, or as detailed as 60 pages.[69]

Trading partner agreements can be a practical solution to the current uncertainty surrounding purely electronic agreements. However, they have many limitations. EDI works well when it takes place between major trading partners. They are less useful in a consumer context.

Enforcement of Electronic Contracts

Jurisdiction

5-25   The rules of private international law and conflict of laws which apply in Canada have generally been developed on the basis of geographic sovereignty over persons and their acts. These rules are difficult to apply to electronic commerce transactions which have no physical manifestations within a territory and which can easily be structured to avoid geo-political boundaries. In many cases, the multi-jurisdictional aspects of a transaction may be entirely inadvertent. For example, a supplier of goods or services over the Internet or other similar network may not know where its customers are physically located. Similarly, the person receiving the products and services may be unable to determine where they originate.

Issues of capacity to contract, contract formation, formal validity, scope of implied or express obligations, illegality and public policy, enforceability and remedies may all depend on the governing jurisdiction. The parties to an electronic contract must also give thought to the appropriate jurisdiction and the procedural rules for hearing any disputes. The parties to an electronic transaction may determine some of these issues by agreement. Generally speaking, choice of law and jurisdiction clauses in a contract are

---

69 See, for example, sample agreement in Jolicoeur, Remsu and Sévigny, "Public Works and Government Services Canada. Contracting with the Government", presented at the *Heading Into the Information Age Conference*, Faculty of Law, University of Ottawa, May 16, 1995.

enforceable in the courts of Canada. However, there may be specific circumstances, such as fundamental breach or unconscionability, which would cause the courts to reject such a clause.

In the absence of an express agreement between the parties regarding the applicable jurisdiction, there are a number of instances in which the Canadian courts will take jurisdiction. A court may have jurisdiction *in rem* or *in personam*. In a contract dispute, a court of a Canadian province will have jurisdiction over the subject matter of the contract (*in rem*) if the contract was formed in that province or if the contract is to be substantially performed within the province. In addition, the court may have jurisdiction over one or more parties to the contract (*in personam*) if the party is resident in the province, carries on business there or has some other "substantial connection" to the jurisdiction.

The Supreme Court of Canada has stated that in tort cases, there must be a "real and substantial connection" between the jurisdiction and the wrongdoing.[70] Where the case is based on negligent or fraudulent misrepresentation, the courts of the location where the statements were received and relied on have jurisdiction.[71]

In defamation cases, the Ontario courts have held that the place where the defamatory statements were published or disseminated is the proper jurisdiction.[72]

The Supreme Court of Canada has recently stated that the law of the place where the activity occurred is the proper law to apply.[73] However, the court also recognised that there are situations where the harm caused by an act may occur in another jurisdiction, or in several other jurisdictions. In those cases, the court has said, other considerations may govern and it may be sufficient simply that a significant portion of the activities were conducted in Canada or a substantial part of the harm was suffered in Canada.[74]

Both the common and Civil Law jurisdictions in Canada permit legal action to be commenced against a non-resident if the contract in dispute was made in that province.

The Ontario Rules of Civil Procedure[75] provide that no special leave of the court is required to serve a party outside Ontario if the contract was made or is to be performed in Ontario, or the breach of contract occurs in Ontario. Ontario courts have jurisdiction if a tort was committed in Ontario or the damage was suffered in the province. The Rules also apply to a person, including a corporation, ordinarily resident or carrying on business in Ontario.

---

70 *Moran v. Pyle National (Canada) Ltd.*, [1975] 1 S.C.R. 393.
71 *National Bank of Canada v. Clifford Chance* (1996), 30 O.R. (3d) 746 (Ont. Gen. Div.).
72 *Jenner v. Sun Oil Co. Ltd.*, [1952] O.R. 240 (Ont. H.C.).
73 *Tolofson v. Jensen*, [1994] 3 S.C.R. 1022.
74 *Libman v. R.*, [1985] 2 S.C.R. 178; in an intellectual property context, see *C.A.P.A.C. v. Good Music, Inc.*, [1963] S.C.R. 136.
75 R.R.O. 194, Rule 17.02.

The Québec Code of Civil Procedure, article 68(2) states that a personal action may be brought before the court of the place where the contract which gives rise to the action was made.

Although a Canadian court may be entitled to hear a dispute, it may decline to do so, applying the doctrine of *forum non conveniens*. This rule has been applied in both the Common Law provinces and in Québec when it is determined that it is more appropriate for the case to be determined in a foreign court.[76] According to the Supreme Court of Canada, the determination of the appropriate forum for litigation is based on weighing the factors that connect the parties and the subject matter of the litigation to one jurisdiction or another. It is not a mechanical exercise of calculating the number of contacts and awarding jurisdiction to the forum with the greatest number.[77]

There do not appear to be any reported cases in Canada which have directly considered the jurisdictional and conflict of law issues relating to electronic commerce or the Internet. Clearly, electronic communications can be received or have an effect in several jurisdictions. In the case of statements made over a computer network (*e.g.*, misrepresentations made with respect to a product or service), the statements may be received and relied on by a number of persons in several locations. Defamatory statements may be published globally with the push of a button. Contracts may be breached or other harm inflicted on persons in remote locations. There have been a number of recent cases in the United States and elsewhere which may offer some guidance for Canadian courts considering these issues. Unfortunately, the courts in other jurisdictions seem to come to conflicting decisions with respect to both the immediate issue of whether they have jurisdiction in a particular case and the more important issue of the appropriate criteria to apply in electronic commerce cases.[78]

Arbitration

5-26   Many electronic contracts and trading partner agreements provide that any disputes arising under or relating to the contract will be resolved by arbitration. Arbitration procedures vary from one province to another.

In addition, most provinces have statutes dealing expressly with international commercial arbitration.[79] The government of Canada has established international commercial arbitration centres in Vancouver, British Columbia, and Montreal, Québec.

---

76 Civil Code of Québec, article 3135 states: "Even though a Québec authority has jurisdiction to hear a dispute, it may exceptionally and on an application by a party, decline jurisdiction if it considers that the authorities of another country are in a better position to decide".

77 *Hunt* v. *T & N Plc.*, [1993] 4 S.C.R. 289; see also *Amchem Products Inc.* v. *BC. Workers Compensation Board*, [1993] 1 S.C.R. 897. For a general discussion of conflict of laws, see Castel, *Canadian Conflict of Laws* (3rd ed., 1995).

78 Sookman, "Electronic Commerce and Conflicts of Law", *Electronic Commerce: Impact of the Digital Age on Commercial Law* (March 25, 1997).

79 International Commercial Arbitration Act, R.S.O. 1990, c. I.9; International Commercial Arbitration Act, S.B.C. 1986, c.14.

Evidence

Hearsay and Best Evidence

The Common Law rules of evidence generally require that facts be proved   5-27
through the oral or written evidence of persons with direct personal knowledge of the facts to be proved. However, the courts have recognised that
modern business practices in general, and electronic record-keeping in
particular, make it virtually impossible for anyone to have direct personal
knowledge of all of the facts of even the simplest commercial transactions.
Courts are generally willing to make an exception to the traditional hearsay
rules where the evidence can be shown to be both necessary and reliable.
Therefore, business records have long been admitted in evidence in Canadian courts, if the record was made by a person with personal knowledge of
the matter recorded and a duty to make the record.[80]

However, the "best evidence rule" requires the production of an original
document to prove its contents. This rule applies to any form of recorded
writing, including information stored in a computer. The original document
is referred to as "primary evidence". Copies of the original and other types
of proof, admissible when primary evidence is unavailable, are referred to
as "secondary evidence". Over the years, courts have struggled to determine
whether a printout of a computer record was an original or a copy.

A reproduction of an original document, such as a digital copy of a
scanned document, is secondary evidence because the reproduction follows
the creation of the original. The original document would be required under
the "best evidence" rule, however, federal and provincial evidence statutes
permit admission of copies of original documents into evidence. In addition,
it is often necessary to produce witnesses who can give evidence of the
authenticity and reliability of the business records.

Canadian courts have demonstrated greater doubts about the reliability of
computer records in criminal cases than in other situations, perhaps because
of the higher burden of proof in criminal cases.[81] Courts seem to have become
more comfortable with computer records over the past 20 years, as computers
have become more familiar to the average person and are now widely accepted
as both necessary and reliable. The courts seem less concerned with technical
questions such as whether the record is an original or copy, and will reject
computer records only when the party objecting to them can demonstrate
substantial doubts as to the accuracy or reliability of the computer records.

---

80 *Ares* v. *Venner*, [1978] 1 S.C.R. 591, S.C.C..
81 See, for example, *R.* v. *McMullen* (1979), 47 C.C.C. (2d) 499 (Ont. C.A.), in which the
   court held that the foundation of computer evidence should be carefully scrutinised for
   reliability; *R.* v. *Rowbotham* (1977), 33 C.C.C. (2d) 411, in which printouts of telephone
   records were rejected because the telephone company employee could not explain how they
   were made; telephone records were also rejected for similar reasons in *R.* v. *Sheppard*
   (1992), 97 Nfld. & P.E.I.R. 145 (Nfld. S.C.T.D.).

The requirements for admissibility in court are stricter than those in administrative proceedings. In Ontario, the Statutory Powers Procedure Act,[82] states that a tribunal may admit as evidence any document relevant to the subject matter of the proceeding and may act on such evidence.

A recent review of the case law concludes, "the preponderance of authority is to admit computer printouts as business records . . . even if the record in question was not made as part of the usual course of business, as long as it concerns a matter in the ordinary and usual course of business".[83]

One of the purposes of introducing public key/private key encryption and the public key infrastructure is to create the conditions necessary to create a presumption that messages using this technology come from the sender, have not been altered and cannot be repudiated by the sender. According to the Final Report of the Legal Issues Working Group of the Information Technology Security Strategy Steering Committee, "It would seem reasonable to presume that the various forms of electronic authentication (*e.g.*, encryption/digital signatures) would be viewed by the courts in a positive light".[84]

Sopinka[85] states that there is no reason why computer-generated records should not be admissible under existing rules of evidence. Nevertheless, the courts have held that there must be sufficient evidence to demonstrate that the computer records are reliable, credible and trustworthy.[86] The standards for electronic evidence developed by the Canadian Information and Image Management Society[87] suggest a number of questions which may be asked when considering both the admissibility of computer records and the weight to be given to the evidence:

- How reliable are the original sources of the data on which the record is based?
- Was the data recorded contemporaneously with the events to which the data relate, or within a reasonable time afterward?
- Was the data regularly supplied to the computer system of the organisation which produced the record and was the data recorded in the usual and ordinary course of business?
- Do the processes by which the data was recorded conform to standard industry practices?
- Do the processes by which the data is stored and processed ensure the integrity of the data maintained by the computer system?

---

82 R.S.O. 1990, c. S.22, section 15.
83 Report of the I.T.S.S. Legal Issues Working Group, chapter 9, citing Ewart, *Documentary Evidence in Canada*, at p. 108, and Sopinka, *The Law of Evidence in Canada* (1992), at p. 214.
84 Report of the I.T.S.S. Legal Issues Working Group, chapter 9.
85 Sopinka, *The Law of Evidence in Canada* (1992).
86 *R. v. Sheppard* (1992), 9 Nfld. & P.E.I.R. 144 (Nfld. S.C.), at p. 148.
87 National Standard of Canada: Microfilm and Electronic Image as Documentary Evidence, CAN/C.G.S.B. — 72.11-93.

- Do the procedures by which the printout of the record was made conform to standard industry practices?
- Does the party producing the record rely on the data for its own internal business purposes?
- Is the data confidential, privileged or protected by some other rule of law or evidence which prevents or limits its disclosure in the subject legal proceedings?

The existence of a formal description of the computer record keeping **5-28** system, produced for the purpose of operating the system rather than for the purpose of litigation, will assist in establishing the reliability of the computer data. Separating the responsibility for entering, maintaining and reproducing records to prevent intended or unintended modification of the data will also help make the records more reliable. So will the use of passwords, fire-walls and other access controls. Finally, the increasing use of digital signatures, encryption and public key certificates may help convince courts that electronic records are the most reliable records available, more reliable, even, than paper records which may be tampered with.

The Canada Evidence Act[88] and equivalent provincial statutes codify the Common Law rules of evidence regarding the admissibility of particular types of records.

Canada Evidence Act

The Canada Evidence Act[89] defines "business" to include any kind of **5-29** business, profession or government operation. "Record" includes any thing on which information is written, recorded, stored or reproduced. "Copy" includes a print from photographic film of the record.

The definition of "legal proceeding" is any civil or criminal proceeding or inquiry in which evidence is or may be given, and includes an arbitration. Section 30 of the Canada Evidence Act governs the admissibility of business records generally. It provides as follows:

"30. (1) Where oral evidence in respect of a matter would be admissible in a legal proceeding, a record made in the usual and ordinary course of business that contains information in respect of that matter is admissible in evidence . . . .

(2) Where a record made in the usual and ordinary course of business does not contain information in respect of a matter the occurrence or existence of which might reasonably be expected to be recorded in that record, the

---

88 R.S.C. 1985, c. C-5.
89 R.S.C. 1985, c. C-5, section 30(12).

court may on production of the record admit the record for the purpose of establishing that fact and may draw the inference that the matter did not occur or exist.

(3) Where it is not possible or reasonably practicable to produce any record described in subsection (1) or (2), a copy of the record accompanied by two documents, one that is made by a person who states why it is not possible or reasonably practicable to produce the record and one that sets out the source from which the copy was made that attests to the copy's authenticity and that is made by the person who made the copy, is admissible in evidence under this section in the same manner as if it were the original of the record . . . .

(4) Where production of any record or of a copy of any record described in subsection (1) or (2) would not convey to the court the information contained in the record by reason of its having been kept in a form that requires explanation, a transcript of the explanation of the record or copy prepared by a person qualified to make the explanation is admissible in evidence under this section in the same manner as if it were the original of the record if it is accompanied by a document that sets out the person's qualifications to make the explanation [and] attests to the accuracy of the explanation . . . .

(5) . . . for the purpose of determining the probative value, if any, to be given to information contained in any record admitted in evidence under this section, the court may, on production of any record, examine the record, admit any evidence in respect thereof given orally or by affidavit including evidence as to the circumstances in which the information contained in the record was written, recorded, stored or reproduced, and draw any reasonable inference from the form or content of the record.

(6) . . . any person who has or may reasonably be expected to have knowledge of the making or contents of any record produced or received in evidence under this section may, with leave of the court, be examined or cross-examined thereon by any party to the legal proceeding.

(7) Nothing in this section renders admissible in evidence in any legal proceeding

    (a) such part of any record as is proved to be

        (i) a record made in the course of an investigation or inquiry,

        (ii) a record made in the course of obtaining or giving legal advice or in contemplation of a legal proceeding,

(iii) a record in respect of the production of which any privilege exists and is claimed, or

(iv) a record of or alluding to a statement made by a person who is not, or if he were living and of sound mind would not be, competent and compellable to disclose in the legal proceeding a matter disclosed in the record;

(b) any record the production of which would be contrary to public policy; or

(c) any transcript or recording of evidence taken in the course of another legal proceeding.

(8) The provisions of this section shall be deemed to be in addition to and not in derogation of

(a) any other provision of this or any other Act of Parliament respecting the admisibility in evidence of any record or the proof of any matter; or

(b) any existing rule of law under which any record is admissible in evidence or any matter may be proved."

Section 30 has been held to apply to computer records, in the same manner as paper records. The definition of "record" includes the whole or any part of any book, document, paper, card, tape or other thing on or in which information is written, recorded, stored or reproduced. This gives very broad scope to the section. The principal criterion for admissibility is that the record was made in the "usual and ordinary course of business". There have been a number of cases which have considered whether computer printouts are original records, to which subsection (1) applies, or copies under subsection (3).[90]   **5 30**

In *Marakis v. Min. of National Revenue*,[91] the tax court stated that computer records of income tax returns were copies rather than originals and refused to admit them in evidence because the originals had been destroyed and there was insufficient evidence to show that the copies were identical to the originals. Nevertheless, in most cases under section 30 of the Canada Evidence Act, the distinction between originals and copies is important only to the extent that it affects the procedure to be followed to introduce the records in evidence.

---

90 *R. v. McMullen* (1979), 47 C.C.C. (2d) 499 (Ont. C.A.); see also *R. v. Hanlon* (1985), 69 N.S.R. (2d) 266 (Co. Ct.).
91 (1986), 86 D.T.C. 1237 (T.C.C.).

Section 29 of the Canada Evidence Act deals specifically with records maintained by financial institutions. It provides that:

"29. (1) Subject to this section, a copy of any entry in any book or record kept in any financial institution shall in all legal proceedings be admitted in evidence as proof, in the absence of evidence to the contrary, of the entry and of the matters, transactions and accounts therein recorded.

(2) A copy of an entry in the book or record described in subsection (1) shall not be admitted in evidence under this section unless it is first proved that the book or record was, at the time of the making of the entry, one of the ordinary books or records of the financial institution, that the entry was made in the usual and ordinary course of business, that the book or record is in the custody or control of the financial institution, and that the copy is a true copy of it, and such proof may be given by any person employed by the financial institution who has knowledge of the book or record or the manager or accountant of the financial institution, and may be given orally or by affidavit sworn before any commissioner or other person authorised to take affidavits.

(3) Where a cheque has been drawn on any financial institution or branch thereof by any person, an affidavit of the manager or accountant of the financial institution or branch, sworn before any commissioner or other person authorised to take affidavits, setting out that he is the manager or accountant, that he has made a careful examination and search of the books and records for the purpose of ascertaining whether or not that person has an account with the financial institution or branch and that he has been unable to find such an account, shall be admitted in evidence as proof, in the absence of evidence to the contrary that that person has no account in the financial institution or branch."

5-31   The definition of "financial institution" in subsection 29(9) includes the Bank of Canada, the Business Development Bank of Canada and any institution incorporated in Canada that accepts deposits of money from its members or the public, and any branch, agency or office of any such Bank or institution. The definition of "legal proceeding" is "any civil or criminal proceeding or inquiry in which evidence is or may be given, and includes an arbitration".[92]

Section 29 makes a copy of an entry in a record of a financial institution admissible as proof of the transactions recorded therein. However, the onus is on the person seeking to admit the record to establish the authenticity and accuracy of the record. For this reason, most of the reported cases involving computer records have involved the consideration of banking records under section 29.

---

92 Canada Evidence Act, R.S.C. 1985, c. C-5, section 29(9).

In *R. v. Bell*,[93] the Ontario Court of Appeal stated that the record may be in any form, and the form in which the information is recorded may change. A record may also be a compilation of other records, such as a bank statement which is compiled from records of individual transactions. The court also concluded that it is possible for a record to exist in more than one form at any given time. For example, the same information may be recorded in different forms for different purposes. Such records may be admissible under either section 29 or section 30 of the Act.

In *R. v. McMullen*,[94] the Ontario Court of Appeal held that a computer printout of bank records was admissible as a business record under section 30 of the Canada Evidence Act and was *prima facie* proof of the transactions recorded therein under section 29.

Ontario Evidence Act

The Ontario Evidence Act[95] is similar to the Canada Evidence Act. The 5-32 terms "business" and "record" are defined broadly, as in the federal statute. The Ontario Act also contains express provisions for the admissibility of records maintained by financial institutions and business records.

Section 33(2) permits a copy of an entry in a record kept in a bank to be *prima facie* proof of the transactions described therein.

Section 34(2) makes photographic prints of bills of exchange, promissory notes, cheques, receipts, instruments, agreements, documents, plans, records or books of entry admissible where they were photographed as part of an established practice to keep a permanent record and the original is destroyed, delivered to another person or lost. In certain circumstances where the original is prematurely destroyed (other than by the government), the court may refuse to admit the copy. This discretion raises potential problems if a program of using paperless technology is not carefully monitored and controlled.

Section 35(2) makes business records admissible. However, the Ontario Evidence Act lacks a provision comparable to those in section 30(3) of the Canada Evidence Act which permits copies of business records to be admitted into evidence.

Accordingly, it may be argued that a copy of a business record is not admissible under the Ontario Act, unless it falls within one of the other provisions of the Act. Nevertheless, as a practical matter, the courts have been willing to admit copies of records if they can be properly shown to be authentic copies of the original.

93 (1982), 26 C.R. (3d) 336.
94 (1979), 47 C.C.C. (2d) 499 (Ont. C.A.).
95 R.S.O. 1990, c. E.23.

New Brunswick Evidence Act

5-33   The New Brunswick Evidence Act[96] was recently revised to expressly allow for the admission in evidence of electronically stored documents.[97] The New Brunswick statute has been criticised as continuing to show a "residual preference" for paper over electronic records.[98]

The statute provides that a printout of a document is admissible in evidence if it is shown that the original document was copied by electronic imaging or a similar process and is stored electronically in the course of an established practice to keep a permanent record of the document. However, the printout of the electronic copy is admissible only if the original document no longer exists and it must be proven to be a true copy of the original document.[99]

If a document was originally created in electronic form, then a printout generated from a computer record or other electronic medium is admissible in evidence in all cases and for all purposes for which the document would have been admissible had it been created in a tangible form.[100]

According to the Uniform Law Conference of Canada's Consultation Paper on the proposed Uniform Electronic Evidence Act, there is a growing view that "the law should be neutral as to the technology that people use to manage their records . . . . The Act should be neutral as to whether the original paper records should be retained, so long as if they are destroyed, this is part of the normal course of business and not in contemplation of litigation".[101]

Civil Code of Québec

5-34   The Civil Code of Québec contains specific rules for the admissibility of computer records, as follows:

- Article 2837 - The data respecting a juridical act are entered on a computer system, the document reproducing them makes proof of the content of the act if it is intelligible and if the reliability is sufficiently guaranteed. To assess the quality of the document, the court shall take into account the circumstances under which the data were entered and the document was reproduced.
- Article 2838 - The reliability of the entry of the data of a juridical act on a computer system is presumed to be sufficiently guaranteed where it is carried out systematically and without gaps and the computerised

---

96 R.S.N.B. c. E-11.
97 An Act to Amend the Evidence Act, Statutes of New Brunswick, 1995, chapter 52, assented to April 25, 1996.
98 Uniform Law Conference of Canada, *Uniform Electronic Evidence Act, Consultation Paper*, March 1997.
99 An Act to Amend the Evidence Act, Statutes of New Brunswick, 1995, c. 52, section 47.1(3).
100 An Act to Amend the Evidence Act, Statutes of New Brunswick, 1995, c. 52, section 47.2(1).
101 Uniform Law Conference of Canada, *Uniform Electronic Evidence Act, Consultation Paper*, March 1997, at p. 6.

data are protected against alterations. The same presumption is made in favour of third persons where the data were entered by an enterprise.

- Article 2839 - The document which reproduces the data of a computerised juridical act may be contested on any grounds.

It has been suggested that these provisions of the Civil Code of Québec do not apply where transactions were originally recorded on paper and then converted to electronic form. However, other commentators have stated that the provisions should apply to all electronic records, regardless of the original form of the data.[102] Article 2680 of the Civil Code specifically permits copies to be admitted where the original cannot be produced.

Record Retention Requirements

Numerous federal statutes and regulations impose requirements on citizens, businesses and government departments to retain specific types of records for various periods of time.[103] A large number of provincial statutes impose similar requirements.   5-35

The Income Tax Act[104] requires particular records to be kept by businesses. Regulation 5800 under the Income Tax Act requires corporations to maintain particular types of records for varying lengths of time. However, the form in which these documents must be kept is not specified in the Act or the Regulations and paper copies of documents are not required to be retained.

Revenue Canada recognises as "books and records", data maintained in a machine-readable format that can be related back to the supporting source documents and supported by a system capable of producing an accessible and readable copy. Revenue Canada also recognises electronic images of books of original entry as books and records of account, provided that the images have been produced, controlled and maintained according to the Canadian General Standards Board standard for Microfilm and Electronic Images as Documentary Evidence.[105]

---

102 Macchione, "Overview of the Law of Commercial Transactions and Information Exchanges in Cyberspace — Canadian Common Law and Civil Law Perspectives", (1996) 13 *C.I.P.R.* 1, at p. 129, citing Ducharme, "Le nouveau droit de la preuve en matières civiles selon le Code Civil du Québec", [1992] *R.G.D.* 5, and Fabien, "La communicatique et le droit civil de la preuve", *Le droit de la communicatique, Actes du colloque conjoint de Facultés de droit de l'Université de Poitiers et de l'Université de Montréal* (1992), at p. 162.

103 The National Archives Act, subsection 5(1); the Canada Business Corporations Act, sections 20 and 22; and the Bank Act, sections 238, 239, and 246; see also sections 243 and 245 of the Income Tax Act and section 230 of I.T. Regulation 5800; Information Circular 78-1   0.R. 2, Unemployment Insurance Act, Canada Pension Plan Act, and Financial Administration Act, section 9, subsection 17(3), and sections 52 and 65.

104 R.S.C. 1985 5th Supp., sections 230 and 230.1.

105 Revenue Canada, Information Circular 78-1 O.R. 2 (S.R.), February 10, 1995, referring to National Standard CAN/C.S.B.-72.11-93, Microfilm and Electronic Images as Documentary Evidence.

ELECTRONIC PAYMENT SYSTEMS

Electronic Fund Transfers

5-36   The Canadian national payments system is administered by the Canadian Payments Association. Its members include the Bank of Canada and all federal chartered banks. Trust and loan companies, credit unions and other deposit-taking organisations are also eligible for membership.[106] The Canadian Payments Association currently operates a national automated clearing settlement system (A.C.S.S.), which in 1996 averaged more than 11-million transactions per day with a daily value of C. $55 billion. Approximately one-half of A.C.S.S. transactions involved electronic fund transfers. However, large-value or one-time transactions involving paper — mainly cheques — still account for more than 90 per cent of the total dollar volume.[107]

The Canadian Payments Association is currently implementing an electronic Large Value Transfer System (L.V.T.S.) to replace the existing A.C.S.S. and the International Interbank Payment System (S.W.I.F.T.), the wire transfer system currently operated by the Canadian Bankers Association. The electronic L.V.T.S. will eliminate the delays and uncertainties inherent in the existing paper-based systems. It will permit most financial transactions to be completed on the same day. Debits and credits will be processed on line by each of the participating financial institutions, thereby guaranteeing finality of payment at each stage of the settlement process. This is currently not the case, since a cheque may take several days to clear and may be returned at any time for insufficient funds.

The Payment and Clearing Settlement Act[108] gives the Bank of Canada the power to act as a central counter-party in the payment system and to guarantee settlement of all electronic transactions in the system. The central bank can also provide short-term loans to facilitate settlement. These powers are essential to the operation of a same-day electronic clearing system. The proposed L.V.T.S. will also comply with the Lamfalussy Standards established by the Bank for International Settlements,[109] thereby ensuring that Canadian financial institutions can participate fully in international electronic fund transfer systems.

Pilot testing of the L.V.T.S. is scheduled to begin in November 1997. Full implementation is expected early in 1998. The C.P.A. has published draft by-laws and rules for L.V.T.S. participants.[110]

---

106 Canadian Payments Association Act, R.S.C. 1985, C-21.
107 McPherson, "The Canadian Payments Association: Large Value Transfer System", *Electronic Commerce, The Impact of the Digital Age on Commercial Law* (1997), at p. 6.
108 S.C. 1996, c. C-6.
109 Bank for International Settlements, *Report of the Committee in Interbank Netting Schemes of the Central Banks of the Group of Ten Countries*, Basle: November 1990.
110 Canadian Payments Association By-Law Number 7, Draft March 1997.

The by-laws provide for the administration of the L.V.T.S. by the Canadian Payments Association and establish the criteria for participation in the L.V.T.S. The establishment of credit limits for multilateral and bilateral transactions within the system will also be governed by the by-laws. The by-laws establish protocols for the exchange and clearing of electronic payment messages, as well as rules for the finality of payments and for dealing with errors in payment messages. The by-laws specifically provide that the general law of mistake, unjust enrichment and restitution continue to apply where payment is made: in error to a person not entitled to receive payment; in an amount other than the amount intended; or as a result of an erroneously duplicated message.[111] If a recipient of a payment message detects an error, he or she is required to return the message. However, recipients have no duty to ensure that errors are detected. As a result, the onus remains on the participants in the system to ensure that the payment messages they send are complete and correct.[112]

Electronic Cash

A number of electronic alternatives to cash are currently available in the Canadian marketplace. The most widespread is the use of debit cards, which are used to make cash payments for products and services through the immediate transfer of funds from the purchaser's bank account to the merchant's account. All of the major Canadian financial institutions offer debit cards. Although debit cards have only been widely commercially available in Canada for a few years, the number and volume of transactions is beginning to approach that of credit and ATM cards.[113]   5-37

In Canada, the existing system of credit and debit cards is based on an interlocking series of contracts between (i) the cardholder and card issuer, (ii) the card issuer and participating merchant and (iii) the cardholder and the merchant.[114] Bank ATM cards are issued under a bilateral contract between the financial institution and its customer, and may be combined with either credit card or debit card features.

Although credit cards have been analogised to pre-existing financial instruments such as cheques, negotiable instruments and letters of credit, Canadian courts and commentators have concluded that credit cards are a *sui generis* financial instrument, governed solely by the applicable contracts. A similar analysis may be applied to debit and ATM cards.

---

111 Canadian Payments Association By-Law Number 7, Draft March 1997, subsection 10.9.
112 Canadian Payments Association By-Law Number 7, Draft March 1997, subsection 10.4.
113 Industry figures for 1996 indicate that debit card transactions now account for almost one-third of all card transactions. The combined credit, debit and ATM card network in Canada processes more than 1-billion transactions per year, with an estimated value of more than C. $100-billion.
114 *Bank of Montreal v. Demakos* (1996), 31 O.R. (3d) 757, at p. 763.

Stored value cards have also been available for some time, in limited roles. For example, research libraries use such cards for photocopying, because it is more convenient to sell patrons a card than to hand out a roll of coins. Cards may also be used for tollbooths, vending machines, and other applications. The Canadian telephone companies also offer a variety of prepaid cards for use in public pay telephones.

Digital stored value cards are physically similar to existing credit or debit cards, but use a computer chip on which stored value is recorded. The user loads the card with a specified amount of money from a special purpose terminal, which may be located at a bank branch or cash machine, in a retail store or at a stand-alone kiosk. The money is immediately deducted from the user's bank account. When a purchase is made, the card is read by the merchant's machine (or by an unattended vending machine) and the amount of the purchase deducted from the card and added to the merchant's account. With some cards, no authorisation code is required to complete the transaction. Payments are the same as cash and, as a result, if the card is lost or stolen it is the same as losing cash. Other systems offer additional security by locking the card in an "electronic wallet", which must be opened with the owner's PIN before the card can be used.

Some commentators have questioned whether electronic cash payment systems are "money" in the conventional sense at all.[115] In Ontario, the Personal Property Security Act defines money as "a medium of exchange adopted by the Parliament of Canada as part of the currency of Canada, or by a foreign government as part of its currency".[116] However, the federal Currency Act merely provides for the denomination of Canadian currency in dollars and cents and stipulates the form of currently circulating bank notes and coins.[117] The Criminal Code also defines money in terms that relate it to official currency and offences such as counterfeiting.[118]

A leading Canadian financial services lawyer has identified five essential characteristics of money which may be applied to electronic payments systems, as follows:

- It must be commonly accepted as a medium of exchange;
- It must not be linked to the credit of the transferor;
- It must be given and received as final payment of the debt, without further right of recourse;
- It must pass freely and be fully transferred on delivery;
- It must be self-contained, with no further requirement for collection, clearing or settlement, and leave no record; and

---

115 Crawford, "Is Electronic Money Really Money?", *Electronic Commerce: The Impact of the Digital Age on Commercial Law* (1997).
116 R.S.O. 1990, c. P.10, section 1.
117 R.S.C. 1985, chapter C-52.
118 R.S.C. 1985, c. C-46, sections 448 *et seq.*

- The transferee in the ordinary course must take free and clear of all claims of prior owners or holders.[119]

Using this analysis, neither credit nor debit cards qualify as forms of money,   5-38
since they both depend on centralised accounting and settlement of all transactions. Neither would single-purpose cards such as those issued by telephone companies or libraries. However, other general-purpose stored value card systems, such as the Mondex card, and some Internet payment systems may satisfy all or some of the criteria.

A number of stored value systems are currently at various stages of development and testing in Canada. For present purposes, the Mondex and VISA Cash systems are described to illustrate some of the relevant legal issues.

Mondex

Mondex is an electronic cash card developed in the United Kingdom and   5-39
currently being tested and marketed around the world. The Royal Bank of Canada and the Canadian Imperial Bank of Commerce, two of the largest national financial institutions, have joined Mondex and began conducting a pilot test of the card in Ontario in 1997. Full nation-wide implementation of the service is scheduled for 1998. The system is designed to replace cheques or cash for typical consumer purchases, such as fast food restaurants, convenience stores, pay phones, vending machines and the like. Unlike other forms of anonymous cash cards, Mondex includes extensive security features to provide authentication and verification capability. Each card maintains a transaction log which can be retained by the user for audit purposes. Transaction terminals can also be programmed to check recent transactions and lock out cards that display unusual usage patterns which may indicate fraud or other tampering. The user can also lock the card with a personal code, to prevent use if the card is lost or stolen.

According to one commentator, "Mondex is heralded as one of the biggest breakthroughs in money since the introduction of cash machines".[120] The Mondex system is particularly noteworthy, because the Mondex system creates value within the existing monetary system of participating countries. In each country, the central bank or a designated commercial bank acts as an originator, to create value in that currency. The originator is also responsible for removing value from the system. Mondex therefore operates within the existing inter-bank payments system and is subject to the same degree of regulatory control.

---

119 Crawford, "Is Electronic Money Really Money?", *Electronic Commerce: The Impact of the Digital Age on Commercial Law* (1997), at p. 4.
120 Chinoy, "Electronic Money: Replacements for Traditional Cash", *Electronic Commerce: The Impact of the Digital Age on Commercial Law* (1997), at p. 3; see also Chinoy, "Electronic Money in Electronic Purses and Wallets", (1996) 12 *B.F.L.R.* 15.

The Mondex system would appear to satisfy the criteria to be considered a form of electronic cash or money because the stored value it represents is centrally originated and can be used for unlimited purposes. No central accounting and settlement is required; all transactions can be completed off-line, without any centralised verification of authenticity. One issue that remains uncertain is who bears the risk of counterfeiting or forgery, the card issuer or the merchant, if there is no recourse against the card-holder. To be truly accepted as money, merchants and vendors must be certain that some authority stands behind the integrity of the payments they accept.[121]

VISA Cash

5-40   The VISA Cash card is also a stored value card, designed for small value transactions. It does not have the security features incorporated in the Mondex card. VISA Cash has been available in Canada since 1995. Disposable cards are issued in denominations of C. $20.

VISA Cash is a centrally accounted system. The card issuer maintains a record of the amount issued to the cardholder, and deducts the amount of each transaction from the account balance. In this way, VISA Cash seems to be more like a debit card than a true cash card.

In addition, in contrast to the Mondex card, VISA Cash is a decentralised origination system. VISA International has established a consortium of financial institutions to develop and implement specifications for an "electronic purse". Both VISA and MasterCard intend to use their existing credit card merchant and cardholder networks to launch digital cash services. The two organisations have agreed to co-operate in the development and implementation of compatible technology. This will enable a variety of financial institutions to issue value and process transactions, with centralised inter-bank settlement capability through the international VISA and MasterCard networks.

Internet Payment Systems

5-41   All of the many Internet payment schemes are available in Canada, but as of the beginning of 1997, most appear to be operating with limited commercial acceptance. Some operate within closed systems that require both merchants and customers to use value tokens that are purchased with "real" money and may be converted back into currency for a fee.[122] Others provide

---

121 Crawford, "Is Electronic Money Really Money?", *Electronic Commerce: The Impact of the Digital Age on Commercial Law* (1997), at pp. 6–14.
122 For example, Digicash Corporation has been testing its "Cyberbucks" system since 1994 and has licensed its ECash to financial institutions.

systems which are functionally equivalent to paper cheques, using digital signature and encryption technology to provide authentication and
security features.[123]

The common thread in all of the systems is the search for features which
make Internet payments transparent to the user while offering levels of
security and privacy required for consumer acceptance. Privacy seems to be
a significant concern. Some advocates of a completely anonymous digital
cash system are concerned that financial institutions, merchandisers, and
others will use smart card technology to obtain vast amounts of information
about users' buying habits. However, other digital cash advocates express
doubts that the public will be willing to pay the extra costs associated with
truly anonymous digital cash.

For digital cash to be untraceable, each unit of currency must be authenticated with a "blind signature". This verifies to the recipient that the money
exists and will be honoured by the authenticating bank, without revealing
who possesses that unit of currency as it is passed from hand to hand. This
imposes extra encryption requirements, which add to the cost of issuing and
processing digital cash.

Meanwhile, law enforcement agencies and financial institutions worry
that digital cash which is not traceable will be used for everything from
tax evasion to money laundering, fraud and counterfeiting. The Canadian
government and financial regulators do not appear to have undertaken any
steps to deal with these issues or to regulate digital cash products and
services.

Role of Financial Institutions

The federal Proceeds of Crime (Money Laundering) Act[124] requires financial   **5-42**
institutions to maintain certain written records, including a signature card
for each account holder and an account operating agreement. The Act also
requires the institution to verify the identity of its customers. The Act,
therefore, restricts the ability of financial institutions to act as intermediaries
in anonymous electronic cash transactions.

Canadian financial institutions have adopted a formal code of practice
for consumer debit card services, which requires each issuer of debit cards

---

123 Examples include Net Cheque, developed by the Information Science Institute of the
University of Southern California School of Engineering in 1996 and ECheck, offered by
the Financial Services Technology Consortium.
124 S.C. 1991, c. 26.

to obtain a "signed request from an applicant".[125] The code also establishes a code of practice for the issuance, use and security of PINs. It sets the general requirements for cardholder agreements, transaction records, and transaction security. The code deals with liability for loss and requires card issuers to establish fair and timely procedures for resolving disputes.[126] Similar rules are expected to apply to the issuance of stored value cards, when those become widely available over the next couple of years.

Despite continuing concerns about security, the majority of commercial transactions over the Internet are still paid for with a credit card. In Canada, the issuance and use of credit cards is governed by the Bank Act[127] and the provincial consumer protection statutes.[128] In a recent decision, an Ontario court noted a "paucity of decisional law in Ontario and Canada dealing with credit cards", but concluded that:

> "The central nerve or core of the credit card is the customer's written agreement with the bank card issuer. The sparse legislation which exists in Canada at the federal and provincial level is largely concerned with creating narrow but specific legislative controls on this contract."

5-43   For example, the court noted that consumer protection statutes prohibit the issuance of unsolicited cards.[129]

In the absence of a written agreement with the customer, therefore, Canadian financial institutions are restricted in their ability to act as financial intermediaries in electronic commerce transactions that involve granting consumer credit.

---

125 Canadian Code of Practice for Consumer Debit Card Services, The Electronic Funds Transfer Working Group, May 1, 1992.
126 The code applies to services which use debit cards and personal identification numbers (PINs) to access automated banking machines and point of sale terminals in Canada. It has been endorsed by the Canadian Payments Association, Canadian Bankers Association, Trust Companies Association of Canada, Credit Union Central of Canada, La *Confederation des caisses populaires et d'économie Desjardins du Québec*, Retail Council of Canada, Canadian Federation of Independent Business, Consumers' Association of Canada, the Canadian Department of Consumer and Corporate Affairs and Department of Finance, Office of the Superintendent of Financial Institutions, and the Consumer Ministries of each Province and Territory.
127 S.C. 1991, c. 46, section 409.
128 Consumer Protection Act, R.S.O. 1990, c. C.31, section 36.
129 *Bank of Montreal v. Demankos* (1996), 31 O.R. (3d) 757, at pp. 762 and 764; citing the Consumer Protection Act, R.S.O. 1990, c. C.31, section 36; see also Ogilvie, *Canadian Banking Law* (1991), at pp. 645-668.

Electronic information rights

Property Rights in Electronic Information

Copyright

Applicability of Copyright to On-line Communications Copyright in Can-   5-44
ada is created by the Copyright Act.[130] The exclusive rights of the copyright
owner relevant to on-line communications include the rights to:

- Produce or reproduce the work;
- Publish the work;
- Perform the work in public;
- Communicate a work to the public by telecommunication; and
- Authorise others to do any of the foregoing.

The author has the moral right to the integrity of the work and to be   5-45
associated with the work or to remain anonymous. These moral rights are
separate from the copyright. They may be waived, but cannot be assigned
or transferred.[131] Electronic commerce poses a threat to the integrity of
copyrighted works as the public is now able to effortlessly transform or
sample portions of works. These capabilities can also result in the disasso-
ciation of original copyrighted works from their authors.[132]

Infringement of Copyright It is possible for an Internet user to violate   5-46
several of the copyright owner's exclusive rights simultaneously. E-mail
messages, which form the vast majority of on-line communication, may
infringe copyright in a number of ways. The sender of the message may
infringe by including a reproduction of a copyright work in the message. The
recipient may infringe by copying it and forwarding it to one or more other
persons. Posting an e-mail message on a public mailing list or newsgroup
may also be considered a communication to the public and infringe the
copyright owner's exclusive right to communicate a work by telecommunication.[133]

The World Wide Web is also a common source of copyright infringement.
Publishing a work on a Web page without the copyright owner's permission
will constitute both an unauthorised reproduction of the work and a communication of the work to the public. If the work was previously unpublished,
it would also constitute an unauthorised publication of the work.

---

130 R.S.C. 1985, c. C-42.
131 Copyright Act, R.S.C. 1985, c. C-42, as amended, section 14.1.
132 Racicot *et al*, *Internet Content-Related Liability Study*, Industry Canada, 1997.
133 "Copyright and the Information Highway", *Final Report of the I.H.A.C. Copyright Subcommittee*, March 1995.

Web pages are frequently copied — or cached — by Internet Service Providers and end-user browser programs to increase the speed at which the pages are accessed and to decrease network traffic. Caching is technically a reproduction of the work and, therefore, an infringement unless it is authorised by the copyright owner, even if the caching is done unwittingly. Knowledge and intent are not relevant to infringement.[134] However, if a copyright owner makes material freely accessible on the Web, there also may be an implied licence to make ephemeral copies by browsing or caching, if such copies are necessary to access the information.[135]

Canadian law does not recognise copyright in a title.[136] The reproduction of another Web page's universal resource locator (URL) will not likely be viewed as an infringement of copyright. A URL is merely a descriptive pointer to the page address, and is analogous to a title.

Amendments to the Copyright Act were introduced in 1996, to implement some of the recommendations in the final report of the Information Highway Advisory Committee's [137] Bill C-32 represents part of the so-called "Phase II" update following a more limited "Phase I" update that took place in the 1980s. However, the government deferred consideration of most electronic copying and digital rights issues to Phase III of the copyright reform program, which is expected to drag on into the next century.[138]

Changes introduced by Bill C-32 that are relevant to electronic communications include the introduction of neighbouring rights to Canada and improved remedies for copyright infringement. Performers, producers and broadcasters will gain the rights to: communicate the performance to the public by telecommunication; fix the performance; rent out a sound recording of the fixation; and authorise such acts by other people. The new neighbouring rights will expand the class of people who may lay claim to copyrights that may be infringed in on-line communications.

5-47   **Acquiring Copyright** No registration formalities are necessary to obtain copyright in Canada. The simple act of the creation of an "original" work by a citizen or resident of a "treaty country" (a Berne Convention, U.C.C., or W.T.O. member state) is sufficient to satisfy copyright requirements. One may register copyrights in Canada, but registration is not necessary. Registration serves an evidentiary function as a presumption of ownership and provides notice of ownership to the public.

---

134 "Copyright and the Information Highway", *Final Report of the I.H.A.C. Copyright Subcommittee*, March 1995.
135 See generally, Racicot *et al, Internet Content-Related Liability Study*, Industry Canada, 1997.
136 *British Columbia* v. *Mihaljevic* (1989), 26 C.P.R. (3d) 184, at p. 190; affirmed (1991), 36 C.P.R. (3d) 445 (B.C.C.A.).
137 *The Challenge of the Information Highway — Final Report of the Information Highway Advisory Council*, Minister of Supply and Services Canada, 1995, September 1995.
138 Bill C-32 was enacted into law in April, 1997.

Ownership of Copyright to On-line Information In 1997, there were two 5-48
class-action cases pending in Canada in which authors were suing newspapers and on-line service providers for republishing their works in electronic
databases. The authors claim they granted only one-time print publication
rights. The publishers have taken the position that the on-line databases are
now an integral part of the newspaper business, that the electronic database
serves as an archive of the print version, and that the industry practice, as it
has evolved over the past decade, amounts to an implied licence to distribute
electronic copies of printed works. The issue is far from settled, however.
Publishers and authors are now negotiating the express allocation of electronic rights in new publishing contracts.

Rights of Copyright User The rights of the user of copyright are granted by 5-49
the owner of copyright in the form of a licence to use or to make a limited
number of copies for specific purposes. There are also statutory exemptions
to copyright infringement, namely, the fair dealing exemption and specific
exemptions.

The Canadian fair dealing exceptions are significantly narrower than the
well-known "fair use" exception to copyright infringement under United
States law.[139] The newly revised section 29 of the Copyright Act provides
that "fair dealing for the purpose of research or private study does not
infringe copyright". The Copyright Act still does not define fair dealing,
however. Sections 29.1 and 29.2 of the Act provide that all fair dealing for
criticism, review, or news reporting do not infringe copyright if the source
and — if given in the source — the name of the author, performer, maker, or
broadcaster are mentioned.

The specific exemption to copyright infringement most relevant to electronic commerce is for single reproductions of computer programs, which
will not infringe copyright when made to ensure compatibility of the
program with a particular computer or for backup purposes.

Bill C-32 expanded the set of specific exemptions to copyright infringement in the Copyright Act. Most notably, it provided for specific exemptions
for educational institutions, libraries, archives, and museums. Exceptions
also exist for incidental inclusion, ephemeral recordings, persons with
perceptual disabilities, statutory and other miscellaneous acts.

Trade Marks

Acquiring On-line Trade Mark Rights There are no special on-line trade 5-50
mark rights. However, one may acquire trade mark rights through on-line
use. The Trade Marks Act provides that a trade mark has been adopted

---

139 United States Copyright Act, 17 U.S.C., sections 101 *et seq.*

in Canada when a person starts to use it in Canada or to make it known in Canada, or when that person files an application for registration in Canada.[140]

A trade mark is used in association with goods if it is marked on the goods; marked on the packages in which the goods are distributed; or associated with the goods in a manner that gives notice to the purchaser of the goods at the time of change of title or possession. A trade mark is used in association with services if it is displayed during the performance or advertising of the services. The use of a trade mark to advertise goods does not constitute use under the Trade Marks Act.[141] Accordingly, trade mark rights may be established by advertising services electronically, but trade mark rights cannot be acquired on-line if the mark is associated only with goods that must be delivered physically.

A trade mark is deemed to be made known in Canada when it has been used in association with wares or services by a person in a country of the Union for the Protection of Industrial Property, or of the World Trade Organisation and wares are distributed in association with the mark in Canada; or the wares or services have been advertised with it in Canada in printed publications or radio broadcasts, so that it has become well known in Canada. Revisions of the Trade Marks Act have been proposed, in which the restriction to advertising in printed publications or radio broadcasts would be removed, allowing any form of advertising to make a trade mark well known in Canada.

The Internet can be viewed as a large advertising medium. Foreign trade mark owners may therefore be able to acquire rights in Canada by advertising their wares or services on the Internet. Trade mark owners outside Canada may also be able to acquire rights in Canada through the on-line distribution of wares coupled with display of the trade mark if such distribution causes the trade mark to be well known in Canada.

5-51   **Infringement**   The registration of a trade mark under the Canadian Trade Marks Act gives to the owner "the exclusive right to the use throughout Canada of the trade mark in respect of those wares or services".[142]

The Act distinguishes between goods (wares) and services. Most electronic commerce transactions include the provision of services. Therefore, advertising those services on-line may constitute an infringement of Canadian trade mark rights, even if the advertisement originates outside Canada.

To the extent that goods may be delivered electronically — for example, software which may be downloaded from a Web site — Canadian trade mark rights would be infringed if the mark is displayed on the goods or included in the transferred data. Contracts concluded completely electronically

---

140 Trade Marks Act, R.S.C. 1985, c. T-13, as amended, section 3.
141 Trade Marks Act, R.S.C. 1985, c. T-13, section 4.
142 Trade Marks Act, R.S.C. 1985, c. T-13, section 19.

may also give rise to trade mark infringement if the courts recognise transfer of title on the basis of the electronic contract, and there is display of the trade mark in conjunction with the contract.[143]

The Trade Marks Act also provides that the use of a confusingly similar trade mark is an infringement of a registered trade mark, and prohibits using a registered trade mark in such a way as to cause depreciation of good will in that mark.[144] Anyone posting content on the Internet that contains another person's trade mark may be liable for direct infringement under sections 19, 20 and 22 of the Act. Others who act as facilitators or intermediaries for direct infringers, such as Internet service providers, may also be liable as vicarious or contributory infringers.[145]

Internet Domain Names

Acquiring Rights   The Canadian Domain Name Registry for the "ca"   5-52 top-level domain is administered by the CA Domain Committee and the University of British Columbia. To obtain a "ca" domain registration, one must fill out and submit a detailed application template to the registry.

The "ca" domain has a hierarchy that follows the political structure of the Canadian federation.[146] The "ca" domain is reserved for national organisations, including the federal government, federally incorporated companies, owners of a federally registered trade mark, and organisations with offices in more than one province or territory. Provincially-incorporated companies, provincially-registered partnerships or proprietorships, and provincial institutions such as universities and/or hospitals and organisations with offices in more than one city qualify for second-level domain names, such as "on.ca" or "bc.ca". The third level is for municipal governments and other local organisations.[147]

One's choice of domain name is not granted automatically. The application template requires the applicant to explain the basis for their entitlement to the requested name. However, the CA Domain Registrar does not independently verify the name. It is up to individual organisations to ensure that they are entitled to use the domain name chosen. Any disputes between the parties will be settled through normal legal methods.

Because of the restrictions imposed on the allotment of the "ca" domain names, many corporations which do not qualify for top-level, pan-Canadian

143 Racicot et al, Internet Content-Related Liability Study, Industry Canada, 1997.
144 Trade Marks Act, R.S.C. 1985, c. T-13, sections 20 and 22.
145 Racicot et al, Internet Content-Related Liability Study, Industry Canada, 1997.
146 The domain hierarchy for a typical e-mail address is name@entity.city.province.ca.
147 For example, the national airline, Air Canada, has the domain name "aircanada.ca" the provincial government of Saskatchewan is "gov.sk.ca" and the Vancouver city public library is "vpl.vancouver.bc.ca". For a detailed description of Canada's domain name structure, see Carroll and Broadhead, Canadian Internet Handbook (1996). Additional information is available from the CA Domain Registry at University of British Columbia, at cdnnet.ca.

domain names opt instead for one of the international "com", "edu", "net", "org", or "gov" international domains allocated by InterNIC. Canadians who wish to obtain these functional domains are subject to the InterNIC rules. All registrants are required to certify that, to the best of their knowledge, the use of the domain name does not violate trade mark or other statutes. The evolving policy of InterNIC has been to allow owners of registered trade marks to claim domain names that are the same as their trade mark, even if someone else has been previously granted them. However, InterNIC registers names world-wide, and InterNIC has been unable to resolve disputes between different owners of the same or similar trade marks in different countries.

5-53   **Protecting Domain Name as a Trade Mark** As of early 1997, there were no reported Canadian cases involving claims of trade mark infringement through the use of a domain name.

However, there has been one reported "passing-off" case[148] where the plaintiff did not have a registered trade mark and applied for an interlocutory injunction restraining the defendant from using the name "pei.net". The plaintiff was unsuccessful. It failed to establish all three elements of the passing-off: the existence of good will; deception of the public due to a misrepresentation; and actual or potential damage to the plaintiff. The court found that the plaintiff had not been "in business under its trade name for such a reasonable time and to such a reasonable extent that it [had] acquired a reputation under that trade name that would prevent the defendants from using a similar name".

The plaintiff also failed to establish misrepresentation to the public; the allegedly infringing name was only in use a short time and the defendant stopped using it almost immediately after notice from the plaintiff. The plaintiff did not show any actual damages from the defendant's conduct, and due to the fact the defendant stopped using the domain name, there were no potential future damages.

This judgment demonstrates the difficulty that Canadian courts have in understanding the new information technology and in adapting existing law to it. For example, the trial judge drew a distinction between the defendant's lower-case domain name "pei.net" and the plaintiff's upper-case company name "PEINET Inc". This distinction is technically irrelevant with respect to domain names. Nevertheless, it seemed to provide the trial judge with a basis for differentiating the plaintiff's corporate name from the defendant's

---

148 *PEINET Inc.* v. *O'Brien* (1995), 61 C.P.R. (3d) 334 (P.E.I. S.C.).

domain registration. The trial judge acknowledged the court's lack of technical expertise, as follows:

"The whole area of the use of the Internet network and its conventions is new to the court. I find that the plaintiff has only made superficial submissions without explaining the Internet system."[149]

The case also illustrates the benefit of registering a domain name as a trade mark. The plaintiff was obliged to meet a higher burden of proof to show passing off. Had the plaintiff owned a registered trade mark in the domain name, it might have been able to show infringement through the use of a "confusingly similar" trade mark contrary to section 20 of the Trade Marks Act.

Patents

Computer hardware and software used in electronic commerce are patent-   5-54
able subject matter under the federal Patent Act.[150] The Federal Court of Appeal, in 1981, declared computer software to be an unpatentable series of mathematical calculations.[151] That is still the leading decision on patentability of software in Canada. However, in recent years, the Canadian Patent Office and the Patent Appeal Board have shown a willingness to allow patents for industrial processes and information processing systems which involve the use of computer software.

The Canadian Patent Office issued a discussion paper in 1993, with new guidelines for computer-related patents. It repeats the basic rule that scientific principles and abstract theorems are not patentable.[152] Computer programs claiming unapplied mathematical calculations or mathematical algorithms per se are not patentable. However, the presence of a computer or a computer program neither adds to nor detracts from the patentability of an apparatus or process.[153]

There are already a number of issued Canadian patents on technology relating to electronic commerce. For example, Public Key Partners, a California partnership, holds the following Canadian patents relating to public key encryption technology:

- The Hellman, Diffie, Merkle cryptographic apparatus and method;[154]

---

149 *PEINET Inc.* v. *O'Brien* (1995), 61 C.P.R. (3d) 334, at p. 338 (P.E.I. S.C.).
150 R.S.C. 1985, c. P-4.
151 *Schlumberger Can. Ltd.* v. *Commissioner of Patents* (1981), 56 C.P.R. (2d) 204 (Fed. C.A.).
152 Patent Act, R.S.C. 1985, c. P-4, section 27(3).
153 Canadian Patent Office Discussion Paper on Patentability of Computer Software Subject Matter, June 1993; following publication of the guidelines, the Patent Office and the Patent and Trade Mark Institute of Canada struck a joint committee, which agreed in 1994 on a revised set of guidelines; these guidelines are continuing to evolve, as the Patent Office acquires more experience with computer software inventions.
154 Canadian Patent Number 1,121,480.

- The Hellman, Merkle public key cryptographic apparatus and method;[155] and
- The Hellman, Pohlig exponentiation cryptographic apparatus and method.[156]

5-55   Public Key Partners also holds United States patents for the above three Hellman patents,[157] for R.S.A., the Rivest Shamir Adleman cryptographic communications system and method,[158] and the Schnorr "method for identifying subscribers and for generating and verifying electronic signatures in a data exchange system".[159] These patents are relevant to Canadian cryptography users because of the close trading ties between Canada and the United States.

In addition to Public Key Partner's patents, the United States government holds the patent for the Digital Signature Algorithm (Kravitz).[160]

Privacy

5-56   The government of Canada has formally adhered to the Organisation for Economic Co-operation and Development's Guidelines on the Protection of Privacy and Transborder Flows of Personal Data (the O.E.C.D. Guidelines). The principles reflected in the O.E.C.D. Guidelines have been adopted by agencies of the federal government. The O.E.C.D. Guidelines are also reflected in privacy legislation passed by the governments of the various provinces and in voluntary codes adopted by a number of industry groups.

The federal Privacy Act[161] and Access to Information Act[162] govern the collection and use of personal information by the federal government and quasi-governmental agencies.

Québec is the only province which has enacted privacy legislation governing the private sector.[163] Within the Québec public sector, the Act Respecting Access to Documents Held by Public Bodies and the Protection of Personal Information[164] applies to approximately 3,600 public bodies, including municipal governments, schools, universities, and health and social services. In Ontario, the equivalent statute is the Freedom of Information and Protection of Privacy Act, 1987.[165] Other provinces have adopted

---

155 Canadian Patent Number 1,128,159.
156 Canadian Patent Number 1,152,592.
157 United States Patent Numbers 4,200,770; 4,218,582; and 4,424,414, respectively.
158 United States Patent Number 4,405,829.
159 United States patent number 4,995,082.
160 United States Patent Number 5,231,668; Canadian Patent Number 2,111,572.
161 R.S.C. 1985, c. P-21.
162 R.S.C. 1985, c. A.
163 Act respecting the protection of personal information in the private sector, S.Q. 1993, c. 17.
164 S.Q. 1982, c. 30.
165 R.S.O. 1990, c. F.31.

similar legislation.[166] While the laws of each jurisdiction vary in their details and procedural requirements, most are based on the O.E.C.D. Guidelines.

Specific statutes in areas of federal jurisdiction (such as banking) or provincial jurisdiction (such as consumer credit reporting) regulate the collection and use of personal information in those industries.[167]

Administrative tribunals have adopted policies and regulations which have either a direct or indirect impact on privacy and electronic commerce. For example, the Canadian Radio-Television and Telecommunications Commission (C.R.T.C.), which regulates telephone utilities, has adopted regulations with respect to the use of automatic dialling devices.

Guidelines established by private bodies, such as the Canadian Bankers' Association and the Canadian Direct Marketing Association, also have an impact on privacy in electronic commerce transactions. While the private guidelines do not carry any force of law, they are generally consistent with the O.E.C.D. Guidelines and with federal and provincial privacy legislation. They are widely followed within the applicable industries, as an informal means of self-regulation. The Canadian Standards Association, in conjunction with business and consumer groups, recently developed a model privacy code which it urges be voluntarily adopted by the private sector.[168] The Information Highway Advisory Council has recommended the development of comprehensive national privacy standards, as follows:

"In order for consumers and users to benefit from electronic information networks, there is a need for a coherent national standard as to what constitutes effective privacy protection in an electronic environment among business, consumer organisations and governments. The Council believes that such a standard can best be achieved through legislation."[169]

Federal Legislation   Various federal enactments regulate on-line business.   5-57 These are examined below.

---

166 Manitoba: Freedom of Information Act; S.M. 1985–86, c. F175; New Brunswick: Right to Information Act, S.N.B. 1978, c. R-10.3, as amended; Newfoundland: Freedom of Information Act, S.N. 1981, c. 5, as amended; Nova Scotia: Freedom of Information Act, S.N.S. 1990, c. 11.

167 See, for example, Bank Act, S.C. 1991, c. 46; Consumer Reporting Act, R.S.O. 1990, c. C-33, R.S.N.S. 1989, c. 93, R.S.P.E.I. 1988, c. C-20; Credit Reporting Act, RS.B.C. 1979, c. 78; The Personal Exemptions Act, R.S.M. 1987, c. P34; Consumer Reporting Agencies Act, R.S.N. 1977, chapter 18; Credit Reporting Agencies Act, R.S.S. 19, c. C-44.

168 Canadian Standards Association, *Draft Model Code for the Protection of Personal Information*, 1996.

169 Final Report of the Information Highway Advisory Council, Industry Canada, 1995, at p. 140; see also Recommendations 10.1 to 10.7.

5-58   *Privacy Act* The Privacy Act[170] applies to each Department or Ministry of State of the federal government, including crown corporations and federal boards and commissions.

The Act restricts the circumstances under which a government institution can gather information concerning individuals and provides controls on the use, sharing and dissemination of that information.

5-59   *Access to Information Act* The Access to Information Act,[171] provides a right of access to information in records under the control of a government institution in accordance with the principle that government information should be available to the public that necessary exceptions to the right of access should be limited and specific and that decisions on the disclosure of government information should be reviewed independently of government. The Act provides specific exemptions for certain personal financial and commercial information.

5-60   *Data Matching Policy* The federal government has also adopted a policy on "data matching" and the use of Social Insurance numbers.[172] The policy, which applies to all government institutions which are subject to the Privacy Act, limits the use of the Social Insurance number as a personal identifier. It is intended to balance the privacy rights of individuals against the desire to optimise the use of personal information for administrative purposes, in particular, to investigate fraud and misuse of government programs.

Individuals must be advised of the purpose for which Social Insurance numbers are collected and the government cannot withhold services due to a refusal to provide Social Insurance number information, unless specifically authorised by statute or regulation. The Privacy Commissioner of Canada has the authority, under the Privacy Act, to examine the collection, use, disclosure, retention and disposal of personal information by government institutions and to investigate compliance with the policy on data matching and use of Social Insurance numbers.

The provisions of the federal Acts, and particularly the restrictions on the use of Social Insurance numbers, may have a direct impact on the proposed Public Key Initiative. Social Insurance numbers have been suggested as a unique identifier which might be used by Certification Authorities. However, concerns have been raised regarding the privacy of information provided to a public key certification authority operated by the federal government or provincial governments or a government agency. The confidentiality and integrity of public and private key information is essential to the operation of a certification authority and the validity of digital signatures.

---

170 R.S.C. 1985, c. P-21.
171 R.S.C. 1985, c. A-1.
172 Treasury Board of Canada, Secretariat, Access to Information and Privacy: Implementation Report number 20, September 1, 1989, File Number A.P.B. 2718-14-3.

The Legal Issues Working Group of the federal Information Technology Security Strategy Steering Committee concluded that if the Public Key Infrastructure (P.K.I.) is a federal government operation, information provided to the P.K.I. will be "under the control of a government institution", and will be subject to disclosure under the Access to Information Act, unless an exemption under the Act protects the information from being disclosed. The Legal Issues Working Group concluded that, if the P.K.I. is not operated by the federal government, but instead is contracted out to a truly independent contractor, the federal Access to Information Act and Privacy Act will not apply unless they are expressly incorporated in the applicable contract.[173] However, the federal Privacy Commissioner has argued in the past that the federal government should not hire independent contractors to perform obligations which would otherwise be subject to those Acts. A court could declare that the federal government is not permitted to contract out of the privacy protection Acts.

Provincial Legislation The various provinces and territories have enacted a number of measures directly affecting on-line transactions.   5-61

Privacy Legislation Québec has the most comprehensive personal privacy protection regime within Canada. The Civil Code of Québec guarantees the privacy rights of individuals and contains general restrictions on gathering personal information. It is supplemented by specific statutes which govern the collection and use of personal information by both public bodies[174] and private enterprises.[175] The Québec privacy statute also contains specific provisions dealing with data matching. Public bodies may release personal information for matching purposes, only if necessary to carry out a provincial statute. There must be a written agreement setting out the terms of the release of data. The agreement is subject to review by the *Commission d'acces l'information* and to government approval and must be made public.[176]   5-62

The Civil Code states it is an invasion of personal privacy to intercept private communications or to observe a person's private life by any means.[177] These provisions, together with limitations on the use of personal information by private enterprises, could have significant implications for electronic commerce in the province. For example, software which tracks access patterns and customises World Wide Web sites according to

---

173 Final Report of the Legal Issues Working Group of the Information Technology Security Strategy Steering Committee, Industry Canada, 1996, chapter 10, Digital Signature, Confidentiality and Public Key Infrastructure.

174 Act respecting access to documents held by public bodies and the protection of personal information, S.Q. 1982, c. 30.

175 Act respecting the protection of personal information in the private sector, S.Q. 1993, c. 17.

176 An act respecting access to documents held by public bodies and the protection of personal information, S.Q., 1982, c. 30, articles 68.1, 69, and 70.

177 Civil Code of Québec, article 36.

the viewer's preferences, without the viewer's knowledge or consent, would appear to violate the law in Québec.

Privacy legislation in other provinces is limited in scope to the collection and use of personal and commercial information by government ministries and agencies, boards, commissions, corporations or other bodies designated in the applicable regulations.[178] In Ontario, this regime has been extended to the collection and use of such information by municipal governments and agencies.[179] Outside Québec, the provincial statutes do not apply to data held by private entities.

The provincial privacy statutes establish administrative requirements which must be followed by institutions with respect to the collection, use and disclosure of specified types of personal information. They establish rights of individual privacy, impose limitations on the use and disclosure of such information, and provide rights of access by individuals to information concerning themselves for the purpose of verifying and correcting the information. The provincial statutes also provide rights for the general public to have access to data held by institutions and impose obligations on the institutions to disclose data, subject to limitations on the disclosure of certain personal and commercial information.

5-63   *Consumer Reporting Legislation* Provincial consumer reporting legislation governs the activities of private entities which collect and distribute credit and financial data of individuals.[180]

In Ontario, the Consumer Reporting Act[181] requires the registration of consumer reporting agencies, regulates the disclosure of data and the contents of credit reports, prohibits the disclosure of certain types of data, and creates rights for consumers to have access to, and to require correction of, data about themselves. The Act also establishes administrative procedures for enforcing the regulations and for investigating complaints with respect to consumer reporting agencies. The statutes in other provinces are generally similar.

---

178 Ontario: Freedom of Information and Protection of Privacy Act, R.S.O. 1990, c. F.31; Manitoba: Freedom of Information Act, S.M. 1985–86, c. 6 — c. F175; New Brunswick: Right to Information Act, S.N.B. 1978, c. R-10.3, as amended; Newfoundland: Freedom of Information Act, S.N. 1981, c. 5, as amended; Nova Scotia: Freedom of Information Act, S.N.S. 1990, c. 11.
179 Municipal Freedom of Information and Protection of Privacy Act, R.S.O. 1990, c. M.56.
180 British Columbia: Credit Reporting Act, RS.B.C. 1979, c.78; Manitoba: The Personal Investigations Act, R.S.M. 1987, c. P34; Ontario: Business Practices Act, R.S.O. 1990, c. B.18; Consumer Protection Act, R.S.O. 1990, c. C.31; Consumer Reporting Act, R.S.O. 1990, c. C.33; Newfoundland: Consumer Reporting Agencies Act, R.S.N. 1977, c. 18; Nova Scotia: Consumer Reporting Act, R.S.N.S. 1989, c. 93; Prince Edward Island: Consumer Reporting Act, R.S.P.E.I. 1988, c. C-20; Saskatchewan: Credit Reporting Agencies Act, R.S.S. 1978, c. C-44; Alberta: Consumer Credit Transactions Act, S.A. 1985, c. C-22.5.
181 R.S.O. 1990, c. C.33.

Regulations under the Ontario Collection Agencies Act[182] prohibit collection agencies from disseminating false or misleading information that may be detrimental to a debtor or any member of his or her family, and provide remedies to individuals in situations where false or misleading information is disseminated. With the exception of Manitoba and Québec, each province has debt collection agency legislation with provisions similar to those in Ontario.

Financial Institutions

Banks and other financial institutions in Canada have a Common Law duty   5-64
to maintain the confidentiality of the financial affairs of their customers.[183]
The rule is not absolute. Information may be disclosed with the consent of the customer, where required by law, or where required in the public interest. Furthermore, the Common Law rule does not restrict the use of the information for the financial institution's own purposes, for example, to market other products or services to the customer.

Bank Act

In recognition of the sensitive nature of the information entrusted to banks,   5-65
the Federal Bank Act requires the directors of a bank to establish procedures for restricting the use of confidential information and for disclosing information to customers of the bank, to monitor those procedures and to satisfy themselves that the procedures are being adhered to by the bank.[184]

The Bank Act requires each bank to maintain various records and to prepare and maintain adequate records showing, "for each customer of the bank, on a daily basis, particulars of the transactions between the bank and the customer and the balance owing to or by the bank in respect of that customer".[185] The bank and its agents are required to take reasonable precautions to ensure that unauthorised persons do not have access to or use of information in the registers and records prepared by the bank.[186]

The Bank Act also requires a bank to maintain and process in Canada any information or data relating to the preparation and maintenance of customer financial records, unless an exemption has been granted by the Superintendent of Financial Institutions.[187] A bank may maintain copies of the records and process data outside of Canada. However, the Superintendent may order all processing to be done in Canada, if the Superintendent is of the opinion that processing or storing records outside of Canada is

---

182 R.S.O. 1990, c. C-14.
183 *Tournier v. National Provincial and Union Bank of England* [1924] 1 K.B. 461; followed *Murano v. Bank of Montreal* (1995), O.J. Number 1451 (Ont. Gen. Div.).
184 Bank Act, S.C. 1991, c. 46, section 157(2).
185 Bank Act, R.S.C. 1991, c.46, section 238(2) (c).
186 Bank Act, S.C. 1991, c. 46, section 244.
187 Bank Act, S.C. 1991, c. 46, section 245; similar restrictions apply to provincially regulated trust companies: Loan and Trust Companies Act, R.S.O. 1990, c. L.25, section 250.

incompatible with the fulfilment of the Superintendent's responsibilities under the Act or the Superintendent is advised by the Minister of Finance that, in the opinion of the Minister, "such maintenance or further processing is not in the national interest".[188]

The Bank Act also gives the government a general power to make regulations governing the use by a bank of any information supplied by customers.[189] Most federally regulated banks have adopted the voluntary privacy code developed by the Canadian Bankers' Association in 1989. The Model Privacy Code applies the O.E.C.D. Guidelines to the collection, possession, protection, use, disclosure, verification and correction of personal information by banks in Canada.

The Model Privacy Code applies to all data that identify and relate to a specific individual, including name, address, age, identification numbers, income, assets, liabilities, credit information and payment records. Under the model code, banks may collect personal information about customers only for specified purposes. They must obtain the customer's consent for any use of personal information for purposes other than those for which it was collected. When the information is no longer required for the purpose for which it was collected, it is to be destroyed or given an anonymous form. Information may be retained in aggregated statistical files, for example. Personal information may be disclosed with the customer's consent, pursuant to legal obligations, where required to protect the bank's interests, or in exceptional cases, where a public duty requires disclosure.

Customers have the right to know whether the bank has personal information about them, to obtain access to the information, to know whether the information has been provided to others and to require the bank to correct erroneous information and to convey the corrections to others.

As a result of the widespread adoption of the C.B.A. Model Privacy Code, no privacy regulations have been adopted under the Bank Act. However, competitive pressures facing the banks and other financial institutions and the development of new electronic products and services have led to greater public concern over privacy of financial information. Concerns have also been expressed over the banks' compliance with the voluntary privacy code. The federal government is reviewing and may revise the Bank Act in 1997. Privacy is one of the matters being reviewed, but it is not known whether the Act will be amended to include mandatory privacy protection.

---

188 Bank Act, S.C. 1991, c. 46, section 245(5).
189 S.C. 1991, c. 46, section 459.

ON-LINE CONDUCT

Regulation of Electronic Communication

Regulation of Broadcasting

Broadcasting is defined in the federal Broadcasting Act[190] as "any transmis- 5-66
sions of programs, whether or not encrypted, by radio waves or other means
of telecommunication for reception by the public by means of broadcasting
receiving apparatus . . .". Prior to 1991, the definition of broadcasting was
limited to radio communication intended for direct reception by the public.
The new definition is significantly broader, capturing any means of wired or
wireless telecommunication.

The 1991 amendments to the Broadcasting Act also include a new
definition of "program" which encompasses "sounds or visual images, or a
combination of sounds and visual images that are intended to inform,
enlighten or entertain, but does not include visual images, whether or not
combined with sounds that consist predominantly of alphanumeric text".
Under the Act, a "broadcasting receiving apparatus" is any device or
combination of devices capable of being used to receive broadcasting, which
would include a computer.

The transmission of World Wide Web pages to the public in Canada
would, therefore, appear to fall within the definition of broadcasting and
would potentially be subject to regulation under the Broadcasting Act.

The Canadian Radio-Television and Telecommunications Commission
(C.R.T.C.) has a dual mandate of regulating broadcasting and telecommu-
nications in Canada and promoting Canadian culture. The C.R.T.C. re-
viewed its role in the regulation of electronic communication in its 1995
Convergence Report to the federal government which urges a policy of "fair,
effective and sustainable competition among facilities and services".[191] In an
Order in Council requesting the C.R.T.C. to report on issues respecting the
Information Highway, the Canadian government stated that:

> "Participants in the Information Highway should make equitable and
> appropriate contributions to the production and distribution of and access
> to Canadian-cultural-content products and services; and government
> should continue to have the tools and mechanisms necessary to promote
> Canadian content."[192]

---

190 S.C. 1991, c. 11, section 2(1).
191 Canadian Radio-Television and Telecommunications Commission, "Competition and
   Culture on Canada's Information Highway: Managing the Realities of Transition", *Report
   to the Minister of Canadian Heritage and the Minister of Industry*, May 1995.
192 Order in Council P.C. 1994-1105.

In its Convergence Report, the C.R.T.C. concluded that the term "broadcasting" should be interpreted broadly and that there should be a consistent regulatory approach to new computer-based services. In particular, the C.R.T.C. has stated that on-line services should be required to contribute to the government's existing Canadian cultural support objectives, possibly through mandated Canadian content or through contributions to existing program development funds. However, the C.R.T.C. has also suggested that some services may be exempted from regulation. These services might include "interactive courses offered by accredited institutions or used by medical institutions, on-line commercial multimedia services and educational multimedia materials directed to schools".

Internet service providers have argued that the nature of the World Wide Web makes Canadian content regulation both impossible and unnecessary.

The members of the Information Highway Advisory Council were divided in their views on regulation of the information highway. In its 1995 report, the Council stated that some members believed that the definition of broadcasting should be narrowed to exclude Internet and other electronic commerce services. Others concluded that the existing legislation and regulations should be interpreted broadly and that the use of the C.R.T.C.'s exemption powers should make legislative changes unnecessary.[193]

The Information Highway Advisory Council has asked the C.R.T.C. to clarify its position with respect to the prospective regulation of interactive multimedia services. In particular, it asked the C.R.T.C. to define the characteristics of services which would fall outside the existing regulatory structure. The C.R.T.C. has not yet taken any further steps to exercise its regulatory authority, however, it is expected to continue to assert jurisdiction over electronic commerce services which are directed at the public, while exercising forbearance in the regulation of such services.

Regulation of Advertising

5-67   Misleading advertising of either goods or services "by any means whatsoever" is a criminal offence under the federal Competition Act.[194] To constitute misleading advertising under the Act, there must be a material and misleading representation made to the public for the purpose of promoting, directly or indirectly, the supply or use of a product, or a business interest. The representation must also concern the price at which the products have been, were or will ordinarily be sold.[195]

Although there have been no cases on the point to date, the wording of the misleading advertising provisions would probably include electronic

---

193 *The Challenge of the Information Highway, Final Report of the Information Highway Advisory Council*, September 1995, at pp. 29 and 30.
194 R.S.C. 1985, c. C-34, section 52.
195 Davies, Ward and Beck, *Competition Law of Canada*, volume 1 (1997), section 6.02.

communications such as over the Internet. The misleading advertising provisions also deem importers responsible for the offence where it is committed outside of Canada.[196]

Because misleading advertising is a criminal offence and the Crown must prove intent to mislead, it has proven to be relatively difficult to secure a conviction under the Competition Act. It has been suggested that the provisions would be more effective if they were dealt with through the mechanism of administrative complaints to the Competition Tribunal. The Director of Investigation and Research of the Bureau of Competition Policy recently proposed the creation of a dual civil and criminal system of sanctions for misleading advertising. The majority of the cases would be dealt with under the civil provisions, while criminal sanctions would be reserved for the more flagrant ones.

Provincial consumer protection statutes also prohibit false or misleading advertising. In Ontario, for example, the Consumer Protection Act provides, "where the Registrar believes on reasonable and probable grounds that a seller or lender is making false, misleading or deceptive statements in any advertisement, circular, pamphlet or similar material, the Registrar may order the immediate cessation of the use of such material . . .".[197] These provisions would apply to advertising or solicitations made over the Internet, although it is unclear whether the jurisdiction of the Ontario Registrar is limited to communications which originate within the province or would extend to any communication which is received in Ontario.

In response to concerns about junk e-mail and advertising directed at children over the Internet, the Canadian Direct Marketing Association is reported to be updating its compulsory code of ethics to include Internet advertising.[198] The Code of Ethics and Standards of Practice is a voluntary code, adopted by the Canadian Direct Marketing Association and its members. The Code includes among other things policies for the collection, use and distribution of personal information about individuals, in an effort to ensure that consumers' privacy rights are protected.

Personal information is not to be included in lists made available for sale or rental, if there is a reasonable expectation on the part of the individual at the time the information was collected that it would be kept confidential. Members are required to delete names and other information from their lists, when requested. The proposed changes to address electronic advertising will presumably deal with such issues as the collection of personal information for the purposes of targeted advertising over the Internet.

---

196 Competition Act, R.S.C. 1985, c. C-34, section 52(2)(f) and (g).
197 Consumer Protection Act, R.S.O. 1990, c. C.31, section 38.
198 *Cyberspace Lawyer*, (1997), volume 2, number 2, at p. 29.

Tobacco Products

5-68   A federal Tobacco Act, which severely restricts advertising of tobacco products in Canada, was passed early in 1997.[199] Previous legislation that prohibited all advertising and promotion of tobacco products was declared unconstitutional by the Supreme Court of Canada in 1995, thereby allowing tobacco companies to advertise their products without restriction.[200]

The new Tobacco Act prohibits any promotion of a tobacco product or a tobacco-related brand element "except as authorised by this Act or the regulations".[201] The Act then establishes very limited circumstances where advertising is permitted. Advertising "that depicts, in whole or in part, a tobacco product, its package or a brand element of one or that evokes a tobacco product or a brand element" is generally prohibited.[202] Advertising in "a publication that is provided by mail and addressed to an adult who is identified by name" is permitted, provided that the advertising is not "life style or advertising that could be construed on reasonable grounds to be appealing to young persons".[203] The Tobacco Act also restricts tobacco sponsorship of persons, entities, activities, or permanent facilities if associated with young persons or if "associated with a way of life that includes glamour, recreation, excitement, vitality, risk or daring".[204] Section 31 of the Tobacco Act prohibits the communication of tobacco advertising or promotional material, as follows:

"(1) No person shall, on behalf of another person, with or without consideration, publish, broadcast or otherwise disseminate any promotion that is prohibited by this Part.

(2) Subsection (1) does not apply to the distribution for sale of an imported publication or the retransmission of radio or television broadcasts that originate outside Canada.

(3) No person in Canada shall, by means of a publication that is published outside Canada, a broadcast that originates outside Canada or any communication other than a publication or broadcast that originates outside Canada, promote any product the promotion of which is regulated under this Part, or disseminate promotional material that contains a tobacco product-related brand element in a way that is contrary to this Part."

---

199 Tobacco Act, S.C. 1997, c. 13; the Act received Royal Assent April 25, 1997.
200 R. J. R. MacDonald Inc. v. Canada (Attorney General) 187 N.R. 1 (S.C.C), declaring the Tobacco Products Control Act, S.C. 1988, c. 20, to be void and of no legal effect.
201 Tobacco Act, S.C. 1997, c.13, section 19.
202 Tobacco Act, S.C. 1997, c.13, section 22(1).
203 Tobacco Act, S.C. 1997, c. 13, sections 22(2) and 22(3).
204 Tobacco Act, S.C. 1997, c. 13, section 24(1) (b).

Although the exception in subsection (2) exempts foreign publications and 5-69
transmissions from the prohibitions of the Act, subsection (3) specifically
prohibits persons in Canada from using foreign media to avoid the application of the Act. This provision would include attempts by persons in Canada
to use electronic communications, such as the Internet, to bypass the
prohibitions in the Act by sending promotional materials into Canada from
outside the country.

Court Orders

Canadian courts have the power, under both criminal and Civil Law, to 5-70
prohibit the publication of information disclosed in court. Publication bans
are frequently used in pre-trial proceedings in criminal cases, to ensure that
the accused can receive fair trial, free from adverse pre-trial publicity.[205]
specifically guarantees the right to a fair trial. However, recent attempts to
impose bans in high-profile criminal cases have illustrated the difficulty of
controlling access to information available over the Internet.

The case of Karla Homolka and Paul Bernardo, an Ontario husband and
wife convicted of brutally kidnapping, sexually assaulting, torturing and killing
two teenage girls, attracted wide media attention, both within Canada and
abroad. Ms. Homolka negotiated a deal with the Crown under which she
agreed to plead guilty and testify against her husband in exchange for a
reduced sentence. At Ms. Homolka's trial in July 1993, the presiding Ontario
Court Justice imposed a temporary ban on publication of information
disclosed in court, to ensure a fair trial for Mr. Bernardo. Breach of the ban
could have resulted in a citation for contempt of court.

Many groups and individuals disagreed with the publication ban and
proceeded to publish details about the trial through the Internet. These
actions led to the issuance of a press release in December 1993 by the
Ontario Ministry of the Attorney General that urged respect for the press
ban and emphasised that the Ministry would make all efforts to enforce it.
Instead of enforcing the ban — which was proving impossible due to the use
of the Internet — the Ministry pleaded with the public to respect it. No one
was ever cited for contempt of court for the publication of trial information
over the Internet.

Hate Propaganda

Under the federal Criminal Code it is an offence to advocate genocide or incite 5-71
hatred. The Criminal Code also provides for the seizure of hate propaganda.[206]

---

205 Criminal Code, R.S.C. 1985, c. C-46, section 486; the Federal Charter of Rights and
    Freedoms, Part 1 of the Constitution Act, 1982, being schedule B of the Canada Act, 1982
    (United Kingdom), 1982, c. 11.
206 R.S.C. 1985, c. C-46, sections 318, 319, and 320.

The Canadian Human Rights Act[207] prohibits the communication of hatred through telephone lines. Regulations under the Canadian Broadcasting Act prohibit broadcasting or distribution of programming that contains abusive comments likely to expose individuals or groups to hatred or contempt.[208]

Complaints were filed in 1996 with the Canadian Human Rights Tribunal, by the City of Toronto Mayor's Committee on Community and Race Relations and a private citizen, alleging that materials posted on a World Wide Web site linked to the notorious Holocaust denier Ernst Zundel expose Jews to hatred or contempt on the basis of their race, religion and ethnic origin, contrary to the Canadian Human Rights Act.[209]

Mr. Zundel, who is a Canadian resident, and the Webmaster of the "Zundelsite", who is a resident of California, have challenged the jurisdiction of the Tribunal because the Web site is not located in Canada. They claim that Mr. Zundel is not personally involved in the publication of the material on the Web site and that there is no illegal activity occurring in Canada. A preliminary motion to prevent the Canadian Human Rights Tribunal from hearing the complaint was denied in December 1996. However, a judicial review of the jurisdictional issues was scheduled to take place in mid 1997.

CONCLUSION

5-72   The law of electronic commerce is evolving very quickly in Canada. However, there is still a long way to go before electronic commerce can be said to be completely integrated into the country's legal framework.

Early indications are positive for the proponents of electronic commerce. Laws of evidence are generally willing to accommodate electronic record-keeping, even though the courts often need help to understand that electronic records can be as reliable as paper documents. Electronic contracts and payment systems are now widely accepted, as security and reliability issues are addressed through both technical and legal means. Canada remains at the forefront of electronic commerce through its federal Public Key Infrastructure project and its involvement in international electronic commerce initiatives.

Nevertheless, many changes are still needed in specific areas of government regulation. These changes may be expected to take place quickly over the next few years. Governments across the country are striving to cut costs

207 R.S.C. 1985, c. H-6, section 13.
208 S.C. 1991, c. 11; Radio Regulations, 1986, section 3 (b); Specialty Services Regulations, 1990, section 3 (b); Television Broadcasting Regulations, 1987, section 5(b) and Pay Television Regulations, 1990, section 3(b).
209 R.S.C. 1985, c. H-6.

and are seizing on information technology as a means to do so. Public demand for more efficient services is also forcing changes in existing laws and regulations which act as impediments to electronic commerce.

Unfortunately, these changes are expected to continue to take place in an *ad hoc* manner, despite the efforts of those inside and outside government who advocate a comprehensive review and amendment of all statutes and regulations.

The pace of change in the law of electronic commerce is such that any description of the law must quickly become incomplete. Some day, perhaps, there will actually be settled law in this dynamic area. In the meantime, those involved in electronic commerce must maintain an active watch on all developments. The author hopes he has contributed in some small way to the understanding of the law of Canada in this area.

Note: The author gratefully acknowledges the assistance of Paul Brown in researching and writing this chapter.

CHAPTER 6

Denmark

Lau Normann Jørgensen
Kromann & Münter
Copenhagen, Denmark

INTRODUCTION

Achieving Information Security

Legal Regime for Electronic Communication in Denmark

Denmark has no legal regime aimed specifically at the regulation of elec- 6-1
tronic communication or commerce. Existing Danish regulation in the fields
of contract law, protection of privacy, consumer protection, etc. is of a
general nature: they will be applied in their present forms to electronic
commerce or marketing. For example, the purchase of goods by way of
electronic communication via the Internet or via EDI will be regulated by
the Promulgation Act on Purchasing in the same way as any other purchase
being made in Denmark, apart from the purchase of real property.

The Contracts Act and the Promulgation Act on Purchasing were drafted
in 1906 and 1917, respectively. They are based on general principles —
comparable to Common Law principles in Anglo-Saxon legal Systems —
rather than sector-specific legislation or provisions based on specific means
of communication. As such, the existing Acts are easily adopted and applied
by the courts in any new area of business such as that of electronic
commerce.

At present, the Danish legal community's general opinion is that it is
preferable to maintain such laws based on general principles rather than
introducing a specific "cyber law", since any such specific regulation in this
field is deemed to become obsolete within a short period of time.

Denmark is a member state of the European Union (E.U.). This obligates
it to incorporate directives adopted within the framework of the Union.
The Directives and other instruments described in chapter 2 of this book, in
the field of copyright and related matters, have been implemented within the
prescribed periods for implementation.

Confidentiality

6-2   As regards confidentiality, the Danish Private Registers Act for the protection of individuals is applicable when electronic data processing is used.

The Danish Private Registers Act, section 1 (1) states that registration comprising personal data that is compiled or stored by electronic data processing, and any systematic registration comprising private or financial data on any individual, institution, association or business enterprise or other data on any personal matter that may reasonably be demanded to be withheld from the general public may be undertaken only in accordance with the rules of Chapter 2, 2a, 2b, 2c, and 3 of the Act.

Section 1(2) defines "personal data"; such data shall be deemed to include data that are referable to identifiable individuals even if such referral presupposes knowledge of individual identification numbers, registration numbers or the like.

The Act prohibits any registration comprising personal data by means of electronic data processing unless registration is specifically permitted by the remaining provisions of the Act.

6-3   **Registrations Made by Companies** As regards companies, section 3(1) of the Danish Private Registers Act states that any business enterprise, trader, institution, association or the like shall be entitled to registration as referred to in section 1 of the Act only to the extent that such registration forms part of the normal operations of any business enterprise in the particular line of business in question.

This provision entitles private copanies to register their employees and customers, but only in so far as so-called sensitive information, *i.e.*, information regarding race and religion,[1] is not registered or derivable from the information registered.

These provisions are highly relevant to trade on the Internet. They prohibit the registration by firms trading on the Internet of sensitive or irrelevant information about their customers. But the provisions are usually applicable only when the company in question is situated in Denmark.

The Act also contains specific rules on electronic registers. Section 6(1) reads:

> "In registers where electronic data processing is used (E.D.P. registers), any data that because of obsolescence or otherwise has lost its relevancy for the purpose of the register in question shall be expunged."

6-4   Also, companies must operate with a checking system to ensure that no incorrect or misleading data is registered, and they must implement safe guards to ensure that no data is wrongfully used or brought to the knowledge of any unauthorised party.[2]

---

1 Private Registers Act, section 3(2).
2 Private Registers Act, section 6(3) and (4).

In relation to Internet trade, the growing practice of placing "cookies" on a customer's disk or other ways of using so-called data mining to identify and trace the customer's purchasing habits and to direct marketing efforts at him will in most instances be contrary to the Act because the Act's formalities are not met. As the Act does not apply to offerors of goods or services that are situated outside Denmark, this is eventually likely to place enterprises situated in Denmark at a competitive disadvantage. This presupposing that the proper authorities will at some point become aware of the said practices and begin to enforce the provisions of the Act.

Section 21(1) of the Danish Private Registers Act prescribes that data that are not permitted to be registered in Denmark[3] may not be collected for the purpose of registration outside Denmark. Under Danish law, the exportation of collected data that are not legally registered in Denmark is thus prohibited.

As regards information other than the information covered by the prohibition, the company in question may not collect the data with a view to having the data registered outside Denmark unless it submits an application and obtains an authorisation for this purpose from the Data Surveillance Authority (D.S.A.).[4]

Section 21(2) further prescribes that the handing over for electronic data processing outside Denmark of data as referred to in section 3(2), *i.e.*, personal data which can be registered only under particular circumstances, is also subject to application to and authorisation by the D.S.A.

The objective of section 21 is to ensure that Danish legislation concerning protection of personal data falls under sectio 21, the principal rule is that data may not be passed on if the data originate from a private register and contain information of a purely private nature.[5] The exprotation of the collected data itself is not directly coverd by the provision. Tather, the Act applies at an earlier stage in such a way that rules regarding collection of data may hinder the exprtation of the material.[6]

Section 21 of the Act only regulates the collection of data regarding persons residing in Denmark. Registers that are established outside Denmark are not affected by the Act even if they contain information regarding Danish citizens.

Scope of the Private Registers Act As with the general provisions, the rules   6-5
are only applicable when the company in question is situated in Denmark. However, section 7 states that the provisions of article 6 will apply also where a register is processed electronically outside Denmark, but on behalf of a company that is situated in Denmark.

---

3 Private Registers Act, section 3(2) as described above.
4 Private Registers Act, section 21(1).
5 Private Registers Act, section 4(1).
6 Karstoft, Elektronisk dokumentudveksling retlige aspekter, 1994, at p. 132.

This limited geographical scope of the provisions of the Danish Private Registers Act complicates the application of the Act when dealing with trade on the Internet, since most companies offering products to customers in Denmark will be situated abroad.

Although the Act prohibits collection and registration of information that is unnecessary or irrelevant for the company in question, ensuring that the Act is not violated will still be an almost impossible task. This is because there are hardly any ways to control the collection and registration of material on the Internet.

The D.S.A.'s possibility to control collection and exportation, as laid out in section 21, is therefore in reality very limited not only when dealing with the Internet but also on other electronic media.

Like other European Union member states, Denmark has ratified the Convention for the protection of individuals with regard to automatic processing of personal data.

Legal Effect of Electronic Signatures

6-6   The validity of a document in Denmark may be ensured by the insertion of an encrypted electronic signature.

An electronic signature is likely to be recognised as evidence by the courts. The Act on Administration of Justice in no way hinders the parties from submitting the necessary proof regarding electronic signatures.

At present, the Danish Parliament is processing a proposal for an Act on Electronic Signatures. It will force public bodies to recognise documents which are submitted and signed in electronic form and it will provide in general terms that wherever Danish legislation requires that something be "in writing" or "signed", these conditions are met when documents are presented in electronic form and signed electronically. The Danish Act is likely to form the basis for a UNCITRAL Model Act on electronic signatures.

It is highly unlikely that Denmark will ever introduce legislation restricting the possibilities of encrypting messages.

ELECTRONIC TRANSACTIONS

Creation of Contracts Electronically

6-7   Electronic transactions on the Internet are governed by the existing Danish legislation. In Denmark a valid agreement can have any form. It is thus possible to have a perfectly valid and enforceable oral agreement.[7] This is

---

7 By contrast, in Russia, a written agreement is required for validity.

important when dealing with electronic transactions on the Internet, since it leaves no doubt as to whether two parties can enter into an agreement using only their computers.

The Contracts Act states in section 1, as regards the formation of contracts, that ". . . the rules of sections 2–9 will apply insofar as not otherwise indicated by the offer or the acceptance or by trade usage or other custom". This implies that it is possible for the parties involved to choose another set of rules to govern their legal relations.

Therefore, it is possible for the parties to agree that an acceptance will be valid only if it is made via the Internet. In the American Bar Association's Model Agreement on EDI, point 1.1., the following rule is found:

> "Any transmission of data which is not a document shall have no force or effect between the parties unless justifiably relied on by the receiving party."

"Document" means a document that has been sent in an EDI format, and   6-8 the rule therefore demands that the parties as a main rule are using only EDI, when they wish to enter into an agreement.

Danish parties may agree that such a rule shall be applied in their internal relationship, and as mentioned above they can choose the Internet as the only proper medium.[8]

The remaining part of this section will deal solely with the Danish Contracts Act. It will describe the rules that are to be applied if the parties have not agreed otherwise.

In general, the presence of a declaration of will is required. That is to say, a statement or equivalent act, whereby the maker thereof and/or other persons incur a legal obligation.[9] Note that, in Danish and Scandinavian law, a declaration of will, once communicated to the addressee, is generally binding. This is unlike Common Law contract law where acceptance would be required for a declaration of will to be binding.

Offer and Acceptance On-line

When an offer is made electronically and a person responds to and accepts   6-9 the offer, the offeror is bound to fulfil the offer. Section 1 of the Contracts Act reads, "a person making an offer or an acceptance shall be bound thereby".

The Act uses, among other terms, the term "reach". In section 3(1), it is stated that where "no time-limit for acceptance is stipulated, acceptance must reach the offeror before expiry of the period which he on making the offer could estimate as being required".

The term "reach" will usually mean that the recipient under normal circumstances has had the opportunity to acquaint himself with the contents

---

8 Einersen, *Elektronisk Aftale-og bevisret*, 1992, at pp. 39–40, note 22.
9 Ussing, Aftaler, 1950, at p. 3.

of the communication. It shall not imply that he has in fact done so or taken cognisance of the contents, or that these had come to his knowledge.

In addition, sections 2(1), 4(1) and 7 address situations where it is decisive for the conclusion of the actual agreement that the message has reached one of the parties. If the acceptance does not reach the offeror within the given time limit, it shall be deemed a new offer.[10]

Regarding commerce on the Internet, it may be concluded that an acceptance has reached the offeror when the message from the person replying with an acceptance is available for the person making the offer. The matter is so far unresolved in Danish law.[11]

Another legal issue arises when the potential receiver of the message deliberately prevents himself from receiving the message, *e.g.*, by turning off his fax machine.[12] However, if we are dealing with electronic mail, then the declaration of will must have reached the receiver when it is available in the receiver's mailbox.

The time it takes to decrypt a message and have the sender's identity verified should also be added. This may not take long, but it can be crucial when deciding whether an acceptance is within the given time limit.[13]

Danish law places heavy emphasis on whether a message has "reached" the receiver. In addition, the Convention for the International Sale of Goods (C.I.S.G.) contains the term in article 15:

> "An offer becomes effective when it reaches the offeree. An offer, even if it is irrevocable, may be withdrawn if the withdrawal reaches the offeree before or at the same time as the offer."

If a firm has its Internet address on its writing paper, then it must be possible for the relevant contractual partners to forward messages to that address in the same way as they may use ordinary mail. The Contracts Act will apply.[14]

Section 7 of the Contracts Act states, "offers or replies which are withdrawn shall lapse if notification of the withdrawal reaches the other party before or at the same time as he has taken cognisance of the offer or the reply".

The main problem as regards section 7 is whether the person receiving offers or replies has taken cognisance of these when they reach the computer or when the person has actually read the messages. When dealing with electronic commerce the chief rule under Danish law is, in this author's opinion, that the person receiving the message in question must have read it before he has taken cognisance of it.

---

10 Contracts Act, section 4.
11 Bryde Andersen, *Lærebog i edb-ret*, 1st Edition, 1991, at p. 405 and Einersen, *Elektronisk aftale- og bevisret*, 1992, at pp. 52 *et seq.*
12 Einersen, *Elektronisk aftale- og bevisret*, 1992, at p. 54.
13 Einersen: *Elektronisk aftale- og bevisret*, 1992, at pp. 56–57.
14 Karstoft, *Elektronisk dokumentudveksling retlige aspekter*, 1994, at p. 114.

However, the situation where there is no need for a person to actually read the message can easily be imagined. For example, where an individual orders flowers, the order is automatically read by the computer in the flower shop receiving the order and thus processed without any delay. The moment of reception, *i.e.*, when the message "reached" the recipient, is thus equivalent to the moment where cognisance is taken.[15]

Mistakes in On-line Contracts

When parties are dealing with each other using the Internet to communicate, **6-10** it may happen that errors occur underway. If two Danish parties are trading on the Internet, the relevant provision, as regards mistakes, will be section 32 of the Contracts Act, which in subsection 1 states:

> "A person who has made a declaration of will which as a result of an error in writing or other mistake on his part has acquired a content other than that intended shall not be bound by the content of the declaration where the person to whom the declaration has been made realised or should have realised that there was a mistake."

Section 32(1) is applicable in situations where the sender of a message has **6-11** declared something different from what he intended to declare. He will be bound by the declaration if the person receiving the declaration acts in good faith. The burden of proof is placed on the sender.

Subsection 1 is also applicable to situations where the technology placing the order is defective, even where the sender or persons working for the sender have not committed any errors. Danish literature on the subject has chosen to place the risk on the sender when electronic media are utilised, since the sender is the person closest to bearing such risk.[16] Section 32(2) of the Contracts Act states:

> "Where a declaration of will has been made which is transmitted by telegraph or conveyed by word of mouth by a messenger, and becomes altered due to a mistake on the part of the telegraph authority or due to incorrect repetition by the messenger, the person making the declaration shall not be bound by the declaration in the form in which it arrived, even though the person to whom the declaration has been made acts in good faith. If the person making the declaration wishes to claim that the declaration is not binding on him, he must, however, give notification thereof without unjustified delay once the declaration comes to his knowledge. If he omits to do so, he shall be bound by the declaration in the form in which it arrived provided the person to whom the declaration has been made acted in good faith."

---

15 Einersen, *Elektronisk aftale- og bevisret*, 1992, at p. 63.
16 Karstoft, *Elektronisk dokument-udveksling retlige aspekter*, 1994, at p. 122.

6-12   If an error occurs during the transmission of a declaration of will, then the question arises whether that situation falls within section 32(2). Section 32(2) deals only explicitly with situations where the declaration is transmitted by telegraph or conveyed by a messenger.[17]

Subsection 2 is not applicable where the Internet is used, since both situations described in subsection 2 are situations where the media forwarding the declaration must do something more than just transmitting the declaration. This means that the messenger must convey and the telegraph operator must receive the declaration and transcribe it for the telegraph. In both situations, the sender of the declaration has no direct influence on the mistakes being made.

This author believes that section 32(2) is not applicable to EDI or commerce via the Internet, but the matter is disputed in Danish law.[18]

Impact of Impostors or Persons without Authority

6-13   Where there is an impact of impostors or other persons without authority, *i.e.*, a situation where the declaration is false, the "sender" will only be obliged in accordance with the false declaration if he has increased the risk through negligence.[19]

On-line Payments

E-Cash

6-14   The use of E-cash entails several advantages. First, E-cash is more convenient and flexible than traditional money and both consumers and businesses can use it as a way to trade on the Internet. Banks that issue E-cash could find it more cost-efficient than handling checks and the paper records that accompany traditional money. Furthermore, E-cash offers privacy to the consumers as compared to the use of ordinary credit cards. However, the disadvantages that are debated in Denmark are the following:

- The uncontrolled growth of E-cash systems could undermine bank and government-controlled money systems, which could result in confusing and inefficient competing systems;
- The social consequences could be that consumers with Personel Computers would have access to acquire E-cash, while those without, many of them being low-income consumers, would not;
- There is an increasing risk of money laundering and tax evasion;

---

17 Karstoft, *Elektronisk dokumentudveksling retlige aspekter*, 1994, at pp. 122 *et seq.*
18 Kofod Olsen, U 1992B402, Lynge Andersen and Jørgen Nørgaard at U 1993B335.
19 Karstoft, *Elektronisk dokumentudveksling retlige aspekter*, 1994, at p. 123. A person does not show negligence by using the Internet.

- Counterfeiters could also create their own personal mints of E-cash that would be indistinguishable from real money and, if the systems are not secure enough, hackers could enter the E-cash systems and simply steal the E-cash.

One of the most recent electronic payment standards is the Secure Electronic   **6-15**
Transaction (SET). VISA and MasterCard have developed it with the participation of Microsoft and others, and it is presently the subject of a pilot test in Denmark. The goal is to protect payment card purchases on any type of open network.

It has been claimed by some Danish authors that the fact that there is a risk if the consumers are paying with credit cards using SET, does not as such affect the consumers in a negative way according to the Danish Act on Credit Cards. It may also be mentioned that the Internet credit card system, First Virtual Holding, lets the consumers use credit cards on the Internet accordingly without fear that their account numbers will be misappropriated. The consumer registers with First Virtual by phone and receives identification numbers in exchange for his credit card number and thereafter he simply supplies his identification number to the merchant.

Yet another solution to provide for safe electronic commerce on the Internet could be to earmark the E-cash, so that the E-cash could only be used for what it has been programmed for.

Problems Regarding Taxation

However, irrespective of whether SET or First Virtual Holding becomes the   **6-16**
future standard, legal problems still remain. In Denmark, the taxation authorities foresee problems regarding the collection of taxes and duties. It is possible, in practice, to trade on the Internet without paying value added tax. The problems are primarily related to computer programs, consultancy services and the like, which can be sent from one country to another by the mere use of the telephone system, and to goods that may be sent by ordinary mail, *e.g.*, music CDs.

Neither the taxation authorities nor the Danish government has so far presented a solution to these issues. Recently, the Ministry of Taxation has appointed a committee to look into the problems and estimate the amount of money that presently is not taxed.

Danish Credit Card Act

Some Danish authors claim[20] that consumers do not assume any risk if they   **6-17**
are paying with their credit cards on the Internet. The argument is as follows.

The Internet is an open network and therefore there is a certain risk. Unauthorised persons could gather the information regarding the credit card

20 Martin von Haller Grønbæk and Kasper Heine.

and use the information to their own advantage. An even larger risk may be that the vendor's employees abuse the information, so that the buyer will be held responsible for purchases which he, himself, has never made.

According to the Credit Card Act, the cardholder is not responsible for unauthorised use, *i.e.*, use made by persons not allowed by the cardholder so long as the personal code has not been used. In other cases, the holder only bears a limited responsibility for unauthorised use.[21] The responsibility in the latter case is limited to an amount of D.K.K. 1,200 (approximately U.S. $200) provided that the cardholder has not acted with gross negligence and that he has not supplied other persons with information regarding the credit card.

Thus, under Danish law, the credit cardholder will not be held responsible for unauthorised use of the credit card on the Internet.

Analogously, if an employee at a petrol station takes note of the information on a customer's credit card while the customer is purchasing goods and he afterwards uses the credit card information to purchase goods on the Internet, the customer never need pay for the purchases made by the employee.[22]

The risk of unauthorised use will thus fall on the issuer of the credit card. From a consumer's point of view, there are hardly any risks.

The Credit Card Act is also applicable when purchases are made outside Denmark. The decisive factor is whether a Danish issuer issues the credit card.

Danish credit card issuers are not allowed to offer their customers the possibility to pay with credit cards on the Internet. The Danish Financial Institutions Payment Service (P.B.S.) will not clear the transactions made on Danish credit cards without the signature of the cardholder. However, it may be difficult for P.B.S. to maintain its point of view in the light of the globalisation of credit card transactions. Today, it is thus possible to use international credit cards in commerce on the Internet when in Denmark. The clearing simply occurs outside Denmark.

The Credit Card Act also applies to payment systems where no card is issued but where consumers can buy their goods at vendors on the Internet who are considering the purchase as made in cash when the buyer draws on a credit set by the operator of the system.

Concerning security when using a card-less payment system, there is a difference as regards commerce on the Internet compared to the ordinary credit card system. The person using a credit card does not need to identify himself while the person using the card-less system must use a code or password.

---

21 Credit Card Act, sections 21 and 22.
22 Heine and von Haller Grønbæk, 1996, *Internetworld*, at p. 18.

The Credit Card Act states that the code or password that is used should be personal and secret.[23] The user of the system and thereby the holder of the code or password has a limited responsibility since he will only be held responsible for an amount up to D.K.K. 1,200 if his code is used by an unauthorised person.

However, this author believes that section 26(e) will apply only when the payment system offered is sufficiently secure. If this is not the case, then the operator of the system will be held solely liable for the economic loss. For example, there are on-line payment systems where no encryption as regards the code is used. The code is thus mailed on the Internet when used for purchases. With respect to such set-ups, it is likely that it will be held in Denmark that the operator is fully liable for any loss that a consumer who has used the system as prescribed may suffer.

Danish Act on Savings Firms and Issuers of Prepaid Credit Cards

Recently, the Danish Parliament adopted the Act on Savings Firms and **6-18** Issuers of Prepaid Credit Cards. The main purpose of the Act is to obtain control over issuers of smart cards, which are used as electronic cash. While the Credit Card Act mainly protects consumers, the new Act is first and foremost aimed at protecting small enterprises which sooner or later will be forced to accept E-cash as payment.

An interesting element in the new Act is that it contains provisions that distinguish between the issuers of prepaid credit cards and firms that establish electronic systems without cards. The issuers of smart cards are met with strict economic conditions prior to establishment,[24] while prepaid payment systems such as e-cash are not covered by the same provisions, but are only met with minor economic conditions.[25] This distinction appears to be unfounded, since the risk by using prepaid payment systems without cards is large compared to prepaid credit cards.

Marketing on the Internet

Danish Marketing Practices Act

The rules governing advertising in Denmark are to be found in the Marketing **6-19** Practices Act. According to section 1(1), the Act applies to private business activities and to similar activities undertaken by public bodies. These activities must be carried out in accordance with proper marketing practices. The Act does not define what is meant by proper marketing practices, but this general clause is supplemented by specific provisions regarding misleading advertising, the prohibition of collateral gifts, discount stamps, prize

23 Credit Card Act, section 26(e).
24 Act on Savings Firms and Issuers of Prepaid Credit Cards, section 8.
25 Act on Savings Firms and Issuers of Prepaid Credit Cards, section 4.

lotteries, and a maximisation of the number of articles for sale per customer as well as the protection of business marks and other business designations and technical drawings.[26]

Violation of the specific provisions of the Act constitutes a criminal offence and the conduct may be enjoined.

The Consumer Ombudsman in Denmark has a supervisory and regulatory function. He supervises observance of the Marketing Practices Act. The Ombudsman has so far issued several guidelines in various areas. The Consumer Ombudsman has taken the view that a Web site where goods are offered, irrespective of its country of origin, falls within his jurisdiction. He has addressed multinational companies such as Kellogg's and Walt Disney, and notified these companies that various games available from their Web sites which are aimed primarily at children are contrary to the Marketing Practices Act and the I.C.C. Guidelines on Interactive Marketing Communications of June 11, 1996. The Consumer Ombudsman argues that the marketing practices of companies such as Kellogg's and Walt Disney raise serious privacy concerns and that there is an increased risk of impulse purchases made by children and young people without their parents' consent. So far, the Consumer Ombudsman has not initiated litigation against the said companies and the jurisdictional aspects of the matter are not yet resolved.

One of the most important provisions in the Marketing Practices Act is section 2(1). It makes it an offence "to make use of any false, misleading, or unreasonably incomplete indication or statement likely to affect the demand for or supply of goods, real or personal property, and work and services".

This rule will, as well as other rules laid down in the Marketing Practices Act, apply when goods are being marketed on the Internet, but the territorial scope of the provisions should also be taken into account. The Act is applicable when the advertising enterprise is situated in Denmark, but not when the advertising is aimed solely at consumers outside Denmark. The Act is applicable when foreign companies operate in the Danish market, and where the advertising made outside Denmark is aimed at the Danish market.[27]

The behaviour of Danish companies on foreign markets will not be covered by the Marketing Practices Act, but in a situation where a given conduct in Denmark is aimed at a Danish competitor on a foreign market, the Act may be applicable.

However, when dealing with commerce on the Internet, in most instances potential receivers will be persons situated in and outside Denmark.

---

26 Dahl, Melchior, and Tamm (eds.), *Danish Law in a European Perspective*, 1st Edition 1996, at p. 426.
27 Palle Bo Madsen, *Markedsret*, 2nd Edition, 1993, at p. 161.

If a Danish company is advertising on the Internet for its products, the Act may be applicable even though the advertisement is in English and primarily aimed at consumers situated outside Denmark. That would be the case with respect to, *e.g.*, Lego's Web site.

Furthermore, the marketing of goods from other European Union Member States cannot be limited in a way that conflicts with the European Community Treaty. In 1984, the European Union adopted the Directive[28] on Misleading Advertising which did not lead to any new legislation in Denmark since the Marketing Practices Act already satisfied the requirements laid down in the Directive.[29]

Trade Secrets and the Marketing Practices Act

Section 9(1) of the Danish Marketing Practices Act states: 6-20

"No person employed by, co-operating with, or performing work or providing services for a commercial enterprise shall, in an improper manner, acquire or attempt to acquire knowledge or possession of the trade secrets of such enterprise."

This provision protects the competitive position of an enterprise, which is   6-21
based, in large measure, on the sum of the knowledge of the production and the sale situation within the enterprise. The protection is granted even though the knowledge is passed on (*e.g.*, to a licensee). The enterprise in question decides for itself what is to be considered a trade secret.[30]

The territorial scope of the Act has been described in the preceding section.

Danish Penal Code and Protection of Trade Secrets

Section 263 of the Penal Code deals with the secrecy of the mail and   6-22
electronic espionage. According to subsection 1:

". . . any person who (1) deprives someone of or opens his letter, telegram or other sealed communication or note or acquaints himself with its contents . . ., shall be liable for a fine, simple detention or imprisonment."

Furthermore, it follows from section 263(2) that any person who unduly   6-23
obtains access to another person's computer-based information or programs designated for use in connection with a computer shall be liable to a fine, simple detention or imprisonment.

In cases involving hacker crimes, Danish scholars have debated whether subsection 1 or subsection 2 should be applied. Thus far, general consensus

---

28 O.J. 1984 L 250.
29 Palle Bo Madsen, *Markedsret*, 2nd Edition, 1993, at pp. 161–162.
30 Eckhardt-Hansen, *Worldwide Trade Secrets Law*, Vol. 2nd Edition by Maclaren, at pp. B7-7 *et seq.*

has been achieved on subsection 2, where the transmitted information is stored or somehow registered in the recipient's computer.[31]

The penalty may be increased for the intruder gaining access to information, if the acts mentioned in subsections (1) and (2) are committed with the intruder's intention to procure or make himself acquainted with information regarding conditions of business or manufacture, documents or records, or in other particularly aggravating circumstances (industrial espionage).[32]

If an unauthorised person adds or erases data during transmission, the unauthorised person will also be held liable according to section 263(2).[33]

Section 279a of the Danish Penal Code deals with computer fraud. A natural person who adds or erases information or programs with fraudulent intent will be held liable according to this provision. The same will apply where a person illegally tries to affect the results of data processing.

Furthermore, it does not matter how the information or programs are stored or whether the information is transmitted.[34] Section 279a will be applied in preference to section 263 where the unlawful act is committed with the purpose of gain.

ELECTRONIC INFORMATION RIGHTS

Property Rights in Electronic Information

Copyright

6-24   **Introduction** The 1961 Danish Copyright Act granted copyright to any person producing a literary or artistic work. A proposal for a new copyright act including various provisions on digital copying was put forward on February 9, 1994, but did not pass prior to the parliamentary elections of September 1994. Therefore, the proposal had to be re-introduced and the Act finally entered into force on July 1, 1995, including the provisions regarding digital copying.[35]

It should be mentioned that the Copyright Act contained provisions regarding copying and the amendment of computer programs already in 1989 and, prior to 1989, computer programs were protected by the Act even though there was no specific provision to that effect.[36] Provisions were implemented in 1992 in accordance with a European Community

---

31 Karstoft, *Elektronisk dokumentudveksling retlige aspekter*, 1994, at pp. 153–154.
32 Penal Code, section 263(3).
33 Karstoft, *Elektronisk dokumentudveksling retlige aspekter*, 1994, at p. 163.
34 Eckhardt-Hansen in *Worldwide Trade Secrets Law*, 2nd edition, Maclaren, p. B7-11.
35 For a short general introduction to Danish intellectual property rights, see Dahl, Melchior, and Tamm (eds.), *Danish Law in a European Perspective*, 1st edition 1996, at pp. 469–481.
36 Schønning, *Ophavsretsloven med kommentarer*, 1st edition, 1995, at p. 109.

Council Directive.[37] The Danish regulation is thus in accordance with the regulation of other European Union Member States.

The Copyright Act bears a strong resemblance to the copyright acts of the other Nordic countries. This is the result of close co-operation among Denmark, Norway, Sweden, Iceland, and Finland during the preparation of the national copyright acts.

In general, all works that meet the originality requirement developed in case law are protected for up to 70 years after the death of the author. Prior to the amendment of the bill in 1995, works were only protected for 50 years, but the bill was amended due to a European Community Council Directive.[38]

The Copyright Act is, in accordance with international practice, based on the principle that a person producing a literary work has a copyright therein regardless of the nature or the appearance of the work. The Act also grants particular protection to catalogues, databases and similar products in which a large number of items of information have been compiled, but which do not meet the originality requirement. This protection lasts for 10 years after the publication of the work.[39] European Community directives on the area are implemented in Danish legislation.

It follows from section 1(1) of the Copyright Act that the person who produces a literary work thereby acquires copyright in the literary work. The term literary work is of interest as a computer program is considered a literary work.[40] The Danish Copyright Act does not define the term "literary work", but the definition developed by the courts is in accordance with the United States Copyright Act,[41] which defines the term as being:

". . . works other than audio-visual works, expressed in words, numbers, or other verbal or numerical symbols or indicia, regardless of the nature of the material objects, such as books, manuscripts, phonograph records, film, tapes disks, or cards."[42]

The presentation can thus be either fictional or non-fictional.[43]

6-25

Computer Programs Computer programs are considered literary work.[44] 6-26
Apart from the originality requirement, which is described below, certain

---

37 European Community Council Directive of May 14, 1991, on the Legal Protection of Computer Programs, O.J. 1991, L 122/42.
38 Council Directive, O.J. 1993 L 290/9.
39 See the Chapter on Denmark in: Hugenholtz and Visser, *Information Management* (European Commission) with the subheading "Copyright on electronic delivery services and multimedia products" and "Copyright problems of electronic document delivery".
40 Copyright Act, section 1(3).
41 17 U.S.C. 101.
42 Bryde Andersen, *Lærebog i EDB-ret*, at p. 185.
43 Schønning, *Ophavsretsloven med kommentarer*, 1st Edition 1995, at pp. 78–79.
44 Copyright Act, section 1(3).

conditions will have to be taken into consideration when evaluating whether a computer program is protected. A computer program is defined under Danish law as a set of instructions or information, arranged in any form or on any medium, with the object to directly or indirectly bring a database to state, perform or achieve a certain function, task or a certain result. In this context, it may be mentioned that computer and video games are also protected. The same is probably the case as regards virtual reality systems.[45]

Preparatory design material is considered a computer program provided that the work is of such character that it can be foreseen that the work will actually result in a computer program. Neither ideas nor principles that underlie any element of a computer program, including those that underlie its interfaces, are protected.

Databases are protected according to section 5 of the Copyright Act, which grants protection for collections of works, or section 71, which grants protection for catalogues. If a database is considered a catalogue, the protection will only last for 10 years. However, if the database is updated, the protection will continue for 10 years after the last update.[46]

6-27 **Originality Requirement** The work also must fulfil the originality requirement. It must be the result of an independent creative and intellectual contribution from the author.

The Council Directive on the legal protection of computer programs contains a provision in article 1(3), according to which a computer program will be protected if it is original in the sense that it is the author's own intellectual creation. No other criteria shall be applied to determine its eligibility for protection. This provision was implemented in the Copyright Act in 1992 and it lays down the conditions under which a computer program will meet the originality requirement.

The Copyright Act protects the work only if humans create the work. Thus, literary works that are created by using only computers, so-called computer generated work, will not enjoy protection under the Act.[47] The rights of the copyright owner are described in section 2(1), which states:

"Within the limitations specified in this Act, the copyright shall carry with it the exclusive right of exploiting a work by producing copies thereof and by making it available to the public, whether in the original or in an amended form, in translation, adaptation into another literary or artistic form or into another technique."

---

45 Schønning, *Ophavsretsloven med kommentarer*, 1st edition 1995, at p. 110.
46 Bryde Andersen, *Lærebog i edb-ret*, 1991, at p. 160 and Schønning, *Ophavsretsloven med kommentarer*, 1st edition, 1995, at pp. 171–172 and 537.
47 Schønning: *Ophavsretsloven med kommentarer*, 1st edition, 1995, at pp. 86–87.

Single copies may be produced for private use,[48] but that right does not **6-28** apply as regards digital-to-digital copying.[49]

It follows from the Copyright Act, section 36 that the person who has acquired the right to use a computer program is entitled to make one back-up. The person entitled to use a computer program may also observe, study or test the functioning of the program to determine the ideas and principles that underlie any element of the program if the person does so while performing any authorised acts of loading, displaying, running, transmitting or storing the program. Section 36 is in accordance with article 5 of the European Community Council Directive on the legal protection of computer programs. Decompilation is allowed under certain circumstances.[50] The provision is in accordance with article 6 of the Directive.

It has been claimed that Danish companies are violating the provisions of the Copyright Act by copying information to their central computers from the Internet and thereby giving the employees of the company access to such information through an internal network. Formally, such use is not in accordance with the provision regarding private digital copying mentioned above, but the issue is of limited practical importance.[51]

The problem in this respect is that a digital storing takes place already when material protected by copyright rules enters the computer. To prevent all Danish surfers from being considered as violating the copyright rules, it is necessary to interpret a licence from all owners of Web sites on the Internet to depart from the prohibition laid out in the Copyright Act. In so far as such Web sites are marketing instruments, this does not present a problem.

Trade marks and Domain Names

The Trade Mark Act The 1991 Trade Mark Act is based on joint prepara- **6-29** tory works of committees in the Nordic countries and European Community Directive 89/104 of December 21, 1988. The Act deals with registered as well as unregistered trade marks and, in all essentials, provides identical protection for both groups.

A trade mark may be established through written application forwarded to the Danish Patent Office or it can be obtained via the European Trademark Office in Alicante. A trade mark right may also be established by mere use.[52]

As regards the Internet, it is of particular relevance that the Danish Trademark Act permits references to a trade mark of another party while selling spare

---

48 Copyright Act, section 12(1).
49 Copyright Act, section 12(2).
50 Copyright Act, section 37.
51 Von Haller Grønbæk, Politiken, September 5, 1996.
52 Koktvedgaard, in: Dahl, Melchior, and Tamm (eds.), *Danish Law in a European Perspective*, 1st edition 1996, at pp. 477 *et seq*; Trade Mark Act, sections 3 and 12.

parts and accessories or the like thereof, provided that the reference does not convey the impression that the spare parts originate from the holder of the trade mark.[53]

According to section 26, a trade mark is valid for 10 years from the day on which the application is submitted and it may be renewed if it still fulfils the condition of sufficient distinctiveness.

Licence rights to trade marks may also be established and they may be recorded in the Danish Registry of Trade marks. Compulsory licences cannot be issued under Danish law.

6-30 **Domain Names and Trade marks in Denmark** Until January 15, 1997, the hostmaster of the DK-domain maintained very restrictive rules with respect to registration. These rules implied that only one domain would be granted per legal person, and evidence of a certain connection to the domain name would be required. For that reason "domain grabbing" and "name piracy" as it is known under the COM-domain was unheard of under the DK-domain.

From January 15, 1997 these rules were changed to the effect that anyone could register anything, and this has already resulted in litigation concerning trade mark protection which in some instances extends to second-level domain names.

With respect to attractive generic names such as "casino.dk" or "sex.dk", Internet Access Providers who had advance knowledge of the new rules took these names on 15 or 16 January, 1997, generally. While this is highly unethical — even in a business which at present is characterised by its high relative number of fast-moving golddiggers — it is unlikely that the Danish courts will find that the registrants are not entitled to these names.

With respect to traditional name piracy which has occurred ("mars.dk" and "toms.dk" were settled out of court), Danish courts will undoubtedly find that domain names are not merely addresses but have the characteristics of significant enterprise marks, and find for a trade mark owner in a dispute with a registrant who has registered a name with the intention of selling it to the proper proprietor.

At present, a matter involving the right to the name "beologic.com" is before the Municipal Court of Copenhagen. It is likely to be held that the registration of that domain corresponding to the company name of Beologic A/S, whose parent company has registered "beologic" as a trade mark in Denmark and the United States, is contrary to section 4 of the Danish Trade mark Act.

With respect to genuine name conflicts, it is likely that the courts will take a different approach. For example, the association of AutoCAD Users (Brugere) in the Construction Industry (*Byggebranchen*) has registered "abb.dk", ABB being the abbreviation generally used for the association.

---

53 Trade Mark Act, section 5.

ABB — Asea Brown Boveri — in Denmark has initiated litigation against the association. At present, it appears that the matter will be settled out of court, although it is generally assumed that the courts would find for the association. Likewise, the principle of "first come, first serve" will apply where alike trade marks are registered in different classes. For example, "Tulip" is the name of both a foodstuffs company and a computer company the domain name "tulip.dk" will undoubtedly belong to whichever company is first to register.

Not only the discussion concerning domain names in connection with trade marks gives rise to problems. There is no doubt that the use of a name or mark on the Internet that may be confused with a trade mark will constitute an infringement of the Trade Mark Act. The enforcement of the Act against the illegal use at present remains unresolved in Danish law.

A possible solution may be to apply principles similar to those established in the judgment delivered by a United States court in *Playboy Enterprises, Inc.* v. *Chuckleberry Publishing, Inc.*[54] There, the court instructed the infringing party to refrain from selling subscriptions in the United States, where the infringed trade mark was registered. Of course, the principles of that judgment do not solve all issues relating to the transnational characteristics of the Internet, but the judgment did provide a reasonable solution to the issue at hand.

The question whether Danish authorities should grant trade mark protection to certain names and marks relating to the Internet has recently been raised. The Danish Patent Office granted an Internet Access Provider, Uni-C, trade mark registration of the word "Web hotel". Other companies were outraged and claimed that the name "Web hotel" does not fulfil the conditions for registration as a trade mark, as it is a generic term, comparable to, *e.g.*, "telephone", at least to users of the Internet. Uni-C later waived the trade mark, and the company would probably have lost if the matter had been brought before the courts.

Patents

In 1978, Denmark acceded to the Patent Co-operation Treaty and as from January 1, 1990, to the European Patent Convention. Hence, patent protection can be obtained via the European Patent Office in Munich as well as from the Danish Patent Office in Copenhagen. Danish patents may be maintained for up to 20 years from the day on which the patent application was submitted.[55]   **6-31**

Regarding licences, the Patent Act includes provisions on compulsory licensing which may be granted particularly because of failure to exercise a patent.[56]

---

54 939 F. Supp. 1032 (S.D.N.Y. 1996).
55 Patent Act, section 40; see also Koktvedgaard, in: Dahl, Melchior, and Tamm (eds.), *Danish Law in a European Perspective*, 1st Edition 1996, at p. 474.
56 Patent Act, sections 43 *et seq.*

Patents may, of course, also be transferred wholly or in part by one's free will to do so. Exclusive licensing agreements may be contrary to the Competition Act, but the administrative practice of the Danish Competition Council is quite lenient in this field. It is considered of far greater importance that Danish licensing agreements may infringe the European Union competition rules, in particular article 85 of the European Community Treaty.

Computer programs are not patentable as such according to the Patent Act, section 1(2) which is in accordance with article 52, section 2(c) of the European Patent Convention.

It is possible to have some computer-related inventions protected, but such protection is granted only where the invention has a technical effect.[57] This practice is in accordance with the practice of the European Patent Office.

If patent protection for a computer program is granted it will, of course, be possible for the holder of the patent to prevent unauthorised persons who have gained access to information regarding the program from reproduction of the same program.[58]

ON-LINE CONDUCT

Regulation of Electronic Communication

6-32   As was described in the beginning of this chapter, electronic communication relating to trade, for example, on the Internet is primarily regulated by existing, generally applicable Danish legislation. A specific "cyber law" has not developed in Denmark so far. Thus, if it — according to Danish law — is prohibited to distribute, e.g., pornography or racist propaganda, it will also be prohibited to distribute such information on the Internet.

A number of leading Danish scholars believe that the Internet is a special forum, and that problems that have not been foreseen by the legislators can easily arise. Legal issues that arise will have to be solved by the courts, which will have to acquire knowledge as regards the media in question.

One legal issue that has recently been raised concerns the Act on Media Liability and the applicability of that Act to news communicated via the Internet. The traditional media, i.e., television, newspapers, etc., are all covered by the Act. The Act applies also to news communicated by databases where a notification to the Danish Press Board is made.[59]

However, as regards databases, besides the fact that notification is required, the Act only applies to situations where there is a periodical communication of

---

57 Håkon Schmidt, *Teknologi og immaterialret*, 1989, at pp. 268–315, especially pp. 283–284.
58 Patent Act, section 3.
59 Act on Media Liability, sections 1(3) and 8(1).

news, and not where the user is connecting to a database, which is updated as soon as a new communication is entered. The area of media liability may therefore be one of the few fields in which a revision of the existing legislation is called for.

Territorial Limits of Jurisdiction

The territorial limits of jurisdiction vary according to particular Danish   6-33 Acts, which are decribed above.

In instances where data transmission is used between two parties entering into a contract within the European Union, *e.g.*, via the Internet, the choice of law is not, on the face of it, a difficult one.[60] Denmark has, as well as other European Union countries, ratified the European Union Convention on the choice of law as regards contractual obligations.

In Denmark, applying the individualised method, whereby a balancing of the individual contract's connection with the countries involved is made, solves issues regarding choice of law in contracts. The law of the country to which the contract's connection is the strongest will apply. The Convention, inclusive of its presumptions to be applied when determining to which country a contract's connection is the strongest, has been implemented in Danish law, the most important of these presumptions being that a contract has the strongest connection to the country where the party rendering the "characteristic performance", *i.e.*, normally the person presenting something other than money, is resident.

The Convention on the International Sale of Goods (C.I.S.G.) will apply to agreements concerning international sales of movable property that fall within the scope of the C.I.S.G. Denmark has also acceded to the European Union Convention on Jurisdiction and the Enforcement of Judgments.

---

60 Karstoft, *Elektronisk dokumentudveksling retlige aspekter*, 1994, at pp. 139 *et seq.*

CHAPTER 7

England

Hugh Flemington
Bevan Ashford
Exeter, England

LEGAL REGIME RELATIVE TO ELECTRONIC COMMUNICATIONS

Like the arena it seeks to regulate, the legal regime relating to electronic **7-1** communication in England is in an embryonic state. English law has always prided itself on its ability to adapt and evolve to meet changing circumstances. The regulation of electronic communication and commerce provides a fresh challenge but one which English law will meet, albeit in conjunction with the rules of other jurisdictions. Many rules under current English law are applicable, either directly or by analogy to the environment of electronic communication. Such regulation spans both the civil and criminal law fields. English law already has specific laws related to information technology, such as those pertaining to telecommunications, computer misuse, data protection, and intellectual property (in so far as it covers items such as software).

Other areas of the law have been extended by piecemeal legislative amendments. For example, the Obscene Publications Act 1959 was amended by Schedule 9 to the Criminal Justice and Public Order Act 1994, so that publication is now defined to include the transmission of electronically stored data which on resolution into user viewable form is obscene.

More and more United Kingdom businesses are embracing on-line communication, especially by using the Internet, if only for basic operations such as e-mail facilities. Domain names are being registered, Web sites set up. Yet it has been estimated that up to 70 per cent of such firms have still to seek legal advice over their Internet operations. Commercially orientated packages are now being established such as "Mondex" (the joint venture between Midland Bank and National Westminster Bank) and Barclays Bank's "Purchase On-line" scheme, the Information Society Initiatives' "Programme for Business", the establishment of "IT Input Output Centres", the proposed ventures of Waterstones and Dillons into on-line trading, the SETS trading service scheduled for October 1997 by the London Stock Exchange, and the Inland Revenues introduction of their Electronic Lodgement Service. These are mirroring larger moves, such as the European Community (E.C.) Recommendation to adopt minimum consumer protection standards for card payments, telephone banking, and electronic cash.

Therefore, far from the on-line environment being anarchic, there are many English laws that affect the medium of electronic communication now and will intensify their impact as its general use as a business medium increases.

Furthermore, basic contractual principles will apply to electronic communication without the need for any tinkering with the rules currently in place.

However, as there are practical problems in regulating this area, such as enforcement among users across various jurisdictions. What may be needed are international regimes or conventions rather than a jurisdiction by jurisdiction approach. For example, the Securities and Investments Board has been urging the International Organisation of Securities Commissions to address the regulatory issues pertaining to operations in the on-line environment in relation to the conduct of investment business; the Board has suggested that recognised "kite-marks" be adopted and attached to Web sites, incorporating standard disclaimers and warnings.

Legal regimes are also only part of a wider picture. Some hope that self-regulation by those at the higher echelons of the relevant information technology infrastructure (e.g., the Internet service providers) will be a key part in the overall solution. The Internet Watch Foundation was established in September 1996 as such a self-regulatory body by the major I.S.P.s; it has introduced hotlines through which users can report findings of illegal material and is working towards a ratings or certificate system for web sites. Much will depend on developments in the technology that have yet to appear.

Finally, it should also be acknowledged that electronic communication also encompasses internal networks (Intranets) within organisations and not just outward on-line communication. The best example of this is the internal e-mail system within the office whereby employees talk and send documents to one another; such systems may raise issues of harassment, defamation and confidentiality just as external e-mail can. The potential risks that a company runs in having e-mail systems was recently demonstrated in the defamation action brought by Western Provident Association against Norwich Union in July 1997; it ended with Norwich Union having to issue a public apology to Western Provident Association and pay it £450,000 in damages and costs. The essential ingredients for on-line libels are the same as for any other libel under English law. Western Provident Association found out that Norwich Union was circulating untrue rumours about it over its internal e-mail system; they applied for and obtained an order that the offending e-mails be preserved and hard copies handed over (unless protected by privilege, e-mail may be discoverable documents). Internal and external e-mail systems may, therefore, be caught and employees should consider whether they will be vicariously liable for the e-mails of their employees. The Defamation Act 1996 has introduced a defence which employers and I.S.P.s may attempt to rely on, i.e., that it took reasonable care (as "publisher") in relation to the publication and did not know, or had no reason to believe, that what it did caused or contributed to the publication, but the scope of this has yet to be tested in an English court.

The laws applicable to on-line commerce and communication are continually to develop with fresh approaches from governmental and other independent organisations, together with case law revision of the court room level. What follows is a discussion of the main issues, and it should not be applied to particular cases; anyone thinking of venturing into the on-line medium to should take specific legal advice.

CONFIDENTIALITY

In electronic communication, there may be both legal and practical ways of attempting to protect the confidentiality of information transmitted. Practical ways include such things as encryption devices and electronic signatures. Legal methods focus on confidentiality laws and the affixing of suitable warning notices to the data concerned.   7-2

Under English law, confidential information is not subject to a statutory scheme of protection. There are Common Law mechanisms (the English law of confidence) and some criminal penalties.

The law of confidence is rooted in basic contractual principles (assuming there is a confidentiality agreement between the parties) and in the law of equity. Thus, protection of such information is on the basis of actual or deemed agreements to keep the information secret; unauthorised use or disclosure may then give rise to a remedy. Examples of information capable of protection include trade secrets, business know-how, software and hardware research and developments, details of computer systems known by programmers and possibly users, marketing strategies, client lists, contracts, personal information and ideas.

In the on-line environment, the law of confidence may offer a potential form of protection to ideas that in their present form cannot be protected by the laws of copyright or patent. For example, copyright protects the expression of an idea whereas the law of confidence may protect the idea itself.

Under English law, a breach of confidence is actionable per se and does not require an established contractual relationship between the parties concerned.[1] Megarry J. laid down the basic requirements for a breach of confidence action in *Coco v. A. N. Clark (Engineers) Limited*,[2] as follows:

- The information must be confidential;

1 *Prince Albert* v. *Strange* 1849 1 Mac & G 25.
2 1969 R.P.C. 41.

- It must have been imparted in circumstances importing an obligation of confidence; and
- There must be an unauthorised use of the information to the detriment of the party communicating it.[3]

7-3   In general, when considering a confidentiality agreement there are a number of issues that should be addressed:

- The parties should be accurately identified;
- Either the agreement will be executed as a deed or consideration will be needed;
- The effective date of the agreement may need to be retrospective, as opposed to the date when it is signed;
- The duration of the obligations should be specified, alongside termination provisions and whether any such duties subsist post-termination and, if so, for how long;[4]
- The subject matter of the confidential information should be defined including pure information (and the media on which it is stored), as well as any physical "information";
- All disclosed information (from whatever source) should be covered by the agreement, although certain information may be expressly exempted from the confidentiality umbrella;
- Express provisions for non-disclosure (except in limited circumstances, such as to employees) and controls on the use of the confidential information must be included;
- General disclaimers as to accuracy of data supplied;
- A statement that no licence to use the information is to be implied (except for those specific rights expressly granted);
- Other obligations may also be imposed on the recipient, including taking particular security measures (*e.g.*, password protected storage or encryption), the return of all information and copies (however stored) and possibly reporting any analysis or findings in relation to the data concerned;
- Other conditions that may need to be placed on the disclosing party include a duty to supply updated information (when available) and that the data should not be given to other third parties while the agreement is in force; and
- The usual boilerplate clauses as to notices, jurisdiction, and governing law should be included.

7-4   Remedies open to an aggrieved party include an injunction, or if the information has already been passed on, an award of damages and possibly a

---

3 This equitable action is discussed further in the section on Trade Secrets.
4 Such time periods may be subject to competition laws.

limited injunction preventing future dissemination. An injunction will only be effective once the third party in question knows the information is confidential. An order may also be made to the effect that the defendant should account for any profits he has made because of the unauthorised disclosure.

Other remedies that may be available lie outside of the law of confidence. They include actions for infringement of copyright or proceedings under the Data Protection Act 1984, which regulates the storage of personal data held electronically.

There also is the potential for criminal liability under the Computer Misuse Act 1990, but much will depend on the precise circumstances. For example, where the Internet is used to publish passwords to allow unauthorised entry into a computer system, the relevant Internet service provider (ISP) itself may be prosecuted under the act. Such ISPs might also face charges of incitement to commit an offence under the Computer Misuse Act 1990; to establish incitement it must be proved that the defendant knew or believed that the person incited had the necessary *mens rea* to commit the offence. As the *mens rea* for an offence under section 1 of the Computer Misuse Act 1990 is merely that the defendant intends to secure access to a programme and knows that such access is unauthorised, this would probably not be too difficult to establish. The service provider might be charged with aiding, abetting, counselling or procuring the commission of an offence. There have been cases where improperly obtained credit card numbers have been placed on bulletin boards thus facilitating the making of fraudulent purchases using the numbers. If the host knew or ought to have known that this was going on, it may have liability as a secondary participant in the crime that is then committed.

Under English law, there is no legislation specifically directed to the dishonest appropriation of pure information, as it is not property capable of being stolen. In *Oxford* v. *Moss*,[5] a university student broke into the Examination Committee's premises and copied the exam papers. He did not remove the original papers. The court held that this was not theft as such confidential information was intangible property and there was no intention to permanently deprive the owner. In *Thompson*,[6] a bank clerk manipulated the bank's computer records so that he debited five customers' accounts and correspondingly credited his own account. Counsel for the prosecution argued that the defendant had stolen a chose in action. However, the Court of Appeal took the view that all that had happened was a case of forgery, that a chose in action did not exist, and that there was therefore no property capable of being stolen. The court felt that this would have been a true reflection of the law before the advent of computers and was equally applicable to the modern day equivalent of the quill pen and accounting ledgers.

---

5 1978 68 Cr. App. Rep. 183.
6 1984 3 All E.R. 565 and 1984 1 W.L.R. 962.

Therefore, specific legislation covering such misappropriation of confidential information may be required as electronic communication becomes widespread, involving the transfer of what can be significant commercial assets. At present, electronic communication is not inherently secure, unless possibly it is encrypted, a view shared by the English Data Protection Registrar. Using such means to transmit confidential information could endanger the secrecy needed for legal protection under the civil laws. Clear notices that the information is confidential, that it should not be disclosed or copied, and is only intended for the named recipient should be attached to each message. This will help establish the equitable obligation of confidence (in the absence of any express contractual duty) in the event of deliberate or accidental interception by a third party. Without such markings it would be probable under English law that an innocent third party recipient would not be bound by any duty of confidentiality.[7]

An employee may internally access confidential information electronically (and then distribute it via an e-mail to anywhere in the world). Obtaining confidential information from an employer without express authorisation may be grounds for summary dismissal. In *Denco Ltd.* v. *Joinson*,[8] the employee used another's password to access another part of the system, which he was not entitled to do. The court held that the employer was entitled to dismiss the employee summarily for this. In *Faccenda Chicken Ltd.* v. *Fowler*,[9] the Court of Appeal laid down some guidelines as to breach of confidentiality actions in the context of the employer/employee relationship, including:

- If there is a contract of employment the employee's obligations must be determined by it;
- If there are no express terms certain obligations will be implied; and
- While a person is an employee they are bound by a basic duty of good faith.

7-5   The scope of this duty might vary from case to case; for example, there would be a narrower obligation on an ex-employee. In general, the duty of confidence owed by ex-employees will be less than that owed by current employees to their employer; and in determining whether an ex-employee was bound by such an obligation the court should consider, *inter alia*, the nature of the employment and the information, whether the employer stressed the confidential nature of the information and whether the information could be easily isolated from other material the employee was free to use.

---

7 See *Malone* v. *Metropolitan Police Commissioner*, 1979 Ch. 344.
8 1991 I.R.L.R. 63.
9 1986 1 All E.R. 617.

ELECTRONIC SIGNATURES

In English law, contracts may be purely oral, in writing, made by deed or be 7-6
implied from the conduct of the parties. Even a party denying the existence
of a contract may be estopped from doing so and may be ordered to perform
its obligations, although this is rare. However, certain types of contract must
be in a particular form and failure to comply with the relevant formalities
may lead to the contract being legally unenforceable. For example, some
contracts must be by deed and, as such, must make it clear on their face that
they are intended to be a deed, and they must be validly executed (*e.g.*,
signed in the presence of a witness and delivered).

Do electronic signatures meet the legal criteria begin with, "Signing"
under English law includes "making one's mark s quite conceivable that
a digital representation of someone's signatu d be compliance with this
relevant contractual formality. Similarly, acts that must be in writing
may probably also be in an electro rm rather than a hard copy.
"Writing" is defined as including "t , printing, lithography, photography and other modes of represen reproducing words in a visible form,
and expressions referring to ng are construed accordingly".[10] The
"visible form" requireme d seem to be capable of including digital
text displayed on a scr

The "Tested Tel e of *Standard Bank London Ltd.* v. *Bank of Tokyo
Ltd., Südwestd Landesbank Girozentrale* v. *Bank of Tokyo Ltd. and
Another*[11] of use in analysing the potential legality of electronic
signatur ree letters of credit were seemingly issued by the Bank of
Tok the signatures were in fact forged. The beneficiary was the
Bank London. The signatures were confirmed by "tested telex",
arently sent by the Bank of Tokyo The fraudsters either sent the telexes
themselves or fooled the Bank of Tokyo staff into sending them. The
Standard Bank London acted in reliance of the telexes and made the relevant
loans. It assigned the proceeds of the second and third letters of credit to
Südwestdeutsche Landesbank Girozentrale In turn, Südwestdeutsche Landesbank Girozentrale asked for tested telexes, which it duly received.

The Standard Bank London sued the Bank of Tokyo for a declaration that
it was entitled to present conforming documents under the first letter of credit,
the Bank of Tokyo being estopped from denying their authenticity. It sued in
the alternate for negligent misrepresentation. Südwestdeutsche Landesbank
Girozentrale sued the Bank of Tokyo for damages for negligent misrepresentation arguing that no funds would have been released to the Standard Bank
London if it had not been for the telexes.

The main issue was the extent to which the Standard Bank London and
Südwestdeutsche Landesbank Girozentrale could rely on the tested telexes

10 Interpretation Act 1978, schedule 1.
11 *The Times*, April 15, 1995.

coming from the Bank of Tokyo as being the statements of the Bank of Tokyo. A "tested telex" is a telex which contains codes or test-keys which are secret as between sender and recipient, and the test-key was thus described as the electronic signature of the bank sending the message. The court presumed that banking systems in general rely on such telexes with total confidence (on the assumption that they avoid arguments in relation to authority).

On the facts, the court found that no one at the Standard Bank London was put on notice of the fraud in the underlying transaction or that fraudsters had produced the telexes. Therefore, the Standard Bank London was entitled to rely on the telexes and present its conforming documents under the first letter of credit. The court also held that the Bank of Tokyo owed a duty of care to Südwestdeutsche Landesbank Girozentrale, having been specifically asked for the telexes by Südwestdeutsche Landesbank Girozentrale and the telexes could not have been sent without negligence on the Bank of Tokyo's part.

It appears that where a system of well-established reliance on electronic signatures is in place, the courts will recognise this and place a relatively light burden on the recipient to investigate the authenticity of the electronic signature. "Wilful blindness", which was indicated as being want of probity rather than mere negligence, would fail to meet this standard. The more usual the circumstances and the clearer the representation appears to be, the less the duty to inquire should be (and the less likely there are to be circumstances which would put anyone on inquiry). The sender carries most of the risk and consequently has the incentive to take every precaution against misuse, fraud, or loss of the relevant test-key.

This potential misuse of an electronic signature lies at the heart of the matter. The above decision is fine as long as we feel the burden has been posited on the right party and to the correct extent. This case was within a purely commercial context. It is hoped that in a consumer context the burden would be on the commercial entity rather than the consumer. The former is better placed to meet the practical implications. However, lost test-keys may prove to be more common where consumers are involved; indeed, it is akin to the lost credit card, where the consumer must notify its card company as soon as possible to remain only with a minimal liability of approximately £50.

Contractual documents have always carried an element of risk, for example, forgery of a signature or tampering with the content of a signed document. Signatures are rarely compared against specimens to confirm authenticity and there is no absolute guarantee that any ink signature can be verified by forensic science. That is why historically the law of contract has attempted to minimise the risks by certain safety procedures, such as the witnessing of a signature.

Under English law, a person's signature may be scanned in and affixed to an electronic document as a mark of that person's consent to the particular contract on the screen. Some systems allow a person to do this by taking a specimen signature, scanning it in and analysing it; subsequent signatures are then compared to the blueprint version to see if they fall within the correct statistical parameters. Authenticity may be expressed as a percentage and the risk is on the recipient to decide whether the percentage confirms authenticity to its satisfaction. Other methods of electronic signature use pure mathematical formulae and codes to mark the document.

The sender will hold a private key, the code of which may be deciphered and confirmed by a public key that it can give to the world at large. Much hinges on the ability of the sender to keep his private key confidential and, like the credit card analogy, who should bear the risk if the sender's key falls into the hands of a third party? Should contracts so signed in its name bind it? In addition, since the private key may need to be stored somewhere (*e.g.*, a smartcard), are the manufacturers of the storage facility liable if it proves insecure? Much will depend on the contractual relations between the parties.

In June 1996, the United Kingdom government announced plans to encourage the development of professional encryption providers to aid the competitiveness of United Kingdom companies within the context of the Global Information Infrastructure (GII). The proposals seek to meet the growing demands to safeguard the integrity and confidentiality of information sent electronically over the public telecommunications networks. The government proposes to license Trusted Third Parties (TTPs) to provide such encryption services to the public, which will encompass digital signature, time stamping of electronic documents, data integrity and retrieval, key management, and the arbitration of claims regarding the origin, receipt, delivery and submission of electronic documents.

However, a balance must be struck between commercial or personal confidentiality and the ability of law enforcement agencies to fight crime; hence, the government proposes that such agencies have access to this type of information.[12]

The government has acknowledged that as in the GII, trust is the linchpin of global electronic trading. The TTPs will be government licensed. The licensing criteria may include fiduciary requirements (*e.g.*, appropriate liability cover), competence of employees and adherence to quality management standards.

It is envisaged that TTPs should be global if true electronic commerce is to be established; to this end, the government will be liaising with other governments both within the European Union and outside it for the introduction of international standards in this area. It has also acknowledged that other more mundane matters will need to be finalised, such as the application of export controls to on-line commerce.

In the United Kingdom, on-line contracting is just starting to impact on the public at large. However, a significant factor that currently prevents

---

12 Potentially similar in procedure to those that already exist for warranted interception under the Interception of Communications Act 1985.

many businesses from using on-line communication is the issue of security. Electronic signatures are one part of this issue. The concept is not a new one. Many United Kingdom citizens use PIN numbers everyday with ATM cards. These are a basic form of electronic signature.

CREATION OF CONTRACTS ELECTRONICALLY

Offer and Acceptance On-line

7-7   Electronic commerce may involve the exchange of contracts via e-mail or Web site interactivity. Developments such as Java are likely to serve to increase Web popularity. Historically, electronically stored information has been supplied between businesses under the auspices of Electronic Data Interchange (EDI). EDI usually uses agreed-form on-line contracts, underpinned by a conventional paper based contract between the parties, dedicated automatic lines and is usually between commercial concerns as opposed to consumer clients. Electronic contracts may be used to deliver physical goods, services, or digitised products.

Under English law, the four main requirements for a legal contract are offer, acceptance, consideration, and the intention to create legal relations. The terms must be certain (although some terms may be determined by the courts under legislative provisions or implied into a contract per se). An offer should be distinguished from a mere invitation to treat, which is more like an advertisement. The offeror must intend to create a legal relationship and this will be judged objectively (unless the advertisement indicates otherwise). The offeree's unconditional acceptance means that it cannot produce its own terms as a valid form of acceptance; traditionally, this has lead to the "battle of the forms", which may yet occur in on-line commerce. To maintain an element of control, sellers ought to attempt to construe any on-line commerce they may venture into on an invitation-to-treat basis (like a shop window or shelf), whereby they are inviting potential buyers to make offers to actually purchase the goods or services (which the seller may then accept or reject).

The time when a contract is made under English law is either immediately when the offeror receives notification of the offeree's acceptance (e.g., when using instantaneous communications mechanisms such as telephone or telex links) or when the offeree actually posts his acceptance (the English Postal Rule). However, a conventional postal system is where the case of time lag may be most acute. Electronic commerce is meant to be instantaneous, but it is possible for a time delay to occur and problems may arise if, during such temporal gap, the offeror may have instead contracted with a third party.

How applicable either of these traditional rules of acceptance are to electronic communications is debatable. A distinction may be drawn between on-line commerce utilising Web sites (where links between servers and end users are instantaneous) and that by way of e-mail (where delays are very likely). Parties will know at once if one server cannot talk to another, but they may not know if an e-mail has either been sent or received. A practical solution is for the relevant parties to stipulate how acceptance is to be communicated and to impose time deadlines, for example, as to when an offer lapses. This also minimises risks of disputes over whether certain conduct indicates acceptance. Historically, English law in this area has developed in response to new delivery systems, the on-line environment being the latest such mechanism. In the case of *Brinkibon Ltd.* v. *Stahag Stahl und Stalhwarenhandelsgesellschaft G.m.b.H.*,[13] Lord Wilberforce stated that "no universal rule can cover all such cases" and "they must be resolved by reference to the intention of the parties, by sound business practice and in some cases by a judgment where the risks should lie". Given these sentiments, it is submitted that much will depend on the outcome of future cases when and if disputes are litigated.

When contracting electronically, parties should be aware of various factors other than issues of offer and acceptance. These will include what terms are to be incorporated, making sure the contract is in the correct legal form, having terms identifying the parties, delivery, method of acceptance and revocation, apportionment of risk and insurance, passing of title, payment, any relevant geographical limitations, exclusion of liability, notice, jurisdiction and governing law. Parties contracting under English law will be subject to relevant statutory requirements under legislation such as the Consumer Credit Act 1974, the Unfair Contract Terms Act 1977, the Consumer Protection Act 1987, and the Unfair Terms in Consumer Contracts Regulations 1994, the Trade Description Act 1968, the Misrepresentation Act 1967, and various guidelines and advertising codes.

Mistakes in On-line Contracts

Mistake under English law may make a contract void, following which the   7-8
parties will be excused from their obligations. Property transferred under the supposed contract may be recovered and no right to damages may arise. Mistake may be unilateral or bilateral.

Mistake on the part of both parties must be fundamental, going to the heart of the contract, for example, as to the existence of the subject matter of the contract[14] or as to the possibility of performing the contract.

Impossibility of performance may attract the attention of special statutory rules if it is in relation to goods of a specific nature that have perished. "Perished" has been defined as a "good" which has been "so changed as to

---

13 1983 2 A.C. 34.
14 See *Associated Japanese Bank (International) Limited* v. *Credit du Nord S.A.* 1988 3 All E.R. 902.

become an unmerchantable thing which no buyer would buy and no honest seller would sell".[15] Conceivably this might include digitised products that have been damaged by a virus. Where the specific goods have perished without the seller knowing when the contract is made, that contract will be void.[16] Where such goods perish before risk passes to the buyer, without fault on anyone's part, the agreement is avoided. Practically speaking, a wide ranging *force majeure* clause will go a long way to helping with such difficulties.

Mistake on the part of just one party will generally not affect the validity of the contract. For example, mistakes as to quality or value rarely succeed in rendering the contract void. However, the agreement will be open to challenge if the mistake was due to the conduct of the other party or where such a party is simply aware that the other person is contracting on mistaken terms. If one party has induced the mistake, the other may have an action for misrepresentation as well as breach of contract.

If the parties are at complete cross-purposes so that it is impossible to agree what the terms are, then the purported contract will be void.

Impact of Impostors or Persons without Authority

7-9   As has been seen in the *Bank of Tokyo* case, tested telexes were issued, directly or indirectly, by impostors but, as long as the recipient had not been put on notice of any fraud, the burden effectively fell onto the bank to ensure that this practice did not occur.

With the use of e-mails, an employee can bind its employer under the basic principles of agency. The test that the courts will apply is whether the employer has held out the employee as having authority to contract on the employer's behalf. The existence of such ostensible authority really turns on the facts of each case. Employers should therefore consider implementing an e-mail user policy to insert in their staff manuals and handbooks. The potential for employees to expose their employers to substantial damages claims has been highlighted by the recent *Norwich Union* case (discussed above).

If someone makes a false statement of fact as to who they are or whom they represent, this may amount to a misrepresentation that induced the other party to contract. The contract is then voidable and may be rescinded. The mere failure to disclose relevant information does not necessarily equate to a misrepresentation unless the contract is one of utmost good faith (such as insurance contracts or partnership agreements). Such a false statement made during negotiations may be seen as a term of the contract (*e.g.*, that a party has authority to contract) or of a separate collateral contract and will consequently give rise to an action for breach of contract as well as misrepresentation.

---

15 *Asfar & Co. v. Blundell* 1896 1 Q.B. 123.
16 Sale of Goods Act 1979, section 6.

Electronic fund transfers

Payment mechanisms for use in the brave new world of electronic commerce   7-10
are constantly developing across the globe. The United Kingdom is no exception.
For example, there has been the increasing deployment of "Mondex" pilot
schemes, an electronic cash joint venture between Midland Bank and National Westminster Bank across England. This is a smart-card-based system
on which is stored electronic money, able to be replenished by a special
terminal. The authenticity of the card is tested by the digital signal it emits
when used.

Electronic fund transfers at the point of sale have been in use in the
United Kingdom since the late 1980s. The buyer instructs its bank to make
payment to the retailer; this instruction is sent electronically through a
terminal in the retailer's shop and this generally means immediate settlement
of the payment obligation. Such terminals involve "swipe cards", which have
particular details encoded on them to allow authentication although, in
some systems, the buyer will sign a receipt slip or enter a PIN.

The current major drawback with electronic fund transfer as a payment mechanism for electronic commerce is the risk of the electronic
payment instruction being intercepted by fraudsters. Hence, new breeds of
electronic cash systems are now being developed. Some use basic electronic
fund transfer principles, while others are a purer form of electronic cash.

The type based on traditional electronic fund transfer principles uses, for
example, the Internet to carry electronic instructions initiating transfers in
conventional bank accounts. Dedicated terminals in the retailer's shop are
therefore no longer required. Essentially, once the consumer has put money
into a bank account, he may then send a payment message to the retailer
accompanied by possible confirmation from the bank. The retailer submits
the payment instruction back to the customer's bank, and the transfer is
initiated. This method operates on a closed system basis — the instructions
that are passing between the parties may only, in theory at least, be used by
the parties themselves.

The "pure cash" systems are closer to the real cash in our wallets than
electronic fund transfer mechanics. A good example in the United Kingdom
is the Mondex system, which enables cash transactions to be effected
electronically via telephone booths, shops and even on public transport
systems. Essentially the customer is credited with so many units of electronic
cash on his card having deposited so much physical money into his bank
account. When he spends the electronic cash, his bank is instructed to
transfer a corresponding amount of their electronic units into a central
clearing house; the retailer makes a separate request to this clearing house
for payment of its bill, firstly by receiving so many units of electronic cash
and secondly by converting the same into hard currency.

By separating the instruction of the customer (to his bank to pay cash
into the clearing house) from that of the retailer (to take cash out of the

clearing house to settle the bill), the retailer can transfer the benefit of these units on to a third party, such as a supplier or an employee. In a sense, units and rights to payment rather than hard currency change hands.

Electronic cash is suited to an electronic commerce environment for many reasons: it is flexible; it has lower transactional costs; the risk of fraud is limited to the value of the transferred units; it can be paid out in various currencies across the globe; and it can be confidential. Low base costs make it suitable for both very small and large payments. Audit trails may be minimal, depending on each system set-up and the organisers' objectives.

A risk of fraud remains. Under the Bills of Exchange Act 1882, hard currency (*i.e.*, notes) have been defined as "negotiable instruments" (instruments in writing), so it is doubtful that electronic cash units would be regarded *prima facie* as negotiable instruments. The advantage of a negotiable instrument is that a third party who acquires it for value and in good faith acquires good title irrespective of any prior defect in title pertaining to it. Electronic cash could conceivably become viewed as such an instrument through "mercantile usage" if such is "notorious, general, certain and reasonable". The more widespread and recognised such systems become, the more likely they are to be viewed as dealing in negotiable instruments. Whether many retailers will want to run the risk of being thwarted by a defect in title "up the chain" has yet to be seen.

Forged electronic cash has not appeared yet in the United Kingdom (although supermarket loyalty cards have recently been the targets for professional fraudsters). It may be that it is undetectable. If it is not, but is only detectable when a person comes to redeem it for hard currency, then they will most likely be the ones who bear the loss. How banks would deal with counterfeited electronic cash is not certain, especially if the clearing-house pools are flooded to such an extent that they know something is wrong, but that it is so perfect they cannot tell it apart from the real electronic cash. To be secure, codes used to create or tag the units must be unbreakable.

Under English law, a party can recover special damages for loss because of late or non-payment.[17] The test is whether it can be inferred from the facts known to the parties as at the date of the contract that the loss resulting from the delay or non-payment was within the parties' reasonable contemplation. Much may depend on the terms of the contract.

Those who issue electronic cash or other money-related services are likely to require authorisation under the Banking Act 1987. Failure to obtain this would be a criminal offence. Companies can get away with issuing prepaid phone cards or luncheon vouchers because under section 5(2) of the Act "money paid on terms which are referable to the provision of property or services" is not caught by the Act (provided such money is repayable only in the event that the relevant property or services are not provided). The need

---

17 *Wadsworth v. Lydall* 1981 1 W.L.R. 598.

for authorisation is embodied in section 3(1) of the Act and focuses on the definitions of "deposit"[18] and "deposit-taking business".[19] Foreign bodies issuing electronic cash must be careful that they do not issue the cash so that they are regarded as accepting deposits within the United Kingdom (or their agent is) as they may then require authorisation under the Act. Such authorised organisations must conduct their business in a prudent manner, which includes ensuring that sufficient capital and liquidity levels are maintained. The European Monetary Institute is pressing for only authorised credit institutions within the European Union be allowed to handle electronic purses.

A further consideration for providers of electronic funds are the Money Laundering Regulations 1993, whereby such organisations must adopt systems to clearly identify their customers, monitor transactions, and be able to report suspicious activities, all of which needs careful record-keeping, analysis, and audit trails.

On-line banking services are beginning to be launched by High Street lenders, including the Royal Bank of Scotland, the Nationwide, and First Direct.

The other potential drawbacks of electronic cash are the potential for it to be used for money laundering and tax evasion as the audit trail such systems can leave may be minimal.

CREDIT CARD PAYMENTS ON-LINE

The main advantage of this form of on-line payment is its popularity, not just in England but worldwide, with international operators such as Visa or MasterCard. The basic card set-up involves a tripartite relationship between the customer, the retailer, and the card company. When using credit cards on-line, the customer will supply the retailer with its card number and expiry date and authorise the latter to contact the customer's instruction to the card company to settle the debt. The card company will then seek to settle the debt. The card company will seek reimbursement from the customer on varying terms dependent on whether it is a credit, debit, or charge card. **7-11**

The card system provides the retailer with an instantaneous guarantee that either the card company or its local bank representative will meet payment. This generally helps the international acceptance of this form of payment, which is obviously important in the on-line environment.

Customers appreciate the card system as it gives them time to meet the debt themselves (albeit with interest added). It may also provide them with

18 Banking Act 1987, section 5(1).
19 Banking Act 1987, section 6.

the practical protection under section 75 of the Consumer Credit Act 1974; it makes the card company (in certain limited circumstances) liable for misrepresentations or breaches of contract on the part of the retailer. This protection is limited to individual consumers (*i.e.*, not corporate or company cards) and only for goods of a value falling between £100 and £30,000. It is not settled in English law whether this protection extends to retailers who are operating outside the United Kingdom. Many major card issuers have, in conjunction with the Director General of Fair Trading, treated such purchases as transactions covered by the section 75 protection, but on a voluntary and *ex gratia* basis.

The credit card payment mechanism has its disadvantages; for example, the card company runs the risk that the customer will default and transaction damages will be levied regardless of the level of the payment in question; some people are simply not eligible for credit cards due to poor credit ratings, and some retailers may find the costs involved in installing a card system prohibitive (although this is unlikely given their current widespread use). Card companies' extensive records mean audit trails and less privacy for the customers.

However, the security risks involved in on-line credit card payments are the main concern. The customer supplies all the details necessary for a fraudster to obtain and use the account to an almost unlimited extent whereas under an electronic cash system, the risk may be minimised to the "units" being transferred at any given time. Encryption is obviously one solution to minimise the risks (but this does not preclude fraud by a rogue retailer) or for the details given to the retailer to be so encrypted that only the card company at the other end of the chain can unscramble them. It is hoped that the SET proposal will go some way toward addressing such security concerns (see text, below).

Where fraud does occur, under English law, much will depend on the provisions of the relevant contracts between card company, retailer, and customer as to where any resulting loss lies. In *Orr* v. *Union Bank of Scotland*,[20] it was established that a bank cannot debit a customer's account following presentation of a forged cheque (although it may have been undetectable). This ought to apply to fraudulent card instructions. The *Orr* principle is limited by certain exceptions where the fraudster has apparent authority or where the forgery has been aided by the negligence of the customer. The principle in *Orr* may be varied contractually, but this may be unlikely given the hurdles imposed by the Unfair Contract Terms Act 1977, the Unfair Terms in Consumer Contract Regulations 1994,[21] the Consumer Credit Act 1974 and the Good Banking Code of Practice.

Retailers must ensure that they comply with the authentication procedures stipulated in their contracts with the card companies to minimise their

20 1854 Macq H.L. (as 512).
21 S.I. 3159.

exposure in receiving fraudulent instructions. Customers must similarly make sure they comply with all the requirements placed on them in their contract with the card company; for example, the card company may stipulate that any on-line payment instructions and card details must be encrypted. Obviously, this is subject to the widespread, low cost availability of the relevant technology.

USE OF ELECTRONIC CHECKS

The use of various electronic security mechanisms is covered elsewhere in   7-12
this chapter. The basic methods of electronic security are use of electronic signatures and encryption. One of the major hurdles to the development of international electronic commerce is the issue of security. The technology may be able to resolve the problem only so far; it will then be up to legal systems to allocate risks.

No doubt many of the issues above will be resolved by the advent of systems such as SET — the proposed Secure Electronic Transactions standard which has been promoted by companies including Microsoft, Visa, MasterCard and Netscape. The aim of such ventures is to provide a single standard of security for on-line commerce. For example, the SET Protocol envisages customers opening accounts with institutions that support electronic payments, whereupon they receive an electronic certificate that includes their public key, together with personal information. Businesses will have similar certificates with their own and the bank's public keys. These are then used in the ensuing transaction by each party to verify the authenticity of the other. Order and payment are also transferred from customer to business with the latter forwarding the payment on to the participating bank. On a final check by the bank, payment is authorised. In essence, SET is designed to work in conjunction with credit card numbers, and it is expected that the necessary software will be widely available; it will keep both the payment and ordering details confidential and aid authentication through the use of digital signatures.

In England, the importation and use of encryption mechanisms is not restricted, and the government has been attempting to establish "Trusted Third Parties" who, it is envisaged, will provide encryption services to the public. In March 1997, the D.T.I. issued a consultative paper focusing on proposals to allow the Security Services, and possibly police forces, to have access to organisations' private keys for the purposes of monitoring electronic communications. However, this has met with a hostile response from groups such as the Business Software Alliance and the British Interactive Media Association who fear that on-line communication and commerce would be stifled by such a "big brother" attitude.

COPYRIGHT

Applicability of Copyright to On-line Communications

7-13   The computer revolution has meant that many different kinds of information may be converted to digital form for electronic transmission. Digital transmission takes place without degradation. This means that every copy is perfect and copies can be made very quickly and cheaply so that a document can be sent over the Internet to potentially millions of people for only relatively low transmission costs. The potential for copyright infringement is massive.

The law of copyright in England is now largely governed by the Copyright, Patents and Designs Act 1988, although different rules may apply to works created prior to August 1, 1959. The European Community Green Paper, "Copyright, The Information Superhighway", has as its main objective a harmonisation of European member state laws in this area.

Information Protected

7-14   Section 1(1) of C.P.D.A. lists the various works that may be protected by copyright subject to certain criteria being met. It should also be stressed that in the on-line environment copyrights may exist in a variety of works that are housed within one product (such as a Web site), including text, sound, graphics, and even the executable code involved.

Under section 17(2) of the C.P.D.A., storing a work electronically may be a copyright infringement as copying includes storing the work in any medium by electronic means; "electronic" is defined as "activated by electric, magnate, electro-magnetic, electro-chemical or electro-chemical energy". Even temporary storage is covered.[22] What should also be remembered is that on-line communication involves the transient storage and copying of the work at various points along the chain.

There are various criteria that works must meet to be eligible to obtain copyright protection under English Law. The work must be recorded in writing or otherwise; "writing" includes "any form of notations or code, whether by hand or otherwise and regardless of the method by which, or medium on which it is recorded". Copyright does not protect mere ideas per se. The work must be "original", which is defined by established case law and essentially a person must demonstrate that some degree of independent skill, labour, or judgment has been used in its creation. In addition, in establishing whether the work is protectable, regard should be had either to the country of first publication, or the author or the place from where the work was broadcast.

---

22 Copyright, Patents and Designs Act 1988, section 17(6).

It is arguable that publication may be held to take place where the publisher actually invites the public to view the work (for example, the server on which he has based the work) rather than the place of receipt (which could be any number of local users' personal computers or terminals). Special rules may apply where the work is being identically published simultaneously on two servers based in different locations.

A qualifying author is defined in sections 145(1) and (2) of the C.P.D.A. and the term also extends to other persons by virtue of such rules as the Copyright (Application to Other Countries) Order 1993, the Berne Convention, and the Universal Copyright Convention.

Whether on-line communications fall within the definitions of "broadcast" or "cable service programmes" (as defined by the C.P.D.A.) is debatable.

Works in electronic form may be copy protected by "any device or means intended to prevent or restrict copying of a work or to impair the quality of copies made". It is an offence to make or distribute a device designed to circumvent such copy protection, knowing, or having reason to believe it will be used to make infringing copies, or merely to publish information to enable such activities to take place. Furthermore, persons who transmit a work over a telecommunications system (which does not include broadcasting or cable), knowing or reasonably believing that reception of the same will lead to infringing copies being produced are themselves infringers; a "telecommunication system" is defined by the C.P.D.A. as "a system for conveying visual images, sounds or other information by electronic means".

Case law in this area will no doubt appear. Already the *Shetland Times* case attracted attention when the Court of Session granted an interim interdict holding that the inclusion of the headlines of one newspaper in the Web site of another newspaper was, *prima facie*, copyright infringement.

Acquiring a Copyright

What are regarded as "works" and how they qualify for protection has been   7-15
discussed above. Every copyright protected work has an author who is, generally speaking, the person who created it. This is further discussed below, as are the various rights that attach to such copyright owners.

Ownership of Copyright to On-line Communication

Generally, the author of a work, the person who creates it, is the first owner   7-16
of any copyright in it. A work of joint authorship is produced by the collaboration of two or more authors in which the contribution of each author is not distinct from that of the other author or authors. The author of computer generated works is the person by whom the arrangements necessary for the creation of the work are undertaken.

Where an employee in the course of his employment makes the work, his employer is the first owner of any copyright in a work subject to any contractual agreement to the contrary. This only applies to employees, not to contractors, so the mere fact that work has been commissioned and paid for does not give the ownership of the copyright to the commissioning party. Therefore, it is important to ensure that the appropriate agreements are in place to deal with the ownership of the rights in contents.

Rights of Copyright Owner

7-17   The copyright owner's exclusive rights include the rights to copy, to issue copies to the public, to perform, show or play in public, to broadcast, to include it in a cable programme service and to make adaptations. As well as such "economic rights", the copyright owner may attract "moral rights"; these were introduced by the C.P.D.A. and may even belong to the author of the work independently of the economic rights. Moral rights include:

- Paternity (the right to be identified as author);
- Integrity (the right to object to the derogatory treatment of the work);
- False attribution (the right not to suffer false attribution of a work); and
- Privacy of photography (the right of a person commissioning photographs not to have copies issued to the public).

Moral rights cannot be assigned but may be waived.

Copyright is infringed by doing any of the prohibited acts in relation to the whole or a substantial part of the work without the consent of the owner. Problems occur in trying to determine whether a "substantial part of the work" has been copied. For example, a single word cannot be the subject of copyright. Case law suggests that the test of substantiality is quality-based rather than quantity based. The test seems to be whether the part taken itself has some originality and merit.

Infringement of a copyright protected work can be by primary infringement (*e.g.*, unauthorised copying), secondary (*e.g.*, sale or distribution of said material) or tertiary (by authorising another to commit an infringing act). Such acts require an element of knowledge or reason to believe that the article was an infringing copy.

Copyright material distributed electronically may potentially be available and copied by the world at large. Given that it would be almost impractical to track down all defaulting end users it may well be that copyright owners seek to protect their interests by attempting to fix liability on an intermediary in the chain of supply, such as an ISP. Indeed, in May 1997, Ignition, the management company of the rock group Oasis, issued formal warnings to unofficial Web sites displaying copyrighted material owned by the band; they threatened legal proceedings if offending material was not removed within 30 days but, on expiry of this deadline, not all sites had complied, and it remains to be seen what action will follow.

The term for which copyright protection may subsist varies with the type of work in question.

Digitised information is much more easily manipulated and adapted and the changes are much harder to detect. Such manipulation can make it very difficult to detect, or to prove, infringement of the copyright in the original work.

A further difficulty is that whereas, for example, the music industry royalties are collected by the Performing Rights Society there is not as yet, in England at least, any such equivalent relating to the multimedia world of on-line communications. There are, of course, immense practical difficulties in making such on-line collections.

Various civil remedies for infringement include an injunction to prevent further infringement, damages or an account of profits, an order for delivery up or destruction of infringing copies in the defendant's possession or control, the right to seize infringing copies found on sale (subject to a number of conditions), an order enabling the plaintiff to seize infringing goods and evidence relating to the infringement[23] and an order for costs. In certain circumstances, the plaintiff may contact H.M. Customs and Excise to prevent importation by having infringing goods labelled as prohibited goods. Their importation will then be prohibited for up to five years and any found by customs will be liable to forfeiture; the on-line environment seems to offer little practical scope for this remedy.

An infringer may attract criminal as well as civil liability. Criminal liability requires either a commercial motive or distribution to such an extent as to seriously affect the copyright owner. Conviction for criminal copyright infringement carries a maximum of two years imprisonment and/or a fine.

Defences to copyright infringement are provided by a number of statutory limitations on the scope of the exclusive rights. For example, fair dealing with some classes of copyright work for research or private study, or for criticism or review, or for the reporting of current events, or the incidental inclusion in another work are not infringements. In addition, educational uses and library activities are exempt from infringement liability.

Rights of the Copyright User

Content providers, ISPs and end users may all look to sue one another for   7-18 copyright infringement or breach of contract, depending on what agreements are in place and simply whether the "target" in question is worth pursuing.

---

23 This is an *ex parte* order authorising the plaintiff or its agents to enter the defendant's premises and remove evidence of copyright infringement, provided the plaintiff can show a strong *prima facie* case that the actual or potential damage to his interests is very serious, that the defendant is likely to have infringing copies of the work in his possession, and that there is a real possibility that if the defendant is forewarned he might destroy the evidence.

Consequently, someone such as a content provider, displaying information via a Web site should check the sources of such information and whether any of it is protected by copyright. The potential for litigation is particularly acute as the information may have come from any number of sources including users, external developers, consultants, and internal employees. If it is protected by copyright, appropriate licences or assignments of rights will be needed to ensure that such content providers do not infringe the copyright.

Any Internet host or access provider who uses or knowingly permits others to use its Internet service to disseminate unauthorised copies of copyright works is in danger of a civil action for infringement. There is also a risk of infringement even if the host or access provider does this unknowingly. In the United States, a number of cases have involved bulletin boards containing copyright material that could be downloaded by accessing the board.

End users should be aware of the potential for copyright infringement and not place works (or even extracts) on-line without first considering the implications and obtaining legal advice if they are unsure. It must be remembered, however, that daily use of on-line communications involves various instances of copying. It is possible for licences to be implied through operation of statute[24] or by the courts. However, users should obviously focus not just on the existence of any licence but its precise scope and duration.

TRADE SECRETS

Acquiring the Rights

7-19   In English law, the terms "trade secret", "know-how" and "confidential information" are used in a variety of often over-lapping contexts. In the context of this chapter, a trade secret is best defined as technical information that gives a business its unique edge. It is the highest form of confidential information. It does not matter that others could compile the same information that the plaintiff is seeking to protect. The law seeks to protect the effort the plaintiff has exerted in compiling the information.

Such pure information is not property under English law. Instead, the law of confidence underlies any rights to legal redress with respect to such trade secrets; it is based in both the law of contract and the rules of equity. The contractual aspects of confidentiality have been discussed above. The law of confidence enables businesses to regard such trade secrets as commercial assets capable of being licensed and somewhat protected.

---

24 Copyright, Patents and Designs Act 1988, section 50.

Rights in such trade secrets are, *prima facie*, acquired via a contractual relationship between the parties concerned. If such a document exists, it will be the first place to refer to for potential rights of action and, hence, remedies. In the absence of such a contract, the potential plaintiff must look to equity and the discretionary remedies that it offers; to have the *locus standi* to bring such an equitable action, a plaintiff must generally prove that:

- The information in question has the "necessary quality of confidence";
- The information was disclosed in circumstances which imported an obligation of confidence; and
- The defendant made unauthorised use of the information to the detriment of the plaintiff.

If the information is "public property and public knowledge", it will have **7-20** the necessary quality of confidence. In its entirety, a "package" of information may be confidential even if some elements may be in the public domain. In *Marshall Thomas (Exports)* v. *Guinle*,[25] Megarry V-C suggested a subjective test for the quality of confidence:

- The owner must reasonably believe that the release of the information would be injurious to him or advantageous to rivals;
- The owner must reasonably believe that the information is secret and not already within the public domain;[26] and
- It must be judged in the context of the usage and practices of the particular industry concerned.

The law of confidence is largely ineffective against innocent third party **7-21** recipients because they will probably not know (and cannot reasonably be expected to know) that the information is confidential. If the information is to be disclosed to another person, it must be under circumstances giving rise to an obligation of confidentiality. This may result from either an express contractual obligation or from an implied obligation arising out of a relationship governed by rules requiring confidentiality on the part of the recipient (*e.g.*, client and lawyer, employer and employee or patient and doctor) where the recipient knew or should have known that the information was confidential and that in the circumstances it should be kept confidential.

An attraction of the trade secret is the fact that, as long as it is kept private, rivals cannot access it (as opposed to published patent information). It does not require any registration formalities and in the absence of a

---

25 1979 Ch. 227.
26 The protection of the law may be lost if the information falls into the public domain, which means either the public at large possessing the information or even if it becomes common knowledge within a particular group (*e.g.*, software companies).

contractual relationship, equity may be invoked. However, it is recommended that a proper written confidentiality agreement be entered into rather than relying on equity.

Once information enters the public arena or becomes the subject of a patent, the protection of the law of confidence is lost. An exception to this is the granting of a temporary limited injunction where the only advantage a defendant has obtained is a head start — commonly known as the "Spring Board" doctrine.

Owner's Rights

7-22   Where an inventor (the original owner) discloses an invention in confidence to a company seeking to develop it, the position of the two parties is relatively clear. The company will owe a duty of confidence to the inventor, who may bring an action based in contract (if there is a contract in place between the two) or in equity (if not).

As commercial assets, trade secrets, know-how and the like are capable of being licensed by their owners to third parties. In *Torrington Manufacturing Co. v. Smith and Sons (England) Limited*,[27] a licensee attempted to argue that it was allowed to use confidential information disclosed to it by the licensor under the terms of a licence to manufacture certain products.

With reference to the contractual agreement, the court held that the licensee could be restrained from obtaining any advantage from the information (received exclusively for the purposes of the contract). Therefore, the courts may imply an obligation on non-owners not to use the information for any other purpose than that expressly contemplated by the parties. Hence, their rights to use the information may not include disclosure to third parties or use for their own commercial benefit (other than presumably that intended under the licence).

If a third party acquires the information (*e.g.*, by way of wrongly addressed e-mail), the position is less clear. If disclosure has occurred in blatant breach of a duty of confidence and the third party knows this, he will probably owe a duty of confidence. If the third party innocently learns of it, he may not owe a duty of confidence unless he subsequently learns that the information is of a confidential nature. The inventor will probably have the requisite *locus standi* to sue the third party, but it is not clear that the company will be able to as the duty of confidence may be owed to the owner rather than non-owner (in the absence of express contractual provisions to the contrary).

The remedies available at equity include an injunction and damages but will be at the court's discretion. Interim injunctions will face the usual tests (*e.g.*, the "balance of convenience" test) applicable to such interlocutory remedies.

---

27 1966 R.P.C. 283.

The Non-Owner's Rights

If an inventor assigns his rights to an entrepreneur and another party intends   7-23
to publish the information on the Internet, the entrepreneur may attempt to
bring proceedings against the other party (*e.g.*, to obtain an injunction). The
entrepreneur is able to do this because he will have stepped into the owner's
shoes and may therefore have *locus standi* to sue. This action will be rooted
primarily in contract though it may be pleaded under equity in the alternative. It may also be advisable to join the inventor as co-plaintiff (or else the
inventor should sue himself).

Where an inventor discloses his trade secret to a company and a third
party subsequently acquires the information, in the absence of a contract,
the company will probably not be able to sue the third party. It would be
prudent for the inventor to raise the action instead, or at least as co-plaintiff.

TRADE MARKS

Acquiring On-line Trade Mark Rights

The United Kingdom Trade Marks Register is divided into 42 classes (34 trade   7-24
marks and eight service marks). Businesses should register on several
classes to fully protect themselves. Signs, sounds, and animated and static
graphics are capable of registration under the Trade Marks Act 1994.
Certain marks may not be capable of registration, including:

- Those devoid of a distinctive character;
- Those which consist exclusively of signs or indications which may
  serve in trade to designate characteristics of the goods or services
  (including their land, quality, quantity, intended purpose, value, geographical origin or time of production);
- Those which are exclusively signs or indications which have become
  used in current language in established trade practices; and
- Those contrary to public policy and those which are identical or similar
  to other registered marks.

Applications are made to the Trade Marks Registry in accordance with   7-25
section 32 of the Trade Marks Act 1994 and the Trade Marks Rules 1994.
One application may be made for registration in more than one class.
Initially accepted applications are published by the Trade Marks Registrar
in the Trade Marks Journal. Anyone wishing to oppose the application may
do so within one month of the publication. Successful marks are initially
registered for 10 years and are renewable for similar periods on payment of
a fee.

Registration may be revoked at any time for one of a number of reasons including non-use for a period of five years from registration or that the mark has become a generic name for the products in question.

Selecting a Mark

7-26 The registration of trade marks is designed to prevent others using that mark. There is no need to show that the applicant has established a business reputation with the mark.

A mark will be registrable unless it is excluded from registration. It is "any sign capable of being represented graphically which is capable of distinguishing goods or services of one undertaking from those of other undertakings".[28] It may therefore include words, designs, letters, numerals, the shape of products or their packaging, logos, jingles, and even single colours, providing they are distinctive of a particular person's products.

Given the delivery of products on-line will not necessarily give a consumer the opportunity to examine the goods before purchasing, much spending will be on the strength of brand image.

Infringement

7-27 Infringement may occur in a number of ways, including:

- Where a third party uses an identical mark for goods or services identical to those of the registered owner;
- Where a third party either uses an identical mark for goods or services that are similar to those of the registered owner or uses a similar mark for goods or services that are identical to those of the registered owner, so that there is a likelihood of confusion among the buying public; or
- Where the third party uses an identical mark that has established a reputation in England for goods or services that are not similar to those relating to the registered mark but which take unfair advantage of or are detrimental to the distinctive character or reputation of the mark.

7-28 To be infringed, a mark usually must be used in the course of a trade or business, as opposed to mere "casual use".

Infringement will occur in each and every country where that Web page may be accessed and where the mark is either registered or has other protection (*e.g.*, rights acquired through use). Therefore, practically speaking, commercial interests in global electronic commerce must be weighed against the potential risks of trade mark infringement.

---

28 Trade Marks Act 1994, section 1(1).

Remedies for infringement include injunctions, damages and accounts of profits. The courts may also order that marks be removed from the products in question (or if they cannot be removed, that the products be destroyed). A number of defences are available such as one party's registered mark is not infringed by another's use of his own registered mark[29] or where a person acting in accordance with "honest practices in industrial or commercial matters" uses his own name or address, indications of the kind, quality, intended purpose, geographical origin, and other identifying factors relating to the product, or simply uses the mark to identify the product as those of the registered proprietor or licensee.

It should also be borne in mind that under English law trade reputation may also be protected by the tort of passing off. This is committed when a defendant supplies products presenting them as the plaintiff's so that the public are capable of being misled and the plaintiff has or is likely to suffer damage as a result. In certain situations, the same act may amount to both infringement of a mark and passing off and the plaintiff may then be able to sue under either or both.

Domain names

Acquiring Rights

Domain names are everywhere — not merely on-line but on letterheads, in magazines, posters, and the like. They are a sign of the commercial impact and importance of electronic communication. Their historical divisions into geographical areas are also diluting, a further sign of their universality. Many companies which have been slower to embrace the world of on-line electronic communication than their competitors have found that their rivals have already registered domain names that would be of use to them. **7-29**

In England, to register a domain name, a person or an organisation may apply to the relevant naming authority, Nominet U.K., which allocates certain names, such as "co.uk"; Nominet dealt with more than 5,000 applications during April 1997 alone. Applicants are required to give further justification if there is no obvious connection between them and the name they are trying to register. No doubt, more detailed application policy statements will appear as new problems arise or old ones continue. As no territorial restrictions are placed on users by Nominet, any foreign body outside the United Kingdom may register a domain name. Likewise, British companies may so register in, for example, the United States with InterNIC, which supervises the allocation of the popular ".com" name. On an application to Nominet a persons domain name will be cleared and delegated (if

---

29 Trade Marks Act 1994, section 11(1).

the application is valid) to the relevant name server. A certificate of registration is then provided. Currently, there is a one-off registration fee and then annual fees which, at the moment, will secure the use of the domain name as long as the fees are paid. Most "name server" organisations will allow a transfer of a specific domain name to another ISP.

Most English organisations register domain names via their service provider, who itself will have a "name server". Turn-around time for valid applications can be relatively short. A prospective applicant may check what names have already been allocated by using the search facilities many ISPs or Nominet itself now make available.

However, being allotted a domain name (unlike a trade mark) does not give a person the legal right to use that name exclusively and, consequently, they may find themselves being sued for infringement of a trade mark or passing off. It is wise to conduct a trade marks search before attempting to register a particular domain name. If someone already has a relevant trade mark registered, it may make commercial sense to attempt to reach an agreement with them regarding the intended allocation and use.

In England, the various categories of domain name that Nominet allots include ".co", ".ac", ".gov", ".nhs", ".ltd", and ".plc". There are rules as to who can or cannot register under such headings.

Protecting Domain Names as Trade Marks

7-30   Once a person or organisation has been allotted a domain name, he or it may seek to protect it by registering it as a trade mark. The name may be so registered if it is used in a business to indicate the source or origin of goods or services, so the domain name should be as prominent as possible on any "packaging" (*e.g.*, Web sites). The Patent Office will ignore such parts of the URL as ".co.uk" and concentrate on the unique front-end segment of the address to see if it alone is sufficiently distinctive to merit the application. If the organisation uses an existing mark as a domain name, then it may not need to consider acquiring further trade mark rights in the domain name itself. Use of an unprotected domain name in the course of business may make it possible to eventually acquire trade mark rights in the fullness of time.

Trade mark protection has its limits. Under English law, no monopoly is conferred to exclusive use of a particular word; instead, the owner of the mark is protected from unauthorised use of it in a manner likely to cause confusion among the purchasing public, thus limiting it to the extent of a particular commercial operation. Furthermore, trade marks only operate within their particular country; thus, anyone contemplating electronic commerce across the world should consider registering in more than just his home jurisdiction; this will protect the domain name and minimise the likelihood of being sued by a third party for infringement of its rights. Care should also be taken in registering in the appropriate range of trade mark classes.

A mark may be particularly computer orientated and, therefore, anyone else trying to use it on-line may be infringing it, whatever their overall activity is. There is also a "dilution" argument that certain widely established marks should not have their impact lessened or diminished through many people using a similar mark, regardless of the type of business run.

The potential commercial significance of domain names has been highlighted by recent cases. The High Court in the *Harrods* case ruled that Harrods Limited (owners of the famous department store) were entitled to prevent United Kingdom Network Services Limited from retaining the domain name "harrods.com"; it was held that the use of the Harrods name in this way infringed the company's trade mark and amounted to passing off. Unfortunately, this case against such "name-jackers" is a weak precedent, as it is based on an uncontested summary judgment.

In *Pitman Training Ltd. and Another* v. *Nominet U.K. and Another* (May 22, 1997) Nominet's policy of "first come first served" for the allocation of ".uk" domain names was upheld by the High Court; this was a case where both parties actually had a legal right to use the name "pitman" in their respective fields of business; the first company, Pearson, had registered the domain name in February 1996 and began preparations to launch a web site. Unfortunately, for unexplained reasons, internal procedures at Nominet resulted in the re-allocation of the domain name to the other company PTC in March 1996. PTC began using the address for e-mail purposes. The domain name was subsequently re-transferred back to Pearson by Nominet, which prompted an action by PTC. The High Court held that PTC had no course of action and that no unlawful act had been committed by Pearson.

Partly in response to such disputes, Nominet launched a new dispute resolution scheme in 1997. It has various stages, beginning with a low-key investigation by Nominet staff, progressing to a suspension of the domain name in question, a referral to an independent expert, a "final" decision by Nominet, followed by a possible choice by either party to utilise the Nominet Alternative Dispute Resolution Service.

PATENTS

Patentability

The patent system is designed to protect inventions, as defined under English 7-31 patents law, and they must be new (including an inventive step), capable of industrial application, and not expressly excluded under the rules. Excluded items include most things protected directly by copyright. In the context of electronic communication, this may encompass software as well as the components of the on-line infrastructure.

In England, a party may consider applying to the United Kingdom Patent Office or its European counterpart. Such applications require expert advice and are time consuming. Patenting means a virtual monopoly of the item, currently for 20 years, after which it is released into the public domain. Applications for patents may be filed at the London Patent Office, including a specification, an abstract, and claims document. The specification describes the invention; the abstract states title and other key details; and the claims document defines the scope of monopoly sought. The filing date is known as the priority date. The applicant has 12 months from this date to decide whether or not to apply for protection in other countries.

The Patent Office then reviews its records for any relevant details and the application may subsequently need amending. Eighteen months later the "A" publication is issued. The Patent Office scrutinises the application further to ensure it conforms to the requirements of the current legislation and hopefully within four and a half years the "B" publication occurs. The patent is initially granted for four years. It may be renewed annually up to a maximum of 20 years from the priority date. Fees become progressively steeper.

Software End Users

7-32   The question of whether software is patentable has highlighted differences between the United Kingdom and European and United States patent systems. In *Merrill Lynch Inc.'s Application*,[30] the Court of Appeal held that the trading system which was the subject of the application was not patentable because it was merely a method of performing a business function. Yet, the patent was granted in an amended form when the method sought to be patented was linked to the physical apparatus concerned. In *Gales' Application*,[31] a ROM-chip was held not to be patentable as it did not have a technical effect. In *Wang's Application*,[32] an expert computer system was also found not to be patentable. In *Raytheon's Application*,[33] the court held that the application in question (for a pattern recognition system) merely related to an everyday computer processing information. A recent leading case has been Patent Application 9204959.2 by Fujitsu Ltd. (Court of Appeal March 6, 1997), where the question of software patentability was examined, and the court felt that patentability should be dependent on substance, not form; in particular it was held that a technical aspect or contribution was needed (as opposed to a mere discovery or invention) and this would be a question of fact in each case.

In contrast, the European Patent Office tends to grant such patents under the doctrine of technical effect. This has significant implications, such as the

30 1989 R.P.C. 561.
31 1991 R.P.C. 305.
32 1991 R.P.C. 462.
33 1993 R.P.C. 427.

fact that developers may seek to go down the European rather than United Kingdom route and those at the other end of the chain should be aware of the possibilities of infringing someone else's patent, even if a search of the Patents Office appears clear.

Developers

In the context of on-line communication, the apparent differences between   7-33
United States, the English, and the European jurisdictions over the patentability of software make it seem sensible for developers to obtain specific advice and to consider patenting as widely as possible or at least in the major jurisdictions. What they should also consider are the practical problems associated with enforcement.

Distributors

Patent owners may sell, license or mortgage such property. Contracts reflect-   7-34
ing the same must be evidenced in writing, signed by both parties and all dealings must be registered at the Patent Office.

Whether an owner may pursue a distributor for infringement depends on the construction and scope of the licence. Licences may also be implied, such as to do acts necessary to repair the object of the patent should it not perform as intended.

Enforcing Patent Rights

The proprietor of a granted patent may be able to sue for infringement from   7-35
the priority date of the original application. Anyone found infringing a patent will be open to an injunction to stop them using the idea, as well as a claim for damages to compensate the patent owner.

However, even after it has been granted, a patent may be found to be invalid, for example, if it is proved that at the priority date the idea behind the patent was not actually innovative, or by the patent owner having inadvertently told a third party prior to filing this application.

The actual ability to enforce patents is a measure of their value. In the on-line world, it may not necessarily be easy to identify or trace the miscreant involved if they are using a re-mailer or "spoofing". One solution which future litigants may opt for is pursuing service or content providers rather than individual end users. However, English courts, as part of the discovery process, have allowed plaintiffs to obtain orders to provide them with the information with which to progress back up the chain to the source of the infringements (*e.g.*, via a "Norwich Pharmacal Order").

Injunctions may be one remedy and, indeed, English courts permitted an injunction (to restrain a foreign user from publishing an alleged libel on the

Internet) to be served with their leave via e-mail[34] where the other possible methods of service (as prescribed in the Rules of the Supreme Court) had either failed or been impossible to utilise; thus the court granted leave for the one remaining avenue — to e-mail it to the defendant at his last known e-mail address. However, it had to be satisfied that this was a sufficiently certain method of bringing it to the defendant's attention.

It is an infringement of a patent to make, dispose of, offer to dispose of, use, keep or import a patented product in a country where the relevant patent already subsists. Plaintiffs will need to be clear where the patent is being infringed, given the global nature of the on-line environment. The Brussels Convention 1968 allows a party to sue someone in the country where they are domiciled, for infringement of intellectual property rights, although this may turn on whether the plaintiff seeks damages or an injunction.

LICENCES

The License and Sale of On-line Rights

7-36   Many view on-line communication as a public domain where information is free. It must be remembered that copyright and other intellectual property rights still subsist. Hence, licences are important to electronic communications. Under English law, licences may be exclusive or non-exclusive, although some have particular requirements (*e.g.*, that they must be in writing and signed by either or both parties). Some forms of electronic licence are already in use, such as Web-wrap licences.

There are horizontal licence strata (*e.g.*, non-exclusive licences to end users) and vertical licence chains (*e.g.*, a copyright owner may grant an exclusive licence to a software publisher who, in turn, will grant non-exclusive licences to the end users). Persons along such vertical chains may require warranties from those up the chain ensuring that they are capable of granting the licences.

In the on-line context, such licences may be a matter of necessity rather than choice because, for example, in order simply to use software, temporary copies may need to be stored in a user's hard disk or back up copies made, both potentially infringing copyright. However, licences, do not need to take any particular form and, indeed, may be implied by the courts or through operation of statute (*e.g.*, under section 50 of the Copyright, Patents and Designs Act) for practical reasons, such as business efficacy.

---

34 *The Times*, April 25, 1996.

Licences will involve both intellectual property law concepts and principles of basic contractual law, often specifying what a licensee cannot do as well as what he is allowed to do. Failure to abide by a licence may then both infringe copyright and breach a contract.

A further practical point is that while conventional mediums of publication or copying are subject to royalty collection by, for example, the Performing Rights Society, few if any collection agencies have extended their remit to include the on-line environment. Yet, potentially, this is where the majority of such royalties may be generated in the near future although the enforced collection of such dues poses immense practical problems, and the issue is one of ongoing debate.

Licences are applicable to many on-line uses such as electronic publishing, on-line databases and software sales. Their need will increase with the spread of true on-line interactivity in the light of recent developments such as Java.

Rights Subject to Licensing

Copyright owners under English law may grant either exclusive or   7-37 non-exclusive licences to do things which would otherwise be an infringement of copyright. The Copyright, Patents and Designs Act 1988 requires that an exclusive licence must be in writing and signed by the licensor.[35] A licence may also be granted in respect of a prospective copyright.[36]

Similarly, a patent owner may also license the use of his patent. Again it may be exclusive or non-exclusive. Exclusive patent licences come within the Block Exemption from the provisions of article 85 of the Treaty of Rome.[37] All dealings with a patent, including licences, must be registered at the Patents Office. Failure to do so may mean the disponee cannot obtain the remedies he is otherwise entitled to if infringement occurs.

The Copyright, Patents and Designs Act 1988 also contains provisions for the grant of licences of right and of compulsory licences. The former covers patents that the owners cannot themselves exploit; owners in such circumstances may apply to the Comptroller of Patents to endorse the Register with a notice that licences to exploit the patent in question are available as of right.[38] Someone who then wants a licence to exploit the said patent must first approach the owner but if no fees can be agreed they may then be fixed by the Comptroller. The renewal fees of such patents are also half the normal rates.

---

35 Copyright, Patents and Designs Act 1988, section 92.
36 Copyright, Patents and Designs Act 1988, section 91.
37 Drafters of exclusive patent licences should avoid all the "black list" terms, which are prohibited.
38 Copyright, Patents and Designs Act 1988, section 46.

Compulsory licences, on the other hand, involve an application to the Comptroller for a licence to exploit a patent that has been under-used or not used at all; applicants will also have grounds if they can show that the failure to grant such a licence has damaged British commercial interests. However, such applications may only be made after three years have elapsed from the initial grant.[39] Under section 55, the Crown may make use of a patent or authorise its use by another person in certain circumstances if it is in the national interest to do so.

Trade marks may be licensed to allow goods sold to be manufactured under licence. They must be registered in accordance with section 25 of the Trade Marks Act 1994. The licensee may require the licensor to bring an action against any third party infringing the trade mark in such a way that affects the licensee's interests under the licence.

An exclusive licence will, in any event, prevent the licensor from using the mark in the manner prescribed by the licence,[40] and the licensee may have the right to bring infringement proceedings himself.[41] The licence must be in writing and signed by or on behalf of the licensor. Unless license otherwise provides, the licensor's successors will also be bound by it.

WHO REGULATES ELECTRONIC COMMUNICATION?

7-38   Electronic commerce and communication is not limited to just one part of English law. It involves civil laws such as those of contract, intellectual property, banking, telecommunications and data protection. It also brings into play criminal offences such as hacking and fraud.

In England, various bodies may be regarded as playing a part in the regulation of the on-line environment. These include the courts, the police, the Data Protection Registrar, the Patents Office, the Trade Marks Registry, Nominet, ISPs, and the Department of Trade and Industry.

When engaging in electronic commerce parties should do as much as possible to be certain of the terms on which they are conducting business. They must be aware of all the various legal pitfalls both nationally and internationally that they may encounter. Self-regulation has as much a part to play as any third-party body.

Territorial Limits of Jurisdiction

7-39   Contracting electronically potentially means an offer to the whole world. There may be sound commercial (*e.g.*, not being able to meet the sheer expected demand) or legal (*e.g.*, being in breach of legislation such as the

---

39 Copyright, Patents and Designs Act 1988, section 48.
40 Trade Marks Act 1994, section 29.
41 Trade Marks Act 1994, section 31.

infamous United States Helms–Burton Bill designed to prohibit trade with Cuba) reasons why a company would seek to limit the territorial scope of its offer. Such scope may be controlled by both indirect methods (such as stipulating that payment will only be accepted in Sterling) and the more direct approach of a jurisdictional clause or an application in a program designed to establish the other party's nationality or location before contracting.

If a dispute arises as to the jurisdiction under which a contract is to be determined, the English courts may apply the proper law of contract doctrine. This means that the courts will seek "the natural forum with which the action has the most real and substantial connection".[42] The courts will have regard to the "interests of the parties and the ends of justice".[43] In short, they will consider a range of factors including the availability of witnesses, convenience, expense and the residence of the parties involved. A stay of proceedings may be granted provided there is another competent and appropriate forum in which the case may be more suitably tried. Even if there are certain procedural difficulties within such a "natural forum", a stay of proceedings may be granted.[44]

Choice-of-law clauses in on-line contracts, as with other forms of international trade, may be affected by such factors as foreign countries' local consumer protection legislation. It may be that such contracts should incorporate warranties and exclusion clauses designed to operate in various different jurisdictions, akin to the varieties of differing jurisdictional clauses often found in shrink wrap licences.

A further impact of electronic contracting and communication has been the apparent ability of plaintiffs to forum shop (*e.g.*, over defamation actions). Under European law, where a harmful tortuous act occurs in more than one jurisdiction, it may be possible for the plaintiff to choose to bring its action in the place of the source of the harm or at any of the other places where the harm has impacted.[45]

There may also be the practical limitation of not knowing either the identity or jurisdiction of the other party because, for instance, they have used a re-mailer or are "spoofing".

Residents and Non-Residents

English courts will consider a variety of factors in determining the optimum jurisdiction to apply to a particular dispute. One such factor will be where the parties are domiciled. The disadvantage of this is that United Kingdom citizens may find themselves in a foreign court where advice is both thin on

7-40

---

42 *The Abidin Dover* 1984 A.C. 398.
43 *Spilada Maritime Corp. v. Consulex* 1987 A.C. 460.
44 *Trendex Trading Corporation v. Credit Suisse* 1982 A.C. 679.
45 *Hannddalswekerij Bier v. Mines de Potasse d'Alsace* 1976 E.C.R. 1735.

the ground and costly. Residency will be further complicated when one seeks to look behind the on-line curtain and discovers that several servers in various locations are involved.

The European Court of Justice considered jurisdiction and residency in the libel case of *Shevill* v. *Presse Alliance S.A.*;[46] it involved a plaintiff "S" who was a United Kingdom citizen domiciled in England. She alleged that she had been libelled by a French newspaper owned by P.A. The offending article had been published in several European states. S. commenced her proceedings in the English courts but P.A. contested their jurisdiction to hear the case. The European Court of Justice ruled that S. could either sue where P.A. were domiciled or where the damages had actually been inflicted (conceivably every place where the article in question had been published).

Foreign (non-United Kingdom residents) must look towards the Private International Law (Miscellaneous Provisions) Act 1995, whereby they may pursue a case in the English courts for acts which are wrongful or tortuous under their own domestic laws, if it is "substantially more appropriate". An exception to this basic approach may be seen in the area of defamation, where the double actionability rule may apply, *i.e.*, an action brought in relation to a tort committed outside the United Kingdom will fail unless the relevant act is also actionable as a tort in the country where it is committed.[47]

Crossborder Transactions and Communications

7-41   Historically, international trade has been subject to geographical and cultural differences, international conventions and business practices. The electronic communications revolution has and will witness a progressive erosion of such boundaries. For this reason, when contemplating the legal implications of electronic communication, regard must be had to levels above and beyond that of an individual country's jurisdiction.

For example, a European approach is rooted in the Brussels Convention on Jurisdiction and Enforcement and Recognition of Judgments in Civil and Commercial Matters 1968 and the subsequent Civil Jurisdiction and Judgments Act 1982. Under article 2 of the Convention, a plaintiff must issue proceedings against a European Union defendant in the courts of the country where the defendant is domiciled. Under article 5(3), a plaintiff may bring an action in respect of a tortious act "in the place where the harmful event occurred". Electronic commerce may cause harmful acts in more than one jurisdiction.

Article 21, on the other hand, apparently gives exclusive jurisdiction to the court first seised of the action, yet this seemingly conflicts with the

---

46 1992 1 All E.R. 409, C.A.
47 *Boys* v. *Chaplin* 1971 A.C. 356.

intended freedom of choice envisaged by article 5(3). In *Marinari* v. *Lloyds Bank Plc*,[48] the courts acknowledged the potential gold mine for litigants that article 5(3) might allow and sought to limit the number of jurisdictions in which an action might be brought (the "forum-shopping" syndrome). The court distinguished between the primary harm (*e.g.*, caused by the initial publication) and a secondary harm (where it is consequential and arising from the original damage occurring elsewhere).

Another example of the higher international levels at work is the European Directive on Distance Selling, adopted on January 23, 1997. It is intended to apply to contracts concluded by "means of communication at a distance" which is further defined as "any means which, without the simultaneous physical presence of the supplier and the consumer, may be used for the purpose of conclusion of a contract between those parties". It will give consumers the benefit of a cooling-off period of seven days from the date of the contract and may consequently affect credit agreements collateral to the purchase. It will require suppliers to provide the buyer with details (*e.g.*, description, price, other costs, payments terms and relevant time periods) in writing or another desirable medium (which ought to include an e-mail). It will also help meet the public's fears over fraud by allowing cancellation of payment by credit card whether a fraud has been perpetrated. It may not, however, apply to the supply of items such as software, audio, and video clips where these are downloaded.

Concepts that are established within more traditional forms of international contracting may also need to be borne in mind when entering the realm of electronic commerce, such as when risk passes, insurance of the goods when in transit, what currency payment should be in, how payment should be made per se and how delivery should be effected. The potential for fraud by electronic communication has been highlighted recently by the collapse of the Antigua-based European Union Bank, an on-line operation which was the subject of an earlier Bank of England alert in October 1996; indeed, a notice in the popular media was really all English authorities could do to alert the public to the risks involved in such offshore trading.

Impact of Penal Law

Penal laws are only really a deterrent if they are enforceable. In electronic   7-42
communication, there are inherent practical problems in identifying possible miscreants (because of, for example, spoofing or re-mailing). However, this does not mean that criminal prosecutions do not occur. In fact, the general awareness of information technology developments and related offences

---

48 1996 2 W.L.R. 159.

within English courts means that more and more cases are being prosecuted. The Computer Misuse Act 1990 houses three main offences, namely:

- Unauthorised access offence under section 1, which carries a maximum sentence of six months imprisonment and/or a fine of up to £2,000;
- The offence of unauthorised access with intent to commit or facilitate the commission of a further offence (such as theft or blackmail) under section 2, which carries a maximum sentence of five years and/or a fine; and
- The unauthorised modification offence under section 3, which carries a maximum sentence of five years and/or a fine.

7-43   It was hoped that the Computer Misuse Act 1990 would act as a deterrent to 90 per cent of those likely to misuse computers, but the findings of the Audit Commission 1994 Report entitled "Opportunity Makes a Thief — An Analysis of Computer Abuse", pointed to an increase in computer misuse. Furthermore, the High Court, in *DPP v. Bignell*,[49] refused to uphold the convictions of police officers under the C.M.A. who had seemingly used their ability to access the Police National Computer for personal rather than professional reasons. The judges discussed whether the integrity of the computer systems or the data itself was intended to be protected and had regard to the possibility of "alternative remedies", internal disciplinary procedures and potential prosecution under data protection laws.

In *R. B. Brown*, the House of Lords quashed another police officer's conviction on the basis that the mere retrieval and display of information on a screen did not amount to use under the C.M.A.

Copyright may be protected by both civil remedies and criminal sanctions. The Copyright, Patents and Designs Act 1988 has within it[50] criminal penalties for "secondary infringements". The Common Law crime of incitement may also be available to combat those who seek to manufacture or market software solely designed to produce infringing copies, even if it is accompanied by a warning that such copying is illegal. Software pirates may also be caught under the Forgery and Counterfeiting Act 1981 or by section 15 of the Theft Act 1968 — obtaining by deception. Both carry maximum penalties of 10 years' imprisonment. Prosecutions by Trading Standards Officers may be brought under the Trades Description Act 1968 with potentially two years' imprisonment or a fine of up to £5,000.

Prosecutions under the Copyright, Patents and Designs Act 1988 are increasing and custodial sentences have been given. The problem for the courts is striking the balance between protecting the interests of those who have invested in such works and not discouraging technical innovation or its availability to the general public via the exploitation of the on-line medium.

---

49 Q.B.D. May 21, 1997.
50 Copyright, Patents and Designs Act 1988, section 107.

A different approach to that of direct penal law has been attempts to encourage self-regulation by those who manage the information superhighway infrastructure, such as ISPs. In England, the Safety Net project has been encouraged, designed primarily to combat the spread of pornography via electronic communication. It is intended that ISPs identify illegal material, trace its source, remove it and put out general warnings notifying other users. Stronger lines of communication with the law enforcement agencies and further categories of offensive (but not strictly illegal) material are also options envisaged under the scheme.

CHAPTER 8

Finland

Pekka Raatikainen
Ahola & Sokka
Helsinki, Finland

INTRODUCTION

The international dimension of information networks creates an obvious need   8-1
for the international harmonisation of national legislation. National legislation,
which is per se valid, can deter the development of networking and the exchange
of electronic information. Obsolete national legislation which fails to respond
to current technical requirements can also lead to circumvention of law or to
an uncontrolled situation. A problem in the harmonisation of international
legislation is its slowness relative to the rapidly evolving technology.

As information networks affect increasingly large segments of the population, there is, however, a growing need to protect the rights of the different
parties operating in the networks. The global nature of information networks make traditional legislative mechanisms obsolete. Merely the supervision of compliance with laws in information networks alone is a hopeless
task on a national level.[1]

Legislative practices should promote the utilisation of information nets
and competition in the various sectors of the infrastructure as well as the
proliferation of electronic services and transactions.[2]

Achieving Information Security

Information security can be classified according to the standard developed   8-2
by the International Standards Organisation:

- Reliable and unfalsifiable authentication of the communicating parties;
- Confidentiality of communication to ensure that information does not
  end up in unauthorised hands;

---

1 Telmo ry, *Tietoverkkotoiminnan pelisäännöt — hyvä verkkotapa* (1968).
2 Tikas Working Group, *Suomi tietoyhteiskunnaksi — kansalliset linjaukset, Report*
(January 1996).

- Integrity of content;
- Non-repudiation of messages transmitted and received; and
- Access control relating to information systems.[3]

8-3   Legislation is the most convenient vehicle for organising confidentiality. Other information sectors are protected where possible by upgrading the technical characteristics of the information network and by ciphered messages. Finnish legislation on electronic information transmission can be broken down into three segments, namely:

- Legislation which regulates teleoperations as a commercial activity;
- Legislation on electronic communications, *i.e.*, regulation of the content of communications; and
- Legislation regulating the physical information network.

ELECTRONIC COMMUNICATION AND LEGAL REGIME

8-4   Electronic communication is recognised in Finnish legislation already in a proclamation dating from 1855 where the electric telegraph was proclaimed the privilege of the Russian government, and in the Senate's telephone decree of 1886 providing for the establishment of telephone companies and building of the telephone network.

Even today, most Finnish legislation dealing with electronic information transmission regulates the building of communication infrastructure. There are very few special regulations on the legal consequences of transmitted communications. The Finnish contractual law gives no special status to an expression of will transmitted electronically. An electronically transmitted expression of will is bound by the same rules as, *e.g.*, a written or oral expression of will.

If the regulations governing electronic mass media are not taken into consideration, the content of electronic communications is regulated in Finland almost exclusively by the Penal Code and the legal provisions which forbid distribution of indecent publications. In fact, the legislation is mainly focused on protecting information transmission, regulating the respective infrastructure and protecting the physical transmission equipment from violation of rights.

Electronic mass communications as well as inspection of films and videos are governed by special laws, such as the Act on the Finnish Broadcasting Company,[4] the Radio Broadcasting Act[5] and Decree,[6] the Act[7] and Decree[8]

---

3 International Standards Organisation, 7498-2.
4 Act on the Finnish Broadcasting Company, Number 1380/December 22, 1993.
5 Radio Broadcasting Act, Number 517/June 10, 1988.
6 Radio Broadcasting Decree, Number 869/September 11, 1992.
7 Act on Cable Television Operations, Number 307/March 13, 1987.
8 Decree on Cable Television Operations, Number 526/May 29, 1987.

on Cable Television Operations, the Act on Inspection of Cinematographic Films[9] and the Act on Inspection of Video and Other Visual Programs.[10] These regulations on mass media communications also include detailed provisions on the communications content. These laws are not extensively discussed in the present chapter.

They can, however, become applicable for instance to multimedia products. The legislation on advance inspection of cinematographic films or videos may become applicable once the increasing use of I.S.D.N. technology permits leasing of films through an electronic network for viewing by home audiences by means of program decoders.

Teleoperations Act

In most European countries, teleoperations have traditionally been the monopoly of a state-owned telecommunications company. They have also traditionally required an operating licence. Due to the development of telecommunications technology, the trend throughout Europe has been towards liberalisation of teleoperations and their opening to competition.[11]   8-5

The new Teleoperations Act came into force in Finland on June 1, 1996. The Act implemented the provisions of the European Union Teleservice Directive[12] into Finnish legislation. The essential objective of the Directive was to encourage the member states to abolish all monopolies connected with telecommunications services with the exception of telephone operations. The European Council Resolution[13] requires that telephone services should also be deregulated by January 1, 1998.

Pursuant to the Restrictive Trade Practices Act,[14] teleoperations are governed by the Teleoperations Act,[15] which came into force in 1987. In Finland, the teleoperations business is subject to a licence. According to section 26 of the Teleoperations Act, teleoperations carried out without a licence or in violation of the Teleoperations Act or any regulations issued thereunder, or the terms and conditions of the licence can be a punishable offence.

The term "teleoperations" means the technical organisation of the telecommunication operations. The Teleoperations Act regulates the activities associated with the physical networks required to carry out electronic communications and with the transmission of messages. The Teleoperations Act is not applied to the implementation, i.e., transmission and reception, of telecommunications or the contents of the communications.[16] "Telecommunications"

---

9 Act on Inspection of Cimematographic Films, Number 229/May 29, 1965.
10 Act on Inspection of Video and Other Visual Programs, Number 697/July 24, 1987.
11 Telmo ry, *Tietoverkkotoiminnan pelisäännöt — hyvä verkkotapa*, 1996, at p. 4.
12 European Community Directive 90/388 E.C.
13 European Council Resolution 93/C213/01.
14 Restrictive Trade Practices Act 122/September 27, 1919.
15 Teleoperations Act, Number 183/February 20, 1987.
16 Teleoperations Act, section 10.

means transmission of communications between electronic terminals in a telecommunications network. "Telecommunications network" refers to the system composed of cable transmission equipment or other equipment where cable or radio can transmit calls or other messages, optically or by means of some other electromagnetic method.

According to the Teleoperations Act, any party has the right to join in general telecommunications networks and lease dedicated lines within the limits permitted by the transmission capacity of the network, using the lines for telecommunications either for that party's own account or offering them further to other operators. The suboperation must not hamper the general teleoperations. The Teleoperations Act also provides for the determination of the fees charged by the public telecommunications operator from its users; the fees must be equitable and reasonable.

Procedural and Administrative Regulations

8-6   The Finnish procedural provisions recognise the electronic transmission of communications. In 1993, Finland adopted the Act on the Utilisation of Electronic Communications and Automatic Data Processing in General Courts.[17] A complaint, a response, and any other document which the interested party can send to a general court by mail can also be delivered to the information system of the court by telefax, electronic mail or through an automatic data processing system. If a document is delivered to the court in an electronic form, the sender always bears responsibility for delivery.

In addition, some other regulations on public authorities recognise the possibility to deliver documents to authorities by means of electronic transmission, or permit the authorities to use electronic printouts of documents.

Freedom of the Press Act

8-7   Pursuant to the Freedom of the Press Act,[18] all newspapers or periodicals must have a responsible editor-in-chief who is liable under criminal law for the published material. An essential provision is section 25 of the Act which sets forth the basic obligation of a paper to publish free of charge a response to an item published in that paper.

The Freedom of the Press Act does not apply as such to electronic publications. If an electronic publication is comparable to a printed paper, *i.e.*, it contains mainly editorial material subject to advance control, the Freedom of the Press Act should be applicable. It should for instance be possible to apply

---

17 Act on the Utilisation of Electronic Communications and Automatic Data Processing in General Courts, Number 594/June 28, 1996.
18 Freedom of the Press Act, Number 1/January 4, 1919.

the Act to the versions of Finnish newspapers distributed on the Internet (World-Wide Web) which resemble traditional newspapers even by their layout.

The Freedom of the Press Act does not apply as such to electronic publications whose publication material consists of readers' contributions. The service provider can become liable also for an uncontrolled publication of the type Bulletin Board, for instance if it is used to distribute indecent material. The liability becomes even more likely if the service is provided for a consideration. The law does, however, not yet address in detail the liability questions concerning the contents of communications sent by such provider of services, *i.e.*, the owner of the server.

The Committee on Freedom of Expression, appointed by the Ministry of Justice, has suggested that the Freedom of the Press Act be replaced by a new general act regulating the exercise of the freedom of expression. The objective would be to create a new general law on the freedom of expression applicable to all types of communications regardless of the modality of communication. The new Act would also include a description of the offences against freedom of expression.[19]

It should be possible to appoint a responsible official for each electronic publication or designate another party comparable to an editor-in-chief. This should also apply to electronic bulletin boards and conversation platforms managed in a responsible way. The editor-in-chief would be responsible for removing any communications infringing on the privacy of individuals from the bulletin boards, conversation platforms or similar media.[20]

Prevention of the Distribution of Indecent Publications

The Act on Prevention of Indecent Publications[21] and the provision in   8-8
chapter 20, section 9, of the Penal Code, dealing with the public violation of sexual morality, can also be applied to material intended for publication by means of electronic communications. Due to the relaxation of society's moral norms, the legislation has become outdated and is seldom applied in practice.

The provisions have been used to prevent the transmission of child pornography from Finland via the Internet. The problem of application is the uncontrolled status of the Internet operators with regard to liability questions. The owners of the server, *i.e.*, the network operator, may not even be aware that their server is used to distribute indecent material. Another problem associated with attempts to prevent the transmission of such material is that it is not always possible to identify the sender and that the material can come from virtually any country of the world.

19 Ministry of Justice 1996, Committee on Freedom of Expression, *Interim Report.*
20 Telmo ry, *Tietoverkkotoiminnan pelisäännöt — hyvä verkkotapa*, 1996, at p. 6.
21 Act on Prevention of Indecent Publications, Number 23/January 28, 1927.

To be able to energetically intervene in the transmission of such material would require an efficient identification of its origins and international co-operation, but to create such control systems is difficult.

Perhaps these objectives can be best achieved by developing an Internet protocol, *i.e.*, international rules for network operating practices. Various national organisations have developed such rules; in Finland, rules have been developed by Telmo ry[22].[23]

Information Security Legislation

8-9   The general Finnish information security legislation includes the Personal Data Files Act[24] and the Personal Data Files Decree.[25] Also, the Teleoperations Act and certain laws governing the activities of banks and insurance institution include specific security provisions.

The Personal Data Files Act regulates the utilisation, collection, storing, and disclosure of personal data on private individuals. By protected personal data the Personal Data Files Act means such personal information which permits the identification of a specific natural person or his or her family. In other words, the Personal Data Files Act does not protect information associated with business activities, or a public office or task. Nor does the Act provide for the compilation, storing, or utilisation of personal data solely for personal or other comparable traditionally private purposes.

Data file means a mass of information, including the previously mentioned personal information processed by means of automatic data processing systems. The Act sets no quantitative criteria; consequently, even the name of an individual or other similar item, temporarily fed into an information network, can create a data file.

According to the Personal Data Files Act, the keeping of a personal data file must be well justified, and it must be possible to anticipate the registration. The keeper of the data file must observe due care and the data file must be adequately protected. Obsolete data files must be destroyed or in certain circumstances filed in archives.

The Personal Data Files Act, section 5, permits the collection and storing of information in a personal data file without the consent of the person concerned in principle only on persons who due to a customer or service relationship, membership or other similar factor have a material connection with the activities of the organisation which keeps the file. This means that it is permitted to store in a data file only such personal information which

---

22 "Telmo ry" is the Telematic Association (www.telmo.fi); *Tietoverkkotoiminnan pelisäännöt — hyvä verkkotapa*, 1996.
23 Www.telmo.fi/telmo/telmo2/pelisaan/pelisa.hty.
24 Personal Data Files Act, Number 471/April 30, 1987.
25 Personal Data Files Decree 476/April 30, 1987.

is necessary for the purpose of the file. In addition, the registering organisation has on request the obligation to disclose the source of the stored data.

According to the Personal Data Files Act, section 18, the information stored in a personal data file can in principle only be disclosed with the consent or on the order of the registered person or pursuant to an Act or a Decree or the regulations issued thereunder, or for purposes where the disclosure of personal data is part of customary information disclosure and provided that the information is not sensitive, as well as for scientific research and statistics.

The rules for disclosure of information used for direct advertising, telephone marketing and address services are broader. Data can be supplied from such registers unless the registered person has explicitly forbidden the disclosure. The Personal Data Files Act also provides for the mass disclosure of personal data and for special restrictions of disclosure of personal identification numbers. The basic principle also forbids the combination of several data files.

According to the Personal Data Files Act, section 41, no one who has learned of the personal circumstances of another person due to his statutory duties can disclose the knowledge to third parties.

According to the Personal Data Files Act, section 42, the keeper of the file is liable for compensating the financial losses caused to the registered person due to improper use or disclosure of the data. This compensation liability arises regardless of negligence. In such case, compensation is also payable for suffering unless deemed insignificant. According to the law, the registered person is also entitled to verify his data in the file and have the incorrect information rectified.

Contractual Law

The general law in Finland governing contracts is the Legal Transactions Act.[26]   8-10
It concerns only legal transactions based on property law and includes provisions on concluding contracts, authorisation, invalidity of legal transactions, and conciliation of unreasonable conditions of contract. Although the Finnish Legal Transactions Act only refers to transactions based on property law, legal practice has taken the view that it is in principle the general law applied to all contracts.

Finland has no special law on standardised contracts. To include standard conditions as part of the contract, legal practice requires that they have been made available to the other party and that an explicit agreement has been reached on their validity. This may be dispensed with if otherwise indicated due to the customary business practice between the parties or generally prevailing in the industry concerned. The banks have recently

---

26 Legal Transactions Act, Number 228/29, Amendment 956/82.

taken the view with regard to the standard conditions of their guarantee contracts that if the standard condition of contract leads to a particularly severe sanction or cannot be anticipated by the bank's customer, to be legally binding the contract negotiations must have explicitly referred to the condition.

The Finnish general contractual legislation is not widely construed on the principles of protecting the weaker party. Therefore, Finland has adopted a number of special laws that aim at protecting the weaker party by means of compelling contractual norms in certain types of contracts. The Insurance Contracts Act,[27] the Tenancy Act,[28] the Hire Purchase Act,[29] the Employment Contracts Act,[30] and the Consumer Protection Act[31] are such laws.

Special laws also have been adopted for certain commonly used types of contract. For instance, the Exchange of Goods Act,[32] as a special law, governs the deeds of transfer of movable goods. This Act provides for the cancellation of deals, the buyer's and the seller's obligations, product defects and liability for risks. The Act applies only if nothing else has been agreed or if the established practice between the parties does not otherwise require. Consequently, the Exchange of Goods Act can be applied also to sale and purchase of goods through the Internet in Finland.

Thus, the Finnish legislation does not accord a special treatment to an electronic offer and its acceptance; these contracts are governed by the Legal Transactions Act and its general legal principles based on the theory of party autonomy. In principle, the execution of a contract is assumed to mean that the content of the expression of will corresponds to the intention of its giver.

The Consumer Protection Act applies to the offering, selling, or marketing of consumer commodities to consumers. As the Consumer Protection Act does not restrict the offering, selling or marketing practice used, it is applicable also to the offering, selling, or marketing of consumer commodities to consumers by means of electronic data transmission equipment.

"Consumer commodities" in the Consumer Protection Act means goods or services provided essentially for private consumption. The Act also applies to the offering, sale, and other marketing of housing by business undertakings to consumers, as well as to consumer credits.

Two decrees dealing with the announcement of prices for consumer commodities in connection with marketing have been issued pursuant to the Consumer Protection Act, namely, the Decree on Information on Consumer Commodities[33] and the Decree on Information Given in Connection with

27 Insurance Contracts Act, Number 132/33.
28 Tenancy Act, Number 653/87.
29 Hire Purchase Act, Number 91/66.
30 Employment Contracts Act, Number 320/70.
31 Consumer Protection Act, Number 38/78.
32 Exchange of Goods Act, Number 355/March 27, 1987.
33 Decree on Information on Consumer Commodities 9/January 13, 1989.

the Marketing of Housing.[34] The Decrees are mandatory provisions dealing with the information which can be given in connection with advertisements or other marketing. The provisions must also be applied to the marketing of the previously mentioned commodities electronically to consumers.

The provisions on door-to-door and catalogue sales contained in the Consumer Protection Act also must be taken into consideration when selling commodities to consumers by transactions through information networks.[35] Door-to-door sales means offering consumer commodities to consumers by telephone or by personal visit in a place other than the premises of the business undertaking, whereas catalogue sales means offering goods which the consumers can order on the basis of a brochure, catalogue or advertisement. In door-to-door sales, the consumer must retain the goods received, or withhold the payment if he has cancelled the order, to enable the seller to collect the delivered goods.

In catalogue sales, the buyer who has cancelled the deal can send the goods back within a reasonable time. If these selling practices are used, the consumer is entitled to cancel the product order if he so wishes. Also, the return of the goods is considered cancellation. In catalogue sales, the notice of cancellation must be sent within seven days from the receipt of the order or the first lot of the ordered goods. In case of cancellation the seller must return immediately the paid amount of the purchase price and compensate for all the costs incurred by the buyer due to the returning of the goods.

In door-to-door sales, the entrepreneur must give the consumer a separate door-to-door selling document. In addition, in door-to-door sales, the consumer has the right to cancel his order in writing within seven days of receiving the selling document, or the ordered goods, or the first lot of goods. More detailed regulations on door-to-door sales and catalogue sales have also been issued by a Decree.[36]

Confidentiality

A prerequisite for the commercial applications of electronic information **8-11** transmission is to guarantee that the information does not fall into unauthorised hands. The confidentiality of information and its regulation in contractual relationships is left to the contracting parties. For this reason, the level of confidentiality varies.

In addition to the Personal Data Files Act, confidentiality regulations with the status of an act are found also in Finnish banking legislation. For

---

34 Decree on Information Given in Connection with the Marketing of Housing, Number 1079/November 18, 1994.
35 Act Number 84/January 8, 1993.
36 Decree Number 1601/December 30, 1993.

instance, the client's electronic account data are protected by the banker's duty of secrecy and can be disclosed to public authorities or third parties only in exceptional cases.

The confidentiality of communications in Finland is guaranteed under penalty, and the most essential confidentiality regulations are found in the Penal Code.

Communications Crimes

8-12   Communications in Finland are confidential regardless of the media used. The Finnish Constitution, section 12, regulates the confidentiality of telegraphic and telephone communications.

The Penal Code provides sanctions for the violation of the confidentiality of telecommunications. According to chapter 38, section 4, and chapter 38, section 8 of the Penal Code,[37] anyone who opens a letter or other closed communication addressed to another party, or by deciphering a code acquires information from a message stored electronically or similarly and protected from outside access, must be punished for violating the security of communications. In addition, the provision criminalises the disclosure of information from the contents of a call, cable, text, picture, or data transmission sent or received through a telenetwork.

The elements of the crime are also fulfilled if someone records in secret the speech of another party that is not meant to be disclosed to the recording party or any other third party. The provision also defines a more outrageous form of violation. If the security of communications is violated by using special equipment designed or modified for committing the crime, this is considered gross violation of the security of communications.

The previously mentioned provision of the criminal law is meant to safeguard the confidentiality of communications. Because the Internet is an open network, the application of the above provision depends on the level of protection of the sent message.

Similarly, the unauthorised possession and use of equipment used for deciphering protected telecommunications are forbidden.[38] This refers to equipment whose purpose is to remove by means of a special technical system the protection of messages transmitted in the electronic network and destined for someone else.

Electronic communications are also protected by the Penal Code, chapter 28, sections 5, 6, and 7, which provide for a punishment of a party who has made himself guilty of wilfully disturbing electronic telecommunications. This provision would, *inter alia*, permit punishing a party who launches a computer virus disturbing communication on the Internet. The party who spreads a computer virus can also be punished for malicious damage.

---

37 Penal Code, Number 578/April 21, 1995.
38 Teleoperations Act, section 29 a.

Unauthorised Access to Information Systems

When someone acquires information of a business secret belonging to another 8-13
party by penetrating an information system protected from access by outsiders
with the purpose of illegally disclosing the secret, the characteristics of corporate
espionage referred to in the Penal Code, chapter 30, section 4[39] are fulfilled.

Unauthorised compilation of data means that a party collects information without due authorisation or exceeding authority. Business secret refers
to a business or professional secret or other similar business information
which is kept confidential by a business undertaking and whose disclosure
would be likely to cause financial losses either to the undertaking concerned
or to another business undertaking.

The Penal Code, chapter 35, sections 1 and 2,[40] provide penalties for
unauthorised use by a party who uses the movable property or immovable
equipment or machines of another party without due authorisation. Also,
an attempt at illegal use is punishable. According to the provision's pream-
ble, it is particularly applicable to computer hackers who penetrate another
information system, *e.g.*, via a telephone line, and use the system illegally.[41]

The Penal Code, chapter 38, section 8,[42] deals with electronic burglary.
A party who penetrates an information system with a user identification
code not belonging to him, or otherwise breaks the security system where
the information is processed, stored, or transferred either electronically or
by another similar technical procedure, or a separately protected part of such
system is guilty of electronic burglary. The criminal characteristics of electronic burglary are fulfilled when the author of the crime gains access to the
information stored or transferred in the information system.

The Finnish legislation on crimes relating to information technology is based
on the Recommendation Number 89/9 on Computer-Related Crime and Final
Report of the European Committee on Crime Problems, Strasbourg (1990).

ELECTRONIC TRANSACTIONS

Creation of Contracts Electronically

According to Finnish legislation, a contract is concluded on the receipt of an 8-14
answer accepting the offer made. If the answer is not fully consistent with
the offer, the differing answer is considered a counteroffer, which requires
the approval of the original bidder. The contract thus leans on the convergence of the parties' wills.

---

39 Penal Code, Number 769/August 24, 1990.
40 Penal Code, Number 769/August 24, 1990.
41 Government Bill to the Parliament, 66/1988, p. 43.
42 Penal Code, Number 578/April 21, 1995.

The form of contracts based on property law is in principle free. Consequently, a predetermined form is not a prerequisite for the validity of a legal transaction unless otherwise stipulated.

The majority of contracts governed by the judicial system can be executed validly by means of any data transmission and storing system as regards their form. Transfers of immovable property and certain consumer credit contracts are the principal exceptions.

Contracts concluded through an information network generally belong to a category of legal transactions whose form is not dictated by any specific regulations; therefore, the use of the information network does not normally cause problems concerning their formal validity.[43]

The main problem with electronic contracts is that their legal security can be compromised unless the expressions of will are documented adequately to make them verifiable. In fact, the problems of producing evidence constitute a significant problem in respect of electronically executed legal transactions.

Electronically made contracts must also take into consideration section 7 of the Legal Transactions Act. It stipulates that an offer or the respective answer which are cancelled are not binding if the cancellation is received by the party to whom the offer or answer was presented before or at the same time as he had learned of the offer or the answer. Legal practice has for instance taken the view that the cancellation of an answer given to an order is still possible if the seller has not yet undertaken definitive measures to fulfil the contract.

Electronic Signatures

8-15   Signing of documents has traditionally been considered a means to document the legal validity of the intentions expressed by the contracting parties and to verify the legal capacity of the parties themselves. The time of signing of a written document is in legal practice considered to be the moment of executing the contract unless evidence exists to the contrary. The time of signing is significant also because the contract negotiations are considered closed at that moment. All the terms and conditions agreed up to that moment have been integrated in the contract, and it is no longer possible to include new terms without amending the contract.

The currently valid Finnish law does not generally require a signature as a precondition for the validity of contracts. It is required that a document must be undersigned if the contract otherwise requires a written form. A signature is a prerequisite of validity in Finland primarily only for legal transactions which must follow a specific form. It can also be an established practice within certain industries to execute contracts in writing. The significance of signature is in the Finnish judicial system impacted by the burden

---

43 Ministry of Transport and Communications, Publication Number 15/92, *Tietoverkon oikeudelliset kysymykset*, Helsinki, 1992, at p. 68.

of proof in situations of forgery, and by the importance given to "graphological" study for the evaluation of evidence.

When the contract is concluded using a telephone, telefax, or other electronic transmission system, an original signature is not possible in the same way as if written on a traditional hard copy of the document. A signature in an electronically transferred document, like indeed the whole document, is a copy of the original document. Thus, the signature of a document sent, *e.g.*, by telefax loses its character indicating originality.

Signature is generally not a prerequisite of validity pursuant to Finnish law, but the objective of originality and correctness is achieved by using the identification and protection protocols created for information transmission systems. Finnish legislation does not currently recognise electronic signatures.

In case of commercial contracts concluded via information networks, the seller must forward the confirmations of contract for further confirmation, for instance, by mail if he wishes to ensure that the buyer becomes bound by the transaction. The seller has the burden of proving that the buyer accepted the offer on the terms and conditions announced by the seller, although this is generally not done in practice. The seller can also minimise his risks by requesting advance payment for the goods; this can be unfair on the buyer before the goods have been inspected.

The problems associated with electronic signature concern in fact more often the difficulty of ensuring the identity of the other contracting party in technically as safe a way as possible rather than the actual signature as such. One alternative is to assign a third party to verify the identities on behalf of the contracting parties, perhaps by means of specific pre-arranged codes.

Already long-established instruments are the on-line payment and credit cards of banks and credit card companies, which have achieved a satisfactory level of security in verifying the cardholder's identity by means of the identification data included in the card and the cardholder's personal code. Automatic cash dispensers have been in use in Finland for many years already, and also the most elementary banking services can today be handled electronically on automatic tellers.

The use of such identifications always involves a risk of abuse. The Consumer Protection Act has, therefore, restricted the consumers' liability in cases where the identification instrument is lost. The liability for the illegal use of the identification transfers to the financial institution from the moment when the consumer reports the disappearance of his identification instrument.

Mistakes in On-line Contracts

The mistakes in connection with the conclusion of contracts can be divided   8-16
into the following types:

- Mistakes relating to a contracting party:
  (1) The contracting party is not legally competent to enter into agreements in his own name;

> (2) The contracting party lacks due authority to enter into an agreement on behalf of someone else;
>
> (3) The contracting party is not the correct party, *i.e.*, identity.

- Mistakes concerning the expression of will:

> (1) The expression of will is not voluntary, *i.e.*, it does not correspond to the giver's will, due to the influence of a third party;
>
> (2) The expression of will was given by mistake, *i.e.*, it corresponds to the giver's will but is given on the wrong grounds;
>
> (3) Mistake of expression, *i.e.*, the expression of will does not correspond to the giver's will due to a mistake.

- Mistakes associated with the transmission of the expression of will, *i.e.*, the content of the expression of will has become distorted during transmission.

- Mistakes of form, statutory restrictions, and compelling regulations.

8-17   All these types of mistakes also can be found in on-line contracts. This chapter does not discuss the problems of interpretation or conciliation of contracts, breach of contract, or legal transactions requiring a specific form.[44]

Lack of Legal Capacity

8-18   According to Finnish law, a person who lacks legal capacity, for instance, due to minority, cannot be bound by legal transactions.

When executing contracts electronically one problem can be how the seller can be ensured whether the other contracting party is legally competent to enter into the agreement. According to Finnish law, a minor can enter into contracts, *e.g.*, to decide on the use of his earnings. Some legal transactions which are considered customary in the circumstances and are of minor significance can be binding also on a legally incompetent party.

Finnish law gives strong legal protection to such legally incompetent persons. The other contracting party bears all the risks for entering into an agreement with such a person. The *bona fides* of the other party are not protected in these circumstances.

Contract Concluded By Mistake

8-19   Finnish law starts from the basic assumption that the contract is binding in its executed form. The Legal Transactions Act, section 32(1) alleviates the basic rule in case of mistaken expression of will. The provision states that the expression of will does not bind the giver if by mistake it has acquired a content different from what was intended. This constitutes a mistake of expression. According to the provision, an expression of will that has been given a wrong content does not as such bind the giver. The provision does not specify whether

---

44 Telaranta, *Sopimusoikeus*, Helsinki, 1990.

the expression of will could be binding on the giver if the content were another (as intended). When examining the question, the contract must be interpreted according to the principles of the contractual law.[45]

For example, if the giver of an expression of will, while ordering a product from a seller via the Internet, orders two units due to a writing error even if he intended to order only one, the order binds him unless the supplier of the product knew or should have known that the order in that form was placed by mistake. The Legal Transactions Act does not recognise mistakes of motive. Mistakes of motive relate to the motives of the person expressing its will. In this case, the will of the giver is correctly expressed as such but the will has evolved on incorrect premises. A party to a legal transaction cannot refer to such mistakes of expression against his *bona fide* contracting party. The contract could, however, be invalid on other grounds.[46]

Transmission Error

The Legal Transactions Act, section 32(2), deals with transmission mistakes. 8-20 Transmission mistake means a situation where the expression of will fully corresponds to the giver's will but its content has become distorted during transmission to the other party. In this case, the expression of will does not come directly to the knowledge of the recipient but is transmitted through intermediaries. In such circumstances, the expression of will does not bind the sender regardless of the recipient's *bona fides*. However, the person expressing its will must inform the recipient immediately after learning that the transmitted expression of will was not received in the same form as it was sent, otherwise he will be bound by the expression of will in the form received by the other party.

The Legal Transactions Act, section 32, can be applied to electronic contracts, if the expression of will is given in accordance with the giver's will but is received with a distorted content, *e.g.*, due to a programming error.

Impact of Impostors or Persons without Authority

If the giver of the expression of will was not free to formulate his will and 8-21 someone has influenced it in an unacceptable way, the opposing party's ability to rely on the legal transaction is determined in accordance with the provisions of the Legal Transactions Act, chapter 3. The binding nature of the legal transaction in these circumstances is affected by the capacity of the giver and by the outrageousness of the influence (*e.g.*, coercion, or other activity).

If the party whom the expression of will concerns has personally been guilty of coercing the giver of fraudulent misrepresentation or extortion, the

---

45 Saarnilehto, *Sopimusoikeuden perusteet*, Helsinki, 1993, 3rd edition, at p. 96.
46 Saarnilehto, *Sopimusoikeuden perusteet*, Helsinki, 1993, 3rd edition, at p. 697.

legal transaction does not bind the giver of the expression of will. If the party guilty of coercing the giver of fraudulent misrepresentation or extortion is someone else, the degree of outrageousness is relevant; if the giver of the expression of will was outrageously coerced to enter into the legal transaction due to use of violence or a threat to his life or health, the expression of will does not bind the giver regardless of whether the recipient knew of the coercion or not. If a third party has influenced the formulation of the will by the giver by using milder coercion or making himself guilty of fraudulent misrepresentation or extortion, the expression of will does not bind the giver if the opposing party knew or should have known that the giver had become the victim of such acts.

With electronic contracts, the lack of personal contact between the giver and the recipient of the expression of will is likely to reduce the recipient's ability to notice defects of the previously mentioned type in the sender's expression of will. The requirement of *bona fides* can then be more readily fulfilled than when executing traditional contracts.[47]

Another risk associated with the transmission of information in general electronic networks is that the transmitted message may have been manipulated or accessed by an unauthorised party. Finland observes the principle of free evaluation of evidence in legal proceedings. In resolving the case, the court is free to decide in each specific case how much value it wants to give to the evidence produced. The court can establish that the more readily the message corresponds to the giver's expression of will, the better the protection of the message and the less likely the influence of a third party.

With electronically concluded legal transactions, it is not as easy as with traditional contracts to verify whether a contracting party is the correct contracting party. According to Finnish law, the legal transaction is only binding if it has been executed personally by the contracting party or by another party legally qualified to execute the transaction on behalf of the former. The party in whose name the legal transaction is executed is in principle not liable for the other party's lack or exceeding of legal competence; the risk in this situation is borne by the other party.

The alleged giver of the expression of will is liable neither for the falsification of origin nor for the falsification of the content of the expression of will. If the other party does not verify the legal capacity of the giver to bindingly express his will, the former must personally assume the risk that he may be unable to enforce the expression of will in relation to the party in whose name it was given, if it can be proved that the party who actually gave it lacked all legal competence to express the will, or that the originally genuine expression of will had been falsified before received by the other party. According to Finnish law, the position of the recipient is not

---

47 Ministry of Transport and Communications, Publication Number 15/92, *Tietoverkon oikeudelliset kysymykset*, Helsinki, 1992.

impacted by his *bona fides* as to the authenticity of the contents of the expression of will and the legal capacity of the giver.

In electronic transmission, several technical procedures can be to verify the identity of the person expressing its will and the integrity of its content or its form; the obtained degree of security can vary greatly, depending on the quality and technological level of the procedure.[48]

On-line Payments

Electronic Fund Transfers

When using a bank transfer, the buyer gives an order to charge a sum to his account. It has long been possible to carry out bank transfers electronically by means of an electronic terminal. In Finland, transfers between different banks have been made electronically since the 1970s on the basis of a clearing system.   8-22

Cheques and bank cards/credit cards are credit orders, which the recipient activates on the basis of the payer's authorisation. Cheques are no longer commonly used in Finland. More convenient bank and credit cards have replaced them almost entirely. A credit card means that the account identification relates to an account with an overdraft facility, whereas a bankcard means an account identification that does not permit overdrafts.

When a credit card or a bankcard is used as means of payment, the buyer authorises a third party, *e.g.*, a credit card company, to charge the payment to his account. The credit card company then makes the payment to the seller. Payment orders and authorities can be issued in hard copy or electronically. In this context, electronic payment refers only to an established payment procedure where electronic transfers have replaced hard copy data transmissions. The actual implementation of the payment as a transfer from the account at the bank has not changed.[49] As technologies are evolving, the transfers are approaching on-line transactions, *i.e.*, when the identification card is read on a terminal in connection with shopping, the debiting, *i.e.*, transfer, is charged at the same time to the cardholder's account.

An efficient technique already exists for the electronic use of credit cards on the Internet. The problem is that the users must acquire separate terminals to read the cards, or otherwise it should be possible to use the cards on public terminals where the net purchases could be paid.

A more likely alternative is that the future standard for shopping in an electronic network will be an electronic signature which will permit risk-free payments directly on the payer's own terminal, once adequate identification and code systems have been developed. Such experiments already exist.

---

48 Ministry of Transport and Communications, Publication Number 15/92, *Tietoverkon oikeudelliset kysymykset*, Helsinki, 1992, p. 70.
49 Reports of the Ministry of Finance 1996:18, *Report of the Working Group on the Regulation of Electronic Money*, at p. 5.

EuNet Finland Oy is currently involved in an experiment where electronic money can be deposited on the hard disk of the payer's own terminal; this is discussed in more detail in the following paragraph.

Electronic Money

8-23   According to the currently valid Finnish legislation, generally used cash payment instruments can only be issued by the Central Bank.[50] However, the Money Act is not applied to electronic payment instruments, and the Bank of Finland as the central bank will probably not start issuing electronic money.

An essential regulatory requirement concerning electronic money is that the system should be able to verify the issuer's ability to honour its obligation to redeem the issued payment instruments in all circumstances. Essential aspects of the regulation of electronic money also include information protection, transferability of electronic money, and possible loading restrictions. The solutions for the information systems required for electronic money are only just beginning to take shape; consequently, no legal provisions with the status of an act exist to date to regulate the system.

The Working Group on the Regulation of Electronic Money suggests that the right to launch a system of electronic money involving considerable public buying power should be restricted to credit institutions and payment instrument corporations. These organisations are required to be sufficiently solvent and possess an adequate technical and organisational security. The payment instrument corporation would be a party permitted only to engage in issuance of electronic money and closely related operations. The legislation on credit institutions would apply to the payment instrument corporation where appropriate.

There is no need to regulate the electronic money systems designed for a single use. Systems with restricted circulation would only need to report the beginning and closing of their operations, and the volume of their buying power in circulation. The regulation of such single-use electronic money systems has not been considered necessary because it would slow down the development of the systems and because the consequences of the issuer's bankruptcy or payment difficulties would be restricted. The qualified suitability of the electronic money issued by such restricted systems also reduces their attraction as a target for abuse.[51]

Electronic money is directly comparable to traditional cash, *i.e.*, notes and coins issued by the central bank. In this case, the payment units representing an economic value and buying power are in an electronic form, and the payment effected with the unit is immediately final in the payer's and the recipient's mutual relationship. The actual money transfer is thus made outside the banking system.

---

50 Money Act, Number 358/April 16, 1993.
51 Reports of the Ministry of Finance 1996:18, *Report of the Working Group on the Regulation of Electronic Money*, at pp. 1–3.

The payment units are stored for instance on the electric circuit of the card or on the hard disc of a home computer. In the card alternative, the payment units are stored or released in direct contact with the issuer's loading equipment, or correspondingly in the payment equipment of the provider of the service in accordance with the so-called face-to-face principle. If, on the other hand, the payment units are stored on the hard disc of a home computer or other similar equipment, both the loading and the payment are made in the information network as an electronic transaction. The card and net money thus differ by the technologies used for transmitting the payment units, and not by the payment instrument.[52]

Today, the differences of net money also include security issues. The technical security of net money is based on technical protection, *e.g.*, cryptography and cipher systems, while the security of card money is also based on the physically protected handling of the card.

Advance payment systems are also similar to electronic money. Under these systems, the user buys payment units in advance loading them for instance on an electronic card and paying their counter-value to the issuer of the units. In this case, the use of payment units is limited only to purchases of the issuer's goods and services or other restricted offerings of goods or services. They are actually advance payments where the payment slips are in the form of electronic entries ready on a microprocessor (*e.g.*, telephone cards). In a legal sense, they do not differ from traditional serial bus tickets or monthly tickets. Due to their restricted purpose of use, such advance payment systems do not fulfil the characteristics of money.

Electronic money combines features from both traditional cash and money deposits and, as with cash and money deposits, the use is ultimately based on trust. There must be the certainty that the buying power of the purchased payment units is retained and that they can be converted into money deposited on an account. Technical security is another basic requirement for an efficient payment instrument.

Electronic money is immaterial in relation to traditional money, and imposes special requirements on safeguarding the authenticity of the money. An advantage of electronic money is its convenience of use and the ready adaptability of the payment to correspond to the smallest useable unit of money. Electronic money is a natural aspect of purchases made in an electronic network.

The operating principle of net money is that an individual user orders from the electronic network a program by which the necessary passwords are delivered to him. Then, the user pays money to the issuer who books a sum of money equivalent to the customer's payment to the customer's net money account. The user can then use the net money in an electronic network drawing against the balance of his net money account. He can then

---

52 Reports of the Ministry of Finance 1996:18, *Report of the Working Group on the Regulation of Electronic Money*, at p. 5.

make payments with the net money in the network to companies that have announced that they accept the issuer's net money; after this, the issuer credits the corporate user with legal tender perhaps in larger instalments.

According to the terms of electronic money, like other banking services, the official supervision in Finland is based on the Credit Institutions Act[53] and the Consumer Protection Act. These laws permit a supervision of both electronic money and card money, because their norms for the scope of applicability do not impose restrictions on the offering, distribution, or marketing channels used.

Today, the provisions that can be applied to abuse of electronic money are those dealing with crimes of information technology, with fraud,[54] and with payment instruments fraud.[55]

Credit Card Payments On-line

8-24   It has been possible for a considerable time already to use the banks' automatic tellers to withdraw money, pay bills and request statements of account by means of bankcards. Credit cards arrived in Finland in the 1950s.[56] The machines have been linked to the systems of the different banking groups to form co-operation groups where the customers have been able to also use machines belonging to another bank.

Credit cards are commonly used in retail trade where the equipment of the retailer, *i.e.*, the payment terminal, creates a coded payment transaction for the payment of the customer's purchase. This is basically a traditional bank card payment where the hard copy document is created by means of a bank card, except that the hard copy document is replaced by direct automatic compilation of data. The customer endorses the payment, either by his signature on the receipt issued by the payment terminal — this is probably the most common way of payment even today — or by feeding his personal identification code into the terminal in a way similar to automatic cash dispensing machines.

If the customer's individual purchase exceeds a certain control limit, the company that accepts the card is required to verify the personal information of the cardholder. On-line technology also permits accessing the list of suspended cards or the information concerning the balance on the customer's account. In case of credit card payments, the authority to make major purchases — the remaining credit limit of the cardholder — is first checked with the credit card company, for instance by placing a telephone call with the card control service.

The subscription fees of bank and credit cards charged on-line are based on the agreement between the bank or financial institution and the cardholder, and that between the bank or financial institution and the business

---

53 Credit Institutions Act, Number 1607/93.
54 Penal Code, chapter 36.
55 Penal Code, chapter 37.
56 Aurejärvi, *Luotto- ja maksuvälineet*, Helsinki, 1986.

undertaking that accepts the card concerning the use of the payment card or credit card. The agreements are based on standard conditions of contract approved by public authorities.

The consumer's liability is restricted in cases where the credit card, *i.e.*, the identification instrument, is lost. The liability for possible illegal use transfers to the credit or financial institution operating as a business undertaking immediately after the holder of the identification instrument has reported the loss of the instrument.[57]

The Visacard may already be used on the Internet by indicating the card number on ordering. The rules for accepting the identification do, however, not yet recognise the use of the identification on the Internet. This means that the business undertaking which accepts the card must still verify the identity of the user, read the identification code and request the user to sign as if the customer used the instrument physically in person. If the business accepts the mere identification number on the Internet, the risk and the burden of proof in case of abuse rests on the business undertaking that accepted the number only. In such circumstances the accepting business undertaking must be able to prove that a contract concerning the transaction was executed.

Today, the biggest credit card companies are developing a so-called SET protocol (Secure Electronic Transactions). The use of a credit card as identification for transactions on the Internet could be secured by means of the protocol. The objective is to create a sufficiently sophisticated ciphering system by means of a key that it is virtually unbreakable. Companies which sell their offerings on the Internet would consent to a strict protocol to ensure the buyer's right to use a specific credit card system for his purchases on the Internet.[58] Some of the problems faced when developing the SET protocol and the security of its ciphering system are associated with the United States, French and Israeli legislation which have criminalised the use of unbreakable ciphering systems, referring to reasons of State security.

From a juridical point of view, the use of a SET key and its verification can probably be compared to the current use of credit cards, and will thus not require new legislative measures in Finland.

ELECTRONIC INFORMATION RIGHTS

The immaterial rights relating to electronic communications are subject to **8-25** the same rules as, *e.g.*, communications carried on radio waves or by means of paper.

---

57 Consumer Protection Act, chapter 7, section 19.
58 Europay Sweden, SET Press release, Stockholm, December 4, 1996.

Finnish copyright is not restricted to any specific type of work. This means among other things that a photographer's right is protected so that no copies can be produced of a photograph without the photographer's permission for commercial distribution for instance by producing electronic copies as part of a multimedia product. Similarly, the provisions on protection of news and quotation rights are applicable to electronic papers published on the Internet.

Electronic networks pose a problem mainly with regard to the financial rights of the authors, because the digital distribution and copying of works is extremely quick, easy, and inexpensive.

The networks carry entirely new products that must also be protected already because of the increasingly commercial aspect of the Internet. For instance, the registration of home page addresses, *i.e.*, so-called domain names, closely resembles traditional industrial rights.

Today, companies use the Internet in their businesses mainly as a marketing tool, informing consumers of their brands, products, and services on the World Wide Web home pages. Technically, the home page is an open file that can be accessed by all net users. It is generally presented graphically and contains the presentation of the owner of the page. To enable net users to access the home page, it must have an address identification. These are called domain names.

To avoid confusion, there can only be one identical domain name in use at a time. Originally, the domain name was just an address comparable to a telephone number. It is easier to find the files if the domain name can be directly associated with the business of the company which owns the home page. It has become a world-wide practice that one element of the domain name is the name or brand of the company.

The registrations of domain names are in principle managed so that each country has a body that receives applications for reservation of a domain name according to a geographical distribution. The United States system is based on an organisation-driven allocation of domain names.

The organisation that registers domain names in Finland is European Union-Net Finland Oy. The registration procedure is based on the rules of F.I.C.I.X., which is the common organisation of companies offering Internet services.

The registration of a specific domain name has not required producing advance evidence in all countries to show that the registered party is indeed entitled to use the name. As a consequence, someone may illegally register the name of a big international company as its domain name in the United States, and when the company tries to register a home page with its name it is not possible, because the name is already reserved for someone else.

If the party that registers such a name *mala fide* in Finland is another company, the Unfair Trade Practices Act is applicable to such action. This name piracy is problematic because the Internet is international and the name of the company can be quite legally registered in the Internet server of another State as a domain name. For this reason, the international registration practice is being updated, and it has been debated whether the registration of the domain names should be entrusted to an international organisation or whether national organisations should have the obligation to examine the registrations of industrial rights in other countries to avoid violations.

According to the Trade Marks Act, sections 5 and 6, a trade mark entitles its holder to prohibit others from using the protected trade mark as a symbol for the same or similar products or services. A trade mark can be used to protect a domain name if the symbol is used in commercial activity. A domain name may also be registered as a trade mark. As the trade mark protection depends on the product categories where the trade mark is protected, it is recommended to protect the trade mark in all the categories essential for the operations of the company and perhaps also in all of the most essential product categories associated with network operations.

Property Rights in Electronic Information

An essential element of traditional copyright is the work that is to be protected.   8-26
Digital data transmission poses problems for the traditional protection of the work. Digitally stored data can be readily transmitted and copied without compromising its quality, or detached from the original work. It is not clear to date whether the transfer of the work in the net is considered producing a copy or whether the copy is deemed as produced only when received via an electronic terminal or shown on a terminal.

The concept of a copy of a work has previously been closely linked with different means of distribution. Electronic transmission has emerged as an entirely new type of distribution. The general trend in transmission of works is from mass distribution towards customised distribution where the works are transmitted along information highways with an "address tag".[59]

According to the copyright law, the works are divided according to type and genre. A new combination of different types of work, multimedia was developed as the result of digital technology, combining all the categories of work which can be produced in digital form. The problem is to decide the category in which a multimedia product containing several different types of work should be placed. To avoid violating the copyrights of the original authors, multimedia production should permit the identification of the various works included in the product, as well as the holders of the respective titles. When the structures become fragmented and the works turn into raw material, the authors lose the ability to control their works

---

[59] Reports of the working groups of the Ministry of Education, 13: 1995, *Tekijänoikeudet informaatioyhteiskunnassa*, Report of the Copyrights Committee on the Impact of Digital Developments on Copyright, at p. 5.

and the producers their productions. In these circumstances, it is necessary to develop markings and identifications.[60]

How to define the actual author is another problem created by the new technology. The digital form of the material permits the processing and alteration of information so that totally new works are created less often and a created new work is simply a modification and combination of existing material. The line between the author and the user of the work has become blurred and the author has become a kind of contributor.

Another reason for the definition problem can also be that, when a work is created on a computer or the work is interactive, users can with their own actions modify the original work communicating with the actual work. Such a work does not necessarily have any permanent form since it changes constantly.

Financial rights, such as the right of the author to distribute his work or produce copies of it, can cause problems as the digital technology increases the value of use and the benefits and speeds up the distribution of the work. A typical example of the right to copy and modify a specific work is sampling, *i.e.*, parts are taken from one or several musical works, combining them in a new way to create a new work.

New ways and situations of use, such as information networks, can require a redefinition of public presentation in a digital environment.

A new immaterial right may be needed, a special digital right which would govern the use of works presented in a digital environment. The existence of digital rights could be required in situations where the technical form of the work changes.

As digital technology permits an easy modification of works, it also increases the risk of violation of moral rights. It may be problematic to identify the original author, especially of multimedia products containing a large amount of material taken from several sources. One solution could be to include a digital identification code in the works. Such identification systems would enable the identification of the original works existing in digital form and their parts, tracing the authors and holders of other rights. Then, it may be possible that the definition of the first author of the work would require a registration of the work. The efficiency of such identification systems requires, however, international agreements and perhaps legislative measures.[61]

Copyright issues play a key role particularly in connection with multimedia products. As a rule, the production of a multimedia product requires sizeable financial commitments and involves a large number of people. The unit price of the actual finished product should not be prohibitive to ensure returns on the financial investments. If the licensing of the authors' copyrights

---

60 Reports of the working groups of the Ministry of Education, 13: 1995, *Tekijänoikeudet informaatioyhteiskunnassa*, Report of the Copyrights Committee on the Impact of Digital Developments on Copyright, at p. 11.

61 Reports of the working groups of the Ministry of Education, 13: 1995, *Tekijänoikeudet informaatioyhteiskunnassa*, Report of the Copyrights Committee on the Impact of Digital Developments on Copyright.

to the multimedia product in favour of the producer with regard to the finished product is not properly managed, the result can be that the financial exploitation of the product becomes impossible due to the royalty claims from various parties. The same applies to the actual raw material for the multimedia product, *i.e.*, its constituent elements, which may be works produced already much earlier.

Copyright — Applicability of Copyright to On-line Communications

Due to their international legal nature, copyrights have been protected for a   8-27 long time already by multinational agreements. The Berne Convention protecting literary and other artistic works was signed in 1886. Finland adhered to the Berne Convention in 1928. The Finnish law governing copyright is the Copyright Act.[62]

According to the Copyright Act,[63] section 1, the author of a literary or artistic work owns the copyright to the work. The work can be a belletristic or descriptive, written or oral presentation, composition or performance, photographic work or other work of visual art, architecture, articraft, or applied art, or presented in some other way. According to subparagraph 2,[64] also maps and other descriptive drawings, or works of graphic or plastic art and computer programs, are considered literary works.

For legal protection pursuant to Finnish law, the work must be independent and original. Independence and originality generally means that no one else who could have undertaken the task would have created a fully identical work.[65]

The threshold of work varies depending on the type of work and is easily exceeded in the case of literary works. Short news, ordinary advertisements, and other similar presentations are excluded from the protection. One criterion can be whether the author has been obliged to follow instructions and models to such an extent that no room is left for independence and originality.[66]

Information Protected

According to the Copyright Act, section 2, copyright confers the exclusive   8-28 right to dispose of the work by copying it and making it available to the public in a modified or unmodified form, in a translation or a variation, in another literary or artistic form, or using a different production method.

---

62 Copyright Act, Number 404/July 8, 1961.
63 Copyright Act, Number 446/March 24, 1995.
64 Act 34/January 11, 1991.
65 Haarman, *Immaterialioikeuden oppikirja*, Helsinki, 1994, at p. 31.
66 Haarman, *Materialioikeuden oppikirja*, Helsinki, 1994, at p. 31.

In practice, the main rule is that a work processed in an electronic form is given largely the same protection as a literary work.[67]

Protection of Databases

8-29 The Copyright Act,[68] section 49, provides for catalogue protection. Catalogue protection refers to a catalogue, table, or other similar work that combines a large amount of data. The catalogue may also enjoy copyright protection if the originality and independence threshold is exceeded.

The legislature's objective has been to protect catalogues which contain large volumes of information, because the compilation of data may have required a considerable amount of work; consequently such catalogues, while not exceeding the threshold of work, are protected by a special statutory catalogue protection. A precondition for catalogue protection, like other copyright categories, is that the catalogue should be in some way distinguishable from other catalogues.

Thus, the catalogue protection protects, *e.g.*, sales catalogues, timetables, address calendars, television program guides, etc. A list of certain addresses compiled from the Internet can enjoy catalogue protection. However, catalogues compiled by agents, *i.e.*, sub-programs, can pose problems because it can be claimed that the production of such catalogues does not necessarily take much time, competence or capital, and that probably virtually anyone could produce a similar catalogue using the subprogram if it is available.

This catalogue protection has, however, been restricted by the regulation that laws, decrees, decisions, and other statements by authorities and other public bodies cannot enjoy copyright. For instance, special provisions on educational activities, libraries, the judicial system, and official publications restrict catalogue protection.

Electronic databases enjoy a similar protection as catalogues or tables containing the corresponding information in a written form.

Limitations of Copyright

8-30 The Copyright Act, chapter 2, stipulates that anyone can produce a few copies of a published work for private use. Notwithstanding, a computer program cannot be copied even for private use. The Finnish copyright legislation has been amended accordingly.[69]

A published work may be quoted in a conventional scope appropriate for the purpose.

---

67 Publications of the Ministry of Transport and Communications 15/92, *Tietoverkon oikeudelliset kysymykset*, Helsinki, 1992, at p. 63.
68 Copyright Act, Number 34/January 11, 1991.
69 European Council Directive 91/250/E.C.

An article dealing with religious, political or current affairs can be taken from a newspaper or periodical and published in another newspaper or periodical unless its reproduction is prohibited.

Ownership of Copyright

According to the Copyright Act, section 1, copyright belongs to the author **8-31** of a literary or artistic work. The copyright is established pursuant to law, and thus requires no registration in Finland. If the authors are more than one and their individual contributions cannot be separated as independent works, they have a joint copyright to the work.

The Copyright Act also contains special provisions on the copyright status of the arranger, translator, and creator of a compiled work as well as on the status of works published anonymously or with a pseudonym.

The Copyright Act,[70] section 40b, concerning computer software stipulates that if a computer program and a closely related work have been created in connection with the author's employment, the copyright to the software and the related work accrue to the employer on the basis of the employment relationship. This also applies to public officials' works, but not to postgraduate teaching and research activities.

Rights of the Copyright Owner

According to the Copyright Act, section 2, copyright confers the exclusive **8-32** right on the owner to dispose of the work by copying it and making it available to the public either unmodified or modified, in a translation or adapted into another literary or artistic form, or by means of another production method.

In addition, the transfer of the original work to an apparatus for reproduction is considered production of a copy. Making the work available to the public means its presentation in public or offering a copy of the work for sale, leasing, borrowing, or other distribution or presentation of the work among the public. Furthermore, presentation to a relatively large restricted audience in connection with a commercial activity is considered public presentation.

Finnish law permits the transfer of all of the above rights to another party without any restriction, *e.g.*, through licensing or selling.

Copyright further includes moral rights, which the author cannot validly transfer to another party. Moral rights consist of the right to be acknowledged as the author and the right to respect. The Copyright Act, section 3(1), deals with the right to be acknowledged as the author. This means that when the financial rights relating to the work are exploited, the author can always

---

70 Copyright Act, Number 34/January 11, 1991, and Number 418/May 5, 1993.

demand that his name must be mentioned in that connection. The Copyright Act, section 3(2), deals with the right to respect, meaning the author's right to oppose any modification or publication of the work which is likely to insult his honour, *i.e.*, the literary or artistic esteem he enjoys.

Period of Validity of Copyright

8-33   According to the Copyright Act, section 43, copyright subsists 70 years from the author's death or, if the copyright belongs to several parties jointly, from the death of the last surviving author.

The copyright to a work which has been published without disclosing the name or a generally recognised pseudonym or *nom de plume* of the author remains in force until 70 years have passed from the year when the work was read. A catalogue, table, program, or other similar work that includes a significant amount of combined work cannot be copied without the compiler's consent until 10 years have passed from the year when the work was published.

CHAPTER 9

France

Philippe Coen
Panthéon-Sorbonne University
Paris, France

INTRODUCTION

The information highways and primarily the Internet are revolutionising the 9-1
way people and companies communicate. In France, the legal framework
concerning on-line transaction is still unclear because of the particularity of
on-line tools.

The World Wide Web is a precious link, information has a commercial
value, and commerce is being more and more virtual and digitised. The Internet
is often compared to a huge library since people from any point of the world
may access to any server.

Costs of intermediaries are decreasing with the advance of on-line
transactions. Consumers are thought to gain bargaining power in this way.
The Internet creates a strange phenomenon for legal experts since it is not
regulated by a centralised authority entitled to control the content of the
data offered on-line.

While Europe is issuing its own currency, a new currency may be created
on the net, with no paper aid. Goods or services purchased on-line in the
near future may be paid for in "Net money". Paper money may become less
used than virtual money and electronic transactions. Traditional cash payment is decreasing, especially with the Web. The cyber system is likely to
change and reduce the notion of national sovereignty.

The Internet may also be an Orwellian nightmare since any person who
accesses a Web site can in turn easily be identified and tracked. Such tracking
is very attractive for corporate marketing departments but may prejudice
individual rights especially where privacy is concerned. The Internet is a step
toward the perfection of mass communication where the law will be the last
barrier — unless technology moves forward more quickly than legal texts.

The on-line transaction issues challenge the definition of privacy under
French law. A French author defines privacy as follows:

"Privacy is the sphere of each individual where no one can intrude without being invited. Freedom of privacy is the recognition of every

person to benefit his own activity area, where the said person is able to prohibit to another person."[1]

9-2   Two concepts are in conflict. The Internet should be widely and freely accessible, or the Internet should be a business forum. In fact, providing information has a cost that cannot be denied. Companies able to compete in the long run will certainly be those holding sufficient content and with sufficient financial and technical resources.

In most developed countries, on-line transactions are on the verge of becoming the most commonly used trans-action system for business transactions. France has a national on-line system (Minitel) accessible to any person equipped with a telephone. Minitel has been operated from the beginning of the 1980s by a company which was, until 1997, state-owned, France Télécom.

The business world's rapid evolution with on-line transactions forces the legal system and the case law related to on-line trans-actions to adapt. To date, the specific issues raised by new technologies have a few answers in French law. International conventions and the French legislature will offer some of the answers, but the major part of the burden of answering these questions will fall on the judges.

ELECTRONIC TRANSACTIONS

9-3   There are many rules relating to electronic commerce, but these rules are not fully adapted to this specific way of concluding contracts. Electronic transactions constitute contracts that are much more peculiar than non-electronic contracts provided by the Civil Code.

A commercial electronic contract arises from the meeting of an offer and an acceptance of goods or services through audio-visual means using an international telecommunication network. The offer and acceptance, therefore, may arise from interactivity.

Creation of Contracts Electronicallys

9-4   For an electronic contract to be validly formed, the wills of the parties must coincide and their valid consent must be given. The physical separation of the parties while concluding a contract raises the issue of identification. As in any contract, identification of the contracting parties is essential to its conclusion in accordance with consumer and audio-visual services law. A difficulty concerning on-line transactions is that an electronic contract is a contract between partners physically separated that can be concluded on an open international

---

1 Rivero, *Libertés publiques* Presses Universitaires de France, 1996 at p. 74.

network where any person could interfere. Persons, consumers and professionals, and companies need to identify the co-contracting parties. Another issue is to avoid contracting with certain persons (*e.g.*, minors) in particular when the transaction concerns alcohol, pornographic or violent messages.

There are many ways to avoid contracting with undesired parties. The most practical way is the secret code for signature (acceptance). The secret code, whether magnetic or microchip (*e.g.*, credit cards), allows identification of the cardholder. The cardholder must keep the card and its secret code, which in no case must be disclosed. The holder is thus informed when he receives the secret code that he must be prudent and not write down his or her PIN-code (Personal Identification Number).

In practice, persons committing credit card of fraud often obtain the code either because it was voluntarily disclosed or was obtained by fraudulent means. The lack of security in this matter is essentially due to the holder's negligence. Fraud may also stem from the flimsy nature of the magnetic strips and their weak resistance to fraud.

A second solution is encryption. This technique allows locking the data by using a password or an integrated system and prevents anyone from gaining access to the data or reproducing data. Until 1986,[2] encryption was considered a second category military device subject to the Law-Decree of April 18, 1939,[3] that sets forth a principle of prohibition. Under Decree 1986, encryption is defined as the use of "equipment or software conceived either to transform information or non-legible signals by using secret conventions, or to carry out the inverse operation". Law Number 90-1170 of December 29, 1990,[4] on the regulation of telecommunications, provides a similar definition replacing the notion of "services" with the words "equipment or software".

Encryption is not only a way to protect the message itself but also to identify the partner with a system of codes and keys to decode the message. It is possible to determine the person entitled to decipher the message. In this context, the main interest of encryption is to allow any intruder to be revealed by using a password, an access number and by providing for confidential information that makes it possible to identify him.

Encryption's former use as a military device during wartime created a legal obstacle. A restrictive French Law of December 29, 1990, its application Decree[5] and two Ministerial Orders of December 28, 1992,[6] have laid down the rules. Article 28-1 of the Law of December 29, 1990, now provides a dual regime. It distinguishes between the formality of preliminary declaration where encryption is used to authenticate a communication or to guarantee its integrity

2 Decree Number 86-250 of February 18, 1986, O.J., February 26, 1968, at p. 3018.
3 O.J., June 13–17, 1939.
4 O.J., December 30, 1990, at p. 16439.
5 Decree Number 92-1358, O.J., at p. 17914.
6 O.J., December 30, 1992, at p. 17916.

and the preliminary authorisation of the Prime Minister in other cases where encryption is used beyond the purpose of authentication.

Criminal sanctions are applicable in case of failure to declare or non-authorisation. To this day, no criminal action appears to have been taken or prosecuted on these bases.

The new Telecommunication Law, Number 96-659 of July 26, 1996,[7] has substantially modified the rules. Contrary to the expectations of the professionals operating on the electronic commerce market, there is no absolute freedom in this matter.

Since July 1996, the use of encryption, in its confidentiality function, is unrestricted if the user provides the keys to decode the message to a "trusted third party" entitled to deliver these to the government on request. Use of encryption is also unrestricted when the sole function of encryption is to authenticate an on-line communication or to secure the integrity of the delivered mail. In all other cases, the mechanism of preliminary authorisation by the Prime Minister remains applicable.

A new system has been created in France — with a limited use up to now — to identify the contracting party when a contract is concluded by phone: the token (*jeton*). The token has been created for banking operations and emits an acoustic message identifying a particular token. A secret code can be linked to the token. It has many advantages because of its personalisation and inviolability and is used as a telephone signature. This solution can be applied to different services (telebanking, audiotel, payment, and fax) and games by phone or pay-per-view television.

Interactivity does not always help or allow negotiation of contracts. In particular, with respect to contracts between a professional and a consumer, on-line transactions are not in practice a way to propose negotiable contracts. French rules on offer and acceptance for common contracts apply to electronic contracts.[8]

Offer

9-5   There is no legislative definition of offer. It may be defined as a proposal sufficient to allow the offeree to agree the conclusion of the contract. It is more than an invitation to tender but less than a promise to contract, even a unilateral one.

A European draft Directive[9] concerning the protection of the consumer in contracts negotiated at a distance defines "offer". An offer is a distance communication including every necessary element for the recipient to conclude immediately a contract.

---

7 O.J., July 27, 1996, at p. 11384.
8 Itéanu, *Les aspects juridiques du commerce électronique,* 1996; Huet, "Le commerce électronique", 1996, *Gazette du Palais,* September 11–12, 1996.
9 [1992] O.J. C156/05, June 10, 1992, at p. 21.

Rules established according to case law state that the offer must be firm. This means it does not reserve the possibility of withdrawal and must contain essential elements of the contract. In the case of sales, the offer must indicate the description of the goods and the price. Recent case law has held that the price may not be pre-defined in the case of the sale of an obligation to perform as opposed to deliver goods.

The offer must always be express, but it need not be in writing. Civil law rules concerning offer are applicable to electronic transactions.

The offer may also be expressly limited for a fixed period of time. Where the limited period of time is not expressly mentioned, it may be inferred from the nature of the contract contemplated and from the time necessary for the offeree to take the decision. In any case, the time period must be reasonable, the duration being subject to the circumstances.

The principle of free revocability of the offer is therefore restricted. The offeror may be held liable if the offer is revoked during the period provided for that purpose. Where no time period is fixed, the offer is freely revocable as long as no acceptance has been made, unless the offer was made to a specific person, in which case a reasonable time period must be granted.

The distance sale is defined by the non-binding Ministerial Act (*Circulaire*) of July 19, 1988,[10] implementing the Ministerial Order of December 3, 1987,[11] concerning the obligation to inform consumers on prices, as a:

> ". . . technique of distance communication through which the enterprises offer their products or services and that enables the consumer to enter into contracts from outside the sale premises."

Sales via telemetric, telephone, video-transmission, multimedia interactive public access terminal and electronic catalogue disseminated on a network[12] are considered distance sales.   9-6

In this respect, the offer in an electronic transaction must comply with the distance sale law since it is a contract "that is executed on a network, which is not the common place to meet clients".[13]

This characterisation's consequences are the application of the Consumer Code,[14] which imposes obligations on the professional co-contractor. These include the obligation to:

- Indicate the name of the company, telephone number, and address;[15] and
- Indicate the price of the product or the service.[16]

---

10 O.J., August 4, 1988, at p. 9951.
11 O.J., December 10, 1987, at p. 14354.
12 Circular of July 19, 1988.
13 Itéanu, *Les aspects juridiques du commerce électronique*, 1996; Huet, "Le commerce électronique", 1996, *Gazette du Palais*, September 11–12, 1996; Bensoussan, *Internet, aspects juridiques,* June 1996.
14 Consumer Code, article L 121-18.
15 Law of January 18, 1992.
16 Ordinance Number 86-1243 of December 1, 1986, article 28.

9-7 A professional association of distance sellers has also set down rules recommending that an offer should be "clear, precise and rigorous and as comprehensive as possible".[17]

Under French law, consumers have the right to revoke within seven days after purchase.[18] Law Number 88-21 of January 6, 1988[19] — embodied in the Consumer Code — concerning all kinds of distance sales allows the buyer, during seven days from the date of delivery, to return the product to the seller for exchange or reimbursement, without any penalties apart from the postage costs. This retraction right appears to delay the definitive conclusion of the contract until the expiry of the seven-day period, the acceptance being in this case only a step in the formation of the contract.[20]

9-8 **Clarity of Offer / Misleading and Comparative Advertising** The obligations concerning clarity and precision must apply to the audio-visual medium, which characterises electronic commerce. All kinds of products or services presentation are involved. The Professional Code of Distance Sales enterprises provides:

> ". . . the enterprises shall ensure that the photos and drawings reproduce loyally the product or the service that is offered, and do not carry any ambiguity as to the particulars of the product, especially those concerning dimensions, weight and quality."

9-9 Moreover, the principle of accuracy governing consumer relationships requires the professional to have recourse to the different presentation techniques of the products (*e.g.*, three-dimensional pictures and technical drawings) in an accurate way.

As any advertising, an on-line offer to consumers must comply with the Consumer Code. Comparative advertising rules are also applicable to on-line advertising for a product or a service.

9-10 **Use of French for Electronic Transactions** Electronic commerce is operated on a network, most often worldwide, such as the Internet network, and the French language is not always used. The "Toubon" Law, Number 94-665 of August 4, 1994,[21] requires the tradesman to draft his/her offer in French or to attach a translation in French whenever it is not the case. This rule is mandatory, which may expose the offender to criminal sanctions.

---

17 Professional Code concerning Distance Sale, published by l'Union Française du marketing direct, December 8, 1993.
18 Consumer Code, article L 121-16.
19 O.J., January 7, 1988, at p. 271.
20 Calais-Auloy, *Droit de la consommation,* 1992.
21 O.J., August 5, 1994, at p. 11392.

However, the practical effectiveness of this rule is jeopardized by the international dimension of the network and by the difficulty of having a comprehensive view of the law when the persons in charge are foreigners and/or non-French speakers. Moreover, a directive proposal of the European Council of May 21, 1992 considered that:

> ". . . a French consumer that responds to an advertisement published in an English journal or to a sales program on television broadcast in German cannot expect to obtain all information in the language of his country of residence. If the media circulates outside his linguistic area and if the consumer decides to order, the linguistic standard must not be an obstacle to this type of transnational contracts."

As a preliminary remark, it should be noted that the 1994 Law has been **9-11** considered compatible with the French Constitution by a Constitutional Council Decision Number 94-345 of July 29, 1994.

The compatibility of the 1994 Law with the European Convention on Human Rights and Fundamental Freedoms has been raised by authors and before first instance courts.[22]

The 1994 law is a criminal law and is applicable when one of the elements constituting the offence has been committed on French territory.[23] There is a contradiction here. On the one hand, criminal law must be strictly interpreted and, on the other hand, criminal law, according to the New Criminal Code, applies widely (as soon as a person situated in France can have access to the on-line data concerned with criminal law).

According to the Supreme Court (*Cour de Cassation*), and in accordance with the *Jehring's* principle, the offence is deemed to occur at "the place of the protected economic interest". The Law protecting French language is also based on economic concerns, therefore, case law should consider that a broad application of this law will be made since most electronic messages or information can be considered as having an economic value.

Article 1(2) of Decree Number 95-240 prohibits advertising that is not made in the French language. The term advertising is not properly legally defined and covers any communication, whatever form is used, aimed at providing goods or services.

This law raises the difficulty of distinguishing between on-line communication and transactions — where transactions subject to commercial and criminal law end, and where privacy of individual rights begin.

Definition of advertising is so wide that any message sent by a potential offeror could be characterised as advertising and thus lead to the application of the law described in this chapter. However, if one compares the Internet with a world library, it appears that a person with access to a library filled

---

22 Court of Paris, *Protection of French Associations* v. *Georgia Tech*, February 24, 1997.
23 New Criminal Code, article L 113-2.

with books is not necessarily subject to advertising law and to the French language protection law. Therefore, decisions to be rendered by the courts are of particular interest.

9-12 **International Aspects** Electronic commerce's characteristic of international dimension makes determination of the relevant applicable law difficult. This problem arises when, in case of dispute, both parties, if they reside in different countries, decide to go before their national courts and have their national law applied.

9-13 *Existence of Conflict of Laws* In contract law matters, there is a conflict of laws if the contract is considered international. Authors define international private law as the law applicable to individuals involved in international legal relationships that concern several states.

French case law does not provide a uniform answer to the conditions to be met for the contract to be considered international. It sometimes suffices that the contract involves the interests of international commerce or that the payment is international. A contract can be considered to have an international character when, for the acts concerning its conclusion or performance, or the situation of the parties regarding their nationality or residence, or the localisation of its object, there are some contacts with more than one legal system.[24]

Since the open and international character of some of the electronic communication networks eases international transfers, the electronic contract often involves two or more persons residing in different countries.

9-14 *Resolution of Conflict of Laws* French conflict of law rules refer to conventions and international agreements which, in any case, are binding in France under article 55 of the 1958 Constitution. The two main conventions are the Rome Convention of June 16, 1980, on contractual obligations in general, and The Hague Convention of June 15, 1955, on international sales of goods.

9-15 *Exclusion of Rules of Conflict of Laws* The search for the applicable law is futile when criminal law or French public order rule are applicable. Under criminal law, French law will be applied if the victim of a crime or an offence is French at the time the offence was committed, without considering the nationality of the offender and the place of the offence.[25]

In the same way, the identification of the applicable law will not prejudice the application of French public order rules. Such a rule — protective

---

24 Battifol and Lagarde, *Droit internationale privé*, 7th edition, 1983.
25 New Criminal Code, article L. 113-7.

of local public and social order — is characterised by mandatory provisions whose application cannot be discarded in France (*e.g.*, most of the Consumer Code's provisions).

Acceptance

Definition   Acceptance and offer are not defined by law. Acceptance is   9-16
understood as assent to an offer, (*i.e.*, the expression of a symmetrical will to the offer).[26] Case law suggests that the offer must comply with certain conditions.

Characteristics   Acceptance must be informed. It requires the full knowledge   9-17
of the person who accepts. French case law considers that everything which is written and apparent is accepted.

Acceptance must be unconditional and address all elements of the offer. If not unconditional, the acceptance will be considered a counter-proposal, a new offer which nullifies the initial offer.

Acceptance must be free. The principle is that no person shall be obliged to accept. However, when an offer is made with a certain time limit, a delay in acceptance by the offeree may constitute a fault, particularly where a good is mobilised for a period of time.

Acceptance can be express, implicit or silent. Implicit acceptance is one that results from facts such as the execution of the contract.

Acceptance can be also silent but only in exceptional cases and special circumstances. Three cases can be considered, namely:

- Where parties have a course of dealing, silence can be interpreted as an acceptance when the new contract offered is of the same nature as the previous one or when it consists of a letter confirming a previous verbal agreement or in case of a renewal of a contract (*i.e.*, a tacit renewal);
- Where parties belong to the same professional sector and silent acceptance is provided by usage or customs; and
- Where an offer is made in the exclusive interest of the offeree.

Apart from these three cases, the principle is that silence is not worth an   9-18
acceptance.

Particular Problems Linked to Electronic Trade   Electronic trade raises a   9-19
number of specific problems such as the nature of acceptance, localising the transaction and identifying the parties.

---

26 Malaurie and Aynes, *Les obligations*, 1996.

9-20   *A "Click" as Acceptance?* There is no legal obstacle under French law for a "click" to be treated as acceptance; however, there is a risk of the acceptor contesting his consent because of lack of proof of acceptance.

To increase the validity of acceptance and reduce the potential claims based on French contract law, acceptance by clicking could be linked to a series of different keyboard operations (*e.g.*, the purchaser first enters his/her name and address and then clicks the mouse for acceptance).

Some on-line product or service sellers will be tempted to employ by-passing techniques to facilitate proof of acceptance of the seller's offer. The seller may allow or require his client to return an order form, which would have been previously downloaded and completed with an original signature. The order would then be confirmed and the paper would establish proof of acceptance without any difficulty.

Another technique consists in inviting the consumer to go to the commercial office of the seller, close to the buyer's residence for the latter to take and pay his order.

9-21   *Identification of the Co-contractor* From commercial and legal points of view, it is particularly important for the seller to identify the other contracting party, particularly when he collects personal information. He is obliged to carry out the obligations defined under the law on computerised databases on individuals.[27]

French law applies mandatorily to any personal data filed in a computerised database whatever the nationality of the data subject if any part of the file is processed on French territory. The law sets down various principles aimed at protecting data subjects and gives them certain rights.

9-22   *Localisation of the Transaction* As with distance sales, determining the time and place where the transaction is concluded presents difficulties when the parties are not physically in each other's presence. The time of execution of the transaction is dependent on the time of the property transfer and the burden of the risks and place contributes to the determination of the applicable law and the competent jurisdiction.

Regarding canvassing by phone or any other similar means, the final formation of the contract is postponed until the consumer has agreed in writing and signed the written acceptance of the offer which the professional must send to him. Therefore, it is the material document (*e.g.*, paper) which is used as a reference and proof in this case.

To solve this matter, two existing theories on the localisation of the contract should be referred to: the theory of emission and the theory of reception.

---

27 "Computer and Freedom", Law Number 78-17 of January 6, 1978, O.J., January 7, 1978.

As the court appears not to have chosen one over the other, both the above mentioned theories must be considered. The contract will be concluded when the message is sent by pushing a key (*e.g.*, "enter") of the computer (emission theory), or at the time of confirmation of the acknowledgement of receipt of the transaction (reception theory).

The legal effects of the contract will depend on the modalities according to which the reliability of the computer hour or the system hour is ensured. Risks of fraud and difficulties of proving them are to be feared.

Advertising

One of the essential conditions for the formation of the contract is the parties' capacity. The material distance of the parties in an electronic contract makes it difficult, even impossible, to be sure of the contracting parties' capacities to contract without defined identification techniques.

9-23

Furthermore, particularly when a professional makes an offer to a consumer, the professional must make an accurate offer, giving precise and clear information to the consumer.

The Internet is a privileged aid to transfer advertising and allows companies to put genuine electronic showcases allowing to make visible products or services. The difficulty is that this type of advertising broadcast like this is open worldwide. However, the regulation in this matter is not the same in all the countries. It will be necessary to determine case by case the applicable law relating to rules of conflicts of laws. The solution would be to harmonise the regulations as they have been carried out within the European Union under Directive 84/450/E.E.C. of September 10, 1984,[28] relating to the legislative regulations and administrative provisions of the member states relating to misleading advertising or the proposal of a Directive by the Council relating to comparative advertising and modifying the aforesaid Directive.

In France, the rules on advertising are strict and are deemed to protect the consumer. They concern both form and the content and they impose an obligation of loyalty on the professional *vis-à-vis* the consumer.

Definition of Advertising

Directive 84/450 defines advertising as:

9-24

". . . all forms of communication made within the framework of trade, industrial, craft activity or liberal profession, to promote the supply of goods and services, including immovable property, rights and obligations."

---

28 [1984] O.J. L250, September 19, 1984, at p. 17.

9-25   Law Number 79-1150 of December, 29, 1979, on advertising considers advertising to be any inscription, shape or image intended to inform the public or to draw attention as well as mechanisms whose main purpose is to receive inscriptions, shapes or images being assimilated to advertising. The Criminal Division of the Supreme Court has defined it as "all means of information intended to allow a potential consumer to make his own decision as to the results that can be expected of the product or the service offered to him".

General information and private messages are excluded, but the precise definition of these concepts is not completely determined.

Concerning electronic trade, it is in some cases difficult to distinguish between offer and advertising. Some authors consider that interactivity would make the difference. It can be concluded that when the service is proposed at the same time as advertising with a possibility of subscription, provisions regulating advertising will be applicable.

Regulation of the Advertising

9-26   While advertising is free in principle, it must be accurate, faithful and must not mislead the public. Misleading or false advertising, defined by the French Consumer Code as being "any allegation or presentation of a misleading nature", is prohibited and severely punished irrespective of the form, nature or medium of the advertising. Misleading advertising is aimed at consumers and if it is "made, perceived or received in France", it will be punished when it appears on any electronic communication network.

As provisions relating to misleading advertising are criminal provisions, they may be interpreted strictly. The prohibition provided by article L. 121-1 of the Consumer Code probably only concerns advertising and not messages intended to inform. However, it is difficult to distinguish these two types of communication in electronic trade, since they are based on the same multi-media aid.

The punishment provided by article L. 213-1 of the Consumer Code is imprisonment ranging from three months to two years and a fine of F.F. 1,000 to F.F. 250,000. Article L. 213-2 provides that punishment is doubled in certain cases, in particular when the advertising has had the effect of making the use of the goods dangerous to human or animal health. Also, according to article L. 121-6 of the Consumer Code, the judge can increase the punishment of up to 50 per cent of the expenses made in advertising.

Article L. 215-5 of the Consumer Code provides that the responsible person is the advertiser. This is the person who sells the product or provides the services and not the person who broadcasts it. As regards telecommunication networks, the access supplier will not be considered liable unless he is considered an accomplice in the misleading advertisement.

Principal On-line Offences

Protection of Computerised Data on Individuals

The Computer and Freedom Law 1978 The principles included in the   9-27
Computer and Freedom Law 1978[29] are as follows:

- Fair and lawful collection of information — The person concerned has a right of control over the information as regards its quantity, use and operations on them.
- Determined purpose — Data must be filed for specific and legitimate aims and may not be used in a manner incompatible with these aims.
- Exactness — Data collected must be exact and up-to-date. The person responsible for the file is obliged to check the veracity of the registered elements.
- Excluded data — Excluded is the collection of certain "sensitive" data, *e.g.*, revealing racial origins, political opinions, religious belief or any other convictions, health conditions, sexual habits and criminal convictions, is prohibited.
- Data security — The person in charge of the file is obliged to take all necessary measures to ensure the survival of the file and the confidentiality of the data.

The application of the Computer and Freedom Law 1978 is controlled and   9-28
ruled by an independent authority, namely, Commission Informatique et
Liberté, the National Computer and Freedom Commission — (*Commission
Informatique et Liberté* — C.N.I.L.).

Rights of Persons Filed Every person has the right to know the existence of   9-29
a file containing personal data of which he is the subject, its purpose, and
the identity and the main establishment of the person in charge of the file.
This is called the right to prior information. The data subject's rights include:

- Right of access — Any person has the right to procure the communication of the data concerning himself to avoid abuses and to encourage transparency.
- Right of amendment — The data subject has the right to demand the amendment of incorrect data relating to him. He can also request deletion of the data.

Any opening of a file must be declared to the C.N.I.L. If the person opening   9-30
the file fails to comply with this formality, he risks a three-year imprisonment and a fine of F.F. 300,000.

---

29 "Computer and Freedom" Law Number 78-17 of January 6, 1978, O.J., January 7, 1978.

Protection of Data Confidentiality

9-31   Confidentiality of data is now protected in a clear and unambiguous way by the "*Loi Godfrain*", Number 88–19 of January 5, 1988.[30] It punishes interference with a data system, intentional infraction defined by article 323-1(1) of the Criminal Code as "intruding" or remaining illegally in all or part of a data system. Two acts are as such punishable: the "access and the maintenance".

9-32   **Fraudulent access** The *Loi Godfrain* punishes fraudulent access whether or not it has an effect on the state of systems.[31] The notion of access means all systems of penetration, such as pirate connection, call of a program without accreditation, or examination of a file without authorisation. If it is an access "without influence", only proof of the access is sufficient. Otherwise, the access and influence on the system will have to be proved.

9-33   **Fraudulent Maintenance and Protection of Data Content** The fraudulent maintenance in a system is also punished by article 323-1 of the Criminal Code. The maintenance corresponds to unusual situations such as connection or visualisation.

Through the *Loi Godfrain*, alteration of data aimed at changing or erasing data in a file is also punishable under the Criminal Code whether or not it was intentional. Unintentional breaches, "which result from an awkwardness or suitable active principles to the system", are punishable by two years' imprisonment and a fine of F.F. 200,000.[32]

Intentional breaches, covered by articles L. 323-2 and 323-3 of the Criminal Code relate to the system or to data. The notion of intentional breaches of the system, *i.e.*, "the fact of hindering the functioning of an automatic data processing system", is extremely wide. It corresponds to any negative influence on the functioning of the system, such as "logic bombs", the occupation of memory capacity or the setting up of codifications, blocks and any other elements postponing normal access.

Functional alteration of the system refers to the modification of the functioning having an influence on programs and data. The introduction of a virus will constitute an alteration of the system's normal functioning. However, the application of article 323-1 to a virus situation comes up against the question of proof: even if it is possible to trace the terminal from which the virus entered, it will still be very difficult to determine the person who introduced the virus into the system.

Intentional alteration of data, punishable by article 323-3 of the New Criminal Code, refers to two breaches: alteration of data and introduction of

---

30 O.J., January 6, 1988, at p. 231.
31 Criminal Code, article 323-1.
32 New Criminal Code, article L. 323-1(2).

"pirate data". Alteration of data corresponds to deletion of data, modification of data, deletion and/or modification of processing methods, and deletion and/or "transmission modification". The material element of the offence is accomplished as soon as there is an unusual influence on data. The introduction of "pirate data" refers to the fraudulent intention to modify the state of the system whatever the consequences. To determine thes origin of such defects is very difficult, particularly with the Internet.

Protection Against Data Content

Protection against data content involves punishing any "immoral offenses" **9-34** and offences against public order. The *Jolibois* amendment, inserted in article L. 227-24 of the New Criminal Code, provides for protection against data content to protect minors against pornographic or violent messages.

Forgery and use of forgery defined in article L. 441-1 of the New Criminal Code are also applicable to computer forgery. Importantly, article L. 323-4 of the Criminal Code covers unlawful associations in computer matters. It provides that "the participation in an association or an agreement established with a view to the preparation, characterized by one or several material facts, of one or several offences provided by articles L. 323-1 to 323-3", is also an offence.

As in the United States, with the N.S.A.'s recent decision ruling that the data provided on-line must comply with the law applicable to publications, French rules on content and expression should be applicable under French law. This is the position of the National Consultative Commission for Human Rights,[33] which adds that a Web server should be considered a publisher. Such an opinion is likely to encourage a server to control the content of transferred data, especially in the case of newsgroups and fora. Screening techniques such as P.I.C.S. can operate control.[34]

In France, there is a special police department, created by an order of February 11, 1994, to discover these offences: the Inquiries Service on Frauds of Information Technologies (S.E.F.T.I.). S.E.F.T.I. has two important tasks, namely:

- To make inquiries on offences aimed at or using computer systems; and
- To give technical support to other services of the Criminal Investigation Department when inquiries are being made by the police.

The content of the data submitted made accessible on the net is subject to **9-35** the rules against libel, slander, defamation and racial speech offences. Such crimes are regulated by the Press Law dated July 29, 1881.

---

33 Commission Nationale Consultative des Droits de l'Homme, "Opinion on the Internet", cited in *Expertises*, Number 200 — December 1996, at p. 416.
34 As recommended by the World Wide Web Consortiu m, December 5, 1996.

In October 1995, the French government proposed to the Organisation for Economic Co-operation and Development (O.E.C.D.) an international charter on the Internet aimed at improving the organisation, management and control of the Internet. This charter articulates three ideas, namely, the commitment of each signatory state to:

- Define a typology of actors and their liability;
- Adapt the national juridical framework of the Member States and to put a behavior code; and
- Develop the judicial and policy cooperation to protect public order and public security.

On-line Payment

9-36   The lack of security for payment, particularly in open and international networks, has obstructed the boom in the electronic trade.

Telepayment (Credit Card and Home Banking Terminal)

9-37   There is a subscription system that consists in giving the details of the bank account to the professional. The account debit will be executed automatically during each purchase. This system is relatively reliable. The system is used by V.P.C. (mail order sale). It consists in asking the customer the characteristics of his credit card for his purchase, information circulating encrypted or unencrypted way on the network. The risks result from misuse of the card number and limitations introduced by the French law on the use of encoding algorithms.

Other systems offer more security, such as "telefact" for the payment of invoices (E.D.F.-G.D.F., French Télécom) or "Facitel" system to a secure payment by credit card from the home with the help of a (microchip) chip card reader.

Companies participating on the Internet have decided to work together to secure electronic payment. The Visa and MasterCard project "secure electronic transactions" would allow consumers and merchants to conclude transactions on the Internet with the same security as in the retail trade.

Virtual Payment

9-38   Electronic trade is no longer content with financial transactions by cards. A new way of payment, virtual money, has emerged. This is called "electronic purse" in France. It consists in purchasing credits from a financial body. The customer debits his/her electronic purse at each transmission of a purchase order by the network. Money circulating in this way becomes virtual. Thus, in the United States, the "cyberbucks", virtual dollars, allow payments to be made on the Internet.

This money has certain advantages such as speed of transactions, fungible money and accessibility but it has one major disadvantage, namely, that it is impossible to follow capital movements since the "issuing bank" is identifiable but not the users.

Virtual money presents a problem regarding the rules on issuing money. In France, this is reserved to the banks, but they cannot be protected in open international networks. No person or regulation will be able to protect banks against the entry of a "non-bank" entity on the market of electronic financial transactions.

Banks are reluctant because of the heavy investments necessary to set up such a system. France is experiencing some use of the electronic purse. Certain banks (the three old banks and the main mutualistic networks), the French post office and the French savings banks reached a common area agreement. The system consists of a pre-paid card that will be available for the public transport networks, parks and private companies (*e.g.*, transportation).

Examples of Secure Payments in France

The Globe ID system originated in France. It seems to be the most sophisti- 9-39
cated system at present and aims at bringing to the customers and sellers a safe, efficient and simple way of making payment transactions on the Internet. It allows customers access to an unlimited number of electronic shops and they may purchase all kinds of services and information. At the same time, it offers the merchants the possibility of proposing and selling all kinds of products.

Globe ID is open not only to large transactions but also to transactions involving small sums. It utilises the existing infrastructure of credit cards. Globe ID is based on the concept of an electronic purse for the customer and the electronic cash register for the seller. It can be only funds transfers between merchants and customers. Globe ID manages purses via a secure data processing system governed by an authorised financial institution. The payment should be secure since secret codes and credit card numbers are encrypted by the use of algorithms.

In the cybercash system, the customer gives his encrypted card number to the merchant with the amount of the operation.

Another solution involves the customer opening an account in a bank partner of the Digicash company. This bank gives the customer software that acts as a virtual purse allowing him or her to pay merchants who are members of the system.

Security and Proof

Protection of Information The "pretty good privacy" (P.G.P.) system, 9-40
which originated in the United States, makes communications inviolable on the Internet and guarantees its users some anonymity. One cannot know the identity or the nationality of the users. Such a protection makes controls

difficult and favors criminality on the open networks, particularly on the Internet. This is certainly the reason for its prohibition in the United States.

In France, P.G.P. that can be used to protect data or mail is prohibited. The French government fears that criminals would use it. Until now, only states own such encryption systems, and commercialised code can be cracked. Therefore, on-line transactions do not provide warranties for privacy and confidentiality.

9-41   **Electronic Signature and Evidence** Under in civil law, rules of proof are, for certain juridical acts, expressly imposed by the law. The law lists exhaustively the means of proof. Article 1341 of the Civil Code requires the production of a written act with a signature for all transactions of an amount exceeding F.F. 5,000 concluded with an individual. This is particularly restrictive in electronic trade matters where the paper aid is not frequent.

Case law holds that the rules of proof are not of public order, so the contracting parties can derogate from them within the framework of their contractual relationship. The parties to an electronic contract can conclude an agreement regarding proof. They can expressly relinquish the obligation of proof by a written act when this requirement is otherwise necessary and they can provide for any other means of proof. However, rules of proof are less strict in trade matters. There, the contract can be proved by any means.[35]

9-42   *Solutions for Better Proof* One of the most effective solutions is the use of acknowledgements in a systematic manner during financial transactions. This allows the existence of the message to be proved and makes it possible to ascertain that it has been received and to determine the sending date.

Swift payment is one example. It is a private and closed international network of electronic transfers of funds where a certain computer formalism has been set up to ensure optimal security.

9-43   *Electronic Signature* According to the law of contract, the original signature is an expression of assent. However, when the contract is electronically concluded, the script signature is excluded and the demonstration of proof of assent is made more difficult.

The law does not define signature, and some authors have debated the identification issue. In a case relating to payment by credit card, the Court of Appeal of Montpellier in April 9, 1987, and then the Supreme Court, in November 8, 1989,[36] admitted the validity of a computer signature consisting of a secret code and presentation of the credit card.

---

35 Commercial Code, article 109.
36 Cassation, 1 Civil Chamber, November 8, 1989, Cases Number 1340 and Number 1341, Appeals Number 86-16-19196 and Number 86-16-19197.

New forms of electronic signature exist today with the "microchip" or "memory chip", which give greater security in the identification of the member. Banks have established their own system, Etabac 5, to secure telecommunications service, signature and proof of transactions.

The intervention of a third-party certifier whose role is to control and trace the accomplishment of electronic transactions is made necessary by the insecurity of telecommunication networks, particularly of the Internet, and by the necessity to retain proof elements of transactions. Such intervention contributes also to the identification of network users. This intervention will be effective only if the third parties' independence and neutrality are guaranteed.

The parties can also designate, by a mutual accord, a third-party "witness" or "certifier", a sort of "electronic notary public", which would allow a reliable identification of parties, ensure data integrity transmitted, keep proof by means of electronic traces, and certify exchanges.

ELECTRONIC INFORMATION RIGHTS

Copyright and Authors' Rights

Distinction between Copyright and Authors' Rights

The copyright concept originated in Common Law systems. The owner of   **9-44**
the copyright attached to a work is the sole owner of the right. Authors' rights grant the author — as defined by domestic law — the right to authorise any transfer of rights attached to his work. Authors' rights include two elements: property rights and moral rights.

The moral right is a perpetual and non-transferable right that exclusively belongs to the author. It allows the author to oppose the way the work is disseminated. Moral rights also grant the author the right to be cited as the author, to demand respect for the integrity of the work and to withdraw his or her agreement on the dissemination of the work. Moral rights may be invoked, for instance, if the work is transformed without the assent of the author.

Authors' Right on Information Disseminated On-line

The authors' rights issues in the present chapter concern pre-existing works   **9-45**
included in an electronic network. Most scholars conclude that authors' rights law, as provided by the Intellectual Property Code (I.P.C.) — applies to works displayed on-line. Authors' rights protection may be granted only if the work in question fulfills a certain number of conditions.[37]

37 Coen and Sivignon, "Multimédia, l'état du droit", *Jurisanté*, September 1994, number 7, at pp. 19–24.

Such an approach is also adopted by the World Intellectual Property Organisation (W.I.P.O.). This led to the Geneva Treaty on December 20, 1996, signed by 160 countries. The treaty will enter into force when 30 countries ratify it.

9-46   **Conditions for Protection**   To be protected by authors' rights, case law has held that a work must be original. Originality is a prerequisite for authors' rights protection and distinguishes it from others. Originality is not related to novelty. In addition, work will be protected only if the following conditions are met:

- The work must be the result of a creative activity that demonstrates that the final result is a voluntary and conscious choice;
- The work must be made concrete and should be perceived by human senses directly or through technical tools; and
- An idea as such cannot be granted protection (contrary to the expression of an idea on a support).

9-47   Digitised work must fulfill the above-mentioned cumulative conditions to be protected. A digitised work displayed on-line must be authorised by the holders of the author's rights to be lawfully accessible on-line. The fact that the work is accessible on-line free of charge does not mean that the express author's authorisation need not be obtained.

Generally, on-line access to an author's work should be deemed a representation of the work as opposed to a reproduction or distribution. The European Commission has suggested this.[38]

After the signature of the 1996 Geneva Treaty, the effectiveness of the protection will depend on the protective procedures and penalties implemented in each signatory state.

9-48   **Work Digitised and Displayed On-line without Authorisation**   Digitisation and/or on-line broadcasting of a work carried out without the express consent of the author may constitute an unlawful reproduction of the work. This may amount to counterfeit under articles L. 335-2 *et seq* of the I.P.C. Counterfeiting a protected work is a criminal offence with penalties of two years' imprisonment and fines of F.F. 1-million.[39] Corporations found guilty of counterfeiting may be liable to five times the fines according to article L. 131-39 of the New Criminal Code.[40]

---

38 Lucas, "Les autoroutes de l'information: enjeux et défis", *Actes des huitièmes Entretiens Rhône-Alpes,* December 5–6, 1996, directed by Frémont and Ducasse, 1996.
39 Law Number 94-102 dated February 5, 1994; see 1996 *Dr. Gubler case,* Paris T.G.I., January 18, 1996, J.C.P. G., number 8, February 21, 1996, at p. 87.
40 Coen, "L'évolution des sanctions en matière de piraterie audiovisuelle", E.F.E. conference, Paris, June 5, 1996.

Article L. 335-3 of the I.P.C. provides that a work is counterfeit if it has been reproduced, represented or broadcast by any means in violation of the author's rights. Printing a protected work is considered as reproduction and opening a computer file and displaying it on a file constitutes a representation of the latter.

Protected work offered on the Internet has been considered for the first time by a first instance judge in a case involving students who digitised songs of Jacques Brel and then offered them on the Internet accessible throughout their Web page. The court held this to be an infringement of the author's rights when the offer of the on-line work was made without the consent of the author.[41]

Authorities entitled to control infringements of authors' rights are agents of the Program Protection Agency (*Agence Pour la Protection des Programmes*) according to article L. 331-2 of the I.P.C.

In the *Jacques Brel* Case, the summary court judge ruled on the minutes of the agents of the Program Protection Agency and concluded that providing a work on a Web page on the Internet should not fall under the free-use exception defined under French law. The judge decided that providing the work on the Internet constituted an unlawful collective use under article L. 122-5-2 of the I.P.C. The judge's decision stated that free use was solely applicable to transfer of digitised work to definite entities (*e.g.*, individual, company, or corporate body). In other cases, when a message is offered to the public, or to a part of it, or if the message is not targeted to specific addressees, then his/her message is characterised as audio-visual broadcasting. A similar decision concerning songs of a French singer Michel Sardou was rendered the same day.

The *Brel* and *Sardou* decisions characterized digitisation as reproduction in accordance with the terms of the I.P.C. Such decisions are consistent with most authors' opinions.

To this day, it is difficult to control on-line author's rights infringements and therefore practical solutions should be sought. The exhaustion of rights principle applied to author's rights is interesting since it limits the control of author's rights infringement to the infringements by the first acquirer of the author's rights.

Advantage of Encoding Due to the royalty losses for authors' rights resulting 9-49 from unauthorised copying, France, like most European Union Member States, favours creating a multi-State database that will provide a code for each author's work. The use of any protected work will then be authorized and licensed by a payment system.[42] Such an encoding system requires a supra-national agreement.

---

41 Tribunal de Grande Instance of Paris, August 14, 1996 (cited in *Expertises des systèmes d'information*, number 197, October 1, 1996, at p. 292 and in *Dalloz*, number 34, October 3, 1996, at p. 49.

42 On this topic, see Gervais; co-author of "Les autoroutes de l'information: enjeux et défis", *Actes des huitièmes Entretiens Rhône-Alpes*, December 5–6, 1996, directed by Frémont and Ducasse, 1996.

9-50   **Remuneration** To make a protected work accessible on-line, authorisation is required and, in most cases, it is necessary to remunerate the author. Under French law, rules relating to remuneration of authors are public order rules that may be invoked against contractual agreements breaching such a rule.

In principle, remuneration is proportionate to the income generated by the sale or use of the work. Fixed remuneration may be granted under French law in the following four cases, as follows:

- Proportional remuneration cannot be determined in practice;
- The number of persons benefiting from the work cannot be determined;
- Costs of control of the use or sale of the work are disproportionate compared to the expected benefits or when the nature or the conditions of use are not appropriate to proportional remuneration; and
- Software creation, press and library edition.

9-51   In other cases, fixed remuneration is prohibited. For on-line exploitation of author's rights, since control of access is not easy, for the time being, fixed remuneration would be appropriate.

9-52   On-line Transmission Control On-line transmission control of a protected work is a critical issue as the person — the author himself or a third party — will not be able to control the use of his/her work made accessible on-line. Encryption is a solution, but the legal framework of encryption limits its use.

The Agency for Program Protection suggests the use of digitised tags on each protected work. A number could direct a person interested in acquiring or using a work toward the relevant state body in charge of centralising author's rights, terms, and conditions.

9-53   **Transfer of Authors' Rights** The transfer of authors' rights must be made under specific rules. The transfer should be made in writing and for proper objects.

The agreement should list the transferred rights and the way the work will be used in the future. Moral rights attached to a work cannot be transferred without the authorisation of the author.

Other Related Rights

9-54   Authors' rights are to be taken into account when digitising and displaying a work on-line; this is also the case for the authorisation of all artists who intervened in the creation of the work.

The "related rights" (*droits voisins*) include rights of musicians, dubbing voice artists, record producers, etc.

Domain Names

Domain names enable a Web site to be identified. The Internet user associates   9-55
the site with the chosen domain name. A domain name may be considered a
distinctive sign of a new kind. New forms of infringement may emerge.

In France, an entity named N.I.C. France, branch of N.I.C. United States
(InterNic), managed in France by the National Institute for Automatic and
Electronic Research (I.N.R.I.A.), assigns domain names and organises the
allocation of names in France. From a legal point of view, domain name
protection by NIC Company is contested. Web or e-Mail addresses (which
address is attributed by the Internet access provider elected by the individual) end with "fr" (e.g., coen@club-internet.fr).

I.N.R.I.A. allocates domain names according to the Internet Architecture
Board (I.A.B.). I.N.R.I.A. proposes a standard name licence contract. It can
be anticipated that conflicts will arise if a name used as a well-known trade
mark or descriptive names is not valid.[43]

A company holding a domain name under the above-mentioned contract
is not protected against misuse or against the fact that the name is already
used. Such contracts are not warranties against any claim relating to the
licensed name.

Trade Mark

The reservation of domain names in the Internet raises trade mark law   9-56
issues. For an entity to be assigned a name address on the Internet, the
practice consists in authorising the choice of the domain name according to
a hierarchical scheme defined in France by N.I.C. France.[44] In France, the
practice consists in having to prove that the entity that files a domain name
request is the holder of rights (e.g., trade mark rights) on the said name. This
is not the case in other countries such as the United States, where a domain
name may be attributed to a party which has no other rights to such a name,
or where a generic term (such as "book") may be granted.

In practice, NIC France refuses to register more than five names corresponding to five trade marks per company. Unlike trade mark registration,
there is no categorisation of the registration of a domain name.[45] However,
the right of the first registration is applicable for domain names since N.I.C.
France refuses to register a name already registered within the French ("fr")
area.

---

43 Comité de la Télématique Anonyme (C.T.A.) rendered decisions when *vis-à-vis* the Minitel
(*e.g.*, Decision 3615 CODEPOSTAL, C.T.A. October 2, 1995: in this case, the name was
only descriptive of the content).

44 Internet Name Charter in France: "Charte de Nommages Internet en France"; for instance,
the letters "fr" at the end means the entity is localised in France.

45 Deprez and Fauchoux, *Le droit des marques et les noms de domaine Internet, Expertises,*
number 200, December 1996.

Under French law, unauthorised use, or misuse of a trade mark constitutes an infringement of the trade mark and article L. 713-3 of the Intellectual Property Code.

ON-LINE CONDUCT

Regulation of Electronic Communication

9-57   Two different state authorities showed their interest in controlling on-line conduct: the Audio-visual High Council (*Conseil Supérieur de l'Audiovisuel*) and the Telecommunication High Council (*Conseil Supérieur de la Télécommunication* — C.S.T.). State independent authorities involved in this field are the State Authority of Post and Telecommunication (*Direction Générale des Postes et Télécommunications*), the National Computerised Database Commission (*Commission Nationale Informatique et Libertés*), the National Commission of Security Interception Control (*Commission Nationale des Contrôles des Interceptions de Sécurité*), the Competition Council (*Conseil de la Concurrence*) and Authors and Artists Societies.

The Law of July 26, 1996,[46] on the regulation of telecommunications conflicts between authorities, created a regulatory authority, the Telecommunication Regulatory Authority (*Autorité de Régulation des Télécommunications* — A.R.T.). A.R.T. is in charge of authorising independent networks and open networks now subject to prior authorisation by the Minister of Telecommunications.

The Minister is entitled to refuse an authorisation if he considers the proposed network detrimental to public order, security, or defence, or if the person or, the requesting company does not demonstrate sufficient financial means.

A.R.T. is granted wide powers and must be consulted before the enactment of any draft law falling within its competence. The first President of the A.R.T., appointed on January 7, 1997, will have to deal with the telecommunication interconnection in preparation for the liberalisation of telecommunications in the European Union on January 1, 1998.

Territorial Limits of Jurisdiction and Impact of Criminal Law

9-58   Under the New Criminal Code, French criminal law is applicable whenever a French national is victim of a crime or misdemeanor and whenever the facts linked to the penal infraction have a connection to French Territory.

---

46   O.J., July 27 1996, at p. 11384.

This jurisdiction rule is very broad. Concerning the Internet, any information accessible from France can be under French criminal law jurisdiction.

Under the New Criminal Code, French criminal law is applicable if any point of the French territory is concerned with the facts in question. Theoretically, most transactions on the Internet are subject to French criminal law jurisdiction.

CHAPTER 10

Germany

Alexander Liegl, Peter Bräutigam, Andreas Leupold
Nörr, Stiefenhofer & Lutz
Munich, Germany

INTRODUCTION

Impelled by the development of commercial on-line services and the World   10-1
Wide Web on the Internet, the on-line wave which has its origins in the
rapidly growing United States market, has swept over Europe and thus also
over Germany. As early as 1996, the number of private users of on-line
connections was estimated to be 1.9-million in Germany, with an additional
4-million users having access to on-line connections at the work place, at
universities,[1] This, however, seems to be only the beginning of a frantic
development. Successful on-line services are said to have enormous growth
rates due to new subscriptions which may even reach 10,000 new subscribers per week.[2]

Besides the big service providers, such as T-Online, CompuServe and
AOL Bertelsmann Online, numerous German enterprises have established
themselves on the on-line market. If a company does not provide services of
its own, it is at least represented by means of its own home page on the
Internet. The Karstadt group illustrates how seriously Germans consider
their new economic situation. At the end of October 1996, the group
launched a Virtual Shopping Mall under the name "My World" on the
Internet". My World" is a unique virtual department store offering 150,000
products and services.[3]

Such commitments are propelled on forecasts predicting further development of the Internet and on-line market in dimensions still unthought of.
Arthur D. Little expects a total turnover of more than DM 100-billion

---

1 Zimmer, "Profile und Potentiale der Online-Nutzung", *Media Perspektiven* 9/96, at
  p. 488.
2 According to Schwarz, in Schwarz (ed.), *Recht im Internet*, Introduction 1-1, at p. 2,
  T-Online, the on-line service of the Deutsche Telekom, has approximately 7,000 new
  subscribers per week. AOL — an on-line service operated by America Online and
  Bertelsmann — registers approximately 10,000 new on-line users per week.
3 Schütz, "Erlebniseinkauf der anderen Art", *Horizont* 41/96, at p. 2.

through multimedia in Europe and in the United States by the year 2000. The situation is seen even more optimistically by the network manufacturer JSB Computer Systems who estimate the turnover volume of goods and services to be upwards of U.S $600-billion.[4]

Andy McGrove, president of Intel, the world's largest chip manufacturer, thinks that the computer will prevail against television in the "War for Eyeballs" and predicts that at the turn of the century the Internet will derive revenues of U.S $5-billion from economic advertising alone.[5]

In view of this development and the forecast for the future, it is obvious that if on-line communication and on-line trading are to be handled safely and efficiently on the free-flying, chaotic Internet, statutory regulations will be urgently needed. Of course, this must not result in over-regulation as this would suffocate the developmental potential of the new market. Due to the global nature of the medium, regulations on an international basis are required.

ON-LINE COMMUNICATION AND COMMERCE

Internet and World Wide Web, from "Pull" to "Push"

The Internet

10-2   The starting point for the development of the on-line market was the chaotic and non-commercial Internet which is neither owned nor organised by any public or private authority.

The United States Department of Defence had the original idea of connecting numerous computers to one decentralised network which was the "birth" of the Internet. By the end of the 60s, the Department of Defence entrusted the Advanced Research Projects Agency (ARPA) with the development of the network ensuring data communication even where individual communication lines are destroyed. This was the beginning of ARPA-Net.[6] In the 1960s and 1970s, other computer networks with different network technologies, so-called LANs (Local Area Networks) and the WANs (Wide Area Networks) were created, inter alia, for the purpose of exchanging scientific information.

The Internet was born when numerous networks that had previously been considered incompatible with each other were cross-linked through special routers and a common protocol. This "Network of all Networks" enabled extensive data communication. The aforementioned network protocol

---

4 Zimmer, "Die Expansion des Online-Marktes in Deutschland; Online-Dienste für ein Massenpublikum", *Media-Perspektiven* 10/95, at p. 476.

5 "Auge um Auge",*Der Spiegel*, Number 6, March 2, 1997.

6 Zimmer, "Online-Dienste für ein Massenpublikum, Die Expansion des Online-Marktes in Deutschland", *Media-Perspektiven* 10/95, at p. 477, with further references.

called "TCP/IP" (Transmission Control Protocol/Internet Protocol) is the software used for the transmission of information on the Internet and is based on the original idea of transferring data by the fastest means possible avoiding destroyed or clogged transmission paths. For this purpose, the data in the transmitting computer are divided into separate packets by means of the Internet Protocol. These pieces of information reach the receiver on different channels and without regard to national boundaries. The chosen route depends on what path offers the fastest possible transmission. The Transmission Control Protocol (TCP) ensures the receiver that the individual information packages are reassembled in the correct order.

The World Wide Web

Today, the Internet has become accessible to 50-million users,[7] while some estimates speak of 80-million. Computers have created a demand for worldwide services, many of which are met by the "World Wide Web". The Web was created in 1989 at the Nuclear Research Centre in Geneva to allow faster communication of research results and enables users to locate private and commercial Web sites to find the information they need.

Uniform Resource Locaters While IP numbers are expressed in binary form and are thus not user-friendly, the 2-million World Wide Web addresses[8] can be retrieved by a specific Uniform Resource Locater (URL) in which a user enters the respective domain he is looking for.[9]

Hypertext Markup Language / Hypertext Transfer Protocol and Web Browser A Web site is encoded in a computer language called HTML (Hypertext Markup Language; this language contains both the text and instructions incorporated into the text).

The Web sites may be requested through World Wide Web (WWW) "browsers", the best known of which are Netscape Navigator and Microsoft Internet Explorer. This can be done via a special protocol known as the Hypertext Transfer Protocol (HTTP).

Hyperlinks The popularity of the World Wide Web is mostly due to its multimedia context and the fact that it allows "surfing" from one Web site to another. "Surfing" is made possible through "hyperlinks" that are contained in a text or graphic chart on each Web page and by which new Web sites and pages may be requested. If the user clicks on a hyperlink, the browser loads the new Web page and the data or programs that are linked to the original page by means of the hyperlink. Under normal circumstances, the page

10-3

10-4

10-5

10-6

---

7 Seeger, "Webcasting", *Global Online* 4/97, at p. 27.
8 Seeger, "Webcasting", *Global Online*, at p. 27.
9 The domain name concept will be subject to an in-depth discussion below.

becomes fully visible so that the user may recognise the new page. The situation will be different if the hyperlink refers only to an optically subordinate part of the page, in which case the new page of the third party appears within the framework of the referring page of the original provider (frames).

The aforementioned features of hyperlinks have caused numerous legal problems notably in cases where the owner of a Web site integrates frames derived from other Web sites into his own Web pages. In addition, the questions of responsibility under criminal law in cases where a hyperlink leads to another Web site containing material on how to create bombs and similar devices has stirred considerable controversy.

E-mail, FTP, Telnet, Gopher

10-7   In addition to the World Wide Web, numerous other Internet applications, such as electronic mail, are available. The tremendously growing number of e-mail sent makes electronic mail a serious competitor of the usual postal delivery services.

"Newsgroups" and "Bulletin Boards" are also important because they allow communications to be uploaded and downloaded visibly for each participant on a given server. The File Transfer Protocol (FTP), on the other hand, allows a transfer of information via structured dictionaries, while Telnet enables the user to remote-control third party computers as if they were his own. Similar to the World Wide Web but somewhat less comfortable to use, Gopher (software named after a burrowing animal of the mammal family) allows file access to computers linked with each other on the Internet. Due to the user-friendliness of the World Wide Web, Gopher has lost popularity, though, and is important only for older data stock not (yet) available in HTML.

From "Pull" to "Push"

10-8   Development has, by no means, come to a halt with the standard achieved with the World Wide Web. The latter requires the user to retrieve the information he needs by a simple mouse click on the respective hyperlink (pull). The long transfer times and the vast amount of unsolicited offers which cannot be mastered even with the help of search engines such as Yahoo, Hotbot, Altavista, and Lycos, have called for new solutions. The hastened development of one medium in which computer, radio, television and telephone grow together, the transition from "pull" to "push" lies ahead in Germany.[10]

As of the time of writing, special software is being developed to search, filter and "push" the information required by the individual user onto his computer, without requiring any action by the user himself. The software of the California Webcasting's market leader Pointcast accesses the Internet at

---

10 Seeger, "Webcasting", *Global Online* 4/97, at pp. 27 *et seq*, in particular p. 28.

determined off-peak hours, collects the latest news from the Pointcast server which is provided with information from CNN, *Wired*, the *Miami Herald* and the *Chicago Tribune*, and "pushes" it onto the subscriber's computer as a screen saver.[11]

Corporate Germany places great hope in the principle of "push" because one must no longer watch idly to see how many "hits" are received on a commercial Web site launched on the World Wide Web. German enterprises do not ignore the trend turning the World Wide Web from a "pull" towards a "push" medium. During the advertising summit in Munich in May 1997, Kabel & Medien Service, a German service provider, delivered the first broadband on-line service. By using the cable network instead of telephone lines, fast access to the Internet is made possible (eight times faster than with ISDN; modems and telephone lines are, of course, used as a return channel).

Additionally, a constantly circulating stream is transmitted to all connected users on a channel in the cable network, covering many different subjects including calendars of events, stock market news, weather forecasts and news reports. All of these technical developments raise new legal issues which have yet to be discussed under German law or considered for legislative initiatives.

Participants

Before it is possible to make a legal evaluation, a brief look must be cast at a few important participants in the Internet and the World Wide Web. The following description of the different service and access providers can of course provide the readers of this monograph only with a basic overview of the relevant entities and individuals involved in on-line communications.   **10-9**

Carriers

The carriers, mostly big telephone companies, have the power to dispose of the network making it available for compensation. According to German telecommunications law, network operators offering telephone services require a licence pursuant to sections 6 and 8 of the Telecommunications Act (T.K.G.).   **10-10**

Although the legal problems in connection with the provision of the infrastructure cannot be dealt with extensively in the following, it may be said that other participants, such as on-line services, are subject to a duty of information towards the authorities pursuant to section 4 of the Telecommunications Act. This, however, applies only if they offer telecommunication services, specifically if they distribute their own or a third-party's content to others.

---

11 Seeger, "Webcasting", *Global Online* 4/97, at p. 28.

Access, Content, and Service Providers

10-11   Anyone who offers services on the Internet and the World Wide Web or on another network is considered a provider. A distinction is made between access, content, and service providers.

Access providers sell the technical access to the Internet and sometimes supply the hardware (modems) and software (browsers) necessary for this purpose. They also lease lines, but do not offer their own content.[12]

Content providers offer their own information on the Internet, without affording their customers access to the network themselves. Content providers include publishing houses, data base operators, newspapers, or agencies which present their own content. The content offered in file format ranges from texts, graphics, and musical offers to video and film clips. Content providers may offer their content to service providers which in turn may act also as content providers.[13] Rather than sticking to the term "Access Provider", "Content Provider" or "Service Provider" alone, it is therefore necessary to determine the provider's offer and the resulting duties by examining the facts of the individual case.

On-line Services

10-12   A special role is played by on-line services, including the German subsidiaries of CompuServe, AOL/Bertelsmann, and T-Online. For a monthly charge, they provide to their subscribers access to the Internet as well as to a great number of proprietary services, including e-mail, data bases, software pools, topical news, and electronic round table discussions. on-line services maintain a network with a closed group of users that is served by means of a host computer (server).[14] The rather high safety standard which is achieved through the closed system, is one reason why home banking is of great importance at T-Online. However, it should be mentioned that there are also banks on the Internet[15] that offer solutions for safe transmission of financial data on the Internet.

Users

10-13   The user of the Internet or World Wide Web not only is a customer and consumer of the content he may find on the Web, but in his capacity as participant in this interactive medium becomes a provider himself. He creates his own home page where he may present information of general interest. When participating in discussions on the USENET (the "blackboard" of the Internet), the user is both the receiver and sender of information.

---

12 Koch, "Rechtsfragen der Nutzung elektronischer Kommunikationsdienste", B.B. 1996, at p. 2050.
13 Koch, "Rechtsfragen der Nutzung elektronischer Kommunikationsdienste", B.B. 1996, at p. 2050.
14 Mayer, "Recht und Cyberspace", N.J.W. 1996, at p. 1784; Sieber, "Strafrechtliche Verantwortlichkeit für den Datenverkehr in internationalen Computernetzen (1)", J.Z. 1996, at p. 431.
15 For example, Advanced Bank, an affiliate of the Bayerische Vereinsbank group.

These "classic" Internet applications notwithstanding, the familiar picture of users actively "surfing the Web" less and less reflects the fast-paced development of this medium. Without doubt, the current transition from a "pull" to a "push" medium redefines the role of the user and calls for a new assessment of the legal consequences resulting therefrom. In the near future, the picture of the user will develop from the active provider of information (so-called desk viewer) to the passive viewer (so-called couch viewer).

Regulation of on-line communication

Statutory Regulation and Netiquette

As a consequence of the increasing commercialisation of the Internet   **10-14** which belongs to no one and for which no one is responsible, the guaranteed protection of the legal interests of its participants has become a point of discussion. Not only are economic assets, in particular protective rights of authors, software programmers, designers, etc. at stake, but also personal interests of users and content providers alike. The frantic technical development and the establishment of this new market place brings along the dangers of unlawful propaganda, dangers to the right to one's name, to registered trade marks and commercial symbols and to the right to informational self-determination. A special software, so-called "cookies", make it possible to trace each individual user of the Internet and thus to determine his preferences and consumer habits. All of these problems require technically practical and feasible regulations.

For a long time, the Internet community has been developing its own codes of ethics for the various services of the Internet. These codes have not yet been subject to regulation and are summarised under the term "Netiquette".[16] It is against Netiquette, for example, if e-mail of an advertising nature is sent to participants without request. Constant capitalisation in e-mail messages or chat forums is considered tantamount to "screaming and yelling" in everyday life and is therefore considered inappropriate.

That existing regulations on the Internet are effectively enforced became obvious in the famous punitive action brought by the Internet community against Canter & Siegel, a United States law firm specialising in immigration law. In this case, the law firm had sent a large number of unrequested e-mail for advertising purposes to potential immigrants all over the world. This violation of Netiquette was immediately punished by so-called mail

---

16 For detailed information on Netiquette, see —
"http://www.screen.com/under-stand/Netiquette.html"; see also the German translation of the classical Netiquette by Rinaldi, July 1994, at NetMayer, address http://www.ping.at/guides/net-mayer/.

bombings.[17] The lawyers were snowed in by insulting letters (so-called "flames") in such number that their link to the Internet broke down.[18]

Even if one considered incorporating these rules of conduct into existing legal regulations through interpretation of general clauses,[19] no general system of self-protection exists that might possibly cover all of the problems.[20]

Since sufficient self-regulation cannot be expected, statutory regulations will be required, at first possibly on a national level, but ultimately on an international level, while over-regulation must be avoided. Statutory regulation should take into account the complexity of the Internet and leave sufficient leeway for the rapid further development of this medium.

Considering these aspects, negative comments on the new statutes[21] have become audible in Germany. Some critics have argued that legal techniques designed to provide a complete and final regulatory framework have proved futile. German authors argued that indeed one should have placed the stake on incomplete regulation strategies that stimulate self-regulation.[22]

Ubiquity of the Internet and the Call for International Regulations

Ubiquity of the Internet in Light of Civil Law, Competition Law, and Criminal Law

10-15   The ubiquity and universality of this new medium is a special challenge to the German as well as every other national legal system. With a simple mouse-click the user can use all services and offers made available by providers on this international market on a world-wide basis.

The difficulties faced by the German legislator with this world-wide market place are described in the following, by discussing the issue of jurisdiction of German courts in case of illegal actions committed on the Internet. At first sight the solution seems to be simple: If one looks on the matter freely, the jurisdiction of German courts should extend only to the territory of the Federal Republic of Germany.

---

17 For further information on on-line vocabulary, see Paul, *N.J.W.-Co.R.* 1996, at p. 62.

18 Gelpin, "Attorney Advertising and Solicitation on the Internet: Complying with Ethics Regulations and Netiquette", *Journal of Computer & Information Law*, 1996, at pp. 73 and 74; Mayer, *N.J.W.* 1996, at pp. 1789 *et seq*; Gummig, in Schwarz (ed.), *Recht im Internet*, section 5.3.1, at p. 19.

19 For example, by inserting the terms "violation of morality" into section 1 of the Unfair Competition Act and section 3 of the Civil Code.

20 Nordemann, Goddar, Tönhardt, and Cychowski, "Gewerblicher Rechtsschutz und UrheberRecht im Internet", *C.R.* 1996, at p. 657.

21 Information and Communication Services Act and Interstate Media Services Convention.

22 Ladeur, "Zur Kooperation von staatlicher Regulierung und Selbstregulierung des Internets", *Z.U.M.* 1997, at pp. 382-384; Ladeur, "Regulierung des Information Superhighway", *C.R.* 1996, at p. 621.

Things are, however, not as simple as that. As of today, German users may call up, almost to an unlimited extent, offers and services uploaded on a server by providers anywhere in the world. Restrictions to the jurisdiction of the courts within the national boundaries are thus no longer possible. Principally, since an international Web sites can be accessed in Germany, there is only one "territory" to which the jurisdiction of German courts extends when it comes to determining the conduct and content of services: the entire world. Under the applicable German international law of procedure, this notably applies to the responsibility of foreign service providers under German Unfair Competition laws, to their liability in tort and to their criminal liability.

Civil Law and Competition Law The international jurisdiction of Ger- **10-16** man courts is basically linked to the registered office residence of the defendant, but in the case of violations of competition and for torts, also the court located at the place where the offence is committed has jurisdiction. This results from section 24(2), sentence 1, of the Unfair Competition Act (U.W.G.) for the right to compete, and from section 32 of the Code of Civil Procedure (Z.P.O.) for torts. According to their phrasing, these provisions regulate only the local jurisdiction. However, according to the established practice of German courts, international jurisdiction lies wherever a court has local jurisdiction.[23]

The place where the offence is committed, within the meaning of section 24(2), sentence 1, of the Unfair Competition Act and section 32 of the Code of Civil Procedure, is both the place where the incriminating act occurred which is the place where anti-competitive content is downloaded on a home page and made available on a server, and the place where the result of this act occurs(*lex loci delicti commissi*). According to the present state of discussion in Germany, the result may occur in all states where the content can be requested. As this is possible in Germany, anti-competitive and/or tortious acts are subject to the jurisdiction of German courts.[24]

This evaluation is consistent with the dominant opinion in connection with a comparable complex of problems. In the case of newspapers and publications, the place of the result is deemed to be the place of publication and any place where such writings are destined to be disseminated.[25] This evaluation might also apply to the cases at issue here because the Internet content available for request must still be called up actively. The same applies to printed matters of which the reader need not know the content but only have access to it.

---

23 B.G.H.Z. 63, at pp. 219 *et seq*; B.G.H.Z. 94, at p. 156; Thomas and Putzo, *Zivilprozeßordnung*, preliminary note, section 1, marginal note 4.
24 Kuner, "Internationale Zuständigkeitskonflikte im Internet", C.R. 1996, at p. 455; Ebbing, "Virtuelle Rechtsberatung und das anwaltliche Werbeverbot", N.J.W.-Co.R. 1996, at p. 244; Peschel, in Schwarz (ed.), *Recht im Internet*, section 5.2.1, at p. 5; likewise, the ruling of the Munich District Court, October 17, 1996, reprinted in C.R. 1997, at p. 156; LG Nürnberg-Fürth, January 29, 1997, reprinted in *AnwBl*. 1997, at p. 226.
25 Thomas and Putzo, section 32, Code of Civil Procedure, note 2.

The universal Internet jurisdiction of German courts which conjures up manifold conflicts of jurisdiction and extensive forum shopping, has so far not been changed by existing international treaties that establish the national jurisdiction of the courts according to the same principles as Germany's International Law of Civil Procedure (Eu.G.V.Ü.).[26]

10-17   **Criminal Law**   The problem of universal Internet jurisdiction has further dimensions: Criminal offences committed on the Internet on a world-wide basis might be subject to the jurisdiction of German criminal courts. Here, the scope of applicability of German criminal law and the jurisdiction of courts and prosecution authorities is governed *inter alia* by the place where the offence was committed.[27]

Under section 9 of the Criminal Code (StGB), the offence is deemed committed at the place where the offender has acted or, in the case of an omission, would have been obligated to act, but also at any place where the final result of the offence occurred or was to occur according to the offender's notion. It is a well-established fact that German courts will have jurisdiction even if the action is committed in a foreign country but the result occurs in Germany — as intended by the offender.[28] If someone is injured or killed in Germany by a bullet fired from the other side of the border, the injury or killing will be deemed to have been committed in Germany. Tortious acts whose activity or result can be localised in Germany (*e.g*, the publication of electronic newspapers instigating netsurfers to commit criminal offences in Germany), especially in cases of acts constituting participation as an accomplice, are therefore principally subject to the jurisdiction of German criminal courts.[29] The global availability of data on the Internet and the international data exchange seems to burst the restrictions to national boundaries.[30] However, German criminal law pursuant to section 9 of the Criminal Code is not applicable to tortious acts committed in a foreign country whose elements are fulfilled without realisation of a result.[31]

Regardless of the place where the offence is committed, criminal offences committed in a foreign country may be subject to the jurisdiction of German

---

26 International Law of Civil Procedure , article 5, number 3: Claims in tort and quasi-tort may be brought "to the court of the place where the damaging event has occurred"; also, international law may not restrict this universal jurisdiction; Kuner, "Internationale Zuständigkeitskonflikte im Internet", *C.R.* 1996, at p. 456, with further references.

27 The so-called principle of territoriality; Criminal Code, sections 3 and 7.

28 *R.G.St.* 11, at p. 22.

29 According to the established practice of the courts, the act committed abroad by any participator in a national offence is deemed to have been committed in Germany, see *R.G.St.* 11, p. 20; *R.G.St.* 67, at p. 139; Tröndle, *Strafgesetzbuch*, 48th ed., 1997, at section 9, marginal note 9.

30 Collardin, *C.R.* 1995, at pp. 619 *et seq.*

31 Ringel, "Rechtsextremistische Propaganda aus dem Ausland im Internet", *C.R.* 1997, at p. 303 and 305.

courts due to the following aspects. Under the principle of protection aimed especially at the self-protection of the Federal Republic of Germany, this may apply to criminal offences that endanger the Constitution.[32] German criminal law further extends to the protection of legal interests that are acknowledged by all civilised states.[33] German courts may, therefore, deal with the dissemination of certain pornographic publications, regardless by whom and in which country these offences were committed.[34] Finally, according to the principle of vicarious criminal justice, as laid down in section 7 of the Criminal Code, national power of sentencing applies to all cases where foreign punitive justice is prevented from criminal enforcement for actual or legal reasons.

According to the described situation, providers and users of the Internet may be confronted with the enforcement under criminal law of German values. The fact that this is not only of theoretical importance is shown in the opinion of the public prosecutors of Mannheim who carried out the investigations against CompuServe and T-Online on the grounds of propaganda activities of Canadian Neonazi Ernst Zuendel. According to newspaper reports, the public prosecutors of Mannheim proceeded on the basis that Zuendel's Internet activities were subject to the jurisdiction of German criminal courts.[35] The inconsistencies with other national criminal law systems and the conflicts of jurisdiction resulting from the extensive application of German national criminal law require an international regulation, or at least a restrictive interpretation of German provisions.[36]

This legal problem cannot be argued away by stating that an effective prosecution and the filing of a legal action and/or the enforcement of the court's decision fail due to the practical problems of criminal and civil law in foreign countries, in particular because of the lack of international co-operation.[37] Ultimately, the difficulties in the prosecution and enforcement are going to show again that a repressive but also preventive control of commerce and communication on the Internet will not succeed without national and international solutions.[38]

---

32 Criminal Code, section 5, number 3.
33 Principle of a world-wide uniform law; see Criminal Code, section 6.
34 Criminal Code, section 6, number 6.
35 *Wall Street Journal Europe*, March 26-27, 1996, at p. 3; in connection with this, Kuner, "Internationale Zuständigkeitskonflikte im Internet", C.R. 1996, at p. 456, in particular note 27.
36 Collardin, C.R. 1995, at pp. 621 *et seq*; Kuner, "Internationale Zuständigkeitskonflikte im Internet", C.R. 1996, at p. 456.
37 Indeed, the investigating competencies of German authorities are limited to the territory of the Federal Republic of Germany; this is why, at present, it is impossible to carry out "on-line searches" of foreign data bases.
38 Sieber, *Baromedia*, at p. 16; Sieber, "Strafrechtliche Verantwortlichkeit für den Datenverkehr in internationalen Computernetzen (1) und (2)", *J.Z.* 1996, at pp. 494 *et seq*; Collardin, C.R. 1995, at p. 621.

Request for International Regulations

10-18   Given this background, it is no surprise that the request in German literature for a European, better yet international, regulation of the legal problems raised by the Internet can no longer be ignored.[39]

Indeed, the introduction of extensive regulations of the Internet has long been considered at a European and international level, such as at the European Community level, within the framework of the Organisation for Economic Co-operation and Development (O.E.C.D.), the Group of Seven Conference, and the World Intellectual Property Organisation (W.I.P.O.). Thus, to mention but a few examples at European Community level, the European Community Commission dealt with the problem of the distribution of punishable material on the Internet following a meeting of the Ministers of Education and the Ministers of Telecommunication in the European Union.[40]

In addition, as early as October 1996, a Green Paper bearing the title "Illegal and Harmful Content of the Internet" was published.[41] The Green Paper summarises proposals for a plan of action against offensive and illegal content on the Internet. The Commission of the European Community has taken the initiative in the copyright field and has, in addition to the adoption of the Data Base Directive, presented the Green Paper "Copyright and Related Rights in the Information Society (*Urheberrecht und verwandte Schutzrechte in der Informationsgesellschaft*)".[42]

Legislative Initiatives in Germany

Constitutional Requirements

10-19   As one of the first countries in the world, Germany has begun to set forth a regulatory framework governing the Internet. Since August 1, 1997, the most urgent legal problems in the Internet have been solved by means of mostly parallel regulations:

- Through the Information and Communication Services Act of the federal government; and
- Through the Interstate Media Services Convention (*Mediendienstestaatsvertrag*)) of the states.

10-20   This dualism of regulations which must be considered unsatisfactory, is understandable only if one bears in mind that the German Constitution sets forth the federation principle. Under the German constitution the regulatory

---

39 Kuner, "Internationale Zuständigkeitskonflikte im Internet", *C.R.* 1996, at p. 457; Kur, "Internet Domain Names", *C.R.* 1996, at pp. 325 and 330.
40 *N.J.W.-Co.R.* 1996, at p. 214.
41 *N.J.W.-Co.R.* 1996, at p. 391.
42 Kreile and Becker, *G.R.U.R. Int.* 1996, at pp. 677 *et seq.*

and legislative powers are divided between the federal government and the individual states.[43] According to the general consensus, the states are competent to regulate the broadcasting within the framework of the constitutionally protected broadcasting freedom.[44] Because this medium required uniform regulations on a national basis, broadcasting was made subject to the control of the states by way of an interstate convention that included all federal states. On this basis, it was possible in the past to respond flexibly to the technical development. By means of cable and satellite broadcasting, this enabled the start of private broadcasting and led to the introduction of the "dual regulation", i.e, the coexistence of public and private television networks.[45]

Digitalisation helped to solve the problem of broadcasting bottlenecks and extend the individual programs existing so far by numerous new special interest channels, pay-per-channel, pay-per-view, video-on-demand or near-video-on-demand (the repeated broadcasting of the same film at different times). Furthermore, the World Wide Web has brought forth many new provider services on the Internet.

While even special interest programs, such as pure sports or news channels, and also near-video-on-demand, are still comparable with the traditional programs, the services on request, such as pay-per-view or video-on-demand and also the numerous services and offers on the Internet, are not perceived as an "integrated whole" having an influencing effect on a mass audience. They rather present themselves as individual communication "piece-by-piece".[46]

It is in particular on the Internet that material previously handled in different media melt together into one uniform multimedia application. The usual point-to-point or individual communication (e.g., e-mail, data transfer and request, voice and picture transmission) is included as "traditional" mass communication (e.g., electronic press and broadcasting). These "classical" communication consequences are followed by completely new possibilities. Now, anyone, rather than only the broadcasting company, may, via the Internet, approach an indefinite general public; thus, participants in an indefinite number may, for example, have discussions with each other in "chat forums".[47]

---

43 Constitution (*Grundgesetz*), articles 33 *et seq*.
44 Constitution, article 51, sentence 2, and article 70; Ladeur, "Regulierung des Information Superhighway", *C.R.* 1996, at p. 618, with further references.
45 Herrmann, *Rundfunkrecht*, 1994, section 7, marginal notes 101 *et seq*; Ladeur, "Regulierung des Information Superhighway", *C.R.* 1996, at p. 614; Eberle, "Digitale Rundfunkfreiheit — Rundfunk zwischen Couch-Viewing und Online-Nutzung", *C.R.* 1996, at p. 193.
46 Bullinger and Mestmäcker, *Multimediadienste, Struktur und staatliche Aufgaben nach deutschem und europäischem Recht*, at pp. 56 and 57.
47 Nitsch, "Die Info-Bahn", *N.J.W.-Co.R.* 1995, at p. 109; Bullinger, "Multimediale Kommunikation in Wirtschaft und Gesellschaft", *Z.Ü.M.* 1996, at p. 750, who refers to these forms as "communication for anyone which is limitless both with regard to its participants and its content"; Eberle, "Digitale Rundfunkfreiheit — Rundfunk zwischen Couch-Viewing und Online-Nutzung", *C.R.* 1996, at pp. 196 *et seq*.

As long as on-line distribution constitutes only a fraction of the total distribution for the existing broadcasting programs, *i.e*, mass communication, it is rightly assumed that the regulations under the existing German broadcasting law are applicable.[48] Web radio or Web television considered broadcasting and is, therefore, subject to the provisions of the German Interstate Broadcasting Convention.

The question remains who is responsible for the statutory regulation of the material and services that are provided on the Internet, such as teleshopping, and which lie somewhere between individual and mass communication. Do the states have the power to regulate these services due to the services' similarity to broadcasting or the federal government, which might derive its legislative power in particular from article 74(1), number 1, of the Constitution (civil law); article 74(1), number 7, of the Constitution (legal protection of minors); article 74(1), number 11 of the Constitution (law of economy), and from the power to regulate copyrights?[49] Initially, the problem of responsibility was overshadowed by the more important question of whether or not the new services should be regulated as strictly as the model applying to broadcasting which is distinguished by a duty to obtain a permit.[50]

Since the multimedia services, in particular the on-demand services with the purpose of transacting businesses, have nothing in common with the nature of traditional broadcasting and its eminent importance to the formation of public opinion,[51] an independent regulation is necessary which does not hinder the development of the multimedia services.[52] The regulation of multimedia services must, therefore, be based on principles of openness rather than on principles of balance, applicable under the existing broadcasting

---

48 Eberle, "Digitale Rundfunkfreiheit — Rundfunk zwischen Couch-Viewing und Online-Nutzung", *C.R.* 1996, at p. 197.
49 Constitution, article 73, number 9; see the suggestions made by Rüttgers, Federal Minister of Education, Science, Research and Technology, "Telekommunikation und Datenvernetzung — eine Herausforderung für Gesellschaft und Recht", *C.R.* 1996, at pp. 51 *et seq*, and *C.R.* 1996, at p. 384; see also Ladeur, "Regulierung des Information Superhighway", *C.R.* 1996, at p. 618.
50 The negative list concerning the term broadcasting adopted by the Conference of the States' Governors on October 26-27, 1995 (published in *Fernseh-Informationen* 1995, at pp. 659 *et seq*), and according to which especially telebanking, telework, electronic mail, and electronic mail-order catalogues were not considered to fall under the term broadcasting. In the opinion of the heads of the states' broadcasting divisions, teleshopping, data services of a different nature (*e.g.*, weather report, stock market, and environmental data) and request services in the audio and video section were at least in part subject to the broadcasting regulations; see Kreile in Schwarz (ed.), *Recht im Internet*, 1996, section 10.2.1, at pp. 8 *et seq*.
51 This aspect is also emphasised in *B.Verf.G.E.* 90, at p. 87.
52 Eberle, "Digitale Rundfunkfreiheit — Rundfunk zwischen Couch-Viewing und Online-Nutzung", *C.R.* 1996, at p. 197; Ladeur, "Regulierung des Information Superhighway", *C.R.* 1996, at p. 621, who thinks that the only possible regulation strategy is "a third-party regulation rather than self-regulation"; Bullinger, "Multimediale Kommunikation in Wirtschaft und Gesellschaft", *Z.U.M.* 1996, at p. 756.

law. The principle of balance under the broadcasting law and its strict regulation regime — it has been suggested[53] — should be limited to such a field in which the broadcasting guarantee can be developed into an institutional limitation of power.

Therein lies the special nature of the power of distribution of programs running according to a fixed time schedule, over individual and public opinion. Only such power over the formation of opinion exercised by the broadcasters justifies the application of governmental approval and supervisory procedures to keep broadcasting free from one-sided state and private influence. The multimedia services which typically offer a large variety of individual pieces of information of an economic or non-economic nature, differ from broadcasting and may not become subject to the regulation under broadcasting law. The application of such regulatory measures will be justified only if the services provide access to a running broadcasting program or offer a complete program running according to schedule.[54]

Compromise between Federal Government and States

In the interest of the business community which requires simple and secure 10-21 regulations, a uniform regulation of the multimedia services by a single German legislator would have been desirable. Given the above-stated constitutional situation in Germany, this could not be politically achieved. In spite of this, the federal government and the states have, following difficult negotiations, agreed on a compromise to avoid a threatening constitutional dispute.[55] On this basis, the entire field has now been regulated in several different acts.

Regardless of the reservation contained in the Interstate Broadcasting Convention that the media services should be subject to regulations under the broadcasting law if they were to be qualified as broadcasts, the above compromise has lead to the multimedia services now being regulated both in a federal law of its own and in a separate interstate treaty on media services.

Tele Services and Media Services It is true that, in principle, the federal 10-22 government has enforced its plan that all new on-line services should be freely accessible, and thus not subject to any permits under current broadcasting law. However, as agreed, federal law now regulates certain multimedia services, whereas others — the so-called media services — are subject to

---

53 Bullinger and Mestmäcker, *Multimediadienste, Struktur und staatliche Aufgaben nach deutschem und europäischem Recht*, at p. 52, with references to *B.Verf.G.E.* 12, at pp. 259 and 260, and *B.Verf.G.E.* 31, at pp. 3254 *et seq.*

54 Bullinger and Mestmäcker, "Multimediadienste, Struktur und staatliche Aufgaben nach deutschem und europäischem Recht", at pp. 57, *et seq*, 174, and 177; dissenting (but erroneous) opinion of Röger, "Internet und Verfassungsrecht", *Z.R.P.* 1997, at p. 205.

55 See press release, *C.R.* 1996, at pp. 509 and 510.

a special interstate treaty which deviates in numerous provisions. According to the phrasing of both the Tele Services Act of the federal government and the Interstate Media Services Convention of the states, the limitation of the scope of applicability is as follows.

Under section 2 of the Tele Services Act,[56] the Federal Law applies to all information and communication services which are determined to be used individually. These services are referred to as tele services, including the field of individual communication, material concerning information and communication, such as data services, distribution of information on goods (unless the formation of public opinion is in the foreground due to their editorial presentation), offers from service providers concerning the use of the Internet and offers of goods and services with the possibility of ordering directly.

The Interstate Media Services Convention applies to so-called media services (*Mediendienste*) that are offered in the form of information and communication services addressed to the public.[57] This includes distribution and services on demand, in which case the individual exchange of performances or the individual data transfer is not in the foreground.

What must be considered is that, where a provider offers a broad range of different services, individual offers may be qualified as tele services or media services, meaning that the same provider may be confronted with two different regulations.[58]

10-23   **Difficulties** The general delimitation provided in the regulations (information and communication services for individual use, on the one hand, and *vis-à-vis* the public, on the other hand) does not make it easier for legal practitioners to differentiate between the respective services because offers aimed at the individual may also be aimed at the public. However, the model enumeration referred to in the above-mentioned acts and the reasons stated in these acts in each case show a practical direction: Information and communication services on demand are subject to federal law. Distribution services whose broadcasting in the form of programs is unilaterally determined by the provider and transmitted to an indefinite number of receivers are to be subject to the Interstate Media Services Convention.[59]

This line has not been pursued strictly because the Interstate Media Services Convention also covers on-demand services,[60] which, according to

---

56 Part of the entire new regulation in the Information and Communication Services Act; see *Bundesrat Drucksache* (Federal Council Printed Matter), June 13, 1997, 420/97, at pp. 1 *et seq.*

57 Interstate Media Services Convention, section 2.

58 Engel-Flechsig, "Das Informations- und Kommunikationsdienstegesetz des Bundes und der Mediendienstestaatsvertrag der Bundesländer — einheitliche Rahmenbedingungen für Multimedia —", Z.U.M. 1997, at pp. 334 and 338.

59 Interstate Media Services Convention, Bayerischer Landtag, Drucksache 13/7716, March 21, 1997, at p. 10.

60 Interstate Media Services Convention, section 2(2), number 4.

the reasons stated in the act,[61] also include "video-on-demand" and "on-line services", such as electronic press and other information and entertainment offers aiming at the public unless they serve the communication between individuals. This is where delimitation problems exist in respect to services on demand which are subject to the regulation of the federal law. This delimitation problem must be solved to the effect that only such services on demand fall under the Convention which lead to a broadcasting program or similarly offer a total event which contributes to the formation of public opinion. What is also unclear with respect to the scope of application of the Tele Services Act and the Interstate Media Services Convention is the question of which regulatory regime shall apply to such future services emerging from the development from a pull to a push medium. Can they be considered distribution services within the meaning of the Interstate Media Services Convention or does communication between individuals prevail?

The problem of a legally uncertain delimitation in some areas has, however, been eased by the fact that, as agreed on between the federal government and the states, regulations identical in their wording or content were used with respect to the crucial points. The identical wording is, however, not used in all cases. This gives reason to examine in greater detail the Tele Services Act as part of the Information and Communication Services Act, the Interstate Media Services Convention, and the Interstate Broadcasting Convention 1997.

Specific Legislation and the German Interstate Broadcasting Convention

The Information and Communication Services Act The Information and 10-24 Communication Services Act (Information and Communication Services Act) which came into force on August 1, 1997, constitutes a so-called article statute (*Artikelgesetz*). This means that the individual articles of this statute summarise entire new Acts or modifications of and amendments to existing Acts. Thus, under articles 4 and 5, for example, the Information and Communication Services Act contains regulations amending the German Criminal Code and the Administrative Offences Act. Under these provisions, the term "writings" which forms part of criminal or administrative offences in these acts has been extended to cover data storage material as well.[62]

Article 6 contains changes to the Act on the Dissemination of Writings Morally Harmful to Minors.[63] This provision is based on a three-stage model designed to protect minors.[64] In the first stage, illegal offers are prohibited under

---

61 Interstate Media Services Convention Bayerischer Landtag, Drucksache 13/7716, March 21, 1997, at p. 10.
62 *Bundesrat Drucksache*, June 13, 1997, 420/97, at pp. 1 *et seq.*.
63 *Bundesrat Drucksache*, June 13, 1997, 420/97, at pp. 1 *et seq.*
64 Bröhl, "Rechtliche Rahmenbedingungen für neue Informations- und Kommunikationsdienste", *C.R.* 1997, at pp. 73 and 77 *et seq.*

criminal law. To avoid undue restrictions on access to information and communication services for adults, the second stage then provides service providers with the possibility to block access for minor users to material morally harmful instead of generally waiving the right to disseminate such material. The Act determines no requirements as to the technical realisation of the ban which may as well be carried out with co-operation of the parents or the persons who have custody of the child. In the legislator's reasoning, the possibilities of coding content and creating closed groups of users with age control are mentioned as appropriate means. Furthermore, it was made clear that the mere order to observe certain times cannot guarantee an effective protection of minors. Finally, providers whose services are offered on a general basis and may contain content morally harmful to minors, must appoint a commissioner who will act as adviser but also as contact for users.

The Information and Communication Services Act not only extends consumer protection to new services through modifications of the Price Indication Act and the Price Indication Ordinance, in article 8 and article 9,[65] but also implements in its article 7 of the European Union Database Directive,[66] thereby modifying the German Copyright Act (UrhG). Unlike all other articles of the Information and Communication Services Act, article 7 came into force only on January 1, 1998, which was still within the period allowed for implementation of the Directive.

In addition to modifications of existing statutory regulations, the core of the Information and Communication Services Act consists of three independent new Acts:

- The Tele Services Act (*Teledienstegesetz*),[67] which provides the legal framework for the conditions governing information and communication services in respect to individual exchange of performances (in particular, the free access to these services) and the question of the responsibility and the transparency of the providers;
- The Act on Data Protection in the Case of Tele Services (*Teledienstedatenschutzgesetz*);[68] and
- The Act Concerning Digital Signatures (*Signaturgesetz*, or "Signature Act" which have been enacted.[69]

10-25   The Signature Act (SigG) aims at bringing about a federally uniform secure infrastructure for digital signatures which is to secure the authenticity and

---

65 *Bundesrat Drucksache*, June 13, 1997, 420/97, at pp. 2, 16, and 17 *et seq.*
66 Directive of the European Parliament and Council, concerning the legal protection of databases, O.J. L77/20, at pp. 20 *et seq.*
67 Tele Services Act; see Information and Communication Services Act, article 1.
68 Act on Data Protection in the Case of Tele Services; see Information and Communication Services Act, article 2.
69 Act Concerning Digital Signatures; see Information and Communication Services Act, article 3.

integrity of declarations. The Signature Act ensures that on the Internet and with its services declarations can be made and exchanged as well as contracts entered into which could be relied on in business dealings. By means of the digital signature based on a coding program, the party signs his communication or declaration with his private key, whereas each participant can verify through his own public key whether the communication or declaration was actually made in this form. This way it can always be clearly established that the declaration stems from the undersigned and was not forged on its way to the receiver.[70] The Signature Act provides that, on application and in case of sufficient identification, each participant receives a private signature key applicable only to him, along with a corresponding certificate. This key can then be verified by the other participants by means of a corresponding key.[71] The Act also provides that foreign signature keys and certificates are acknowledged if they both originate from a Community member state or from a member state to the European Economic Area, as well as from a third-party country in the case of a corresponding supranational agreement.[72]

Compared internationally, the Signature Act has gone far to enable legal relations on the Internet. It is striking that the Signature Act says nothing about the legal transactions in which the digital signature is to replace the written form and/or other qualified formal requirements. Through introduction of the Act it has become possible to only apply optionally the digital signature where no formal requirements must be observed, *i.e*, where an oral conclusion meets the requirements. Although this Act has wrongly been referred to as "a toothless shark",[73] it must be considered that the German legislator is already examining in which of the 3,800 cases of formal requirements under German law it is possible to replace the requirement of the written form by digital signature or even by simple electronic transmission.[74]

Originally, the Signature Act was rejected in its present form by the higher house of the German parliament (*Bundesrat*) because in its opinion the Ministries of Justice of the individual states had not agreed with the concept of certification through private providers,[75] who require only a licence to be obtained from public sources. The states considered the identification and allocation of signature keys to be a public function that could be delegated only to authorities, courts, or notary publics as holders of a public position. In its first statement, the *Bundesrat*, therefore, recommended

---

70 Act Concerning Digital Signatures , section 1, *Bundesrat Drucksache*, 420/97, June 13, 1997.
71 See the following text dealing with "electronic transactions".
72 Act Concerning Digital Signatures , section 15.
73 Mertes, "Gesetz und Verordnung zur digitalen Signatur — Bewegung auf der Datenautobahn?", *C.R.* 1996, at p. 771.
74 So-called compliance with the likewise proposed "text-form", see text, below.
75 Act Concerning Digital Signatures , sections 3 and 4 *Bundesrat Drucksache*, at p. 10.

that the Act should be taken from the overall Information and Communication Services Act and revised again separately. The states felt encouraged in their first recommendation particularly because, according to the Signature Act, restrictions of the legal scope and statements on a third party's power of attorney could be inserted in the certificates[76] and because the draft made only insufficient provisions for the reliability of screening for private institutions. The states also argued that there existed no adequate liability rule in case of professional misconduct.[77]

Despite the aforesaid reservations, the *Bundesrat* did not thwart the enactment of the Signature Act and, hence, of the entire Information and Communication Services Act.

10-26   **Interstate Media Services Convention** The Interstate Media Services Convention entered into force on August 1, 1997, replacing the Interstate BTX Convention (*BTX-Staatsvertrag*) previously applicable.[78] The Convention sets forth the regulatory framework for media services, *i.e*, services aiming at the public.[79] As shown, media services include mostly distribution services which transfer to a certain number of receivers and whose broadcasting time is unilaterally determined by the provider, such as teleshopping.[80] Also included pursuant to section 2(2), number 4 are services on demand, in cases where the individual communication is in the background as is the case with electronic press.

Crucial provisions of the Convention, such as freedom of access,[81] basic principles of responsibility,[82] the transparency of providers,[83] and the provisions concerning data protection[84] are consistent, in part, as to the wording and, in part at least, as to the content, with the regulations at the federal level.

Since the media services (for example, the electronic press) may influence the formation of public opinion, meaning that they come "close to broadcasting", the Convention contains numerous provisions which are known from related fields of law, such as press law and broadcasting law. These provisions go beyond the regulations of the Information and Communication Services Act.

Thus, section 6(2) of the Convention contains qualified requirements as to the transparency of providers in cases where material is presented in a

---

76 Act Concerning Digital Signatures , section 5(2).
77 *Bundestagsdrucksache*, 13/7385, Ann. 2, opinion of the *Bundesrat*, at pp. 58 and 59.
78 Interstate Media Services Convention, section 22(2).
79 Interstate Media Services Convention, section 2(1).
80 Interstate Media Services Convention, as amended, January 1 to February 7, 1997, Bayerischer Landtag Drucksache, 13/7716, March 21, 1997, at pp. 1 *et seq*, section 2(2), number 1-3, and reasons, at p. 4.
81 Interstate Media Services Convention, section 4.
82 Interstate Media Services Convention, section 5.
83 Interstate Media Services Convention, section 6(1).
84 Interstate Media Services Convention, sections 12 to 17.

journalistic or editorial fashion which are similar to the masthead obligation under the press law. Section 7, which sets the minimum standard in respect of the content of media services, provides under (2) that the persons responsible for distribution services are obliged to observe the following journalistic principles. Editorials must be separated from reports, news concerning current events of the day must be reviewed in respect to their content, origin and truth. Since the Convention is orientated towards press and broadcasting law, it is also not surprising that it sets further provisions concerning the presentation of advertising and sponsoring,[85] an obligation to make a counter-statement,[86] and a right to information.[87]

What deserves special attention is the regulation concerning the protection of minors under section 8, together with sections 5, 18, and 20, of the Interstate Media Services Convention. The states argued that the protection of minors at the federal level concerning information and communication services did not go far enough because distribution and advertising restrictions according to the Information and Communication Services Act did not apply before such services were put on an index. According to the opinion of the states, it was necessary to issue a preventive ban on sites which were obviously morally harmful to minors in cases of fast-moving, short-lived electronic media, rather than providing for a repressive indexation.[88]

This is consistent with section 8 of the Interstate Media Services Convention referring in particular in (1) to sites that are without exception impermissible. This includes, for example, such sites that incite racial hatred,[89] glorify violence[90] or war,[91] or are of a pornographic nature,[92] or are capable of severely endangering minors.[93] In addition to further bans on the distribution of material under (2) and (3), section 8(4), which is similar to the regulation at the federal level, provides that any service provider be obligated to appoint a commissioner in charge of the protection for minors if morally harmful material is to be distributed to minors. In the case of a contravention of these prohibitions, the supervisory authority (*i.e.*, the authority responsible for the protection of minors in the states), entrusted under section 18(1) with controlling the observance of the provisions relating to the protection of minors, has the power to intervene and may, notably, prohibit or block sites.[94]

---

85 Interstate Media Services Convention, section 9 — in particular the principle of separation of advertising and program in section 9(2).
86 Interstate Media Services Convention, section 10.
87 Interstate Media Services Convention, section 11.
88 Kuch, "Der Staatsvertrag über Mediendienste", Z.U.M. 1997, at pp. 225, *et seq*, 229, and 230.
89 Interstate Media Services Convention, Number 1.
90 Interstate Media Services Convention, Number 2.
91 Interstate Media Services Convention, Number 3.
92 Interstate Media Services Convention Number 4.
93 Interstate Media Services Convention Number 5.
94 Interstate Media Services Convention, section 18(2), sentences 1 and 2.

10-27   **Interstate Broadcasting Convention**   The third legal code to be considered is the Interstate Broadcasting Convention (*Rundfunkstaatsvertrag* 1997 — RStV), which came into force on January 1, 1997. Media service providers need a permit under state law pursuant to section 20(2) of the Interstate Broadcasting Convention, if and to the extent that the media service offered is attributable to broadcasting. If the media institution of one state, in agreement with all other state media institutions, determines that these preconditions are met, the provider must file within six months following the notification of this determination an application for admission or offer the media service in such a manner that it is not attributable to broadcasting. The requirement of an admission under broadcasting law entails far-reaching consequences: In addition to the regulations of the states' media laws, the approval procedure of sections 20 *et seq* of the Interstate Broadcasting Convention 1997 is fully applicable.

Thus, the media service is subject to the new provisions under the media concentration law.[95] According to the market share model underlying sections 25 *et seq* of the Interstate Broadcasting Convention, the enterprises, together with the programs attributable to them, are permitted to achieve a market share in viewers of up to 30 per cent. Media-relevant related markets, such as the field of print media or on-line services, that do not satisfy the term "broadcasting" must also be considered. If 30 per cent have been achieved, the provider cannot obtain any further permits pursuant to section 26(3) of the Interstate Broadcasting Convention. Within the framework of the application proceedings, the state media institutions enjoy rights to information and powers of investigation to find out about the facts. In addition, media services requiring admission are subject to the disclosure provisions in section 22 of the Interstate Broadcasting Convention. As soon as media services fall within the "broadcasting" term as set forth in the Interstate Broadcasting Convention, they will no longer benefit from the clearly more favourable Tele Services Act or from the Interstate Media Services Convention.[96]

To avoid — as far as possible — unpleasant consequences due to the fact that the term "broadcasting" is not precisely defined in the Interstate Broadcasting Convention, the competent state media institution should be approached in borderline cases and a certificate of non-objection under section 20(2), sentence 3, of the Interstate Broadcasting Convention should be applied for.[97] The solution of doubtful issues depends on the interpretation of the broadcasting terms.

---

95 Kreile, "Der neue Rundfunkstaatsvertrag, Neue Wege bei der Vielfaltsicherung im Rundfunk", *N.J.W.* 1997, at p. 1334.
96 Kuch, "Der Staatsvertrag über Mediendienste", *Z.U.M.* 1997, at p. 227.
97 Bröhl, "Rechtliche Rahmenbedingungen für neue Informations- und Kommunikationsdienste", *C.R.* 1997, at pp. 73 and 75.

Further Considerations

At the federal level, legislators are considering to adopt further provisions **10-28** to regulate on-line communication and on-line trade. What must be mentioned are the Text-form Law (*Textformgesetz*) and the Crypto Law (*Kryptogesetz*).

Text-form Law In February 1997, the Federal Ministry of Justice transmit- **10-29** ted to authorities, associations and interested circles a draft discussion of an Act by means of which the common obligation under civil law to make declarations in writing was to be replaced in numerous cases by a new formal requirement, the "text-form".[98]

This "text form" is intended to make it possible that declarations still requiring written form today may be made effectively by means of electronic transmission as well. This is to be accomplished through the introduction of the so-called "Text-form" into section 126a) of the Civil Code. This text-form requires a fixation of the communication or legal declarations in readable letters, and makes a personal signature as well as a printout on paper redundant; as an additional measure, numerous regulations of the Civil Code, as well as of the Commercial Code, which now require the written form, shall be amended in accordance with the Text-form Law to the effect that compliance with the "text-form" will suffice for effective and legally binding declarations.

The intended deregulation of the "text-form" is to replace the written form in all cases in which the personal signature is an unreasonable formal requirement, and which presently still excludes the use of electronic media in an unjustified manner. A number of existing legal provisions will be affected by the proposed Text-form Law which provides in several articles for the amendment of numerous laws, for instance the provisions of the Tenancy Law.[99] To mention a final example, the compliance with the text-form also must apply to the one-week right to revocation, exercised by the consumer in cases of credit transactions and door-to-door dealings.[100]

In cases where the written form is needed for warning and evidence purposes, the formal requirements will not be relaxed according to the draft.[101] Thus, the reform does not affect, for example, section 766 of the Civil Code, which provides that for the protection of the guarantor the assumption of the guaranty must be in writing.

---

98 Letter from the Federal Ministry of Justice, February 27, 1997, at p. 3, together with a draft act concerning the modification of the Civil Code and other Acts, as per January 31, 1997, here referred to as the "Text-form Law".

99 Draft act for the amendment of the Civil Code and other laws, as per January 31, 1997, article 1, at pp. 3 *et seq*, and article 8, at pp. 8 *et seq*.

100 Draft Act for the amendment of the Civil Code and other laws, as per January 31, 1997, article 7, at p. 6, article 9, at p. 8.

101 Draft Act for the amendment of the Civil Code and other laws, as per January 31, 1997, at p. 18 (reasons).

The plans of the German legislator, however, reach far beyond the introduction of the Text-form Law described above. Thus, with respect to the remaining circumstances under which the requirement of written form will still apply, it is intended to review whether in addition to the written form, a signature in digital form should be allowed. Finally, it has even been considered, after experiences have been obtained from the substantive law, to relax the formal requirements in the field of law of procedure.[102] It is absolutely expedient not to exclude the law of procedure from the reform. German courts have already proven to be very progressive in this field, when one looks at the relaxation of formal requirements accepted by the courts in cases of filing certain written statements through telefax,[103] by telegram, telex,[104], or BTX communication.[105] The latest relaxation of the formal requirements came with a decision of the Federal Social Court which found that the requirements of the written form were met in the case of the filing of an appeal, if the appeal was transmitted directly from computer through a modem via the telephone line to the court, without the computer fax requiring a signature.[106]

10-30   **Crypto Law**   Much more controversial than the changes to the formal requirements are the considerations of the federal government, more accurately the Federal Ministry of the Interior, in connection with the "crypto policy" which may even result in the introduction of a crypto law. The question is in which framework of conditions it is possible to exchange news or legally binding declarations in a coded form via the Internet to ensure secrecy.

As already stated, the transfer of messages through electronic mail is as unprotected from unauthorised reading as a postcard sent in the traditional manner, even if the e-mail is transferred into individual packages through different routers to the receiver.[107] Unauthorised third parties may, with the use of special programs (so-called "packet sniffers") intercept, filter, tap and copy to their computers the information held in each router, from the transmission lines as well as from the target computer.[108]

To avoid unauthorised persons reading data, the users may use efficient coding programs that are offered for sale. The coding methods have reached such a degree of sophistication that coded messages cannot be decoded by third parties even with the help of the latest technical means. Thus, according

102 Letter from the Federal Ministry of Justice, February 27, 1997, at p. 3 (not published).
103 BSG (German Federal Social Court), *M.D.R.* 1995, at p. 1053; BGH (German Federal Supreme Court), *Vers.R.* 1996, pp. 778 *et seq*; BGH, *Fam.R.Z.* 1995, at pp. 1135 *et seq*; BGH, *N.J.W.* 1994, at pp. 1881 *et seq*.
104 BVerwGE (Federal Administrative Court) 81, at p. 35; BFH, *N.J.W.* 1996, at p. 1432.
105 BVerwG, *N.J.W.* 1995, at p. 2121.
106 BSG Order, October 15, 1996; BSG, *W.I.R.*, section 151, *S.G.G.* 1/95, at pp. 235 *et seq*, with short commentary by Huff.
107 See the warning statement by Taylor and Resnick, "Better Safe", *Internet World*, February 1995, at p. 33: "It is a good idea not to post anything on the Internet you would not want to see on the front page of the *National Enquirer*".
108 Graff, "Der Krypto-Komplex", *Süddeutsche Zeitung*, May 9, 1997, at p. 13.

to experts, an unauthorised decoding of the most popular data-coding program PGP (Pretty Good Privacy) is impossible even for the best-equipped organisations.[109] The coding by means of the aforementioned PGP software is based on an asymmetrical method (the so-called "public key method"). Under this procedure, each party generates a pair of keys which consists of a public and a private key. To code his message, the sender needs the public key of the receiver. The coded message can then be decoded by the receiver, but only with the private key. Even the sender can no longer produce the plain text.[110]

The use of this asymmetrical coding method is not prohibited in Germany. What is rather striking in this connection is that the federal government did not provide for any restrictions in the case of the regulation of the digital signature which is based on the use of asymmetrical coding. Instead, it was expressly determined in the Signature Act under section 5(4), sentence 3, that the storage of the private signature key at the place of certification is not permitted.[111] Of course, there are technical and legal differences between coding and digital signature, in that the digital signature is generated by the private key of the sender and that any third party may verify the integrity and authenticity of the signed message by means of the public key.[112]

However, as early as 1996, the Federal Ministry of the Interior was responsible for the formation of a "Task Force" which was to consider a state-controlled cryptography (coding) within a national and international framework. According to press releases and public statements made by Manfred Kanther, the Federal Minister of the Interior, at the end of April 1997, concrete considerations were made to regulate coding by an Act providing for an obligation to deposit the key. This is to ensure that security authorities (the Office for the Protection of the Constitution and secret services) are able to investigate coded messages in cases of suspicion.[113]

These attempts have met with broad opposition in Germany from enterprises, scientists, and controllers for data protection and German "netizens".[114] The regulation of the coding has also been contested within the federal government. The Minister of the Interior (supported by the Federal Office for the Protection of the Constitution) is currently confronted with opposition from his fellow cabinet members Rüttgers (Education, Science

---

109 Stallings, *Datenzeichensicherheit mit PGP*, 1995, at p. 74; Kuner, "Rechtliche Aspekte der Datenverschlüsselung im Internet", *N.J.W.-Co.R.* 1995, at p. 414.
110 Kuner, "Rechtliche Aspekte der Datenverschlüsselung im Internet", *N.J.W.-Co.R.* 1995, at p. 414.
111 Mertes, "Gesetz und Verordnung zur digitalen Signatur — Bewegung auf der Datenautobahn", *Z.R.* 1996, at p. 774.
112 Bieser, "Bundesregierung plant Gesetz zur digitalen Signatur", *C.R.* 1996, at p. 565.
113 "Einen Dietrich für den Staat", *Süddeutsche Zeitung*, April 17, 1997, at p. 4; Graff, "Der Krypto-Komplex", *Süddeutsche Zeitung*, May 9, 1997, at p. 13; Lütge and Siegele, "Was darf geheim sein?", *Die Zeit*, May 9, 1997, at p. 4.
114 The excerpt from the written statement by the Kryptography initiative, c/o Dipl.-Ing. Dr. Wolfgang Schreiner, *C.R.* 1996, at pp. 190 *et seq.*

and Research), Rexrodt (Economy), and Schmidt-Jortzig (Justice), who warn against over-regulation in this field. These ministers advocate the idea that the user himself should have the responsibility for ensuring effective protection and secrecy on the Internet.[115]

As far as coding is concerned, the government faces a dilemma: If it tolerates the fact that crypto technology is being used in an uncontrolled way by a vast number of people, Cyberspace becomes a safe haven for criminals. If the government rejected coding, the increased use of the Internet and notably electronic money transactions by German businesses would also be put at risk. One must wait and see in which direction these considerations will develop.

At present, data coding programs can be used under German law without limitation; only the export of data coding software has been restricted on the European Union level.[116]

ON-LINE CONDUCT

Access and Responsibility

Freedom of Access

10-31   In contrast to the obligatory admission under the broadcasting law, both the new federal law and the new Interstate Media Services Convention provide for the free- dom of access and application of the tele and/or media services. Of course, the freedom of access does not entail that the application and admission requirements under general laws, in particular the industrial and commercial laws, no longer apply; this expressly follows from the reasons in respect to section 4 of the Tele Services Act. This express clarification seems to be superfluous; it is due to the fact that, in the course of the negotiations between the federal government and the states, several states held that on-line services similar to broadcasting services should at least be registered. The fact that no approval or registration under the broadcasting law is necessary, such as in the case of the Interstate BTX Convention, shows the remarkable success of the compromise between the federal government and the states.

Of course, the Interstate Broadcasting Convention (*Rundfunkstaatsvertrag*) 1997 has dampened the spirits of private on-line providers. By means of a clause contained in section 20(2) of the Interstate Broadcasting Convention 1997, according to which the offering of services is subject to approval if they are attributable to broadcasting, the states have found a possibility to judge certain providers by measures under broadcasting law, notwithstanding the applicability of the Interstate Media Services Convention.

---

115 Graff, "Der Krypto-Komplex", *Süddeutsche Zeitung*, May 9, 1997, at p. 13; Lütge and Siegele, "Was darf geheim sein?", *Die Zeit*, May 9, 1997, at p. 4.
116 Kuner, "Rechtliche Aspekte der Datenverschlüsselung im Internet", *N.J.W.-Co.R.* 1995, at p. 413 *et seq*, at p. 414.

This results in a certain legal uncertainty for private enterprise, even if the regulations on the tele and media services come into force.

Responsibility

The regulation of the responsibility and any obligation to identify one's own **10-32** Web site content and to make counter-statements has a substantial influence on a provider's conduct. The new regulations in Germany deal specifically with this issue.

Basic Principle of Responsibility The previous legal situation was marked **10-33** by great uncertainty in respect to the scope of liability for service providers under civil, copyright and criminal law. Due to the urgent need for clarification, both the German federal government in the Tele Services Act (*Tele-dienstegesetz — TDG)* and the German states in the Interstate Media Services Convention laid down the responsibility of the providers in a new regulation which, to a large extent, refers to the media and tele services. These provisions introduce that a review should be made before bringing the facts under the rule of criminal or civil law. If the preconditions of responsibility are met under these Acts, the further consequences (as to criminal liability or liability for damages under civil law) are also to be determined by the applicable legal system.[117]

Section 5(1) sets forth with the same phrasing as in the Tele Services Act and in the Interstate Media Services Convention the principle of the provider's responsibility and clarifies that the latter are responsible for "their own content offered for use according to general laws". Accordingly, the content provider is liable for his own Web site content.

In respect to offers of media services, as well as tele services, the responsibility of the service providers for the third-party content are worded identically as follows. Service providers are jointly responsible for third-party content made available by them, "if they have knowledge of such content and if it is technically possible to and can reasonably be expected of them to prevent third-party use".[118] What is additionally striking is that the larger scope of interpretation involved with the terms "technically possible" or "reasonably" is, above all, restricting the liability to acting with intent. This term exists in Germany and is used in criminal, but not in civil law.[119] In view of the organisers' and publishers' liability developed by the courts, many critics argue that the definitional element of the positive knowledge is too narrow. Therefore, proposals have been made to the effect that the preconditions of

---

117 Engel-Flechsig, "Das Informations- und Kommunikationsdienstegesetz des Bundes und der Mediendienstestaatsvertrag der Bundesländer — einheitliche Rahmen- bedingungen für Multimedia —" *Z.U.M.* 1997, at p. 236.
118 Tele Services Act, section 5(2).
119 Bröhl also refers to this point in "Rechtliche Rahmenbedingungen für neue Informations- und Kommunikationsdienste", *C.R.* 1997, at p. 75.

liability should be linked to negligent lack of knowledge. In such cases, the element of organisational possibility to control the networks concerned should be considered a new regulative tool.[120]

The service provider who only provides access is not responsible for illegal third-party content pursuant to section 5(3) of the Tele Services Act and of the Interstate Media Services Convention. In addition, the operators of proxy cache servers, such as the access providers, are not responsible for third-party content, because the "automatic and short-time presentation of third-party content due to the request by the user serves the procurement of access".[121] This is appropriate because operators of such servers cannot reasonably be expected to control the automatic and intermediate storage of information. Users mostly return to the Web sites that are stored automatically and for only a short period of time on proxy cache servers which would otherwise involve expensive connections to the actual host computer if they were called up without this intermediate storage. If the frequency of the request for certain Web sites declines, the sites are automatically deleted on the proxy cache servers. It is not practical to regulate responsibility in connection with this because the users may access the Web sites where the information originated.[122]

In contrast to the federal regulation, the Interstate Media Services Convention provides under section 5(3), sentence 2, in conjunction with section 18(3), a no-fault authorisation to intervene against access providers and providers of proxy cache servers if it is impossible to take action against the original party responsible according to (1) and (2). The authorisation laid down in section 18(3) of the Interstate Media Services Convention demands a ban on illegal or offensive material, provided that it is technically possible and can be reasonably expected. However, federal law makes it clear that, under (4), most existing laws shall remain unaffected.[123]

In summary, it can be said that, by means of the enacted regulations for the responsibility of tele and media service providers, together with section 5 as *lex specialis*, a level of examination under liability law has been introduced. It is followed by a review of whether the preconditions of the individual elements of liability under the civil or criminal law are met. A high standard of liability has been introduced, owing to the fact that responsibility for Third Party content is linked to the requirement of wilfulness. The

---

120 Bortloff, "Verantwortlichkeit von Online-Diensten", Z.U.M. 1997, at p. 169, with reference to the decision by the BGH, June 19, 1956, "Tanzkurse", BGH G.R.U.R. 1956, at p. 516.
121 Section 5(3), sentence 2, of the new Regulations.
122 Sieber, "Strafrechtliche Verantwortlichkeit für den Datenverkehr in internationalen Computernetzen (1)", J.Z. 1996, at p. 433.
123 Engel-Flechsig, "Das Informations- und Kommunikationsdienstegesetz des Bundes und der Mediendienstestaatsvertrag der Bundesländer — einheitliche Rahmen- bedingungen für Multimedia —", Z.U.M. 1997, at pp. 236 and 239.

terms "necessary" and "reasonable" require interpretation and allow flexibility of the courts, while entailing legal uncertainty for on-line providers.

Even though the proposed regulations do not expressly regulate a provider's liability for the various services he offers, the same services are covered by the aforementioned provisions of the Interstate Media Services Convention. The question as to the liability of such providers is determined on the basis of a review of the individual offering that is which concrete area of responsibility is concerned: If the individual service of the program offered is only to provide access, section 5(3) will be the relevant regulation. If the responsibility for the provider's own content is at issue, section 5(1) will be applicable. The individual offers of service providers may be qualified as tele services and others as media services.[124]

Duty of Identification and Duty of Counter-Statement Section 6 of the Tele   **10-34**
Services Act and of the Interstate Media Services Convention sets forth in each case identical phrases for the provider's duty to identify his material through name and address. In addition to consumer protection and the safeguarding of transparency, it is also explained in the law that the duty to state the identity and address shall serve the prosecution as a connecting factor.[125] Thus, the idea of responsibility rests with the duty of identification which is subject to an administrative fine in case of contravention: each provider is responsible for his content.

Section 6(2) of the Interstate Media Services Convention concerning electronic press contains a provision that is orientated towards the masthead regulation according to media law. According to this, providers of material of a journalistic or editorial nature, in which the content of periodical publications or texts in a periodical order are distributed, are required to furnish the name and address of the persons responsible. Only those persons that have their permanent abode in Germany and have not lost their capacity to hold public offices through judicial decision[126] may be subject to criminal prosecution. The purpose of this provision is to determine who is to be held responsible for the content of the service.

Moreover, since the introduction of the Interstate Media Services Convention, providers of editorially prepared offerings have been obligated pursuant to section 10 to "immediately insert into their material counter-statement of the person or authority affected by the facts that were asserted in the original material, without cost to the person concerned".[127]

---

124 Engel-Flechsig, "Das Informations- und Kommunikationsdienstegesetz des Bundes und der Mediendienstestaatsvertrag der Bundesländer — einheitliche Rahmenbedingungen für Multimedia —", Z.U.M. 1997, at pp. 234 and 238.
125 Interstate Media Services Convention as amended December 12, 1996, reasons in respect of section 6, at p. 8; Tele Services Act, reasons in respect of section 6, *Bundesrat Drucksache* 966/96, at p. 23.
126 See the future section 6(2), sentence 3, of the Interstate Media Services Convention.
127 Interstate Media Services Convention, section 10(1), sentence 1.

The claim to a counter-statement by the person concerned is dealt with in greater detail in the following paragraphs of section 10. To enforce the claim, reference is made to (3) of the decisions of the courts of ordinary jurisdiction in civil and criminal matters and to the proceedings of preliminary injunctions. For tele services that provide individual exchanges, the Information and Communication Services Act does not provide for a corresponding duty of counter-statement, but establishes that provisions under press law are definitely to remain unaffected.[128] It may be rightly argued that a claim to a counter-statement may be derived from the media laws to be loosely interpreted in the case of on-line offerings attributable to electronic press.[129]

Responsibility under Criminal Law

10-35   **Elements of the Offence — "Writings"** In Germany, pornography, libel, and extremist propaganda on the Internet have also raised the question of the responsibility of the participants under criminal law. It has been suggested that crimes committed on the Internet should be summarised under the new term "multimedia criminality".[130] The sensational criminal investigations conducted by the Munich public prosecutors against CompuServe at the end of 1995 led to an indictment of the firm's managing director, Felix Somm, and show the uncertainty presently prevailing in Germany when it comes to dealing with these problems. It is hoped that the new regulation of responsibility, also applicable to criminal law, contributes to legal clarity.

Even before the introduction of the new section 5(1) of the Tele Services Act which expressly states the principle of the provider's own responsibility, the one who offers criminal content on the Internet (the content provider) was already punishable. Numerous offences may be thought of, such as the dissemination of pornographic writings.[131] Defamatory offences, such as insult,[132] slander, or libel,[133] and defaming someone's reputation by knowingly making false statements,[134] as well as other offences such as the disparagement of the President of the Federal Republic of Germany, defamation of the state and its symbols, or of constitutional bodies are also considered to be punishable.[135] German criminal law punishes racist or right-extremist propaganda that glorifies violence. Incitement to hatred or violence against segments of the

---

128 Tele Services Act, section 2(4).
129 Lerch, "Der Gegendarstellungsanspruch im Internet — Findet der Gegendarstellungsanspruch auch auf die "elektronische" Presse Anwendung?", C.R. 1997, at pp. 261 *et seq.*
130 Vassilaki, "Multimediale Kriminalität, Entstehung, Formen und rechtspolitische Fragen der 'Post-Computer-Kriminalität' ", C.R. 1997, at pp. 297 *et seq.*
131 Only special acts are subject to punishment, such as "hard core" pornography, particularly the depiction of sexual child abuse or sodomy. Criminal Code, section 184; Stange, "Pornographie im Internet, Versuche einer strafrechtichen Bewältigung", C.R. 1996, at p. 424).
132 Criminal Code, section 185.
133 Criminal Code, section 186.
134 Criminal Code, section 187.
135 Criminal Code, sections 90, 90a, and 90b.

population or publishing insults directed at them[136] is punishable by imprisonment of up to five years. Also punishable are the depiction of violence[137] public incitement to criminal offences,[138] approving criminal acts,[139] giving directions how to commit criminal offences,[140] disturbance of the public peace through threat of criminal offences,[141] and the distribution of propaganda by means of unconstitutional organisations.[142]

As far as these crimes include the distribution of writings, these offences were already punishable according to the current definition of "writings" under section 11(3) of the Criminal Code. The provision was already expanded in 1974 with respect to the extended use of various media and equates "sound and visual recordings, pictures and other illustrations" with "writings". In the case of on-line communication, the physical manifestation of intellectual content for a certain period of time which is considered necessary by the prevailing opinion[143] can be seen in the storage of data on a service providers' computer.[144] The extension of the term "writings" to include stored data, provided for in article 4 Information and Communication Services Act, deserves approval. Thus, it has been made clear by the legislator that, in addition to the content on data carriers, such as CD-ROMs or hard disks, such content existing on electronic main memories[145] is covered as well.

Most of the offences mentioned above are not precluded from punishment by the mere fact that a "distribution" in the legal sense requires the precondition of a physical transmission of concrete writings. The criterion is not fulfilled in the case of on-line communication.[146] It has been rightly pointed out that these criminal acts can also be realised on-line without physical transfer by distributing[147] but also by making accessible the material[148] or the commitment of a criminal offence in public.[149]

---

136 Criminal Code, section 130.
137 Criminal Code, section 131.
138 Criminal Code, section 111.
139 Criminal Code, section 140 number 2.
140 Criminal Code, section 130 a.
141 Criminal Code, section 126.
142 Criminal Code, section 86 a.
143 Tröndle, *Strafgesetzbuch*, 48th ed., 1997, section 11, marginal note 44.
144 Sieber, "Strafrechtliche Verantwortlichkeit für den Datenverkehr in internationalen Computernetzen 82", *J.Z.* 1996, at p. 228; see also OLG (Higher Regional Court) Stuttgart, *N.St.Z.* 1992, at pp. 38 *et seq.*
145 Engel-Flechsig, "Das Informations- und Kommunikations-dienstegesetz des Bundes und der Mediendienstestaatsvertrag der Bundesländer", *Z.U.M.* 1997, at p. 237.
146 Tröndle, *Strafgesetzbuch*, 48th ed., 1997, section 84, marginal notes 13 and 23; *B.G.H.St.* 18, at p. 64; BGH, *N.J.W.* 1977, at p. 1965.
147 Sieber, "Strafrechtliche Verantwortlichkeit für den Datenverkehr in internationalen Computernetzen (2)", *J.Z.* 1996, at pp. 494, 495, and 496.
148 Like, for example, Criminal Code, sections 131(1), number 3, 184(1), number 184(3), number 2.
149 Like, for example, Criminal Code, sections 86 a(1), number 1, 90 a(1), 90 b, 140 number 2, 186 *et seq.*

10-36   **Responsibility for Third-Party Content** German prosecuting authorities are especially uncertain when it comes to establishing whether on-line services or service providers that provide access to third-party offerings of criminal content stored on the Internet or on the service provider's own server can and must be held responsible under criminal law. The same applies to the responsibility of providers or users whose home pages contain hyperlinks referring to third-party Web sites with punishable content.

In 1995, the Munich public prosecutors became world-famous by instigating criminal investigations against the on-line service CompuServe Deutschland G.m.b.H., based on the suspicion of distributing pornographic "writings" involving children. Such "writings" were stored within the framework of newsgroups on the server of CompuServe Inc. in Ohio, and they could be accessed in Germany through the Munich network junction point. When enforcing a search warrant on November 22, 1995, the police discovered a list of 250 forums for examination. CompuServe blocked all listed newsgroups without examining the content more closely. This action caused a stir, not only in Germany but also around the world. The United States was especially disturbed because among the blocked newsgroups were forums that had a scientific content and also served self-help groups.[150] In February 1997, Munich public prosecutors brought charges against the managing director of CompuServe Deutschland G.m.b.H., Felix Somm, who had just resigned. Somm was accused of allowing pornographic depictions of children and animals from newsgroups to be distributed without hindrance in 1995 and 1996.[151]

Regardless of the revision of the responsibility of service providers on the network, a service provider is, according to applicable German criminal law, probably not responsible for third-party content on the Internet or on chat forums not presented by him.[152] An on-line service or service provider who neither presents newsgroups with criminally relevant content nor offers criminal material of his own may only be charged with neglecting to carry out control measures and not with an active transmission which consists here only in the provision of the connection and in the offering of storage capacity. Criminal liability for neglect would, however, require.[153] that the service provider be responsible that no offence is being committed. Such guarantor's obligation is not discernible. It neither results from dangerous preliminary conduct in breach of duty, as it is socially adequate and lawful to provide the possibility of communication and storage nor from an obligation to control hazards.

---

150 Jäger and Collardin, "Die Inhaltsverantwortlichkeit von Online-Diensten", *C.R.* 1996, at p. 236; Stange, "Pornographie im Internet, Versuche einer strafrechtlichen Bewältigung", *C.R.* 1996, at p. 425.

151 Kuner, "Internet-News", *N.J.W.-Co.R.* 1997, at p. 252; Rubner, "Internet — ein juristisches Minenfeld", *Süddeutsche Zeitung*, June 6, 1997, at p. 1.

152 Sieber, "Strafrechtliche Verantwortlichkeit für den Datenverkehr in internationalen Computernetzen (1) und (2)", *J.Z.* 1996, at pp. 429-442, and *J.Z.* 1996, at pp. 494 and 507.

153 Criminal Code, section 13.

In respect to the possibilities of misuse, the Internet does not differ from other modern methods of computer communication. For this reason, one is unable to establish any increased hazards that would involve duties of control. Moreover, a guarantor's obligation no longer exists in cases where third parties are acting illegally in their own responsibility. The lender of a dangerous tool is no guarantor for a murder committed by the third party by means of such tool. This is also the case for a service provider who is not punishable for an illegal third-party content to which he only provided access.[154] For want of a guarantor's obligation, the preconditions of responsibility are not met under the applicable criminal law. An exception may perhaps apply only to cases where the provider presents its own content and in case of the operation of a FTP server with uncontrolled upload and download functions.[155] Furthermore, it is questionable whether or not punishment is excluded because the on-line service concerned is not able to prevent the distribution of pornography on the Internet due to users having the possibility to obtain access to its content through alternative means. Finally, the service providers may be expected only superficially and subsequently to control third parties' content.

Thus, a punishment would fail because the provider cannot reasonably be expected to prevent the result. In this connection the computer-controlled solutions (such as developed by PICS — "Platform for Internet Content Selection"), which evaluate and block Internet pages at the server level according to categories, must be considered. Such categories include sex and violence. Programs such as "Surf-Watch" or "Cyber Patrol" do not, however, ensure complete control because in contrast to the aforesaid alternative, they only make it possible for parents to block Internet pages not suitable for their children.

Besides the lack of objective elements of the offence, the deliberate intent of the offence is also missing. Service providers are still not liable for third party content according to the applicable criminal law. The new rules concerning responsibility confirm the view that the service provider cannot be held responsible for content on the Internet to which he provides access according to section 5(3) of the Information and Communication Services Act. Service providers also cannot be held responsible for content in case of services offered for use.[156] Positive knowledge of the illegal content and reasonableness in respect of the prevention of the result will mostly be missing.

Another well-known case that has triggered public discussion in Germany about the responsibility under criminal law regarding the use of

---

154 Sieber, "Strafrechtliche Verantwortlichkeit für den Datenverkehr in internationalen Computernetzen (2)", *J.Z.* 1996, at pp. 499 *et seq*, 501, and 502.

155 Sieber, "Strafrechtliche Verantwortlichkeit für den Datenverkehr in internationalen Computernetzen (2)", *J.Z.* 1996, at p. 502.

156 Responsibility pursuant to the Information and Communication Services Act, section 5(2), applies only in case of positive knowledge of the illegal content and in case of a reasonable possibility to prevent the use.

hyperlinks was the charge and the proceedings brought against the former deputy P.D.S. party leader Angela Marquard. She was charged with aiding the instruction of criminal offences.[157] and with the approval of criminal offences.[158] The charge, brought before a local court in Berlin, was based on the fact that the politician used a hyperlink in her home page which led to the Web site of the left-wing newspaper *Radikal*. The page contained reports on acts of sabotage against the rail service due to the Castor (nuclear waste) transports and a "short guide to obstructing rail transports of any kind" (an instruction on paralysing railway lines). The politician is accused of having committed an offence by making such criminal content accessible by means of the hyperlink.

The provider of a hyperlink is not chargeable as a perpetrator of criminal offences committed by the content of the third-party Web site.

It is conceivable to participate in a crime by means of aiding the criminal offence of a third party. Section 27 of the Criminal Code provides that anyone who is wilfully aiding an unlawful act wilfully committed by another shall be liable to be punished as an aider and abettor. It is not relevant on which means the participation in the form of aiding and abetting is based. If a guarantor's obligation exists, participation by means of aiding and abetting may be realised also through mere neglect.[159]

A distinction must be made to answer the question as to whether the provider of a hyperlink fulfils the objective elements of aiding and abetting. If the hyperlink leads directly to a third-party provider's pages containing criminal content, then the elements of aiding and abetting will be deemed fulfilled. The hyperlink provides easy access to pages with criminal content for a large number of people, whereby the distribution of unlawful content is unquestionably furthered. The objection that hyperlinks only help users in their search for information is of minor validity.

While this does not change the fact that the principal offence is furthered, other users may, nevertheless, reach the incriminated pages accidentally.[160] A different conclusion would apply if the hyperlink did not directly refer to the third-party pages with criminal content, but when such Web sites are reached only by clicking on further hyperlinks on the third-party Web site. In cases where the user reaches the criminally problematic content of a page only through several third-party Web sites, the elements of a supporting offence will not be fulfilled, provided that the first page reached by a hyperlink has a lawful content. In such cases, the crucial point of the charge under criminal law does not lie in the actions, but in the omission to control whether further

---

157 Criminal Code, sections 27 and 130a.
158 Criminal Code, sections 27 and 140; Kuner, "Internet-News", *N.J.W.-Co.R.* 1997, at p. 123; Rubner, "Internet — ein juristisches Minenfeld", *Süddeutsche Zeitung*, June 6, 1997, at p. 1.
159 Tröndle, *Strafgesetzbuch*, 48th ed., 1997, section 27, marginal note 2.
160 Ernst, "Rechtliche Fragen bei der Verwendung von hyperlinks im Internet", *N.J.W.-Co.R.* 1997, at p. 228.

hyperlinks lead from the lawful Web site to pages with punishable content. As stated, the preconditions of aiding through omitting are met only if a guarantor's obligation exists. This is not the case. Such an obligation may not be derived from dangerous conduct which results in a breach of duty, because the use of hyperlinks on pages with criminally unproblematic content on the World Wide Web is customary and not unlawful. It is neither possible nor can it reasonably be expected of each provider of hyperlinks to pursue the chain of interlinked third-party Web sites to the end. No punishable offence is committed by the person who refers to a legal page of a third party via hyperlink, and through the access to yet another party's illegal Web sites.

Whenever a direct connection is made by means of a hyperlink to a page with criminal content as depicted above, this will be considered "aiding" while the subjective elements of the offence must be reviewed very carefully in each individual case. Aiding will be only punishable if the offender has acted with at least conditional intent. This applies to persons who knowingly and wilfully support the distribution by third parties of unlawful Web sites, or at least accept the consequences of their actions. It will frequently be impossible to prove that the provider of hyperlinks had knowledge of the punishable content, especially in cases of extensive linked third-party Web sites.

It will also be difficult to furnish evidence in support of a wilfully committed act if it is stated that the content relevant under criminal law was adopted only after installation of the hyperlink on the third-party Web site. If a user links his Web page to a third-party page knowing that such other Web site includes criminal content, it will be virtually impossible for him to evade liability under criminal law. If one links one's page to a third-party page knowing its unlawful content, it will be practically impossible to evade one's liability under criminal law. This applies even if one expressly rejects such content.[161]

Competition Law and Separation of Advertising from Program Content

Importance of Advertising on the Internet

As stated in the introduction, "Netvertising"[162] is of great importance to the economic enterprises concerned. As long as no established billing system for Web site users exists and as long as parts of the Internet community continue to resist subscription fees for commercially offered services, advertising will be the only source of refinancing for most enterprises.[163]

10-37

---

161 Ernst, "Rechtliche Fragen bei Verwendung von hyperlinks im Internet", *N.J.W.-Co.R.* 1997, at p. 228.
162 This term has been registered as a trade mark by a Berlin agency, see Gummig, "Rechtsfragen bei Werbung im Internet", *Z.U.M.* 1996, at pp. 573 and 575.
163 A well-known case is the boycott of "Hotwired", a formerly popular Web site which was no longer visited by a major part of the netsurfers after it had become known that plans existed for the development of a subscription fee.

In contrast to radio and television, the surfer on the World Wide Web is not passively "showered" with advertising. Instead, he moves actively on the network when he moves via hyperlink from Web site to Web site. It is obvious that the users will respond to this new situation. To provide incentive for the active decision in favour of certain advertisements, advertising messages may be packaged editorially.[164] This would have the advantage that the loss of a target group which happens in all media, would be reduced to a minimum by means of suitably attractive editorial contributions which are closely linked to advertising.

This economically enforced development of "advertainment" and "infomercials" may come into conflict with requirements under competition law, especially regarding the principle of separation of advertising and program. At present, in Germany and elsewhere, it cannot be foreseen which consequences will be involved with the gradual transition to "push" technology, where the user will get an individually tailored selection of offerings and programs on his computer.

Competition Law

10-38   **Applicability of German Competition Law** German competition law, in particular, the Unfair Competition Act (UWG), is of decisive importance for the evaluation of the admissibility of content and conduct on the network. It has already been explained that pursuant to section 24(2) of the Unfair Competition Act, German courts have jurisdiction over all competitive acts occurring in their district. Due to the global nature of the Internet medium, this entails a universal jurisdiction of German courts.

It is quite a different question which has so far neither been solved by the case law nor by the German legislators, whether the evaluation of a case relevant under competition law qualifies under German law. No provision exists in German private international law which regulates the applicability of German competition law to competitively relevant actions performed on an international basis.[165] The constant line of decisions by the highest German courts has long established the principles of application which also apply here. The decision proceeds on the basis of the principle of the place where the market is situated and, accordingly, the competition law of the country must be applied in whatever market the competitive conflict of interest occurs.[166] In respect to the distribution of products and services, the question of which law is to be applied always depends on the market in which the concrete products and services are distributed to the consumer. In

---

164 Kur, "Internet Domain Names", C.R. 1996, at p. 326, footnote 5.
165 Ebbing, "Virtuelle Rechtsberatung und das anwaltliche Werbeverbot", N.J.W.-Co.R. 1996, at pp. 242 and 244.
166 BGH N.J.W. 1962, at pp. 37 et seq, "Kindersaugflaschen"; BGH N.J.W. 1964, at pp. 969 et seq; BGH N.J.W. 1977, at pp. 2211 et seq; BGH N.J.W. 1988, at pp. 644 et seq.

the case of international advertising, the relevant market shall be determined according to the advertising market which is to be influenced.[167]

All discussions on the application of German competition law to on-line transactions and competitive measures on the Internet are being held on this basis. Evaluating the international marketing activities already causes great problems. Products and services that are distributed by foreign companies to German consumers fall under the evaluation of the German competition law. Exceptions should apply if the distribution offers made by foreign enterprises are not accessible on the German market or are "noticed rather in a scattered way and by chance" by the German consumer if the share in the total sales of the product distributed is small.[168] The evaluation of advertising of foreign enterprises on the Internet has not been clarified yet. Due to the ubiquitous nature of the information on the Internet which may be called up anywhere in the world and thus also in Germany, each advertisement appears on the Internet as multistate advertising.

This means that the advertising must meet the requirements under competition law of all countries, in particular Germany. Now and then, in literature, the suggestion was made that the application of German competition law should be restricted. It should prevail only if the foreign enterprise holds a certain share of the German market. This means the advertising is noticeable in Germany or the advertising is aimed at German customers.[169] The latter may, however, be assumed as a rule if an enterprise deliberately uses the Internet. It would then be accessible on a world-wide basis for advertising purposes, in particular if the advertisement were provided in English — the language of the Internet.

All in all, the situation of the legal practitioner in regards to Internet law is now unsatisfactory. In the end, it is the responsibility of the courts or the legislators to develop delimiting elements which are suitable for an evaluation, for example, the exact definition of the term "noticeable".

Brief Survey Presupposing the applicability of German competition law, actions in business dealings for competitive purposes on the Internet must be compared with the pertinent case law relating to sections 1 and 3 of the Unfair Competition Act. The evaluation is made in the same way as in traditional business dealings. Violations are the same, and are only transferred to a new medium.[170]   **10-39**

In section 1 of the Unfair Competition Act, the main general clause covers all competitive actions contrary to public policy. Such actions are followed by cease-and-desist claims, claims for removal and, in case of fault,

---

167 Peschel, in Schwarz (ed.), *Recht im Internet*, chapter 5.2.1, at pp. 10 *et seq.*
168 Peschel, in Schwarz (ed.), *Recht im Internet*, chapter 5.2.1, at p. 13.
169 Peschel, in Schwarz (ed.), *Recht im Internet*, chapter 5.2.1, at p. 14.
170 Nordemann, Goddard, Tönhardt, and Czychowski, "Gewerblicher Rechtsschutz und Urheberrecht im Internet", *C.R.* 1996, at p. 653.

damage claims. In the course of time, five major scenarios in connection with section 1 of the Unfair Competition Act have been developed. These examples are, of course, incomplete, but they include:[171]

- Touting for customers and concealed advertising;
- Impeding competitors — a subordinate case being the prohibition of comparative advertising applicable in contrast to other legal systems (for example, in Switzerland and the United States);
- Exploitation, such as benefiting from another person's performance and advertising as freeloader;
- Disturbance of the market; and
- Gaining a lead through a breach of the law if, for example, lawyers present themselves on the Internet contrary to professional law or if businessmen do not comply with the advertising bans as written in German and European Community law.

10-40 Apart from section 1 of the Unfair Competition Act and the very specific provisions of competition law, attention should be paid to section 3 of the Unfair Competition Act, the so-called "small general clause". This provision deals with misleading statements for business situations of any kind. Any contravention of this law involves cease-and-desist claims and claims for removal.

10-41 **Competition Law on the Internet: E-mail Advertising, Hyperlinks, and Frames**
The "Internet community" accepts some generally applicable rules of conduct in the form of Netiquette. Even though this code of ethics is very incomplete, these widely accepted rules should also be considered for the purpose of interpreting and defining uncertain legal terms, such as the term "violation of morality" in section 1 of the Unfair Competition Act.[172] The unsolicited dispatch of e-mail with an advertising content does not only constitute a contravention of Netiquette, but is simultaneously an act of unfair competition, within the meaning of section 1 of the Unfair Competition Act, and is against public policy.[173]

The result of this contravention is consistent with the evaluation aspects applied by the courts to unsolicited telefax and BTX advertising.[174] Unsolicited telefax advertising is considered to be against public policy because it results in an unreasonable nuisance for the addressee. The same applies to

---

171 Baumbach and Hefermehl, *Wettbewerbsrecht*, 19th ed., 1996, section 1, marginal notes 60 *et seq.*
172 Nordemann, Goddard, Tönhardt, and Czychowski, "Gewerblicher Rechtsschutz und Urheberrecht im Internet", *C.R.* 1996, at p. 657.
173 Gummig, in Schwarz (ed.), *Recht im Internet*, chapter 5.3.1, at p. 19.
174 OLG Frankfurt, *W.R.P.* 1992, at p. 823; BGH *N.J.W.* 1996, at pp. 660 *et seq.*; see also Baumbach and Hefermehl, *Wettbewerbsrecht*, 19th ed., 1996, section 1, Unfair Competition Act, marginal note 69b.

undesired BTX advertising which ties up the addressee's phone line and involves an expenditure of time for its deletion. This evaluation is also applied to advertising e-mail sent to the addressee without his consent. Time is required to delete undesired mail. It also causes an unreasonable nuisance. In cases where large quantities of undesired e-mail arrive, the storage capacity of the receiving computer may be impeded. This circumstance is referred to as "net-marketing-overkill".[175]

Under German competition law, the use of hyperlinks might principally be permissible. The World Wide Web thrives on the fact that different Web sites are linked, so that it is possible to surf comfortably from one Web site to another. If the use of hyperlinks alone was considered to be anti-competitive, this would strike the World Wide Web in its heart. Anyone who presents himself on the Internet expects references and accepts the same as a typical consequence of the network. In exceptional cases, however, a different evaluation under competition law may apply. This is when references are made to third-party Web sites to recommend the goods or services offered on the original Web site.[176]

A further problem under competition law arises if a provider of a hyperlink refers to a new page of a third party, but the third party's page appears within the framework of the original provider. The anti-competitive exploitation of a third party's performance may be considered to be contrary to public policy within the meaning of section 1 of the Unfair Competition Act, and may involve cease-and-desist claims as well as damage claims. It is true that it is not contrary to public policy if a person directly assumes a third party's performance in such a manner that the person assuming the performance saves an expenditure of his own and deprives the person actually rendering the performance of the fruits of his work. In such a case, however, the requirements as to the fulfilment of the other elements of unfairness are lower. Thus, the requirements are met if the assumption of a third party's performance is followed by deceit about the origin. This constitutes the exploitation of another person's reputation or unlawful impediment.[177]

In cases where frames are used, the page that is connected to the hyperlink and appears on the click is considered in the absence of corresponding indications to be the page of the frame provider. Thus, the requirements of an identical assumption of the performance are met. This strengthens the frame provider's position as a competitor, without involving any considerable performance of his own. This aspect is followed by an avoidable deceit about the Web site origin. The use of frames without any indication that the page was not prepared by the frame provider is in breach of section 1 of the

---

175 Hoeren, "Internationale Netze und das Wettbewerbsrecht", *U.F.I.T.A.*, at p. 46.
176 Baumbach/Hefermehl, *Wettbewerbsrecht*, 19th ed., 1966, section 1, marginal notes 547 *et seq* and 552 *et seq*; Ernst, "Rechtliche Fragen bei der Verwendung von Hyperlinks im Internet", *N.J.W.-Co.R.* 1997, at pp. 224 and 226.
177 Baumbach and Hefermehl, *Wettbewerbsrecht*, 19th ed., 1996, section 1, marginal notes 495 *et seq*, 500, and 501.

Unfair Competition Act, provided that the page connected by a Link has relevant characteristics under competition law.[178]

Separation of Advertising and Program Content

10-42 **Basis and Meaning of the Separation Principle** The principle of separation for advertising and program content and editorial sections is a constitutional requirement. It is very important to German competition law and has already been mentioned within the framework of the statutory regulations of the Internet by the German states. The separation principle was enacted to protect the constitutionally guaranteed freedom of press and broadcasting[179] by safe-guarding the independent reporting of the press and of broadcasting against direct and indirect influences by the advertising industry.[180]

Numerous legal provisions define the requirement for separation of advertising and editorial sections. The press laws of the German states provide that commercial texts published in newspapers and journals for payment of a fee must be identified as advertisements. Under the rules of the Broadcasting Convention (Interstate Broadcasting Convention), television and radio commercials must be clearly identified as such. They must also be contrasted by optical and acoustical means from other programming.

In addition to the regulations at the state level, the courts have established a protection of journalistic independence under competition law, and consider editorial advertising to be against public policy in accordance with section 1 of the Unfair Competition Act.[181] The courts have found that section 3 of the Unfair Competition Act gives rise to cease-and-desist claims in cases where consumers are misled by advertising disguised as editorial contribution.[182]

10-43 **The Separation Principle on the Internet** In respect to media services aimed at the public, especially through the electronic press, the prohibition of mixing advertisements and programming on the Internet results directly from section 9 of the Interstate Media Services Convention which entered into force on August 1, 1997. If traditional broadcasting programs are offered on the Internet and World Wide Web, which may soon be the case, the existing regulation under the Interstate Broadcasting Convention will apply.[183]

One must be aware of the fact that advertising on the Internet and the World Wide Web must meet the requirements of section 1 and section 3 of

---

178 Ernst, "Rechtliche Fragen bei der Verwendung von Hyperlinks im Internet", *N.J.W.-Co.R.* 1997, at p. 226.
179 Constitution, article 5(1), sentence 2.
180 BGH, *G.R.U.R.* 1990, at p. 615; Gummig, *Z.U.M.* 1996, at p. 577.
181 BGH, *G.R.U.R.* 1996, at p. 615 — "Wer erschoß Boro?"; OLG Hamburg, *W.R.P.* 1994, at p. 129; OLG München, *W.R.P.* 1993, at p. 424.
182 BGH, *W.R.P.* 1967, at p. 363; OLG Düsseldorf, *Af.P.* 1987, at p. 418.
183 Bullinger, "Multimediale Kommunikation in Wirtschaft und Gesellschaft", *Z.U.M.* 1996, at p. 754; Eberle, "Digitale Rundfunkfreiheit zwischen Couch-Viewing und Online-Nutzung", *C.R.* 1996, at p. 197.

the Unfair Competition Act. Since the ban on the misleading mixture of editorial sections and advertising may be enforced within the framework of the foregoing provisions, the separation principle must be considered in the case of advertising measures on the Internet and the World Wide Web.

This law applies whether the Internet content is evaluated as electronic press or as broadcasting.[184] The Central Association of the German Advertising Industry thinks that the separation principle is a "vital element for the presentation of content" for on-line services. The industry should avoid the irritations of the user which are caused when the latter notices after a period of time that he has been reading a commercial advertisement.[185]

Consequences — Duty of Information, hyperlinks, Automatic Animation, 10-44 Push The case law in Germany has not yet dealt with the question of the concrete requirements resulting from the separation principle for advertising on the Internet or the World Wide Web. In view of the continuing technical development of presentational forms of the Internet, and of the possibilities to present advertisement — for example, animation programs which make it possible for graphics or characters to be projected on a requested Web page where they may attract attention through sound signals and movement.[186] The following paragraphs can only summarise the discussions conducted so far and offer possible solutions.

The print media, as well as radio and television channels, observe the separation principle by identifying the commercial content as an advertisement by clearly contrasting it with a program. A corresponding identification of advertising on Web pages could be achieved if the commercial content is specially framed, identified in another manner, or if it were referred to as an "advertisement". Repeated identification on a single Web site would seem useful, especially in cases where a longer editorial text is continuously interrupted by commercial advertisements. A single identification of advertising is, however, considered sufficient where the Web site is characterised by entertainment and games, and if the user expects no objective information.[187]

Obviously, the requirements will not be met, however, if, at any point information such as ".com" is given in the provider's domain name. The domain names, first of all, are supposed to contain the addresses of the persons and enterprises represented on the Internet. Subordinate pages are systematically

---

184 Hoeren, "Internationale Netze und das Wettbewerbsrecht", *U.F.I.T.A.* 1996, volume 137, at p. 51.

185 ZAW Communication 8/1995, at pp. 1–3, "Multimedia: ZAW mahnt zu Realismus"; Zimmer, "Online-Dienste für ein Massenpublikum?", *Media-Perspektiven* 1995, at pp. 476 *et seq* and 486.

186 Gummig, "Rechtsfragen bei Werbung im Internet", *Z.U.M.* 1996, at p. 580.

187 Gummig, in Schwarz (ed.), *Recht im Internet*, 1996, chapter 5.3.1, at pp. 14 and 16,l with reference to the evaluation made in the decision by the BGH *G.R.U.R.* 1994, at p. 822, "Preisrätsel Gewinnauslobung I"; BGH *G.R.U.R.* 1994, at p. 824, "Preisrätsel Gewinnauslobung II".

identified at the subordinate levels of the domain description. This also serves for orientation and order. The user expects no additional indications. The mere indication in the domain does not take into account a separation of editorial and advertising content on the page itself. Therefore, the information of the commercial content of the new page is useful only on the page itself and not in its domain name.[188] The courts must be open to relevant technical developments when applying the separation principle to this medium. A mere transfer of the solutions developed for print media and television involves the risk that opportunities suitable to the new media will not be seized and that further development will be hindered.

This idea certainly applies when it comes to evaluating hyperlinks. Some critics doubt the legal permissibility of hyperlinks within editorial content if such links lead to a new Web site containing advertisements. The automatic reference from a text of a journalistic nature to a commercial page via a hyperlink must be considered, so it is argued, a contravention of the separation principle. Furthermore, if this were to be allowed, it was argued, the information provider would assume the marketing functions of a businessman.[189]

This view is rightly rejected by the argument that the special advantage and nature of the World Wide Web services lies in the fact that one may easily reach other Web sites via hyperlinks in unlimited cross references. This principle must not be rashly sacrificed to falsely protect a consumer.[190]

One may think of interim solutions which take into account the separation principle, without throwing the baby out with the bath water. The hyperlink might be provided with the additional bracket "commercial", "advertisement" or with some other special identification. This way it would be clear to the user that after clicking on the Link, he would land on a page with advertising content. Alternatively, it would be possible to interrupt the direct connection between text and advertisement pages though an information page, thus separating advertisements and programs.[191] In the case of using hyperlinks, the technical possibilities to secure the separation principle should be freely developed in cases of advertisement by means of automatic animation or via "push". If, on browsing a site by means of "scrolling", an advertisement appears as soon as a certain point of the respective Web site is reached, the separation principle might be observed when the advertisement appears on a field which is visibly separated from the editorial content.

188 Gummig, Z.U.M. 1996, at pp. 580 and 581; Gummig, in Schwarz (ed.), *Recht im Internet* 1996, chapter 5.3.1, at pp. 17 and 18.
189 Hoeren, "Internationale Netze und das Wettbewerbsrecht", U.F.I.T.A. 1996, Volume 437, at p. 52.
190 Gummig, "Rechtsfragen bei Werbung im Internet", Z.U.M. 1996, at p. 582.
191 Gummig, "Rechtsfragen bei Werbung im Internet", Z.U.M. 1996, at p. 582.

Canons of Professional Ethics

In addition to the requirements under competition law, certain professional **10-45** groups are subject to a ban on advertising because it is contrary to professional ethics. These ethics might conflict with advertising content and presentations on home pages. This ban is, by international comparison, enforced rather strictly. The extensive advertising restrictions apply to German medical doctors, lawyers and tax advisers. These professionals may not evade the restrictions by placing their home pages on a foreign Internet surfer. If the Web site is called up by a German user, this would result in an unfair and therefore illegal competitive advantage.[192]

German courts have had to deal with contravention of the ban on advertising because lawyers and medical doctors had presented themselves on the Internet. It has been pointed out that in special cases the enforcement of the comparably strict German ban on advertising[193] entails serious competitive disadvantages and thus a disadvantage to German professionals. This must be met by internationally uniform regulations or, as a less favourable solution, by an adaptation of international standards.[194] The court decisions available and the dominant opinion in literature apply, for the most part without any modification, to the national advertising rules for the presentation of lawyers and medical doctors on the Internet. Some of the first signs of a hesitant liberalisation are recognisable, but judging from the present developments in the case law, these changes seem unlikely to be enforced.

Advertising Restrictions

Physicians   In Germany, the conduct of physicians is governed by the **10-46** provisions applicable in each German state by the respective professional codes. In all federal states, medical doctors must observe extensive advertising bans. The Trier Regional Court was the first German court to deal with the conflict between the advertising ban and the nature of the presentations on the Internet.[195]

A dentist in Rhineland-Palatinate created a home page on the World Wide Web, in which he stated his address, his admission to health insurance and substitute dentists in case of holidays and illness. He also presented his medical team and services, offered a guest book, made recommendations for dental care products and made medical statements. He presented artistic

---

192 OLG Düsseldorf, *N.J.W.* 1994, at p. 869, "Anwaltswerbung in den Niederlanden"; Schopen, Gumpp, and Schopen, "Präsenz einer deutschen Anwaltskanzlei im Internet, kein Verstoß gegen 43b, BRAO", *N.J.W.-Co.R.* 1996, at p. 115.
193 Gilpin, "Attorney Advertising and Solicitation on the Internet: Complying with Ethics Regulations and Netiquette", *Journal of Computer & Information Law*, 1996, at pp. 73 *et seq.*
194 Ebbing, "Virtuelle Rechtsberatung und das anwaltliche Werbeverbot", *N.J.W.-Co.R.* 1996, at p. 247.
195 LG Trier, September 19, 1996, *Z.U.M.* 1997, at pp. 147 *et seq.*

works on his home page and organised a game in which the Internet user was requested to look for a toothbrush hidden on a Web page. The offered prize was an electric toothbrush with the value of DM 260. This game was intended to motivate the user to browse informatively through the dentist's Web site. On application of the State Dentists Association of Rhineland-Palatinate, the Trier court held that the dentist was not permitted to offer his guestbook on the home page, to make recommendations on dental care products for sale or to present artistic works. He was likewise prohibited from organising games.

In support of its decision, the court held that the prohibited practices were attributable to obtrusive commercial advertising which is regarded as unsuitable for the medical profession of dentistry.[196] In addition to the statement of his address and the information on substitute dentists, the court considered it permissible for the medical doctor to introduce his medical team and his services on the home page and provide information on dental care. These details were in accordance with the constitutionally permitted factual information for professional activities furnished to non-medical persons.[197] The structure and presentation of the advertising dentist's home page, especially the insertion of illustrations and a site plan into the presentation, was not opposed by the court since, so it was argued, there existed no special regulation under the professional code or recommendations for advertising on the Internet.

In its reasoning, the Trier court pointed to a liberal way of thinking to take into account the fact that this new medium demands laws of its own. The court stated that "It must be considered that each medium has characteristics and special possibilities of presentation which influence its style. In view of the internationality of the medium and its global range, an adjustment to the German ways of thinking of internationally used standards seems to be justified".[198]

In the meantime, the Higher Regional Court of Koblenz[199] has taken a more restrictive approach. The court held that, according to section 13 of the professional code for dentists, dentists were not completely prohibited from making advertisements, but that a dentist was not allowed to use advertising methods that were usual in commercial industry. The decision reads as follows:

"The advertising launched by the respondent (the dentist — author's note) on the Internet is inconsistent with the principles and professional image of the dentist. What is not decisive for the evaluation of the court is which kind of medium is used as an advertising vehicle. It is rather the kind and nature of the outside presentation that gives offence."[200]

---

196 LG Trier, September 19, 1996, Z.U.M. 1997, at pp. 147 and 148.
197 LG Trier, September 19, 1996, Z.U.M. 1997, at p. 148.
198 LG Trier, September 19, 1996, Z.U.M. 1997, at p. 148.
199 OLG Koblenz, February 13, 1997, 6 U 1500/96.
200 OLG Koblenz, February 13, 1997, 6 U 1500/96, at pp. 11 et seq, in particular at p. 12 (unpublished).

Dissenting from the decision of the regional court, the appellate court also **10-47** held that the presentation of the medical team and of the services had a strong advertising character and was, therefore, not acceptable for a dentist.[201] Even if the decision of the appellate court does not share the liberal view of the Trier court, it does not prohibit the presence of dentists or medical doctors on the Internet in general, if the information on the performance of the physicians is provided in a factual and objective manner.

In the case at hand, the dentist is permitted to present his dental practice on data networks together with a statement of the academic degrees and medical titles, his business and private address with telephone and telefax number, the admissible health insurance and his substitutes during holidays and illness. Although the State Dental Association demanded a ban on these issues, the court ceased to consider the application any further.

Lawyers and Tax Advisers Lawyers are subject to advertising restrictions in **10-48** Germany. On the basis of section 43b of the Law for Revision of Lawyers' and Patent Attorneys' Professional Code of September 2, 1994,[202] the principles developed by the Federal Constitutional Court were defined in the Federal Rules for Lawyers (*Berufsordnung für Rechtsanwälte*) which came into force in March 1997. Section 43b of the Federal Rules for Lawyers provides that the advertising by lawyers is permissible only to the extent that it informs of the form and content of the professional activity and is not aimed at procuring clients in individual cases. This principle is in accordance with the regulations of the new professional code in sections 6 *et seq..*[203] Under the principles established by the German Constitutional Court on the basis of these new rules, advertising methods are deemed to be impermissible when they are misleading.[204]

It was considered permissible by the German Constitutional Court to present lists of practising lawyers and to participate in lawyers' location services.[205] Section 6(2) of the new Federal Rules expressly allows the information of the public by way of practice brochures, circular letters and other comparable information means which may also indicate the lawyers' main fields of interest and activities. Section 7 of the Federal Law provides that not more than five main fields of interest and activities must be mentioned. Only three main fields of activity shall be named in each case.[206] It is impermissible to provide information on success rates or earnings or about clients or a client's case unless the client has given his express consent.[207]

201 OLG Koblenz, February 13, 1997, 6 U 1500/96, at p. 16.
202 B.G.Bl. (*Federal Law Gazette*) I, at p. 2278; this revision was expressly necessary according to the order by the BVerfG of July 14, 1987, *N.J.W.* 1988, at p. 194.
203 Federal Chamber of Lawyers Communication, 1996, at pp. 241 and 242.
204 BVerfG, Order, February 18, 1992, *N.J.W.* 1992, at p. 1614.
205 BVerfG, decision dated February 18, 1992, *N.J.W.* 1992, at p. 1614.
206 Federal Chamber of Lawyers Communication, 1996, at p. 242.
207 Federal Rules for Lawyers, section 6(3); Federal Chamber of Lawyers Communication, 1996, at p. 242.

On the basis of the principles developed by the German Constitutional Court and on the basis of the provisions of the Federal Rules, it is deemed to be legally permissible in Germany for German lawyers to be presented in an on-line list of lawyers such as HIEROS GAMOS, lists of lawyers at universities or at associations such as the German Lawyers Association and to provide a professional description on a home page.[208]

The Regional Court of Nürnberg-Fürth found that the Internet presentation of a tax adviser by means of a home page is legally permissible.[209] A presentation which is confined to a factual communication is legally unproblematic. It was stated by the court that it was permissible if the presentation contained an e-mailbox in which users could leave their address or other data, should they wish to contact the tax adviser as this was not in conflict with section 57a of the Act Relating to Tax Advisers (St.Ber.G.), which permitted advertising only to the extent that it informed of professional activities in a factual manner as to form and content and was not aimed at gaining individual cases.[210] Since section 57a of the Act Relating to Tax Advisers is almost identical to section 43b of the Federal Rules for Lawyers, the statements made by the Nürnberg-Fürth Regional Court may be used as a basic guideline for the use of home pages in the case of lawyers.

It is obvious that the presentation as to content and optical impression of home pages for lawyers is subject to numerous restrictions. The dominant opinion, in accordance with the strict national view, considers obtrusive recommendations, music and video clips, or hyperlinks to irrelevant Web sites to be just as impermissible as advertising for a concrete retainer. The latter applies to cases where potential clients can fill out power of attorney forms made available on-line and transmit them to the lawyer directly by e-mail or telefax.[211] Given this background, it is not surprising that the Munich regional court prohibited a provider from publicly requesting the participants in his forum "Recht on-line" to contact the "Online Lawyer" and from advertising an initial appointment for advice at a flat rate fee of DM 35, including value-added tax.[212] This result is correct because the recommendation of a single law office as an "Online Lawyer" is misleading

---

208 Schopen, Gumpp, and Schoppen, "Präsenz einer deutschen Anwaltskanzlei im Internet, kein Verstoß gegen 43 b Berufsordnung für Rechtsanwälte", *N.J.W.-Co.R.* 1996, at pp. 114 and 115; Ebbing, "Virtuelle Rechtsberatung und das anwaltliche Werbeverbot", *N.J.W.-Co.R.* 1996, at p. 246.

209 LG Nürnberg-Fürth, January 29, 1997 —, 3 O 33/97, *AnwBl.* 1997, at p. 226.

210 Act Relating to Tax Advisers, section 57a, was amended by the 6th Act for Revision of the Act Relating to Tax Advisers (*B.G.Bl.* 1994, part 1, at p. 1387) and came into force on July 1, 1994.

211 Schopen, Gumpp, and Schopen, "Präsenz einer deutschen Anwaltskanzlei im Internet, kein Verstoß gegen 43 b Federal Rules for Lawyers", *N.J.W.-Co.R.* 1996, at pp. 114 and 115; Ebbing, "Virtuelle Rechtsberatung und das anwaltliche Werbeverbot", *N.J.W.-Co.R.* 1996, at p. 246.

212 LG Munich I, Order, March 25, 1996, 1 *H.K.O.* 5953/96 — (unpublished), brief notification, together with the communication of the application, *C.R.* 1996, at p. 736.

within the meaning of section 3 of the Unfair Competition Act and furthers the professional misconduct of the lawyer concerned, as does the procurement of concrete retainers for the purpose of rendering advisory activities.

Confidentiality

Section 203(1), numbers 1 and 3, of the Criminal Code provides that **10-49** medical doctors, lawyers, and tax advisers are liable to a term of imprisonment not exceeding one year or to a fine if they disclose a client's confidential information or a trade or business secret which was confided to them because of their professional position or of which they learned in another way without authorisation. One can proceed on the basis that most of the facts communicated in the correspondence between a lawyer or physician and his client or patient, respectively, are known only to a limited circle of persons, and that the persons concerned have a personal interest in secrecy.[213]

While a punishment presupposes the existence of a business secret and its wilful and unauthorised disclosure, the provisions of the professional codes go beyond the scope of protection under criminal law. Thus, the lawyer's duty to observe secrecy pursuant to section 43 a(2) of the Federal Rules for Lawyers, in conjunction with section 2 of the Federal Rules enacted on March 11, 1997, includes anything that the lawyer learned as a consequence of performing his professional duties. Pursuant to section 113(1) of the Federal Rules for Lawyers, negligent contravention is sanctioned with measures under the lawyers' professional code. These include a warning, reprimand or fine.[214]

Both in the case of a betrayal of secrets under criminal law and in the case of the professional duty to observe secrecy,[215] the question arises as to whether or not the transmission of e-mail of a confidential nature constitutes "unauthorised disclosure" of secrets which must be evaluated as negligent conduct in breach of professional law or even as wilful conduct punishable as a contravention of section 203 of the Criminal Code.

The preconditions of disclosing a secret will be satisfied if both the secret and the concerned client's identity are imparted to a third party. The communication may be made through conduct implying intent or through omission.[216] Since a guarantor's obligation, and thus duty to avoid the disclosure of a secret,

---

213 *B.G.H.Z.* 40, at p. 292; *R.G.St.* 74, at pp. 110 and 111; Schönke and Schröder-Lenckner, *Criminal Code*, 24th ed., 1991, section 203, marginal note 19.

214 Kleine-Cosack, Federal Rules for Lawyers, 2nd ed., 1996, section 43a, marginal note 3.

215 The element of "unauthorised disclosure" is relevant also to determine a breach of confidentiality by the lawyer; see Feuerich and Braun, *Federal Rules for Lawyers*, section 43a, marginal note 11.

216 Schönke and Schröder-Lenckner, *Criminal Code*, 25th ed., section 203, marginal notes 19 and 20; Tröndle, *Criminal Code*, 48th ed., 1997, section 203, marginal note 26; Lackner, *Criminal Code*, 20th ed., 1993, section 203, marginal note 17; Jähnke, *Leipziger Kommentar*, 10th ed., 1989, section 203, marginal note 44, with further references.

results from the fact that lawyers and physicians, due to their positions, qualify as offenders within the meaning of section 203 of the Criminal Code,[217] It would be irrelevant concerning the responsibility under criminal law whether the charge is linked to the action, transmission of the e-mail or to the omission to encrypted messages of a confidential nature. The decisive question, however, is whether the transmission of an e-mail of a confidential nature without encryption, constitutes a culpable disclosure or a reprehensible omission to avoid unauthorised reading.

It is true that, in the case of previous communication means (letter, telefax, telephone), the preconditions of a culpable disclosure of a secret were principally not met because the content could become known only by the unlawful conduct of third parties or, in rare exceptions, through intervention by the German government.[218] Some authors suggested that, due to the possibility of telephone interceptions by the German government, lawyers should be careful with confidential phone calls and inform their clients with the inherent risks of such means of communication.[219] In the field of e-mail communication, it must be considered that e-mail without encryption (like postcards in the case of traditional mailing) may be copied and read on any computer on which a final or intermediate storage is made. Due to these circumstances, each lawyer or physician must be aware of the fact that confidential information is easily accessible and thus disclosed to third parties.

It is likely that, in the future, the courts will evaluate a transmission of confidential information via e-mail as a failure to observe the duty of reasonable care and thus as negligent conduct, unless the content has been encrypted before being sent.[220] A negligent breach of confidentiality is sanctioned under the professional code applicable to lawyers. This cannot be objected to by arguing that due to the amount and volume of data of electronic mail on the Internet and for want of predictability of transmission channels, through which the e-mail divided into individual packets flow, one must not expect that the content is read by unauthorised persons.[221] In view of the existence of the special programs which may, purposefully, intercept data packets, recompile them and thus enable the reading of a third party's e-mail, this objection is not suitable for refuting the negligence charge.

A final question is whether or not the charge must be based also on wilful and, thus, punishable conduct pursuant to section 203 of the Criminal Code. Under the constant line of decisions, this would be the case only if the lawyer had transmitted an e-mail while being aware of the high risk of unauthorised reading and accepted the possible consequences of his action, thus acting with

---

217 Jähnke, *Leipziger Kommentar*, 10th ed., 1989, section 203, marginal note 44.
218 Wagner and Lerch, "Mandatsgeheimnis im Internet", *N.J.W.-Co.R.* 1996, at p. 383.
219 Zuck, in Lingenberg, Hummel, Zuck, and Eich, *Kommentar zu den Grundsätzen des anwaltlichen Standesrechts*, 2nd ed., 1988, section 42, marginal note 27.
220 Wagner and Lerch, "Mandatsgeheimnis im Internet?", *N.J.W.-Co.R.* 1996, at p. 384.
221 Edenhofer, "Internet für Anwaltskanzleien", *C.R.* 1997, at p. 121.

conditional intent.[222] In individual cases, it must be considered whether, instead of conditional intent, the preconditions of wanton negligence are met. In the latter case, the offender, although he is conscious of the possibility of unauthorised reading, relies on the fact that this result will not occur. However, it has been pointed out that the great importance of the confidential relationship between the lawyer or physician and client or patient, respectively, as well as the great publicity of the technical background, speak against such a view.[223]

To avoid these difficulties, it may be recommended, especially to lawyers in Germany, that they should draw their clients' attention to the risks of e-mail communication and obtain their express consent to correspondence via e-mail.[224] Lawyers and their clients must agree on the use of coding programs which are currently very efficient. From a German point of view, this is still legally unproblematic. The situation could, of course, change if the regulations of cryptography as proposed by the Federal Minister of the Interior were to come into effect.

ELECTRONIC TRANSACTIONS

Creation of Contracts Electronically

Offer and Acceptance On-line

Declarations of Intention Declarations of intention can also be made   10-50
electronically, for example, in the form of an e-mail, a posting in the USENET or a corresponding page in the World Wide Web. These examples relate primarily to the Internet, but any form of communication in any data network may constitute a declaration of intention. Whether it is to be viewed as such must be determined in accordance with the same requirements that apply also to non-electronically transmitted declarations of intention. The fact that the declaration is made by electronic means does not give rise to any special circumstances whatsoever.

The following remarks are restricted to e-mail and World Wide Web in the Internet as the presently most important forms of electronic communication. However, the remarks apply also analogously to all other forms of communication in different data networks.

It should be pointed out that also the question as to the existence of a legally binding declaration must be answered according to the same rules that apply generally. Consequently, a World Wide Web page on which certain products are offered for sale will not normally be able to be construed as a

---

222 *B.G.H.St.* 36, at p. 1; *B.G.H.St.* 21, at p. 283.
223 Wagner and Lerch, "Mandatsgeheimnis im Internet?", *N.J.W.-Co.R.* 1996, at p. 383.
224 Wagner and Lerch, "Mandatsgeheimnis im Internet?", *N.J.W.-Co.R.* 1996, at p. 383 and 385; Edenhofer, "Internet für Anwaltskanzleien", *C.R.* 1997, at p. 121.

binding offer, but rather as a so-called *invitatio ad offerendum*.[225] In this case, if in doubt, there is no legally binding declaration, the situation is equivalent to that of an advertisement in a newspaper. In addition, in the latter case, the seller will not want a binding offer because he thereby exposes himself to the risk, without any effort on his part, of entering into a multiplicity of contracts, of which he is able to fulfil only some. As for the rest, he makes himself liable for damages. Moreover, the seller will not normally be willing to enter into a contract with just anyone (*e.g*, owing to the insolvency, unknown to him, of the other party). The situation is precisely the same, for example, in the case of a posting in a newsgroup or a discussion forum in the World Wide Web because, there too, the circle of addressees is basically unlimited.

As far as binding offers are concerned, therefore, the means of the e-mail will enter primarily into consideration. Yet, an HTML form which is filled out on the screen may also represent a binding declaration of intention (*e.g*, when an order form is filled out).

In the case of the automated processing of an order form filled out over the World Wide Web with an automatically generated answer from the offeror, this might constitute a declaration of intention. Thus, for example, if an on-line order form is filled out on the World Wide Web and the offeror's server automatically checks whether the desired product is still in stock, whether the customer's name is on a blacklist and whether complete credit card information has been given, a message is generated to the shipping department to ship the ordered product and the orderer is informed that he will be receiving the product.

Some have argued that an automatic answer to a customer's inquiry cannot represent a declaration of intention even if it was generated in response to a specific inquiry because such a declaration of intention can be made only by a true representative of the offeror but never by a machine.[226] Here, however, he overlooks the fact that, in this case, the machine is merely the means of transmitting the declaration of intention. According to the present level of development of computer technology, a computer system is not able to make real decisions or to form an intention. Rather, such an answer always represents a statement that is generated on the basis of the previously determined execution of a program. Consequently, in putting such a mechanism into operation, the operator has expressed his intention, say, to accept the offer of a contract whenever the conditions required by the computer program for a positive answer are satisfied. No one would doubt that the person signing a letter has made a declaration of intention simply because he has used a computer system to write the letter and has inserted an automatic calculation from a spreadsheet program. Therefore, a declaration that is generated

---

225 OLG Oldenburg, *C.R.* 1953, at p. 558; Eckert, *D.B.* 1994, at pp. 717 and 718; Wagner, *W.M.* 1995, at p. 1129.
226 Ernst, "Der Mausklick als Rechtsproblem — Willenserklärungen im Internet", *N.J.W.-Co.R.*, 1997, at p. 165.

automatically in accordance with fixed rules may always be viewed as a declaration of intention on the part of the operator.[227]

However, if the entire contract is created electronically, it is also possible to apply the rules that were developed for sale by automatic vending machines, *i.e*, the principles of offering *ad incertas* personas.[228] Accordingly, one is dealing here with an offer that is subject to the condition subsequent that products are still available. Such an offer may then, on the grounds of implied waiver of receipt pursuant to section 151 Civil Code (Civil Code), be effectively accepted even without the involvement of a human recipient or receiving agent.[229] This, however, can apply only if the contract is actually completed, *i.e*, if performance and counter-performance are made immediately since only then is the situation equivalent to that existing in the case of such an offer *ad incertas personas*.

In the case of contracts involving payment, given the present state of technology, this will be the case only in exceptional circumstances, namely, when payment can be made immediately using so-called cyber cash. The circumstances will not be deemed sufficient if merely credit card information is transmitted to permit the offeror subsequently to collect payment by that method. In such a case, the offeror is not protected to the same extent as in the case of immediate payment. The assumption of a legally binding declaration in the case of an offer *ad incertas personas* is made precisely because of the immediate payment.

This is of interest in the case of a contract that does not involve payment, such as the free-of-charge use of an FTP server through so-called anonymous FTP. Here, one will be able to see, in the making available of downloadable files, an offer *ad incertas personas*, with the consequence that the actual fact of downloading gives rise, even without receipt of acceptance, to the creation of a contract. Of course, this will apply only if, according to the intention of the operator, the use of the server is designed to be not merely a favour or kindness standing outside of legal transactions. Since, however, the operators of such servers frequently impose General Terms and Conditions for use, in such cases, one must assume a legally binding declaration, with the result that a contract may come into being by which, say, the modalities of use are regulated.

Making of the Declaration of Intention According to general rules, a 10-51 declaration of intention has been made if the declarer has done everything to enable the declaration to become effective.

---

227 Heun, "Die elektronische Willenserklärung", *C.R.*, 1994, at pp. 595 *et seq*.; Fritzsche and Malzer, "Ausgewählte zivilrechtliche Probleme elektronisch signierter Willenserklärungen", *D.Not.Z.*, 1995, at p. 7.

228 Fritzsche and Malzer, "Ausgewählte zivilrechtliche Probleme elektronisch signierter Willenserklärungen", *D.Not.Z.*, 1995, at p. 7; Ernst, "Der Mausklick als Rechtsproblem — Willenserklärungen im Internet", *N.J.W.-Co.R.* 1997, at p. 165.

229 Palandt-Heinrichs, Civil Code, 56th Aufl., 145 Rn. 7.

In the case of a declaration of intention which does not require receipt by the other party to become effective, it is clear that such a declaration of intention has been made once the constituting elements of a declaration have been satisfied. In the field of electronic communications, the only cases that will enter into consideration in this regard are the acceptance of the offer of a contract not requiring receipt pursuant to section 151 of the Civil Code and the public offer of a reward pursuant to section 657 of the Civil Code.

The case, important for practical purposes, of the execution of a privately written will, pursuant to sections 1937-2247 of the Civil Code (*e.g*, in the form of a written will by e-mail) is not relevant here because this is bound, under existing law, to fail on the relevant formal requirements.

Of greater practical significance is the case of a declaration of intention which requires receipt by the other party to become effective. Such a declaration of intention has been made if the declarer intentionally directs his declaration at the recipient in such a manner that, assuming normal circumstances, receipt can be expected.

In the case of an e-mail, therefore, the declaration will normally be considered to have been made when the "Send" function of the mail program is activated and, in the case of the filling out of an HTML form, when the form is sent off by using the "Transmit" or "Send" function.

Accordingly, no declaration is made if this function is activated by mistake. In such a case, however, a liability of the "declarer" from *culpa in contrahendo* or section 122 of the Civil Code enters into consideration by analogy, as also in the event of a so-called "lost declaration of intention".

10-52   **Receipt of the Declaration of Intention**   Whereas a declaration of intention which does not require receipt by the other party becomes effective as soon as it is made, a declaration of intention which requires receipt must indeed be received to become effective.

If the recipient of the declaration is not in the same place as the maker of the declaration, a physical declaration of intention becomes effective by receipt when the declaration has entered the sphere of influence of the recipient such that the recipient is able to take cognisance of the declaration of intention and that, under normal circumstances, such taking of cognisance can also be expected.[230] In the field of the World Wide Web, the conclusion of the contract accomplished by way of declarations of intention between absent persons can be assumed, especially as section 147(1), sentence 2, of the Civil Code presupposes, for example, in the case of a declaration transmitted by telephone, that this declaration is made directly from person to person. As far as the receipt of declarations of intention via e-mail is concerned, therefore, what is decisive is when the declarer can normally expect the recipient to collect the mail. Business people in the field of electronic marketing will read their mail

---

230 So-called receipt theory; see, for example, *Münchner Kommentar*, Förschler, at p. 130, R. 3 *et seq*.

once a day at normal business times; it is more difficult to determine the time of receipt in the case of private citizens, since there are no established customs whatsoever as regards the reading of mail.

In the case of a non-physical declaration of intention, moreover, it is required that the declaration has entered the sphere of influence of the recipient and that the recipient has also correctly understood the declaration. To date, this case group has been of relevance only with regard to the use of telephone answering machines or receiving messengers.

Therefore, it must first be clarified whether electronic declarations of intention are physical or non-physical declarations.

Physical declarations of intention made between persons who are present are received under the same circumstances as those made between persons who are absent since prevailing opinion applies section 130(1) of the Civil Code analogously; they enter the sphere of influence of the recipient and, under normal circumstances, the taking of cognisance thereof can be expected. Consequently, a letter which is handed over is normally deemed to have been received immediately since, as a rule, it can be expected that cognisance will be taken immediately.

Conversely, according to the prevailing theory of perception, non-physical declarations of intention are received only if they have been correctly perceived since the risk involved in non-physical transmission is to be borne by the person who chooses that method.

Agreement   As regards the question as to whether an agreement has come   10-53
about, the same rules that apply generally apply also in the case of the electronic exchange of declarations of intention. It should, however, be pointed out that whether on-line offers can be accepted is normally judged in accordance with section 147(2) of the Civil Code, since offers between absent persons are the rule. Thus, the offer can be accepted as long as "the applicant can, under regular circumstances, expect the answer to be received".

Different rules apply only in the rare case in which there is an offer between persons who are present, *e.g*, in the case of the exchange of declarations of intention in the IRC or other chat services. In such cases, an offer that is made can only be accepted immediately.[231]

With regard to the filling out of order forms, *e.g*, in the World Wide Web, it will normally be assumed that the offer is between absent persons, even if it is possibly automatically processed and accepted immediately. An offer between persons who are present can be accepted only if the applicant knows about the automatic processing. The practical relevance of the problem, however, is slight since, in the case of automatic processing, there is always a reply which may possibly be negative. Thus, the offer is rejected and, in that case, later acceptance no longer enters into consideration anyway.

---

231 Civil Code, section 147(1).

10-54   **Contestation of Electronic Declarations of Intention** Electronic declarations of intention can be contested under precisely the same conditions as conventional declarations of intention. Even the process of contestation may, in turn, be effected electronically, *e.g*, by e-mail.

However, there are a number of failures of intention which occur typically in conjunction with electronic declarations of intention and with regard to which the question is raised as to whether there is then a right of contestation.

The simplest case is that in which the declarer merely strikes a wrong key when typing the declaration. In such a case, however, there is clearly a declaration error which gives rise to the right of contestation pursuant to section 119(1) 2. Alt. Civil Code. Namely, there is no discernible reason why the situation should be treated any differently from that in which the declarer strikes a wrong key on a typewriter when typing a declaration of intention.[232]

More interesting is the case in which the declaration is falsified while being transmitted through systems belonging to the telecommunications infrastructure. In this case, there is basically a transmission error pursuant to section 120 of the Civil Code which gives rise to the right of contestation. The only problem is whether the situation does not become different if the error occurred on a part of the telecommunications infrastructure to be attributed to the declarer. Section 120 of the Civil Code regulates the transmission risk in the case of declarations of intention. However, there can be no talk of transmission until the declaration has left the sphere of control of the declarer which, at that time, however, was not yet the case. Therefore, a right of contestation pursuant to section 120 is to be ruled out in such cases. However, the practical relevance of this problem is slight because, in such a case, contestation on the grounds of declaration error pursuant to section 119(1) 2. Alt. Civil Code enters into consideration.[233]

Should, however, a declaration be deficient because the technical devices used for generating the declaration are defective (*i.e*, in the case of hardware defects or software errors) or because incorrect output data was used then, in general, it will have to be judged that there is no right of contestation. Namely, the right of contestation affords protection basically not against mistakes in the formation of the intention, but only against errors in the expression and transmission of that intention.[234] However, this view may go too far. Namely, for the event of a so-called calculation error (which is comparable), the Hamm Higher Regional Court ruled that, in the case of the incorrect entry of data that, without further human intervention, becomes — in processed form — the subject of a declaration of intention, there is a right of contestation pursuant to section 119(1) 2nd Alternative Civil

232 Heun, "Die elektronische Willenserklärung", *C.R.*, 1994, at p. 596.
233 Heun, "Die elektronische Willenserklärung", *C.R.*, 1994, at p. 596.
234 Heun, "Die elektronische Willenserklärung", *C.R.*, 1994, at p. 597.

Code on the grounds of declaration error.[235] This opinion is based on the view that it must not make any difference whether an incorrect entry modified by calculation or the incorrect entry itself becomes the subject of the declaration.

Conversely, the prevailing opinion fears that, in this case, the distinction between relevant declaration error and irrelevant motive error is made blurred and therefore fundamentally rejects the right of contestation.[236]

Depending on how one wishes to decide here, there is, in the case of the incorrect entry of data which is a basis for calculation and therefore also in the case of incorrect programming of the calculation algorithm of the software, a right of contestation pursuant to section 119(1), 2nd Alternative, of the Civil Code. The view held by the Hamm Higher Regional Court likewise deserves consideration in this connection.

Inclusion of General Terms and Conditions   To make General Terms and   10-55
Conditions an effective part of a contract, it is necessary to make express reference to the Terms and Conditions at the time of conclusion of the contract and to grant the purchaser a reasonable opportunity to take cognisance thereof.[237] Insofar as skeleton contracts are concluded and effective reference is made to the application of the General Terms and Conditions and their inclusion is agreed, the requirements of section 2 of the Civil Code are satisfied. Problematic in this connection is the inclusion of General Terms and Conditions of which the user is able to gain knowledge merely by way of electronic retrieval. In the rulings of the courts, the view is held that the reading of extensive General Terms and Conditions cannot reasonably be expected owing to the long transmission time.[238]

In the literature it is stated that the inclusion of General Terms and Conditions is inadmissible because the creator of the General Terms and Conditions is able unilaterally to amend them by reprogramming, including after the conclusion of the contract, and the recipient is inasmuch disadvantaged.[239] This view cannot be supported because, within the World Wide Web, the orderer is at liberty to download the General Terms and Conditions of the user onto the computer or proxy server, to print them and read them at his leisure. No additional transmission costs are thereby incurred. The text of the printed General Terms and Conditions can subsequently also be used as evidence in so far as the user retrospectively changes the General Terms and Conditions that would constitute fraud and would be a criminal offence.

---

235 OLG Hamm, *N.J.W.* 1993, at p. 2321.
236 Palandt-Heinrichs, Civil Code, 56th Aufl., 119 Rn. 18 *et seq.*
237 Civil Code, section 2(1).
238 LG Freiburg, *C.R.* 1992, 93; LG Wuppertal, *N.J.W.-R.R.* 1991, at pp. 1148 and 1149.
239 Wolf, Horn, and Lindacher, *AGBG*, 3rd Aufl. 1994, 2, Rn. 24.

10-56   **Applicable Law** Which law is to be applied to the conclusion of a contract is determined according to the general rules of private international law. The fact that contract-constituting declarations are exchanged through data networks does not result in a judgment any different from that in the case of an exchange of declarations, say, by telefax.

Effect of Electronic Signatures, Impact of Impostors or Persons without Authority

10-57   In the interim, the German legislature has passed the Law Regulating the Standard Terms and Conditions for Information and Communication Services (Information and Communication Services Act); this law has been in force since August 1, 1997. Section 3 of this law caused the Law on Digital Signatures (Act Concerning Digital Signatures) to become effective on the same date. With these laws, the Federal Republic of Germany is apparently the first country in the world to have created a legal basis for dealing with the issue of digital signatures.

Under German law, legally binding declarations may basically be made also without conformance to any formal requirements. With regard to certain legal transactions, however, the law provides that these must be effected in compliance with defined formal requirements. The law provides, in particular, for the written form required by law or by dint of agreement,[240] authentication by a notary,[241] and certification by a notary public.[242]

Under section 126 of the Civil Code, the issuer in his own hand must sign a document by signature or by means of notarised manual sign. If this is not done, the legal transaction is null and void on the grounds of defect of form.[243] Also ineffective is a declaration of suretyship if it is not made in the legally required written form.[244] In addition, there are formal requirements which, if not complied with, do not result in the invalidity of the entire legal transaction. For example, in the case of fixed-term rental contracts which, pursuant to section 566 of the Civil Code, require the written form, the consequence of non-compliance with the written form is that the rental contract is to be viewed as being not of fixed term. In the case of section 4 of the Consumer Credit Law (VerbrKrG), the consequence of non-observance of the formal requirements is that the cancellation period laid down in section 7(1) of the Consumer Credit Law does not start to run. The transaction remains provisionally ineffective because cancellation is still possible even after a lengthy period of time.

---

240 Regulated in Civil Code, sections 125 *et. seq.*
241 Civil Code, section 128.
242 Civil Code, section 129.
243 Civil Code, section 125.
244 Civil Code, section 766; unless the declaration of suretyship was made by a registered trader; Commercial Code, section 350.

The Act Concerning Digital Signatures regulates the signing of data by means of a so-called public key procedure. In this procedure, a type of "checksum" is calculated on the data to be signed by a specific mathematical procedure using a secret private key. Using the public key, a counterpart to the private key, anyone can check whether this "checksum" was calculated using the corresponding private key or not.

For this purpose, the public key is calculated from the private key in such a way that it becomes impossible to calculate back from the public key to the private key, according to current mathematical knowledge.

Starting from the assumption that only the user himself can make use of his private key, one can then conclude from a positive result of a checking procedure that, on the one hand, the data originate from the user in question and, on the other hand, that they come from him in exactly the form received.

Such a signature thus aids in maintaining the security of data, *i.e*, in answering the question of whether these data actually originate from the stated sender or originator. In addition, it also guarantees the integrity of the data since the "checksum" would no longer be correct if the data had been changed subsequent to signing.

The most significant problem arising in such procedures has been whether a particular public key truly is one of a pair of keys belonging to a particular user, or whether it has actually been put into circulation by a third party, cannot be determined with certainty. In this case, such a third party can circulate statements that give rise to the impression that they originated with the supposed key owner. PGP, for example, attempts to solve this problem by having individual users sign the public keys of other users when they are certain that they truly belong to the user in question. If a sufficient number of such signatures from trustworthy persons are present, one can then assume that the signed key is authentic. This is referred to as a web of trust because, ultimately, a network of reciprocally signed public keys is formed.

The Act Concerning Digital Signatures goes beyond such personally responsible authentication by the users themselves since it is still associated with certain risk factors. Instead, in accordance with the Act Concerning Digital Signatures , a guarantee that a key belongs to a particular user will be given by granting the user a certificate from sites to be created for this purpose. If a key is guaranteed by such a site, it is then clear that the corresponding key truly belongs to the stated user.

In the future, the procedure will be that an interested user must first apply for such a certificate. Note in this context that certificates can only be assigned to natural persons[245] which, after all, goes without saying since legal persons themselves cannot make legal statements, but rather only

245 Act Concerning Digital Signatures , section 2(3).

natural persons designated as their representatives on their behalf. On application, the interested person must first reveal his identity, generally by presentation of an official identity document. The granting of a certificate under a pseudonym can also be applied for at this time. It is also possible, furthermore, to possess an unlimited number of certificates simultaneously. The applicant is then informed by the certification site concerning procedure under Act Concerning Digital Signatures and available technical devices.

The so-called signature key certificate itself essentially only confirms that the corresponding signature key belongs to the named person. In addition, however, section 7(1), number 7 Act Concerning Digital Signatures permits inclusion of a statement that can limit use to particular applications and/or a particular extent. Furthermore, according to section 7(2) Act Concerning Digital Signatures , additional statements concerning professional and other licensing can be included, as well as statements of the extent to which a user has representative authority for other persons; however, such statements are only permitted by permission of those persons.

This last possibility is expected to be used particularly when the key owner has executive representative authority for a legal person. However, it must be pointed out that it is by no means necessary for the signature key of the representative to contain such a statement for effective agency when submitting a manifestation of intent in electronic form. The question of effective agency is to be answered using the general principles of agency law. The presence of such a statement also does not mean that power of agency actually exists at the time of submission. Since the law does not tie any good faith effect to this statement, it is effectively legally meaningless.

Both the licensing statements and those concerning any power of agency may also be the subject of so-called attribute certificates.[246] These are independent certificates that make reference to a signature key certificate and contain additional statements.

The user can either generate his signature key himself, or the certification site can provide it. After granting, the certificate is recorded in a certificate registry which must be open to inspection by everyone at all times via publicly accessible telecommunications institutions;[247] in practice, this will most likely only occur via the Internet.

The actual "signing" of data will occur in such a way that the user can sign his data using his private key. The precise general technical conditions for this purpose are only roughly sketched out in section 14 of the Act Concerning Digital Signatures . The details are to be spelled out in regulations issued by the federal government in accordance with section 16 number 6 Act Concerning Digital Signatures . Section 14 Act Concerning Digital Signatures itself merely states that the facilities used for creation, storage, and testing of digital signatures and signature keys must be such

---

246 Act Concerning Digital Signatures , sections 2(3) and 7(2).
247 Act Concerning Digital Signatures , section 5(1).

that they guarantee sufficient security against manipulation. Section 14(2) Act Concerning Digital Signatures is also important in this context and states that when signing is being performed, the facility must indicate precisely which data are designated for signature and that the facility will now be signing them.

The procedure is planned to be regulated in the as-yet drafted Signature Regulations (SigV) in such a way that the private key is stored on a chip card from which it cannot be copied. In this way, the danger of misuse is minimised since only the card user can make use of the key. If the card is lost, it is obvious that the key is no longer completely secure against misuse, and as long as the rightful user has the card, it is obvious that no one else can use the key. This does have the disadvantage that all terminals intended for such use must be equipped with appropriate card reading devices. But otherwise there is the danger that the private key could be replicated and stored permanently in the system. This would greatly increase the danger of misuse, for example, by making it possible for hackers to copy it from the system.

Similarly to the use of an ATM, the mere possession of the card is not sufficient to initiate the signature procedure. Instead, the user must also identify himself as the rightful user by entering a PIN or a password. As long as the user takes measures to keep it secret, misuse is largely impossible. Including biometric characteristics for identification can create additional levels of security. However, this quickly reaches its limits in practice since the necessary hardware for recording such characteristics is expensive and every terminal intended for such use would have to be so equipped.

Once the user has authenticated himself using the password, a suitable signature program forms such a "checksum". Using the same technical resources required for signing, the receiver can then check, using the certified public key, whether or not the data truly were signed with the corresponding private key.

Under section 8 of the Act Concerning Digital Signatures , a certificate that has been issued can later be blocked to exclude the possibility of misuse. However, retroactive blocking is impossible.

In addition, the Act Concerning Digital Signatures provides that the certification sites shall attach so-called time stamps to digital data on request.[248] This is a digitally signed certification by the site that this data were present at that site at a particular time. However, the question is still open as to what legal effect will be connected with the presence or absence of such a time stamp.

The certificates will not be distributed by official sites themselves, but rather by private sites under official supervision. Section 4 Act Concerning Digital Signatures lists the requirements placed on such sites. In principle, the operation of such a certification site is to be permitted on application

---

248 Act Concerning Digital Signatures , section 9.

according to section 4(1) Act Concerning Digital Signatures , unless reasons for denial of permission according to section 4(2) exist. Permission is to be denied when it can be assumed that the applicant lacks the necessary dependability or technical ability to fulfil this task. It must also be denied if it can be expected that the prerequisites for operation, as described in sections 5 *et seq.* Act Concerning Digital Signatures and to be regulated in the regulations (SigV) to be issued by the federal government, will not be fulfilled on start-up of the activity. Under section 4(3), anyone whom it can be assumed will comply with the relevant provisions of the law is to be considered dependable. To guarantee that the regulations will be complied with, the applicant must submit a security plan that will be examined with this in mind.

Under section 4(5) Act Concerning Digital Signatures , the public authority itself shall issue certificates for the signature keys that are to be used for the creation of certificates for the individual user; no further distribution of certificates from public bodies is provided for.

It is possible to deduce from section 1(2) Act Concerning Digital Signatures that, in the future, signatures according to the Act Concerning Digital Signatures will also be sufficient to adhere to any form which may need to be observed. This will occur where that the use of such a signature is expressly recognised as legally valid by regulation. However, at this time it is not possible to state clearly when and to what extent digital signatures are planned to be made equivalent to other forms. Nevertheless, the prospect has been raised that a first step may still be made in the current legislative session *i.e*, by the end of 1998. For the present, even signatures according to the Act Concerning Digital Signatures will never create a legally valid written document that may be required; instead, despite the Act Concerning Digital Signatures , effective manifestations of intent may only be submitted at such places where they would be possible nonetheless, even without providing a legally valid written form.

Where the effectiveness of the statement is not connected to adherence to the form, but other legal consequences are, the use of a digital signature according to the Act Concerning Digital Signatures does not provide the legally valid form, so that the legal consequences that the law provides in connection with the lack of a written form will occur.

Currently, the Act Concerning Digital Signatures can only acquire significance in the area of the probatory force of digital "documents". Within the framework of the Act Concerning Digital Signatures , the legislature found itself unable to also modify the Code of Civil Procedure; digitally signed documents still can only be taken into account in a case within the framework of free evaluation of evidence by the court according to section 286 of the Code of Civil Procedure.[249]

---

249 Geiß, *C.R.*, 1993, at pp. 653 *et seq.*

On the other hand, a digitally signed document cannot be seen as a private document in the sense of section 416 of the Code of Civil Procedure, with the consequence that it is not granted the enhanced probatory force given to such documents. The reason for this is that section 416 of the Code of Civil Procedure could only apply if the maker signed the document, but according to the Act Concerning Digital Signatures , a digital signature is not generally equivalent to a written signature. The federal government is currently investigating to what extent the Code of Civil Procedure should be modified for this purpose. On the one hand, the digital signature might be made equivalent to a written signature in section 416 of the Code of Civil Procedure, so that a document so signed is granted the full probatory force of a private document. On the other hand, a separate statutory definition of an electronically signed document might be introduced into the law of evidence.

Within the framework of free evaluation of evidence by the court, however, the Act Concerning Digital Signatures will probably only result in a relatively minor improvement since the presence of a digital signature already results in significantly improved probative value for the signed data. The value is possibly impaired by the fact that judges typically lack background knowledge to correctly evaluate a digital signature. Actually, the only objection that can be raised concerning the accuracy of digitally signed data is that either the key used for the signature did not belong to the putative issuer at all, but rather only his name was used, or that the key was wrongfully used by a third party.

However, with signatures according to the Act Concerning Digital Signatures , the first objection is almost completely excluded since when a signature key certificate is issued in accordance with the Act Concerning Digital Signatures , it is almost impossible for an applicant to successfully masquerade as someone else; an identity check is performed as part of the issuing procedure. Without a doubt, this provides *prima facie* evidence that the corresponding data in their concrete form originated with the key holder. In practice, a rebuttal from the key holder's side will hardly be possible.

However, it is still possible to object that a third party wrongly used the signature key. Since the Act Concerning Digital Signatures provides no standard at all as to which security measures are to be used in the protection of the private key, one cannot necessarily assume that the prerequisites for a *prima facie* argument of proper use are present. After all, general life experience shows that many users will be careless in their storage of the key, *e.g*, the chip card, and many use either insecure passwords (*e.g*, name of spouse) or make note of them or a PIN in an easily accessible form.

We must wait and see whether future adjudication will impose the burden of proof on the key holder for wrongful use of a key when a digital signature is present as *prima facie* evidence.

It must be noted that the Act Concerning Digital Signatures will probably lead to increased awareness on the part of judges with regard to the probative value of digital signatures which is really very high. Furthermore, the person named in the certified key as the holder can no longer successfully argue that he was in reality not the holder at all.

Finally, it should be pointed out that the Act Concerning Digital Signatures expressly permits the use of other procedures for digital signatures.[250] However, when in the future the digital signature is made equivalent to other forms in individual cases, this will only apply to signatures in accordance with the Act Concerning Digital Signatures . Therefore, the practical significance of other procedures in legal practice will be greatly reduced in the future. In certain circumstances, a different signature could play a role within the framework of free evaluation of evidence by the court according to section 286 of the Code of Civil Procedure since even such a signature makes the integrity and authenticity of the signed data more credible than without the presence of a signature.

We must wait and see to what extent the signature procedure according to the Act Concerning Digital Signatures will gain practical significance in a larger context, even though initial signs are already visible.[251]

Confidentiality

10-58   **Using Only One Provider's Communications Infrastructure** When information is transmitted through one single provider, such as an e-mail between customers of the on-line service (*e.g*, CompuServe or AOL), it is guaranteed that the data will pass only through computers of the provider. However, the provider or its employees may read the data in plain text. No other persons have access to this data, unless they have gained access to the computer systems of the provider. Therefore, as long as one has confidence in the discretion and soundness of the provider and its employees and considers it capable of preventing unauthorised access to its computer systems, there is no security problem.

It can further be assumed that the provider is greatly at pains to ensure the confidentiality of the data entrusted to it because, in the case of culpable neglect of duty, it makes itself liable for damages, at least on the grounds of positive violation of contractual duty. Here, too, section 282 of the Civil Code may be applied by analogy, so that the burden of proof is distributed by areas of risk or responsibility, with the result that the provider — if there is a violation of duty — must prove that it is not responsible.[252] If the data gets into the wrong hands, then it is certain that a violation of duty has been committed either by the provider itself or by persons whose liability-creating behaviour is, pursuant to section 31 of the Civil Code (usually by analogy) or section 278 Civil Code, attributable to the provider. The reversal of the burden of proof relating to responsibility then represents a major facilitation for the damaged party, it not being possible, however, at this point to predict when the courts would deem

---

250 Act Concerning Digital Signatures , section 2(2).
251 See also in this context the comments on the creation of a text form law under paragraph number 1-57.
252 Palandt-Heinrichs, Civil Code, 56. Aufl, 282 Rn. 8.

the evidence in exoneration to have been furnished. To the extent to which this is apparent, there have not yet been any decisions regarding this problem area.

On the other hand, however, the majority of providers will take pains to limit their liability as far as possible, at any rate to contract out of liability for negligence. Since the latter is possible also by way of General Terms and Conditions, even *vis-à-vis* non-traders, the claim for damages has, for practical purposes, relatively little value. Yet, even if liability of the provider does not enter into consideration or enters into consideration merely to a limited extent, a provider will, to safeguard its reputation, surely be at pains to safeguard the confidentiality of the data entrusted to it.

Using Various Providers' Communications Infrastructure Conversely, the   10-59
situation is different if use is made of networks whose infrastructure is maintained by a plurality of providers, particularly when using the Internet. In this case, there is a great probability that the information will be routed through computer systems of various operators. If using TCP/IP (Transfer Control Protocol/Internet Protocol) as in the Internet, owing to the associated dynamic routing, it is not even possible to predict which computer systems the data will pass. Consequently, it is completely unclear who will have access to the data while it is on its way to the recipient. A particular risk results from the fact that, owing to the technical possibilities, even the automatic "interception" of the data streams with filtering-out of the relevant data is possible.

To be sure, the risk should not be overestimated since, in practice, it is not the case that everyone who has the technical know-how and corresponding possibilities of access is desirous of spying out the data of other people. However, there can be no talk of confidentiality with regard to the transmission of data in such networks. Therefore, an old rule for the use of the Internet is the sentence: Don't post anything to the Internet you would not want to see on the front page of the 'National Inquirer'. Although the successful targeted spying-out of data is rare, it can under no circumstances be ruled out.

Use of Cryptography Both the residual risk when using a single provider   10-60
and also the greater risk of using the Internet can be virtually ruled out by means of strict cryptography. An example of this is PGP (Pretty Good Privacy) which is now widespread in the Internet. This is based on a method that makes use of the mathematical problem of breaking down a number into prime factors. By the present-day level of mathematical science, it can be considered certain that this encryption technique cannot be "broken". The only possibility of attack is represented by so-called brute-force attacks, *i.e*, to a certain extent the trying-out of all possible keys (an intelligent attack would proceed somewhat more efficiently than to try out all possibilities one after the other). If use is made of a key length of 1024 bits which is now

generally customary, there are so many possibilities that, on the basis of the computing power presently in existence world-wide, the chance of success of such an attack is virtually zero. Any other form of attack on the relevant data at the sender's or receiver's end would appear to be more promising. In particular, the method is far more secure than a telephone call or a fax transmission.

The other advantage of PGP is that it is a method of asymmetrical cryptography. This means that one pair of keys is generated for each user. One is the public key which is made accessible to everyone, and one is the private key which must be kept secret. This key can then be used to encrypt data to send it to the holder of the private key. The encrypted data can be read only by using the private key, with the result that interception by third parties is out of the question; not even the sender is able to decrypt the message once it has been encrypted. This has the advantage that there is just one pair of keys for each user, whereas, with symmetrical cryptography (in which both parties use the same key), a separate key is required for every two users wishing to communicate. If, for example, 10 users wish to communicate with each other, then, with asymmetrical cryptography, they need just one pair of keys each, *i.e*, a total of 10 pairs of keys, 11 pairs of keys for 11 users, etc. Conversely, if using symmetrical cryptography, each user must agree on a separate key with each other user. This means that 45 keys are required; even 55 for 11 users; 66 keys for 12 users, etc. With symmetrical cryptography, therefore, the number of keys required rises astronomically as the number of users grows, as a result of which the method becomes unmanageable in practice. In addition, these so-called public key systems allow the public keys to be transmitted also via non-secure channels since anyone may read them; only the private key must be kept secret. Conversely, with symmetrical cryptography, the key must be exchanged via a secure channel.

From a legal viewpoint, it should be noted in this respect that the use of even strict cryptography is not subject to any legal restrictions whatsoever in Germany. However, the present Minister of the Interior has spoken of a regulatory framework. He has in mind a system which, similarly to the key escrow formerly planned in the United States, allows only the use of specific cryptography systems and obliges the users to deposit the private keys with agencies which, under certain conditions, will grant certain authorities access to those keys, with the result that the data in question can be read by them. However, this legislative project is given little chance of succeeding. There is already resistance within the government. Both the Ministry of Justice and also the Ministry of Economics have rightly rejected the proposal.

To be sure, the possibility of encryption is a problem of internal policy if it is used for criminal or even terrorist purposes. However, corresponding legislation promises no success whatsoever. Namely, criminals will hardly be so stupid as to deposit their private keys. Since, however, the monitoring of compliance with cryptography legislation is virtually impossible because the supervision of all data streams is almost impracticable and it is also technically impossible automatically to establish whether specific data has been encrypted or not, it will not be possible to prevent illegal communications. Consequently, restrictions on cryptography are not suitable for combating crime.

On the other hand, however, key escrow means that those people who wish to use cryptography for legal purposes will have less confidence in the security of their data. Industry, in particular, has a justified interest in safeguarding company secrets, etc. as effectively as possible. Regardless of the question of the trustworthiness of the deposit agencies, every transmission of the private key increases the risk of its falling into the wrong hands, be it merely by mistake and without evil intent. Finally, in every country, even in the Federal Republic of Germany, it is appropriate for there to be a certain degree of mistrust *vis-à-vis* means of government supervision which are liable to misuse. Furthermore, whether such legislation might not constitute a violation of the right to informational self-determination which is acknowledged by the German Federal Constitutional Court as a product of the general right to personal privacy, is not clear.

On-line Payment

Credit Card Payments on-line

The simplest method of electronic payment is to employ already known **10-61** types of money transfer. The most important possibility in this connection is that of paying by means of credit card, the card data required by the payee being exchanged over the data network.

Transmission of Card Data Here, there are no special circumstances what- **10-62** soever as compared with the old-established system of payment by credit card over the phone, by letter or by fax. In this case, the customer merely communicates his credit card information, enabling the other party, by the use of that information, to collect his money less the commission charged by the credit card company. The credit card company then on-debits the payment to the customer.

There is a problem with regard to the confidentiality of the transmitted data. Owing to the already mentioned problems of security with the Internet, there is the risk that, on its way to the payee, the information may be intercepted and later misused.

As regards the question of whether, in the event of loss, the customer is guilty of contributory negligence or whether he has violated a contractual duty *vis-à-vis* the card-issuing company, attention should be drawn to the following:

Even the Internet cannot be classed as such a non-secure medium that the cardholder can be accused of gross negligence if he transmits his card data by that means. Namely, in that case, virtually any use of the card would be grossly negligent since it is always associated with the risk that the card data will pass into the wrong hands; one can never know who at the premises of the payee will have access to the payment vouchers. Furthermore, one only needs to refer to so-called dumpster diving, *i.e*, people looking for thrown-away credit card vouchers in garbage cans, say, near restaurants, etc. For the average criminal, this is considerably easier than intercepting such data on the Internet.

Moreover, it should be pointed out that, in spite of non-secure transmission routes, the greater risk is that the data security of the destination systems on which the data is stored will not be adequate.[253]

Moreover, the card holder does not normally have any contractual duty *vis-à-vis* the card-issuing company to ensure that his card data is kept secret because this is not usually agreed in the relevant General Terms and Conditions. Whether such a duty exists as a collateral duty under the terms of the credit card agreement is extremely doubtful and the answer is probably no.

10-63   Other Methods of On-line Payment Using Credit Cards   The problem of security in the transmission of the card data can be solved by cryptography. The aim of such developments is to get round the problematic use of programs such as PGP and to ensure the reliable encryption of the data in a more user-friendly form. Ideally, such mechanisms are transparent in operation, and the user is completely unaware that the data is being transmitted in encrypted form.[254]

Of course, this is not a solution to the problem of attacks on the destination systems, where the guaranteeing of adequate security is exclusively under the control of the respective system operators.

No particular legal problems are associated with these methods in Germany, at any rate not as long as the use of cryptography is not subject to any restrictions there.[255]

The most important example of such technology is the SSL system developed by Netscape Communications which is integrated in its Netscape Navigator or, in future, Communicator.

More innovative is the system developed by CyberCash which ensures that the credit card data does not remain with the payee, but is transmitted immediately, with indication of the amount owed, to CyberCash, from where the conventional accounting procedure is initiated. In this connection, reference should be made also to the system developed by First Virtual. Its special feature is that the credit card information is available only to First Virtual itself and payment can be initiated by the user in that he sends the payee a special identification code with which the payee can obtain payment

---

253 The most successful attack to date on such systems, perpetrated by Kevin Mitnick, who "got away with" 20,000 data records containing credit card information from the company Netcom has been reported by Reif and Kossel, "Bits statt Bares", *c't report* 2, at p. 177.
254 For technical details: Reif and Kossel, "Bits statt Bares", *c't report* 2, at pp. 177 *et seq.*
255 See above.

from First Virtual which then debits that amount to the customer's credit card. A side effect of this system is that payment can also be made to vendors who do not accept credit cards. However, the system belongs really in the realm of genuine cyber cash; at least, the boundaries in this regard are fluid.

Reference should further be made to methods which are intended to ensure that payments can also be made to vendors who themselves do not (cannot) accept credit cards. Thus, for example, CheckFree provides its services as a broker that can be instructed to pay a specific amount to any payee. The company then debits the amount to the credit card account of the person giving the instruction and passes on the money by the means most convenient to the payee. From the legal viewpoint, this presumably must be judged according to the rules for bank transfers (without an intermediate bank). Since, however, a legal appraisal is in no way related to the problems of electronic data communications (the same system is also conceivable with the use of telefax), it is not further discussed here.

Electronic Fund Transfers

The use of credit cards in transactions has the disadvantage that, for the vendor, payment is associated with greater uncertainty than, say, in the case of cash payment. Furthermore, the vendor may possibly object to the commission he must pay to the credit card company (costs are also incurred in the case of electronic fund transfer, only it is not yet clear how high they will be and who is to pay what proportion of them). Finally, the use of credit cards is necessarily associated with the storage of personal data of the cardholder at the premises of the payee, although the cardholder might prefer to remain anonymous. It is the aim of the system of electronic fund transfer to overcome these disadvantages. Conversely, it appears utopian to imagine that this might provide an on-line payment facility also for those people who, for lack of financial soundness, do not qualify for a credit card.

10-64

Since credit cards are presently available to broad masses of people and since cyberbanks, too, will probably only be interested in financially sound customers, those persons who presently are unable to be issued with credit cards will also have great difficulties in opening a cyber account. Nevertheless, this may happen in individual cases, for example, if a normal commercial bank wishes to offer cyberbanking to all its chequeing account customers. This might also have further significance in conjunction with under-age chequeing account holders, who do not qualify for a credit card but who, in this manner, will nevertheless be able to participate in on-line payment transactions.

Genuine electronic fund transfer — in which it is not merely a question of transmitting data with the aid of which payment is handled by conventional means — is still in its infancy world-wide. Probably the only significant practical type of implementation to date is the fact that inter-bank payment transactions are now in large part handled via the SWIFT network operated by the banks. Otherwise, however, there are virtually no genuine on-line fund transfers because the appropriate mechanisms do not (yet) exist. The only system that can be subsumed under the heading of electronic fund transfer is the up-and-coming system of electronic cash which is based on the Eurocheque card and a secret number.[256] In contrast to this, the ever more frequently encountered system of direct debit, using account data from the ec card, with the form then being signed by the customer, is not a system of electronic fund transfer. Namely, in this case, payment is subsequently handled using the conventional system of debit-transfer order. Even as regards the presentation of transfer orders to the bank in electronic form by data carrier (*e.g*, using the so-called magnetic-tape clearing system) or on-line (*e.g*, "home banking" using an on-line service), one cannot really speak of electronic fund transfer. In this case, use is merely made of electronic transmission methods to initiate actions (usually a transfer) which were previously initiated using written documents. Indeed, the paperless contracting of banking business does not automatically mean that there is the genuine electronic transfer of funds.

To be sure, owing to the necessary storage and transmission of personal and confidential data, the last-mentioned methods, too, may, as compared with the conventional methods, represent a problem with regard to data protection[257] and also with regard to security.[258] Since, however, this is not a question of on-line payment within the meaning of the present chapter, these aspects are not to be discussed here.

10-65   **Methods for Paying Large Sums of Money**   As regards electronic money, the idea is that a specific bit string of any length has a specific monetary value, just as is the case with a bank note. Consequently, each such bit string would be a virtual bank note or coin with a specific value.

The purpose of such methods is, first, to overcome the disadvantages associated with payment by credit card (*e.g*, big commission for the credit card company, risk of misuse) and, second, to make commercial transactions anonymous, which appears desirable to protect the private sphere of users since, otherwise, a further step would be taken on the way to the glass consumer.

The problem in this regard is that it must be ensured that each of these bit strings is unique, just as in the same way each bank note must be unique. Whereas the duplication of bank notes can be prevented relatively effectively by printing-related means, this is very difficult in the case of bit strings

---

256 For further details see Werner, "Datenschutzprobleme des elektronischen Zahlungs-verkehrs", *C.R.*, 1997, at p. 48.
257 As regards problems relating to data protection, see, for example, Werner, "Daten-schutzprobleme des elektronischen Zahlungsverkehrs", *C.R.*, 1997, at p. 48 *et seq.*
258 With regard to security-related problems, see, for example, Birkelbach, "Sicheres Homebanking — Ist der Kunde zukünftig das Hauptrisiko?", *W.M.*, 1996, at pp. 2099 *seq.*

because digital data of any kind can be duplicated in any quantity without loss of quality, with virtually no costs being incurred.

This problem can be solved in that use is made only of special hardware which denies the user direct access to the data and thereby effectively prevents copies being made of such bit strings.[259]

Steps toward such a system can be found in the CAFE[260] project of the European Union Commission and in the technology being propagated by the British company Mondex. Both systems have in common the fact that they store the money on chip cards and employ corresponding read/write devices for transfer. On the other hand, there are differences with regard to data protection: whereas CAFE ensures, to a certain extent that transactions cannot be traced, Mondex is in part open to the criticism that the last 10 transactions remain stored on the card and are very easy to read.[261]

Finally, it should further be pointed out that, in principle, both systems are intended to replace cash transactions in everyday life and not to serve as means of payment in computer networks. However, this does not mean that they could not be used for that purpose. The connection of corresponding read/write devices to the participating computers would permit a form of money transfer which does not exist in the case of conventional bank notes since bank notes cannot be dematerialised and transmitted electronically.

Considerably more interesting is the second possible solution to the problem of the copying of such bit strings because this approach does not require any special hardware and each bit string can only be used once in payment transactions. If, therefore, a user makes copies of such a string, they will not be of any use to him later, because that string has already been used once for a payment transaction.

In practice, what would happen is this: the customer obtains such bit strings from his "cyberbank" and pays for them in the conventional manner. Later, he can pass on such a bit string to someone else, who then has the corresponding amount credited to him at the "cyberbank". Through this act of crediting, the bit string is then blocked for any further use. Of course, prior to each transaction, it would be necessary immediately to check whether the bit string in question is not already blocked.

Once again, there are different approaches to the implementation of such a system. One might mention NetCash from Software Agents, Digi-Cash from the company of the same name and the project of the Mark Twain Bank. From a German viewpoint, interest is attached above all to Digi-Cash, since Deutsche Bank is presently preparing a pilot project with Digi-Cash.[262]

259 For technical details in this regard see Reif and Kossel, "Bits statt Bares", *c't report* 2, at p. 180.
260 Conditional Access for Europe; information on this on the Internet at —
http://www.cwi.nl/projects/cafe.html.
261 Reif and Kossel, "Bits statt Bares", *c't report* 2, at p. 181.
262 For details of these systems see Reif and Kossel, "Bits statt Bares", *c't report* 2, at p. 182.

It is still completely unclear which system will ultimately be able to establish itself on the market. At present, none of the systems is of any practical significance. To date, experiments conducted with the systems have merely permitted the purchase of digital information of little economic value since, as yet, no vendor has apparently had the courage to entertain the risk of such a trial while rendering higher-value services.

It should also be noted that the concept of the once-only use of such bit strings is of necessity associated with the drawback that the use of the money must be communicated immediately to the agency handling the payment transaction, to rule out any repeated use. Since this can never be done absolutely instantaneously, the risk of repeated use is even then still quite high. If one attempts to remedy this situation by registering the users of the money, then this, in turn, is problematic with regard to data protection because it would then be quite simple to trace which user spent what money when and on what. This is, of course, unacceptable because, after all, the purpose of the system is precisely to maintain secrecy with respect to such information, as is the case with the use of cash.

Work is also in progress on the solution to these problems. However, it will be some time before the systems are suitable for everyday use.

10-66   **Methods for Paying Extremely Small Amounts (Cyber Coins)** In practice, however, the above-mentioned methods can function only where the amounts being transferred are of such magnitude that the associated expense is worthwhile. The immediate crediting of an account for a bit string can only be implemented if there is a permanent reliable on-line connection to the paying agent. To exclude the possibility of repeated use of the bit strings, an inquiry must be made to the paying agent prior to the transaction and, simultaneously with the transaction, the bit string must be blocked for further use.

Consequently, it would be advisable only to credit several amounts at a time, so that there is a reasonable relationship between the associated expense and the amount credited. In addition, cryptographic methods which appear justified in the case of large transfers are, in relation to the amount of the transfer, nonsensical in the case of extremely small amounts because this would require too much computing power. To date, however, there have been no studies into where the limit of profitability lies precisely for the "big" methods.

Of course, this is not a problem for those methods that are based on special hardware, such as the previously mentioned CAFE system. Such systems are, therefore, also suitable for the payment of extremely small amounts.

The approaches adopted to the creation of such micro-payment methods have in common the fact that a certain degree of non-security with regard to payment is accepted since individual losses can be tolerated owing to the small amounts involved. Such approaches employ only relatively simple cryptographic methods and only group credits for several micro-payments are envisaged.[263] Although fraudulent practices are possible in certain respects with these systems, the fraud can, as a rule, be found out relatively easily because illegal transactions can be traced and the perpetrator can be excluded from further use. If, however, such mechanisms are provided, there is no longer any anonymity of the payment transactions.

Approaches to such systems are, for example, Payword, Micromint, Millicent from DEC, GlobeID from GCTech, and CyberCoin from Cyber-Cash. However, all these systems, too, are still at an early stage of development, with the result that one cannot say which systems will ultimately become established in practice.

Legal Problems of Genuine on-line Payment The first problem in this regard 10-67 relates to whether such an electronic form of payment has the effect of performance within the meaning of section 362 of the Civil Code or whether it is not merely on account of performance, such as the presentation of a cheque. In this connection, it must be stated that, of course, there is performance if such a form of electronic payment is explicitly what is owed. If, however, there is an unspecified obligation to pay money, this question cannot yet be answered from a present-day perspective. Such an answer will not be possible until it can safely be assessed how secure such a form of payment is for the payee, this probably differing from system to system. As far as can be seen, there is as yet no information available about who, in the eyes of the system developers, is to bear what risks with regard to on-line fund transfer.

Closely related to this is the question as to whether such a payment constitutes a performance within the meaning of the enrichment law. With reference to the situation of performance in the case of a bank transfer, one will be able to say, even from a present-day perspective that the answer to the question is yes. Accordingly, one will have to accept that there is a performance by the "cyberbank" to its customer, in that it honours the bit string, and a performance by the customer to the payee, although the direct transfer of money is from the "cyberbank" to the payee. If there is the involvement of intermediate "cyberbanks", this represents a further stage of performance; however, the situation is equivalent to that of a bank transfer with the involvement of intermediate banks.

Within the meaning of the enrichment law, the account of the payee is deemed to have been credited starting from the time at which such crediting can, under normal circumstances — as also in the case of a bank transfer — be classified as an abstract acknowledgement of debt[264] on the part of the "cyberbank".

---

263 For technical details see Reif and Kossel, "Bits statt Bares", *c't report* 2, at pp. 183 *et seq.*
264 Civil Code, section 780.

Since cyber money under the above systems will have to be regarded materially as deposit money, it is necessary, for the control of government monetary policy[265] to apply to cyber money the same rules and regulations as to deposit money. Since, however, cyber money is not deposit money, it may be necessary here to introduce corresponding legislation.

The most interesting and important question in this connection appears to be whether the Banking Law (KWG) is applicable to cyber money transactions. Operating as a cyberbank could be viewed as a banking business within the meaning of section 1(1), number 9, of the KWG if such activity by the cyberbank were to be counted toward the implementation of cashless fund transfer. One will have to say that this is the case since the payment transaction when using cyber money is equivalent to a bank transfer, even if, after several intermediate stations with different users, the bit string is ultimately credited to someone.

There is, therefore, no need to extend the list of banking businesses as called for by some authors,[266] rather, the activity as a cyberbank is already under existing law a banking business, with the result that the Banking Law (KWG), with its control mechanisms, is wholly applicable thereto.

A further question is whether, with the operation of cyberbanks, there is not also a need for monetary control mechanisms. Once again, the answer is probably yes, and it would be conceivable to allow the bit strings to be issued only by the central bank or to introduce another form of careful government supervision of such cyber money transactions. Namely, if the relevant business circles were given a free hand here, there would be the risk of the money supply no longer being adequately controllable. Such control mechanisms are in existence for deposit money (such as the minimum-reserve policy). If necessary, such mechanisms would have to be created for the materially comparable cyber money. With regard to the fact that foreign-currency accounts at German banks are also subject to monetary-policy access by the Bundesbank, Gramlich assumes that cyberaccounts, too, may be held in any currency. Furthermore, he points out that, owing to the internationalisation of business, the monetary-control options of an individual central bank are ever more decreasing.[267] At European level, however, this problem will be partially solved by the introduction of the Euro and control by the European Central Bank.

Owing to the storage of personal data which is unavoidable in the case of electronic fund transfer, there is also a problem with regard to data protection. As stated previously with regard to the description of methods for electronic fund transfer, some systems are already attempting of their own accord to implement anonymisation.

---

265 Gramlich, "Elektronisches Geld", *C.R.*, 1997, at p. 18.
266 Gramlich, "Elektronisches Geld", *C.R.*, 1997, at p. 18.
267 Gramlich, "Elektronisches Geld", *C.R.*, 1997, at p. 18.

Regardless of such efforts, the following must be stated in general with regard to electronic fund transfer:

First, cyberbanks, too, must be made subject to the obligation of banking secrecy. Since no express legislation has been established for banking secrecy, it can be assumed that this requirement would be met under already existing law. Even if the application of banking secrecy does not emerge expressly from the contract with the bank, it is still assumed in general that banking secrecy applies. The legal institution of banking secrecy is anchored in the Constitution. On the side of the customer, it is by the general right to personal privacy and the therein contained right to informational self-determination[268] and, on the side of the bank, by the right of freedom to choose a profession or trade from article 12 Constitution (Constitution) which right is impaired if there can no longer be confidence in the bank's discretion.[269] Furthermore, the application of banking secrecy can also be based on the right of banks to general freedom of action under article 2(1) Constitution (Constitution), but not on the general right to personal privacy under article 1, 2 Constitution (Basic Law)since this right, by its nature, is not applicable to legal entities.[270]

Therefore, it remains to be stated that, also in "cyberbank contracts", the application of banking secrecy is agreed, by implication at least. This will — in so far as such transactions are not effected by "real" banks under application of the General Terms and Conditions for Banks — at any rate be the normal case at the beginning since, if in doubt, the operators of cyberbanks will not be interested in granting customers any legal status through their General Terms and Conditions.

Beyond the subject of banking secrecy, it should be pointed out that, of course, any storing of data is subject to the restrictions and requirements set forth in the Data Protection Law (BDSG).[271] This is of significance, first because banking secrecy provides protection only against the data being passed on by the cyberbank to third parties, whereas the bank-internal storage and use of the data is possible without restriction. Second, data is also stored, for example, on the premises of the payee, who, of course, is not subject to banking secrecy.[272] Essentially, it follows therefrom that the

---

268 The right to informational self-determination must, under Constitution, article 19(3), also protect bank customers who are domestic juristic persons.

269 See Werner, "Datenschutzprobleme des elektronischen Zahlungsverkehrs", *C.R.*, 1997, at p. 50.

270 Jarass and Pieroth, Constitution, 3rd Aufl., article 2, Rn. 31, it would be conceivable for there to be protection under the general right to personal privacy in the case of banks which are operated in the legal form of a partnership and in which at least one personally liable partner is a natural person — a case which exists virtually only with a few small private banks. The one-man operation of a bank is, under section 2a KWG (Banking Law), not permitted in any event.

271 Data Protection Law, particularly sections 27 *et seq.*

272 Werner, "Datenschutzprobleme des elektronischen Zahlungsverkehrs", *C.R.*, 1997, at p. 50.

storage and processing of personal data within the framework of electronic fund transfer must be reduced to the absolute minimum. The safeguarding of this principle is, therefore, also a fundamental requirement to be satisfied by any system which aspires to achieve practical significance.[273]

To summarise, it can be stated that the problems relating to data protection can be fully answered under existing law. The Data Protection Law provides a sufficient basis therefor and the obligation of banking secrecy must apply also to cyberbanks. Consequently, there is inasmuch no need for legislation. However, the Data Protection Law cannot effectively ensure that the systems on which the data is stored are adequately secured against attacks from outside. Requiring the operators of such systems to comply by law with the highest possible security standards appears an attractive solution to this problem.[274] Furthermore, discussion is required, however, as to what level of security can be required in such cases without causing the costs of such measures to rise disproportionately.

If the system of electronic fund transfer is to increase in significance, then it must also be asked whether the criminal law as it stands provides sufficient protection against manipulation and misuse with regard to cyber money. The definition of fraud as laid down in section 263 of the Criminal Code may not be sufficient. It will probably be advisable, to cover the duplication of such bit strings or the generation of bit strings suitable for payment, to create a separate criminal offence which could be based on the counterfeiting of money under section 164 of the Criminal Code.[275]

It should also be noted that, to promote electronic commerce, it is desirable for legislation to be introduced to create a virtual "negotiable instrument" comparable with a cheque or also to permit the electronic issuing of cheques. By means of strict cryptography — the use of which could be made a formal requirement — it can be guaranteed that the signer can be reliably determined. An advantage over an electronic civil law payment order which is already possible under existing law would, in particular, be that the beneficiary from the cheque would then be able more easily to assert his rights in cheque payment enforcement proceedings — a legal procedure which ought also to be made admissible for the enforcement of electronic cheques.

It would be desirable for such an extension of cheque-related law to take place at international level, in order, also in this field, to achieve the extensive internationalisation of cheque-related law.

In addition, the question of whether there is a need for a virtual bill of exchange which could be accepted and discounted, i.e, which could be used

---

273 For details see Werner, "Datenschutzprobleme des elektronischen Zahlungsverkehrs", *C.R.*, 1997, at p. 51 *et seq.*

274 Werner, "Datenschutzprobleme des elektronischen Zahlungsverkehrs", *C.R.*, 1997, at p. 53.

275 Such a need is seen also by Gramlich, "Elektronisches Geld", *C.R.*, 1997, at p. 18, without, however, making any specific proposals.

also for credit transactions, should be examined more closely. However, such an examination would go beyond the scope of the present chapter.

COPYRIGHTS

While the previous sections have shown that Virtual Shopping Malls and payment systems will significantly change the traditional exchange of goods and services, perhaps the greatest challenge of the on-line revolution lies in the protection of intellectual property in the vastness of the allegedly "anarchic" cyberspace. One of America's most prominent copyright scholars, David Nimmer, correctly called the Internet "one gigantic copying machine".[276] Although at first this remark may appear rather pessimistic from the point of view of an author, the fact is that it has never been easier to make unauthorised use of copyrighted works without any danger of detection, let alone prosecution.

10-68

Any picture, be it a photograph or painting, or any musical or literary work can easily be digitised and put on a Bulletin Board System (*B.B.S*) or offered for downloading on a Web site. Of course, the piracy of copyrighted works has always been a problem since works of authorship have been created. However, the ease and speed and, perhaps even more importantly, the quality with which even inexperienced users can copy or alter protected works has given rise to serious concern among authors and record companies alike. What aggravates the situation is the lack of public awareness when it comes to the protection of copyrighted works on the Internet — a large number of "netizens" still take the view that everything available on the Internet is considered within the public domain. Are we, therefore, as one author[277] rather drastically put it, "dancing on the grave of copyright"?

Although the suggestion that copyrights have become obsolete in the digital age has repeatedly been made in recent months. Copyright protection is not only alive and kicking in the Information age, but the challenges of the Internet[278] can be met if the traditional vocabulary of copyright protection which was originally developed to protect authors and artists in an analogue world, is amended by a new set of terms that aptly mirror the legal implications of the digital media without running the risk of becoming outdated all too soon because of being too technologically specific. This

---

276 *The Economist,* July 27, 1996, at p. 59.
277 Barlow: "Selling Wine without Bottles. The Economy of Mind on the Global Net", in Hugenholtz (ed.), *The Future of Copyright in a Digital Environment,* at pp. 169 and 174 *et seq.*
278 While this chapter will primarily focus on the legal implications of the Internet, the crucial questions discussed in relation to copyright protection arise in commercial on-line services such as AOL or Compuserve ("on-line service providers" or OSPs) as well. When the need arises, differences between the use of copyrighted works on the Internet and commercial on-line services will be dealt with separately.

chapter looks primarily at the challenges to copyright protection from a German perspective, but the principle of territoriality must eventually give way to a more global approach to copyright protection. This approach has already gained considerable momentum with the adoption of the European Union's Database Directive and the findings of the diplomatic conference on certain copyright and neighbouring rights questions held in Geneva in December 1996.

Before venturing any further into the various aspects of copyright protection in light of the Internet, it will be necessary to deal briefly with the crucial question of which law applies to copyright infringements on the Internet and to take a closer look at the specific rights covered by the German Copyright Act of 1965 and the applicability of the respective provisions to on-line communications. The Acquisition of Rights in digitised works of authorship from the various German collecting societies and notably the newly founded Clearingstelle Multimedia (CMMV, one of Europe's first multimedia copyright clearance centres) will be discussed in a separate section. Apart from copyright protection, an increasing number of corporations and institutions in the past few months have been facing the problem of "domain name grabbing" to which German case law has just started to respond. The protection of domain names and trade marks on the Internet will therefore be subject to an in-depth discussion in the final section of this chapter on the law of electronic commerce in Germany.

Applicability of Copyright Protection to on-line Communications

10-69   Similar to the Anglo-American copyright system, German copyright law has traditionally distinguished between the author's "economic rights" and his so-called *droits moral* or moral rights which together form an integrated whole and are often intertwined.[279]

Works Protected by the Copyright Act

10-70   Of the works protected under section 2(1) of the Copyright Act, mainly literary works, including computer programs, musical works, artistic works, photographs, and motion pictures are most likely to be transferred onto the Internet and, therefore, be subject to unauthorised copying. Unlike section 102 (a) of the United States Copyright Act of 1976, copyright protection

---

279 For an in-depth review of the various economic and moral rights conferred on the author and/or performing artist by the German Copyright Act see Liegl, Leupold and Bräutigam, "Copyright Protection in Germany", Campbell (ed.), *The Comparative Law Yearbook of International Business, Special Issue 1997, Copyright Infringement;* as well as *Amtl.Begr.*, printed in Haertel and Schiefler, "Urheberrechtsgesetz und Gesetz über die Wahrnehmung von Urheberrechten und verwandten Schutzrechten", *Textausgabe mit Verweisen und Materialien,* 1967, at p. 146; and Schricker-Dietz, *Urheberrecht,* section 11 marg. note 1.

under the German Copyright Act subsists in all works of authorship, fixed or unfixed. Under section 2(2) of the Copyright Act, however, only personal, intellectual creations are to be considered protected works under the Copyright Act. Ordinary business e-mail is therefore not subject to copyright protection, but the transmission of a scientific treatise or a poem certainly satisfies the personal intellectual creation test.

The question under which category multimedia productions employing sound, video, computer-generated graphics and text must be classified cannot be answered in any generally binding way, but must be tackled with respect to each part of such works and on a case-by-case basis. In this context it is important to note that contrary to traditional wisdom,[280] photographs and motion pictures within the meaning of section 2(1), numbers 5 and 6, of the Copyright Act are no longer necessarily the result of a chemical reaction on light-sensitive film but are increasingly made with digital (still) video cameras. It is therefore a self-evident truth that copyright protection is not restricted to chemical film and photography, but extends to video, as well as all types of digitally rendered screen designs, provided they reach the degree of creation required by section 2(2) of the Copyright Act.[281]

Rights Granted to the Author by the German Copyright Act of 1965

Under section 15 of the Copyright Act, the author has the exclusive right to exploit his work in any tangible form, including the right of reproduction and the right to display his work in public. The aforementioned right of reproduction in turn comprises the right to: (1) perform the protected work in public[282] (2) the right of broadcasting as regulated in section 20 of the Copyright Act(3) the right to communicate the work to the public by means of sound or visual recordings,[283] as well as (4) the right of communicating broadcasts of the work to a public audience.[284]   **10-71**

The so-called "moral rights" are covered by sections 12-14 of the Copyright Act and comprise: (1) the right of publication,[285] under which the right to communicate or describe a previously unpublished work to the public is reserved to the author (2) the right of attribution set forth in section 19 of the Copyright Act and (3) the right to prohibit any distortion or other impairment of a protected work.[286]

---

280 Fromm, Nordemann and Hertin, *Urheberrecht*, 8th ed., section 72, marginal note 4.
281 Schwarz, *Recht im Internet*, section 3-2.1, at p. 9.
282 Copyright Act, section 19.
283 Copyright Act, section 21.
284 Copyright Act, section 22.
285 Regulated in the Copyright Act, section 12.
286 Copyright Act, section 14.

The Implementation of the European Database Directive into German Copyright Law

10-72   Directive 96/9/E.C. of the European Parliament of March 11, 1996 on the Legal Protection of Databases[287] for the first time addressed the specific legal implications of electronic media. Complying with its obligation to bring the Directive into force before January 1, 1998, the lower house of the German parliament has passed a revision of the Copyright Act which will significantly extend the degree of protection offered to databases.[288]

Section 4(2) of the Copyright Act as revised by article 7 Information and Communication Services Act defines a "database work" as "a collection of data or other independent elements arranged in a systematic or methodical way and individually accessible by electronic or other means" and provides that a computer program used in the creation of the database or for the purpose of gaining access to the elements of a database does not form part of the database itself". This wording closely abides by the definition in article 1 (2) of the Database Directive and makes it clear that electronic, as well as non-electronic, databases are protected. A multi-volume dictionary, such as the *Encyclopedia Britannica*, will therefore enjoy the same degree of protection under the amended Copyright Act as its digital counterpart. The revised section 4 of the Copyright Act does not distinguish between on-line and off-line databases, from which it follows that data published on the Internet will principally be treated in the same way as data stored on a CD-ROM or DVD.

Contrary to the first draft of the German government submitted to the lower house of the German parliament in April 1997, which regulated the rights of the maker of a database right after the provisions on the protection of computer programs in sections 69a) *et seq* of the Copyright Act, the revised Information and Communication Services Act now inserts the relevant changes into sections 87a) *et seq* of the Copyright Act which form part of a newly introduced section 6 of the Copyright Act. Section 87 a) of the Copyright Act contains a separate definition of databases[289] by providing that a database within the meaning of the Copyright Act is a collection of data or other independent elements arranged in a systematic or methodical way and individually accessible by electronic or other means, the obtaining, verification or presentation of which requires a qualitatively or quantitatively substantial investment. Under section 87 a)(1), sentence 2, of the Copyright Act, a database which has been materially altered in its character or size is regarded as a new database if the changes made required a qualitatively or quantitatively substantial investment. A "maker of a database" in turn is

---

287   O.J. L 77 of March 27, 1996, at pp. 20 *et seq.*

288   Information and Telecommunications Services Act (Information and Communication Services Act), Bt. Drs. 420/97 of June 13, 1997, at pp. 1 *et seq.*

289   Not to be confused with the definition of the so-called "database works" in section 4 of the Copyright Act.

defined as the individual or entity who made the investments necessary for its creation, under section 87a)(2) of the Copyright Act.

Similar to the Database Directive, the revised Copyright Act consequently distinguishes between databases which, due to the selection or arrangement of the contents constitute the author's own intellectual creation and are therefore protected as such by copyright[290] and databases which are not amenable to copyright protection but are, nevertheless, protected by the new *sui generis* right codified in section 87b)(1), in connection with section 87a) of the Copyright Act. Section 87 b)(1) of the Copyright Act grants the maker of a database the exclusive right to copy or distribute the database or any qualitatively or quantitatively substantial part of it and to communicate it to the public. The repeated copying, distribution or communication to the public of insignificant parts of a database is reserved to its creator as well, provided that such copying runs counter to a normal use of the database or unduly impairs the legitimate interests of its creator.

Section 87 b)(2) of the Copyright Act significantly limits the application of the first-sale doctrine by providing that section 17(2) of the Copyright Act shall apply *mutatis mutandis* to databases. From this it follows that once a database has been put into circulation within the territory of the European Union or a contracting state of the European Economic Area by sale, it may be re-distributed as long as it is not hired out against payment. Since section 17(2) of the Copyright Act refers to "the original or reproduction" (*Vervielfältigungsstücke*) of a protected work, it is clear that only the distribution of physical copies leads to an exhaustion of rights. Consequently, on-line transmission of databases via the Internet always require the prior consent of their creator.

This restriction of the first sale doctrine to the distribution of physical copies which corresponds to recital 43 of the Database Directive so far has not been subject to any criticism from German authors. As the exclusion of section 53 of the Copyright Act, in section 69l), this restrictive approach can be justified with the ease of copying by electronic means. Yet again, the question arises whether the on-line transmission of a computer program from a German software distributor to his French customer is really any different from the sale of a shrink-wrapped package in a store in Paris. In addition to this application of the exhaustion principle set forth in section 17 of the Copyright Act, section 87 b)(2) also refers to section 27(2) and 3 of the Copyright Act from which it follows that in case a sold copy is rented out to the public, the maker of a database is entitled to an appropriate compensation. Since article 7(2), sentence 3 of the Database Directive provides that public lending is not regarded as an act of extraction or re-utilisation and the rules on public lending have not yet been harmonised

---

290 So-called "database works" within the meaning of section 4(2) of the Copyright Act.

on a Union-wide level, the German legislator was free to grant the maker of a database the right to ask the lender for such an appropriate compensation.

Not surprisingly, section 87 c)(1) of the Copyright Act significantly restricts the fair-use principle regulated in section 53 of the Copyright Act for conventional works of authorship by expressly limiting the private use exemption to the copying of a qualitatively or quantitatively substantial part of a non-electronic database only. The revised section 53 of the Copyright Act now provides, in subsection (5), that the private use exemption set forth in section 53(1) of the Copyright Act does not apply to databases the elements of which can be accessed individually by electronic means.

Under section 87c)(1), numbers 2 and 3, of the Copyright Act, the reproduction of electronic databases is only permitted (1) for scientific use if and to the extent that such use is justified by the scientific purpose to be achieved and always provided that the reproduction is not made for a commercial purpose or (2) for use in schools and non-commercial training colleges to the extent necessary. In the latter two cases referred to in section 87c)(1), numbers 2 and 3, of the Copyright Act, the reproduction must always contain a clearly visible reference to the original source, section 87c)(2), last sentence, of the Copyright Act. Finally, section 87c)(2) of the Copyright Act permits the reproduction, distribution and communication to the public of a substantial part of a database for a proceeding before a court of law, an arbitration panel or administrative authority or, more generally, for the purpose of public security.

The restriction of the fair-use principle for private copies in the digital domain has been justified with the increased vulnerability of digitised works which can be copied with a simple key stroke. Although there is certainly something to be said for this argument if one considers the relative ease with which copies of digitised works are distributed and the resulting difficulties in keeping track of such copies, the question whether this total ban of private copies is indeed a necessary change to traditional fair-use principles has not yet received the attention it deserves. If one leaves aside the small inconvenience caused by the necessity to use a copying machine, the reproduction of printed matter has been almost as easy to make and hard to control as digital copies of protected works. In addition, the reason for granting the private use exemption in section 53 of the Copyright Act for analogous works were very much the same as the ones that could justify the application of a similar rule to works in the digital domain.

According to the legislative intent, the introduction of section 53 of the Copyright Act was based on the insight that a ban of copying for private use would not be enforceable under practical considerations.[291] With the steady progress of the modern industrial society, the private use exemption seemed

---

[291] *Amtl.Begr., BGDrucks.* IV, at p. 71.

all the more justified and even necessary to ensure the continuing growth of the economy, as well as the arts and sciences.[292]

While the latter aspect is taken care of by section 87c)(1), numbers 2 and 3, of the Copyright Act, one potential problem still remains. Early on, the German legislator recognised the fact that while the promotion of science and technology made it necessary to create the fair-use exemption set forth in section 53 of the Copyright Act, it did not require that the private or other personal use be free of charge. Section 54 of the Copyright Act therefore provides that in case a protected work is likely to be subject to copying, the author is entitled to an appropriate compensation from the manufacturer of the devices and recording materials used in the reproduction process.[293] Section 87b, according to which sections 54-54h) of the Copyright Act apply *mutatis mutandis* to the database maker's entitlement to remuneration if the specific form of the database he created makes it likely that substantial parts might be excerpted from it, has been abandoned in the legislative procedure, the question remains whether computer-generated or digitised works in general fall under section 54 of the Copyright Act. If this were the case, the imposition of a collective fee on hard drives and all other kinds of computer storage material such as CD-Rs, magneto-optical floppies and rewritable DCDs would be inevitable.

The question of whether computer hard drives fall under section 54 of the Copyright Act has not yet been answered by German courts. The view that the grant of a additional compensation under section 54 of the Copyright Act apart from the licensing fee paid by the supplier of a protected work on the Internet (*e.g.*, the operator of a bulletin board or newsgroup) would not be warranted because the use of such work would be permitted under section 53 of the Copyright Act and therefore be lawful on the whole,[294] can no longer be upheld in its entirety since the copying of electronic databases is now expressly exempted from the scope of section 53 of the Copyright Act. Besides, it appears likely that the limitation of the private use exemption that applies to databases will apply to other kinds of digital works, as well.

The current wording of section 54 of the Copyright Act which merely speaks of "devices" and "recording material" would certainly cover such an extension of its scope of application. The introduction of a collective fee for computer storage materials would nevertheless give up the careful balance that section 53 of the Copyright Act, on the one hand, and sections 54 *et seq* of the Copyright Act, on the other, once struck for analogue works. Under certain restrictions, private copies are free, but manufacturers of photocopiers and recording

---

292 AmtlBegr. for the amending law of 1995, *Bundestagsdrucksache* 10/837, at p. 20, and Schricker-Loewenheim, section 53, marginal note 1.
293 For a detailed review of section 54 of the Copyright Act, see Nordemann, "Die urheberrechtliche Leerkassettenvergütung", Z.U.M. 1985, at p. 57, and Schulze, "Vervielfältigungsrecht der Urheber von Werken der Literatur und Kunst zum persönlichen Gebrauch", U.F.I.T.A. 93 (1982), at p. 73, as well as Schricker-Loewenheim, *Urheberrecht*, section 54 of the Copyright Act, marginal notes 1 *et seq*.
294 Schwarz, in Schwarz (ed.) *Recht im Internet*, section 3-2.2, at pp. 34 and 35.

devices are obliged to indemnify the author for the losses resulting from the use of such devices. If section 54 of the Copyright Act were to be applied to computer hard drives, manufacturers of such devices would have to pay a collective fee despite the fact that the revised Copyright Act prohibits private copies of electronic databases in whole or in part and the author would be entitled to compensation from both the manufacturer of copying devices and the legitimate user himself. The very fact that the private use exemption does not apply in the digital domain therefore lets it appear appropriate not to grant authors an additional compensation under section 54 of the Copyright Act. As new technological developments will soon permit the transmission of feature-length films and sound recordings on the Internet, it will be interesting to see which stance collection societies will take in this matter.

Unlike conventional works of authorship which may be edited freely under section 23 of the Copyright Act if the edited versions are not published, editing of modifying computer software requires the express consent of its creator, section 69c), number 2, Copyright Act. The same holds true under section 23 2. sentence for cinematographic adaptations of a work as well as the execution of plans and sketches of an artistic work or copies of an architectural work. The Information and Telecommunication Services Act (Information and Communication Services Act) applies this principle to database works within the meaning of section 4(2) of the Copyright Act by amending section 23 of the Copyright Act accordingly. In its revised version, section 23 of the Copyright Act requires the consent of the creator of a database work before it can be edited or modified in any way. The only exception to this rule may be found in the newly inserted section 55 a) of the Copyright Act which allows the modification of a database work to the extent that such modification is necessary for a normal use.

The *sui generis* right granted in section 87b) in connection with section 87a) of the Copyright Act runs 15 years from the creation of the database irrespective of the date of publication, section 89 of the Copyright Act. If the database is made available to the public within the 15-year period, the term of protection expires 15 years after its publication. At first sight, this term of protection seems somewhat limited, but in most cases it will last much longer than 15 years. The reason for this lies in the second sentence of section 87a)(2) of the Copyright Act which provides that any substantial change to the character or size of a database results in the creation of a new database provided that such change requires a qualitatively or quantitatively substantial investment. Although the wording of section 87d) of the Copyright Act deviates significantly from the original wording of the Database Directive,[295] it has the intended effect to extend the term of protection to infinity for all practical considerations.

---

295 Database Directive, article 10(3) reads as follows: "Any substantial change, evaluated qualitatively or quantitatively, to the contents of a database including any substantial change resulting from the accumulation of successive additions, deletions or alterations which would result in the database being considered to be a substantial new investment, evaluated qualitatively or quantitatively, shall qualify the database resulting from that investment for its own term of protection".

To counterbalance the reinforced position of the maker of a database, section 87(1) of the Copyright Act declares any contractual obligations which seek to exclude a lawful user's right to reproduce, distribute or communicate to the public qualitatively or quantitatively insignificant parts of a database without the consent of the rightholder as null and void, provided that these acts do not run counter to a normal exploitation of the database and do not unreasonably prejudice the legitimate interests of the maker of the database. This self-evident condition has also been codified in article 9 (2) of the Revised Berne Convention for regular works of authorship.

The amended section 108(1) of the Copyright Act now makes the illegal exploitation of a database a criminal offence subject to imprisonment of up to three years and the revised section 119(3) of the Copyright Act permits the execution of money claims on technical devices used in the copying of databases only to the extent that the creditor is entitled to use the database with the help of such devices.

The beneficiaries of the *sui generis* right granted by section 87b) of the Copyright Act are circumscribed in section 127a) of the Copyright Act. Significantly deviating from article 11 of the Database Directive,[296] section 127 a)(1) of the Copyright Act now provides that only such makers of a database shall enjoy *sui generis* protection under section 87 b) of the Copyright Act which are either German nationals or, in case of corporations, have their seat in Germany. Section 127a)(2), number 1, of the Copyright Act extends the protection granted by the *sui generis* right to companies formed in accordance with the law of a member state and having their registered office, central administration or principle place of business within the member state or contracting state of the European Economic Area. If, however, only the registered office is located in the aforementioned territory, the operations of the respective company must be genuinely linked on an ongoing basis with the economy of the member states or contracting states.

Other foreign citizens or corporations only enjoy protection under section 87b) of the Copyright Act as provided for by international treaties concluded by the Federal Republic of Germany or the European Union. Consequently, section 127a) of the Copyright Act gives up the principle of national treatment laid down in the Revised Berne Convention in favour of the principle of reciprocity. The reason for this approach which is in accordance with article 11 of the Database Directive, may well be the United States Microchip Protection Act.[297]

---

296 Database Directive, article 11(1) reads as follows: "The right provided for in article 7 shall apply to databases whose makers or rightholders are nationals of a member state who have their habitual residence in the territory of the Community".

297 Lehmann, "Die neue Datenbankrichtlinie und Multimedia", *N.J.W.-Co.R.* 1996, at pp. 249 and 251, and Koch, in Lehmann (ed.), *Rechtsschutz und Verwertung von Computerprogrammen*, 1993, at pp. 342 *et seq.*

The express restriction to German nationals in section 127a)(1) of the Copyright Act, however, does not violate the European Community Treaty since section 120(2) of the Copyright Act expressly states that nationals of other member states of the European Union or the European Economic Area are equal to German citizens. From this it follows that a British citizen enjoys the same degree of protection for the database he created as a German national. For the sake of clarity it should nevertheless be mentioned that a member state national who acquires a database which was created outside the European Union does not acquire a *sui generis* right to protection under section 87c) of the Copyright Act because the Database Directive does not provide for a derivative acquisition of the *sui generis* right by means of an agreement with the maker of the database. The reference to "rightholders" in article 11(1) of the Directive is therefore redundant and the German legislator consequently refrained from incorporating it into the Copyright Act.

Finally, section 137g) of the Copyright Act contains a transitional arrangement for databases created before January 1, 1998, to which section 23, sentence 2, section 53(5), and section 55a)(1), sentence 2, of the Copyright Act apply, as well. Likewise, sections 87a)-87d) of the Copyright Act apply to databases the making of which has been completed between January 1, 1983, and December 31, 1997. In this case, the term of protection starts to run on January 1, 1998.

Classifying on-line transactions under Traditional Copyright Terms

10-73   Although the problems posed by the emergence of on-line communications and digital media may not be unheard of and can therefore, to a large extent, be handled by applying already existing provisions to new uses of copyrighted material, it would be short-sighted to think that no amendments to the current legislation are required. Quite to the contrary, the question must be raised whether the traditional notions of "publishing", "distribution" and "broadcast", which have long-served their purpose in a pre-digital world where books and magazines together with radio and television-broadcasts were the mediums of choice, are still the right tools to cope with on-line transactions. Even the introduction of satellite broadcasting and Cable Television did not require a redefinition of the term "broadcast" as used by section 15(2) of the Copyright Act. The use of interactive services via the so-called "Information Super Highway" or "Infobahn", however, will change this.

It appears questionable whether or not digitising photographs or paintings with a scanner can be considered a "reproduction" within the meaning of section 15(1), number 1, of the Copyright Act which only grants the author the exclusive right to exploit his work in tangible form. One could therefore argue that the process of digitising conventional artistic works does not result in a physical copy of the respective work and can consequently not be considered as a violation of the author's exclusive right of reproduction. This, however, would be wrong since German courts as well as German literature have taken the opposite view.[298] Regardless of the fact that digitalisation in itself does not immediately result in a tangible copy of the converted work, it cannot be contested that it renders the work perceptible to the human senses, either by means of an on-screen display or a regular printout, and this must remain the ultimate yardstick when it comes to determining the applicational scope of the right of reproduction conferred on the author by section 15(1), number 1, of the Copyright Act.[299]

Long before the so-called "Infobahn" became part of colloquial German, the prevailing opinion among German scholars assumed that the storage of a copyrighted work in a computer's main memory (Random Access Memory — RAM) — even if it occurs only for a minimum period of time — must be considered as a reproduction in the legal sense,[300] and takes the view that any storage of a work of authorship in a computer's RAM "for more than a short period of time" should be considered a reproduction within section 15 of the Copyright Act. Assuming for the time being that this view is correct, it is only logically consistent to treat any uploading or downloading to one's own server connected to the Internet as a reproduction within the meaning of section 16 of the Copyright Act which principally requires the consent of the author. Likewise, the transmission of a protected work from one personal computer (or a server for that matter) to somebody else's Bulletin Board System (*B.B.S*) or FTP site[301] is generally considered to involve multiple reproductions of the relevant work.[302]

Although, from a legal point of view, this approach appears entirely correct, it almost inevitably leads to the conclusion that even the most transitory storage of copyrighted works on any server used in the transmission of said work to its final destination entails a reproduction. The potential pitfall becomes apparent if one considers that by simply surfing the "World Wide Web", anyone who dares to take a look at a new site consequently

---

298 OLG Düsseldorf, *G.R.U.R.* 1997, 75 — "Elektronisches Pressearchiv"; Lehmann, "Digitalisierung und Urhebervertragsrecht", in Lehmann (ed.), *Cyberlaw*, at pp. 57 *et seq.*; Vahrenwald (ed.), *Recht in Online und Multimedia*, section 6.1, at p. 4; Schwarz, *Recht im Internet*, section 3-2.1, at p. 14.

299 Schricker-von Ungern-Sternberg and Loewenheim, *Urheberrecht*, section 16, marginal note 9.

300 Fromm, Nordemann and Vinck, *Urheberrecht*, 8th ed., section 16 marginal note 1; Ulmer, *Urheber- und Verlagsrecht*, 3rd ed., 1980, section 45 IV and *G.R.U.R.* 1971, at pp. 297 and 300 *et seq.*; Katzenberger, *G.R.U.R.* 1973, at pp. 629 and 632; Schwarz, in Schwarz (ed.), *Recht im Internet*, section 3-2.2, at p. 14; Vahrenwald, in Vahrenwald (ed.), *Recht in Online und Multimedia*, section 6.1, at p. 6.

301 FTP stands for File Transfer Protocol. This Protocol enables Internet users to both download files from remote computers and upload files to computers to which they have access.

302 It should be noted that although it is becoming increasingly popular to speak of "data" or "files" being transferred on the Internet, one must not forget that said data more often than not eventually amount to an original work of authorship which deserves every bit of protection as conventional (non-digitalised) works under the 1965 Act.

becomes a potential copyright infringer. As of today, this problem has largely gone unnoticed by German literature, perhaps because it questions the quickly adopted view that effective copyright protection makes it mandatory to treat even temporary storage in a computer's memory as "reproductions" in the legal sense. The objection that unlike sending works by "snail mail", works transmitted via the Internet are sent in several packages of data rather than in a single package and rarely, if ever, are stored in their entirety on intermittent servers located between the sender and the addressee of a file does not lead to a different outcome.

The reason for this lies in the fact that copyrighted works are not only protected in their entirety but in any part that constitutes an original work of authorship.[303]

The view that even temporary browsing of the World Wide Web may result in reproductions of copyrighted works is further corroborated by national as well as supranational law. Firstly, section 69c), number 1, of the Copyright Act grants the owner of rights in a computer program the exclusive right to permit or prohibit the permanent or temporary reproduction of a computer program, or parts thereof, by any means and in whatever form. The European Union proposal for a protocol to the Berne Convention states:

". . . contracting parties confirm that the permanent or temporary storage of a protected work in any electronic medium constitutes a reproduction within the meaning of article 9 (1) of the Berne Convention. This includes acts such as uploading and downloading of a work to or from the memory of a computer."

10-74 While this approach has already stirred considerable controversy in the United States[304] it must be said that due to the increased vulnerability of digitised works which results from the ease and speed of copying by means of a simple key stroke, it is necessary to consider the uploading and downloading of copyrighted works to or from a server as a process which intervenes with the author's exclusive right of reproduction.

The question remains, therefore, whether the well-established principle of fair use as codified in sections 45-53 of the Copyright Act has really become obsolete in the digital domain. After all, striking a balance between the legitimate interests of authors and publishers, on the one hand, and the general interest of the public, on the other, has always been one of the primary goals of copyright protection. Since the European Database Directive already

---

303 Hubmann, *Urheberrecht*, 7th ed. 1991, at p. 21 V, and Bortloff, "Tonträgersampling als Vervielfältigung", *Z.U.M.* 1993, at pp. 476 and 477.

304 Samuelson, "Big Media Beaten Back", *Wired*, March 1997, at pp. 61 *et seq.*, describing the opposition of United States telephone, computer, software and on-line service companies against article 7 (2) of the W.I.O.P. copyright treaty adopted during the W.I.O.P. conference of December 2-20, 1996 in Geneva.

created a veritable "fait accomplit" in this regard, the only viable solution to the browsing problem appears to lie in the creation of a legal presumption that anybody offering his works on the World Wide Web without password protection agrees to the temporary storage of his Web page in a computer's RAM as long as it serves the exclusive purpose of viewing said Web page with a browser.[305] For the sake of clarity, however, it would be highly desirable to create an express exemption in the Copyright Act which would at least allow users to view Web pages not protected by a specific password without running the risk of infringing on someone else's copyright.

The on-line transmission of copyrighted works does not infringe on the author's exclusive right of distribution since section 17 of the Copyright Act always requires the production of a physical copy of the respective work. If a protected work is transmitted via a computer network, however, neither the original nor any copy of it is being moved from the place where it is kept.[306] Rather than receiving the original or a copy made by the author or a third party, the individual who "surfs the net" obtains another copy which is made at the very moment he accesses the respective Web site.[307]

One of the most controversial issues discussed in connection with on-line transmissions of copyrighted works involves the right of reproduction in intangible form and notably the Broadcasting Right granted in section 15(2), number 2, of the Copyright Act. Section 20 defines the Broadcasting Right as the right to render the work accessible to the public by wireless broadcast such as radio or television transmission by cable[308] or similar technical devices. The legislative intent to section 20 of the Copyright Act states that a wireless broadcast is any transmission of signs, sounds or images by electromagnetic waves which are emitted from a broadcasting station and can be accessed by any number of receivers and re-transformed into signs, sounds or images.[309] A broadcasting station is any organisation which carries out the transmission of public broadcasts, be it by wireless radio waves, satellite, cable or telecommunications.[310]

Although the term "wireless broadcast" therefore principally includes all types of transmissions regardless of the technical means employed, the majority of German scholars have taken the view that on-line communications do not fall under the traditional notion of "Broadcasting" within the

305 Schwarz (ed.) in: *Recht im Internet*, section 3 2.2, at p. 23 and Schwarz, "Urheberrecht im Internet" at http://www.jura.uni-muenchen.de/Institute/Internet II.html.
306 Schwarz, *Recht im Internet*, section 3-2.2, at p. 17.
307 Correctly, Vahrenwald, *Recht in Online und Multimedia*, section 6.1.2, at p. 2.
308 Although the actual language of the law reads "by wire", the meaning is the same.
309 *Amtl.Begr. zum Copyright Act*, at p. 50, reprinted in *U.F.I.T.A.* 45 (1965), at pp. 240 and 265; see also *B.G.H.Z.* 79, at pp. 350 and 353 — "Kabelfernsehen in Abschattungsgebieten".
310 Vahrenwald, *Recht in Online und Multimedia*, section 6.1.3.1, at p. 2.

meaning of section 20 of the Copyright Act. The main arguments against such an interpretation of section 20 of the Copyright Act are:

- Unlike radio and television, the Internet is not a passive medium but an active, or even interactive, one and companies or individuals offering their services or works on the Internet are not broadcasting "programs" in the traditional sense;[311] and
- The term "broadcast" in section 20 of the Copyright Act demands that the work be made publicly available to a large group of people at once (the audience).

10-75   Although intriguing at first glance, the latter argument is not a strong one. Section 15(3) of the Copyright Act does not require any transmission to a multitude of people at the same time but simply states that the reproduction of a work is public if it is destined for an audience, unless this group is personally connected to each other or the organiser of the underlying event. In addition, it has been pointed out correctly that the wording of section 20 of the Copyright Act does not demand that the public be reached by the respective transmission. The Viewdata Systems (BTX) of the 1980s have consequently been considered to entail a public reproduction within the meaning of section 20 of the Copyright Act.[312] The "sequential communication to the public" triggered by on-line transmissions of protected works coincides with the author's exclusive right to reproduce his work in public, as any regular television broadcast does.[313] The Austrian Federal Supreme Court has also adopted this view in the late eighties.[314]

This does not mean that the current legal framework provided for by the copyright laws of European Union member states does not require any changes and/or amendments in this respect. In its Green Paper on Copyrights and Related Rights in the Information Society[315] the Commission showed justified concern that there is no definition of the word "public" in current intellectual property law which tackles the issues raised by on-line communications. If the Information Society is to progress, the definition of the term "communication to the public" needs to be applied in a uniform way. If this task is left to the member states, there certainly will remain an undeniable risk that some of them may leave on-line transmissions in the public domain

---

311 Dreier, "The Cable and Satellite Analogy", in Hugenholtz (ed.), *The Future of Copyright in a Digital Environment*, at pp. 57 and 58.

312 Fromm and Nordemann, *Urheberrecht*, 8th ed., at p. 20, marginal note 6, and Katzenberger, *G.R.U.R. Int.* 1983, at pp. 895 and 902.

313 Taking the same view Schwarz, "Der urheberrechtliche Schutz audiovisueller Werke im Zeitalter der digitalen Medien", Becker and Dreier (ed.), *Urheberrecht und digitale Technologie* 1994, at pp. 118 *et seq.*

314 OGH OBl 1987, 82 and *G.R.U.R. Int.* 1987, at p. 609; see also Walter, "Zur urheberrechtlichen Einordnung der digitalen Werkvermittlung", *Medien und Recht* 1995, at pp. 125 and 126.

315 COM 95 382 of July 19, 1995.

while others might make transmissions to the public subject to an exclusive right.[316] The fact alone that this issue is still largely disputed not only in Germany but in a great number of other member states of the European Union and in the United States as well should be reason enough to harmonise national copyright laws on a Union-wide level.

The first argument against considering on-line communications public broadcasts which relies on the different characteristics of on-line communications as opposed to entirely passive/receptive television broadcasts, is somewhat more convincing. Supporters of this view will nevertheless soon be in for a surprise. Industry giants such as Microsoft and smaller enterprises such as PointCast are about to bring us the most radical change in our perception of new and old media by the introduction of so-called "push" services. Although such services have already taken up operation at the time this chapter is being written, "surfing the web" today is by and large tantamount to retrieving information with the help of "search engines" such as Yahoo or Alta Vista and the archetypal browser framed on a two-dimensional hypertext page. The user needs to click on hyperlinks to access the information he is looking for which may then be downloaded to his computer — if he is lucky. In other words, the user pulls the information from a Web site or an FTP server, whereas a television program is being pushed to its viewers.

The new "push" media will change all that and ultimately lead to the convergence of networks and broadcasts. While "push" will have many faces in the not so distant future, one of the first manifestations of this new medium has been introduced with a subscription system offered by PointCast, in which news flashes and other types of information related to specific topics are delivered directly to the screen of the subscriber's computer whenever it is not being used for another application. Unlike with simple screen savers, the subscriber has instant access to additional information on a given topic on his screen. Assuming that compression techniques continue to improve at the current speed, a user will soon be able to read an article on hurricanes and tornadoes and run across a link to the feature film *Twister* which will provide him with a much more vivid description of what tornadoes are like than any text-based information ever could. Another user may want to learn more about health food and read a study on various diets only to be interrupted by a commercial on cereals. Contrary to its predecessor — the World Wide Web as we know it today — "push" media will arrive automatically at our desktops, in e-mail, and on pagers and "Personal Digital Assistants". "Push" media will always be on and can, therefore, only be turned off rather than accessed in an interactive search session.[317] Traditional

---

316 Puller, "The Green Paper on Copyright and Related Rights in the Information Society — Is it all a Question of Binary Numbers?", *E.N.T.L.R.* 1996, at p. 80 and 88.

317 Kelly and Wolf, "Kiss Your Browser Goodbye: The Radical Future of Media beyond the Web", *Wired* March 1997, at pp. 1 and 12 *et seq.*; see also Seeger, "Webcasting — Volles Programm auf allen Kanälen", *Global on-line* 4/1997, at pp. 26 *et seq.*

boundaries between written information and sounds and moving images give way to a combined "push-pull" experience which will enable Home Scholars,[318] or employees of large companies as well as a multitude of individual users to watch their "Web Programs" over small and middle scale "individual" broadcast networks.

This scenario should make it abundantly clear that in the digital era on-line communications may no longer be denied broadcast status simply on the grounds of their nature as "interactive media". The fact is that there is no such thing as "the transmission of copyrighted works on the Internet". Instead of taking a generalist approach to on-line communications, we will need to distinguish between the various manifestations of the Internet.

The Law Applicable to Copyright Protection on the Internet: the Emitting-State Principle

10-76   The rise of "push-pull" media will fuel the ongoing controversy with regards to the direct or analogue application of the European Community Cable and Satellite Directive.[319] According to its legal intent, the Directive was originally designed to create a uniform legal framework "for crossborder broadcasts within the Community, notably by Satellite and cable".[320] Due to the fact, however, that satellite broadcasts raised much of the same questions as on-line transmissions do today, namely, whether a broadcast shall be governed by the laws of the emitting state or by the laws of the receiving state as well, the question arises if the Cable and Satellite Directive should be applied *mutatis mutandis* to on-line transmissions.

While the Directive itself does not provide for a definition of the terms "broadcast" or "program", article 1 (2) makes it clear that a satellite broadcast relevant under copyright law must be assumed to exist if the program-carrying signals are introduced into an uninterrupted chain of communication and are also emitted from the satellite to the public. From this it follows that with respect to a satellite broadcast, the programming signals can be transported via one or more intermediate satellites or via several terrestrial radio link stations before the satellite transmission, and this will still be treated as a uniform act of broadcasting if no interruption

---

318 Fromm and Nordemann, *Urheberrecht*, 8th ed., section 15, marginal note 4, as well as Schricker-v. Ungern — Sternberg and Loewenheim, *Urheberrecht*, section 16, marginal note 40, correctly point out that regular lectures held in universities are public events; see also BGH, *G.R.U.R.* 1983, at pp. 562 and 563 — "Zoll und Finanzschulen", in which the German Federal Supreme Court took the view that the reproduction of protected works in schools are "public" within the meaning of section 15(3) of the Copyright Act.

319 European Community Directive 93/83/EEC of September 27, 1993, on the co-ordination of certain rules concerning copyright and rights related to copyright applicable to Satellite Broadcasting and Cable Retransmission, O.J. L 248, October 6, 1993, at p. 15 (Cable and Satellite Directive).

320 See recital 3 of the Directive.

has occurred and if the broadcast is made accessible to the public.[321] Although data on the Internet never travel in a single package but are always divided into several packages by the Internet protocol currently in use, the definition of broadcasts in article 1(2) of the Directive applies to on-line Transmissions especially if one takes into account that ordinary Web Pages, as well as the "push-pull" media described above, will soon be transmitted via satellites as well.

Such a direct or analogous application of the Directive would have far-reaching consequences. The reason for this lies mainly in article 1(2)(b) of the Directive according to which the communication to the public occurs solely in the member state where, under the control and responsibility of the broadcasting organisation, the program-carrying signals are introduced into an uninterrupted chain of communication leading to the satellite and back down towards the earth. This means that the broadcast may be authorised or prohibited in the broadcasting state alone. With respect to broadcasts from outside the European Union, article 1 (2) (d) fictitiously relocates the place of satellite broadcasts within the territory of the European Union if the copyrighted act has been carried out in a non-Community state where the law on satellite broadcasts does not live up to the standard provided in the Directive. This country-of-origin principle will soon be implemented into national German law by a new section 20a) of the Copyright Act which largely adheres to the language of the Directive.[322] While said principle may offer a viable solution for conventional satellite broadcasts, its application to on-line communications would prevent an effective enforcement of copyrights in the digital domain. First, the national copyright laws of the member states are far from offering an equal degree of protection, and electronic commerce is still largely unregulated. It has therefore rightfully been pointed out that before the country-of-origin principle may be applied to on-line communications, it would be a *conditio sine qua non* to first harmonise the relevant laws of the member states with regard to the protection of Digital Transmission Acts, the level of rights to be granted and the categories of rightholders.[323]

Apart from possible friction caused by different levels of protection in national copyright laws, the application of the country-of-origin principle would make it much more difficult for authors and rightholders to enforce their rights in countries not belonging to the European Union. The copyright law of the United States, for example, may offer the same degree of protection to works transmitted electronically as German copyright law, but it would put a considerable burden on the copyright holder if he were to sue

---

321 For a more detailed review of the respective provisions of the Directive, see Liegl, Leupold and Bräutigam, "Copyright Protection in Germany" in Campbell (ed.), *The Comparative Law Yearbook of International Business, Special Issue 1997 Copyright Infringement.*

322 See the bill of the federal government of the 4th Law to Amend the Copyright Act, *Bundestagsdrucksache* 13/4796 of June 4, 1996, at p. 4.

323 Vandoren, "Copyright and Related Rights in the Information Society", in Hugenholtz (ed.), *The Future of Copyright in a Digital Environment*, at pp. 153 and 159.

an infringer before a court in Texas rather than in Cologne. Lastly, the country-of-origin principle would also disadvantage the copyright holder within the European Union with regards to the calculation of damages. Due to the difficulties in determining the actual losses suffered from unauthorised copying, German courts have traditionally allowed the infringing party to pay an appropriate licensing fee.[324] If a copyrighted work is directed into a German *B.B.S* from a small member state such as Luxembourg, the licence fee will be considerably lower under the country-of-origin principle because the licensing fee always corresponds to the size of the respective territory whose laws govern the infringing act.[325] Not the laws of the emitting state where the broadcast emanates from, but the law of the receiving state should therefore govern on-line transactions.

Acquisition of Rights

10-77   The question of whether or not the principles guiding cable and satellite broadcasts should be applied to on-line communications is also closely intertwined with the acquisition of rights. The draft section 20b of the Copyright Act, which implements article 9(1) of the Cable and Satellite Directive, provides that the exclusive right to authorise or refuse to authorise the cable re-transmission may only be exercised by a collecting society or, in accordance with the exception made in article 10 of the Directive, a broadcasting organisation. The idea of a mandatory exercise of rights by collecting societies in the digital domain, however, has already been rejected by a number of authors claiming that this concept would have the twofold disadvantage that the rights in a digital work could no longer be granted on an exclusive basis, and that any licensing fee would have to be calculated in a general manner for certain groups of works and/or types of uses. Under this view, the administration of digital works by collecting societies would exclude individual remuneration in relation to the particular commercial value of a particular work with regard to a particular use.[326] This argument is certainly valid and needs to be considered carefully. First, of all, it should be mentioned that the Commission has already rejected the concept of compulsory licensing in its Green Paper on Copyrights and Related Rights in the Information Society, and rightly so. A compulsory license would be irreconcilable with article 2 of the Revised Berne Convention which only concedes the contracting states the option to permit the reproduction of protected works "in certain special cases" and under the express condition

---

324 BGH, *G.R.U.R.* 1990, at pp. 1008 and 1009 — "Lizenzanalogie"; BGH, *G.R.U.R.* 1975, at pp. 323 and 325 — "Geflügelte Melodien", and *B.G.H.Z.* 26, at pp. 349 and 352 — "Herrenreiter — Fall".

325 Vahrenwald, in Vahrenwald (ed.), *Recht in Online und Multimedia*, section 6.1.3.1.

326 See, *e.g*, Dreier, "The Cable and Satellite Analogy", in Hugenholtz (ed.), *The Future of Copyright in a Digital Environment*, at pp. 57 and 60.

that such reproduction does not conflict with normal exploitation of the work and does not unreasonably prejudice the legitimate interests of the author. While a *mandatory* exercise of rights by collecting societies would not intrude on the author's rights as severely as a compulsory licence, it would nevertheless significantly curtail the author's leeway by depriving him of the possibility to grant exclusive licences to his works.

Furthermore, one must take into account that, in the near future, "digital watermarks" will allow the exact identification of digitised works regardless of whether they are sold "offline" on a CD-ROM or DVD or transmitted on-line via the Internet. As for conventional CDs, record companies are already applying a Source Identification Code (SID) which allows them to trace the factory which manufactured a specific CD.[327] New identification and encryption technologies[328] will certainly permit the author a much better control over his work than in the pre-digital era.

The flip side to this regained control, however, lies in the difficulties encountered by producers of multimedia products who wish to acquire the rights in the works they use. An average multimedia CD-ROM often carries many sound clips, video sequences and texts, and the producer needs to obtain a licence from every author of even the shortest video clip if he wants to avoid potential cease-and-desist and/or damage claims from third parties. With the fast progress of compression techniques and the use of cable and satellite transmissions, the same, and even more elaborate multimedia works that are today offered on CD-ROMs will soon be available on-line. Already, it is virtually impossible for publishers who want to transfer back volumes of scientific journals from the past decades onto CD-ROMs to obtain the necessary permissions from the respective authors. Under German copyright law, the distribution of copyrighted works onto CD-ROMs constitutes a new use within the meaning of section 31(4) of the Copyright Act and is therefore not covered by license agreements concluded before 1985. In this connection, it has been pointed out that "at the present time, the greatest risk would seem to come at a corporate level, from publishers and systems integrators who push to introduce (multimedia) products without clearing the use of the material they are including".[329]

---

327 Liegl, Leupold and Bräutigam, "Copyright Protection in Germany", in Campbell (ed.), *The Comparative Law Yearbook of International Business, Special Issue 1997, Copyright Infringement.*

328 For a detailed description of the proposed Electronic Copy Management System (ECMS), see Wand, "Dreifach genäht hält besser! — Technische Identifizierungs- und Schutzsysteme", *G.R.U.R. Int.* 1996, at p. 897; in Germany, Dr. Eckhard Koch of the Fraunhofer Institute for Graphical Data Processing in Darmstadt has developed a system for electronic copyright protection (SysCoP); Scheuerl, "Rechtlicher Schutz durch die digitale Signatur der Werke", *Blick durch die Wirtschaft*, February 18, 1997, at p. 10, and Rinke, "Bildergeschichten — Digitale Wasserzeichen unterstützen den Urheberrechtsschutz im Internet", *c't report* 8/1997, at pp. 162 *et seq.*

329 Gumsey, *Copyright Theft*, 1995, at p. 126; see also Melichar, "Verwertungsgesellschaften und Multimedia", in Lehmann (ed.), *Internet und Multimedia Recht, Cyberlaw*, at pp. 207 and 208.

Recognising this problem, the European Community Commission has suggested that the collecting societies create a "one-stop-shop-intermediary" in its Green Paper on Copyright and Neighbouring Rights in the Information Society.[330] The introduction of a centralised database containing all the relevant data which is needed for obtaining a licence in the respective work (name and address of the author and/or the collecting society which has been entrusted with the exercise of rights, amount of the licence fee) would ultimately complement the use of technical identification systems rather than counteract them. In June 1996, the German collecting societies[331] have responded to the growing need for such a centralised information system and founded the "Clearingstelle Multimedia" or Clearance Centre Multimedia (CMMV) which will begin operations in the fall of 1997. The CMMV will operate as an electronic clearing system and provide producers of multimedia products with a special database that can be accessed via the Internet and will deliver information on all types of work falling within the area of responsibility of its members.[332]

While the foundation of the CMMV certainly satisfies a long overdue need for multimedia producers and authors alike, it is only a first step in the right direction and must ultimately lead to the creation of a true "one-stop-shop" which not only provides its users with the information necessary to obtain a licence, but also grants licenses itself. In all likelihood, the CMMV will take on this task as soon as the current information system has proved to be successful and the authors and industry players represented by the various collecting societies have given their approval to such centralised authorisation of rights. Until recently, most European collecting societies did not dispose of the right to authorise the use of works in the digital domain.

Among the first to authorise on-line transmissions of musical works were the British Collecting societies MCPS — Mechanical Copyright Protection Society — and PRS — Performing Right Society — which are granting

---

330 COM (95), 382 final, at p. 76.
331 These are GEMA (*Gesellschaft für musikalische Aufführungsrechte und mechanische Vervielfältigungsrechte*), which grants licenses to musical works; GVL (*Gesellschaft zur Verwertung von Leistungsschutzrechten*), which represents the interests of performing artists and record companies, as well as film producers; VG Wort (*Verwertungsgesellschaft Wort*), which exercises the rights of authors and publishers of literary works, VG Bild-Kunst (*Verwertungsgesellschaft Bild-Kunst*), which represents, among others, the rights of photographers and cartoonists; VFF (*Verwertungsgesellschaft für Film und Fernsehgesellschaften m.b.H.*); VGF (*Verwertungsgesellschaft für Nutzungsrechte an Filmwerken m.b.H.*); GWFF (*Gesellschaft zur Wahrung von Film- und Fernsehrechten m.b.H.*), and GÜFA (*Gesellschaft zur Übernahme und Wahrnehmung von Filmaufführungsrechten m.b.H.*), which all represent the interests of movie producers as well as broadcasting stations, and the AGICOA (*Urheberrechtsschutz G.m.b.H.*), which represents national and foreign film producers in connection with cable re-transmission.
332 The database may be accessed at http//www.promedia.de or contacted at the following address: CMMV, Rosenheimerstrase 11, 81667 Munich, Germany.

licenses to the Cerberus Digital Jukebox.[333] In the United States, the BMI and ASCAP (Association of American Publishers) are also licensing musical works for on-line uses.[334] In Germany, the aforementioned GEMA[335] has recently revised its agreement with authors and publishers of musical works. It now expressly mentions the right to include musical works (with or without text) in databases, documentation systems, or similar storage systems and to transmit the works electronically.[336] Furthermore, the agreement covers the right to use these works — with or without text — for the making of motion pictures and any other multimedia product and their use by means of databases or other storage systems allowing an interactive use of such works.

Despite this broad wording, the new agreement does not make it mandatory for authors and publishers to let GEMA exercise their rights. It makes the acquisition of rights subject to the condition that the author and/or publisher does not inform GEMA within four weeks of obtaining knowledge of a grant of on-line rights by the aforementioned collecting society in a written notice that he wishes to exercise his rights himself. This should enable authors and publishers of sound recordings to exercise their rights in the most appropriate manner, depending on the circumstances of each individual case, provided that they are duly informed about their right to reclaim control over their work. Collecting societies who wish to follow GEMA's lead will still must establish the licensing fees to be charged for on-line transmissions of copyrighted works.[337] At this time, no precise figures have been fixed for such uses.

Liability of Service Providers and Unauthorised Users for Copyright Infringements

Until recently, the liability of service and access providers as well as of content **10-78** providers was predominantly discussed in connection with the proceedings instituted against the service provider CompuServe by the Munich district attorney in 1995. The United States landmark decisions of *Playboy Enterprises* v. *Frena*,[338] *Sega Enterprises* v. *Maphi*,[339] and notably *Religious Technology Centre* v. *Netcom Online Communication Services*,[340] as well as the

---

333 Melichar, "Verwertungsgesellschaften und Multimedia" in Lehmann (ed.), *Internet- und Multimediarecht (Cyberlaw)*, p. 205, 213.
334 Kreile and Becker, *G.R.U.R. Int.* 1996, 677, 685 *et seq.*
335 Paragraph number 1-77.
336 Section 1 lit. h of the agreement.
337 Gackelick, "Gema pocht auf on-line Rechte", *Screen Multimedia* 1/1997, at p. 80.
338 839 F.Supp. 1552 (MD Fla. 1993).
339 857 F.Supp. 679 (MD Cal. 1994).
340 907 F.Supp. 1361 (ND Cal. 1995).

Information and Communication Services Act[341] however, caused a number of German authors to discuss the liability of users and access as well as service and content providers under civil law and notably their responsibility for copyright infringements.[342] The following explanations will provide an overview of the most recent case law regarding the liability of service and content providers to re-examine it in light of section 5 Information and Communication Services Act which, for the first time, codifies principles for ISP and OSP liability.

European and American Case Law Regarding on-line Service Provider Liability

10-79   The first cases that dealt with the liability of on-line providers were, as anyone might have expected, decided by American courts and, until recently, remained the only judicial decisions in this new field of law.[343]

In *Playboy Enterprises* v. *Frena*[344] the United States District Court for the Middle District of Florida had to decide whether the posting of unauthorised copies of Playboy's "Playmate" pictures on a *B.B.S*, infringed on Playboy Enterprises' copyrights. George Frena, the bulletin board operator, claimed that he could not be held liable for copyright infringement because:

- He himself had not uploaded the pictures onto his server;
- He had no actual knowledge of the fact that said pictures were stored on his server; and
- He had blocked the site from further access as soon as he was notified regarding the infringing material.

10-80   The court, however, rejected Frena's claims and came to the conclusion that Frena was liable for direct infringement of the plaintiff's exclusive right to display and distribute the photographs in dispute because he had made

---

341 Act for the Regulation of the Basic Conditions for Information and Communication Services, *Bundestagsdrucksache* 966/96 of December 20, 1996, at p. 1(Information and Communication Services Act).

342 From an American perspective see, *e.g*, Rieder, "Copyrights im Cyberspace — Copyright Probleme im Internet aus U.S.-amerikanischer Sicht", *W.R.P.* 1996, 859; more generally Schwarz, "Urheberrecht im Internet", http://www.jura.uni-muenchen.de/ Institute/internet II.html; Koch, "Rechtsfragen der Nutzung elektronischer Kommunikationsdienste", *B.B.* 1996, at p. 2049; Spindler, "Deliktsrechtliche Haftung im Internet — nationale und internationale Rechtsprobleme", *Z.U.M.* 1996, 533; Vahrenwald in Vahrenwald (ed.), *Recht in Online und Multimedia*, section 6.2.6.4, at pp. 1 *et seq.*; Waldenberger, "Zur zivilrechtlichen Verantwortlichkeit für Urheberrechtsverletzungen im Internet", *Z.U.M.* 1997, at p. 176.

343 For a concise summary of the following cases see also Hagen, "On-Line Service Provider Liability: The latest United States Copyright Conundrum", 7 *RENT LR* 1996, at pp. 274 *et seq.* and the statement of William J. Cook before the House Judiciary Committee Courts and Intellectual Property Subcommittee, reprinted in 12 CLSR (1996), at pp. 150 *et seq*, as well as Rieder, "Copyrights im Cyberspace, — Copyright Probleme im Internet aus U.S.-amerikanischer Sicht", *W.R.P.* 1996, 859.

344 839 F.Supp. 1552 (MD Fla 1993).

available storage space on his server and enabled users of his *B.B.S* to gain access to the pictures. The court also emphasised that intent or knowledge is not an element of infringement, and thus even an innocent infringer is liable for infringement penalties.

A somewhat different approach was taken by the United States District Court for the Northern District of California in *Sega Enterprises Ltd* v. *Maphia* in which the operator of a *B.B.S* had actively solicited his users to upload illegal copies of Sega's video games onto his server. From there, the games could be downloaded by anybody who was willing to pay the requested fee, as well as to anybody who had purchased the defendant's hardware equipment which was designed for the use of the illegal copies of the plaintiff's games. Regardless of the fact that the defendant did not know exactly when the games were uploaded to or downloaded from his *B.B.S*, the court held that due to the defendant's role in the copying and his provision of facilities, direction, knowledge and encouragement of his customers to upload the infringing material onto his server, he had to be considered a contributory infringer of Sega's copyrights in the games.[345]

In *RTC* v. *Netcom*[346] the Church of Scientology instituted legal proceedings against a former member of the church who had posted "secret" and hence previously unpublished works of L. Ron Hubbard on a newsgroup where it could be read and downloaded for free by anybody owning a personal computer and a modem. When the access provider refused to remove the unauthorised copies from the *B.B.S*, RTC sued the former church member's Internet access provider, as well as the actual operator of the bulletin board from which the copies were retrieved. The United States District Court for the Northern District of California enjoined the former Scientology member from further posting the works under dispute on the *B.B.S*, but disagreed with the *Sega* decision and held that ISP and *B.B.S* operators cannot not be considered direct infringers. Furthermore, the court granted Netcom's move for summary judgment and dismissed RTC's claim that Netcom as well as the *B.B.S* operator be held liable for vicarious infringement because no evidence had been delivered that they had a direct financial interest in the postings.[347] The court did not render a final ruling on the question of contributory liability because it still needed to be clarified whether or not the defendants knew that Hubbard's works were offered in their newsgroup.

---

345 Under United States copyright law, contributory infringement can be assumed whenever the infringer had actual knowledge of the infringing activity and induced, caused, or materially contributed to the infringing conduct of another; see *Gershwin Publishing Corp.* v. *Columbia Artists Mgt, Inc.*, 443 2d 1159 (2d Cir. 1971).

346 907 F.Supp. 1361 (DND Cal. 1995).

347 Under United States copyright law, the concept of vicarious infringement liability relies on the tort concept of *respondeat superior* and can be assumed whenever the infringer disposes of the right and the ability to supervise the infringer while having an obvious and direct financial interest in the exploitation of copyrighted materials, see *Shapiro, Bernstein & Co.* v. *H. L. Green Co.*, 316 et seq. 2d 304, 307 (2d Cir. 1963).

In the Fall of 1995, the Church of Scientology's fight against unauthorised postings of Hubbard's writings on the Internet arrived in Europe. In
Scientology v. Providers and Karin Spaink,[348] RTC sued a Dutch citizen and
22 Internet providers for copyright infringement before the District Court
of The Hague.[349] Spaink had posted the "Fishman Affidavit", which had
been deposited during a judicial proceeding against former Scientology
member Steven Fishman, on her home page where it could be accessed by
users via the above-mentioned ISPs. The affidavit contained substantial
parts of a previously unpublished work entitled "Operating Thetan" (OP)
as well as a book entitled Ability, which had been published in the United
States as well as in The Netherlands. After its deposition in the United States
Court, the affidavit had been publicly available for sale.[350] When asked to
remove the affidavit from her home page, Spainks edited her home page and
henceforth only displayed single passages of the Fishman affidavit together
with personal comments. RTC requested that the defendants stop infringing
on its copyrights in the works posted by Spaink and specifically required the
Internet access providers to:

- Remove all infringing documents from their servers as soon as they
  have been notified of its existence;
- Disconnect the user who uploaded the unauthorised copies to their
  services; and
- Provide them (RTC) with the names and addresses of third parties who
  had published said copies either through their own computer system
  or through computer systems that were under their control.

10-81   The court followed Spaink's argument that the passages under dispute fell
under her "right to quote" described in article 15A of the Dutch Copyright
Act and rejected RTC's claim that the works "OT" and "OT III" were
previously unpublished and, therefore, not quotable by taking the view that
there was no reason to assume that judicial depositions may not be regarded
as "publications" within the meaning of article 15A of the Copyright Act.

With respect to Internet access providers, the court held that such
providers did nothing more than provide their customers with the opportunity of publication and that they "are unable to exert influence over or have
knowledge of what a person who gains access to the Internet through them
will supply". The court concluded that there was — at least in principle —
no reason to hold Internet access providers liable for copyright infringements

---

348 G.R.U.R. Int. 1997, at p. 556.
349 This judgment may be retrieved in English from Karin Spaink's Internet site at
http://www.xs4all.nl/~kspaink/cos/verdleng.html. For a detailed review of the facts of the
case, see also Bortloff, "Neue Urteile in Europa betreffend die Frage der Verantwortlichkeit
von Online-Diensten", *Z.U.M.* 1997, at pp. 167 and 170 *et seq.*
350 Bortloff, "Neue Urteile in Europa betreffend die Frage der Verantwortlichkeit von
Online-Diensten", *Z.U.M.* 1997, at pp. 167 and 170 *et seq.*

committed by third parties. At the same time, however, the court conceded that a responsibility might be assumed in a situation where "it is unequivocally clear that a publication of a user is wrongful and where it may be assumed with reason that this is known to the access provider, for instance because someone has notified the provider thereof".

In *Societé Art Music France et Societé Warner Chappell France* v. *Ecole Nationale Superieure des Telecommunications et al*,[351] Warner Chappell of France and other plaintiffs brought an action against Xavier Bergot, a student of the French Academy of Telecommunications (ENST), who had digitised several songs of Michel Sardou and other French musicians and later posted them on his private home page on the Academy's server where they could be downloaded for free. Warner Chappell sued not only the student who had posted the songs but also the head of the Academy's computer department and the Academy itself. The professor in charge of the administration of the computer department claimed that he did not have any responsibility whatsoever for the different services offered on the Academy's servers.

The Academy, in turn, took the view that Mr. Bergot had been granted a private space on its servers which the Academy was not willing to censor. Since Mr. Bergot had signed a declaration that he would not make any abusive use of his server space, the Academy claimed that only Mr. Bergot himself could be held liable for the uses he made of his server space. The Academy pointed out that it had taken "conservatory measures" by rendering the disputed Web site inaccessible to the public as soon as it had received the court's subpoena. The student claimed that the illegal reproduction of a copyrighted work demanded that it be made with the intent to make it available for public use and that he never had this intention since he merely stored the songs in his "private domicile" on the Academy's server. According to Mr. Bergot, the creator of a Web page does not in any way "broadcast" its content. Consequently, only the users visiting the site are making reproductions of its content without having been invited to do so.

The court dismissed the application for an injunction against the head of the computer department without reasoning its decision. As for the Academy, the court held that it had satisfied its obligations under French law by closing down the site and informing its students accordingly. Considering the fact that the student had placed the relevant songs on his home page, the court nevertheless held him liable for copyright infringement since anyone who permits third parties to visit his Web site readily accepts any public use of his reproductions stored on that site. The fact that the defendant had not engaged in any act of "broadcasting" the songs was regarded as irrelevant

---

351 *Revue Internationale du Droit d'Auteur* 1996, at pp. 361 *et seq*; the authors wish to thank the head of the International Department of GEMA, Mr. Nils Bortloff, for providing them with a copy of the court's ruling.

because the court took the view that the right to visit his site contained the implicit consent to make copies of its content.[352]

Liability of Service and Access Providers under the Information and Communication Services Act of 1996

10-82   The first distinction that must be drawn with respect to the question of liability for copyright infringements in the digital domain is the one between service and access providers. While service providers such as AOL or CompuServe are offering their own "channels"[353] simple access providers restrict themselves to offering their customers access to the Internet. Section 5 Information and Communication Services Act regulates the responsibility of both types of providers.

First, section 5(1) of the Tele Services Act provides that service providers are responsible for their own content in accordance with the general laws. According to the legislative intent,[354] the term "responsibility" refers to the service provider's direct liability. A service provider who makes available his own content or adopts content created by a third party as its own, may consequently be held liable if such content infringes on somebody else's rights. The reference to "civil laws" in section 5(1) of the Tele Services Act covers not only torts under the general provision of section 823 of the Civil Code but copyright infringements as well.[355] The opposite view[356] misjudges the clear wording of section 5 Information and Communication Services Act and fails to provide a convincing reason why copyright infringements should be excluded from the scope of this provision.

This liability for one's own content corresponds to the consistent case law of the German Federal Supreme Court, according to which anyone who uses a copyrighted work must make sure that the person from which he acquired his licence was entitled to authorise such use.[357]

This does not mean, however, that service providers may be held liable for every file that may be downloaded from their servers as section 5(2) of the Information and Communication Services Act makes it clear that service providers are responsible for somebody else's content only to the extent that:

- They have actual notice of such content;
- They dispose of the technical means to prevent others from accessing such content; and

---

352 *Revue Internationale du Droit d'Auteur* 1996, at p. 368.
353 AOL offers a comprehensive list of servicing areas such as "computers and software" which, *inter alia*, contains software ready for downloading, a "newsstand" with digital versions of major newspapers and magazines, and "the people connection" by which users can join chat rooms to communicate with other members, to name but a few.
354 Bundestagsdrucksache 966/96 of December 20, 1996, at p. 21.
355 Correctly, Vahrenwald in Vahrenwald (ed.), *Recht in Online und Multimedia*, section 6.2.6.1, at p. 2.
356 Waldenberger, "Zur zivilrechtlichen Verantwortlichkeit für Urheberrechtsverletzungen im Internet", *Z.U.M.* 1997, at pp. 176 and 183.
357 BGH *G.R.U.R.* 1959, at pp. 331 and 334, and BGH *G.R.U.R.* 1960, at pp. 606 and 608.

- They can be reasonably expected to block the respective site from other users. The latter condition acknowledges the fact that service providers, as a rule, do not have any control on what is being posted in the myriad of newsgroups they offer. In addition, it would be unreasonable to demand that the entire data on a given server be erased if only specific sites stored on that server are actually carrying illegal content. The requirement of actual rather than constructive knowledge of infringing content, however, might encourage service providers and bulletin board operators to be intentionally ignorant of infringing activities.[358] In this respect, the standard of liability set forth by section 5(2) of the Information and Communication Services Act deviates from the general rules regarding the liability of direct and contributory or vicarious infringers set forth in section 97 of the Copyright Act and reflected in the case law of the German Federal Supreme Court.

To assess the potential liability of service and access providers properly, one **10-83** must distinguish between the forbearance of future infringements, on the one hand, and damage claims, on the other. Under section 97(1) of the Copyright Act, anyone who unlawfully infringes on someone else's copyright may be subject to a cease-and-desist claim from the author or copyright holder. German law therefore applies the same standard of liability as the United States District Court for the Middle District of Florida, in *Playboy Enterprises* v. *Frena*,[359] as far as the forbearance of future infringements comes into play". While the service provider himself cannot be considered a direct infringer in relation to Third Party content published on his servers, he may well be regarded as a vicarious infringer if one takes into account that the German Federal Supreme Court has repeatedly taken the view that indirect liability ensues from any act by which the infringer provides a third party with the technical means and/or facilities to copy protected material without the permission of the copyright owner or rights holder.[360] By permitting the use of his server, the provider adequately causes the infringements by a third party and may, therefore, be compelled to stop such infringing activities.

    Contrary to these general principles of liability developed by the German Federal Supreme Court, section 5(2) of the Information and Communication Services Act suggests that a service provider must have had *actual* knowledge of the existence of infringing material on his server before he can be compelled to remove it. In practice, however, this deviation from the

---

358 See the report of President Clinton's working group on intellectual property rights ("White Paper"), at p. 122 and Hagen, "OnLine Service Provider Liability: The Latest United States Copyright Conundrum", 7 *E.N.T.L.R.* 1996, at p. 274 and 278.

359 839 F.Supp. 1552, where the court held that "intent or knowledge is not an element of infringement, and thus even an innocent infringer is liable for infringement.

360 *B.G.H.Z.* 42, 118—"Personalausweise beim Tonbandgerätekauf" as well as BGH *G.R.U.R.* 1961, at p. 91—"Tonbänder Werbung" and BGH *G.R.U.R.* 1964, at p. 94—"Tonbandgeräte-Händler".

aforementioned case law will not have severe consequences because, even under the current wording of section 5(2) of the Information and Communication Services Act, a provider will be obliged to delete any infringing material from his server as soon as he has been informed accordingly by the author or copyright holder, provided that it is technically feasible for the provider to remove only the infringing material while his other services remain unaffected. The latter restriction should not create a significant obstacle to the enforcement of the author's claim since it will be the exception rather than the rule that infringing content cannot be removed from a server without blocking or deleting other data.

For damage claims to be justified, German courts have always required the plaintiff to show that the defendant either wilfully or negligently infringed somebody else's copyright and that, as a consequence of such infringement, the copyright holder suffered a monetary loss.[361] Negligence within the meaning of section 97(1) of the Copyright Act may be assumed whenever the infringer had constructive knowledge, i.e, knew or had reason to know that he committed a copyright infringement.[362] The German Federal Supreme Court has traditionally applied rather rigid standards when it came to the question of whether an infringer acted negligently. Under the pertinent case law, publishers of non-periodical printed matters such as novels, as well as editors of periodical printed matters such as newspapers and magazines, are obliged to check whether the respective novel or article is indeed an original work of authorship of their client or whether it was licensed to them by a copyright holder who is entitled to grant sublicences.[363] The same holds true for printing works,[364] video printing laboratories[365] and television stations.[366] The question, therefore, is whether an Internet service provider may be treated in the same way as publishers or editors of printed matters or broadcasting stations.

The authors of this chapter take the view that the answer to this question must clearly be negative. Service providers do not and cannot exercise the same kind of control, if any, over postings from their users as publishers and editors do with their books and magazines. In addition, it has correctly been pointed out that unlike publishers, service providers do not "cause" specific content to be published,[367] but merely grant their customers access to server

---

361 BGH, *G.R.U.R.* 1960, at p. 606—"Eisrevue II"; KG, *G.R.U.R.* 1959, at p. 150—"Musikboxaufsteller"; Schricker, *Urheberrecht*, section 97, marginal notes 50 *et seq.*; Fromm and Nordemann, *Urheberrecht*, 8th ed., section 97, marginal notes 31 *et seq.*

362 Schricker, *Urheberrecht*, section 97, marginal note 52.

363 BGH, *G.R.U.R.* 1959, at pp. 331 and 334 — "Drei Groschen Roman II"; *B.G.H.Z.* 14, at pp. 163 and 178 — "Constanze II".

364 LG Berlin, *G.R.U.R.* 1950, at p. 339.

365 OLG Köln, *G.R.U.R.* 1983, at p. 568.

366 KG, *U.F.I.T.A.* 86 (1980), at pp. 249 and 252 *et seq.*; see also Schricker, *Urheberrecht*, section 97, marginal note 52.

367 OLG Düsseldorf, *N.J.W.* 1980, at p. 71.

space.[368] The suggestion that service providers are similar to kiosk owners[369] is similarly erroneous since the latter make an active choice as to which newspapers and magazines they wish to sell to their customers, while the former do not have any possibility to select the contents of the news groups they offer.[370] Furthermore, the view that service providers may be compared to kiosk owners and, therefore, be held liable for any infringing material on their servers, overlooks the fact that the German Federal Supreme Court has early on taken the view that one would expect too much of a simple kiosk owner if one were to ask him to check the multitude of magazines and newspapers he sells for their content.

Considering all of the above, the deviation from the constructive knowledge standard of liability as codified in section 97 of the Copyright Act is ultimately justified. Section 5(2) of the Information and Communication Services Act strikes an acceptable balance between the interests of content and service providers and does not prevent an author from asserting damage claims against a provider who refuses to remove infringing material from his server after being informed about the existence of such material by the author or copyright holder or any other person, provided that the infringing material may be removed without affecting other non-infringing content on the same server (which should be the rule rather than the exception). To give a practical example, the Internet service providers in *Sega Enterprises Ltd. v. Maphia*,[371] who refused to comply with Sega's request to remove pirated video game programs from their servers- would be liable for damages under section 5(2) of the Information and Communication Services Act.

The actual knowledge standard now adopted by section 5(2) of the Information and Communication Services Act was also applied in a recent settlement concluded between the American music publisher Frank Music Corp. and CompuServe. According to United States literature, CompuServe committed itself to use "reasonable best efforts" to avoid future infringements but assumed no subsequent liability for any infringement unless CompuServe had actual knowledge of its subscriber's activities.[372] Furthermore, there is a certain likelihood that the actual knowledge standard might be adopted by the United States Congress, which is discussing proposals for an amendment of the 1976 Copyright Act with regards to on-line transmissions

---

368 Waldenberger, "Zur zivilrechtlichen Verantwortlichkeit für Urheberrechtsverletzungen im Internet", *Z.U.M.* 1997, at pp. 176 and 186.
369 Rütter, *jur-pc* 1992, at pp. 1812 and 1221.
370 Correctly, Waldenberger, "Zur zivilrechtlichen Verantwortlichkeit für Urheberrechtsverletzungen im Internet", *Z.U.M.* 1997, at pp. 176 and 186.
371 857 F.Supp. 679 ND Cal. 1994.
372 Keller, "Conducting the Intellectual Property Audit in Cyberspace", in *Conducting Intellectual Property Audits* 1996, at p. 483, as cited by Hagen, "On-line Service Provider Liability: The Latest United States Copyright Conundrum", 7 *E.N.T.L.R.* 1996, at pp. 274 and 278, footnotes 78 and 75.

of protected material.[373] In a statement before the House Judiciary Committee,[374] it has been suggested to introduce a duty for Internet service providers to remove materials on notice from copyright owners that such material infringes on a copyright.

Access providers who do not offer any original content but merely enable their users to gain access to the Internet obviously cannot assume any responsibility over the myriad of Web pages already on offer since they have neither placed them nor do they have the technical means or even the right to remove them. This fact is aptly mirrored by section 5(3) of the Information and Communication Services Act, which provides that service providers[375] may not be held liable for third-party content to which they convey access. Under section 5(2), sentence 2, of the Information and Communication Services Act, an automatic and short-term storage of third-party content is considered as conveying access to such content. This means that the customary, and automatic, storage of highly frequented Web sites in proxy servers maintained by service and/or access providers does not have the consequence that such Web pages are being offered by the provider who stores them only temporarily on his server. The legal intent of section 5, subsection 3, of the Information and Communication Services Act, however, emphasises that a "temporary storage" is one of "a few hours — not of days".[376]

Finally, section 5(4) of the Information and Communication Services Act provides that the obligation to block access to unlawful content as set forth in the general laws will remain unaffected if the service provider, while complying with the secrecy of telecommunications laid down in section 85 of the Telecommunications Act, obtains knowledge of such content, provided closing off the infringing site is technically feasible and reasonable. This provision seeks to make it clear that access providers do not only enable their customers to access the Internet, but also to perform telecommunications services and would, therefore, violate their secrecy obligations if they were to ask their employees to check (*i.e*, read and disclose to their superiors) the content which has been transmitted individually in point-to-point communication, *e.g*, by e-mail. To stop unlawful private communications (*e.g*,

---

373 S. 1284, 104th Cong., 2nd Sess. (1995); H.R. 2441, 104th Cong, 2nd Sess. (1995); see also Hagen, "Online Service Provider Liability: The Latest United States Copyright Conundrum", 7 *E.N.T.L.R.* 1996, at p. 274.

374 Statement of William J. Cooke before the House Judiciary Committee Courts and Intellectual Property Subcommittee continued hearing on the NII Copyright Protection Act of February 8, 1996, 12 C.L.S.R. (1996), at pp. 150 and 153 *et seq*.

375 Although section 5(2) of the Information and Communication Services Act refers to "service providers" (*Diensteanbieter*), it really means "access providers" within the meaning used in this chapter; this becomes clear from the legal intent in *Bundestagsdrucksache* 966/66, at p. 22, which compares "service providers" to telecommunications companies because they simply serve as a conduit for third-party content without having any possibility whatsoever of influencing such content.

376 Bundestagsdrucksache 966/96 of December 20, 1996, at p. 22.

the regular mailing of unauthorised copies of computer software via FTP to private individuals), either the author or copyright holder himself or public authorities must, therefore, inform the provider that illegal material is being stored in the cache memory of his server(s).

As the diverging case law of European courts demonstrates, it will be necessary to develop common rules for the liability of Internet service and access providers on a supra-national level if the emergence of safe havens for copyright pirates is to be avoided. Given the fact that the Internet is a medium that knows no national boundaries, the ideal framework to establish common standards for ISP liability would be the next W.I.O.P. conference which should lead to an amendment to the current treaties.[377]

PROTECTION OF DOMAIN NAMES

Due to the ever increasing commercialisation of the Internet, domain names **10-84** have become valuable economic goods, just like all other intellectual property. The fact that the registration of domain names is still unregulated and therefore not governed by any codified law, but conducted by an organisation which, until recently, could not even be considered a legal entity, stands in sharp contrast to the importance of domain names in the realm of electronic commerce. For readers not yet familiar with the domain name concept, the following introduction will describe the meaning and structure of domain names before discussing the legal implications of the "domain grabbing" under German law.

The Domain Name Concept

Put simply, domain names are the digital equivalent to an individual's or **10-85** company's address in the real world. A software company having its headquarters at 55 Cambridge Parkway in Cambridge, Massachusetts, may therefore be visited under its physical address or under its World Wide Web address http://www.lotus.com. This address consists of the top-level domain (.com) and the sub-level domain (.lotus). The top-level domain indicates the nature of the organisation that operates the host computer under this specific address. In our example, the top-level domain ".com" indicates that the owner of the address "lotus.com" is a commercial company. Other top-level domains include the acronyms ".edu" for schools and universities, ".gov" for governmental departments, ".net" for network operators, ".mil" for military and ".org" for other organisations.

---

377 Bortloff, "Neue Urteile in Europa betreffend die Frage der Verantwortlichkeit von Online-Diensten", *Z.U.M.* 1997, at pp. 167 and 175, who points out that this issue has expressly been omitted from the agenda of the recent diplomatic conference in Geneva in December 1996.

It is important to note, however, that apart from the increasingly popular domain ".com", the aforementioned top-level domains are almost exclusively used in the United States. In Germany as in other (European and non-European) countries, top-level domains only indicate the geographical location of the server, such as ".de" for Germany, ".uk" for the United Kingdom and ".fr" for France. It has been suggested that this lack of differentiation is partly responsible for the deadlock situation that has occurred in the solution of domain name disputes. The second-level domain (in our example ".lotus") stands for the user's name and may be chosen freely. In addition to the top-level and second-level domains described above, a domain may contain various sub-level domains that lead the prospective customer to specific products or offers. The Web site of the German car manufacturer "BMW", for example, may be accessed under the address "BMW.de" but motorcyclists may prefer to go directly to BMW's motorcycle pages under "motorradBMW.de".

The Registration Process

10-86   Since a specific Internet domain may only be used by one company or individual, domain names need to be registered. The registration of new domain names was first conducted by the Internet Assigned numbers Authority (IANA) at the University of Southern California, but later was delegated to various Network Information Centres of which the InterNIC registers all descriptive domain names. Locative domain names, on the other hand, are allocated by the *Reseaux IP Européens* in Amsterdam which, in turn, delegated its registration powers to National Network Information Centres (NICs) in which local service providers are organised. For Germany, the *Interessenverband Deutsches Network Information Centre eG* (IV-DE-NIC) operates the primary name server for all domain names below the top-level domain ".de" at the University of Karlsruhe's Computation Centre.

The collection of registration fees has been delegated to a limited liability company, the IntraNet G.m.b.H.[378] To register a given domain name, the user must file an application with his ISP, and submit it to DE-NIC which in turn makes sure that the domain name has not already been allocated to another user before registering it. As in other countries, domain names are basically allocated on a "first-come, first-served" basis without any examination of the intended use of the domain name or the registrant's entitlement to register.

---

378 DE-NIC's home page may be accessed at "http://www.nic.de/"; the IntraNet G.m.b.H. may be e-mailed at "denicinkasso~intra.de".

Domain Name Dispute Policies

Unlike trade mark ownership which is governed by the German Trade Mark 10-87
Act of 1995, the allocation and use of Internet domain names is not
regulated by any codified law, and the registration process itself is left to an
omnipotent co-operative which is not subject to any scrutiny by public
authorities. While this in itself gives rise to serious concerns with regards to
a possible violation of German and European anti-trust law which cannot
possibly be discussed in this chapter, the lack of any clear-cut rules for the
solution of domain name disputes creates additional confusion.

Network Solution's Domain Name Policy

Increasingly faced with litigation over domain names, the NSI adopted its 10-88
own domain name dispute policy to escape potential liability for registering
a given name.[379]
    Under this policy, which was substantially revised in September 1996,
the applicant must represent that the registration of the domain name
selected does not interfere with or infringe on the rights of any third party,
and that the domain name is not being registered for any unlawful purpose.
Under article 5 of the policy, a domain name dispute is initiated by NSI's
notification that a registered domain name violates the legal rights of a third
party which is generally assumed if a second-level domain name is identical
"with a valid and subsisting foreign or United States Federal Registration
trade mark or service mark that is in full force and effect and owned by
another person or entity".
    To succeed with his claim and get the domain name removed from NSI's
register, the complainant must deliver a certified copy of the (foreign or
United States) Trade Mark Registration which must not be older than six
months. Furthermore, the complainant must inform the registrant about his
claims and provide NSI with a copy of such notice. NSI then determines the
date of registration of the respective domain name. If it turns out that the
respective domain name has been registered after the date of first use of a
complainant's identical trade mark or the effective date of the trade mark
registration, NSI will ask the registrant to prove his ownership of the domain
name by submitting a certified copy of his own trade mark registration. If
the registrant fails to provide such evidence of his ownership of a protected
trade mark or if the registrant's domain name has been "activated" after the
date of first use and registration of the complainant's trade mark, NSI will
put the registrant's domain name on a hold status after a transitional period
of 90 days, during which the registrant will be allowed to use both the old
domain name which has been challenged by the trade mark owner, and the

379 Network Solution's domain name solution policy may be accessed on the World Wide Web
at "http://www.internic.netldomain. policy".

new one which will be assigned to him by NSI. If the registrant does not comply with NSI's request for proof of ownership of a trade mark identical to the domain name within 30 days of NSI's request or simply refuses to rescind its use of the respective domain name, NSI will place the domain name on hold status right away. In both cases, the hold status — during which neither the registrant nor the complainant may use the name — remains in force until NSI receives either "a properly authenticated temporary or final order by a Federal or State Court in the United States having competent jurisdiction and stating which party is entitled to the domain name" or "other satisfactory evidence from the parties of the resolution of the dispute", section 6 (f) of the NSI policy.

The registrant, however, may effectively prevent NSI from putting his domain name on hold status simply by filing suit in any court of competent jurisdiction in the United States and providing NSI with a file stamped copy of his action.[380] Likewise, NSI will not put the domain name on hold status if the complainant files suit against the registrant. While section 7 (c) of the NSI policy states that regardless of being named as a party to the proceeding, NSI will abide by all temporary or final court orders directed at either the registrant or the complainant, the policy also makes it clear that NSI does not act as an arbiter of disputes between registrants and complainants and that the policy merely contains "guidelines" which may be applied by NSI in case of domain name disputes without conferring any rights to registrants or third-party complainants. Network Solution's domain name dispute policy can therefore be considered a non-binding "soft law".

The Situation in Germany: Not Even a Dispute Policy

10-89   Unlike its American counterpart, the DE-NIC has not yet adopted any true Domain Name Dispute Policy. The only statement regarding such disputes may be found in the general information to ".de"-domains published by the IntraNet G.m.b.H..[381] Section 2 of this information states that the organisation filing the application for the registration of a domain name "is responsible for the rights to the name being respected and any conflicts with registered or protected names which may arise must be resolved". The statement continues to declare that the applicant confirms that, to his knowledge, no rights of third parties are being violated by the application and that neither DE-NIC nor its bookkeeping office may be held responsible for any conflicts regarding domain names. If such conflicts arise, DE-NIC expressly reserves the right to refrain from assigning the respective domain name.

---

380 Section 7 (a) of the NSI policy.
381 An English version of this information may be retrieved under "http://www.intra.de /englishinfo.htm".

Legal Basis for Cease-and-Desist Claims in Domain Name Disputes under German Law

While Network Solution's policy is a far cry from what is really needed to   10-90
protect the legitimate interests of American as well as foreign corporations
in their name, the lack of even the most basic guidelines for disputes over
second-level domain names in Germany certainly did not make it any easier
to bar a registrant from reserving a company's name for the sole purpose of
selling it back to its rightful owner. As in the United States, a number of
German companies discovered that their names had already been registered
by individuals who seized the opportunity to acquire the respective domain name before the company did. Among the most prominent victims
of this variety of on-line piracy was Germany's leading bank, Deutsche
Bank A.G. which (temporarily) lost its domain name equivalent to
Wordchannel, an American domain trader. In one of the most recent
cases, German Sports Television (DSF) brought suit against Con:action,
a limited liability company which had registered not only the domain
"DSF", but also the designations "Eurosport" and "Sportschau" before
DSF could register them.

   Since there is no codified law which explicitly regulates the registration
and use of domain names and the NSI policy merely contains non-binding
guidelines, German courts had to revert to general provisions of the Civil
Code, as well as to trade mark and unfair competition law. A corporation
wishing to regain control over its domain name which has already been
registered by a third party, may base its cease-and-desist claim regarding any
future use of its name as an Internet domain on section 12 of the Civil Code,
as well as section 17 of the Code of Commercial Law (HGB), which regulate
the right to bear a name, sections 4 and 5 in connection with sections 14 and
15 of the German Trade Mark Act and finally sections 1 and 3 of the German
Law against Unfair Competition (Unfair Competition Act). The following
paragraph will discuss these provisions and their application to Internet
domains in light of the recent case law, as well as the forthcoming introduction of new top-level domains.

Right to Bear Name under the Civil Code and the Commercial Code

In section 12, the Civil Code grants the owner of a name the right to ask a   10-91
third party which infringes on his legitimate interest in his name by challenging his right to use said name or by using the same name without being
authorised to do so to eliminate any interference with his interests resulting
therefrom. If further interference is imminent, the owner of the name may
file an injunction suit against the unauthorised user. While the extensive
case law that interpreted this provision will not be discussed indetail in this

context,[382] it shall be noted that a given denomination serves as a name within the meaning of section 12 of the Civil Code if it is suitable for distinguishing one individual or legal entity from another and is consequently considered as the name of its holder.[383] The use of a name may be considered "unauthorised" if and to the extent that said use creates a likelihood of confusion as to identical names or the danger of dilution of a famous business name.[384] The following discussion of the pertinent case law will show that these primary functions of a name in the legal sense, are well fulfilled by domain names as well.

10-92   **The Heidelberg.de Case**   The first lawsuit over a domain name that came before a German court was filed by the city of Heidelberg, which claimed that the use of the domain "Heidelberg.de" by a small software company infringed the right to bear its name under section 12 of the Civil Code.[385] Originally, the defendant had informed city officials that it intended to create an on-line database which would contain information on the Rhine-Neckar region and could be retrieved by tourists seeking up-to-the-minute information on local events before their trip. When the city indicated that it was not interested in possible co-operation, the software company registered the domain and later refused to release it by claiming that:

- Internet users did not expect the domain "Heidelberg.de" to be identical with the city's home page and that the disputed address was not used as a name within the meaning of section 12 of the Civil Code;
- The city of Heidelberg could choose a slightly different domain name such as "Stadt-Heidelberg.de";
- There are two other places bearing the name "Heidelberg" in Germany; and
- There are more than 400 families in Germany bearing the name "Heidelberg" from which it must follow that the city of Heidelberg cannot claim an exclusive right to the domain "Heidelberg.de".

10-93   The Mannheim District Court rejected all of the defendant's arguments and held that the city could ask the software company to refrain from any future use of the domain "Heidelberg.de" on the grounds of a violation of section 12 of the Civil Code. The court took the view that anyone surfing the Internet would not only expect information about the city of Heidelberg

---

382   For an in-depth review of the various decisions of the German Federal Supreme Court as well as lower courts see Klippel,"Der zivilrechtliche Schutz des Namens" and the commentary on section 12 of the Civil Code, in Staudinger, *Civil Code.*

383   *B.G.H.Z.* 11, at p. 217; *B.G.H.Z.* 79, at p. 270; Palandt-Heinrichs, section 12 of the Civil Code 2.c (aa).

384   BGH *N.J.W.-R.R.* 1988, at p. 553 and BGH *N.J.W.* 1966, at p. 344.

385   Judgment of the Mannheim District Court of March 8, 1996, reprinted in *C.R.* 1996, at p. 353, and *B.B.* 1996, at p. 2484.

under the corresponding Uniform Resource Locator (URL) but also information from the city of Heidelberg. The mere fact that other largely unknown places as well as a certain number of individuals bear the same name, on the other hand, was not considered essential by the court because, even if this were true and known to a user, the latter would not assume that the domain "Heidelberg.de" would be used by individuals which do not bear the name "Heidelberg" nor have their residence in Heidelberg. Perhaps the most interesting aspect of the court's decision lays in the fact that the court did not have any doubt that domain names serve as a reference to their owner and are, therefore, used as a name within the meaning of section 12 of the Civil Code. Although the Court did not state this explicitly, it rightfully dismissed the defendant's claim as irrelevant that domains are not used as "names" because a user would never access a previously unknown Web site by simply punching in the address in the uniform resource locator (URL) but almost always use a search engine which, in turn, retrieves the relevant site automatically. The court's reasoning that Web sites are not only retrieved with search engines, but published in Internet directories (Yellow Pages) as well was further complemented by the fact that a user who came across the defendant's Web site for the first time would clearly associate the city of Heidelberg with the disputed address.

Kerpen.de In its ruling of December 17, 1996,[386] the Cologne District Court **10-94** arrived at an entirely different conclusion with regard to the function of domain names as names within the meaning of section 12 of the Civil Code although the facts of the case were quite similar to the ones underlying the case decided by the Mannheim District Court. The defendant had registered the domain "Kerpen.de" and the City of Kerpen had applied for an injunction against the registrant which was granted but subsequently revoked by the court after the defendant had filed an objection. The Court took the view that the denomination "Kerpen.de" did not serve as a name within the meaning of section 12 of the Civil Code because the combinations of numbers and letters which make up domain names can be chosen freely and are not necessarily related to the names of their users. For this reason, the court found that domain names may be compared to telephone numbers, bank code numbers or postal zip codes. The court also emphasised that it did not overlook the fact that domain names may serve as an orientation guide to find a specific user on the Web since domain names are often related to the name and function of its user.

According to the court, however, all of this did not make domain names susceptible to protection under section 12 of the Civil Code because this function of domain names to serve as a reference to a specific user is neither a common habit nor is it prescribed by law or commercial practice. If cities

---

386 File number 3 O 477/96, still unpublished.

and other communities were obliged to use a specific domain name, then it would be justified to expect that the municipality of the same name owns the domain.

10-95 **Inadequacy of the Decision of the District Court of Cologne** The authors of this chapter are firmly convinced that this reasoning entirely misses the true meaning of domain names and fails to recognise their primary purpose in on-line transactions. The mere fact that there are currently no fixed rules that prescribe the use of specific domain names does not justify the conclusion that domain names are not generally associated with specific legal entities if they are identical to the regular names. This is more often the case than not if one considers the fact that corporations and small to medium-size businesses usually choose their company's name as their domain name precisely because they want it to be easily retrieved on the World Wide Web. If a maker of camping equipment were allowed to name its Web site "BMW.com", confusion as to the identity of the user of this domain would inevitably occur.

At least in principle, the same holds true for other legal entities, such as cities and local communities since they too want to choose their true name as their domain name to be easily retrievable on the World Wide Web. Internet domain names may indeed be compared to telephone numbers, but not to the ones used in Germany and other European countries, which merely consist of a number of digits, but to the 1-800 numbers used in the United States which usually feature the name of the subscriber.[387] These toll-free numbers indeed serve a similar purpose as Internet domain names in that they are chosen for the same reason: to be easily remembered by consumers. What also speaks strongly in favour of the applicability of section 12 of the Civil Code to Internet domains is the fact that German courts granted telephone numbers as well as teleprinter codes protection under trade mark and naming regulations long before the rise of the Internet.[388]

Considering all of the above, it cannot be seriously contested that domain names serve similar purposes as regular names and are consequently protected under section 12 of the Civil Code. In addition, it has been largely ignored in German literature that section 17, in connection with section 34 of the Commercial Code, protects commercial businesses, *i.e*, single merchants as well as corporations against an unauthorised use of their name as an Internet domain. For the sake of completeness, it should also briefly be mentioned that the suggestion that domain names may not be protected

---

387 *E.g*, 1-800-4-A-DODGE to receive information on that American car manufacturer or 1-800-GO-CLARION for product information from the car audio manufacturer Clarion.

388 BGH *G.R.U.R.* 1953, at p. 290 — "Fernsprechnummer" and OLG Hamburg, *G.R.U.R.* 1983, 191 — "Fernschreibkennung"; see also Kur, "Namens- und Kennzeichenschutz im Cyberspace", *C.R.* 1996, at pp. 590 and 591.

under section 12 of the Civil Code because they merely denominate a certain host server rather than a specific person or entity[389] does not deserve acknowledgement. This becomes clear if one recalls the example of toll-free telephone numbers mentioned in the preceding paragraph: Nobody ever suggested that these numbers designate a specific telephone company, and domain names do not designate the host server used in the transmission of data but always refer to the holder of said domain.[390]

Trade Mark Protection for Internet Domains

Domain names may also be protected as trade marks under the Trade Mark   **10-96** Act of 1995 (*MarkenG*). Section 14(1) of the Trade Mark Act grants the owner of a trade mark the exclusive rights to the respective trade mark and section 14(2) of the Trade Mark Act bars third parties from using an identical or similar sign for identical or similar goods or services as well as from using an identical or similar sign for other goods or services if the protected trade mark is well known and its use by a third party either dilutes its distinctiveness or unfairly exploits the good-will associated with that trade mark. Likewise, section 15 of the Trade Mark Act grants the owner of a business name the exclusive right to use said name or a similar name in the course of business in such a way that it is likely to be confused with the name of its true owner. From this, it becomes clear that trade mark protection for domain names is only available if certain prerequisites are fulfilled.

Use of Protected Trade Mark in the Course of Business First of all, trade   **10-97** mark protection requires the use of a protected trade mark in the course of business. Under the Trade Mark Act of 1995, trade mark protection may be acquired by registering a trade mark with the Federal Patent Office or, without registration, if the trade mark has acquired secondary meaning, section 4, numbers 1 and 2, of the Trade Mark Act, respectively. Such trade mark is used in the course of business whenever it is not used for private purposes but for commercial transactions. Although this condition is certainly fulfilled in cases where one corporation uses another company's name for a Web site on which it advertises its products or services to the public, the question remains whether this is also the case if a private individual registers a specific domain name for the sole purpose of selling it back to its rightful owner.

The authors of this chapter take the view that the answer to this question must be yes as long as the registrant draws some kind of commercial gain from this transaction. Any other solution would ignore the ongoing emergence of

389 Kur, "Namens- und Kennzeichenschutz im Cyberspace", *C.R.* 1996, at pp. 590 and 591.
390 Correctly, Böhm, "Verfügbarkeit und Schutz von Domain Names", see —
    http://www.fu-berlin.de/jura/pages/seminare/seminare/ws96boehmO2.htm.

domain name traders that advertise their services on the Web and charge considerable amounts of money for transferring a particular name to their customers.[391]

The days when private individuals reserved the domain names of famous companies such as Toyota[392] or Deutsche Bank without actually using them, on the other hand, are practically over since DE-NIC in February 1997 abolished the option to make reservations for domain names. It would be premature, though, to assume that the phenomenon of "domain name grabbing" will vanish entirely because of this change of policy. The fact is that the misappropriation of domain names has become more difficult, but individuals who want to make money with Internet domains will probably be able to find a front man who will use the name for his own Web site.

10-98   **Use of a Domain Name as a Trade Mark for Particular Goods or Services**
Under the Trade Mark Act of 1965, only the use of a protected trade mark as a reference to specific goods or services was considered a violation of the exclusive rights of the trade mark owner. With the passing of Directive 89/104 and its transformation into national law by the Trade Mark Act of 1995, the question of whether this principle still applies became controversial. While part of German literature takes the view that trade marks must still be used in relation to particular goods or services to justify any cease-and-desist claims from their owner,[393] the prevailing opinion has given up this criterion.[394]

Although the German Federal Supreme Court has not yet ruled on this issue, the prevailing opinion deserves approval since the requirement that the trade mark must be used in relation to particular goods or services can neither be deduced from the wording or legal intent of the Directive nor from sections 14 and 15 of the Trade Mark Act.[395]

In the end, however, the practical importance of this unresolved question for domain name disputes is rather small since domain names which are used for commercial gains are almost always derived more or less directly from a company's name and are, therefore, associated with that company's goods or services to no lesser degree than the same name in a traditional print advertisement. Home pages of commercial businesses serve very much the

---

391 A comprehensive list of more than 300 ".de" domain names currently offered for prices of up to DM 25,000 can be accessed at "http://www.domain-markt.de"; for a similar domain name trading site dealing in domain names under the top-level domain ".com" see "http://bestdomains.com".

392 See below.

393 See notably, Sack, "Sonderschutz bekannter Marken", *G.R.U.R.* 1995, at pp. 81 and 93 *et seq.* and Keller, "Die zeichenmäßige Benutzung im Markenrecht", *G.R.U.R.* 1996, at pp. 607 *et seq.*

394 Teplitzky, "Abschied von der zeichenmäßigen Verwendung", *G.R.U.R.* 1997; Fezer, "Rechtsverletzende Benutzung einer Marke als Handeln im geschäftlichen Verkehr", *G.R.U.R.* 1996, at p. 566, and Fezer, *MarkenG*, section 14, marginal notes 21 and 31 *et seq.*; Starck, "Markenmäßiger Gebrauch — Besondere Voraussetzung für die Annahme einer Markenverletzung", *G.R.U.R.* 1996, at p. 688.

395 Kur, "Namens- und Kennzeichenschutz im Cyberspace", *C.R.* 1996, at pp. 590 and 591 *et seq.*

same purpose as more traditional ways of advertising with print ads, as well as radio spots which increasingly contain a reference to the manufacturer's Web site address.[396]

Creation of Likelihood of Confusion as to Source of Goods or Services   10-99
Under section 14 of the Trade Mark Act, third parties may not (1) use an identical trade mark for identical goods or services; (2) use an identical or similar trade mark for identical goods or services if said use creates the danger that consumers may confuse the respective goods or services, including the danger that the trade mark used by a third party may be associated with the protected trade mark; and (3) use an identical or similar trade mark for goods or services which are not similar to the ones for which the trade mark enjoys protection if said trade mark is a well-known trade mark in Germany and the use of a similar or identical trade mark by a third party dilutes its distinctiveness or tarnishes its reputation. If the registrant of an identical domain name conducts his business in the same industry, section 14(2), number 1, of the Trade Mark Act therefore grants the owner of a registered trade mark the right to enjoin the registrant from using the domain for goods or services sold under said trade mark. In cases where the registrant uses an identical or similar domain name for similar goods or services, section 14(2), number 2, of the Trade Mark Act grants the trade mark owner the same relief.

It is important to note, however, that the rather strict standard German courts traditionally apply when it comes to examining the likelihood of confusion in trade mark law cannot be applied *mutatis mutandis* to the domain name problem because it would unduly limit the options for registering a different domain name which looks and sounds partly identical to the one already registered. In this context, it has been proposed by some authors,[397] that section 23 of the Trade Mark Act might hold a solution since it provides that the owner of a trade mark or business name may not prevent a third party from using his own name or address in the course of business. This view suggests that if one is willing to concede that the term "address" in section 23 of the Trade Mark Act not only covers regular addresses but Internet addresses as well, the use of a domain name which has been derived from the registrant's own name, company name or trade mark cannot be prohibited even if the domain name closely resembles the protected trade mark.

---

396 Bettinger, "Kennzeichenrecht im Cyberspace: Der Kampf um die Domain Namen", *G.R.U.R. Int.* 1997, at pp. 402 and 409 *et seq*, who distinguishes between the use of a domain name as a simple address on the Web and the use of the same name as a catchword on the respective home page, corporate stationery or even the goods themselves and correctly assumes that the domain is being used as a trade mark in both cases.

397 See, *e.g*, Kur, "Namens-und Kennzeichenschutz im Cyberspace", *C.R.* 1996, at pp. 590 and 593.

Whether this approach really offers a viable solution to the problems caused by the application of traditional trade mark law to Internet domains remains questionable if one considers the fact that section 23 of the Trade Mark Act — unlike its predecessor, section 25 of the 1965 Act — does not create an exception for the use of company names but only permits the use of a regular family name.[398] Besides, section 23 of the Trade Mark Act permits the use of (family) names or addresses, rather than the use of an Internet address derived from a company name. There is no doubt, however, that in case section 23 of the Trade Mark Act does indeed not apply to Internet domains (which will be up to the courts to decide), trade mark owners will have to accept the use of domain names by third parties which would normally, *i.e*, outside the digital domain, be considered an infringement of their trade mark.[399]

The fact that trade mark law does not provide a universal remedy for domain name disputes becomes clear, however, if one tries to resolve the remaining cases in which the registrant uses a domain which is identical or closely similar to a protected trade mark for entirely different goods or services. Here, the trade mark owner is only protected if the requirements set forth in section 14(2), number 3, of the Trade Mark Act are fulfilled, *i.e*, if his trade mark is a well-known one. In principle, corporations such as Siemens or Daimler-Benz could therefore effectively prevent third parties from using their trade marks for products other than cars or household appliances, computers and electronic consumer goods, but smaller businesses with less-known trade marks would be left standing in the rain and could not use its company name or trade mark as an Internet domain. In this context, it has been pointed out that the registration of a domain and its subsequent use for goods or services not similar or identical to the ones offered under a protected trade mark cannot be considered unfair competition within the meaning of section 1 of the Unfair Competition Act nor a tort within the meaning of section 823(1) of the Civil Code .[400]

Likewise, section 15 of the Trade Mark Act does not provide a solution for cases in which two competitors have used the same business name in different regions if both want to use this name as their Internet domain as well. The traditional view that the legitimate interests of a company in its business name are only infringed on if a third party uses the same name or a similar name within the same geographical region does no longer hold true in the digital domain where every content provider is ubiquitous on the Internet. Apart from the application of section 23 of the Trade Mark Act to such cases as well, no other solutions have been offered to reconcile this

---

398 *Amtl.Begr.* to section 23 of the Trade Mark Act, reprinted in *Blatt für P.M.Z., Special Edition* 1996, at p. 74.

399 Correctly, Bettinger, "Kennzeichenrecht im Cyberspace: Der Kampf um die Domain Namen", *G.R.U.R. Int.* 1997, at pp. 402 and 415.

400 Bettinger, "Kennzeichenrecht im Cyberspace: Der Kampf um die Domain Namen", *G.R.U.R. Int.* 1997, at p. 402.

clash of interests. By simply applying the "first-come first-served" principle to companies which have used the same business name in different geographical regions for years without hampering each other would not be satisfactory.

That trade mark law can only partly solve the problems triggered by the registration of Internet domains becomes all the more clear if one considers a recent decision of the Frankfurt Court of Appeal[401] in which the defendant had used the domain "wirtschaft.online.de" (the English equivalent would probably be "business.online.de") for a Web site containing business information derived from the defendant's various business newspapers and magazines such as the *Handelsblatt, Wirtschaftswoche,* and *DM.* The plaintiff asked the defendant to refrain from any further use of the above-mentioned domain on the grounds of an analogous application of section 8(2), numbers 1 and 2, of the Trade Mark Act which excludes the registration of generic trade marks.

Although the court acknowledged the fact that the registration of a generic domain name confers the registrant a factual monopoly over the respective domain and therefore shows some similarity to the cases regulated by section 8(2), numbers 1 and 2, of the Trade Mark Act, which seeks to avoid that single individuals gain a legal monopoly over generic terms, it arrived at the conclusion that this alone does not justify the application of section 8 of the Trade Mark Act. The court pointed out that both cases are not entirely comparable since the registration of a domain name only prevents others from registering (and using) the same name, whereas section 14(2), number 2, of the Trade Mark Act prevents third parties from using similar (and not just identical) trade marks as well. Even more importantly, the court stressed that the main reason why section 8 of the Trade Mark Act cannot be applied *mutatis mutandis* to Internet domains lies in the fact that the legal consequences it provides for applicants which ignore the commonly accepted principle that generic terms are not subject to trade mark protection (refusal to register, deletion of the generic trade mark from the trade mark register) require a state-run examination and monitoring system which is currently not yet available for domain names.

From this it follows that to smooth out the friction caused by the peculiarities of the domain name system, it is necessary to change the system itself rather than the law. The International Ad Hoc Committee (IHAC) recently took the first steps to initiate such a change by submitting to the parties concerned its recommendations for the administration and management of generic top-level domains together with a set of guidelines for the establishment of Administrative Domain Name Challenge Panels.

401 Order of the court of February 13, 1997, reprinted in *W.R.P.* 1997, at p. 341.

Unfair Competition Law

10-100   Apart from trade mark law and section 12 of the Civil Code, cease-and-desist claims can also be supported by section 1 of the Law against Unfair Competition (Unfair Competition Act) which prohibits all actions in the course of business that are irreconcilable with good manners. The typical cases of "domain name grabbing", in which the registration is made for the sole purpose of selling the domain to its rightful owner, clearly fall under this provision. A typical example may be seen in the (still unpublished) decision of the Munich District Court of January 9, 1997.[402] In this case, German Sports Television (DSF) had filed suit against Con:action, a sport news trader which had registered the domains "Eurosport", "Sportschau" and notably "DSF" before DSF itself could register them. The court held that the registration of the aforementioned domain names had obviously been made to compel the plaintiff to enter into a co-operation agreement with the defendant. The defendant's argument that it had registered the domain "DSF" for a charity bearing the name *Deutsch Slowenische Freundschaft* (German-Slovenian Friendship) was rejected because the court arrived at the conclusion that this charity did not, in fact, exist.

The court further emphasised that even if such an organisation existed, the defendant's conduct would still violate section 1 of the Unfair Competition Act because the average user who enters the domain "DSF" into his browser expects to receive sport news from plaintiff's home page rather than information from the defendant's "German Slovenian Friendship". *Bona fide* users are consequently misled to a Web site they never wished to access and the good reputation of the plaintiff is being tarnished if said users blame German Sports Television for not being retrievable on the World Wide Web under its household name.

The latter argument in fact stresses the so-called "channelling" effect already discussed in the relevant literature.[403] The view that this "channelling" function of Internet domain names would also justify it to prohibit the registration of generic domain names, however, appears too far-fetched because the simple fact that such generic domain names can only be registered once is due to the technical peculiarities of the registration process rather than any violation of the good manners in the course of business.[404]

Notwithstanding the fact that other German courts have granted preliminary injunctions against domain name grabbers on grounds of a violation of section 1 Unfair Competition Act[405] this provision is only of

---

402 File number 4 *H.K.O.* 14792/96.

403 Notably Kur, "Internet Domains — Brauchen wir strengere Zulassungsvorschriften für die Datenautobahn?" *C.R.* 1996, at pp. 325 and 330.

404 Bettinger, "Kennzeichenrecht im Cyberspace: Der Kampf um die Domain-Namen", at pp. 402 and 413.

405 See the unpublished order of the Landgericht Frankfurt am Main (Number 2-06 711/96) of January 8, 1997 — "citroen.de" and the Order of the Cologne District Court of June 14, 1996 — "toyota.de", in which the auto manufacturers obtained injunctions against individuals who had registered their domain names.

secondary importance because it applies only if the plaintiff and defendant are competitors in the same branch of business. Whenever this requirement is fulfilled, however, the plaintiff will also own a trade mark identical to the domain name registered by the defendant which gives him the cease-and-desist claims provided by sections 14 and 15 of the Trade Mark Act.

Liability of Service Providers and DE-NIC

Anyone who reads his way through the ever-increasing German literature dealing with domain name disputes will soon realise that, as of today little, if anything, has been said about the liability of the organisation responsible for the allocation of domain names and service providers. **10-101**

Apparently, it is still largely assumed that once a domain name has been released by its registrant, the re-allocation of the respective name represents a mere formality which does not raise any material problems. In practice, however, things are sometimes more difficult than expected. Since the registration of a ".de" second-level domain is carried out by the registrant's service provider, the release of a disputed domain name and its subsequent re-registration always involves two providers, *i.e*, the one of the original registrant and the one of the domain name challenger. The re-registration of a domain name can be a tedious process if the registrant's provider and/or DE-NIC does not respond to the challenger's request for a fast change in ownership of the disputed name. The question of if and how the organisation ultimately responsible for registering domain names (IV-DENIC) may be held liable for any unwarranted refusal to honour the challenger's request for re-registering a domain name in his favour is, therefore, not only theoretical although, as of to date, no such case had reached a German court.

DE-NIC's Liability for Domain Name Registration If one examines the relevant provisions of the German Trade Mark Act of 1995 and the Act against Unfair Competition (Unfair Competition Act) which usually form the legal basis for cease-and-desist claims in domain name disputes, one might at first draw the conclusion that neither the providers themselves nor IV-DENIC may be held liable for the violation of the challenger's rights in a specific domain name if one considers the fact that they do not use the desired domain themselves nor do they keep said name in their register for their own commercial gain or to foster the original registrant's business. More often than not, the reason for delaying the release and subsequent re-registration of a disputed domain name may be found in the desire to escape potential claims from the original registrant or in simple negligence. Section 5 Information and Communication Services Act only regulates the liability of service and access providers for content which is being stored on their servers with their knowledge but leaves any liability for domain name registrations unregulated. **10-102**

10-103 **IV-DENIC as an Infringer under Trade Mark and Unfair Competition Law**
Under German trade mark and unfair competition law not only the individual or legal entity which actually used someone else's trade mark or company name in the course of business but also any third party of which one
must fear that he will intentionally contribute to someone else's illegal
behaviour and thereby adequately cause a violation of another party's rights
in a given (domain) name may be considered an "infringer", provided that
he has the actual possibility of preventing the infringement of the name.[406]
Under this rule, a co-infringer must not act for competitive reasons or use
the domain name in the course of business himself.

Likewise, it is of no importance what kind of contribution he made and
whether he had any competitive interest in violating someone else's rights.[407]
In BGH *G.R.U.R.* 1986, 683 the German Federal Supreme Court made it
clear that a publisher makes a significant contribution to the distribution of
a false allegation because he had the power to prevent its publication. Also,
in BGH. *G.R.U.R.* 1957, at p. 352 (Pertussin II), the German Federal
Supreme Court held a carrier of trade marked goods liable for trade mark
infringement because any further distribution of the goods which were
bearing someone else's trade mark would not have been possible without his
transportation services.

If one applies the aforementioned case law to the DE-NIC in cases where
it ignores the superior rights of trade mark owners in a disputed domain by
maintaining the domain name registration for the original registrant, it is
safe to say that not only the registrant himself but DE-NIC which actually
carried out the registration may be subject to cease-and-desist as well as
damage claims from the owner of an identical trade mark or company name.
By keeping the domain registered, DE-NIC enables the infringer to use it in
the course of business and due to its factual authority in the registration and
maintenance of domain names, it undoubtedly has the technical means as
well as the possibility to at least prevent any trade mark infringements in the
future by putting the disputed domain name on a "hold" status or by
re-registering it for the complainant.

Since its re-organisation as a co-operative under the Co-operative Societies Act,[408] DE-NIC itself has acquired the legal capacity to sue and to be
sued in court, section 17(1) of the GenG, so the enforcement of cease-and-
desist as well as damage claims does no longer fail because of formal reasons.

---

406 *B.G.H.Z.* 14, at pp. 163 and 176 — "Constanze II"; BGH *G.R.U.R.* 1957 at pp. 352 and
353 — "Pertussin II"; BGH *G.R.U.R.* 1976, at pp. 257 and 258 "Rechenscheibe"; BGH
G.R.U.R. 1986, at p. 683—"Ostkontakte"; BGH *G.R.U.R.* 1990, at pp. 463 and 464—I
"Firmenfortführung" and Baumbach and Hefermehl, *Wettbewerbsrecht*, 19th ed., Einl.
UWG, marginal notes 327 *et seq.*
407 BGH *G.R.U.R.* 1990, at pp. 373 and 374—"Schönheits-Chirurgie"; BGH *G.R.U.R.* 1976,
at pp. 256 and 257— "Rechenscheibe".
408 "Genossenschaftsgesetz", (GenG), reprinted in *B.G.Bl. I* of August 19, 1994, at p. 2202.

New Developments

On February 4, 1997, the International Ad Hoc Committee (IAHC) submit-   **10-104**
ted its "Recommendations for the Administration and Management of
Generic Top-Level Domains" ("Proposal") together with its "Proposed
Guidelines Concerning Administrative Domain Name Challenge Panels"
("Guidelines"). The aforementioned Proposal in turn resulted in the establishment of a Memorandum of Understanding on the Generic Top-Level
Domain Name Space on the Internet Domain Name System ("Memorandum"). The primary goal of these new recommendations is the extension of
the current number of domains together with a re-distribution of the
registration powers currently held by the InterNic to a much larger number
of registries.

Introduction of New Generic Top-Level Domains

Article 3 of the Proposal recommends the introduction of seven new generic   **10-105**
top-level domains consisting of three to five letters designating a specific
activity or service offered under such domains. The new top-level domains
are:

> ".firm" for businesses or firms in general;
>
> ".store" for businesses offering merchandise for sale (*e.g*, a department store);
>
> ".web" for entities focusing their activities on the World Wide Web (*e.g*,
> a company offering a search engine);
>
> ".arts" for entities engaged in cultural and entertainment activities (*e.g*,
> galleries or museums);
>
> ".rec" for entities emphasising recreational and/or entertainment activi-
> ties (*e.g*, a gym);
>
> ".info" for entities providing information services such as a tourist board; and
>
> ".nom" for (private) individuals who wish to use their own name on the web.

Whether the introduction of this new set of generic top-level domains will   **10-106**
alleviate the current clash of interests between companies which have the
same name but are offering different goods or services in different areas of
business remains to be seen. However, it is safe to say that the new domains
will not make it easier for businesses to choose the one that most fittingly
reflects their field. A major car dealer, for example, might register its home
page under the ".com" domain. Alternatively, he might also register under
the extension ".firm" or ".store"since he offers tangible goods for sale.
Customers, in turn, may look for the dealer's Web site under the top level

domain ".firm" but be unable to locate it because he could not register under this domain too. An art gallery may register under the top-level domain ".com" since it offers works of art for sale but will probably be better accommodated under the ".arts" domain. The claim that the introduction of the above-mentioned top-level domains will only cause owners of existing ".com" domains to register under the ".firm" and ".store" domains is nevertheless too pessimistic since this problem can be taken care of by allocating only one generic top-level domain to one and the same entity.

Reorganisation of the Registration Process

10-107 Section 7 of the Memorandum calls for the establishment of a Council of Registrars (CORE) under Swiss law and makes it mandatory for registrars to become a member of this Association. Under section 7 lit. e) of the Memorandum, each registrar may assign second-level domains in any generic top-level domain covered by the Memorandum on a fair use, first-come, first-served basis. Article 4 of the Proposal originally suggested that a total number of 28 entities be selected as registrars of domain names and provides that the selection shall be made by means of a regional quota mechanism according to which four applicants will be selected from seven global regions. The regions were to be defined by the World Trade Organisation (W.T.O.) and comprised North America, Latin America, Western Europe, Central and Eastern Europe, the Baltic States and the Commonwealth of Independent States, Africa, the Middle East and Asia.[409] Applicants who wish to acquire a domain registry were obliged to take part in a lottery and satisfy certain financial conditions to become eligible. In addition, each applicant had to pay a U.S $20,000 fee.

It was notably this provision that attracted considerable criticism from the European Commission, which rejected any raffling of registration powers and complained that not a single European company or governmental authority was represented in the IAHC, which consists entirely of American entities and individuals predominantly selected by other American entities and organisations.[410] The Interim Policy Oversight Committee (I.P.O.C.) eventually gave way to this criticism by passing a resolution in May 1997 according to which the financial and technical qualification criteria for becoming a registrar would be maintained but the limit on the number and geographical location of registrars sharing registration activities for generic top-level domains would be removed. When this chapter was completed, details for this new arrangement had not yet been written into a formal proposal.

---

409 A detailed list of the countries belonging to these regions can be retrieved at "http://www.iahc.org/docs/countries.html".
410 *Blick durch die Wirtschaft*, April 29, 1997, at p. 19.

Allocation of Sub-Level Domains and Dispute Resolution Mechanisms

Like section 7 lit. e) of the Memorandum, article 6.1.3 of the Proposal   **10-108**
declares that the allocation of sub-level domains on a "first-come, first-
served" basis shall be maintained. Article 6.2 of the Proposal, however,
declares that:

> ". . . it is desirable that a domain name application include sufficient
> information regarding the applicant and the applicant's intended use of
> the domain name to ensure applicant accountability and to ensure that
> sufficient information is available to enable trade mark owners to assess
> the need for a challenge to the proposed sub-level domain."

One might add here that such information is also necessary to expose   **10-109**
domain name grabbers who do not really have the intention to use the name
for their business but merely seek to register it to sell it back to its rightful owner.

Mediation and Arbitration

Article 7.1 of the Proposal has for the first time established a mandatory   **10-110**
mediation and arbitration process by providing that every application must
contain a clause whereby the applicant agrees:

> ". . . to participate in On-line mediation under the rules of the Arbitration
> and Mediation Centre of the World Intellectual Property Organisation.
> Such mediation is initiated by a copyright holder who wishes to challenge
> the domain name applicant's right to hold and use the second-level
> domain name."

Likewise, each applicant must agree: **10-111**

> ". . . to participate in binding arbitration under the corresponding rules of
> the W.I.O.P. Arbitration and Mediation Centre. Such an arbitration is
> initiated by a copyright holder who wishes to challenge the domain name
> applicant's right to hold and use the second-level domain name."

Whether trade mark owners will, in fact, make use of this option remains to   **10-112**
be seen. Since article 7.1.1 is not in any way binding on the party challenging
a registrant's right to a domain name, trade mark owners will, in all
likelihood, apply for an injunction before their national courts rather than
engaging in a binding on-line arbitration procedure, the outcome of which
may be doubtful and may effectively prevent him from suing the registrant
before a court in his own country once the arbitration panel has rendered its
verdict.

Introduction of Administrative Domain Name Challenge Panels

10-113   Section 2 of the Memorandum provides:

> "... a policy shall be implemented that a second-level domain name in any of the CORE-generic top-level domains which is identical or closely similar to an alphanumeric string that, for the purposes of this policy, is deemed to be internationally known, and for which demonstrable intellectual property rights exist, may be held or used only by, or with the authorisation of the owner of such demonstrable intellectual property rights. Appropriate consideration shall be given to possible use of such a second-level domain name by a third party that, for the purposes of this policy, is deemed to have sufficient rights."

10-114   To ensure the implementation of this policy, section 8 of the Memorandum of Understanding calls for the introduction of so-called "Administrative Domain Name Challenge Panels", the composition and operation of which is regulated in the proposed Guidelines. While it would go beyond the purpose of this chapter to discuss the various indefinite terms used in section 2 of the Memorandum in detail, the most important provisions of the proposed Guidelines shall be dealt with briefly. Section 33 of the Guidelines provides that a challenge procedure shall be initiated with the transmission of a completed form to the W.I.O.P. Centre together with a fee. Once the W.I.O.P. Centre receives a complaint, it immediately posts it on its home page, as provided by section 35 of the Guidelines.

Under section 36 of the Guidelines, if a complaint is lodged within 15 or 30 days from the date on which the registration was first published, then the disputed domain name will be automatically suspended until the challenge procedure is completed, provided that the challenger pays a bond. Subject to the payment of this additional fee, the challenge will be put on a "fast track" and decided within 30 days from the date it was lodged. According to section 74 of the Guidelines, a successful challenge will typically result in a decision that the allocation of the disputed domain name should be excluded from registration and transferred on the challenger if the latter so requests. In special cases, *e.g*, if the respective domain name is identical or closely similar to a trade mark which has been registered "worldwide", the domain name may not only be excluded from registration under its original top level domain but also from registration under several or any other top-level domain over which the Council of Registrars has control, as provided by section 77 of the Guidelines. Once the administrative domain name Challenge Panel has reached a decision, it may be appealed to an Appeals Panel consisting of two or three (the final number of members has not yet been determined) members appointed by the W.I.O.P. Centre from the list of potential members of the panel of first instance and one or two individuals appointed by the Policy Oversight Committee (P.O.C.).

While the creation of common standards for domain name challenges and their definition in the proposed Guidelines is certainly welcome, its dispute resolution potential is somewhat limited. This becomes clear if one takes a closer look at section 6 of the Guidelines, which clearly states that the administrative domain name Challenge Panels does not constitute a legal authority and does not have jurisdiction over persons or over the interpretation and enforcement of national or regional intellectual property laws. In addition, section 7 of the Guidelines states that the challenge procedure cannot preclude resort to a national or regional court. Section 9 of the Guidelines reiterates this restriction to the decision-making powers of the panel by expressly stating that "any case may be brought at any time before, during or after the administrative challenge procedure, to a national or regional court which would hear the dispute under its normal jurisdictional and substantive rules".

Although it would be both impossible and undesirable from a legal perspective if a number of private or semi-official organisations with no clear backing from national or European legislators were to prevent domain name challengers and registrants from enforcing or defending their rights before a court in law, the question remains whether the envisaged panels will not be considered "toothless sharks" which only delay a final and binding verdict on the permissibility of a domain name registration. In addition, section 11 of the Guidelines expressly states that "this policy is binding only with respect to top-level domains which fall in the purview of the Memorandum". The dispute resolution process set forth in the Guidelines, therefore, does not apply to "national" (ISO 3166) top-level domains like ".de" for Germany or ".uk" for the United Kingdom. Furthermore, the panels do not even have any dispute resolution power over the generic top-level domains ".com", ".org" and ".net" until these domains are shared among the CORE registrars. Already existing registrations are only covered by the Guidelines once they are renewed.

The composition of the panels gives rise to concern as well. According to section 32 of the Guidelines, panels shall consist of only one member and only be enlarged by two additional members if one party to the proceeding so requests. In this respect, it is easy to predict that most parties will opt for a three-member panel since a panel with only one member cannot be considered a true "panel" at all. Besides, the Guidelines do not contain any clear provisions on the selection of panel members but merely state in section 31 that "panel members shall be chosen from a list of international experts who are knowledgeable in both fields of trade marks and Internet domain names".

The approach taken by section 43 of the Guidelines which provides that hearings before the panels shall exclusively be conducted via Internet chat software, e-mail or (failing this) by telephone conferences is certainly a courageous one and aptly reflects the change in communications brought about by the medium. Although it will probably take some time before domain name challengers will adapt to this kind of proceeding, it will eventually prove to be a much more practical solution to conduct hearings on-line, rather than ask a party to travel from a remote location where it happens to have its principal place of business to a panel hearing scheduled in Switzerland or elsewhere.

The biggest problem that will still be subject to an extensive discussion and cannot simply be left to the resolution of the ad hoc committee, however, undoubtedly lies in the definition of the somewhat dubious terms "demonstrable intellectual property rights" and "identical or closely similar" contained in sections 65 to 69 of the Guidelines. Section 64 of the Guidelines determines that a domain name shall be deemed to be protected by demonstrable intellectual property rights if the challenger submits documentary evidence in the form of an intellectual property registration certificate (*i.e*, trade mark registration certificates), a search report from a reputable search firm, a court order or authoritative government opinion showing the existence of intellectual property rights or any other "declaration or attestation of relevant government authorities".

As anyone familiar with the protection of trade marks will know, trade mark protection not only ensues from registration but from the use of a mark in the course of business and the acquisition of secondary meaning for that trade mark as well. For Germany, this has been expressly set forth in section 4(2) of the Trade Mark Act. Since such trade marks are not considered a "demonstrable intellectual property right" under the Guidelines, they are excluded from the panel's decision-making powers which is an undesirable consequence of the IAHC's effort to simplify things. The definition of what is to be considered an identical or closely similar domain name necessarily, one must say, deviates from the traditional standards set forth in the national trade mark laws from which it follows that a domain name challenger who failed to obtain a favourable decision from the panel will have a good reason to try his case before a national court of law.

Conclusion

10-115 The above-described difficulties and potential pitfalls notwithstanding, the proposed Guidelines for the resolution of domain name disputes by special administrative panels should be taken as a valuable effort to get such disputes under control by developing a set of commonly accepted rules for their solution. As long as the composition of the *ad hoc* committee is not truly international and the European Union as well as other confederations of states are not involved in the process of developing such rules for the Internet community, however, no acceptance of any memorandum or guidelines may seriously be expected.

Apart from the participation of all relevant public and private bodies in the formation of new structures for the Internet, the next logical step would be the creation and implementation of a truly binding set of terms for the registration and cancellation of domain names which must be respected by national courts as well. This, of course, will certainly prove to be difficult since the principle of territoriality has only started to give way to a more global approach in the protection of trade marks. In this respect, it will be interesting to see what the future holds in store for "netizens" and commercial businesses alike.

CHAPTER 11

Italy

Giovanni Carcaterra and Matteo Bascelli
Studio Legale Fondato da F. Carnelutti
Milan, Italy

INTRODUCTION

Legal Regime

Beginning in 1989, both the European Community (E.C.) and Italy enacted **11-1**
a number of rules governing information technology, including on the keeping
and transfer of information and data in general through information systems.

A decree issued by the Italian government on February 15, 1989, established in Italy for the first time a policy for the co-ordination and development of information systems in public offices.

Law Number 70 of February 21, 1989, enacted new rules to reflect E.C.
Directive Number 87/54 of December 16, 1986, concerning the protection of
semiconductors. This involves a form of special protection based on the "Semi-
conductor Chip Protection Act" issued by the United States of America in 1984.

Law Number 98 of February 21, 1989, authorised the President of the
Republic to ratify Convention Number 108 Concerning the Protection of
Individuals in the Automated Processing of Personal Data (Strasbourg, January 28, 1981). The impact of the above ratification in Italy will be more
exhaustively described below.

Legislative Decree Number 322 of September 6, 1989 launched a reform
of the national statistics system (S.I.S.T.A.N.) and of the Central Statistics
Institute (I.S.T.A.T.).

With a view to circulating and making all information available to
citizens as easily and expeditiously as possible, Circular Number 2 of
January 25, 1990, of the Ministry of Health set out operating rules for the
adoption of a personal access code to be used by citizens in their relations
with the Italian National Health Service.

Circulars Number 46666 of March 2, 1990, and Number 8636 of March
5, 1991, issued by the Public Service Department commenced and carried
out a procedure whereunder special funds would be provided to local

authorities and other public agencies for the implementation of automation projects having such features and using such technologies as to ensure proper interconnection with the information systems of other public offices.

The Public Service Department, by Circular Number 51223 of May 21, 1990, focused on the problem of harmonising and standardising all information technologies in public offices by encouraging a uniform approach towards information and telecommunication technologies to be acquired and by removing those restrictions that could impede the interconnection of the various systems and the transfer of data among public offices.

As to the means through which "electronic communications" shall be transferred, a Ministerial Decree of the Ministry of Post and Telecommunication dated April 6, 1990, approved the National Telecommunications Regulations, in which a new operating structure for telecommunications in Italy was outlined.

A first important innovation is represented by the definition of telecommunication services contained in article 2 of the National Telecommunications Regulations, which classifies these services as follows:

- Carrier services, *i.e.*, services offered by the network which ensure interconnection among several terminal units, *i.e.*, points to which users can have access;
- Teleservices, *i.e.*, telecommunication services that are subject to international uniform procedures (essentially, the telephone service and the teleprinter exchange service);
- Ancillary services, *i.e.*, services which have no autonomous nature and can only be used in association with the above services (such as caller identification, collect calls, meter reading, and intermediate links); and
- Applicational and/or value added services, *i.e.*, all services, other than those listed above, which include higher level functions than those of carrier services and which will be the real "computerised communication channels" (such as e-mail, video telephone, facsimile and videotext).

11-2   Article 3 of the above Regulations specifies that carrier services, teleservices, and ancillary services will be provided through a franchised company, as these services are included in the state monopoly, whereas the applicational and/or value-added services will be offered by specialised companies under free competition conditions.

Articles 4 *et seq.* concern the network. They outline four possible "network architectures" through which the above "computerised communication channels" may be organised on a national basis (connecting network; common channel signalling network; intelligent network; management network). This architecture will result from the various functions differently combined in switching centres and in other network nodes, through connections of various kinds.

Ministerial Decree Number 260 of August 7, 1990, of the Ministry of Post and Telecommunication (concerning the "PRESTEL service") defines this service[1] and sets out[2] the terms for the operation of the electronic mail public service. The user can have access to this service using interactive procedures or other procedures[3] through a personal computer or public computer terminals or authorised teller systems.[4] Delivery may be made through either messengers or electronic mail box[5] and the rates payable will be fixed by a ministerial decree.[6] The limits for the contents of the correspondence to be exchanged[7] are established in article 11 of Presidential Decree Number 156/73 to which this ministerial decree expressly refers.

Many are the provisions of law with which Italy is endeavouring to regulate and develop electronic-computerised data transfers among public offices.

Within the scope of Law Number 407 of December 29, 1990 (General Provisions for the Implementation of 1991–1993 Finance Acts), article 4 provides that the government is authorised to resort to a legislative decree to regulate the terms on which public offices shall have access to the computer system of the tax records office; it specifies, *inter alia*, that once access is obtained, all public offices will be bound to secrecy.

Circular Number 83245 of December 16, 1991, by the Public Service Department contains rules for the standardisation and interconnection of the records and files of public offices. In this context, the fiscal code, which is automatically assigned to each newly born citizen, is the legal factor that ensures interconnection among the various public records offices with a view to arriving at an integrated information system. This is a "personal identification number", which in this case will identify each individual and not magnetic cards. The data banks concerned are the "municipal registries", the records of the Chambers of Commerce, the National Social Security Office (I.N.P.S.), Ministry of Finance and National Health Service, as well as court records and police files.

The following three principles which, although they only apply to local government units, are innovative for the Italian legal scenario concerning electronic data transfers, were introduced by article 6 *quater* of Law Number 80/91, based on Law Number 241/90, concerning new administrative proceedings:

- Any data input and data reproduction transaction must be accompanied by the mention of the source and of the operator;

---

1 Decree Number 260 of August 7, 1990, article 1.
2 Decree Number 260 of August 7, 1990, article 2.
3 Decree Number 260 of August 7, 1990, article 3.
4 Decree Number 260 of August 7, 1990, article 5.
5 Decree Number 260 of August 7, 1990, article 6.
6 Decree Number 260 of August 7, 1990, article 7.
7 Decree Number 260 of August 7, 1990, article 10.

- Wherever a signature is required for a document to be valid, such signature is suitably replaced by the name of the operator affixed electronically to the document generated by a computer system; and
- Wherever a document has been signed electronically, the said document is automatically accepted subject to judicial challenge only.

11-3   In addition, legislative Decree Number 39 of February 12, 1993, sets out rules for the engineering, development and management of automated information systems in public offices. The purpose for introducing the use of these systems is, *inter alia*, to ensure transparency in public services and provide stronger information supports to public decisions. Article 3 of Decree Number 39 is very innovative. It establishes the principle that electronic documents are valid in every respect for administrative purposes.

Within the scope of the various legal issues associated with computerised data and electronic data processing, particularly important for the advanced position taken by Italy, are environmental matters. In this respect, the European Union has appointed Italy to create a data bank, collecting the laws and court decisions of the member states relating to any legal restrictions on the use of natural resources, with a view to maximising the circulation of this information among international authorities.

Finally, Law Number 675 (Protection of Individuals and Other Entities in Relation to Personal Data Processing), which is of paramount importance to both private and public sectors, was passed on December 31, 1996. The provisions of this law are the final version of a government bill dating back to 1984.

The Law not only implements E.C. Directive Number 46/95 but also makes it possible to officially ratify the aforesaid Convention number 108 of the Council of Europe (Strasbourg Convention). The final ratification by each Contracting State of this Convention was conditional on the adoption of such legal measures as to properly protect the principles stated therein, and these measures are contained in the aforesaid Law. Similarly, Italy is now in a position to ratify the Schengen Agreement of June 14, 1985, for the gradual abolition of customs controls between the signatory countries. The Common Declaration of June 16, 1990 on the protection of personal data, attached to the Convention for the implementation of the above Agreement expressly states that Italy:

"... undertakes to adopt any and all measures as are necessary to complete Italian law in accordance with the Convention of the Council of Europe dated January 29, 1981."

11-4   Considering the importance and complex contents of Law Number 675 of 1996, the most important provisions contained therein are dealt with in detail in the following paragraphs.

Confidentiality

One of the most important and much-discussed questions is the problem of **11-5** safety, both on-line and of the network. Safety on-line means the safety measures offered by the network to protect files in transit, and "network safety" means warranties on the provision of network services for the circulation of information flows and computer products and services. To ensure on-line safety the following main operating requirements must be satisfied:

- Integrity, *i.e.*, the information must be received in the same form and contents as those it originally had when it was transmitted;
- Authenticity, *i.e.*, the identity of transmitters and recipients must be certain;
- Accessibility, *i.e.*, access to all on-line information must be warranted;
- Confidentiality or secrecy, *i.e.*, the information must be received only and exclusively by the intended addressee and any and all personal data must be processed, transferred and recorded in such a manner as to ensure that they do not become public knowledge.

"Confidentiality", intended as a correct and genuine receipt of the data **11-6** transferred, has strictly technical implications. These concern mainly technological solutions and legal measures adopted to protect the confidential nature of the information exchanged between computer users and to punish hacking as a criminal offence.

In this connection, it is striking how the computer system has become a vital centre for the collection of interests, whether strictly personal or of a professional nature, as a projection of the individual's personality.

Fortunately, the European Community and Italy have taken notice of the increasing importance of computer systems and, consequently, the risks deriving from their vulnerability. Italy finally enacted Law Number 547 of December 23, 1993 (Amendments and Supplements to the Provisions of the Penal Code and of the Code of Penal Procedure Governing Computer Crimes), to satisfy the citizens' requests for protection from unlawful acts connected with the use of computers.

Article 4 of Law Number 547, section IV, chapter II, title XII, of the second book of the Penal Code (Intrusion on Another's Dwelling) has been supplemented with three new provisions: article 615 *ter* (Unauthorised Access to an Information or Computer System), article 615 *quater* (Unauthorised Keeping and Circulation of Access Codes), and article 615 *quinquies* (Circulation of Programmes Intended For Damaging or Interrupting an Information System).

The new rules complete, through a technological updating, those contained in the following provisions of the Penal Code: article 614 (Intrusion on Another's Dwelling); article 615 (Intrusion on Another's Dwelling by a Public Official); and article 615 *bis* (Infringement of Privacy).

Equally, the interception, hindrance, or unlawful interruption of computer or telematic communications;[8] the installation of devices aimed at intercepting, hindering or interrupting computer or telematic communications;[9] and the falsification, alteration or suppression of the contents of computer or telematic communications[10] have been included in section V, Chapter III, Title XII, of the second book of the Penal Code (Crimes against the Inviolability of Secrets) as crimes against the freedom and secrecy of telecommunications.

Confidentiality in processing, transferring and storing personal data in Italy was first brought to the public eye with Law 241 of 1990, which was followed by regulations ensuring access by the public, through terminals, to the records of public offices entered in electronic data banks.

Clearly, this provision of law gave rise to the problem of protecting the privacy of individuals while creating electronic data banks and circulating information relating to them.

All discussions immediately focused on the need to make a distinction between "sensitive data" and "non-sensitive data" according to the type of personal data to be recorded; "sensitive data" are those that under the laws of almost all of the industrialised countries cannot be freely processed through computer systems (and are those which relate to the religion, health, race, sex and criminal records of an individual). As far as all other data are concerned, there are different opinions.

In fact, those who state that nobody can enter any data in a data bank, even if such data bank is intended for personal use, without the prior authorisation of the person concerned, are opposed by those who believe that personal data can be freely processed whenever they are not intended for use by third parties.

In Italy, the Law on Protection of Persons in Relation to Personal Data Processing (P.D.P. Law), which was enacted on December 31, 1996, is very important. Its main purpose is to protect privacy rights relating to all personal data entered in data banks. The Law's main provisions can be summarised as follows:

- Prior to processing personal data, the written consent of the person to whom such data relate must be obtained; this consent must then be reiterated if such data are to be divulged;
- More severe criteria are established for the processing of the so-called "sensitive data", *i.e.*, those which affect the most intimate sphere of an individual (health, religion, political opinions, etc.); in this case, it is

---

8 Penal Code, article 617 *quater.*
9 Penal Code, article 617 *quinquies.*
10 Penal Code, article 617 *sexies.*

not enough to obtain the consent of the person concerned: in fact, a special authorisation of the competent Authority is also required;

- Notification to the competent Authority must be effected whenever personal data are to be transferred to non-European Union (E.U.) member states (the transfer cannot take place before 15 days have elapsed from notification) and whenever "sensitive" data are to be transferred to another Country (the transfer cannot take place before 20 days have elapsed from notification).

The Law provides for some exceptions in favour of physicians and reporters: **11-7**

- Physicians can — within certain limits — process data relating to their patients' health without the authorisation of the competent Authority;
- Reporters need not obtain the consent of the individual concerned, except for information relating to the health and sexual life of the said individual.

The P.D.P. Law does not apply to data processed by individuals exclusively for   **11-8** personal purposes, provided that such data may not be disclosed to pre-determined persons on a regular basis and that it shall not be intended for public circulation.[11] However, any such processing is subject to the obligation provided by law that appropriate safety measures be adopted to protect the data recorded;[12] that any damages suffered from the processing of personal data be compensated;[13] and to criminal punishment in the event that the measures required to ensure that such data are safely stored have not been adopted.

Article 5 of the P.D.P. Law also provides that "the processing of personal data by other means than electronic or automated systems is subject to the same rules as those governing data processed through such systems".

Particularly important is the provision with which the Italian legislator has, with an intervention which is significantly innovative for Italy, made moral damages indemnifiable, damages which were formerly awarded solely if a crime had been committed.

In other sectors, there have been heated discussions on the terms for collecting, storing and circulating data through electronic means; with respect to health data, reference must be made to the Recommendation dated January 23, 1981, issued by the Ministers' Committee of the Council of Europe. It recommended that the government of each member state prepare regulations embodying the principles contained in the Annex to the Recommendation. This Annex, which is composed of eight points, clearly:

- Provides that regulations governing each data bank as to reflect the purposes of each such bank are to be issued;

---

11 Law on Protection of Persons in Relation to Personal Data Processing, article 3.
12 Law on Protection of Persons in Relation to Personal Data Processing, article 15.
13 Law on Protection of Persons in Relation to Personal Data Processing, article 18.

- Sets out the publicity requirements for health data banks; and
- Lists the essential provisions to be included in the aforesaid regulations (purposes, classification of information, user, persons operating the data bank, controls and remedies, access, notices to persons concerned, safe keeping of data and installations, connections with other banks, if any).

11-9   All of the above provisions show that absolute priority is given to the protection of privacy rights over any other organising or scientific purposes; these purposes are permitted and can be served, but the individuals concerned must remain unidentified.

The Recommendation and the Annex thereto had a considerable impact on the laws subsequently enacted in the various member states.

In Italy, Law Number 135 of June 5, 1990, concerning the protection of patients affected by AIDS provides:

- For the right to secrecy in case such infection is diagnosed;
- For anonymity in case of a general screening made for statistical purposes;
- That the results can be delivered only to the individual concerned; and
- That employers are prohibited to make seroposivity investigations on employees.[14]

11-10   In light of the confidentiality requirements to be met in processing personal data, other measures have been adopted to update certain provisions of law already in force, such as the Workers' Statute, the Law on Abortion, drug laws, and laws on handicapped persons.

Legal Effect of Electronic Signatures

11-11   Traditionally, the control of the full original contents (integrity) of a document and of its objective source, *i.e.*, of its evidential value — is based, respectively, on the existence of a material support and of a signature.[15]

"Material support" means a substance to which the graphic signs in which the document is expressed are affixed. To be valid as evidence, any such support must be indelible or, at least, retain marks of any alterations made, so that any modification is detectable.[16]

"Signature" means the manual affixing of one's own name at the foot of a document, authorship of which is taken.[17] Handwriting is assumed to be unique to each individual and, as such, hardly reproducible and, in any event, inalterable and not re-usable, as it is indissolubly embodied in the support.

---

14 Law Number 135, article 5.
15 Zagami, "Firme digitali, crittografia e validità del documento elettronico", *Diritto dell'informazione e dell'informatica*, 1996, at p. 151.
16 Carnelutti, "Documento — teoria moderna", *Novissimo Digesto Italiano*, VI, 1957, at p. 85.
17 Carnelutti, "Studi sulla sottoscrizione", *Rivista di Diritto Commerciale*, 1929, at p. 513.

Therefore, a paper-based document duly signed is considered certain and reliable, as it is difficult to alter it and, if altered, any alteration can be detected through scientific or handwriting examinations.

The problem of signature has been discussed for a long time[18] on the basis of the fact that the new technologies are making this traditional means inadequate to serve as a principle for identifying the author of a document.

The principles for checking the integrity and source of a document based on a material support and signature are demonstrably inadequate whenever electronic documents are concerned because, as a general rule, the data recorded in any such document can be deleted and no mark of any alterations is retained.

In addition, an electronic document cannot be signed in a traditional manner, *i.e.*, by affixing the author's full name manually.

The above clearly shows that those purposes which are typical to a manual signature, *i.e.*, those of serving as identification, attribution and evidence, are not immediately satisfied by an electronic document.

These difficulties, which have up to now prevented an electronic document from being recognised as having full evidential value, can be overcome by adopting the new encryption technologies. In fact, under certain conditions, digital signatures can suitably replace a manual signature, and give to an electronic document the same evidential value as that recognised to a traditional paper-based document.

A "digital signature" is a group of alphanumerical types deriving from complex mathematical operations of encryption made in an electronic document by a computer. To encrypt a text or a signature means to apply to such text or signature an algorithm which, by way of a given variable (encryption key), transforms it into another text which is unintelligible and cannot be decoded by a person who lacks the relevant key.

In principle, digital signatures can therefore satisfy the three purposes that, according to Italian academic commentators, are typical to manual signatures, namely:

- Identification purpose;
- Attribution purpose; and
- Evidence purpose.

Each digital signature includes a code that identifies the relevant encryption key and, consequently, the person to whom it belongs.   **11-12**

Notwithstanding the above, some commentators believe that manual signatures and digital signatures cannot be perfectly equivalent, as the latter satisfy only partly the requirements that are traditionally met by a manual signature according to the Italian jurisprudence and the existing decisions of law.

---

18 Irti, *Idola libertatis*, Milano, 1985, at p. 75.

In fact, a digital signature meets the "written form" requirement only if an electronic document is considered a written document.[19] The encryption key, which is personal and exclusive to the person to whom it belongs, replaces personal handwriting. Moreover, a digital signature cannot meet the requirement of being "readable", as non-readability is the very warranty offered by encryption.

Finally, digital signatures do not meet the requirement that the signature be affixed at the foot of a document. In fact, a digital signature is even safer than a manual signature because it covers the entire document and makes it impossible to alter the document so signed in any way. No manipulations, such as the unauthorised completion of an incomplete document or of a signed blank document, can occur.

Based on the foregoing, it is unreasonable to state that a digital signature cannot be considered equivalent to a manual signature in that any or several of the above requirements are not met, or are met only partly or in a peculiar manner. However, considering that, presently, there are no specific provisions of law governing this matter, an Italian judge is quite unlikely to unconditionally accord full evidential value to a document bearing a digital signature, as he would do in respect of a manual signature.

To make a digital signature as effective as a manual signature, regulations should be issued to serve:

- The identification purpose, thus warranting that the encryption key actually pertains to a given person by regulating the issue of encryption keys and their certification by authorised persons or organisations and, in addition, by prohibiting that encryption keys' use by any person other than their respective owners, and by requiring the owners to keep such keys in a safe and secret place;
- The attribution purpose, by providing that a digital signature is an acknowledgement of authorship of the contents of the electronic document to which it has been affixed, with all consequences in terms of legal obligations and effects arising out therefrom;[20] and
- The evidence purpose, i.e., to ensure that an electronic signature be strictly linked to the person to whom the encryption key pertains, by providing for shifting the burden of proof and establishing the (rebuttable) presumption that the source of a digital signature is the person to whom the encryption key pertains.

11-13 Many academic commentators hold that, failing an express provision of law, the force to be accorded to digital signatures could derive from contract

---

19 Giannantonio, *Manuale di diritto dell'informatica*, Padova, 1994, at p. 338; Borruso, *Computers e diritto*, I, 1988, at p. 275.

20 Civil Code, article 2702, which establishes for manual signatures that, subject to certain conditions, the statements contained in a signed document must be considered as originating from the signer.

arrangements between the parties concerned. These would be arrangements similar to the so-called "interchange agreements" which are used in the Electronic Data Interchange (EDI) field and can be defined as an exchange of business data between computers.[21]

Such agreements, as far as their evidential value is concerned, would fall within the provisions of article 2698 of the Civil Code. They would provide, by mutual agreement of the parties, for shifting the *onus probandi* by creating a *juris tantum* presumption that a digital signature (and, accordingly, the electronic document so signed) comes from the person to whom the encryption key used to make the relevant control pertains. It would be the burden of this person, if and when a digital signature is determined by a court to be his, to provide rebutting evidence thereof, *i.e.*, evidence that the encryption key with which such signature was calculated had been lost or stolen and then used by an impostor.

As to formal requirements, these agreements would fall within the scope of article 1352 of the Civil Code, which provides that the parties can enter into a contract in any form whatsoever, even in a form which is different from those expressly provided by law.

Failing specific provisions of law and failing an express understanding between the parties under a contract, the force of digital signatures in legal proceedings would be very limited, as all this matter would be left to the probatory initiative of the plaintiff who, together with an electronic document bearing a digital signature, would be required to give evidence of the defendant being the source thereof and of the integrity of its contents, without having the benefit of a legal presumption and/or a shifting of the burden of proof.

For the time being, the presence of a certified digital signature is only an aid which, together with other evidence, may serve to persuade a judge.[22]

To conclude, reference to digital signatures has been made in a resolution passed by the Authority for Computer Systems in Public Offices (A.I.P.A.) on July 28, 1994, concerning the keeping of administrative records on WORM (Write Once Read Many) optical supports. In addition, as far as digital signatures in administrative documents are concerned, as already said in commenting on Law 80/91, the content of a document signed electronically is valid until and unless its validity is challenged.[23]

Further references to digital signatures are made in two bills recently introduced: a draft bill concerning computerised documents prepared by the

---

21 Fadda, "L'electronic data interchange nella normativa italiana e straniera", *Rivista dell'informazione e dell'informatica*, 1994, at p. 22 — Finocchiaro, "Documento elettronico", *Contratto e Impresa*, 1994, at p. 433.

22 Code of Civil Procedure, article 116.

23 Minerva, "L'atto amministrativo in forma elettronica e la sicurezza dei sistemi informativi pubblici", *Rivista dell'informazione e dell'informatica*, 1995, at p. 939.

Electronic Data Processing Department of the Court of Cassation[24] and a bill for the recognition of electronic documents prepared by the regulatory group Ediforum.[25]

In light of the foregoing, we can say that, if duly inserted in a regulatory framework (which presently does not exist) or in a contract framework, an electronic signature satisfies all the conditions required to be considered a means that is sufficient (or even essential) to give evidence of the source and of the integrity of an electronic document and that "[e]xcept for signature, nothing is required by and nothing is useful to the judge for him to determine the author of a document".[26]

ELECTRONIC TRANSACTIONS

Creation of Contracts Electronically

Offer and Acceptance On-line

11-14   A great number of legal issues arising from the so-called "electronic transactions" — business deals made through electronic processors — have been discussed by Italian scholars since the end of the 1970s.[27]

Before the limits within which the traditional rules and institutions apply to the new computer means are examined, it may be worthwhile describing how a computer can be used to carry out negotiations and legal transactions in general in light of the newly enacted provisions of Italian law. Electronic data processors are mainly used:

- For merely informational purposes (in this case, the function of a computer remains in the inner sphere of the user, which means that such use does not necessarily appear from outside);
- For communicating a will already formed (therefore, if so used, they can be assimilated to the traditional means of communication, such as a telegram or a telex, by which the parties' will, previously formed, is officially made known);
- As a means that directly affects the process of formation of the parties' will (when the user puts in the computer the data and algorithms that will govern the whole negotiation, so that such data and all consequent decisions are processed by the computer); and

---

24 Court of Cassation, "Presentazione di uno schema di disegno di legge sul documento informatico", *Rivista dell'informazione e dell'informatica*, 1994.
25 Gruppo normativo di Ediforum, *Presentazione di uno schema di disegno di legge per il riconoscimento del documento elettronico.*
26 Carnelutti, "Studi sulla sottoscrizione", *Rivista di diritto commerciale,* 1929, at p. 513.
27 Parisi, *Il Contratto conluso mediante computer*, Milan, 1987; Finocchiaro "I contratti d'informatica", *I contratti del commercio, dell'industria e del mercato finanziario*, Torino, 1995, at p. 1609.

- As a place where the parties' will, previously formed, meet (whenever the computer becomes a place or means in which or by which several different and opposite intents previously formed by separate parties are collected and connected with each other (the so-called "electronic market").

The most immediate problems mainly arise from the use of computers as **11-15** referred to in the last three paragraphs above. In these cases, the computer is no longer used for information purposes, *i.e.*, for the personal purposes of the user, but for "telematic purposes", which result in the processing of data and instructions and their subsequent communication to third parties.

In this connection, the matter of the so-called "cyberspace", *i.e.*, an immaterial aggregation of communication networks, telematic links, and operating systems through which digital information can be transmitted, located and stored without any space and time restrictions which joins and replaces territorial space, is being discussed also in Italy.[28]

All transactions made in this new context are between electronic entities (and not physical entities) situated in different and distant places, even in different countries, each having a separate and distinct legal system, and are settled with digital money.[29]

In addition, this "new mode of negotiating" gives rise to the most interesting problems of interpretation, which affect not only the preliminary stage in which the parties' will is formed, but also the subsequent stage in which the contract is concluded.

Article 1326(1) of the Civil Code provides that "a contract is formed at the moment when who made the offer is informed of the acceptance of the other party". According to article 1335 of the Civil Code,

". . . an offer and the acceptance thereof . . . are deemed to be known at the moment they reach the intended recipient at his address, unless the intended recipient is able to give evidence that, without his fault, it was impossible for him to have notice thereof."

The presumption of knowledge established by article 1335 of the Civil Code **11-16** might also be applied to any offer and acceptance on-line, as the condition that makes the above presumption enforceable could be satisfied by the fact that the proposal and the relevant acceptance have been recorded in the memory of the computer and, accordingly, knowledge thereof can be acquired by the offeree and/or the offeror through terminals.

---

28 White Book by Delors of December 5, 1993, *Crescita, competitività ed occupazione: le sfide e le opportunità del XXI secolo.*
29 Imperiali D'Afflitto, *Il diritto alle prese con la società dell'informazione*, Milano, 1996, at p. 1.

Even the more peculiar case of cross-offers having nearly identical content could be solved similarly: each would at the same time be an offer and an acceptance, and the contract would be formed on receipt by their intended addressees.

In fact, the contracts that are more eligible for being concluded by computer generally concern business deals, a sector in which expeditiousness are fundamental requirements. Based on the foregoing, an on-line offer may be deemed to contain the implicit will of each offeror to consider the contract formed if and when his proposal comes across another proposal having substantially equal contents stored in the same computer.

Mention should be made of the authors of such communications; in this respect, the computer has often been compared to a voluntary representative of the person for whom it is operated. This argument appears untenable in that, on the one hand, there are no provisions of law covering this matter and, on the other hand, a computer can in no way be compared with a human mind, as it is not endowed with its own independent decision-making powers.

It could instead be reasonably argued that representation powers are conferred by each user on the person in charge of the operations of the computer, on whom the complex technical activities that characterise the operation of the machine are incumbent. This person would act as representative of all the users who intend to conclude a contract by computer by submitting thereby and storing therein an offer for that purpose. Accordingly, all responsibilities for the operation of the computer would pertain to such person, who should also be legally liable for the provision of the relevant service. Therefore, a contract would be deemed formed when the computer, operated by such representative in the name and on behalf of the single users, receives instructions, based on the offers submitted by the contracting parties, to execute the contract according to the information contained therein.

Although on the basis of the above guidelines, the moment in which a contract is formed can be determined, the awkward problem of determining the place where such on-line contract is formed is still to be solved. This problem is closely linked to that of determining the law governing a contract so concluded. According to Italian jurisprudence, there are two possible solutions.

If a contract is deemed to be formed when the latter offer having the same subject matter and containing similar terms is received, the place where the on-line contract is formed should be the place where the party who made the former offer is when knowledge of the latter offer can be acquired by him through a terminal.[30]

On the contrary, if the contract is deemed concluded by means of a representation power conferred on the person who operates the computer, the place where the contract is concluded should be the place where the memory of the computer through which the contract has been made is situated.

---

30 In this case, the presumption provided for in the Civil Code, article 1335, applies.

Some problems, which are strictly connected with the electronic — abstract — nature of an on-line contract, arise from the provisions of articles 1341 and 1342 of the Civil Code.

Standard Conditions

The time when "electronic transactions", *i.e.*, transactions made through data processing systems, will make it necessary to use standard conditions of contract,[31] prepared by either contracting party and freely accepted or refused by the other contracting party is forthcoming. The first sentence of article 1341 of the Civil Code immediately gives rise to a problem where it provides: **11-17**

"Standard conditions of contract prepared by one of the contracting party are effective on the other party if at the time of the formation of the contract the latter knew of them or should have known of them by using ordinary diligence."

Obviously, knowledge of the standard conditions of contract contained in a paper-based document can more easily be acquired by whoever examines them than those set out in an on-line contract. In fact, one can reasonably doubt that an electronic document, the full text of which cannot be contained in a sole screening, may be read only partly and that the most burdensome clauses may go unnoticed.   **11-18**

Digital signature techniques might solve this problem. This kind of signature, which is calculated on the basis of the whole contract text, would cover all the document and would prevent the offeror party from subsequently making any fraudulent amendment or additions to the original text of its offer and/or the offeree party from inaccurately examining the offer received.

An equally serious problem arises from the wording of the second paragraph of article 1341 of the Civil Code. This provides that so-called "unfair contract terms" are ineffective on the party against whom they are enforceable unless they have been "expressly accepted in writing by the said party".

Unless an electronic signature, however affixed, is assumed to validly satisfy the written form required by law, the approval of any "unfair contract terms" cannot be validly expressed on-line.

Further discussions arise from article 1342 of the Civil Code which, in the first paragraph, provides, "clauses added to a form or formulary shall prevail over those printed on the original form or formulary wherever any such added clause is incompatible with the original one".

This prevalence is based on the assumption that the former are easily detectable, because everybody can distinguish *ictu oculi* the original clauses

---

31 Civil Code, article 1341.

of a form from those subsequently included. But, in the case of an electronic form, any amendments and/or deletions are undetectable.

Adopting appropriate techniques for an "electronic impermeabilisation" of the original text could solve this problem, so that the said text would become inalterable after the conclusion of the contract.

Particularly important, as is shown by the serious approach of the Italian legislator to the matter of electronic contracts, is legislative Decree Number 50 of January 15, 1992, implementing E.C. Directive 85/577.

This provision of law, although it specifically covers "contracts for the supply of goods or services entered into outside business premises", can reasonably be considered as the first acknowledgement by Italian law of "on-line sales". In fact, article 9 of Decree Number 50 expressly provides that the rules set out therein also apply to contracts concerning the supply of goods made through computer and telematic systems.

All of the rules established for the above contracts are closely connected with the provisions governing the right of withdrawal. Article 4 of Decree 50 gives any consumer who buys goods by telemarketing the right to withdraw from the contract. This right can in no event be waived.[32]

As far as electronic contracts and transactions are concerned the principle established in Law Number 59 of March 15, 1997, is of paramount importance. Article 15(2) reads:

"Any acts, data and documents prepared by public offices and private persons by using computer or telematic means, any contracts made in that form, as well as their storage and transmission through computer systems, are valid and binding for all purposes of law."

11-19   For the implementation of the above provision, paragraph 2 also provides:

". . . the principles and terms for the implementation of the provisions of this paragraph are set out, both for public offices and for private persons, in special regulations to be issued within 180 days of the coming into operation of this Law . . .".

11-20   The above is only a principle and, for the time being, nobody can imagine how it will be applied.

Mistakes in On-line Contracts

11-21   A point to be attentively examined is the presence of any mistakes[33] in on-line contracts. A so-called "impedimental mistake", *i.e.*, a divergence between the parties' will and its expression, can be detected only when the parties'

---

32 Decree 50 of 1992, article 10.
33 Civil Code, articles 1427 *et seq.*

will is addressed to third parties; a "fundamental mistake" — which affects the process of formation of the parties' will — can go back to the moment in which the system programming was made.

The potential deficiencies in the process of formation of the parties' will through a computer system include, in addition to those created or deriving from misrepresentations at the time when the system programming is made, those that are more specifically connected with the use of the computer.

The latter are any deficiencies of the will connected with and caused by malfunctioning of the electronic components of a computer which, as a result thereof, does not fairly reflect the original will of the parties and/or those caused by logical errors in the system programming.

The view that both types of error, wherever any such error is essential and detectable, make the transaction voidable pursuant to the provisions of articles 1428 *et seq* of the Civil Code appears correct.

In addition, with respect to any damages suffered by the contracting parties as a result of any malfunctioning of the electronic components of a computer and/or any mistake made by the programmer, problems may arise in determining who will be liable for any such malfunctioning or software error. For this purpose, general civil law rules can reasonably be applied.

Impact of Impostors or Persons without Authority

Cases in which a person acts as representative of another person without having such authority or in excess of the powers received are rather common in on-line contracts where the parties often avail themselves of the services of computer operators.   **11-22**

As a principle, Italian law provides that any transaction concluded by a person without authority is not binding on the contracting parties and is ineffective. To become effective, such transactions must be ratified in accordance with the provisions of article 1399 of the Civil Code.

Such ineffective transactions may cause damages to third parties if any such third party, having innocently relied on the validity of the transaction, incurred any expenses in relation thereto or renounced other opportunities or assumed any consequential obligations. On the basis of the legal provisions governing pre-contractual liability, the person who acted without authority must compensate such damages.[34] The benefits and losses that — had the contract been validly concluded — would have been obtained or would not have been suffered and, on the other hand, the benefits and losses that — had the damaged party abstained from entering into contract negotiations — would have been obtained or would not have been suffered will be taken into account.

---

34 Civil Code, article 1337.

Since, in Italy, there are neither legal provisions nor court decisions concerning "impostors" or "persons without authority" in the conclusion of electronic contracts, it seems that the the aforesaid provisions are also applicable to any persons who, without having been vested with representation powers or acting in excess of their powers, carry out on-line negotiations and conclude on-line contracts so deceiving unaware third parties.

Of course, this requirement is proportional to the safety level that one wants to offer to electronic transactions in general.

On-line Payments

Electronic Fund Transfers

11-23   In Italy, the tendency to have the means traditionally used to transfer funds replaced by the new systems of electronic fund transfer (EFTS) is increasing.

An electronic fund transfer can be summarily described as a special technical manner to perform an obligation, under which "A" (the debtor) gives instructions to "C" (a bank with which "A" holds a current account) to transfer a certain sum of money to "B" (the creditor of "A") at the bank with which "B" holds a current account. The bank "C", on receipt of the payment order, operates the "EFTS" through which the account of "A" is debited and the account of "B" is credited with the agreed amount.

As the above is a tripartite relationship where "A" is the debtor-transferor, "C" is the transferring bank and "B" is the creditor-transferee, this scheme falls within the scope of delegation as covered by articles 1268, 1269, 1270 and 1271 of the Italian Civil Code; in the event that the creditor ("A") and the debtor ("B") hold a current account with the same bank ("C"), such transaction could even be defined as an "electronic clearing transaction".[35]

The only difference would be that, whereas a traditional bank transfer, made on instructions of the holder of a current account, consists in a credit item being manually transferred from one account to another, an electronic bank transfer is made by means of electronic impulses.

The Court of Verona confirmed the affinity between the two systems of payment by holding that the provisions governing traditional bank transfers also apply to electronic bank transfers.[36]

Since in the EFT the order is generally given by means of electronic impulses — coming from the user directly or through the bank operator, a pre-requisite for the validity of the said electronic order is that a contract be expressly made for that purpose whereunder the bank and its client agree that all credit and debit transactions must be made through a computer system.

---

35 Giannantonio, "Trasferimento elettronico di fondi e adempimento", *Foro Italiano*, 1990, V, at p. 165.

36 Judgment in *Banca Antoniana di Padova e Trieste* v. *Bauli* rendered on February 16, 1990.

In Italy, electronic fund transfers are considered a unilateral act, as provided in articles 1334 and 1335 of the Civil Code, with which the transferor expresses its will to pay a sum to a third party through a bank.[37]

Whether electronic fund transfers have discharging effects is another issue closely linked with electronic fund transfers.

Considering that, where intended as performance of the transferor's obligation towards the transferee, electronic fund transfers fall within the scope of articles 1173–1200 of the Civil Code governing the performance of obligations in general, one could wonder whether an electronic fund transfer can be reasonably considered perfectly equivalent to a payment made in legal tender.

Problems may arise from the wording of article 1197 of the Civil Code. It provides that "a debtor cannot discharge his obligation with a performance which is different from the one due . . . unless the creditor so agrees". Article 1277 of the Civil Code provides that "[p]ecuniary debts are paid with money which is legal tender in the State . . .". These provisions, if combined, accord discharging effects to electronic fund transfers only if the creditor's consent is previously obtained.

Otherwise than as outlined above in abstract terms, Italian bank practice considers electronic fund transfers to fully effectively discharge payment obligations, on the basis of the provisions of law-Decree Number 143 of May 3, 1991 (Anti-Laundering Decree). Article 1 of this Law-Decree prohibits any delivery of legal tender in excess of the sum of L. 20-million. It provides that any such transfer must be made through intermediaries duly authorised by law using such payment means as are listed in the Law-Decree, including credit cards and payment cards. As far as payment cards are specifically concerned, it may be worthwhile recalling that E.C. Recommendation Number 88/590 defines these cards as "the means which permits the user to make electronic fund transfer transactions".

Credit Card Payments and Electronic Checks

Credit card payments and electronic checks may be jointly discussed for **11-24** Italy, referring to the very recent European program Secure Electronic Commerce (S.E.C.). This now includes 38 banking organisations, among which eight are Italian.

Purchases and sales on the Internet are developing exponentially. In the year 2000, it is believed that the "net of the nets" will bear commercial exchanges up to U.S. $32-billion, by the year 2005 the volume of trades may be over U.S. $186-billion. This growth has not always been supported by an equal increase of the safety devices that are to protect the discretion of financial transactions.

---

37 Giannantonio, "Trasferimento elettronico di fondi e adempimento", *Foro Italiano*, 1990, V, at p. 165.

For the sake of filling these gaps, "Visa" has started a pilot project called "safe electronic trade on open nets" or "SEC" (Secure Electronic Commerce). The initiative is based on "SET" (Secure Electronic Transactions) standards, worldwide safety standards developed by the main operators in the credit cards sector (Visa, Master Card, and American Express), with the co-operation of the giants of the computer sector (Microsoft, IBM, and Netscape). These standards comply with essential requirements, such as discretion, integrity, and genuineness of the message and "inter-operability".

Discretion secures the holder the secrecy of the place where he does his shopping and of the amount of money spent; integrity assures the holder that an order remains qualitatively and quantitatively identical with the one originally formed. Authentication grants all parties involved in the transaction the certainty of dealing with the tradesman or the legitimate owner of the card. Inter-operability is granted by a common operational standard used by all involved parties.

The system operates as follows. When the credit cardholder wants to make a payment on Internet, he requests from his bank a "digital certificate" which enables him to make Visa payments on an open net. The bank that issued the credit card to the holder undertakes the role of guarantor (a sort of authority) for the issuing of certificates. The retailer who wants to receive the payment will have to obtain an authenticity certificate from his own bank. The holder of the card, once he has obtained the digital certificate, will look for a virtual window he likes.

If this window belongs to a retailer who also has the certificate and is enabled to use the "SET" program, he can send and receive messages to that site, being totally sure that both parties are legitimate operators. Once the agreement is settled, the holder places his purchase order and all the details of the transaction are first kept secret under a public key and then sent to the retailer's server; afterwards, the message, still secret, is sent to the retailer's bank. At this time, the message is not secret anymore, and the operation enters in the normal process for requesting the payment authorisation. After this, the authorised message returns to the retailer's server, is made secret again and, through the open net, is brought to the holder's server. The holder will thus know that the payment authorisation has been issued. The holder of the credit card and the retailer affix their digital signature to confirm the purchase and the acceptance of the transaction, which is thus concluded.

Electronic information rights

Property Rights in Electronic Information

11-25   The Italian legislature's sporadic interventions on this matter are principally due to the wish to adapt Italy's national legal provisions to the trend that emerges from five E.C. Directives (Directive Number 91/250 on Computer

Programs, Directive Number 92/100 on the Rental Right, Directive Number 93/83 Amending Copyrights and Rights Connected to Artists and Performers, Directive Number 93/98 on the Duration of the Copyright Protection, and Directive Number 96/9 on Data Bank Protection.

Even if the legislative production is not rich, sometimes the decisions of the Italian courts have acknowledged the possibility that "a data bank containing commercial information may be protected as an original work".[38]

Although these are unbinding precedents, it must be highlighted that the protection of data banks as original works seems to be the most recurring thesis in Italian doctrine.

Copyright protection is enforced only when the collection of data meets the requirements stated in article 1 of Law Number 633 of April 22, 1941: "the originality of the form in which the work is made" and the "intelligibility" or the "external comprehensibility".

The requirement of "originality" for data bases — as for all collective works — concerns selection, choice or organisation of materials: accordingly, the copyright does not protect the "series of data" collected, but the "system used to collect, process, file and use these data". When this "organising system" has a certain originality, it will most likely be protected by the Copyright Law and by articles 2575 *et seq* of the Civil Code.

Unfair Competition

Finally, also the general discipline stated by article 2598, point 3, of the Civil Code, concerning "unfair competition", could be usefully applied in the relations between "rival data banks", potentially exposed to the risk of reproductions and counterfeiting. It states: **11-26**

> "Acts of unfair competition are performed by whoever avails himself directly or indirectly of any other means which do not conform with the principles of correct behaviour in the trade and are likely to injure another's business."

The possibility of this extension requires that this prohibited activity and behaviour be found in the subjects and not in the particular kind of goods or objects of the single act of unfair competition. A recent decision of the Court of Cassation[39] stated that even: **11-27**

> ". . . the unlawful reproduction of data collected and published in different magazines is to be considered unfair competition and is a violation of articles 2598 *et seq* of the Civil Code and Law 101 [on Copyright]."

---

38 *Pretura* of Rome, December 14, 1989.
39 Court of Cassation, January 18, 1993, Number 5346.

11-28   Similarly reproductions of data collected and divulged with data banks should be considered acts of unfair competition.

ON-LINE CONDUCT

Regulation of Electronic Communication

11-29   In Italy, no authority, entity, or institution has been established by law to oversee the electronic communication. Law Number 675 of December 31, 1996, provided for the setting up of the authority for personal data protection.

Such authority will attend to the regulation of the data banks and of the electronic and traditional transmission of personal data. The correct working of the electronic instruments depend on the setting up of the competent authorities.

Territorial Limits of Jurisdiction

11-30   In Italy, territorial limits of jurisdiction, residents and non-residents, and crossborder transactions and communications are regulated by Law Number 218 of May 31, 1995 (The Reform of the Italian International Civil Law).

Article 3 of Law Number 218/95 provides, "The Italian jurisdiction applies when the defendant has his place of residence in Italy or has in Italy a representative having authorities to enter judicial proceedings". Moreover, on the basis of the rules provided by sections 2, 3, and 4, title II, of the Brussels Convention of September 27, 1968, implemented in Italy by Law Number 804 of June 21, 1971, and its amendments, as follows:

> "Italian jurisdiction applies even if the defendant has not his place of residence in a contracting country, when it refers to one of the areas of law falling within the scope of application of the Convention."

11-31   This means that the Brussels Convention provides that the court having jurisdiction over the illicit conduct (torts) be alternatively the court where the defendant has his place of residence or the court where the damage is suffered. This latter concept is interpreted by the most authoritative Italian authors so to allow the plaintiff the option to start legal proceedings in anyone of the place where the damage is suffered or in the place where the fact generative of such damage takes place.

As regards the applicable law for contractual obligations, article 57 of Law Number 218/95, provides that "the contractual obligations are always governed by the Rome Treaty of June 19, 1980, implemented by Law Number 975 of December 18, 1984, without prejudice to the other international treaties as applicable".

Impact of Penal Law

The enforceability of the Italian criminal law has territorial and temporal   **11-32**
limits. As regards the present subject matter, the main problems of interpretation and of application refer to the territorial enforceability of Italian
criminal law. Disputes about the determination of the applicable law may
arise in the case of crimes committed by means of computers.

Italian law adheres to the general rule of "territoriality", which states that
the scope of application of the criminal law is defined by the country's
borders and binds the people therein, both foreign and stateless.[40]

This means that if the crime is wholly committed in Italy, the place of the
crime's commission is where the illicit act occurred. If the crime is partially
committed in Italy, it is considered committed in Italy when the act or the
omission — wholly or partly — happened in Italy or if the result took place
in Italy.

From the above rules, it can be said that for crimes committed via
computers the place of the hardware must be taken into account to determine the *locus commissi delicti.*

---

40 Criminal Code, articles 3 and 6, and Introductory Law, article 28.

CHAPTER 12

Luxembourg

Yann Baden
Etude Georges Baden
Luxembourg

INTRODUCTION

The general class of commercial issues arising from electronic media includes   12-1
many problems dealt with by "normal" commercial rules and regulations.
Although electronic commerce is not limited to the Internet, this tool provides
the prime example of electronic commerce all its problems connected.

Commerce via electronic media has existed for quite some time now,
even prior to the popularisation of the Internet, but in such a restricted way
that there was no specific need to regulate it via special legislation. The Internet
has changed this and provides an internationally widespread medium.

Technical evolution in Luxembourg lags behind the evolution in larger
countries such as the United States. The electronic revolution, as it has occurred
in North America, has not yet reached Luxembourg in its full extent. As
recently as 1995, there were few serious Luxembourg Internet providers.
Today, this number is growing in proportion to the population of the country.
Thus, the Internet and its specific problems as to commerce via electronic
media are relatively new to Luxembourg. There are nearly no specific solutions
to the problems unique to Luxembourg. However, Luxembourg's legal
regulations have their specific importance, as anybody is able to deal directly
with a Luxembourg resident, so that Luxembourg regulations might become
applicable.

Legal Environment

A recent law of 1991 purports in general to provide legislation and regula-   12-2
tions for electronic media. However, this law does not seem to be applicable
to electronic computer media as the Internet. The law's scope is limited to
television and radio broadcasting. The same law organises a *Conseil National des Programmes*, which is meant to assist the Government in passing
legislation. This body, although making recommendations concerning the
Internet to the relevant authorities, considers itself to have no competence

whatsoever over Internet problems. Similarly, no particular government agency considers itself as having competence for these questions. It is thus a technical evolution that has outpaced the legislation.

Since there are no specific regulations concerning both commerce via electronic media such as the Internet and general dealings by use of the same medium, general law will be applicable.

General criminal law will be applicable for any criminal offences. It may be difficult to find in the existing criminal laws definitions which apply to dealings over the Internet or in general over electronic support; these are technically very new and modern problems whereas criminal law is fairly old and in general dates back to the original Criminal Code of 1810, except for more recent laws and amendments.

As criminal law is to be construed in a restrictive way, many offences committed by way of electronic media slip through the criminal definitions because they are not worded to cover the use of electronic media. For example, indecent or obscene publications committed by way of electronic media may be difficult to pursue under existing criminal law, because the existing legal definition refers to a publication by way of writing or printing. Nevertheless, and from a moral point of view, it seems obvious that an indecent or obscene publication committed over the Internet system is an offence and should be considered as such under positive criminal law.

To date in positive law, there is no specific criminal offence concerning electronic media. However, there are no specific offences with respect to software viruses, to unauthorised or "illegal" access to a computer system, or theft of data. These offences, however, depending on the specific circumstances, may be viewed as criminal offences regulated by "general" criminal law. As for normal commercial and civil law, one must go back to Common Law and analyse its applicability to electronic media.

One of the main problems with respect to general law is the system of legal evidence. This system provides that in civil matters, save for exceptions, evidence in court must be administered by way of written documents, and oral testimony is not admissible. By contrast, in commercial matters courts in their discretion may accept all means of evidence so there is no absolute requirement of written evidence.

Confidentiality

12-3   The right to confidentiality and protection of private life is protected by the Constitution and by the European Convention on Human Rights. This protection is not as wide as similar protection in some other countries.

Thus, it is a criminal offence for anyone and in particular employees of the Postal Authorities to open or destroy letters or telegrams. However, as these offences refer specifically to letters or telegrams, they should be inapplicable to any kind of electronic mail. Again, save for general criminal offences, and a few computer-related offences, no specific criminal law protects electronic mail, whether from destruction or from violation.

Listening into telephone communications is prohibited. Due to the nature of the Internet system and the normal access of the end user via telephone line, it may be argued that this criminal offence is applicable to Internet communications. However, questions may arise as to whether this specific criminal offence may be applicable to anyone who is listening into a communication by tapping into the dedicated transmission lines of the Internet. A further complication is the fact that a telephone connection with the provider is not a regular telephone conversation and that in case software "tapping" occurs, this happens generally outside the provider-end-user connection. Furthermore, the physical location of the offence may be very difficult to determine and may be outside of Luxembourg, thereby making, at least to a certain extent, application of Luxembourg criminal law more difficult or even impossible.

The prohibition of listening into telephone conversations is also applicable to Luxembourg authorities who need special authorisations by court to proceed to a telephone tapping.

There are no other specific criminal offences provided for by Luxembourg criminal law with respect to commerce via electronic media, although the European Convention on Human Rights requires the Luxembourg law-making authorities to define in laws to be enacted further and more complete legal environment to protect communications by way of electronic media.

As to Civil Law, the non-respect of the private sphere and of confidentiality of information and communication gives rise to actions in the law of torts, but damages are generally very low.

The violation of computer security and the penetration into a computer by unauthorised persons is specifically prohibited by criminal law relating to computers or electronic supports. Such a breach can also be prosecuted if it fits into more general definitions and laws, irrespective of the technical means by which it has been committed.

For instance, it may be considered as a breach of trust (*abus de confiance*) if the person obtains a material benefit under false pretences qualified as "manoeuvres". Depending on the circumstances, other criminal categories and definitions may be applicable, but many are not specific to the use of electronic supports or media.

Legal Effect of Electronic Signatures

Electronic signatures, *i.e.,* those derived from a mathematical formula   12-4
enabling a party to recognise the identity of the other party which, for all
practical purposes cannot be reproduced by a third party and constitute a

means of identification similar to a normal hand-written signature are not provided for under Luxembourg law. Likewise, there is no case law as to such electronic signatures.

Traditionally and for administering legal proof, a signature is required for any documents. Traditionally, a signature is the name or other identification by which the author is known in the public, affixed to a document by hand and in the author's own handwriting. While written evidence is required in principle in litigation involving civil matters, evidence is free under the control of the courts in commercial matters and even in civil matters when the amount in dispute is below a certain level (presently L.F. 100,000) or in other situations where the law provides for exceptions to written evidence. For instance, in commercial matters, an agreement may be evidenced without any written document if it is shown to the satisfaction of courts that an offer was tendered and that this offer has been duly accepted.

For all those cases where evidence may be freely administered and where no written statement signed by the parties is required, an electronic signature may be deemed sufficient by a court, although there is no known corresponding precedent in Luxembourg case law. Indeed, to prove a contract, the parties will have to be positively identified and their agreement must be documented beyond any doubt. If a signature by electronic means were challenged, the courts might consider any evidence tendered and resort to expert evidence.

International Private Law

12-5   Due to the lack of national specification as to electronic media and to the problems arising from the principle of legal proof, it is obvious that private international law will be of major importance in dealings over the Internet. Due to the small size of the Luxembourg territory and its population, conflict of law issues will probably arise much more regularly than in larger countries. Briefly, it may be stated that as soon as an end user in Luxembourg is concerned, it is very likely for Luxembourg courts to have jurisdiction, as any kind of transaction over the Internet will necessarily imply some kind of information as to the end user available in Luxembourg.

Likewise, Luxembourg law will be applicable as soon as a Luxembourg-resident end user is concerned. Even if there are non-Luxembourg law provisions in the agreement, and in the case where this content may be proven, Luxembourg law on the protection of the end user will be applicable.[1]

---

1 Loi relative . . . la protection juridique du consommateur du 25 août 1983.

ELECTRONIC TRANSACTIONS

System of Legal Proof

First, a distinction is to be made between evidence in civil matters and **12-6**
evidence in commercial matters. Whereas in civil matters and as against civil
defendants written evidence is required in principle, in commercial matters
and as against commercial defendants evidence is basically within the
discretion of the court.

The rules with respect to evidence to be administered in court state both
a principle and certain exceptions. The exceptions will be of particular
importance to dealings over the Internet.

Civil Evidence

Principle

Article 1341 of the *Code Civil* prescribes that for contracts involving **12-7**
amounts equal to or in excess of L.F. 100,000, legal proof may only be
admitted in writing. This implies evidence by documents and more often than
not by written contracts signed by both parties, and containing their obligations under the agreements.

If there is no evidence, the parties' rights will not be sanctioned by a court
ruling. If there is written evidence, no proof contrary to or in addition to this
written evidence may be admitted save by another document in writing. It
would thus appear impossible in civil matters to have a written contract
modified via e-mail and Internet communications.

Exceptions

When the value of the transaction is less than L.F. 100,000, proof may be **12-8**
freely admitted under the discretionary control of the court. Thus, an
electronic contract may be accepted in court, provided there is a clear
identification of the parties and the court is satisfied in its discretion that
there has been no forgery, neither of the contents nor of the signatures. It
seems obvious that a positive identification of the parties may not be
deduced from the e-mail addresses as these do not contain sufficient information as to the contracting person and may too easily be forged.

The Civil Code also provides for exceptions to the requirement of legal
evidence when either written evidence is available authored by the defending party and that makes the alleged fact likely as opposed to certain
(*commencement de preuve par écrit*) or when the court is satisfied that
under the circumstances it was materially or morally impossible for the
party to obtain evidence in writing at the time of the alleged fact, or if it is
proven that the written evidence was lost or destroyed due to an act of
God.

Commercial Evidence

12-9   In commercial matters, being transactions and contracts concluded for the sake of the commerce of both merchant parties, proof may be freely admitted under the control of the court.

Certain frequently relied on rules in commercial matters hold that an invoice that has not been duly challenged within a reasonably short period provides enough evidence for the existence of the contract and the execution thereof and thereby for the justification and accuracy of the invoice. A normal written or faxed invoice would be sufficient if there is strong enough evidence that the invoice was indeed received by the purchaser.

Such a proof is generally to be considered as present if the invoice has been sent by registered mail. However, an invoice sent via Internet will certainly not be considered sufficient to administer any kind of proof, as the recipient, the date of receipt and the contents of the invoice are not proven.

Electronic Contracts

12-10   There is no specific law as to electronic contracts. It follows that generally applicable law governs these contracts. These contracts must be concluded according to the forms stated above.

This is not necessary for their validity and binding effect, but to be able to bring evidence before a court and to obtain by court the relief in connection with the contract.

Offer and Acceptance

12-11   Under Luxembourg Civil Law an agreement is reached as soon as an offer meets an acceptance. This principle is true both in "normal" dealings and dealings via the Internet.

An offer is considered legally valid as soon as the seller is identified and his offer is specific as to the product, service or merchandise and to the price asked.

On the other hand, an acceptance is given as soon as the purchaser, being clearly identified, accepts the offer, which means that there is agreement as to the product and the price. Save for a very few exceptions, the acceptance must be explicit. One of the major exceptions is a continuos commercial relationship between the parties.

From the moment that an offer meets an acceptance, the contract is concluded and valid. Thus, if a seller offers to sell various products via on-line, the transaction will be concluded as soon as the user accepts this offer. The seller will be liable if he is unable to deliver the product. Since the electronic media are available world-wide, there is a risk that too many customers will accept at one given moment an offer made via webpage; the seller may not be able to deliver. For this reason, it would be wise for the seller to state explicitly that the offer to contract is not an offer in the legal sense, but only an offer to start negotiations about the sale of a specific product.

Regarding mistakes possibly made in the conclusion of an on-line commercial transaction, clarification and interpretation would be a specific problem of administering legal proof as the legal proof extends not only to the evidence of the existence of a transaction, but also of its contents.

Legal evidence is nearly impossible to supply by means of electronic commerce or at any rate very difficult to conceive, so that the details of a transaction may be very difficult to prove.

If, however, the contents have been proven sufficiently, and there are mistakes in an agreement, it is the common intention of the parties which should be taken into consideration as required by the general rules of interpretation, whatever the form of the agreement may be.

Lack of Authority

It is clear that the lack of authority of a person to enter into a contract has   **12-12** very little impact as Internet documents are generally deemed insufficient to prove the actual agreement.

If a transaction has been concluded with a person without authority to contract and where the transaction has been proven in court, Luxembourg law provides that under certain very strict conditions the appearance of authority of a person would be sufficient to validly bind the party represented by the person without authority.

Thus, for instance, a single member may represent a company normally represented by its board of directors in the case of an electronic offer if the contracting party is in a position where he may generally consider the representative to have the necessary authority. Thus, an appearance of authority has been created which is sufficient to bind the company.

Payments

Electronic Fund Transfers

A distinction is to be drawn between digital cash and electronic fund transfers.   **12-13**

Digital cash may be defined as a virtual currency unit that may be used electronically for debits and credits. It is obvious that digital cash is no legal tender and that payments made via digital cash depend solely on the agreements concluded between the user, the merchant and the bank.

Electronic fund transfers are those made by cash cards and which correspond to immediate and simultaneous movements of funds from one account to another. This method of payment is relatively new to Europe and there are only two such systems in Luxembourg ("Bancomat" and "Postomat").

A payment via electronic fund transfer works like any ordinary fund transfer done by a bank, but is made electronically and the owner's account is debited immediately when the order of transfer is recorded by the use of the cash card. Although there are no specific rules for such a payment to be made over the Internet or any assimilated system, it is relatively widespread in commercial transactions. Therefore, it may be easily imagined that the actual working system may be transposed to the Internet. However, today's system is built in such way that the user must enter a confidential code for the transfer to take place. It would be highly unwise for the user to send this code via Internet, even over a secured line, the risk of abuse being too large.

The specific regulations of this way of payment are largely regulated by the agreement between the merchant and the bank, on one hand, and the bank and the user, on the other hand.

Credit Cards

12-14 As a matter of principle, payments by credit card in Europe need a specific signature on the voucher of the credit card, which must be identical to the signature on the credit card.

In general terms, it is again the agreement between user and bank, on one hand, and bank and merchant, on the other, which regulates the payments by credit card.

It must, however, be stressed that an unsigned credit card voucher is very fragile both relative to proof and to effective payment. Indeed, if challenged by the cardholder, the user may not use such a payment to prove the execution of the agreement, as it does not necessarily imply an active payment. Furthermore, the user may normally challenge these debits after having received his monthly bank statement. It is then usually the bank's responsibility to sort this out.

It has thus been decided that a credit card voucher where the signature was forged must be assimilated to a forged cheque and that the bank may not pay the merchant because he has a legal obligation to check the signatures on such documents.

Electronic Cheques

12-15 The user does not sign electronic cheques in the normal hand-written fashion. As a consequence, Luxembourg law does not provide for electronic cheques. Indeed, according to the legal definition, the payer must sign cheques; otherwise, they are not valid as cheques. Again, the operation may at its best be considered as a digital cash process.

ELECTRONIC INFORMATION RIGHTS

Copyright

12-16 The Berne Convention of September 9, 1886, and the European Agreement of December 15, 1958, are applicable in Luxembourg. National laws of March 29, 1972, and of September 23, 1975, have ratified them, respectively.

The rules resulting from the international agreements are applicable to electronic creations on the Internet or Internet-like media. Indeed, all productions whatever the form of expression are protected as copyright.

For present purposes, it may be sufficient to say that under Luxembourg law there is no need to register a specific creation to obtain a copyright protection. Indeed, no specific registration is possible and the author of the "creation" has the copyright on condition that he is the first person to have created this specific item. If somebody using a production protected by copyright as a starting point creates a derivative production, he may acquire copyright protection over the derivative, although the primary author's copyrights may not be violated.

There are different exceptions to copyright law where reproduction of a protected creation is allowed. Apart from a quotation of statements or books, an end-user is allowed to make his own reproduction of any protected creation for his own purposes. Obviously, this user may not use this reproduction in any commercial or non-commercial activities or in general for non-private purposes, except if authorised by the copyright owner.

Trade Secrets

Trade secrets are not specifically protected in Luxembourg. They may be protected if they comprise copyrights or patents.   **12-17**

Trade Marks

Trade marks are regulated by the Benelux Convention of March 19, 1962, which was fully integrated into national law on December 7, 1966. The Treaty on the Paris Union of March 20, 1883, as well as the European Union Council Regulation 94/40/E.C. of December 20, 1993, also regulate them.   **12-18**

Trade marks must be registered to be protected. The registration is valid for 10 years and may be renewed indefinitely. Registration does not by itself provide the protection of the trade mark, as there may be other prior registered trade marks having the specific rights on this sign. It is obvious that trade marks as published on the Internet are fully protected and that violations are sanctioned both on a civil and on a criminal basis.

Domain Names

Domain names have no specific protection. Copyright law may protect them as long as they constitute an independent creation. It is obvious that the protection will be very restrictive and that it may not be extended to similar sounding domain names, as the originality of such a domain name is restricted.   **12-19**

If a domain name represents a registered trade mark, it will obviously benefit from the normal trade mark protection.

Patents

12-20   The Agreements of Strasbourg of November 27, 1936, as well as of Washington of June 19, 1970, and of Munich of October 5, 1973, are applicable in Luxembourg. The national law dates to July 20, 1992. The normal protection of patents is both of a civil nature and/or a criminal nature.

   The protection of software is not obtained via patent protection, but via copyright protection. Indeed, the specific definition of patents excludes the protection of software programes.

   Thus, the applicable law on copyright will be applicable to software creations. The owner of the creation will obviously be the first author of the product, although there may be agreements between a software company and its software engineers regarding the acquisition of the engineer's copyrights. Again, a licence may be given to any specific person. This licence may be a licence as distributor or as final user.

   It is thus generally considered that the sale of a software program is not a sale of a product or indeed not a sale at all, but a licence given to the end user to use the product. This definition is not entirely accepted by case law.

Unfair Trade Practices

12-21   Although the national law on unfair trade practices is not part of the law on patents, copyright or trade mark protection, and is only subsidiary to the patents or trade marks, it might be very useful in protecting certain rights.

   Indeed, this law states among other things that no merchant may try to confuse the public as to the product to be sold or as to the personality of the merchant. The sanctions are civil and criminal.

Miscellaneous

Who Regulates the Internet?

12-22   To date, no regulating body in Luxembourg has any authority over the Internet. The primary domain name "lu" is registered by "restena.lu". This organisation, which is a semi-public school, regulates registration and inscription of secondary domain names. The regulation has no legal effect whatsoever.

Territorial Limits of Jurisdiction

12-23   Generally, Luxembourg courts will have jurisdiction if the defendant is a resident of Luxembourg. There are obviously exceptions to this rule. Save for international treaties, Luxembourg courts will also have jurisdiction if one of the parties is a Luxembourg citizen. In contractual matters, they will have jurisdiction if the implementation of the main litigated obligation should have taken place on the Luxembourg territory. The Brussels Convention of September 25, 1968, for European Union member states and the Lugano Convention of 1980, for European Union and European Economic Area member states specifically regulate this.

As to criminal matters, Luxembourg courts have jurisdiction as soon as the criminal offence or a vital element has been committed in Luxembourg.

Distinction between Residents and Non-Residents

There is no distinction to be made between Luxembourg and non-Luxem- **12-24** bourg citizens residing in Luxembourg.

Crossborder Transactions and Communications

Except for the problems arising out of private international law and legal **12-25** proof, there are no restrictions whatsoever.

Impact of Criminal Law

It must again be stressed that there are no specific criminal offences relating **12-26** to commerce via computers or electronic media. As there are no specific provisions, the generally applicable law for criminal offences will be applicable as far as possible. Criminal offences are construed in a restrictive way.

A specific offence which is applicable to electronic media and which may be useful to the authorities is the offence of fraudulent transactions, wherein the defrauder obtains monies from the victim under false pretences. There are a few computer-related offences which deal with breaking into computer systems, alteration of data, forgery of digital documents, and modification of system functions (*e.g.*, by virus).

Law of Torts and Contractual Liability

The law of torts will be applicable to the Internet and like media and this **12-27** both in contractual and non-contractual matters. The victim may seek damages in case he suffers damage from a wrongful act. The victim must have suffered a prejudice in relation to the wrongful act.

CHAPTER 13

The Netherlands

Rob van Esch
Rabobank
Utrecht, The Netherlands

INTRODUCTION

Legal Regime Relative to Electronic Communication

No Dutch legislation relates especially to electronic communication of data,   **13-1**
but some Dutch statutes and legislative initiatives that are relevant for
electronic communication can be mentioned.

The construction, the maintenance and the operation of telecommunication infrastructures necessary for electronic communication are governed by
the Telecommunications Act (*Wet op de telecommunicatievoorzieningen* —
W.T.V.). The W.T.V. is licence-based. In the past the Dutch Post Telegraph
and Telephone operator (P.T.T.) was the only organisation that had a licence
for operating a telecommunications infrastructure. The W.T.V. explicitly
prohibited others to transport data via the telecommunications infrastructure
of the Dutch P.T.T. thus granting it an exclusive right on the transportation
of data. In addition thereto the Dutch P.T.T. had the statutory obligation to
transport data over its infrastructure.

Although the W.T.V. is a very recent Act,[1] several telecommunications
directives of the European Union have forced the Dutch legislature to amend
it both with respect to the telecommunications infrastructure and telecommunications services. A statutory framework for offering pan-European
public mobile telecommunication networks and services different from
those offered by the Dutch P.T.T. pursuant to its licence has been created
covering both G.S.M. services and paging services. Furthermore, the restrictions with respect to the transport of data via the telecommunications
infrastructure of the Dutch P.T.T. have been removed by an amendment of
section 5 of the W.T.V. resulting in a completely liberalised market for data

---

1 Telecommunications Act, *Law Gazette*, Number 551.

transport services.[2] The liberalisation of the Dutch telecommunications market is still in process. Liberalisation of telephony services will be realised in 1998.

On July 14, 1994, an amendment of the General State's Taxes Act (*Algemene wet inzake rijksbelastingen*) to adapt the administrative obligations relating to the collection of taxes and related amendments of certain other laws (adaptation of administrative obligations) came into force.

The General State's Taxes Act contains provisions that are common to all State taxes except for customs and excise.

Before the amendment of the Act, the primacy of writing was laid down in the Act. The amendment replaced sections 47 up to and including section 56 by new sections. Throughout the text the words "books and other documents" have been replaced by the words "books, documents and other data carriers". Data and information are to be provided at the choice of the tax inspector orally, in writing or by other means. The tax inspector has the right to make copies, readable printings, or abstracts of the data carriers that are handed over to him for inspection. The word "bookkeeping" has been replaced by the word "administration".

The obligation has been introduced to organise the administration and keep the data carriers in such a way that the tax inspector can inspect them within a reasonable period. The holder of the administration is under the obligation to give the necessary support and the necessary information about the organisation and functioning of the administration to the tax inspector. By Ministerial Regulation, the Minister of Finance can lay down rules with regard to the way in which the administrative work must be done.

A new paragraph was added to section 52. It provides that data kept on a data carrier may be copied to and kept on another data carrier under the condition that the data are correctly and completely copied and will be available during the complete storage time and can be reproduced in a readable form within a reasonable period. A similar paragraph was added to the Civil Code (*Burgerlijk Wetboek*).[3] The duration of the accounting obligation was not changed in Civil Law or in tax law; it still is 10 years.

The Customs and Excise Act (*Algemene wet inzake de douane en accijnzen*) was amended on January 1, 1990, enabling importers and exporters that have obtained a licence from the tax authorities to electronically declare the import or the export of goods. The information system set up by the Dutch tax authorities to exchange electronic declarations with importers and exporters is called S.A.G.I.T.T.A.[4]

---

2 Act of June 16, 1994, [1994], *Law Gazette,* Number 628.
3 Civil Code, section 3:15a, in conjunction with section 2:10. See Van Esch, "Nieuwe wet inzake de civielrechtelijke bewaarplicht", *Computerrecht* 1994/2, at p. 70.
4 Van Esch, "Enige Juridische aspecten van Sagitta", *Computerrecht* 1991/3, at p. 153, and Van Esch, "Wijziging AWDA in verband met SAGITTA", *Computerrecht* 1990/4, at p. 214.

In 1993, the Dutch government published a preliminary draft of an act regulating the use of cryptography. The preliminary draft contained a prohibition of the use of cryptography without a licence from the State. It furthermore contained the obligation of licensees to deposit their keys with a governmental body. The preliminary draft was highly criticised, because of its material adverse affect on business practice.[5] The criticism induced the government to withdraw its preliminary draft.

Confidentiality

Confidentiality of electronic data is secured by the Dutch Penal Code **13-2** (*Wetboek van Strafrecht*).

The present Dutch Data Protection Act (*Wet persoonsregistraties*) in general protects personal data that have been stored in a personal data file. It regulates issues such as:

- The object of the personal data file;
- The use of personal data;
- The disclosure of personal data to third parties;
- The right of access of the data subject;
- The right of the data subject to demand rectification or erasure of personal data;
- The liability of the holder and the processor of the file; and
- The notification to the Registrar (*Registratiekamer*) of the existence of the personal data file.[6]

The Act does not specifically deal with the transfer of personal data through **13-3** a telecommunications network. Section 49 of the Act prohibits the disclosure of personal data to or the obtaining of personal data from a data file outside the Netherlands to which this Act does not apply if by way of a General Regulation[7] such disclosure or obtainment has been declared to have a severe adverse affect on the privacy of the data subjects involved. A new act is drafted to implement the Data Protection Directive of the European Union.

Pursuant to section 125g of the Code of Criminal Procedure (*Wetboek van Strafvordering*), the examining judge conducting a judicial inquiry is authorised to demand that data communication through a telecommunications infrastructure or a public telecommunication device will be tapped or recorded by a criminal investigator if he suspects that the criminal suspect uses this infrastructure or device. Section 64 of the Telecommunication Act

---

5 "Dossier Cryptografie", *Computerrecht* 94/4 138.
6 Berkvens, Van der Horst and Verkade (editors), *Wet Persoonsregistraties*.
7 A General Regulation is promulgated by the Council of Ministers. The power to promulgate a General Regulation is regulated by section 89 of the Dutch Constitution.

provides that the owner of the telecommunications infrastructure or the public telecommunication device has the obligation to assist the criminal investigator in tapping or recording the communications. The Minister of Transport and Communications has sent a letter to the Dutch Lower House expressing his intention to include in the Dutch Telecommunication Act a section providing that the owners of telecommunication infrastructures and public telecommunication devices have the obligation to install in their infrastructure or device such facilities as are necessary to make it susceptible to tapping.[8]

Legal Effect of Electronic Signatures

13-4   Dutch legislation lacks a definition of 'signature'. A definition of this notion that is commonly accepted is that "someone's hand-written name expressed in letters, with or without one's first name or initials, which enables individ-ualisation of the signatory". The use of a facsimile or a stamp which produces an exact copy of the signature of the signatory by a person authorised to use the facsimile has been accepted in Dutch case law as a legal equivalent of a written signature.[9]

The formal requirement of a signature does not occur many times in Dutch legislation. For the legally valid performance of certain legal acts, such as the transfer of the ownership of land[10] or the creation of a pledge on receivables,[11] a notarial deed or a private deed is required. Both deeds require the signature of the parties involved. Moreover, the notarial deed also needs the signature of the notary public. The legal status of the electronic signa-tures under Dutch law is uncertain.

Where no statutory formal requirements must be fulfilled to perform a certain legal act, the court will probably accept an electronic signature as a valid instrument for identification of the person that has made the declaration to which the electronic signature is related and as a means of expressing one's will to be bound by the message the electronic signature relates to. If a statutory requirement of a signature explicitly or implicitly exists with respect to a specific legal act, the court will probably not be ready to accept an electronic signature as an alternative for the written signature. Conse-quently, those legal acts cannot validly be performed electronically.

Dutch case law shows a few examples of court decisions equating certain electronic documents and "electronic signatures" with the legally prescribed signed written documents. For instance, the Dutch Supreme Court has

---

8 Tweede Kamer der Staten-Generaal 24679, number 1. Van den Hoven van Genderen, "Aftappen, een kostbare zaak voor de telecommunicatie onderneming", *Computerrecht* 1995/6, at p. 253.
9 Supreme Court, February 2, 1920, *Nederlandse Jurisprudentie*, 1920, at p. 235. See Pitlo/Hidma-Rutgers, *Bewijs, Gouda Quint*, 1995, at p. 62.
10 Civil Code, section 3:89.
11 Civil Code, section 3:239.

decided in several cases that a faxed writ is valid although the relevant statutory provision prescribed a signed written writ.[12] The examples relate to procedural law. The impact of these court decisions on other fields of law, such as private law in general and the law regarding legal acts in particular, is uncertain.

Some amendments in administrative law have come into force accommodating the use of electronic documents and electronic signatures. These amendments mainly relate to tax law, such as the introduction of the electronic tax return.[13] No changes in private law regarding the use of electronic documents and electronic signatures to perform legal acts have been implemented yet.

Dutch legal scholars have raised objections against the general unconditional legal equalisation of electronic documents and electronic signatures with writings and signatures. Some would be willing to accept an electronic signature as an alternative for the hand-written signature if the method used to generate the electronic signature performs the same functions as the traditional signature.[14]

ELECTRONIC TRANSACTIONS

Creation of Contracts Electronically

Most contracts under Dutch law require no set formalities. These contracts **13-5** are valid and enforceable when entered into by electronic means. Some contracts require writing. Examples of such contracts are the insurance contract,[15] the hire-purchase contract,[16] the transfer of the ownership of land[17] or the creation of a pledge on receivables.[18] Pursuant to section 3:39 of the Civil Code, such contracts are invalid if they are entered into

---

12 Zwanikken, "Volmacht per fax", *W.P.N.R.* 94/6135, at p. 327, and Van Esch, "Elektronische rechtshandelingen", *De notaris en het elektronisch rechtsverkeer, Koninklijke Vermande Lelystad*, 1996, at p. 55.

13 Act of December 6, 1995, *Law Gazette,* Number 606.

14 Vandenberghe, "De betekenis van de handtekening bij het elektronisch betalingsverkeer en teleshopping", Schutte and Stuurman (ed.), *Elektronisch betalingsverkeer en teleshopping,* 1988, at p. 23; Kaspersen, "Telematica", Recht en Computer, Franken and Others (ed.), *Recht en computer,* 1992, at p. 154; Kemna, "Juridische aspecten van identiteit, authenticiteit en integriteit bij EDI", Esch van en Prins (ed.), *Recht en EDI*, 1993, at p. 21; Pitlo/Hidma-Rutgers, *Bewijs, Gouda Quint,* 1995, Number 47; De Vries, *Juridische aspecten van huistelematica: telewerken en consumeren in het informatietijdperk*,1993, at p. 181; Prins, *Overtollig recht inzake informatietechnologie, Inaugurale rede Tilburg 1995,* 1995, at p. 26; Van Esch, "Elektronische rechtshandelingen", *De notaris en het elektronisch rechtsverkeer, Koninklijke Vermande Lelystad*, 1996, at p. 51.

15 Commercial Code, section 255.

16 Civil Code, section 7A:1576i.

17 Civil Code, section 3:89.

18 Civil Code, section 3:239.

electronically, unless the law provides otherwise. An example of such a divergent statutory provision is the Governments Account Act (*Comptabiliteitswet*). Pursuant to section 30 of this Act, all private contracts entered into by the Dutch State must be in writing if the financial interest is higher than an amount set by the Minister of Finance. Section 31 explicitly provides that the validity of a contract is not affected if the formal requirements set by section 30 are not met.[19]

Offer and Acceptance On-line

13-6   Under Dutch law, offer and acceptance are regarded to be unilateral legal acts. Pursuant to section 3:37 of the Civil Code, offer and acceptance have legal effect from the moment they have reached the addressee. If an offer or an acceptance does not reach the addressee due to an act of the addressee or of a person for whom the addressee is liable, such as an employee or an event that can be imputed to the addressee, such as a computer break-down, the offer or the acceptance have legal effect from the moment it would have reached the addressee if the act had not been performed or the event had not occurred.[20]

It is uncertain how these statutory provisions will have to be applied on electronic mailboxes. Probably, an electronic message that has been sent to an electronic mailbox will be regarded to have reached the addressee at the moment it is downloaded from the mailbox to its information system. If the addressee does not empty his mailbox in a reasonable period of time, the message will be regarded to have reached him at the moment he should have emptied the mailbox.[21]

Some scholars are of the opinion that an offer regarding a formal contract requires the same formalities as those set by law for such contract.[22] This means that an offer to enter into a hire-purchase agreement must be in writing.

Section 6:221 of the Civil Code provides that an oral offer expires if it is not accepted immediately and a written offer expires if it is not accepted within a reasonable period of time. How this provision must be applied to an electronic offer is uncertain.

Mistakes in On-line Contracts

13-7   If a mistake in the communication of an offer or an acceptance occurs that the receiver did not discover or should not have discovered, the offer or acceptance as received by the addressee is binding on the sender unless the

---

19 For a general discussion of the requirement of a writing and the use of electronic means of communication, see Van Esch, "Elektronische rechtshandelingen", *De notaris en het elektronisch rechtsverkeer, Koninklijke Vermande Lelystad*, 1996, at p. 46.

20 Civil Code, section 6:224.

21 Van Esch, "EDI en het Nederlandse recht: een inventarisatie van problemen", *Computerrecht* 1993/6, at p. 237.

22 Asser-Hartkamp II, *WEJ Tjeenk Willink Zwolle*, 1993, Number 220.

recipient has prescribed the means of communication.[23] This provision is based on the assumption that the sender will choose the means of communication and therefore must bear the risk of a miscommunication. Parties can agree otherwise.[24]

In an electronic environment, it will not always be easy to answer the question whether or not the recipient has prescribed the means of communication. Such a situation might occur if the recipient informs the sender that it will no longer trade with the sender unless the sender uses a certain means of communication, like Electronic Data Interchange (EDI).

Impact of Impostors or Persons without Authority

If an impostor or an unauthorised person sends an offer or an acceptance   13-8
misusing the identification code of another, the question arises if the owner of the identification code is legally bound by such an offer or acceptance. The decision of the Dutch Supreme Court in the case *Stichting Centraal Orgaan Voorraadvorming Aardolieprodukten* v. *Banque Generale du Luxembourg (Suisse) SA and Internationale Nederlanden Bank N.V.* [25] is of overriding importance.

The Internationale Nederlanden Bank had granted the Stichting Centraal Orgaan Voorraadvorming Aardolieprodukten (C.O.V.A.) a credit facility. C.O.V.A. would send payment orders to the bank by telex. The bank and C.O.V.A. had agreed on C.O.V.A. adding an identification code to the telex message. The identification code had to be derived from a code list supplied by the bank.

In 1984, one of the employees of C.O.V.A. committed fraud. He sent a payment order to the bank, ordering the bank to transfer an amount of approximately N.L.G. 9-million to a bank account held with Banque Generale du Luxembourg (Suisse). The telex message contained the agreed identification code. The employee was not authorised to use the identification code. As the message contained the agreed identification code, the bank assumed that it originated from an authorised employee and executed the payment order.

In this case, C.O.V.A. pleaded that, as a general rule, the "owner" of an identification code is not bound by a message that contains its code if the code was used by an unauthorised person, even though it was quite reasonable for the receiver of the message to assume that the message originated from an authorised person. The Dutch Supreme Court decided against C.O.V.A. It took into consideration that adopting the view of C.O.V.A. would in principle produce an inequitable result where the person that had misused the identification code was an employee of its owner. In an *obiter*

---

23 Civil Code, section 3:37.
24 Katus, "De aansprakelijkheidsaspecten van EDI en het Ediforum Contract", *Computerrecht* 92/2, p. 59.
25 *Nederlandse Jurisprudentie* 1994, November 19, 1993, at p. 622.

dictum, the Supreme Court went into the situation that the owner of the identification code and the receiver have not contractually allocated the risk of misuse of the identification code. It decided that the question who should bear the risk of an unauthorised use of an identification code must be answered taking into account all circumstances of the case, whereby it is in particular relevant to establish who can be held responsible for the fact that the code had come to the disposal of an unauthorised person.

If the unauthorised person was an employee of the owner or otherwise had a relationship to the owner that meant he had more easy access to the code than others, then as a general rule the owner is legally bound by the message; it may be assumed that the misuse was a result of his own negligence. If the owner of the identification code can prove that he has fulfilled his duty of care with respect of his identification code, the risk shifts back to the receiver of the message.

Although the decision of the Supreme Court relates to telex messages and secret telex keys, it also applies to electronic signatures.[26] The sender and the receiver can agree that the sender bears the risk of misuse of an identification code and is legally bound by any message containing its identification code. A court can set such a contractual arrangement aside if it is unfair taking into account all circumstances.[27] One of the relevant circumstances would probably be the security measures taken to prevent misuse of the identification code.

On-line Payments

13-9   The Civil Code distinguishes two kinds of payments of a monetary debt: payment by circulating currency and payment by giro. Pursuant to section 6:114 of the Civil Code, a debtor has the right to fulfil its monetary obligations by transferring the amount owed to the creditor to an account of the creditor, unless the creditor has validly prohibited such a payment by giro.

The question whether or not the creditor has the right to exclude a payment by giro depends on the facts of the case. If the debtor pays his debt by money transfer the payment is deemed to be completed when the account of the creditor is credited for the amount transferred.[28]

Electronic Funds Transfer

13-10   Electronic funds transfer is a very common means of payment in The Netherlands. A client having a bankcard can make a cash withdrawal or give an electronic payment order using the card in combination with a secret PIN-code. The PIN-code is communicated to the computer of the bank in an encrypted form. The computer recalculates the PIN-code and compares

---

26 Van Esch, *Computerrecht* 1994/4, at p. 167.
27 Civil Code, section 6:248.
28 Civil Code, section 6:114.

this code with the code received from the cash dispenser or the point-of-sale terminal. If they match and the balance of the account is sufficient to execute the withdrawal or electronic payment order, the computer of the bank will send an acknowledgement to the cash dispenser or the point-of-sale terminal.

Dutch law does not have a special statute relating to electronic funds transfer. The relationships between the creditor, the debtor, and the banks are based on general conditions.

The general conditions governing the relationship between the card-holder and its bank are the Cash Dispenser and Point-of-Sale Terminal Conditions (*Voorwaarden Geld- en Betaalautomaten*). These conditions are the result of negotiations between the Dutch banks and Dutch consumer organisations. The obligations of the bank are described in article 2 of these general conditions. The bank will endeavour to have its hardware, software and infrastructure operate uninterrupted as far as possible. The bank under-takes towards its cardholder to exercise due care when executing payment orders of the cardholder and in performing other agreements with the client and to take the cardholder's interest into account to the best of its ability.

The bank is liable towards the cardholder for any loss suffered as a result of any shortcomings in the execution of such payment orders if such shortcoming is caused by its negligence. Finally, the bank undertakes to keep operational a reporting point 24 hours a day, seven days a week, enabling the cardholder to report the loss, the theft, the unauthorised use or the forgery of its card.

The obligations of the cardholder are laid down in article 3 of the general conditions. It provides that the cardholder must observe due care with respect to the card and the PIN-code. The cardholder is responsible for (the use of) his card and PIN-code. The PIN-code is strictly personal and non-transferable. The cardholder has the obligation to keep the PIN-code secret and is not allowed to write the code on the card. If it assumes that its PIN-code has become known to third parties, the cardholder must immedi-ately give notice to the bank.

Article 6 of the general conditions contains the provisions relating to the liability for unauthorised use of the card and the PIN-code. The cardholder is liable for damage suffered as a result of unauthorised use up to a maximum amount of N.L.G. 350. The limitation of the liability of the cardholder does not apply in certain situations, for instance if the cardholder has not immediately reported the theft of its card to the bank. The card-holder is not liable for any damage sustained after it has reported the loss, the theft, the unauthorised use or the forgery of its card to the bank, unless the bank can prove that the cardholder has acted intentionally or with gross negligence.

Article 5 of the general conditions provides that the payment order is irrevocable from the moment the cardholder has performed all the acts necessary to give the payment order.[29]

In the general conditions applicable to the relationship between the creditor and its bank, the bank guarantees towards the creditor that its account will be credited with the amount of electronic payment orders issued for its benefit.

Most Dutch banks have their own telebanking system. Clients that have entered into a contract with a bank offering such telebanking services can give payment orders to the bank electronically. The payment order is generated by the computer of the client and is sent to the bank through the telecommunications infrastructure. The relationship between the client and the bank is governed by special general conditions. Unlike the general conditions for cash dispensers and point-of-sale terminals, each bank has drafted its own general conditions applying to telebanking services.

The Dutch banks have jointly developed a payment system for the Internet called I-Pay. If the client wants to participate in the I-Pay system an I-account is opened. The client can transfer money from its regular account to the separate I-account. During the experiment, the maximum balance of the I-account amounts to N.L.G. 250. From his I-account the client can give an electronic payment order to his bank. The payment order includes a digital signature that has been calculated on the basis of the data of the payment order and a secret password by software on a special key-disk. The payment order is sent to the creditor (the company providing services or offering goods on the Internet) that adds his digital signature to the electronic message and sends this message to Interpay, a company owned by the Dutch banks (except the Dutch Postbank). Interpay verifies the digital signatures and transfers the amount of the payment order from the I-account of the client to the I-account of the creditor. The creditor can dispose of the balance of its I-account by transferring the money to its regular account.

The I-Pay General Conditions govern the relationship between the client and the bank. Article 5 of these general conditions provides that the client must observe due care with respect to the I-Pay software, the secret password and the key-disk. The client must inform the bank immediately of the loss or theft of its key-disk. The client must immediately give notice to the bank of its presumption that a third party has obtained the secret password. Pursuant to article 8 of the general conditions, the bank shall set up and maintain a report centre. Article 9 provides that the client is liable for any damage suffered as a result of the unauthorised use of the I-Pay software, the password or the key-disk before it has given notice to the bank in accordance

---

29 Van Esch and Berkvens, *Giraal Betalingsverkeer/Elektronisch betalingsverkeer*, 1988, at p. 127; Knobbout-Bethlem, *Konsumentgericht elektronisch betalingsverkeer*, 1992.

with article 5. Article 6 provides that the payment order is irrevocable as soon as the client has performed all the acts necessary to give the order.[30]

The latest development is the introduction by the Dutch banks of the prepaid card or the electronic purse. All payment cards that are issued in the Netherlands are multifunctional. They have a magnetic stripe for electronic payments and a chip for the electronic purse. The chip can be charged using the same PIN-code as the code used for giving electronic payment orders or withdrawing money from a cash dispenser. Payments can be made without using the PIN-code. If a client has charged his chipcard, the amount of the charge is transferred from his account to an account of the bank (the so-called "Float"). When a payment has been made the amount of the payment is transferred from the Float to the account of the creditor.

The relationship between the cardholder and the bank is governed by general conditions called the "Voorwaarden Chipknip". The contents of these general conditions are similar to the General Conditions Cash Dispensers and Point-of-Sale Terminals.[31]

Credit Card Payments On-line

Dutch credit card organisations have adopted with respect to credit card payments on-line the same conditions as the banks apply to electronic funds transfers.   **13-11**

Use of Electronic Checks

Due to the high level of development of payments systems in The Netherlands checks are only used in international trade transactions.   **13-12**

The Commercial Code (*Wetboek van koophandel*) contains several provisions relating to checks.[32] From these statutory provisions it is clear that the legislature has presumed that a check is a paper signed by the drawer. The rights under a check to the order of a person can be transferred by handing over the check and writing an endorsement on the reverse side of the cheques.

Given this, it is not certain if a Dutch court will recognise an electronic check as being a valid check in the sense of the Commercial Code.

ELECTRONIC INFORMATION RIGHTS

Copyright

In the Netherlands copyrights are protected by the Copyright Act 1912 (*Auteurswet* 1912). The creator of a work acquires a copyright in such work   **13-13**

---

30 Van Esch and De Rooy, "Juridische aspecten van Internetbetalingen", *N.J.B.*, 1996/41, at p. 1741.
31 De Rooy, "De chipknip: een (juridische) verkenning", *N.J.B.*, 1996/14, at p. 511; Van Esch, "De Chipknip: het virtuele geld", *Computerrecht* 1996/4, at p. 126.
32 Commercial Code, sections 178–229e.

by force of law. Section 10 of the Copyright Act 1912 contains a non-exhaustive list of works that are protected by copyright. This list includes computer programs and their preparatory material (such as a flow chart).

A work is protected by copyright if it is expressed or can be expressed in a perceptible form. The underlying ideas are not protected. Furthermore, a work must bear the personal mark of the creator. This means that the creator when creating the work must have been presented with choices when giving expression to his ideas. The creator of a non-personal work (such as a telephone book) is only protected against mere copying of its work. Non-personal computer programs are explicitly excluded from this protection.[33]

Section 7 of the Copyright Act 1912 provides that if the creator is an employee and has created the work in the performance of his duties under the employment contract, the copyright in the work belongs to the employer.

The owner of the copyright has the exclusive right to distribute and reproduce the work. Reproduction includes acts such as translation and adaptation of the work.

Digital or digitised works are susceptible of protection by copyright because they can be expressed in a perceptible form by means of computer hardware and computer programs. It is not certain whether under Dutch law technical reproductions of (parts of) a digital work that are made in the network while transporting the data through the telecommunications infrastructure without the approval of the owner of the copyright in that work are an infringement of copyright. As technical reproductions of computer software, such as the loading and the execution of the program, explicitly fall under the scope of the Copyright Act,[34] it is perceivable that a court will decide that technical reproductions of a digitised work, made for transmission purposes, are also covered by this Act.

When a reproduction of a work has been distributed, the copyright with respect to that reproduction is exhausted. An exception is made for computer programs. The owner of a copyright in such a computer program has the right to control further rental of the reproduction.[35]

Some Dutch scholars are of the opinion that the exhaustion of copyright does not apply to reproductions communicated through an on-line network because the concept of exhaustion is restricted to reproductions made on a physical data carrier.[36]

In case of an infringement of a copyright the owner of the copyright can request the court to issue an injunction prohibiting the infringing acts. Furthermore, he can claim damages.[37] He can also claim the turn over of any profit

---

33 Copyright Act 1912, section 10(1).
34 Copyright Act 1912, section 45i.
35 Copyright Act 1912, section 45h.
36 Brunt and Schellekens, "Auteursrecht in DigiWorld", *Intellectueel eigendom in digitaal perspectief*, 1996, at p. 34.
37 Copyright Act 1912, section 27.

the infringing party has made out of the infringement.[38] Finally, he can attach those goods that have been distributed or reproduced in violation of his copyright.[39]

In the case *Scientology* v. *Xs4all*,[40] the question was raised whether the network access provider could be qualified as the distributor of documents of the Church of Scientology that had been published by a subscriber of the provider without the prior approval of the owner of the copyright in those documents. The Presiding Judge decided that it merely solicited the distribution of the documents and was not itself a distributor. In its capacity as an access provider it was not responsible for the infringement of the copyright of the Church of Scientology.

In another case, *Bridgesoft* v. *Lenior*,[41] the court decided that the defendant (Lenior) had distributed software in which the plaintiff (Bridgesoft) had a copyright by enabling others to download this computer program from its Bulletin Board System. The decisive factor here was that Lenior had adapted the Title Allocation Table of the computer program to facilitate the downloading of the computer program from its bulletin board.

It is uncertain whether an Internet provider can be regarded as reproducer of a work that is distributed through the network. The answer to this question depends on whether a technical reproduction of such a work can be qualified as a relevant reproduction and an infringement of the exclusive right of the owner of the copyright in such work.

Trade Secrets

Under Dutch law, trade secrets are primarily protected by the Penal Code.   13-14
Section 272 of the Penal Code provides that he who intentionally violates a secret that he has obtained in his profession is punishable by imprisonment for a maximum of one year and six months or a fine of up to a maximum of N.L.G. 25,000 if he knows or reasonably should have known that he should keep the secret. Violation of the secret can take place by publishing the secret through a network.

Pursuant to section 273 of the Penal Code, anyone who intentionally discloses a detail regarding a trade company that he is or has been employed in, is punishable by imprisonment for a maximum of six months or a fine of up to a maximum of N.L.G. 25,000 if he by disclosing such detail violates a duty of confidentiality towards that company. Disclosure of such detail can occur by making the detail available to third parties through a network.

Pursuant to this section, the same penalty can be imposed on a person that discloses data relating to a trade company or that uses such data himself

---

38 Copyright Act 1912, section 27a.
39 Copyright Act 1912, section 28.
40 Presiding Judge of the Court of The Hague, *Computerrecht* 1996/2, at p. 73.
41 Court of Rotterdam, *Informatierecht/AMI*, 1996/5, at p. 101.

for pursuit of profit if these data are obtained by felony from an information system of that trade company and are not generally known to the public, provided that such disclosure can cause damage to the company. Felonious acquiring of data from an information system, for example, occurs when these data are obtained by computer trespass and the trespasser has gained access through the public telecommunications infrastructure or a public telecommunication construction.[42] Data can be disclosed by publishing them through a network.

It is very unlikely that a network provider will be punishable for being an accessory to the criminal offence in the sense of the aforementioned sections 272 and 273 of the Penal Code. Section 48 of the Penal Code requires for complicity that the accomplice intentionally solicits the crime or intentionally provides the means or the information to commit the criminal offence.

Supplementary to the provisions in the Penal Code, section 7:678 of the Civil Code provides that an employer has the right to dismiss an employee summarily if that employee has disclosed details regarding the company of the employer that he should have kept secret.

The person that wrongfully discloses a trade secret thereby causing damage to the owner of the trade secret commits a tort. Pursuant to section 6:162 of the Civil Code, that person is under the statutory obligation to compensate the owner of the trade secret for any damage suffered as a result of that tort. The same applies to a third party that has encouraged the wrongful disclosure of a trade secret and has profited from such disclosure. An example would be when a competitor has induced an employee to disclose a trade secret of his employer.

It is not certain whether the provider of a network through which a trade secret is disclosed is liable for the damage suffered by the owner. Probably, the network provider shall only be liable if it knew that its network was used for wrongfully disclosing a trade secret and has not taken any measures to prevent this, such as disconnecting the person that is distributing the information.[43]

Trade Mark

13-15   Trade marks are governed by the Uniform Benelux Act on Trade Marks (*Eenvormige Beneluxwet op de merken*). The Act covers both trade marks for goods and services. Marks can only serve as a trade mark if they have a distinguishable capacity.[44]

---

42 Penal Code, section 138a.
43 *Scientology* v. *Xs4all*, Presiding Judge of the Court of The Hague, *Computerrecht* 1996/2, at p. 73. Compare Ottow and Grootenhuis, *Intellectueel eigendom in digitaal perspectief*, 1996, at p. 85.
44 Uniform Benelux Act on Trade Marks, section 1.

A right in a trademark on a good or service is created by first registration of that trade mark with the Benelux Trade Mark Bureau in The Hague in the public trade mark register.[45] After the registration the owner of the trademark has the exclusive right to use the mark.[46]

To register a trademark the applicant must fill out a form in writing, sign this form and send this form in quadruplicate together with the required enclosures to the Benelux Trademark Bureau.[47] The Benelux Trademark Bureau will draw up a deed of registration and will register this deed in the public trademark register. As an on-line application through a network does not meet the formal requirements as laid down in the implementation order, the Benelux Trade Mark Bureau will not take up such an application.

The registration expires after a period of 10 years has elapsed.[48] Expiration of a right in a trademark can be prevented by renewal of the registration.

The owner of a right in a trademark can request the deletion of the registration.[49]

The exclusive right in a trademark also expires if the owner has not actually made a normal use of the trademark for a period of five years in the area of the Benelux (*i.e.*, Belgium, The Netherlands, and Luxembourg) without a valid reason.[50] Normal use of a trademark means that the owner or a licensee uses the trademark commercially outside its own enterprise with respect to goods or services offered by it thus distinguishing these goods or services from those of others. A court deciding whether an owner has made a normal use of its trademark will take into account all circumstances, such as:

- The character of the enterprise;
- The character of the goods or services that the trademark relates to; and
- The frequency and the scale of the use.

The use of a trademark on a public network such as the Internet can be regarded   **13-16**
as a use of the trademark. Even if the Web site on which the trade mark is published is located outside the Benelux, one can say that the trade mark has been used within the area of the Benelux if the Internet users within the Benelux can open this Web site. Whether such a use on the Internet can be qualified as a normal use depends on the above-mentioned circumstances.[51]

---

45 Uniform Benelux Act on Trade Marks, section 3.
46 Uniform Benelux Act on Trade Marks, section 13.
47 Uniform Benelux Act on Trade Marks, sections 6 and 41 provide that the application must fulfil the formal requirements laid down in an implementing order. The present implementing order dates from November 20, 1995, and requires a signed written document.
48 Uniform Benelux Act on Trade Marks, section 5, in conjunction with section 10.
49 Uniform Benelux Act on Trade Marks, section 5.
50 Uniform Benelux Act on Trade Marks, section 5.
51 Wefers Bettink, "Merken en domeinen in digitale omgeving", *Intellectueel eigendom in digitaal perspectief*, 1996, at p. 69.

Registration of a trademark does not lead to a creation of a right in that trademark if the trademark was maliciously registered.[52] A malicious registration is a registration by a person that knows or should have known that a third party acting in good faith has made a normal use of a similar trademark in the preceding three years in the area of the Benelux for similar goods or services and has not acquired the prior approval of that third party for the registration of the trademark. The use of a trademark on a public network such as the Internet can be a preceding use blocking the valid registration of a trademark by another.

Malicious registration requires that the person registering the trade mark knew or should have known the preceding use of that trade mark by somebody else. Presumably, under Dutch law, this requirement has been met if the trademark is regularly published on a Web site that is easily accessible by Internet users within the Benelux area and such users frequently visit the Web site.[53]

If a third party infringes the right in a trademark by commercially using a similar trademark for similar goods or services, the owner of that right can request the court to issue an injunction prohibiting the subsequent commercial use of the similar trade mark by that third party. Furthermore, the owner of the right that has been infringed can claim compensation for any damage suffered as a result of such infringement. Finally, he can claim the turn over of any profit the infringing party has made out of the infringement.[54]

Use of a similar trademark for similar goods or services on a public network such as the Internet can result in an infringement of another's right in a trade mark under the laws of any country in which the network is accessible. This might lead to a court order in such country to remove the infringing trademark from the worldwide Web site.[55]

Domain Names

13-17   In the Netherlands, domain names for the Internet are issued by a foundation called *Stichting Internet Domeinregistraties NL*. The Internet providers that participate in the foundation make applications for users' domain names. According to its rules, the foundation has the right to refuse the registration of a domain name if it contains general names or generic names

---

52 Uniform Benelux Act on Trade Marks, section 4.
53 Wefers Bettink, "Merken en domeinen in digitale omgeving", *Intellectueel eigendom in digitaal perspectief*, 1996, at p. 67.
54 Uniform Benelux Act on Trade Marks, section 13.
55 Wefers Bettink, "Merken en domeinen in digitale omgeving", *Intellectueel eigendom in digitaal perspectief*, 1996, at p. 71.

and therefore can give rise to misunderstandings. The foundation does not examine whether the domain name infringes rights of third parties such as a right in a trademark.[56]

Case law in The Netherlands shows that the use of an Internet domain name can result in the infringement of another's right in a trademark or a tradename.

In the case *Kok and Franken v. van As*,[57] the court denied the request for an injunction prohibiting the use of the domain name "flevonet.nl" because the plaintiffs had failed to register the trademark "Flevonet". Presumably, the court would have issued the injunction if a registration of the trademark had been made.

In the case *NTG XLINK v. XXLink Internet Services*, the court also denied the request for a court order prohibiting the use of the domain name "xxLink.nl". The court decided that no infringement of the right of the plaintiff in the trademark and tradename "XLINK" had occurred because the services of the plaintiff differed too much from the services of the defendant.[58]

In the case *Ouders On-line*, the plaintiff, VNU (publisher of the magazine *Ouders van Nu*), requested the Court of Amsterdam to prohibit (i) the use of the name "Ouders On-line", used by the defendant as the name of an Internet Web site, and (ii) the use of the domain name "ouders.nl".[59] The plaintiff alleged that the use of these names infringed its right in the trademark *Ouders van Nu*. The court rejected the request with respect to the name *Ouders On-line* because the word *ouders* had insufficient distinguishing capacity. The request regarding the domain name was denied because the complete domain name "http://www.ouders.nl" had not enough similarity with the trade name.[60]

Finally, the use of a domain name can infringe the right of another in a trade name under the Trade Name Act (*Handelsnaamwet*) if such use can cause confusion with the public about the origin of products or services offered.[61]

Patents

Patents are regulated by the Patent Act 1995 (*Rijksoctrooiwet*). Patents can be taken out in respect of new inventions that can be applied in the field of   **13-18**

---

56 Wefers Bettink, "Merken en domeinen in digitale omgeving", *Intellectueel eigendom in digitaal perspectief*, 1996, at p. 73.
57 Presiding Judge of the Court of Zwolle, *Kort Geding* 1996, at p. 250.
58 This case is referred to in Wefers Bettink, "Merken en domeinen in digitale omgeving", *Intellectueel eigendom in digitaal perspectief*, 1996, at p. 82.
59 Presiding Judge of the Court of Amsterdam, *Kort Geding* 1996, at p. 334.
60 Wefers Bettink, "Merken en domeinen in digitale omgeving", Intellectueel eigendom in digitaal perspectief, 1996, at p. 81.
61 Verkade, "Internet-domeinnamen, merkenrecht en handelsnaamrecht", *Computerrecht* 1997/1, at p. 3.

industry, agriculture included.[62] An invention is new if it is not a part of the state of the art of technology.[63] An invention creates a solution to a technical problem that was not obvious for an expert given the state of the art of technology.[64] The Patent Act 1995 explicitly excludes software from the notion of invention.[65] This means that under Dutch law software itself cannot be patented. Software-based products, such as computer-controlled machines, are still patentable.

The patent will be granted to the applicant. The applicant is presumed to be the inventor.[66] The applicant does not have a right to a patent if the contents of his application are derived without the prior approval of such third party from something that has already been produced by someone else or a design, description or a model of someone else. Such third party keeps his right to the patent.[67]

If the invention was made by an employee, the employer is entitled to the patent if the employee is under a duty under the employment contract to use his special skills for making inventions of the same nature as that to which the patent application relates to, unless explicitly agreed otherwise in writing between the employer and the employee. The employee, making an invention that has been patented by his employer, has a right against his employer to a reasonable compensation if his wages cannot be considered to compensate him for the lack of the patent.[68] If an invention is made jointly by more than one person those persons will have a joint right to the patent.[69]

Patents are issued on application by the Bureau for Industrial Property (*Bureau voor de industriele eigendom*). The application is registered by the Bureau for Industrial Property in the Register of Patents.[70] Although the Act does not explicitly provide that the application must be in writing, the wording of the Act implies that a written application must be filed with the bureau. The inventor can apply for the granting of a patent without examination of the state of the art of technology[71] or with such examination.[72]

---

62 Patent Act 1995, section 2.
63 Patent Act 1995, section 4.
64 Patent Act 1995, section 5.
65 Patent Act 1995, section 2.
66 Patent Act 1995, section 8.
67 Patent Act 1995, section 11.
68 Patent Act 1995, section 12.
69 Patent Act 1995, section 13.
70 Patent Act 1995, section 31.
71 Patent Act 1995, section 33.
72 Patent Act 1995, section 36.

The patent issued without examination of the technological state of the art will expire after a period of six years has elapsed from the date of filing the application.[73] If the patent has been issued after such examination it will expire after 20 years.[74]

The patentee has the exclusive right to:

- Produce, use, traffic, sell, rent, deliver or otherwise trade, offer, import or have in stock the patented product; or
- Apply the patented process in its company and use, traffic, sell, rent, deliver or trade the products directly obtained by applying the process.[75]

A patent can be enforced against anyone that performs an act that is part of   **13-19**
the exclusive right of the patentee without the approval of the patentee. Damages can only be claimed in case of a wilful infringement of the patent. In addition to damages the patentee can claim the turnover of any profit the infringing party has made out of the infringement.[76]

Licensing

A person that is the owner of a copyright, a right in a trademark or a patent   **13-20**
can grant to a third party a licence to perform one or more of the acts that are part of his exclusive right. Thus, for example, a holder of a copyright in a computer program can give a third party the right to make reproductions of the computer program. The owner of secret know-how can enter into a licence agreement with a third party giving that third party the right to use this know-how.

The Copyright Act 1912 does not include provisions regarding the licensing of copyrightable works. This means that a licence agreement with respect to a copyright is governed by the general rules of the law of contract as laid down in the Civil Code. There are no formal requirements with respect to a licence regarding a copyright. Therefore, a copyright licence can be granted electronically.[77]

Pursuant to section 45j of the Copyright Act 1912, the rightful owner of a computer program has by force of law a licence to make a reproduction of the computer program necessary for the intended use of such program, unless parties have agreed otherwise. The making of a reproduction as part of the loading of the computer program, the displaying of the program on a

---

73 Patent Act 1995, section 33.
74 Patent Act 1995, section 36.
75 Patent Act 1995, section 53.
76 Patent Act 1995, section 70.
77 Thole, *Software en novum in het vermogensrecht*, 1991, at p. 157; Verkade and Spoor, *Auteursrecht*, 1993, at p. 362; Van Schelven and Struik, *Softwarerecht*, 1995, at p. 121.

screen or the correction of errors cannot be prohibited by contract. The making of a backup copy is not considered to be a reproduction.[78]

Pursuant to section 11 of the Uniform Benelux Act on Trade marks, a licence agreement regarding a trademark must be entered into by notarial deed or private deed. If this formal requirement is not met the agreement is invalid and unenforceable against the counterpart. To be enforceable against third parties, the notarial deed or private deed containing the licence agreement or a declaration regarding the licence signed by the licensor and the licensee must be registered in the public trademark register. In case of an infringement of the right in the trademark the licensee has the right to intervene in the lawsuit between the owner of the right in the trademark and the infringer to claim compensation for the damage suffered as a result of this infringement.[79] A licensee can only file a claim for compensation against an infringer independently from the owner of the right in the trademark if he has explicitly stipulated that right.

A licence with respect to a patent is an informal agreement. The licence includes all acts covered by the exclusive right of the patentee and is considered to be granted for the complete duration of the patent unless agreed otherwise. The licence is enforceable against third parties after registration of the title of the licence in the register of patents.[80] Pursuant to section 57 of the Patent Act 1995, the Minister of Economic Affairs is authorised to grant a licence with respect to a patent to a third party if the public interest requires this. Before granting such a compulsory licence the Minister must investigate if the owner of the patent is willing to grant a licence voluntarily under reasonable conditions. The court has the authority to grant a licence to a third party if the owner of the patent or a licensee has not used the patent for a period of three years after the date of the patent without justification.[81]

ON-LINE CONDUCT

Regulation of Electronic Communications

13-21   Dutch law legislation does not know any statutes that specifically relate to electronic communications.

The Civil Code and the Commercial Code primarily cover the private law aspects. The Ministry of Justice is responsible for these acts. At this moment these acts do not contain any specific provisions that address the legal aspects of electronic communications. This means that the contents of the private legal relationships between the participants of electronic

---

78 Copyright Act 1912, section 45k.
79 Uniform Benelux Act on Trade Marks, section 11D.
80 Patent Act 1995, section 56.
81 Patent Act 1995, section 58.

communications are dominated by the contracts that those participants have entered into between themselves and the general conditions that are applicable to those contracts.

The Telecommunications Act regulates telecommunications. The Ministry of Transport and Communications is responsible for applying the Act.

Privacy aspects of electronic communications are covered by the Data Protection Act. This Act comes within the area of responsibility of the Ministry of Justice.

The Penal Code lays down rules regarding the penal aspects of electronic telecommunications. The Code of Criminal Procedure covers the criminal procedure aspects of electronic telecommunications. The Ministry of Justice is responsible for the application of both Acts.

Copyright aspects are dealt with in the Copyright Act 1912. This Act falls under the responsibility of the Ministry of Justice.

Trade marks are governed by the Uniform Benelux Act on Trade Marks. This Act is based on a treaty between Belgium, The Netherlands, and Luxembourg. The Ministries of Foreign Affairs of the participating countries are responsible for this treaty. The Ministry of Economic Affairs is responsible for applying the Patent Act 1995 that regulates patents.

Territorial Limits of Jurisdiction

Dutch legislation does not provide a systematic or exhaustive regulation **13-22** regarding private international law. The General Provisions Act (*Wet Algemene Bepalingen*) contains some provisions on this subject. Section 6 of this Act provides that statutes regarding the rights, the status and the powers of persons bind persons with Dutch nationality even if they are abroad. Pursuant to section 7 of the General Provisions Act, the laws of the country or the place where they are located govern immovable properties. Section 8 provides that penal regulations are binding on anyone situated in the territory of the Netherlands.

According to section 9 of the General Provisions Act, Dutch private law is equal for foreigners and persons having the Dutch nationality unless provided otherwise. Section 10 provides that the form that is required for certain legal acts must be determined in accordance with the legislation of the country in which the act is performed. Because the General Provisions Act dates from 1829, it has lost much of its importance.[82]

Under Dutch private international law, parties to a contract are in principle free to choose the law that will be applicable to the contract, even if the chosen law conflicts with imperative rules of the law that would have been applicable in the absence of a choice of the parties to the contract.[83]

---

82 Strikwerda, *Inleiding tot het Nederlandse internationaal Privaatrecht*, 1995, at p. 26.
83 Supreme Court, May 13, 1966, *Nederlandse Jurisprudentie* 1967, at p. 3.

There are exceptions to this general rule. The right to choose the applicable law is restricted to contracts having an international character. Furthermore, parties are not free to choose the law applicable to their contract if this is contrary to Dutch legislation.

If, for example, Dutch law prohibits the transfer of moneys to a certain country, parties cannot circumvent this rule of law by declaring the laws of another country applicable that does not contain such a prohibition. Finally, foreign priority rules can set aside the choice of law of the parties to the contract.

It is uncertain when a contract should be regarded to have an international character. Criteria that are relevant in this respect are the domiciles of the parties, their nationality, the place of the act and the location of the goods involved, if any.[84] One may assume that a contract entered into by exchange of electronic messages through an international network between parties residing in different countries has an international character. Under Dutch law, parties to such contracts are in principle free to choose the applicable law.

If parties have not made a choice of law, the laws of the country in which the party that must make the characteristic performance under the contract is domiciled will be applicable.[85] In the case of a transport agreement, for example, the laws of the country in which the transporter has its domicile will be applicable to the contract.

On September 1, 1991, the European Union Treaty of June 19, 1980, concerning the law applicable to obligations arising out of contract (Treaty of Rome) came into force in the Netherlands. As of this date, the rules of this treaty are decisive for answering the question as to which law is applicable to obligations arising out of contracts, with the exception of those contracts that have been explicitly excluded from the scope of the treaty.[86]

Under Dutch law, the laws of the country where the tort has taken place (*lex loci delicti*) govern a claim arising out of tort in general. There are exceptions to this general rule. One exception relates to the situation in which both parties involved reside in another country than the country in which the tort was committed and the consequences of the tort completely occur in that other country. In that case the laws of the country of consequences prevail.[87]

If, for example, a person residing in the Netherlands infringes the copyright of a Dutch company in a computer program by publishing this computer program on an electronic bulletin board accessible in Germany,

---

84 Strikwerda, *Inleiding tot het Nederlandse internationaal Privaatrecht*, 1995, at p. 23.
85 Supreme Court, October 27, 1972, *Nederlandse Jurisprudentie* 1973, at p. 121; Supreme Court, April 6, 1973, *Nederlandse Jurisprudentie* 1973, at p. 371. See Strikwerda, *Inleiding tot het Nederlandse internationaal Privaatrecht*, 1995, at p. 184.
86 For more information, consult the chapter in this book regarding International Treaties and Conventions.
87 Supreme Court, November 19, 1993, *Nederlandse Jurisprudentie* 1994, at p. 622; Strikwerda, *Inleiding tot het Nederlandse internationaal Privaatrecht*, 1995, at p. 201.

the *lex loci delicti* rule will probably be set aside and Dutch tort law will be applicable to the claim for damages filed by the copyright owner against the infringer. A second exception to the general rule sees to the case in which a tort is closely connected to another legal relationship. If, for example, an employee discloses a trade secret of its employer by publishing it on the Internet, any claims arising out of tort filed by the employer against the employee will be governed by the law that is applicable to the employment contract.[88]

In case of unlawful competition, the question whether the competition was unlawful must be answered on the basis of the laws applicable in the market where the competition took place. If, for example, a Dutch company publishes on the Internet untrue statements regarding the products sold by this company in the United States, the laws of the United States are decisive as to the lawfulness of such behaviour. On the other hand, it is conceivable that the Dutch court will apply Dutch law on a claim for damages filed by the producer against its competitor.[89]

Pursuant to section 10 of the General Provisions Act, the laws of the country in which the contract was entered into (*lex loci actus*) set the legal formalities that must be observed to make a contract valid. Under Dutch law, the agreement is considered to be entered into at the place that the offeror receives the acceptance of his offer. If the acceptance is contained in an electronic message that is sent through an electronic telecommunication network to the offeror, the contract is entered into at the place the message reaches the information system of the offeror.

The Dutch Supreme Court has decided, however, that section 10 of the General Provisions Act is not imperative and that parties may also observe the formalities laid down in the law that materially governs such contract.[90] Dutch law does not contain a systematic statutory regulation regarding jurisdiction.

In general, under Dutch law, a Dutch court has jurisdiction if the defendant has its domicile or its permanent residence in The Netherlands. If the defendant is a legal entity, the place where it has its registered office is decisive. If a legal entity that has its registered office abroad has an establishment in The Netherlands, the Dutch court will find itself competent in a case against such legal entity brought before it.

If the defendant has no domicile or permanent residence in The Netherlands, a Dutch court will nevertheless find itself competent in cases where the plaintiff has its domicile in The Netherlands.[91]

---

88 Strikwerda, *Inleiding tot het Nederlandse internationaal Privaatrecht*, 1995, at p. 202.
89 Strikwerda, *Inleiding tot het Nederlandse internationaal Privaatrecht*, 1995, at p. 205.
90 Supreme Court, April 2, 1942, *Nederlandse Jurisprudentie* 1942 , at p. 468.
91 Strikwerda, *Inleiding tot het Nederlandse internationaal Privaatrecht*, 1995, p. 239.

In international situations, parties are free to attribute jurisdiction to a Dutch court or deprive a Dutch court of its jurisdiction by contract, unless such a choice of court contradicts with treaties or statutory provisions that are part of Dutch law.[92]

On February 1, 1973, the European Union Treaty regarding jurisdiction and the execution of judgments in private and commercial cases (Brussels Convention 1968) came into force. On January 1, 1992, the Treaty of Lugano came into force.[93]

Residents and Non-Residents

13-23   Pursuant to section 9 of the General Provisions Act, Dutch private law is equal for foreigners and persons having the Dutch nationality, unless provided otherwise. Dutch private law in general does not distinguish between residents and non-residents. An example of an exception to this general rule is the Financial Relations with Foreign Countries Act 1994 (*Wet Financiële betrekkingen buitenland*). This Act covers primarily financial transactions between residents and non-residents. Residents are persons having their domicile in The Netherlands and legal entities that are established in The Netherlands. The nationality of the payer and the payee are irrelevant for the application of this Act.

Pursuant to section 7 of the Act, every resident is obliged to supply information and data to the Dutch Central Bank that are of interest for the composition of the national balance of payments. The Dutch Central Bank has laid down rules elaborating on this statutory obligation to report on payment transactions between residents and non-residents. Transactions must be reported if they exceed an amount of N.L.G. 25,000.[94]

According to section 47 of the present Data Protection Act, its provisions apply not only to personal data files situated in the Netherlands but also to such files situated abroad in as far as the holder of that file has its residence in the Netherlands and that file contains personal data of residents of The Netherlands.

Crossborder Transactions and Communications

13-24   Dutch law does not contain many provisions that specifically relate to crossborder transactions and communications.

The Dutch Civil Code contains a paragraph relating to general conditions. Pursuant to section 6:233 of the Dutch Civil Code, general conditions can be declared null and void by a court at the request of the counterpart of

---

92 Strikwerda, *Inleiding tot het Nederlandse internationaal Privaatrecht*, 1995, at p. 242.
93 For more information about the contents of these two treaties, consult the chapter in this book with respect to International Treaties and Conventions.
94 Rank, *Geld, Geldschuld en betaling*, 1996, at p. 88.

the party using the general conditions if these general conditions, taking into account all circumstances, are unfair or the counterpart has not had a reasonable opportunity to take cognisance of the contents of these general conditions. In principle the user must hand over the general conditions to its counterpart beforehand. It is uncertain if this requirement can be met by providing the general conditions in electronic form, for example, by publishing these conditions on the computer terminal of a person that wants to enter into a transaction through the Internet or another network.

The paragraph contains a list of general conditions that are assumed to be unfair (the grey list) and a list of general conditions that are unfair (the black list). These lists apply if the counterpart of the user of the general conditions is a consumer.

Section 6:247 of the Dutch Civil Code provides that the provisions of the general conditions paragraph of the Dutch Civil Code are applicable to a contract if both parties act in the exercise of their profession or their business and are both established in the Netherlands, irrespective of the law applicable to the agreement.[95] If either of these parties is not established in The Netherlands, the provisions of this paragraph do not apply. If the counterpart of the user of the general conditions is a consumer and such consumer has its residence in The Netherlands, the statutory provisions regarding general conditions are always applicable, regardless of the law applicable to the contract.

Pursuant to section 49 of the present Data Protection Act, the disclosure of personal data to or from a foreign data file to which that Act does not apply is prohibited if by General Regulation such disclosure is declared to have a severe adverse effect on the privacy of the data subjects involved.

Impact of Penal Law

An amendment of the Penal Code came into force on March 1, 1993, **13-25** implementing the so-called Computer Crime Act. Among others a new section 138a was added attaching a penalty to computer trespass. Gaining unauthorised access to another's information system is punishable by imprisonment for a maximum of six months or a fine of up to a maximum of N.L.G. 10,000 if this is realised by:

- Overcoming some security;
- Using false signals or a false key; or
- Adopting a false identity.

---

95 "Established in The Netherlands" means having its head office in The Netherlands or having an establishment in The Netherlands that must make the performance under the contract.

13-26   The maximum penalty is higher (imprisonment for a maximum of four years or a fine of up to a maximum of N.L.G. 25,000) if the offender has copied data from the records of the computer or has gained access through the public telecommunication infrastructure or a public telecommunication construction and has subsequently used the processing capacity of the computer.

Sections 139b and 139c of the Penal Code cover among other things the unauthorised tapping or recording of data exchanged through the telecommunication infrastructure.

Simultaneously, the Code of Criminal Procedure (*Wetboek van Strafvordering*) was amended to reflect the increasing application of modern information technology. Sections 125i–n were included in the Code of Criminal Procedure. These sections relate to the examination of data in information systems. Pursuant to section 125i of the Act, the examining judge conducting a judicial inquiry can order anyone that he may reasonably expect to have access to electronic data that are relevant for the inquiry, to provide him access to such data or provide such data to him.

Section 125k requires that person to provide the examining judge with those details regarding the security of the information system that the judge requires to gain access to the data. Section 125j relates to a house search. It provides that from the place the house search is conducted data in information systems located elsewhere can be examined provided that the persons that live, work, or stay in the house in which the house search is conducted have access to such data with the approval of the proprietor of the information system concerned. This provision is important in cases of telecommunication networks.[96]

---

96 Kaspersen, "Wetsvoorstel Wet Computercriminaliteit", *Computerrecht* 1992/5, at p. 226; Kaspersen, "De Wet computercriminaliteit is er-nu de boeven nog", *Computerrecht* 1993/4, at p. 134; Franken, "De implicaties van de Wet computercriminaliteit", Van Esch and Prins (ed.), *Recht en EDI*, 1993, at p. 225.

CHAPTER 14

New Zealand

Paul Barnett, Melanie Noble, and Cassie Nicholson
Chapman Tripp Sheffield Young
Wellington, New Zealand

INTRODUCTION

Legal Regime Relative to Electronic Communication

The regulation of electronic communication in New Zealand is made up **14-1**
of two regimes contained in the Telecommunications Act 1987 and a
small number of specific regimes relative to the subject matter of various
pieces of legislation such as filing income tax returns and various procedures
under the customs legislation. Outside the specific and very narrow statutory regimes, regimes contained in more general and traditional legislation
together with the Common Law must be consulted.

Certain sections of the commercial community have regulated their
own activities as with the banking industry pursuant to that industry's code
of conduct, backed by a network of paper based agreements.

At the highest level, New Zealand has not legislated to recognise on a
general basis the growing (but still relatively small) number of commercial
transactions between onshore entities and New Zealand-based and offshore entities. At an intermediate level, legislation only superficially addresses the concept of electronic communication and electronic commerce.
Commercial entities are endeavouring to use the technology available by regulating themselves.

To rely on a legal structure based on technologies which are now cen-
turies old is potentially dangerous. To nurture the use of electronic technologies, New Zealand will have to introduce new legislation to deal with,
among other things, the traditional concepts attaching to offer and acceptance.

Confidentiality

14-2   Briefly, breach of confidentiality of on-line information in New Zealand can potentially give rise to actions in contract (depending on the terms of the contract in question), equity or under the Privacy Act 1993.

First, if an obligation of confidentiality between the parties to a contract is imposed by the terms of that contract, an action can be brought for breach of contract.

Secondly, an equitable action for breach of confidentiality could also be brought, provided that the necessary ingredients of such an action were met. For such an action to succeed, the information must have the necessary quality of confidence, must be imparted in circumstances importing an obligation of confidence, and must have been used in an unauthorised manner to the detriment of the party communicating the information. It may well be that the nature of the medium on which the information is communicated electronically, and the security afforded to the communication, will affect the availability of an equitable remedy.

An action in tort for breach of privacy appears to be slowly emerging,[1] based on a line of United States case law. Any such action is in an inchoate state at the moment.

Finally, New Zealand also has specific legislation in relation to privacy of personal information (*i.e.*, information about an identifiable individual), the Privacy Act 1993. This statute, and its application to electronically held or communicated information, is discussed under the "Electronic Information Rights" heading below.

Legal Effect of Electronic Signatures

14-3   Several New Zealand statutes require certain documents to be signed (*e.g.*, the Life Insurance Act 1908, the Bills of Exchange Act 1908, the Land Transfer Act 1952 and the Securities Transfer Act 1991). The legal effect of electronic signatures and, more particularly, whether electronic signatures meet such statutory requirements, is not dealt with by any legislation in New Zealand.[2]

---

1 *Tucker* v. *News Media Ownership* Ltd [1986] 2 N.Z.L.R. 716; *TV3 Network Services* v. *Broadcasting Standards Authority & Another* [1995] 2 N.Z.L.R. 720.

2 Some statutes, however, allow electronic transmissions to be used, in specific instances, as alternatives for documents which would otherwise require signing under the relevant statute; see, for example, the Births, Deaths and Marriages Registration Act 1995, sections 4 and 47; the Finance Act (Number 2) 1994, section 4; and the Racing Act 1971, sections 8 and 67. Also, in the taxation context, filing of returns can be undertaken by electronic means, although a hardcopy transcript of the transmission must be signed and retained by the taxpayer and it is this signed transcript which constitutes the tax return itself; see Tax Administration Act 1994, section 36.

Any argument that electronic signatures meet such requirements would, therefore, need to rely on the Common Law. The Common Law has given a broad interpretation to the concept of signature. For example, initials[3] and thumbprints[4] have been held to suffice. The Common Law also does not require signatures to be hand-written — printed[5] and stamped[6] signatures have been accepted by the courts.

On the basis of the Common Law and the degree of confirmation of authenticity conferred by electronic signatures, several commentators have argued that electronic signatures should be accepted by Common Law courts as meeting statutory requirements for signing.[7]

On the other hand, while the Common Law has given the term "signature" a broad interpretation, the courts may well refuse to extend that meaning to electronic signatures, given the technical nature of such authentications, and defer to Parliament on that issue. In any case, the legal effect of electronic signatures in New Zealand will remain unclear until the courts address it.

ELECTRONIC TRANSACTIONS

Creation of Contracts Electronically

Before parties to a commercial arrangement use EDI as a basis for formation of their contract, they should consider the subject matter of the contract and whether any applicable legislation demands that it be in writing and/or signed.   **14-4**

In New Zealand, the Contracts Enforcement Act 1956 and the Property Law Act 1952 are the principal pieces of legislation setting out various types of contract which must be signed and be in writing. These Acts repealed and replaced the United Kingdom Statute of Frauds, which had applied in New Zealand. Section 2 of the Contracts Enforcement Act 1956 provides that no contract for the sale of land; to enter into any disposition of land, which disposition is required by statute to be made by deed or instrument or in writing or to be proved in writing; or to enter into any mortgage or charge on land; or by any person to answer to another person for the debt, default or liability of a third party, shall be enforceable by action unless the contract or some memorandum or note thereof is in writing and is signed by the party to be charged therewith or by some other person lawfully authorised by him.

---

3 *Taylor v. Dobbins* (1720) 1 Stra 399, 93 E.R. 592.
4 *Re Finn's Estate* [1935] All E.R. 419.
5 *Schneider v. Norris* (1814) 2 M&S 287, 105 E.R. 388.
6 *Chapman v. Smethurst* [1909] 1 K.B. 927.
7 Reed, *Computer Law,* 2nd edition, 1993, at p. 271; Edwards, Savage and Walden, *Information Technology and the Law,* 2nd edition, 1990, at p. 240; and Ng, "EDI and Contract Law", December 1994, 26 *Computers and the Law* 8.

14-5   Section 49A (1) of the Property Law Act 1952 also provides that no interest in land may be created or disposed of except by writing, signed by the person creating or conveying that interest, or by that person's agent.

Many other New Zealand statutes also provide that a specific type of contract will be void unless in writing and signed (*e.g.*, certain types of insurance contracts).[8]

Both the Copyright Act 1994 and the Securities Amendment Act 1996 (which amends the Securities Act 1978) have given broad definitions to the terms "writing" and "written". The Copyright Act defines these terms as including "any form of notation or code, whether by hand or otherwise and regardless of the method by which, or the medium in or on which, it is recorded". This definition would be wide enough to include electronic messages. The Securities Amendment Act goes even further and expressly recognises as "writing" a "display of words by any form of electronic . . . communication", provided that the message can be stored in permanent form and retrieved.

It remains unclear in New Zealand law whether electronic messages will meet the requirements for "writing" where such a broad definition is not set out in the relevant statute. Common Law cases have held that the requirement for "writing" does not necessitate a handwritten paper document. The courts have accepted the products of mechanical instruments such as telegrams as "writing".[9] However, whether electronic messages constitute "writing" has not been conclusively determined by any New Zealand court.

To bring electronic messages within the term "writing" in New Zealand may be more difficult than would be the case in the United Kingdom. The Acts Interpretation Act 1924 restrictively defines "writing" and "written" as including "words printed, typewritten, painted, engraved, lithographed, or otherwise traced or copied". The United Kingdom equivalent in the Interpretation Act 1978 defines "writing" as including "typing, printing, lithography and other modes of representing or reproducing words in visible form".

Thus, although "writing" might be interpreted more broadly than its literal sense, the use of EDI to form such contracts may still leave the contract at some risk of being held unenforceable or void. Furthermore, while some broad interpretations of the word "signature" have also been expressed in relevant case law, it is not certain that electronic signatures would meet a statutory requirement for signature. Unfortunately, there has been no legislative movement at a general level in New Zealand to resolve these problems with respect to EDI and the formation of contracts.

---

8 Life Insurance Act 1908, sections 43 and 44; Marine Insurance Act 1908, sections 23–26. Other legislation containing requirements for writing and signatures include the Bills of Exchange Act 1908, the Land Transfer Act 1952 and the Securities Transfer Act 1991.

9 *Welsh v. Crawford* (1906) 25 N.Z.L.R. 361.

Offer and Acceptance

Where the contract is not required by statute to be in writing or signed, an   **14-6**
enforceable contract will be formed when the parties agree on the terms of
the contract, by way of offer and acceptance. Offer and acceptance can be
communicated in a number of ways including by electronic means.

The legal principles of offer and acceptance arise from the Common Law.
The New Zealand position reflects that in other Common Law jurisdictions.[10] The basic principles of offer and acceptance under Common Law
are:

- An offer remains open for the period expressed in or with the offer, or
  if no such period is expressed, for a reasonable time or until accepted,
  rejected or validly withdrawn;
- An offer may be withdrawn before acceptance (unless the terms of the
  offer state or imply otherwise), but any withdrawal will only take effect
  once it is received;
- A counter-offer terminates the original offer and comprises a new offer;
  and
- When accepted, the contract is formed.

For a contract to be formed, the parties must intend to enter into the contract   **14-7**
and must agree the terms — *i.e.*, there must be a true "meeting of the minds".
The commercial exchange of messages by way of EDI does not require
human involvement. A purchase order may simply be automatically generated by the purchaser's computer and sent electronically to the supplier's
computer through a network. Similarly, the supplier's computer may automatically generate a message of acknowledgement. In these circumstances,
it may be arguable that offer and acceptance has not taken place, there
having been no "meeting of the minds" — any "offer" would be confined to
the automatic generation of an order by a computer and any "acceptance"
would similarly occur without human intervention.

Arguably, an interchange agreement would have to be in place between the
parties to govern their electronic commercial relationship and to express the
parties' intention to be bound by the automatically generated communications.

Assuming for the moment that there is such a meeting of the minds,
where the communication of acceptance is instantaneous, the contract will be
completed when and where the message is received by the offeror. This principle
would generally hold in relation to communication of acceptance by EDI.[11]

---

10 For a New Zealand analysis of the law of offer and acceptance, see Burrows, Finn, and
   Todd, *Law of Contract*, 1997, at pp. 31–86.
11 By analogy to contracts concluded by telex; see *Entores Limited* v. *Miles Far East Corp*
   [1955] 2 Q.B. 327, and *Brinkibon Limited* v. *Stahag Stahl GmbH* [1983] 2 A.C. 34. For
   a full discussion of offer and acceptance in the EDI context, see Reed, *Computer Law,*
   2nd edition, 1993, at pp. 258–263, which analysis is equally applicable in New Zealand.

However, if, for example, the network through which the message is transmitted stores the acceptance, then arguably the "postal rule" would apply, *i.e.*, acceptance would occur and the contract would be completed when the acceptance message is received by the network used by the offeree. The effect of the application of the postal rule is that the time of acceptance will be the time at which the network used by the offeree receives the message and the place of acceptance will be the jurisdiction in which that network so receives the message. Where the part of the network that receives the message is not in the jurisdiction of either the offeree or the offeror, the contract could conceivably be governed by the law of a third jurisdiction, that in which the network receives the message.

A further potential difficulty in respect of the postal rule arises from the rules as to revocation. While an acceptance is effective when sent, a revocation of an offer is only effective once received by the offeree. Thus, where delays occur between the transmission and receipt of messages, a revocation of an offer will be ineffective if the offeree has sent an acceptance message before receiving the revocation. The offeror, on the other hand, may not receive that acceptance message for some time after the actual time of acceptance.

Some commentators have raised the possibility that the postal rule may not apply in some instances of delay in transmission.[12] The commercial and computing practice of the parties to the contract may imply that the parties did not intend the postal rule to govern the time and place of acceptance. The parties may have adopted a standard practice of acknowledging their receipt of messages and this practice might arguably imply that the parties intended their messages to be effective only once received and acknowledged. However, those commentators also point out the uncertainty surrounding such a submission and emphasise the need for the parties to expressly stipulate the time and place of acceptance.[13]

Whether or not the postal rule applies at Common Law where delays occur in transmission, the parties can exclude the Common Law position by stipulating in their contractual arrangements the acts which will constitute acceptance and when and where acceptance is to have effect. Most such stipulations involve acceptance occurring when and where the message of acceptance is received by the offeror.

Notably, New Zealand has a model agreement that can be adopted by parties entering into an EDI relationship — the Electronic Data Agreement (the Model Agreement). The New Zealand Electronic Data Interchange Association Incorporated (N.Z.E.D.I.A.) produced it in 1990. The N.Z.E.D.I.A. has now been absorbed by another association, the Telecommunications Users Association of New Zealand Inc. (T.U.A.N.Z.), which has published a checklist for use

12 Myburgh, "Bits, Bytes and Bills of Lading: EDI and New Zealand Maritime Law" [1993] *N.Z.L.J.* 324, at pp. 326–327.
13 Myburgh, "Bits, Bytes and Bills of Lading: EDI and New Zealand Maritime Law" [1993] *N.Z.L.J.* 324, at p. 327.

in producing such interchange agreements.[14] The T.U.A.N.Z. checklist suggests issues that should be dealt with by parties to interchange agreements and reflects many of the matters dealt with in the Model Agreement. The T.U.A.N.Z. checklist also raises some matters not dealt with in the Model Agreement.

The Model Agreement is based on that of the United Kingdom and adopts the E.D.I.F.A.C.T. standard (although the parties can use a substitute standard if preferred). It includes those provisions that the N.Z.E.D.I.A. considered "minimal but essential requirements to be included in any contract between trading partners entering into an EDI relationship". Unlike the United States and Canadian models, the Model Agreement does not provide terms specifically in relation to the underlying commercial contract to be entered into via EDI (except to the extent that it imposes an obligation on the parties to accord electronic messages the same status as paper ones). In particular, the New Zealand model does not include provisions dealing with contract formation and the terms and conditions of the underlying contract. It is left to the parties to decide these issues as part of the negotiation of the underlying contract. Notably, however, the T.U.A.N.Z. checklist raises as matters that should be addressed by the parties:

- Recognition of the legal status of the electronic messages; and
- The point at which a message is deemed received by the recipient and the point at which the contract becomes irrevocable.

14-8 Given the problems that can arise from the application of the postal rule, it is important that the parties stipulate the acts that constitute acceptance and the law that will govern the contract.

Mistakes in On-line Contracts

14-9 **Common Law** Mistakes as to contractual terms can arise in respect of any contract, where one or more parties do not appreciate the meaning of the terminology used in the contract. In the context of contracts executed on-line, mistakes can also arise as a result of corruption of the electronically transmitted messages of offer and acceptance. At Common Law, a mistake in a contract executed on-line and affected by corruption could lead to two possible outcomes:

- If the corrupted message received is in substantially different form from that in which it was transmitted, the misunderstanding may prevent an enforceable contract from arising;[15] and

---

14 "Checklist for Electronic Commerce Participation Agreement Between Trading Partners (Purchasers, Suppliers) and Network Providers (HUB,VAN)", prepared by Elizabeth Longworth of Longworth Associates and appearing in the T.U.A.N.Z. Special Report, June 1996.
15 *Raffles v. Wichelhaus* (1864) 2 H.&C. 906; Walden and Savage, "The Legal Problems of Paperless Transactions" (1989) *J.B.L.* 102, at p. 109.

- The offeror may be *prima facie* bound by the corrupted message received and accepted by an offeree who is unaware of the corruption.[16]

14-10 In the first case the contract will be held to be unenforceable, while in the second case the sender of the corrupted message will be bound. Which analysis will apply appears to depend on whether the terms received were so fundamentally different from those which were sent that objectively — *i.e.*, from a reasonable third party's perspective — there could be no intention on behalf of either party to sign the version of which they had no knowledge. If so, the first principle will apply. If not, the second principle will apply and the mistaken party who led the other party to reasonably believe that an agreement existed will not be able to avoid the concluded contract on the basis of the mistake. If a reasonable bystander would conclude from the actions of the parties that an agreement had been made, then the contract will be enforceable.

14-11 **The Contractual Mistakes Act 1977** The Contractual Mistakes Act was introduced to overcome the inequitable position arising from the application of the Common Law to mistakes in contracts, *i.e.*, that the contract would either be found valid or void with any loss arising from the mistake falling entirely on one or other party. The Act replaces the Common Law where the mistake is one that falls within the Act's scope. Otherwise, the Common Law still applies. Under section 7 of the Act, the Court may grant such relief as it thinks just and, in particular, may:

- Declare the contract valid;
- Cancel the contract;
- Vary the contract; or
- Grant relief by restitution or compensation.

14-12 The party seeking relief, where the corrupted contract was held to be binding, would generally be the sender of the message.[17]

To obtain relief under the Contractual Mistakes Act, the following four requirements must be satisfied:

- The mistake must fall within one of the categories listed in section 6(1)(a);
- The mistake must not be a mistake as to the "interpretation of the contract", as provided by section 6(2);
- An inequality of consideration must have arisen consequent on the mistake;

---

16 *Smith* v. *Hughes* (1871) L.R. 6 Q.B. 597.
17 For a full discussion of the Contractual Mistakes Act, see Burrows, Finn, and Todd, *Law of Contract*, 1997.

- The contract must not place on the applicant an obligation to bear the burden of any risk arising from the mistake.

While the Act could, therefore, possibly offer some relief to a mistaken party   **14-13** to an EDI contract, it may be difficult to bring within the Act mistakes arising from corruption of messages transmitted via EDI, for the reasons discussed below.

Category of Mistake First, the mistake may not be seen to fall within the   **14-14** categories listed in section 6(1)(a). Section 6(1)(a) lists the three types of mistake situation to which the Act applies:

- A party makes a mistake that influences that party's decision to enter into the contract. The other party knows the mistake at the time at which the contract is entered into;
- All parties to the contract make the same mistake and the mistake influences each of the parties in its decision to enter into the contract;
- The parties make a different mistake about the same matter of fact or law and the parties are both influenced to enter into the contract by their respective mistakes.

Notably, section 6(1)(a) does not include, within the application of the Act,   **14-15** mistakes made by one party and not known to the other at the time of execution of the contract. Corrupted EDI messages will not generally fall within the first two categories of mistake listed above. As is the case under Common Law, in respect of the first category, if the recipient knew of the error, then arguably there would be no meeting of the minds and no contract would be created to dispute. In respect of the second category, no single mistake is made by both parties. The category which will usually be raised where a contract says something other than what one party intended and where the other party was unaware of the first's mistake, is the third category: *i.e.*, where different mistakes are made by the parties as to the same subject matter.

Early cases on the Act would have allowed mistakes arising from corrupted EDI messages to fall within the third category; under the decision in *Conlon v. Ozolins*,[18] the parties would be treated as having made different mistakes about the same subject matter. The sender would be mistaken as to the content of the message in relation to the subject matter of the mistake, while the recipient would be mistaken as to the sender's intention in regard to the subject matter of the mistake.

Most legal commentators believe the decision to be erroneous.[19] In reality, the mistakes relate to different subject matters, *i.e.*, the sender's

18 [1984] 1 N.Z.L.R. 489.
19 McLauchlan, "Mistake as to Contractual Terms under the Contractual Mistakes Act 1977", (1986) 12 N.Z.U.L.R. 123.

mistake is as to the content of the message, while any mistake which could be said to have been made by the recipient would relate to the sender's intentions. Really only one party has been mistaken as to the contractual terms, *i.e.*, the sender. As far as the recipient is concerned, the contractual terms received and accepted reflect exactly the intentions and beliefs of the recipient.

Subsequent cases have also cast doubt on the decision although they have been decided on a different ground, *i.e.*, that such mistakes are as to "the interpretation of the contract".

14-16 *Mistakes as to interpretation of the Contract*   In *Shotter* v. *Westpac Banking Corporation* [20] and *Paulger* v. *Butland Industries Limited*,[21] it was held that mistakes as to the terms which are finally included in a contract are mistakes as to the interpretation of the contract itself so that relief under the Act is denied by section 6(2). Again, many legal commentators have argued that these decisions are flawed, as section 6(2) of the Act was intended by Parliament to have a far narrower effect than that expressed in the decisions.[22] The decisions of the courts continue to plague attempts to bring such mistakes within the Act.

14-17 *Inequality of Consideration*   It may also be difficult in the particular circumstances to prove an inequality of consideration that is consequent on their mistake.

14-18 **Risk of Errors in Transmission**   The Act will not apply where it is express or implicit in the contractual relationship (which may be guided by previous dealings and customary practices) that one or other party has taken on the risk for errors in transmission. Such assumption of the risk may be expressed in the contract. Further, arguably the use of verification procedures in EDI, which are specifically used to minimise or prevent corruption, may influence the court's decision whether or not to grant relief under the Act. In particular, a party who does not comply with the adopted procedures may have impliedly assumed the risk of errors in the transmission in question.

Thus, while it may be possible for relief to be granted by the Court in the context of corrupted EDI messages, many obstacles stand in the way of such relief. If no relief can be obtained under the Act, the aggrieved party is left with the position at Common Law. The parties can provide in their interchange agreements for the consequences of such corruption. New Zealand has a Model Agreement that can be adopted as a contractual basis for parties entering into EDI based relationships. The T.U.A.N.Z. checklist can be used as a guide to amending the Model Agreement as appropriate and also provides certain additional terms the parties may wish to consider.

20 [1988] 2 N.Z.L.R. 316.
21 [1989] 3 N.Z.L.R. 549.
22 McLauchlan, "The Demise of Conlon v. Ozolins: "Mistake in Interpretation" or Another Case of Mistaken Interpretation?", (1991) 14 *N.Z.U.L.R.* 229.

The Model Agreement and the T.U.A.N.Z. Checklist First, clause 4 of the **14-19**
Model Agreement provides that the message must identify the sender and
the recipient as provided in the user manual and must include a means of
verifying the completeness and authenticity of the message, either through a
technique used in the message itself or by some other means provided for in
the adopted protocol (usually EDIFACT).

The Model Agreement also provides that generally the sender of a
message will be liable for any error in the message it transmits, even if the
error is the result of the third party network provider's acts and omissions
(clause 5.3). If the sender is aware of the corruption, it must retransmit the
message as a corrected message and must reference the original message
(clause 5.2). The rule that the sender is liable for errors in transmission is
varied, however, where the recipient knows or ought reasonably to know that
the transmission is incomplete or incorrect. In such a case the recipient must
immediately inform the sender.

Clause 6 provides that except where receipt of messages is automatically
confirmed, the sender of a message may request the recipient to confirm receipt
of the message. If such a request is made, the recipient must confirm its
receipt without unreasonable delay. As discussed above, if the parties decide
to adopt such procedures, a decision by a party not to use those procedures
may imply that that party is assuming the risk of errors in the communication.

Where a party uses the services of a third party network provider for the
transmission, the provider is deemed to be an agent of the instructing party
(clause 8). Furthermore, if either party mandates the use by the other of the
services of a specific network provider, then the mandating party is responsible to the other for the network provider's actions and omissions. Clause
8.3 places an obligation on a party giving such instructions to ensure that
the third party network provider is obliged to make no change in the
substantive data content of the message. Thus, if the parties adopt the Model
Agreement, the following principles will apply:

- The parties must use the adopted verification procedures to ensure the
  completeness and authenticity of all messages;
- If the recipient could not reasonably know of the corruption, the sender
  will generally be responsible for the completeness and accuracy of the
  message;
- Where the sender is aware of the corruption, it must retransmit the
  message with a clear indication that it is a corrected message and referencing the original message;
- If the recipient is aware of the corruption, the recipient must immediately inform the sender. The sender is not liable for errors in transmission of which the recipient should reasonably have been aware;

- If the corruption is due to an act or omission of a third-party network provider, the risk of such corruption will lie with the party instructing the third party;
- If a party mandates the use of a third party network provider, corruption caused by the acts or omissions of that third party will be at the risk of the mandating or instructing party; and
- The instructing party will also be obliged to ensure that the third party does not change the substantive data content of the messages.

14-20   These guiding principles will determine who bears the risk of errors in transmission in the process of formation of a contract.

The T.U.A.N.Z. checklist reflects the matters dealt with in the Model Agreement, by asking the parties to consider whether certain matters as to verification procedures and distribution of liability have been addressed in their contract.

Problems of Evidence

14-21   In disputing the contents of the contract, in any case relating to mistakes made in electronically transmitted messages, problems of evidence will inevitably arise. The parties will wish to adduce computer generated-evidence of the contents of the contract. There are two types of computer-related evidence:

- Information which a human inputs into a computer; and
- Records such as purchase orders that are generated automatically by a computer.

14-22   The law of evidence in New Zealand has not yet fully evolved to deal with the admissibility of electronic records evidencing the contents of a contract. The two rules that are problematic when attempting to adduce computer-generated evidence are the "hearsay rule" and the "rule of best evidence".[23]

Broadly, the hearsay rule provides that facts may only be proven if witnesses with personal knowledge of those facts provide testimony. In the context of documents, a document is not admissible as evidence unless the person who created that document is present to testify as to its contents.

The best evidence rule provides that the existence and contents of a document can only be proven if the original document is available for inspection. The original ensures the highest level of authenticity. In the context of electronically created documents and the best evidence rule, there is a significant risk that the information contained in a record can be changed without trace. However, checks in the system or the record itself (such as system logs and digital signatures) will allow the record to be authenticated. One of the

---

23 For a detailed analysis of these rules, see *Cross on Evidence*, 6th edition, 1985.

best methods of ensuring authenticity is for the parties to have a third party such as the network operator maintain a log which will show any changes to the message.

It may be, therefore, that technical evidence of measures within the system or the message itself will be accepted by a court as sufficiently authenticating the message for the purposes of the best evidence rule. The hearsay rule is, perhaps, more problematic.

The rule as to documentary hearsay evidence is now set out in section 3 of the Evidence Amendment Act (Number 2) 1980. That section provides that where direct oral evidence of a fact would be admissible, any statement made by a person in a document and tending to establish the fact is admissible as evidence of that fact if the document is a business record and the person who supplied the information for the composition of the record:

- Cannot reasonably be identified; or
- Is unavailable to give evidence; or
- Cannot reasonably be expected to recollect the matters dealt with in the information he supplied; or
- In the case of civil proceedings, the maker of the statement had personal knowledge of the matters dealt with in the statement and undue delay or expense would be caused by obtaining his or her evidence.

The Act defines "documents" as including "any information recorded or **14-23** stored by means of any tape recorder, computer, or other device; and any material subsequently derived from information so recorded or stored". Thus, computer-generated records are clearly "documents" for the purpose of section 3.

Section 3, although allowing some computer-related evidence to be adduced, is too confined to adequately deal with computer-generated evidence. Records generated by a computer will not be statements "made by a person in a document" and will consequently not be able to be adduced in court, notwithstanding the evidential importance of the records.

The New Zealand Law Commission is currently considering changes to the evidence legislation to deal with these issues.[24] The Law Commission has proposed a regime whereby computer-generated evidence would be admissible provided it met certain tests as to its relevance. Once admitted, its reliability would also be tested.

The proposals are already being criticised by some legal commentators as ignoring the need to also consider the prejudicial effect of the evidence. Those commentators have also criticised the proposals for dealing with the reliability of the evidence only by way of presumption or inference after

---

24 "Evidence Law: Documentary Evidence and Judicial Notice" (Discussion Paper), New Zealand Law Commission Preliminary Paper, Number 22, Wellington, *N.Z.L.C.* 22, 1994.

the evidence has already been admitted.[25] Because of the inadequacies in the law of evidence, parties often provide terms in their interchange agreements to the effect that:

- The parties will treat evidence of electronic messages as admissible; or
- The parties will not contest the admissibility of the electronic data; or
- The parties will treat the electronic data as having the same evidentiary weight as that of signed written documents.

14-24   All of these measures are intended to overcome the potential evidential problems arising from the use of EDI.

In the New Zealand context, the Model Agreement contains certain terms aimed at preserving and, perhaps, increasing the evidentiary value of EDI messages. First, the Model Agreement requires a transaction log to be kept by each party containing complete records of the EDI communications between the parties. Each party must ensure that the person responsible for the data processing system of that party certifies that the log and any reproduction made from it is correct. These matters are dealt with in clause 7 of the Model Agreement and go some way to ensuring the authenticity of the record in question. However, the Model Agreement does not explicitly state that the messages will be treated as admissible or that the parties will not dispute the admissibility of the message as evidence. Clause 5.1 simply states that:

"... each party accepts the integrity of all messages and agrees to accord these the same status as would be applicable to information sent by other than electronic means, unless such messages can be shown to have been corrupted as a result of technical failure on the part of machine, system or transmission line."

14-25   Notably, the T.U.A.N.Z. checklist asks the parties whether they have provided for the recognition of the legal status of the electronic messages in their agreement.

In any event, even if the parties have agreed not to contest the admissibility of the message, such agreement cannot preclude a court from exercising its discretion to exclude the message as evidence if it does not, in the court's opinion, meet the hearsay and best evidence requirements.

Impact of Impostors or Persons without Authority

14-26   The impact of impostors or persons without authority will fall into two broad categories:

- Where impostors interfere with the message for mischievous or malicious purposes, but still allow the message to be received and

---

25 Perry, "Technology on Trial — Admissibility of Computer Generated Visual Presentations", (1995) 1 N.Z.B.L.Q. 183.

accepted by the intended recipient and the considerations to pass between sender and intended recipient; and
- Where impostors intercept the offeror's message and purport to accept it on the offeree's behalf — this scenario usually involves the absconding of the impostor with funds or other subject matter of the contract.

Impostor Causing Mistakes In the first instance, the interception of the impostor will create a mistake in the contract and the analysis in the previous section will apply. In particular, if the changes made are substantial, it is likely that there will be no objective meeting of the minds and the contract will be held unenforceable.   **14-27**

The New Zealand Model Agreement requires the sender or the party mandating the use of a specific network provider to be responsible for the acts and omissions of the network provider used. Moreover, clause 8.3 imposes an obligation on the party instructing the particular network provider to ensure that the network provider does not alter the substantive data content of the message and that the messages are not disclosed to any unauthorised person. Thus, where the acts or omissions of the network provider lead to mistakes in the contract, the party mandating the use of the network provider, or the sender if there is no such mandating party, will be liable for losses arising from the errors.

Impostor Defrauding the Parties The second scenario described above is where an impostor intercepts a message and purports to accept it. Section 8 of the Telecommunications Act 1987 makes it an offence for any person to knowingly give a fictitious order, instruction, or message in using a telecommunications device. Persons committing the offence are liable on summary conviction to imprisonment for a term not exceeding three months or a fine not exceeding N.Z. $2,000.   **14-28**

This provision still leaves open the status that the law would give to the fraudulently completed contract itself. The status of the contract will depend on whether the offeror intended to supply the subject matter of the contract — for example, goods — to the offeree only, or whether the offeror would have sold the goods to anybody with the offeree's attributes. That is, if the identity of the offeree, as opposed to his or her mere attributes, is vital to the seller's decision to sell, then no title will pass to the fraudster and the contract will be void.[26] However, if it is only the attributes of the offeree which are important to the offeror, then a voidable title will pass to the fraudster — *i.e.*, the offeror can avoid the contract at any time before title is passed by the fraudster to a *bona fide* purchaser for value.[27]

---

26 *Cundy v. Lindsay* (1878) 3 App. Cas. 459.
27 *Midland Bank plc v. Brown Shipley and Co. Limited; Citibank N.A. v. Brown Shipley and Co. Limited* [1991] 1 Lloyd's Rep. 576, (140 N.L.J. 1753).

This state of affairs may cause significant difficulties in the EDI context, where orders are automatically processed by computers. The defrauded party may not become aware of the fraud until well after the fraudster has absconded with the goods.

The provisions of clause 8.3 of the Model Agreement would go some way to shifting the risk in such a scenario — the party instructing a network provider who allowed the unauthorised access would be liable for the loss occasioned. That party could then bring an action against the network provider (however, in most contracts between network providers and users, the network provider seeks to severely curtail its liability).

Moreover, the user manual referred to in the Model Agreement and forming part of that agreement is intended to set out security measures designed to minimise the possibility of such intrusion occurring. The notes to the Model Agreement provide that the user manual should set out such matters as:

- The number and names of those persons authorised to have access to the system;
- How senders and recipients will be identified;
- How messages will be verified in respect of their completeness and authenticity;
- The passwords which are to be used, the situations in which passwords will be required and how frequently passwords will be changed;
- The situations where encryption and other special protection may be required;
- The encryption devices to be used at either end of the process; and
- The protection that is required if otherwise than by encryption.

14-29   Further, clause 4.1 of the Model Agreement provides that all messages must identify the sender and recipient as provided for in the user manual and must include a means of verifying the completeness and authenticity of the message either through a technique used in the message itself or by some other means provided for in the adopted protocol (generally EDI-FACT). The T.U.A.N.Z. checklist reflects these provisions with respect to mistakes in on-line contracts.

On-line Payments

Electronic Fund Transfers

14-30   In contrast to countries such as the United States, New Zealand has no legislative framework in respect of Electronic Funds Transfer or EFT. This position can be contrasted with that in relation to cheques, where long-standing legislation exists (the Bills of Exchange Act 1908 and the Cheques Act 1960).

In the absence of such a legislative framework, the relationship between an issuing bank and a cardholder must be governed by contractual terms. The principal legal issues that must be addressed by the contractual terms relate to:

- The distribution of liability between the parties to the EFT transaction where the cardholder's card and/or personal identification number (PIN) are used in an unauthorised transaction; and
- The responsibilities of the parties for ensuring the security of the EFT system and the cardholder's card and PIN.

In New Zealand, any contract between a service provider and a personal **14-31** customer must comply with certain consumer and individual rights-based legislation (*e.g.*, the Fair Trading Act 1986, the Consumer Guarantees Act 1993, the Human Rights Act 1993 and the Privacy Act 1993). In addition, Common Law and equity may have some impact — in particular, the law relating to inequality of bargaining power and unconscionable bargains may be relevant.

Moreover, in the EFT context, the member banks of the New Zealand Bankers' Association have provided rules in relation to their standard terms and conditions with cardholders, by way of self-regulation. These rules are contained in the Code of Banking Practice (the Code).[28]

The Code regulates, among other things, the terms and conditions on which cardholders enter into agreements with banks for EFT services. The member banks (which comprise the banks currently providing personal banking services in New Zealand) have formally endorsed the Code and are bound by its terms in relation to contracts entered into with cardholders. Thus, the terms and conditions that the bank imposes on a cardholder in respect of EFT must be consistent with the Code (clause 5.5.8). The EFT market in New Zealand is very competitive, and such competition and market forces also go some way to regulating the provision of EFT services in New Zealand.

Terms of the Code The Code sets out the standards of good banking practice **14-32** that the member banks agree to observe when dealing with cardholders in New Zealand. It should be noted that the Code does not apply in respect of commercial (*i.e.*, non-personal) customers. In respect of those customers, the contract negotiated between the bank and the customer will prevail. The application of the Code to personal customers is intended to address the imbalance in bargaining power between banks and individuals. From a review of the standard terms and conditions of several issuing banks, it appears that the banks are currently complying with the Code as those standard terms and conditions clearly reflect the provisions of the Code.

---

28 Code of Banking Practice, 2nd edition, November 1996.

14-33   **General undertakings of the Bank** First, the Code provides that the member banks must make certain general undertakings to all personal customers (whether or not cardholders). In clause 1.7.2 the banks undertake, in providing any banking service to personal customers:

- To provide timely and adequate information with respect to accounts and banking services;
- To ensure the security and integrity of banking systems and technology;
- To have full regard to the customer's legal rights; and
- To act fairly and reasonably towards customers in a consistent and ethical manner.

14-34   Clause 2 of the Code relates to privacy of customers' personal information. The banks undertake to observe and apply the Privacy Act 1993 and, specifically, the 12 privacy principles set out in the Act. The banks also undertake to:

- Have all employees, contractors and agents of the bank sign declarations of secrecy;
- Endeavour to ensure that all personal information held about customers is accurate — the clause also provides that customers should inform the bank of any changes to their personal information, such as addresses, phone numbers or fax numbers;
- Provide bankers' references only with the prior consent of the customer in question;
- Act responsibly in the use of direct marketing — the banks also undertake not to send marketing material if the customer has advised that it does not wish to receive such material.

14-35   **Clarity and Availability of Terms** From the bank's point of view, it is important that terms and conditions relating to the provision of banking services are made available to the customer prior to the bank's supply of the services, as the customer's inability to consider the terms may affect the enforceability of the contract.

It is also important that those terms and conditions are clear to the customer, for the same reason. Clause 3.2 provides that the bank will inform its customers, on request, of the terms and conditions of any banking service and that where such terms and conditions are in writing, plain language will be used.

14-36   **Provisions Specifically Relating to EFT** Clause 5 deals specifically with cards, PINs and passwords and is consequently specifically applicable in the case of EFT.

14-37   *Issue of Cards, Pins and Passwords* Clause 5.1 deals with the issuing of cards, PINs, and passwords. In the interests of security, the Code provides that where a card, PIN or password is issued to a cardholder personally, the bank will check the identity of an applicant before allowing the card to be used and will obtain a signed acknowledgement of receipt from the cardholder. Where not issued personally, the bank must issue the PIN or password separately from the card and the cardholder will not be liable for any losses occurring before receipt of the card or the PIN/password. In terms of evidence, the Code provides that if the parties are in dispute about the receipt of cards, PINs or passwords that are mailed to the cardholder, the bank cannot rely on proof of despatch to the cardholder's correct address to prove receipt by the cardholder.

Clause 5.1 also deals with notification to the cardholder of changes in the terms and conditions relating to the card, PIN, or password. The bank must give the cardholder at least 14 days' notice of any such variation, except for variations in respect of interest rates or other variations that are subject to market fluctuations, in which case the variation is notified, under clause 3.6, by:

- Direct communication with the cardholder;
- Advice on display in branches; or
- Statements in the media.

Transaction records and use of cards Clause 5.2 provides that banks must   **14-38** inform cardholders that they cannot stop transactions initiated by cards. The banks must also warn cardholders of the risks involved if card transactions are authorised in advance of the receipt of goods or services.

Clause 5.2 also sets out matters that will be included on printed transaction records that are offered or produced. Such records assist cardholders in identifying unauthorised transactions, allowing the cardholder to check the transaction records against statements provided at regular intervals by the bank and identify any inconsistencies arising. The information provided on such printouts includes:

- The amount of the transaction;
- The date of the transaction;
- The type of transaction;
- Data enabling identification of the cardholder and transaction;
- Where relevant, the name of the person or account to whom payment or deposit of funds was made; and
- Non-specific information to enable the cardholder, but not an unauthorised person, to identify the accounts being debited or credited.

Security of Cards and PINs and Passwords The Code also requires that banks   **14-39** warn cardholders of acts that may compromise the security of EFT transactions. Clause 5.3 deals mainly with selection of PINs and passwords and warnings given by banks to cardholders to ensure security of PINs and passwords. First, banks must warn cardholders not to write down PINs and passwords selected and must emphasise the cardholders' responsibilities for safeguarding cards and memorising PINs and passwords. Banks must also warn cardholders against:

- Keeping records of PINs and passwords or writing them on cards;
- Being negligent in the use of cards and PINs and passwords — for example, by allowing some other person to identify a PIN while the cardholder is keying it at a terminal; and
- Disclosing PINs and passwords to any person including family members or persons with apparent authority (including bank staff) — such a warning deals with the type of scenario that arose in *Ognibene v. Citibank N.A.*[29]

14-40   Clause 5.3 also places obligations on the cardholder. The cardholder must not select PINs which the bank advises are unsuitable — for example, birth dates, sequential numbers, parts of personal telephone numbers and other easily accessible personal data, or number combinations that are easily identified. A similar obligation is imposed in respect of passwords.

The bank undertakes to conform to internationally accepted standards for methods of generation, storage, and terminal security relating to PINs and passwords, to ensure confidentiality and security. The bank also undertakes to encourage third parties to maximise PIN and password security and to ensure that equipment used in EFT facilities is of a type that maximises PIN and password security.

14-41   *Reporting Loss or Theft*   To avoid losses further to those that have already occurred, it is important that cardholders notify banks of any circumstances that might compromise the security of cards, PINs or passwords. Prompt notification will usually also impact on the cardholder's liability for losses. Clause 5.4 places responsibility on the cardholder to notify the bank as soon as the cardholder becomes aware of:

- The loss or theft of cards;
- The unauthorised use of cards; and
- The actual or possible disclosure to other persons of PINs or passwords.

14-42   The bank undertakes to log such reports so that the parties can ascertain when the notifications were made, for the purposes of assessing cardholder liability, if any.

---

29 (1981) 446 N.Y.S. 2d 845, where a fraudster convinced a cardholder that he was checking the malfunctioning of a machine and asked for the cardholder's number. The cardholder gave him the number and the fraudster withdrew a substantial amount of money from the cardholder's account. While, in this United States case, the cardholder succeeded in his claim, under the Code, such a transaction would be an authorised one, and the cardholder would have no claim against the bank.

The bank must also provide and publicise toll-free phone numbers for reporting such matters. If the facilities are unavailable, the bank will be liable for "any actual card transaction losses due to non-notification", provided that the bank is notified within a reasonable time of the facilities being restored. The reference to "actual card transaction losses" is intended to limit the bank's liability to any amounts obtained by an unauthorised person through use of the card, PIN, or password. Thus, it seems that the bank does not accept liability for any consequential loss, although nothing in the Code prevents the cardholder seeking to claim such consequential losses in the event of a dispute.

Cardholder Liability One of the most important functions of any regula-   **14-43**
tory regime in relation to EFT is that of determining the liabilities of the parties in respect of unauthorised transactions. Clause 5.5 sets out the extent to which the cardholder is liable for any losses arising from such transactions.

Clause 5.5.1 provides that the cardholder is not liable for loss caused by:

- Fraudulent or negligent conduct by employees or agents of the bank or parties involved in the provision of electronic banking services;
- Faults that occur in the machines, cards or systems used, unless the faults are obvious or advised by message or notice on display;
- Unauthorised transactions occurring before cards, PINs or passwords are received by the cardholder; and
- Any other unauthorised transaction, where it is clear that the cardholder could not have contributed to the loss.

The cardholder will be liable for all loss if he or she has been involved in any   **14-44**
fraudulent act giving rise to the loss (clause 5.5.2).

In addition, the cardholder may be liable for some or all of the loss arising from an unauthorised transaction if the cardholder has contributed to or caused the loss (clause 5.5.3). The Code provides examples of how a cardholder might cause or contribute to such loss. These include:

- Selecting unsuitable PINs or passwords;
- Failing to reasonably safeguard cards;
- Keeping written records or disclosing or parting with PINs, passwords and cards;
- Failing to take reasonable care when keying in PINs or using passwords; and
- Unreasonably delaying notification of loss, theft or actual or possible disclosure of PINs or passwords to another person.

Several rules come into play in determining the extent of the cardholder's   **14-45**
liability. First, if losses, thefts, and disclosures are promptly notified to the

bank, the cardholder is not liable for loss occurring after notification unless the cardholder has acted fraudulently or negligently.

Secondly, where the loss occurs prior to notification, and the cardholder has not acted fraudulently or negligently and has not contributed to or caused the loss, the cardholder's liability is limited to the lesser of:

- N.Z. $50, or such other sum as specified in the relevant terms and conditions;
- The balance of the cardholder's account, including any pre-arranged credit; or
- The actual loss at the time of notification to the bank.[30]

14-46   Thirdly, if the cardholder has not acted fraudulently or negligently but has contributed to or caused losses from unauthorised transactions, the cardholder may be liable for some or all of the actual losses occurring before notification, but will not be liable for:

- Any portion of the losses incurred on any one day that exceeds the daily transaction limit applicable to the card or account in question; or
- Any portion of the losses incurred that exceed the balance of the account accessed, including any pre-arranged credit.

14-47   Importantly, the bank undertakes that it will not avoid liability to the cardholder by reason of the fact that the bank is a party to a shared EFT system. Thus, the bank assumes liability for all losses caused by the system, notwithstanding that the acts of another party to that system may have been responsible for the loss.

14-48   **Statements and Audit Trails**   Clause 10 deals with records of account transactions, which the bank must provide on a regular basis to the cardholder. Such records are vital for the cardholder to ensure that transactions made in relation to that cardholder's account are authorised. Regular statements allow timely identification of any irregularities in respect of the account.

The bank must provide records, in printed or electronic form as agreed, of all account transactions since the previous statement unless the cardholder agrees otherwise. The statements must show:

- For each such transaction, the amount, date and type of transaction and a transaction record number or other means by which the account entry can be reconciled with a transaction record. Where relevant, the name of the person making or receiving payment to or from the account should also be specified;

---

30 Notably, the Code specifies that the limitation of liability may not apply to stored value cards or the stored value function of a multi-function card.

- Any charges relating to the transactions; and
- The address or telephone number to be used for making enquiries or reporting errors in the statement.

Complaints Finally, clause 14 of the Code establishes a comprehensive, **14-49** cost-free procedure for handling complaints.

First, the bank investigates the complaint under its own internal complaints review procedure, which procedure must be documented, accessible to cardholders and must provide for speedy resolution of disputes in a fair and equitable manner. The Code makes it obligatory for banks to put in place such internal complaints procedures (clause 14.1).

If the cardholder is unhappy with the bank's decision, he or she may refer the complaint to the Banking Ombudsman for further consideration. The Banking Ombudsman may then independently review the complaint. Cardholders must exhaust all internal procedures of the bank before they can have recourse to the Banking Ombudsman's scheme. The bank must inform the cardholder of all of the procedures available.

The Banking Ombudsman Scheme

Independence The Banking Ombudsman Scheme provides a free and inde- **14-50** pendent body for dispute resolution in respect of personal banking. The Banking Ombudsman is appointed by the Banking Ombudsman Commission, which is chaired by a retired Court of Appeal Judge and also comprises two consumer representatives and two banking representatives.

The independence of the Banking Ombudsman is largely ensured by the make up of the Commission. He is accountable to the Commission for decisions made.

Jurisdiction Complaints involving loss or damage of up to N.Z. $100,000 **14-51** can be taken by a cardholder to the Banking Ombudsman. In addition to the actual loss arising from the unauthorised transaction, any incidental expenses that are reasonably incurred by the complainant in making or pursuing the complaint may also be awarded.

Notably, however, the Banking Ombudsman has no jurisdiction to consider any complaint relating to a commercial judgment by the bank in its decisions in respect of lending, securities, interest rate policies, or any practice or policy of a bank that does not itself breach an obligation or duty owed by the bank to the cardholder.

Nature of Dispute Resolution and Matters Relating to Evidence Disputes **14-52** submitted to the Banking Ombudsman are resolved on the basis of fairness rather than on the basis of strict legal rules. The Banking Ombudsman's Terms of Reference require the Banking Ombudsman to make recommendations or awards on the basis of what is, in his or her opinion, fair in the circumstances. However, applicable rules of law and general principles of good banking practice must also be taken into account by the Banking Ombudsman. The Banking Ombudsman is not bound by any previous decision he or she has made.

The Banking Ombudsman is also not bound by rules of evidence. He or she can consider any material from both sides of the dispute which is considered relevant. Further, the bank must provide to the Banking Ombudsman any information relating to the complaint which is, or is alleged to be, in its possession. If it possesses such information, it must disclose the information to the Banking Ombudsman unless the bank certifies that (a) the disclosure of such information would place the bank in breach of its duty of confidentiality to a third party, and (b) the bank has used its best endeavours to obtain that third party's consent. If any party supplies information to the Banking Ombudsman and requests that it be treated as confidential, the Banking Ombudsman cannot disclose that information to any other person except with the consent of the person providing the information.

These rules assist the cardholder for reasons mentioned earlier. The cardholder may not be able to present evidence in support of its claim, as certain matters will not be within the cardholder's sphere of knowledge. The Banking Ombudsman's scheme allows a more inquisitorial approach to be taken than would be the case in a court.

14-53   **Acceptance of settlements by cardholder** If the Banking Ombudsman comes to a settlement or recommendation involving the bank compensating the complainant, then the Banking Ombudsman's proposal must, unless the bank has otherwise requested or agreed, state that it is only open for acceptance by the complainant if he or she accepts it in full and final settlement of the claim. If the complainant accepts the recommendation or settlement, but the bank does not, the Banking Ombudsman can make a binding award against the bank.

If the claim is outside the Banking Ombudsman's jurisdiction (*e.g.*, if the claim is for a sum greater than N.Z. $100,000) or if the Banking Ombudsman considers the matter better heard in a court, then the Banking Ombudsman may refuse to consider the complaint.

Effect of Other Contractual Arrangements of the Bank in Respect of EFT

14-54   The contract between the cardholder and the bank is not the only contractual arrangement involved in the provision of EFT services. The bank, in its capacity as issuer of the relevant debit or credit card, will usually also have a contract with a provider of EFT settlement services (the "EFT service provider"). The EFT service provider will usually own or control the system through which EFT transactions are made.

The EFT service provider may limit its liability to the bank in respect of erroneous transaction authorisations to circumstances where the EFT service provider has wilfully or negligently failed to observe any authorisation procedures agreed between the parties. The EFT service provider may also seek to limit any other liability, to losses arising from wilful acts, omissions, or default of the provider or its employees, servants or agents.

Notably, most of such agreements in New Zealand also place an obligation on the bank to observe the terms and requirements of the Code. If the particular bank is not a party to the Code, the agreement will often provide that the bank shall observe the requirements of the Code as if it were a party to it. Thus, the agreement between an EFT service provider and a bank may in fact bring within the scope of the Code, banks that are not party to the Code. At present, there are only two E.F.T.P.O.S. systems in New Zealand and the contractual terms are quite similar.

Credit Card Numbers Communicated On-line

Persons purchasing goods or services by way of credit card need not produce   **14-55** the card itself. All that is required is for the cardholder to give the merchant the cardholder's card number, along with any requisite information intended to verify the authenticity of the transaction.

This type of credit card payment method has been used for some time in respect of mail order purchases or orders by telephone. Shopping on the Internet is now well established, and payments for goods purchased on the Internet are generally effected by the cardholder communicating his or her credit card number on-line to the merchant. The electronic communication of the number creates an exposure of the transaction to interception and can lead to unauthorised transactions being made by impostors using the communicated card number. The Internet currently lacks sufficient security measures to represent an effective payment channel in all instances. While public key cryptography has been implemented to some extent by some of the large players in the industry, significant risks of interception and unauthorised use still exist in many such transactions.

Because of these exposures, the New Zealand chapter of the International Association of Credit Card Investigators (A.I.C.C.I.) has recently approached Internet service providers to assess the risks and security measures in place for credit card payments on the Internet.[31] The A.I.C.C.I.'s membership includes representatives from banks, other credit card operators, and telecommunications suppliers.

The major banks in New Zealand do not generally have any terms in their standard contracts with cardholders specifically governing the communication of credit card numbers on the Internet. Credit card use is covered at a general level by the Code, which will govern the allocation of liability for unauthorised transactions. Thus, provided the cardholder notifies the

---

31 Bell, "Credit Card Industry to Investigate Internet Security", *The Independent*, June 7, 1996, at p. 29.

bank as soon as he or she becomes aware of any interception or unauthorised usage of the card number, the following rules will apply:

- The cardholder will not be liable for loss occasioned by an unauthorised transaction, where it is clear that the cardholder could not have contributed to the loss (clause 5.5.1);
- The cardholder will be liable for all loss if he or she has taken part in a fraudulent act giving rise to the loss (clause 5.5.2);
- The cardholder may be liable for some or all of the loss if the cardholder has contributed to or caused the loss, for example, by "failing to reasonably safeguard cards" (clause 5.5.3);
- Provided the cardholder has not acted fraudulently or negligently, the cardholder will not be liable for loss arising after the time of notification — (clause 5.5.4);
- In respect of losses occurring prior to notification, where the cardholder has not acted fraudulently or negligently and has not contributed to or caused the loss, the cardholder's liability will be limited as provided in clause 5.5.5; and
- In respect of losses occurring prior to notification, where the cardholder has not acted fraudulently or negligently but has contributed to or caused the loss, the cardholder may be liable to the extent set out in clause 5.5.6, which is also discussed above in relation to EFT.

14-56   Notably, clause 5.2.2 provides that banks issuing cards must inform cardholders of the risks involved if card transactions are authorised in advance of the receipt of goods or services.

Where liability becomes an issue at any stage, the web of contracts between the card issuer, merchants and the cardholders will dictate who ultimately bears any loss. Each merchant will have a contract with the card issuer, as part of the contractual chain existing between the parties to the on-line transaction. If the merchant has not complied with security measures specified in its contract with the issuer (such as asking for certain identifying information of the cardholder), and that non-compliance has caused or contributed to the loss, liability may ultimately be borne by the non-complying merchant.

Electronic Cheques

14-57   On-line payments over media such as the Internet could also be made by electronic cheques, *i.e.*, by communicating on-line to a merchant all information contained in a paper-based cheque, combined with the use of electronic signatures.

Such electronic cheques are not currently used in New Zealand to the writers' knowledge. The Code may require extension to accommodate electronic, as well as paper-based, cheques within its terms, as appropriate.

Notably, however, some statutory movement has occurred in respect of electronic inter-bank clearing systems, *i.e.*, the electronic presentation and payment of cheques between paying and collecting banks.[32] This legislative recognition of electronic inter-bank clearing in respect of cheques perhaps signals that legislative changes to accommodate electronic cheques will ultimately be forthcoming in response to pressures from the commercial community.

ELECTRONIC INFORMATION RIGHTS

Copyright

Applicability of Copyright to On-line Communications

No legislation specifically addresses the copyright protection of on-line communications in New Zealand. Accordingly, the generic provisions of the New Zealand Copyright Act 1994 must be applied to that form of communication.   **14-58**

Information Protected

The Copyright Act protects original works that come within the specified categories in section 14 and qualify for protection by the nationality or residence of the author,[33] the country of first publication[34] or the place of transmission.[35]   **14-59**

As with non-electronic forms of communication, there is no copyright in on-line facts or information *per se*. The protected categories of works include literary, dramatic, musical and artistic works, irrespective of the form in which the data is held. Sound recordings, films, and cable programmes are also protected by copyright and may be relevant to protection of on-line communications.

Electronic and other databases are protected because of the definition of "compilation", which includes compilations consisting, wholly or partly, of works or parts of works, and extends to include "a compilation of data other than works or parts of works".[36] This literary copyright will subsist independently of any copyright in the component "works" provided there is sufficient originality in the database compilation in terms of the structure, arrangement, and selection of the works or data.[37]

---

32 Bills of Exchange Amendment Act 1995, and in particular, the amendments that Act made to sections 7A and 7D of the Cheques Act 1960.
33 Copyright Act, section 18.
34 Copyright Act, section 19.
35 Copyright Act, section 20.
36 Copyright Act, section 2.
37 Moon "New Zealand's New Copyright Act Ensures Protection for Multimedia" (1995) 13 (2) *International Technology Newsletter* 11.

The broad definition of "compilation" also ensures that multimedia works (which may consist of a number of different types of works, such as films, sound recordings and literary works) are protected as literary works.[38]

Computer programs are protected as literary works. There is no definition of "computer programs". Accordingly, it is hoped that the Copyright Act will remain current with technological developments. The Copyright Act does not resolve the question of whether copyright subsists in the "look and feel" of a computer program, or whether the copyright in a program extends to cover "look and feel". The issue of whether program copyright extends to program structure and database definition has also not been resolved.[39]

Acquiring Copyright

14-60   Copyright exists automatically on the creation of an original work. There is no requirement for registration.

Ownership of Copyright in On-line Information

14-61   In general, the first owner of a copyright work is the author.[40] The author of a work is the person who creates it.[41] In the case of a computer-generated work, this is the person who makes the necessary arrangements for the creation of the work.[42]

There are exceptions to the general rule. If the work was made in the course of employment, the employer of the author is the first owner of the copyright in the work, subject to any agreement to the contrary.[43] In addition, in the case of certain categories of works that have been commissioned (including computer programs, drawings, diagrams, films and sound recordings), the person who commissioned and pays or agrees to pay for the work is the first owner of the copyright in the work, subject to any contrary agreement.[44]

Rights of Copyright Owner

14-62   The owner of the copyright in a work has a number of exclusive rights to do or authorise others to do "restricted acts". These acts include:[45]

- The right to copy the work;
- The right to issue copies of that work to the public;
- The right to adapt the work;

---

38 Moon "New Zealand's New Copyright Act Ensures Protection for Multimedia", (1995) 13(2) *International Technology Newsletter* 11; Bandey "An Analysis of the Copyright Anatomy of Multimedia Works" (1996) 1 *N.Z.I.P.J.* 52.
39 Moon "New Zealand's New Copyright Act Ensures Protection for Multimedia", (1995) 13(2) *International Technology Newsletter* 11.
40 Copyright Act, section 21(1).
41 Copyright Act, section 5.
42 Copyright Act, section 5(2)(a).
43 Copyright Act, section 21(2).
44 Copyright Act, section 21(3).
45 Copyright Act, section 16 and part II.

- The right to perform the work in public; and
- The right to include the work in a cable programme service.

Right to Copy the Work The exclusive right to copy a work is not **14-63** media-specific. The right is broadly defined to include "reproducing or recording the work in any material form".[46] Accordingly, the copyright owner has the exclusive right to download and copy or store a copy of the work. In addition, a temporary copy of the on-line work is made by a computer to enable it to be presented on the screen.

Technically, therefore, merely accessing on-line information without the copyright owner's consent is also a restricted act. Commentators have argued that this action is more equivalent to browsing through a library's shelves than the act of making a permanent copy of a work. On this view, accessing on-line information should not be treated as a breach of copyright for policy reasons.[47] This issue will need to be clarified by case law or statutory amendment.

The initial copying by a service provider of a work for inclusion on the Internet or some other on-line service will also infringe the copyright owner's exclusive right to copy the work.

Right to Include a Work in a Cable Programme Service It has been argued **14-64** by at least one New Zealand commentator[48] that the Internet or another on-line service may be a "cable programme service" and, therefore, that inclusion of a work on the on-line service may also infringe copyright under section 33. The definition of a "cable programme service" is a complex one.[49] Essentially, an on-line service will qualify where a telecommunications system (other than a wireless system) is used to transmit visual images, sounds, or other information for reception by different users.

The definition of "cable programme service" is subject to a number of exceptions. In particular, it does not include a service an essential feature of which is that it be interactive (*i.e.*, the receiver of the service may transmit information on the same service back to the service provider). Therefore, in many cases web pages on the Internet or other on-line services will not qualify as cable programme services.

If a work is included in a "cable programme service" under the Copyright Act without the copyright owner's permission (*e.g.*, a non-interactive web page on the Internet), the person providing the cable programme service may have breached copyright in the work.[50] Three persons may arguably be the person "providing the cable programme service". The provider may be the

---

46 Copyright Act, section 2.
47 Harrison and Frankel, "The Internet: Can Intellectual Property Laws Cope?", (1996) 1 *N.Z.I.P.J.* 60.
48 Harrison and Frankel "The Internet: Can Intellectual Property Laws Cope?", (1996) 1 *N.Z.I.P.J.* 60.
49 Copyright Act, section 4.
50 Copyright Act, section 33.

person to whom the web page belongs, the person on whose server the web page resides or the system operator who provides the means for transmission of the programme service. It is logical that the infringer should be the web page provider, who controls the content of the web page and puts arrangements in place for its transmission. The issue is not yet settled in New Zealand law.

14-65   Right to Perform a Work in Public In relation to a literary, dramatic or musical work, the performance of a work in public is also a restricted act.[51] A "performance" is defined to include any mode of visual presentation of a work[52] and accordingly would cover the display of protected works on a computer screen.

Since broadcasting and including a work in a cable programme service are dealt with elsewhere as restricted acts, where a work is performed, played or shown by electronic means, the Act provides that neither the person who transmits the information nor the "performers" shall be regarded as responsible.[53]

Cross-Border Communications

14-66   Cross-border on-line communications may severely limit the rights of a copyright owner in practice. While the on-line service may easily transcend borders and it is largely irrelevant to users where information originates, New Zealand copyright protection will likely only apply where an infringing act occurs in New Zealand. Reproduction will only occur in the country where the work is accessed, downloaded or copied, regardless of whether the work was transmitted from New Zealand. Inclusion in a cable programme service arguably only takes place where the web page is compiled.[54]

Reciprocal protection under the Berne Convention or the Universal Copyright Convention, both of which New Zealand is a member, may be available in other member states. Equally, New Zealand provides copyright protection for those member states under the Copyright Act.

Moral Rights

14-67   In addition, an author (as opposed to a copyright owner) has a number of moral rights. These moral rights are in brief:[55]

- The right to be identified as the author of a work;
- The right to object to derogatory treatment of a work;

---

51 Copyright Act, section 32.
52 Copyright Act, section 2.
53 Copyright Act, section 32(3).
54 Harrison and Frankel, "The Internet: Can Intellectual Property Laws Cope?", (1996) 1 N.Z.I.P.J. 60.
55 Copyright Act, part IV.

- The right not to have a work falsely attributed to him or her as author; and
- The right not to have a work falsely represented as the adaptation of a work of which the person is the author.

A person who has commissioned photographs or films for private and domestic purposes also has the right to enforce the privacy of those photographs or films, even if he is not the copyright owner.

Rights of Copyright Users

Aside from where there is a contract between the copyright owner and the user that permits use of the work, or where the copyright owner has expressly stated that users may copy the work, the rights of copyright users essentially depend on the extent of the copyright owner's exclusive right to do the restricted acts, subject to the exceptions set out in the Copyright Act.   **14-68**

It is still unclear under the Copyright Act whether copyright users may legitimately browse through on-line information, or whether the act of accessing on-line information will be found to breach copyright in the work.

It has also not yet been decided by New Zealand courts or legislation whether the act of placing a work on an on-line service such as the Internet impliedly authorises users to copy the work.

The restricted acts relate to the whole or a substantial part of a work.[56] "Substantial" relates essentially to the quality, rather than the quantity, of the part of a work that is copied or used in relation to the whole work.[57] This limit on the copyright owner's rights is still not likely to permit any more than a minimal copying of on-line copyright works.

There is no exception in New Zealand law specifically for electronic uses of protected works. The Copyright Act sets out a large number of specific exceptions to copyright. The most important of these in the context of on-line services are:

- The fair dealing exception for research, private study, criticism, review or news reporting;[58]
- The exceptions for copying for educational purposes;[59] and
- The exceptions for copying by libraries and archives.[60]

These and other similar exceptions are all technical and circumscribed. Notably, in relation to computer programs, there is no exception for decompiling   **14-69**

---

56 Copyright Act, section 29.
57 *Longman Group Ltd & Ors v. Carrington Technical Institute Board of Governors & Anor* [1991] 2 N.Z.L.R. 574.
58 Copyright Act, sections 42 and 43.
59 Copyright Act, sections 44 to 49.
60 Copyright Act, sections 50 to 57.

for the purposes of producing an interoperable program. Copyright in a computer program will be infringed by copying, conversion into another language or code, storage in any medium and decompilation for any purpose.

The extent of intermediaries' rights to provide copyright works to others is also still undecided under New Zealand law. Even when intermediaries, such as bulletin board operators or access providers, do not themselves copy a work by placing it on an on-line service, by providing access to works for users through on-line services they may be responsible for authorising others to copy works. In addition, sections 35–39 of the Copyright Act prohibit certain other acts which if committed without the licence of the copyright owner and with a suitable state of mind (*e.g.*, knowledge) amount to "secondary infringements" of copyright.

Trade Secrets

14-70   The ease of access to information held on on-line services inevitably raises issues as to the information provider's ability to protect the confidentiality of on-line information. Traditionally, one way in which persons may protect their intellectual property is to maintain its secrecy. In New Zealand, this secrecy may be protected by an action in equity or contract for breach of an obligation of confidentiality.[61]

The advantage of the protection afforded to confidential information in New Zealand is that it can extend beyond the rights and remedies provided by the statute-based protection of copyright, and is without the registration and disclosure requirements of patent protection. The information need not be in any particular form. Accordingly, in principle, the protection clearly covers on-line information. However, the Internet and other such on-line services may jeopardise the practical and, in some cases, legal efficacy of these mechanisms.[62] Arguably, the nature of on-line services such as the Internet is inconsistent with keeping information confidential.

In addition, the privacy of "personal information" contained in on-line services may be preserved under the New Zealand Privacy Act 1993, although New Zealand commentators appear to differ on how appropriate the Privacy Act is to protect on-line information. On the one hand, the Privacy Commissioner, Bruce Slane, has maintained that the privacy principles are broadly sufficient for the protection of e-mail. On the other hand, Elizabeth Longworth, a specialist in privacy legislation, has stated that "the

---

61 In New Zealand, the term "trade secrets" is generally used interchangeably with the term "confidential information" and the two are not usually distinguished: see Katz, *Laws NZ*, Intellectual Property, Confidential Information (1995) paragraphs 12–15.
62 The large number of practical issues as to the security of information placed on on-line services are not covered here.

Privacy Act is not designed to address the specific issues of telecommunication interceptions and electronic messaging".[63]

Acquiring Trade Secret Rights

Breach of Confidentiality To protect on-line information as a trade secret   **14-71**
or as confidential information in New Zealand, a person will have to establish that the recipient of the information was subject to an obligation to respect its confidentiality.

This obligation will generally be founded in contract or equity. A contractual confidentiality obligation will exist where the obligation is expressly or impliedly contained in the contractual relations between the parties.[64] The obligation may arise, quite independently of contract, in equity.[65] An equitable obligation will exist where:

- The information has the necessary quality of confidence; and
- The confidential information was imparted in circumstances importing an obligation of confidence.

Where there is then an unauthorised use of that information to the detriment   **14-72**
of the party communicating it, that equitable obligation will be breached.[66] Information that is of a trivial nature, obvious or is generally available to the public cannot be regarded as confidential.[67] However, novelty in the sense required for a patent is not necessary for information to be protected.[68] Rather, the court is recognising the skill and effort involved in creating the information when it protects confidentiality.[69]

In addition, information that has been released into the public domain will not be protected as confidential. Whether or not publication of information has been sufficiently extensive to destroy a confidence is a question of degree.[70]

Information disseminated over the Internet in an unencrypted form might almost immediately cease to have the necessary quality of confidence. Arguments by overseas commentators that this is very likely to be the case

---

63 Dennis "Legal Roadblocks to Internet Business", March 1996, *Management Technology Briefing* 11, at pp. 13 and 15.
64 *Seafresh Fisheries (New Zealand) Ltd* v. *Rodney Fletcher,* Unreported, High Court Wellington Registry March 13, 1995, C.P. 33/95.
65 *AB Consolidated Ltd* v. *Europe Strength Food Co. Pty Ltd* [1978] 2 N.Z.L.R. 515 (C.A.).
66 *Coco* v. *AN Clark (Engineers) Ltd* [1969] R.P.C., 41, at p. 47, per Megarry J; *AB Consolidated Ltd* v. *Europe Strength Food Co. Pty Ltd* [1978] 2 N.Z.L.R. 515 (C.A.), at p. 520.
67 *SSC & B: Lintas New Zealand Ltd* v. *Murphy* [1986] 2 N.Z.L.R. 436.
68 *AB Consolidated Ltd* v. *Europe Strength Food Co. Pty Ltd* [1978] 2 N.Z.L.R. 515 (C.A.), at p. 520.
69 *House of Spring Gardens* v. *Point Blank Ltd* [1985] F.S.R. 327, at p. 335.
70 *Attorney-General* v. *Wellington Newspapers* [1988] 1 N.Z.L.R. 129 at 175 (C.A.) and Katz, *Laws NZ,* Intellectual Property: Confidential Information (1995) paragraphs 93–95.

where information is placed on a bulletin board on the Internet are equally convincing in New Zealand.[71] Even the use of e-mail has been said to be "analogous to sending messages by postcard" and as such is less likely to have been imparted in circumstances imposing an obligation of confidence.[72] Encryption of messages would likely import an obligation of confidence. It is even arguable that the ability to decode encryption is an inherent risk of the Internet and so the information provider cannot complain if the information is decoded.

Conversely, it is arguable that transmitting confidential information on the Internet without taking steps to maintain its secrecy (such as encryption), would breach a duty of confidence.

The New Zealand courts have not yet addressed the specific issue of the confidentiality of information available on the Internet and other on-line services.

14-73   **Privacy Act 1993** On-line information which contains "personal information" as defined in the New Zealand Privacy Act 1993[73] may also be protected from unauthorised use and disclosure. "Personal information" is information about an identifiable individual.

The Privacy Act does not specifically mention on-line or electronic information, but the courts in an analogous context have broadly interpreted "information" as "that which informs, instructs, tells or makes aware".[74] Accordingly the principles under the Privacy Act may be applied to protect the privacy of the individuals concerned.[75]

Rights of Trade Secret Owner

14-74   **Rights over Confidential Information** The owner of confidential information must be able to establish a breach or potential breach of an equitable obligation of confidentiality or of a contractual obligation. The usual range of remedies is then available to the owner of the confidential information. The ability to obtain an interim injunction to prevent disclosure of the information is generally crucial.

As with other interim relief available in New Zealand, an interim injunction is discretionary.[76] The normal remedies and actions for breach

---

71   McGinness "The Internet and Privacy — Some Issues Facing the Private Sector", June 1996, *Computers & Law* 25; Newton "The Law and the Internet in Europe", May 1996, *Managing Intellectual Property* 34.

72   McGinness, "The Internet and Privacy — Some Issues Facing the Private Sector", June 1996, *Computers & Law* 25.

73   Privacy Act 1993, section 2.

74   *Commissioner of Police* v. *Ombudsman* [1988] 1 N.Z.L.R. 385, at p. 402, in relation to the Official Information Act 1982.

75   Dennis "Legal Roadblocks to Internet Business", March 1996, *Management Technology Briefing* 11.

76   *American Cyanamid Co.* v. *Ethicon Ltd* [1975] A.C. 396; [1975] 1 All E.R. 504; *Klissers Farmhouse Bakeries Ltd* v. *Harvest Bakeries Ltd* [1985] 2 N.Z.L.R. 129.

of confidence are a permanent injunction and some form of monetary compensation, either damages or an account of profits.[77]

Rights over Personal Information   If a person places information on an on-line service which is linked to specific and identifiable individuals, or which enables the identification of an individual, the Privacy Act may apply.   **14-75**

The Privacy Act imposes certain broad information privacy principles (I.P.P.s) which entitle the person that the information concerns to complain about the breach of his or her privacy.[78] In summary, the Privacy Act imposes:

- Restrictions on the purpose for which and manner in which agencies may collect information about an individual (I.P.P.s 1, 2 and 4);
- A requirement that certain information be supplied to the individual from whom information is collected, including information as to the manner in which the collected information will be held and the person's rights of access to and correction of that information (I.P.P. 3);
- A requirement that the agency holding the information protect it, by such security safeguards as are reasonable in the circumstances to take, against loss, unauthorised access, use, disclosure, or misuse (I.P.P. 5);
- Limits on the use and disclosure of personal information (I.P.P.s 10 and 11); and
- An obligation on agencies to permit an individual to access and correct that information (I.P.P.s 6 and 7).

Accordingly, the Privacy Act may affect (for example) the way in which personal information is stored on on-line services or requested from individuals over on-line services, and whether employers or others can monitor e-mail.   **14-76**

Rights of Non-Owner of Trade Secret

Rights of Non-Owner of Confidential Information   The rights of a non-owner of trade secrets to use trade secrets will be determined by whether the information is confidential and the circumstances in which the information was disclosed to that person.   **14-77**

Where the information is simply a compilation of publicly available information, a person may be able to use it. However, even in this case, if the owner of the information has expended skill and effort either in combining that information in a particular manner or in analysing it and using it in

---

77 Katz, *Laws NZ*, "Intellectual Property: Confidential Information" (1995), paragraphs 144–166.
78 Privacy Act, sections 6 and 66.

a manner that is of value, the courts are likely to protect that information as involving sufficient skill and labour to be confidential.[79]

In addition, the confidentiality obligation will not generally cover information once it has been published, even if the initial disclosure was made by a third party and through no fault of the owner of the information. However, publication by a third party will not necessarily release a confidant from an obligation of confidence. The courts will examine all the circumstances. In certain circumstances, the courts have held that, even once information has been made public, once a person has received information in confidence he or she is not free to exploit any advantage that person has over other members of the public by having had advance knowledge of the information.[80]

14-78   **Rights of Non-Owner of Personal Information**   The Privacy Act applies to all agencies (broadly defined in section 2 as any person or body of persons in the public or private sector, with certain exceptions) in New Zealand. In addition, the Privacy Act is expressly extraterritorial in relation to information concerning New Zealanders. Section 10 provides that personal information held by an agency covered by the Act includes information held by that agency outside New Zealand. I.P.P.s 5 and 8–11 only apply when the information has been transferred out of New Zealand.[81] However, the access and correction principles (I.P.P.s 6 and 7) cover all personal information held outside New Zealand by that agency.[82] This extraterritoriality is particularly relevant to cross-border on-line communications.

Specific exceptions to particular I.P.P.s include where a particular action is authorised by the individual concerned. General exemptions include where the action is authorised or required by or under law[83] or where the Privacy Commissioner authorises the action due to public interest reasons or a countervailing benefit to the individual concerned.[84] In addition, the I.P.P.s do not apply to personal information which is collected or held by an individual solely or principally for the purposes of, or in connection with, that individual's personal, family or household affairs.[85]

The rights of a person who collects, uses or wishes to disclose personal information turn on a two-stage test. A privacy complaint may only be upheld if both limbs are satisfied. First, the proposed action must breach an information privacy principle set out in the Privacy Act. Secondly, the proposed action must cause an interference with the privacy of that individual by

---

79 *AB Consolidated* v. *Europe Strength Food Co.* [1978] 2 N.Z.L.R. 515, at p. 523.
80 The "springboard doctrine" set out in *Aquaculture Corporation* v. *New Zealand Green Mussel Co. Ltd and Others* (Number 1) (1985) 5 I.P.R. 353.
81 Privacy Act, section 10(1).
82 Privacy Act, section 10(2).
83 Privacy Act, section 7.
84 Privacy Act, section 54.
85 Privacy Act, section 56.

damaging the individual's interests in some way set out in section 66 of the Privacy Act. A complaint as to a breach of privacy is likely to be made to the Privacy Commissioner who has a jurisdiction to investigate or mediate the matter or refer the matter to the Complaints Review Tribunal. A range of remedies is available to the injured individual.

Trade Marks

In New Zealand, no technology-specific legislation relates to trade marks. **14-79** Accordingly, the general trade mark law must also be applied to on-line trade marks.

New Zealand law recognises two types of trade marks, registered and unregistered. Trade marks for goods or services may be registered under the Trade Marks Act 1953. The expanded definition of a "trade mark" because of recent amendments to the Trade Marks Act is particularly relevant to on-line trade marks. A trade mark now means "any sign or any combination of signs, capable of being represented graphically and capable of distinguishing the goods or services of one person from those of another person". Accordingly, it may even encompass colour and smells. Registration confers a statutory right to sue for infringement, without the need to prove reputation relating to the trade mark, in New Zealand.

It is not compulsory to register trade marks in New Zealand. Unregistered trade marks, rights to use them and to prevent others from using them are obtained solely through use. Both registered and unregistered trade marks may be protected in an action for passing off or under the provisions of the Fair Trading Act 1986.

Selecting an On-line Trade Mark

As a trade mark registration confers a monopoly over the word or logo in relation **14-80** to the goods or services in respect of which registration is granted, New Zealand trade mark legislation is designed to prevent (and courts have been reluctant to permit) any one trader from obtaining a monopoly over words or devices that competitors might fairly want to use in relation to their goods or services.

To be registrable, a trade mark must be one in the terms of the Trade Marks Act 1953, either inherently distinctive, adapted to distinguish or capable of distinguishing the goods or services in relation to which it is used.[86] In selecting a trade mark, this requirement, and the other criteria for registration, should be borne in mind. The following are examples of trade mark features that are usually held to be non-distinctive:

- The generic name of the goods or services such as "soap" should not be registrable as a trade mark for soap;

---

86 Trade Marks Act, sections 14 and 15.

- Laudatory words, such as "best", "quality", and "perfection";
- Descriptive words which refer directly to some quality or characteristic of the goods or services which other traders may want to use when legitimately describing their goods or services;
- Surnames, except in the case of rare surnames, which may be registrable;
- Geographical names, unless the place name is relatively insignificant in relation to trade;
- Letters in ordinary form (single letters) and unpronounceable combinations of two or three letters;
- A descriptive device, such as a picture of the goods or services provided;
- Words and devices common to the trade; and
- Ordinary borders, common geometric devices, such as circles, triangles, or stars, which are not distinctive on their own.

14-81   Trade marks can include certain non-distinctive features, as long as the trade marks as a whole are registrable. For example, a mark that is not distinctive may become registrable if it is stylised or made visually distinctive in some way. In these cases, the applicant may be required to disclaim any monopoly rights in relation to the non-distinctive features.[87] Other general criteria for registration should be taken into account when selecting an on-line trade mark. In particular, the following trade marks are unregistrable:

- Deceptive marks;[88]
- Offensive marks;[89]
- Marks prohibited by the Trade Marks Act (such as A.N.Z.A.C.);[90]
- Flags and symbols of foreign countries;[91] and
- Marks which are confusingly similar to existing registered marks, to prior applications for registered marks or to marks which have been in use prior to the mark in question.[92]

14-82   Even if the trade mark is not to be registered, the above issues in selecting a trade mark remain very important. If the chosen mark conflicts with an existing mark, the user may be prohibited from using that trade mark in New Zealand in an action for passing off, under the Fair Trading Act or in a trade mark infringement action. In addition, distinctiveness will be an important element in being able to protect even an unregistered trade mark.

---

87 Trade Marks Act, section 23.
88 Trade Marks Act, section 16.
89 Trade Marks Act, section 16.
90 Trade Marks Act, section 21.
91 Trade Marks Act, section 21.
92 Trade Marks Act, section 17.

Acquiring On-line Trade Mark Rights

As discussed above, trade mark rights may be acquired either through the   **14-83**
registration of a trade mark under the Trade Marks Act 1953 or by sufficient
use of a trade mark on which to base a passing off action or an action for
breach of the Fair Trading Act 1986.

In brief, the process of obtaining a trade mark registration involves filing
an application in the New Zealand Trade Marks Office.[93] The application
will be examined by an examiner who will issue an examination report that
either accepts the trade mark for registration or objects to the registration of it.
If objections are raised, it may be possible to overcome these by legal submissions and/or the provision of evidence of use of the trade mark. On acceptance
of the trade mark for registration the application is advertised in the Patent
Office Journal. During a three-month period (or a longer period if the Commissioner allows it) other persons may oppose the registration of the trade
mark. If the application for registration of the trade mark is not successfully
opposed then registration will proceed on payment of registration fees.

Registration is backdated to the date of application and is for an initial
period of seven years. It may be renewed for further successive periods of
14 years.[94] The trade mark does not need to be in use when the application
is made — a genuine intention to use the mark in the foreseeable future is
sufficient — although use may be relevant in establishing the distinctiveness of
the mark.

Although registration of a trade mark confers the exclusive right to
prevent others from using that mark in New Zealand in relation to the goods
or services for which it is registered (subject to any imposed limitations), it
does not necessarily entitle the registered proprietor to use the trade mark
as a domain name on the Internet. That right must be obtained independently
under the procedure outlined below for domain names. Conversely, registration
of a domain name does not necessarily entitle a person to use that name if it
would infringe a registered trade mark in New Zealand. These issues are largely
untested by the courts in New Zealand at present.

In New Zealand, a trade mark may be protected by an action in passing
off or under the Fair Trading Act 1986, or by an action under both heads.
Briefly, passing off occurs in New Zealand where a trader makes a misrepresentation in the course of trade which damages the goodwill of another
trader. To succeed in an action for passing off, and so establish a right to
prevent use of the trade mark by another, the trader must demonstrate that
it has a goodwill in the trade mark, and that this goodwill is or is likely to
be damaged, as a result of the misrepresentation involving that trade mark.[95]

---

93 Trade Marks Act, sections 26–28.
94 Trade Marks Act, section 29.
95 *Dominion Rent A Car Ltd.* v. *Budget Rent A Car Systems Ltd.* [1987] 2 N.Z.L.R. 395;
   Wineworths Group Ltd v. *Comite Interprofessionel du Vin du Champagne* [1992] 2
   N.Z.L.R. 327.

To bring an action in passing off in New Zealand, the trade mark owner will need to show sufficient reputation and business connection with New Zealand to establish goodwill relating to the relevant trade mark.

To protect its trade mark under the Fair Trading Act, the trader will need to show misleading or deceptive conduct on the part of another. In order for conduct to be misleading or deceptive or likely to mislead or deceive it will generally be necessary for the trade mark owner to establish a reputation in the country connected with the relevant trade mark.

New Zealand courts have drawn a distinction between goodwill (required in a passing off action) and the lesser requirement of reputation (which is sufficient under the Fair Trading Act).[96] New Zealand courts at this stage require "something more" than mere reputation in New Zealand for a plaintiff to have goodwill in New Zealand. Accordingly, advertising on the Internet alone may not be sufficient use to establish trade mark rights in a passing off action. However, advertising, combined with the sale of goods and/or services throughout the Internet will generally be sufficient. Where a business has an international reputation, then not much business activity in New Zealand is required to establish goodwill in New Zealand. In this case, something less than the sale of goods (such as negotiations to establish a New Zealand branch or franchise) may be sufficient.[97]

In an action for passing off, a range of different types of damage are recognised by the New Zealand courts. These include the most obvious, such as loss of profits, but in certain cases may extend to dilution of the goodwill associated with the trade mark.[98] This head of damage will be particularly relevant to on-line trade marks where there is not yet any sale of goods or services in New Zealand and where, consequently, it would be difficult to establish loss of profits arising from the misrepresentation. One of the advantages of bringing an action under the Fair Trading Act is that damage is not necessary. It is sufficient if it is likely to occur.[99]

Remedies for an action in passing off include damages, an account of profits and injunctions prohibiting the offending use. The remedies under the Fair Trading Act are set out in part V of the Act, and include injunctions and damages.

Infringement of On-line Trade Marks

14-84   The general principles of trade mark law are likely to be applied to uses of the trade marks on the Internet or other on-line services.

---

96 Morgan "Local Business Connections: Passing Off and section 9 of the Fair Trading Act" (1995) 1 *N.Z.I.P.J.* 28.

97 *Dominion Rent A Car Ltd.* v. *Budget Rent A Car Systems Ltd.* [1987] 2 N.Z.L.R. 395; *Midas International Corp.* v. *Midas Autocare Ltd* (1988) 2 N.Z.B.L.C. 102,915.

98 *Taylor Bros. Ltd.* v. *Taylors Group Ltd.* [1988] 2 N.Z.L.R. 1; *Midas International Corp.* v. *Midas Autocare Ltd.* (1988) 2 N.Z.B.L.C. 102,915.

99 Fair Trading Act 1986, section 41.

In New Zealand, a registered trade mark will be infringed where any person uses, in the course of trade:

- An identical sign in relation to any goods or services in respect of which the trade mark is registered; or
- An identical sign in relation to any goods or services that are similar to any goods or services in respect of which the trade mark is registered, if such use would be likely to deceive or cause confusion; or
- A similar sign in relation to any goods or services that are identical with or similar to any goods or services in respect of which the trade mark is registered, if such use would be likely to deceive or cause confusion, if the sign is used as a trade mark or if the use of the sign is on or in relation to goods or services in a manner that refers to someone having the right, either as proprietor or registered user, to use the trade mark.[100]

The most relevant limitations to bringing an action for infringement of a   **14-85** trade mark by on-line use are that the infringing sign must be used in the course of trade and in a trade mark sense. "In the course of trade" is construed very broadly. The need to use the mark in a "trade mark sense" before it will infringe is particularly problematic in the case of domain names.

The other main limitation on trade mark law in relation to on-line services is that a trade mark registered in New Zealand only protects the use of the mark in New Zealand. Accordingly, the proprietor of a registered trade mark in New Zealand may have limited rights to protect that mark on on-line services in other parts of the world.

The main challenge imposed by infringement by on-line services, in addition to proving the infringement, is finding the offending use and preserving the evidence. Currently, only textual material can be searched on the Internet. Consequently, infringements occurring only in graphic or photographic form must be found by human review. However, technology may provide new search engines that will enable this to be done on command. Once infringing uses have been located, they should be preserved immediately by printing out the relevant page and attaching them to an authenticating affidavit or declaration. Preservation of the evidence is crucial because the infringer may destroy the evidence by editing the on-line service, an easier task than removing a sign or reprinting a product's labels.

Provided a trader is able to establish the requirements of an action in passing off the trader will be able to prevent use of a trade mark on the Internet.

In addition, the New Zealand Fair Trading Act 1986 provides a further cause of action for an on-line trade mark owner. This Act prohibits misleading or deceptive misrepresentations in the course of trade (principally under section 9 and under sections 10 and 11). False representations including those

---

100 Fair Trading Act 1986, sections 9 and 10.

of endorsement, approval or affiliation are also prohibited.[101] These actions have the advantage of not requiring the trade mark owner to prove goodwill or any business connection with New Zealand if the conduct misleads consumers or amounts to a false representation in the manner prohibited by the Fair Trading Act. Advertising by using a trade mark on the Internet will be sufficient to breach the Fair Trading Act if the advertising is misleading or deceptive or falsely represents an endorsement, approval, or affiliation.

Domain Names

Acquiring Rights to Domain Names

14-86   Registration of a trade mark does not necessarily allow the registered proprietor to use that mark as a domain name. The registered proprietor must obtain domain name approval independently of registering the trade mark.

To obtain a domain name, a person must apply to the Internet Society of New Zealand Inc. There is no statutory basis for this registration system. The Society's policy for registration is that registration is a listing service, operated on a first-come, first-served basis.[102] The Society does not check whether the applicant has the right to use the name and it is the applicant's responsibility to ensure that it is entitled to do so. The applicant in lodging the request for a name informs the Society that they are asserting a claimed right to a name.

The Society has stated that it will not adjudicate where objections are made to domain name registration. Accordingly, in the case of conflicting name requests between an applicant and an existing listing, it is left to the parties concerned to resolve such matters by negotiation or through the courts, and report to the Society if the resolution includes a change of registration detail.

Protecting Domain Name as a Trade Mark

14-87   Domain names arguably function as trade marks.[103] In principle, ordinary trade mark law should apply to this situation. To infringe a registered trade mark, a sign must (among other things) be used "in the course of trade" and in a trade mark sense. It would probably be difficult for a commercial organisation to argue that it was not using a domain name "in the course of trade", but it may not necessarily be using it in a trade mark sense. Arguably, domain names feature as addresses and not as trade marks. However, this argument is likely to be given short shrift in New Zealand.

---

101 Fair Trading Act 1986, section 13.
102 "Internet Society of New Zealand Inc: Domain Name Registrations", September 2, 1996 http://www2.waikato.ac.nz:81/isocnz/nz-domain/DNSopinion.html.
103 Harrison and Frankel, "The Internet: Can Intellectual Property Laws Cope?", (1996) 1 N.Z.I.P.J. 60.

The most difficult question in protecting a domain name as a trade mark is whether the use of that name takes place in New Zealand and can consequently be protected under trade mark law in New Zealand. If a foreign company uses its trade mark on the Internet from a site based overseas, it is arguably not using that trade mark in New Zealand. The issue is by no means clear in New Zealand, yet.[104]

It may also be possible to bring an action in passing off or under the Fair Trading Act in relation to use of a domain name. In this case, the central issue will be whether the use of the domain name is a misrepresentation injuring the goodwill of a trader in its trade mark, or likely to confuse or deceive the public.[105]

Patents

Patentability of On-line Information

There is no specific legislation for patents for software or other on-line information. On-line information will be patentable in New Zealand where it meets the generic requirements of the New Zealand Patents Act 1953. In short, these are that the idea or concept be a new invention that is not obvious to anyone skilled in the field.

14-88

The key requirement for an idea to be an "invention" is that it be a "manner of new manufacture". The Patents Act does not exclude particular categories of subject matter from patents. Rather, case law must be used to determine what constitutes patentable subject matter according to this definition. Traditionally, new ideas of a non-technical nature have not been patentable. Accordingly, methods of doing business and mere principles or theorems have not been patentable. However, software is now patentable in New Zealand due to a decision of the Commissioner of Patents which adopted the Australian test for patentability: "does the invention claimed involve the production of some commercially useful effect?".[106]

Under this test, a method-type claim must define a method that, either directly or by implication, embodies the commercially useful effect. A claim to a mathematical algorithm in itself is not patentable, because it does not produce a commercially useful effect. A commercially useful effect may only

---

104 Harrison and Frankel, "The Internet: Can Intellectual Property Laws Cope?", (1996) 1 N.Z.I.P.J. 60.

105 The Domain Name Company Limited recently tested these issues in New Zealand by obtaining domain names such as Sanyo, Cadbury and Xerox. These three companies brought a test case. The case was never decided by the court as the defendant consented to giving up the domain names and to the transfer of them to the relevant plaintiff companies. However, prior to the settlement of the matter, the High Court briefly indicated its preliminary view that the defendant had no right to use the names and that it did not matter that the Court was dealing with a new medium.

106 Unreported decision of the Commissioner of Patents, *In re Application by Hughes Aircraft Co.* (Application Numbers 221147, 233797 and 233798), May 3, 1995.

arise when the mathematical algorithm is implemented in some manner to produce a result. A claim to a mathematical algorithm when used in a computer is patentable provided a commercially useful effect is produced. Under this broad test, computer software will often be patentable.[107]

Software End Users, Developers and Distributors

14-89   The person entitled to apply for a patent is the inventor and any person to whom the inventor assigns its rights. In the case of software, this person will be the software developer and its assignees.

Enforcing Patent Rights

14-90   The Patents Act 1953 does not contain a definition of "infringement". The form of patent prescribed by the legislature indicates the extent of the rights granted to the patentee.[108] Accordingly, a patent confers an exclusive monopoly over the idea or concept embodied in the specification. The scope of a patent is defined by its claims.

It is monopoly prevents software end users, developers, and others from copying patented software or even from independently developing the same software. Accordingly, developers will have to conduct the necessary searches to ensure that software they develop does not infringe any existing patents. A person may make some experimental use of a patented invention during the life of the patent without infringing it. However, it is not permissible to experiment in such a way as to derive a commercial advantage by doing so. Distributors are also affected by the extension of patent protection to computer software, particularly as suppliers often indemnify licensees. The term of a patent is 20 years. This period cannot be extended.

Licensing

License or Sale of On-line Rights

14-91   As there is no specific legislation for intellectual property rights and electronic information, the ability of an owner of on-line information to license or sell its rights will be dependent on the general provisions of copyright, trade secret, trade mark, and patent law.

Rights Subject to Licensing or Sale

14-92   **Copyright** Under the Copyright Act, ownership of copyright in on-line work may be assigned in writing.[109] An assignment of copyright may be limited so as

---

107 Moon, "Software Inventions Now, Patentable in New Zealand", (1995) 13(2) *International Technology Newsletter* 12; Terry, "Software Patents: Good or Bad?", (1995) 1 *N.Z.I.P.J.* 10.
108 Patents Regulations 1954, 3rd Schedule, Form A.
109 Copyright Act 1994, section 114.

to apply to one or more, but not all, of the things that a copyright owner has exclusive rights to do, and to part only of the period for which the copyright exists.[110] A licence granted by a copyright owner is binding on every successor in title to that person's interest in the copyright, except a purchaser in good faith for valuable consideration without notice of the licence.[111]

Trade Secrets Confidential on-line information may be licensed or sold   **14-93**
under contract.

Trade Marks The rights to a registered trade mark may be assigned. The ability   **14-94**
to assign or license unregistered trade marks will depend on the extent to which the underlying business relating to those trade marks is also assigned. Traditionally, at least, unregistered trade marks may not be assigned separately from the goodwill that they represent.

For similar reasons, the ability to license trade marks, whether registered or not, traditionally depends on the licensor's ability to retain quality control over the business in which that trade mark is used. Recent amendments to the Trade Marks Act 1953, however, indicate that the required level of quality control has decreased.

Domain Names The registration is a listing service and it does not create a   **14-95**
property right. A person will be able to sell or license a domain name by agreement and subsequent notification of the change in registration.

Patents The owner of patentable on-line information may sell or license that   **14-96**
patent under the provisions of the Patents Act 1953.[112] The assignee of a patent must apply to the Commissioner of Patents to be registered as the proprietor of the patent. Licensees have a right to terminate the licence by three months' notice on the expiry of the patent, regardless of the terms of the licence.[113]

ON-LINE CONDUCT

Regulation of Electronic Communication

There is still little legislative recognition of electronic commerce in New   **14-97**
Zealand. The result is that statutes designed to deal with traditional paper-based commercial transactions have had to be interpreted to apply to the

110 Copyright Act 1994, section 113.
111 Copyright Act 1994, section 111.
112 Patents Act 1953, section 84.
113 Patents Act 1953, section 67.

new technology. Where statute law is not of assistance, the Common Law has had to be manipulated and applied.

There is growing pressure from the commercial community for certainty to be introduced to completion of transactions by electronic means. That certainty is still some way off.

Legislative

14-98   Parliament has been involved only to a relatively minor extent in the regulation of electronic communication in New Zealand. A handful of Acts deal specifically with electronic communication or electronic commercial transactions.[114] With the exception of the Telecommunications Act, even this legislation does not regulate electronic communications on a widespread basis but is restricted to dealing with it in the context of the subject matter of each Act. The Telecommunications Act is the principal piece of legislation which in two provisions[115] deals with interference with networks[116] and use of a telecommunications device to give a fictitious order, instruction or message.[117]

Apart from the traditional areas in which electronic communication has been regulated for many decades (essentially telecommunications and radio broadcasting), Parliament has taken little action to update the New Zealand law to reflect the adoption of new technology concepts such as electronic data interchange or electronic funds transfer.

Self-Regulation

14-99   Outside of Parliament, which is the only entity in New Zealand that can regulate with the force of law, a number of groups of commercial entities have regulated for themselves. The principal group is the banking industry, which in terms of its banking code[118] provides for the rights of the industry and its customers in respect of E.F.T.P.O.S. and interchange arrangements that the customers have with their bankers.

The T.U.A.N.Z. organisation, which originally represented the interests of users of telecommunications in New Zealand, has recently assumed the function of the now defunct N.Z.E.D.I.A. In 1990, N.Z.E.D.I.A. published a model interchange agreement (see the Model Agreement and the T.U.A.N.Z. checklist discussed above). T.U.A.N.Z. has now promulgated for member and general use a checklist of EDI or electronic commerce considerations for use in parties' interchange agreements.[119]

---

114 Telecommunications Act 1987; Customs and Excise Act 1996; Finance Act (Number 2) 1994; Tax Administration Act 1994.
115 Telecommunications Act 1987, sections 6 and 8.
116 Telecommunications Act 1987, section 6.
117 Telecommunications Act 1987, section 8(2)(b).
118 Code of Banking Practice, 2nd edition, November 1996.
119 T.U.A.N.Z. Special Report, "Electronic Commerce: Eliminating the Paper Trail".

At the lowest level, organisations and individuals may by contract regulate the terms of electronic communication between themselves but the terms of such agreements would not normally bind third parties.

Territorial Limits of Jurisdiction

The New Zealand Parliament has jurisdiction over everything within the   **14-100** boundaries of New Zealand. It also has the power to provide for the punishment of acts and omissions committed outside the territory and territorial waters of New Zealand.[120]

Section 2 of the New Zealand Boundaries Act 1863 (United Kingdom) defines the boundaries of New Zealand to "comprise all territories, islands, and countries lying between the 162nd degree of east longitude and the 173rd degree of west longitude, and between the 33rd and 53rd parallels of south latitude". This has been expanded to cover the Kermadec Islands,[121] Tokelau,[122] and the Ross Dependency,[123] although there is some doubt regarding the extent to which this and subsequent measures have made the Ross Dependency part of New Zealand.

By the Crimes Act 1961, New Zealand's principal penal statute, "New Zealand" is defined as including all waters within the outer limits of the territorial sea of New Zealand. Section 3 of the Territorial Sea (Contiguous Zone) and Exclusive Economic Zone Act[124] defines the territorial sea, which is measured from a baseline around the New Zealand land mass.

Section 3 of the Judicature Act 1908 constitutes and establishes (together with sections 16 to 23) the jurisdiction of the High Court of New Zealand "for the administration of Justice throughout New Zealand".

Section 3 of the District Courts Act 1947 reconstitutes and establishes (together with section 4) the jurisdiction of District Courts in New Zealand. The High Court and the District Court are the principal courts that would act in matters involving commercial transactions, at first instance.

Section 5 of the Crimes Act 1961 establishes the jurisdiction of the New Zealand courts in respect of specified activities that constitute the offences the subject of the Act. Those activities are described as being "done or omitted in New Zealand".[125] The Act also, in section 8, provides a jurisdiction "in respect of crimes on ships and aircraft beyond New Zealand". The perpetrators or victims of the crimes do not need to be New Zealand citizens although there must be a connection to either:

- The British Commonwealth (in the case of a ship);

---

120 Constitution Act 1986; Crimes Act 1961, section 8.
121 Letters Patent, January 18, 1887, passed under the Great Seal of the United Kingdom.
122 Tokelau Act 1948.
123 Order in Council, July 30, 1923 (*Gazette*, 1923, volume II, at p. 2211).
124 Territorial Sea [Contiguous Zone] and Exclusive Economic Zone Act 1977.
125 Crimes Act 1961, section 5(2).

- New Zealand (in the case of aircraft);
- Arrival in New Zealand of the person "acting or omitting", at the end of the journey in which the act or omission occurred;
- The status of a British subject within the territorial waters of any Commonwealth country.

14-101 Other subject specific enactments, such as section 8(2)(b) of the Telecommunications Act 1987 (in using a telecommunications device, knowingly gives any fictitious order, instructions or message) contain offences relative to their subject matter but all relate to within "New Zealand" as the focus of jurisdiction.

The Common Law fills the gaps in and expands on the statutory jurisdiction. New Zealand closely follows the English Common Law and extraterritorial operation could be available by applying the principle in *Joyce* v. *DPP*.[126]

Residents and Non-Residents

14-102 The issues of choice of law and forum, where these are not identified in any hard copy agreement between the parties, are identified pursuant to the Common Law as applied by the New Zealand courts. The law of New Zealand provides that where residents contract with non-residents and the contract does not identify the *lex fori* or the arbitral forum, the court will meet "the omission from the contract of the designation of location of the seat of arbitration by application of the established principles for determining *forum conveniens*".[127]

In determining *forum conveniens*, the court must "identify the forum in which the case can be suitably tried for the interests of all the parties and the ends of justice".[128] Relevant considerations include:

- Convenience and expense;
- Places where parties reside or carry on business;
- Law governing the transaction;
- Natural forum (that with which the action has the most real and established connection); and
- Whether a New Zealand forum offers the plaintiff a "legitimate personal or juridical advantage".[129]

---

126 [1946] A.C. 347; [1946] 1 All E.R.
127 *Impac Australia Pty Limited* v. *Cavalier Bremworth Limited*, Court of Appeal of New Zealand C.A. 102/96, September 9, 1996 per Gault J (unreported).
128 Lord Goff of Chieveley, in *Spiliada Maritime Corp* v. *Cansulex Ltd* [1987] A.C. 460, adopted by the Court of Appeal of New Zealand in *Club Mediterranee NZ* v. *Wendell* [1989] 1 N.Z.L.R. 216.
129 Eiselen, *The EDI Law Review* 2, Number 1: 9-27, 1995.

Cross-Border Transactions and Communications

The application of New Zealand statutes when issues of private interna-   **14-103**
tional law arise is somewhat haphazard.[130] Provisions regulating the scope
of a statute appear in some Acts[131] but not in others. The drafters of New
Zealand statutes appear to turn their minds to the question principally where
the statute is based on a foreign model that contains such a provision. No
recent reported New Zealand cases discuss the application of New Zealand's
recent contract statutes to an international transaction. Comment has been
made that in some situations a New Zealand court would apply provisions
in our contract statutes that would not be applied by a foreign court
considering the same dispute.[132]

The Sale of Goods (United Nations Convention) Act 1994 incorporated
the Vienna Convention on the International Sale of Goods 1980 in the law
of New Zealand. The Act came into force on October 1, 1995, but without
application to the Cook Islands, Niue and Tokelau. The Convention deals
only with the sale of goods and not any other type of commodity or service.
No other New Zealand legislation specifically addresses cross border commercial transactions or communications undertaken by electronic means.[133]

As the Convention does not deal with validity of contracts, or the effect
of some misrepresentations or mistakes, New Zealand law will remain
applicable, if the application of principles discussed under "Residents and
Non-Residents" above, finds that New Zealand is the *forum conveniens*.

In many New Zealand statutes, it is far from clear whether a New
Zealand court would apply the statute to a dispute concerning a contract that
does not have New Zealand law as its proper law. It is also unclear whether
the statute would be applied to a dispute concerning a contract which does
not have New Zealand law as its putative proper law, *i.e.*, the law that would
be the proper law of the contract if the contract was validly concluded.[134]
This position could be clarified by expressly stating the limits of each statute's
application.[135]

If a dispute is litigated outside of New Zealand, and an issue in that
dispute is characterised by any of:

- Whether a contract has been formed;
- Its interpretation;
- Its validity;

---

130 Goddard, Law Commission Report, Number 25, *Contract Statutes Review*, at p. 239.
131 Frustrated Contracts Act 1944; Credit Contracts Act 1981, section 7; Commerce Act 1986,
  section 4.
132 Goddard, Law Commission Report, Number 25, *Contract Statutes Review*, at p. 240.
133 Webb, "A New Set of Rules for International Sales", *New Zealand Law Journal*, March
  1995, at p. 85.
134 Dicey and Morris, *The Conflict of Laws*, 11th edition, 1987, rules 180 and 181.
135 Goddard, Law Commission Report, Number 25, *Contract Statutes Review*, at p. 243.

- The nature of the obligations arising under it; and
- Whether it has been discharged and whether any restitutionary obligations arise in connection with it.

14-104 The proper law or putative proper law of the contract is not New Zealand law; a foreign court will almost certainly not apply New Zealand law (even if, for example, the contract was entered into in New Zealand and all the parties are resident there). This is clearly undesirable as the principal goals of private international law are to avoid that result, increase certainty in commercial relations, and discourage forum shopping.[136] Methods proposed to achieve this outcome by allowing New Zealand law to be applied by a foreign court are:

- To define in New Zealand statutes "court" to mean ". . . in relation to any matter, the court or arbitrator by or before whom the matter falls to be determined";[137] and
- To prescribe in considerably greater detail the consequences of, for example, the cancellation of a contract or other matters dealt with by the statutes.[138]

14-105 Clearly, the only method that can be pursued by parties to a contract in electronic form would be the second of the above proposals.

Impact of Penal Law

14-106 The New Zealand penal law has undergone little adaptation to recognise offences committed by unauthorised access or other electronic on-line means. The result is that the existing law must be applied and in many instances 'stretched' to accommodate the factual circumstances of the new technology.

Unauthorised extraction of data will not, of itself, be regarded as 'theft', 'larceny' or stealing' as the essential elements of deprivation of property and an intention to permanently deprive are absent.[139] Such actions could constitute breach of copyright.

Where data is stored electronically, it will in some circumstances be found to be a "document" and, therefore, within the ambit of the penal legislation, but in other circumstances it is not.

"Document" is defined in section 263 of the Crimes Act 1961 for the purposes of sections 263 to 279 (forgery and related offences). This definition expressly includes "any material derived, whether directly or by means

---

136 Goddard, Law Commission Report, Number 25, *Contract Statutes Review*, at p. 240.
137 Frustrated Contracts Act 1944.
138 Goddard, Law Commission Report, Number 25, *Contract Statutes Review*, at p. 250.
139 Hughes, *Electronic Funds Transfer Services Legal Issues for Providers, Merchants & Users*, Business Law Education Centre, at p. 49.

of any equipment, from information recorded or stored or processed by any device used for recording or storing or processing information". The following criminal offences, for example, may consequently be committed in relation to a document stored electronically:

- Forgery;[140]
- Uttering forged documents;[141]
- Altering or reproducing a document with intent to defraud;[142]
- Using an altered or reproduced document with intent to defraud;[143]
- Procuring the execution of a document by fraud;[144] or
- Drawing a document without authority.[145]

"Document" is not otherwise defined. Where the term is used in sections   **14-107** outside of sections 263–279 it carries its normal meaning of a thing that conveys information. Whether it will apply to information stored electronically will depend on the circumstances of each case. The High Court of New Zealand held, in *Nicholson v. Police*[146] that "document" for the purposes of section 253 included a computer disk. *Adams on Criminal Law*[147] states in relation to section 229A that data held solely in electronic form is not a document. In light of this uncertainty, it is difficult to say with any certainty whether or not the following crimes may be committed in relation to information stored electronically:

- Taking or dealing with certain documents with intent to defraud;[148]
- Fraudulently destroying any document;[149]
- Compelling execution of documents by force;[150]
- Extortion by certain threats;[151]
- Obtaining by false pretence;[152]
- False accounting by an officer or member of a body corporate;[153]
- False accounting by an employee.[154]

---

140 Crimes Act 1961, section 265; however, see *R v. Gold* [1988] 2 W.L.R. 94, [1988] 2 All E.R. 186.
141 Crimes Act 1961, section 266.
142 Crimes Act 1961, section 266A.
143 Crimes Act 1961, section 266B.
144 Crimes Act 1961, section 270.
145 Crimes Act 1961, section 272.
146 Unreported McGechan J, High Court Napier, November 1986, ref M 148-85.
147 *Adams on Criminal Law*, 1992.
148 Crimes Act 1961, section 229A.
149 Crimes Act 1961, section 231.
150 Crimes Act 1961, section 236.
151 Crimes Act 1961, section 238.
152 Crimes Act 1961, section 246.
153 Crimes Act 1961, section 252.
154 Crimes Act 1961, section 253.

14-108 However, the Evidence Amendment Act (Number 2) 1980, section 3 provides that where direct oral evidence of a fact or an opinion would be admissible (both in criminal and civil proceedings) but the statement maker is unavailable to give evidence, information which is stored on a computer is a document which is covered by the "business records" exception to the hearsay rule.[155] This may, depending on the factual circumstances, allow electronically stored data to be used in prosecuting the above crimes.

The definition of document in the Companies Act 1993 includes information stored on a computer, so that any criminal offences in the Companies Act[156] which relate to documents (such as under section 25(1)(b), documents signed by the company creating a legal obligation) can be committed in relation to information stored electronically.

---

155 Adams, *Criminal Law*, 1992, volume 2, at p. 101.
156 See section 25(5).

CHAPTER 15

Portugal

Susana Albuquerque and Paulo Marques
A. M. Pereira, Sáragga Leal, Oliveira Martins,
Júdice e Associados
Lisbon, Portugal

INTRODUCTION

Electronic commerce in Portugal is regulated through the application of various   15-1
regimes. These include the personal automated data protection regime and
the computer crime regime, as well as the relevant provisions of the Portuguese Civil and Penal Codes. These will be examined in the present chapter.

Achieving Information Security

Legal Regime Relative to Electronic Communication

The current Portuguese regime on personal data protection related to   15-2
electronic data processing begins at the level of the Portuguese Constitution.
The provision of its article 35 prohibits the use of electronic data processing
to keep records regarding political and philosophical beliefs, party or union
membership, religious conviction or private life. Exceptions are made for the
processing of statistical data that is not individually identifiable.

In accordance with article 35, each citizen has access to any data or
computer registers relating to him or her. They are entitled to demand the
record's updating and rectification, except when such would compromise
State secrets or legal privileges.

Third-party access to registers and logs and their interconnection are
generally not allowed, save for cases where it is specifically permitted under
statute.

Personal Automated Data Protection

Law 10/91 of April 29, 1991, as amended by Law 28/94 of August 29, 1994,   15-3
sets out the personal automated data protection legal regime. It adopts the
principles internationally in force, in particular those laid down by the International Convention on Protection of Automated Data 1981, which was subsequently ratified by Portugal in 1993.

This certification aims to ensure that the use of electronic data processing is made in a transparent manner with strict respect for privacy and fundamental rights.[1] It regulates the establishment and maintenance of automated files, databases, and personal databases as well as of electronic data processing support means regarding juridical persons and similar entities when such files contain personal data.[2]

Law 10/91 adds to the list of issues that cannot be electronically processed set out by article 35 of the Portuguese Constitution. These excluded topics include ethnic origin, any prior criminal convictions, any suspicions regarding the conduct of illegal activities, personal health condition and financial situation.

However, under the provisions of both the Constitution and Law 10/91, electronic data processing of the issues listed above is allowed in the following situations:

- For statistical and research purposes, provided the data supplied is not individually identified;
- When the information concerning such data is provided to institutions by the individuals with full understanding of the use and aim of such data processing; and
- To ensure the compliance of legal or contractual obligations.

15-4   Data collection must be carried out in accordance with its specifically identified purpose and it cannot be deceitful.[3]

The automated files, databases, and data banks must have safety devices preventing unauthorised access, modification, destruction, and the intentional or unintentional detouring of such data.[4] The interconnection of personal data files is not allowed.

Conversely, public data files may be interconnected. Public data are defined as "all the personal data contained in official public documents which is not confidential".

Confidential data are the name, address, occupation, and other information that may be deemed of a confidential nature by the public entities concerned.

The control of the automated data processing in strict compliance with the protection of fundamental rights is effected by the National Commission for Informatic Personal Data Protection (C.N.P.D.P.I.), which was created by Law 10/91.

15-5   **Transborder Personal Data Flows** The above described legal regime is fully applicable to transborder personal data flows (either processed or not).

---

1 Law 10/91, article 1.
2 Law 10/91, article 3(1).
3 Law 10/91, article 12.
4 Law 10/91, article 21.

Transborder personal data flows may be allowed by the C.N.P.D.P.I., if the destination State assures similar protection to the one granted by Portuguese internal law.[5]

Thus, transborder personal data flows are forbidden when such flows are effected with the intention of circumventing the legal requirements with which they should comply.

Handling of Personal Data by Public Authorities The public authorities 15-6
keeping automated files must comply with specific regulations on the handling of the personal data held by them.[6]

Such regulations prescribe, in general terms, that data collection should be accurate, *i.e.*, restricted to the exercise of the competencies of the relevant authorities and for the specifically identified purpose of the collection.

The relevant authorities may provide information on the data held to each other within the scope of their competencies and activities.

Currently, the following public authorities possessing personal databases specifically governed by the Ruling Decree of the Council of Ministers are:

- *Guarda Nacional Republicana* (National Guard);[7]
- *Policia de Segurança Pública* (National Police Force);[8]
- *Serviço de Estrangeiros e Fronteiras* (Foreigners and Borders Service);[9]
- *Sistema Integrado de Informação Aduaneira Anti-Fraude* (Integrated Information System Against Customs Fraud);[10] and
- *Polícia Judiciária* (Criminal Investigation Police).[11]

Juridical Persons Databases The protection of data bases containing infor- 15-7
mation on juridical persons and entities of a similar nature, *e.g.*, an unincorporated society, is governed under Ruling-Decree 27/93 of September 3, 1993.

Such databases are created with the aim of organising and keeping up-to-date the information relating to juridical persons that may be deemed necessary by the public authorities, *e.g.*, tax authorities. These data may be accessed by private entities such as financial institutions under certain specific conditions, *e.g.*, for statistical purposes.

The data relating to juridical persons that should be presented for collection for automated processing are the following:

- The name or designation adopted;
- The identification of business activity and of its nature;

---

5 Law 10/91, article 33, number 2.
6 Law 10/91, article 44.
7 Ruling-Decree 2/95 of January 25, 1995.
8 Ruling-Decree 5/95 of January 31, 1995.
9 Ruling-Decree 4/95 of January 31, 1995.
10 Ruling-Decree 22/95 of August 23, 1995.
11 Ruling-Decree 27/95 of October 31, 1995.

- The address, registered offices or domicile;
- The number and date of the entrepreneur or company's identity card; and
- The date of commencement and of termination (if applicable) of activity.

15-8   Juridical persons are entitled to acknowledge the data file contents, as well as to store such data, and may also demand correction or deletion of unlawfully filed data.

The supervision of the collection, maintenance and access of juridical person's databases is effected by the Bureau of Studies and Planning of the Ministry of Justice.

Penalties

15-9   The infringement of the legal regime on data protection may be deemed to constitute one of the following criminal offences:

- Illegal data use;
- Obstruction of access to data;
- Unlawful interconnection of data;
- Creation of data bases for false purposes;
- Improper access;
- Unlawful disabling and destruction of data;
- Unlawful interruption; and
- Breach of legal confidentiality.

15-10   The above-listed crimes are punished by either imprisonment or the payment of fines. These fines are calculated on the basis of multiples of fixed rates. The fixed rates are equated to daily rates. The multiplicators range up to a maximum of 240 days. The alternative terms of imprisonment can be up to a maximum of two years. Additionally, the court may order the publication of the judgment rendered.

Unauthorised acts or conducts in the area of informatic/electronic communications in general (and not only in what relates to personal data) are typified as criminal conducts under Law 109/91 of August 17, which sets out the specific regime of computer crimes, as well as under the Portuguese Penal Code,[12] which will be subsidiarily applicable.

Law 109/91 punishes the following acts or conduct:

- Falsehood related to electronic data processing;
- Damage to electronically processed data or software;
- Sabotage related to electronic data processing;
- Unauthorised access to computer systems or networks;
- Unauthorised interference in computer communications; and
- Unauthorised reproduction of software;

---

12 Law 109/91, articles 193–196.

The penalties applicable to individuals for the commission of the above   **15-11**
crimes may be either the payment of fines (calculated on a fixed daily amount)
up to a maximum of 600 days or imprisonment up to a maximum of five
years.

When juridical persons commit such crimes, the penalties applicable are
a formal rebuke, a fine, or even the dissolution of the entity concerned.

The provisions of the Penal Code may be subsidiarily applicable when
the unauthorised act or conduct is not deemed to constitute any of the above
crimes. Thus, such act or conduct may be deemed to constitute one of the
following crimes, being punished in the described terms:

- The unauthorised access or disclosure of data through computer means
  is punished with either the imposition of a fine (calculated on the basis
  the daily multiplicand) up to a maximum of 240 days, or imprisonment
  up to two years;
- The violation of correspondence or telecommunications is punished
  with either the imposition of a fine (calculated on the basis the daily
  multiplicand) up to a maximum of 240 days or imprisonment up to a
  maximum of one year;
- Breach of confidentiality is punished with either the imposition of a
  fine (calculated on the basis the daily multiplicand) up to a maximum
  of 240 days or imprisonment up to a maximum of one year;
- The unauthorised use of secret or confidential information is punished
  with either the imposition of a fine (calculated on the basis the daily
  multiplicand) up to a maximum of 240 days or imprisonment up to a
  maximum of one year.

Confidentiality

Protection of Confidentiality

Confidentiality of personal automated databases is protected by the regime   **15-12**
of penalties.

A specific duty of confidentiality is also imposed on professionals and
public entities handling personal automated data. If they breach this duty of
confidentiality, it will be punished by either imprisonment up to a maximum
of two years or by the imposition of a fine up to a maximum of 240 times
the daily multiplicand. Additionally, the court may also order the publication of the court judgment rendered.

Confidentiality of computer and electronic communications is protected
under the regime.

The operations of electronic commerce carried out by credit and financial
institutions are also protected by the specific duties of confidentiality which are
imposed on the members, representatives, and employees of such institutions.

Exceptions to Confidentiality

15-13   In general, the duty of confidentiality regarding information kept by computer may be overridden for the combat of drug trafficking[13] or money laundering.[14]

Moreover, the duty of confidentiality protecting data obtained through the realisation of electronic commerce operations effected by credit and financial institutions may also be set aside either with consent of the person or entity concerned or when the disclosure is specifically authorised by law. Delivering information to the supervisory entities of the financial and banking market (Bank of Portugal and the Securities Commission) or to the Deposits Security Fund, or when a higher court expressly orders such disclosure are examples of the latter.

LEGAL EFFECT OF ELECTRONIC SIGNATURES

15-14   There is no resort in Portugal to the use of electronic signatures to complete or execute transactions as its probative value is not recognised under law.

ELECTRONIC TRANSACTIONS

Creation of Contracts Electronically

Offer and Acceptance On-line

15-15   **General** Until January 1997, although the number of contracts concluded on-line increases every day, no specific legislation on offer and acceptance on-line had been promulgated in Portugal. The general regime, set out by the Portuguese Civil Code, articles 217 *et seq*. remains applicable.

Under the Civil Code's general regime, on-line offer is a declaration that constitutes a contractual proposal, provided the following requirements are fulfilled:

- It must have the same legal form of the contract to be entered into;
- It must convey an unequivocal intention to contract; and
- It must be complete. That means that it must contain the essential elements of the contract, *e.g.*, object or subject matter and price.

15-16   The receipt of such offer by its addressee grants him the right to accept it, the contract being perfected by the declaration of acceptance.

---

13 Decree-Law 15/93 of January 22, 1993.
14 Decree-Laws 313/93 of September 15 and 325/95 of December 2, 1995.

When the offer does not comply with the above-listed requirements, it is deemed to constitute an invitation to contract. Conversely, such an invitation does not confer on the offeree the right to conclude the contract by issuing its acceptance.

On-line Offers to the World at Large When an offer or contract proposal is not destined to anyone in particular, it may be accepted by any counterparty. The contract is, similarly, concluded on receipt of acceptance by the offeror. **15-17**

Mistakes in On-line Contracts

The occurrence of mistakes may constitute a ground for annulling the contract on the initiation of the party who concluded the contract on the basis of the mistake, provided such party may prove that the mistake is included in one of four categories established by the Civil Code. **15-18**

Lack of Consciousness of the Declaration The issuer of the declaration is not aware that he is making a contractual declaration. **15-19**

Mistake in the Declaration The intention declared does not correspond to the actual/real intention of its issuer. **15-20**

Mistake in the Transmission of the Declaration When the mistake occurs due to the undue interference of the third party responsible for the transmission of the declaration. **15-21**

Mistake concerning the Subject Matter or Object of the Contract When the subject matter or object of the contract does not correspond to the one intended by the party concerned which determined the issuance of a contractual declaration. **15-22**

Impact of Impostors or Persons without Authority

Impostors The acts of impostors may constitute one of the above-listed criminal offences, and are subject to the corresponding penalty. **15-23**

Persons without Authority The lack of authority to conclude an on-line contract is governed by the provisions of article 245 of the Civil Code on "Anserinus declarations". **15-24**

According to article 245, if the person without authority makes the contractual declaration in such circumstances that he or she expects that the addressee of such declaration understands the non-existence of a real intention to contract, the contractual declaration shall not produce any effects.

The burden of proof is on the person making the contractual declaration without authority.

Conversely, should the contractual declaration be made in circumstances which would justifiably induce its addressee to accept its seriousness, *i.e.*, the existence of a real intention to contract, the addressee is entitled to claim the damages caused by such declaration.

The burden of proof is on the addressee of the contractual declaration made without authority.

ON-LINE PAYMENTS

Electronic Fund Transfers

15-25   In Portugal there are two types of electronic fund transfers (EFT): consumer-related EFT and non-consumer-related or institutional EFT.

Consumer-Related Electronic Fund Transfers

15-26   Consumer-related electronic fund transfers can comprise cheque guarantee card services, cheque authorisation services, automated teller machine services, and point-of-sale systems.

15-27   **Cheque Guarantee** Where consumer-related electronic fund transfers comprise cheque guarantee card services, the bank will issue and deliver to a client a card, legible by a computer, similar to a credit card. When the client purchases assets or services, he or she will sign a cheque for payment and will present the guaranty card.

The card is read by the terminal computer, obtaining the on-line confirmation from the bank that the payment may be effected by cheque. The bank assumes the liability for the payment of the cheque, pre-authorised debits and credits, and home-banking or in-home financial services.

15-28   **Cheque Authorisation** Where consumer-related electronic fund transfers comprise cheque authorisation services, the bank merely confirms on-line whether the cheque has provision or not, not assuming any liability for its payment, home-banking or in-home financial services.

15-29   **Automated Teller Machines** With respect to automated teller machines (ATMs), the client will insert a card containing a magnetic band, previously codified as to enable the performance of the transactions and will carry out them, which may be withdrawals, payment of services, and change of the personal code, which must be supported by a receipt that will constitute the proof of the transaction effected for all legal purposes. Simpler versions are cash dispensing machines or cash dispensers.

15-30   **Others** Point-of-sale systems have similar functioning to ATM, but perform transfers from one bank account to another for the payment of assets and services in shopping facilities.

Pre-authorised debits and credits will be processed via electronic means. The transfer will occur in a moment previously established with the bank, such as wage payments.

Home-banking or in-home financial services means that banking transactions may be ordered and executed via telephone, provided each transaction is correctly provided.

Electronic mail enables transfers between accounts. It is a privileged channel for home shopping when combined with a credit card number.

Consumer-related EFTs are governed by the relevant contracts entered into between the consumer and the relevant entity. Such contracts must comply with the regime of General Contractual Clauses set out by Decree-Law 446/85 of October 25 as amended by Decree-Law 220/95 of January 31, 1995. This implemented Directive 93/13/E.C.[15] on unfair terms in consumer contracts and wire transfer services.

Non-Consumer-Related Electronic Fund Transfers

Non-consumer related EFTs comprise cheque truncation and automated clearing houses: **15-31**

Cheque truncation   Cheque truncation is an electronic transmission of information, replacing paper-based information, cancelling the cheque processing due to lack of funds.   **15-32**

Automated Clearing Houses   Automated clearing houses (ACH) collect data from the credit operations of various credit or financial institutions, combine these data with other relevant data for the operations of financial compensation and send the results to the institutions concerned. These data may be sent by "batch" or on-line systems.   **15-33**

Wire transfers   Wire transfers are used to transfer large sums of money between banks or between companies.   **15-34**

In the absence of specific legislation governing the institutional fund transfers, the referred services/transactions are governed by the contracts and arrangements entered into between the institutions.

Credit Card Payments On-line

Under Decree-Law 166/95 of July 15, 1995, which sets out the regime of credit cards issuance, credit card payments on-line are regulated under the "General Conditions of Use of Credit Card" to be drafted by the credit card issuing entity.   **15-35**

The General Conditions of Use of Credit Card must comply not only with the regime of General Contractual Clauses already mentioned, but also

---

15 1995 O.J. L95/29.

with the recommendations issued by the European Union, in particular, Recommendation 88/590/E.E.C. concerning payment systems and the relationship between card holder and card issuer.

Additionally, the contracts of credit card use (drafted by the issuing financial institutions) must comply with the requirements of Regulation Number 4/95 of the Bank of Portugal of July 28, 1995. This Regulation provides that the credit card use contracts must be made in writing. They must specifically mention all the rights and obligations of the contractual parties as well as the consumer's liability before notification of loss or misuse of a credit card and must refer the terms of alteration of the contract.

The credit card issuers, which are authorised financial institutions, are under the supervision of the Bank of Portugal. They should send it a copy of their General Conditions of Use of Credit Card (and of its subsequent alterations) as well as of the standard form of the contract of use of credit card.

Use of Electronic Cheques

15-36   The use of electronic cheques has not been formally introduced in Portugal until now.

ELECTRONIC INFORMATION RIGHTS

Property Rights in Electronic Information

15-37   Under Portuguese law, property rights in electronic information are governed by the regime of legal protection of computer software, which is laid down by Decree-Law 252/94 of October 20, 1994. This Decree-Law implemented Directive 91/250/E.E.C.[16]

The software created (and all the material used to create it) is protected in the same manner as literary works. This means that the creator of the software has the copyright.

The exception to such principle is when an employee creates the software. Then, there is a legal presumption that the copyright belongs to the employer. Such presumption may be set aside by express agreement of the parties in that respect. Copyright lasts for 50 years from the death of the work's author.

The regime under this law also describes the contents of the rights granted to the copyright owner, the copyright user, and the copyright author.

---

16   1991 O.J. L 122/42.

Copyright Owner

The copyright owner is entitled to reproduce and alter the software;[17] to **15-38** circulate the original or copies of the software program, as well as to rent each of the copies.

Users of Copyright Works

Users of copyright works are entitled to make back-up copies to observe, **15-39** study, or analyse the software operability, to decompile the various parts of the software that may be deemed necessary for the interoperability of the software program.

Software Author

The software author is entitled to have his name inserted in the software **15-40** program and to claim the authorship of the program.

The protection of computer software programmes is also effected by the express reference in Decree-Law 252/94 to the applicability of the provisions of Law 109/91 (see "Penalties", above) relating to "Illegal Reproduction". Illegal reproduction constitutes a criminal offence punishable by imprisonment up to a maximum period of three years or, alternatively, with the imposition of a fine.

International Legal Protection

The recognition of the international legal protection of computer software **15-41** depends on material reciprocity. This means that the same protection that would be conferred in the state of origin of the computer software is granted, provided the protection granted under Portuguese law would be recognised by such State in the inverse situation.

---

17 Decree-Law 252/94, article 5.

CHAPTER 16

Spain

Javier Cremades
López, Lozano, Cremades & Sánchez Pintado
Madrid, Spain

INTRODUCTION

The Law of Information Technology

The evolution of information technology — the science of automated   16-1
processing of information and its growing utilisation during the last decade
— have decisively influenced the rapid social change which we are experiencing. However, the growing popular use of information technology implies neither that it is understood, nor that it is applied with the minimum
conditions required for its possibilities to be beneficially exploited.

In the juridical sphere, the application of modern technical means will
provide precision and clarity to the legal profession's comprehension and application. The new technologies will eventually change the methods and
structures of how lawyers think.

Consequently, the interest in regulating all aspects of information technology and of taking advantage of its potential applications to the law has
grown beyond expectation. The impact that information technology can
have over our society is so large that we cannot easily imagine living without it.

Information technology is not alien to the law. For this reason, it is present
in all social and economic relations created as a consequence of the introduction
and development of all activities intrinsic in the new information technologies. Such relations give rise to a number of different types of conflict, such as:

- The necessity of a juridical relationship between the rights and obligations inherent in the creation, distribution, exploitation, and/or utilisation of hardware and software, with possible protection under the laws
  of industrial property and intellectual property;
- The rights and obligations of the creators, distributors, and users of
  legal databases;
- The large scope for contracting for information technology goods and
  services with their factual and legal characteristics, including the direct

agreements relating to information technology between states and indirectly through the elements incorporated in the computer programs;.

- The so-called "laws of data protection", which develop the legal protection of the rights of persons against the potential aggressiveness of information technology in respect of the automated processing of personal data;
- The responsibilities, rights, and obligations derived from the electronic transfer of funds or data nationally or internationally, with different legal regulations, and the consequent responsibilities of chain operations by means of communication networks linked to different territories and under dissimilar legal regimes;
- The probative validity of the documents generated through information technology, or susceptible to its operation;
- The so-called "information technology offence", which refers to offences committed by means of information technology;
- The rights of buyers and customers in general against the dominant position of some information technology multinationals; and
- The legal protection of software against "software piracy".

16-2   These and many other aspects have configured what today is known as information technology law. This is understood as the legal regulation given to all aspects of information technology.

Use of Information Technology and Data Protection

16-3   Article 18 of the Spanish Constitution of 1978 provides that:

"The law will limit the use of information technology so as to guarantee the honour, personal and familiar intimacy of all citizens and the full exercise of their rights."

16-4   A text was already included in the Constitutional Draft in which the possible negative effects of information technology on all rights and freedoms were considered. The Draft stated:

"The law will limit the use of information technology so as to guarantee the honour and the personal and familiar intimacy of all citizens."

16-5   Much like the Spanish Constitution, the Agreement for the Protection of All Persons as Regards the Automated Processing of Personal Data of January 28, 1982,[1] in article 1, guarantees to all physical persons that their rights and fundamental freedoms will be respected and, especially, their right to privacy,

---

1 Signed in Strasbourg by the Spanish Plenipotentiary on January 28, 1982, and published in the *Boletin Oficial del Estado* (B.O.E.), Number 274, of November 15, 1985.

as regards the automated processing of data of a personal character concerning them. As an international treaty that has been ratified and published, this agreement is an important part of Spain's national law.[2]

Subsequently, the European Commission submitted a draft directive to the European Council on the protection of persons regarding the processing of personal data. The establishment and the functioning of the internal market with the free movement of persons, goods, services, and capital means the circulation and exchange of personal data between the member states.

This exchange of data will have to be undertaken with similar legal security in respect of the holders of the data and with an equivalent level of protection in the different member states. This requires legislative harmonisation as regards the protection of the fundamental rights recognised and guaranteed by the member states in relation to the treatment of personal data susceptible to computerised processing.

A new law for the protection of persons regarding the treatment of their personal data localised in files susceptible to computerised processing has been recently published. The Law for the Protection of Data, which develops the legal protection of the rights of persons against the potential aggression of information technology in respect of computerised processing of personal data, constitutes the epicentre of the denominated "information technology law".

ELECTRONIC TRANSACTIONS

Electronic Creation of Contracts

Contracts are created electronically through the utilisation of certain electronic elements when these are directly incidental to the formation or development of the agreement.   **16-6**

The number of transactions realised through this method grows daily due to their general acceptance in today's society. Still, this type of contract involves certain problems of a judicial and technical nature.

The legal difficulties are a direct consequence of the supremacy of written paper in the majority of regimes. Consequently, the law obliges the issue and retention of documents on paper. A legal power resides in the manuscript characteristic of the signature. This is considered necessary to satisfy the conditions for a document's validity or negotiation and, in many cases, for accounting or fiscal requirements. In other cases, it is the written character of a document that lends it evidential value.

The use of electronic data transfer, when information technology is used in the formation of contracts, allowing distant contracting parties to finalise

---

2 Spanish Constitution, article 96(1).

a contract, creates the problem of identifying the applicable law. Furthermore, in the case of differing interpretations, the problem of identifying the jurisdictional organ competent to determine the differences originating from the new legal relationship arises.

Entity Verification and Contractual Errors

16-7   When contracting through an electronic medium, an error can be committed in respect of the identity of the other contracting party. In the case of contracting in person, the person as such can be identified by his signs and physical appearance, as well as by his personal data and the signature in the document. In the case of contracting between absent contractors, the person can be identified by his signature and his domicile. However, in the case of contracting via electronic mediums further difficulties arise.

Those contracts that the Spanish legal system requires to be finalised in a written form will not be valid if made via an electronic medium. Both the Civil Code and the Code of Commerce express, as a general rule, the freedom of choice of a contractual form; however, some contracts require, as an exception, writing and other formalities, such as a public (notarised) document and registration in a certain register for the creation of a right. This is the case for mortgages. Their inscription in the register of real property has a constitutive character; the right is not created until the right is inscribed in the register.

There can be an identification error of the issuer and/or the recipient. Certain controls can be established that certify that the issuer is the terminal or equipment that identified or accepted. This guarantee of issuer or recipient terminal equipment cannot guarantee the contents of the message or identify whether the sender or the receiver are authorised to send or receive messages.

As far as the security of the received data is concerned, a document can be sent in a certain format and with determined information. This information can be submitted to a modifying process, which can lead to the acceptance of contracts that were not desired. This is more likely where the sent messages are saved on a magnetic carrier that needs to be read again to send it to the addressee, for example, in a written form.

The difference between error and fraud is intention, but the result could be the same from the point of view of the authenticity of the information and the identity of the user. These cases raise the question as to the extent to which the documents received via telematic media and processed by a computer are an objective reflection of the intention originally stipulated. These documents may be liable to two types of risks, namely:

- All problems derived from a failure in the communication and equipment infrastructure; and
- Fraud (which is intentional), given the possibilities for manipulation in a message sent via an electronic medium.

Such errors are less likely to occur given the evolution of information technol-   16-8
ogy and its security methods, but they remain possible. Fraud is not only
possible, but it is happening more frequently in the use of documents and
data via computer. Error and fraud represent very important risks in respect
of the identification of the message and the sender.

Scope for Electronic Contracts

Both legislation and doctrine in Spain consider the contract a concurrence   16-9
of intentions between two or more persons aimed at creating one or more
obligations. Similarly, an electronic contract is an agreement of intentions
where the parties are two or more persons with a commitment to carry out
an obligation to give or do something. The only difference in this case is that
the commitment is executed via an electronic medium.

The intervention of a computer terminal in the contractual process raises
certain issues. In some circumstances, the only function of the computer is
to transfer information containing a contractual intention. This transfer will
form part of a valid legal transaction.

In principle, all the valid requisites in the creation of the volition, the
offer, and the acceptance are complied with in the contract that is concluded
electronically. The Civil Code provides, in article 1254, that the contract
exists from the moment that one or various persons bind themselves to one
or several other persons to give them something or render them a service.

The contract is independent from the computer. The basic requirement
is that a binding intention exists to render a service. The Civil Code provides
the following as to the way a contract should be agreed:

> "Contracts are binding, whatever the form in which they have been agreed,
> the only requirement is that the essential conditions for its validity are
> present."[3]

Similarly, applying the principle of contractual autonomy reflected in the   16-10
Civil Code, it is provided that:

> "The contracting parties may establish all the agreements, clauses and
> conditions which they think fit, save those which are contrary to law,
> morals or public order."[4]

In this way, an agreement of conditions can be reached between the contract-   16-11
ing parties when both of them have previously accepted that the transactions
can be concluded via electronic mediums. Therefore, contracts can be
entered electronically based on the free will of the contracting parties.

---

3 Civil Code, article 1278.
4 Civil Code, article 1255.

Conclusion of the Contract

16-12 The contract will be concluded via electronic mediums and in compliance with the Civil Code when the acceptance reaches the offeree.

The Code of Commerce provides that all commercial contracts concluded by mail will be binding on the contracting parties from the moment acceptance is communicated by the offeree.[5] Similarly, those contracts finalised via electronic mediums will be concluded once the acceptance is transmitted through the computer or any other electronic medium and it is no longer possible for the offeree to alter that acceptance.

Where the Contract Is Concluded

16-13 The place where the contract is concluded is of great importance to determine which law is applicable or to resolve questions of jurisdiction.

In the case of contracts made electronically, the place where the contract is celebrated, once the competent judge has confirmed it, is the place where the offer was made. The place of the conclusion of the undertaking is also the place where the offer was made.

Effects of a Contract Made by Unauthorised Person

16-14 Each contracting party will have to take the necessary security measures so as to ensure that only authorised persons are able to send the messages within which the legal acts are included.

The acceptance given via a computer in response to an offer sent by the same method will constitute the acceptance by both parties of the contractual relationship, without taking into account who has sent the order of offer or acceptance or who has been the person to manipulate the computer system. Each party will have to take the necessary measures so an unauthorised transmission does not take place.

Information Technology Contracts

16-15 A distinction must be made between contracts relating to information technology goods or services and contracts made via electronic mediums.

An information technology contract must be understood as the undertaking involving information technology goods or services, while a "contract made via electronic mediums" involves the undertaking to supply any other good or service which is made via a computer or any other information technology element.

---

5 Code of Commerce, article 54.

An information technology contract is either any contract the object of which is an electronic good or service — or both — or the inclusion of any kind of an information technology element in the rendering of a service by one of the parties. Information technology goods can be defined as:

- All the elements that form the system, as far as hardware is concerned, being either the central system or the peripheral;
- All the equipment which has a direct correlation with these elements and which, taken as a whole, forms the physical support of the information technology element; and
- The immaterial goods which supply the orders, procedures, data and instructions in the automated processing of information and which taken as a whole form the logistical support of the information technology element.

Information technology services are all those which support and comple-   **16-16**
ment the information technology activity in a direct relation with it. Given the latitude of the definition, one should concentrate on the main or auxiliary services which posses a particular identity linked to the automated processing of information.

Electronic Payments

Electronic transfer of funds can be analysed with respect to its implications   **16-17**
for information technology contracts, to its impact on data protection and telematic transmission, and to electronic payment.

All those payment operations that are made via electronic mediums may be deemed electronic payments. The use of electronics in economic activity is not reduced to only payments. It is also possible to withdraw money or make deposits by using cards or other electronic means. These are not payments in the narrow sense, but they can be considered in the same legal matrix of electronic payments.

Electronic payments can be defined as "any payment operation made with a magnetic card or with an incorporated microprocessor on terminal equipment of electronic payment (T.E.E.P.) or a terminal sales point (T.S.P.)".[6]

In Recommendation 88/590/E.E.C. of November 17, 1988, the European Commission distinguishes between payment made via electronic mediums that involve the use of payment cards and payments made via electronic mediums made by individuals without using the card. The best example of the latter is a banking transaction made from one's own home.

---

6 Recomendation 88/590/E.E.C. of November 17, 1988.

Electronic Funds Transfer

16-18   A universal definition of electronic fund transfer (E.F.T.) is difficult to arrive at. There are many definitions accepted in different contexts and covering the different possibilities and appreciations of a phenomenon with various intervenors.

Electronic Fund Transfer Systems for Professional Fields

16-19   The professional world has learned how to use the advantages that the new telematic developments offer. Transfers are a way of payment widely used not only by large corporations but also by small enterprises. These operations clearly affect the relationships between companies and banks and the direct relationships between banks.

Intrabank relationships, which affect only one bank, and interbank relationships, which require a minimum of two banks, can be distinguished. Certain funds transfers require specific treatment. These include those between credit entities, or those that arise as a result of stock exchange operations.

The core of these transfers is constituted by the clearing systems , which involve both electronic transfers and operations where paper work is admitted at some stage.

Mass Electronic Funds Transfer Systems

16-20   The applications that have an effect on the general public are also of general interest to the banking sector. The different services offered by E.F.T. are:

- Automated distributors of bank notes (A.D.B.);
- Sales point terminals (S.P.T.);
- Telebank; and
- Teleshopping.

Automated Distributors of Bank Notes

16-21   The A.D.B. can be unifunctional or multifunctional. The former act only as cashpoints while the latter, as well as having this function, offer services ancillary to the distribution of cash among which are:

- Balance enquiries;
- Last operations;
- Deposit receipt;
- Fund transfers to third persons;
- Start transfers between accounts belonging to the same client; and
- Information on the stock exchange.

Sales Point Terminals

The S.P.T. systems are fund transfers made from the client's account to the   **16-22**
buyer's account in each point from which the consumer desires to obtain goods
or pay for services. The payment is made via a telematic connection from the terminal installed in the merchant's store. The transfer by the consumer requires a
series of preventative actions such as authenticity and solvency controls.

Telebank

The Telebank system offers the possibility to use banking services from one's   **16-23**
own home. The services are multiple:

- Balance of account;
- Stock exchange information; and
- Funds transfers from funds belonging to the same user or third party.

These services operate from terminals installed in the user's home or via a   **16-24**
telephone connected to the user's personal computer.

Teleshopping

Teleshopping is understood as the aquisition of products shown on televi-   **16-25**
sion by the use of a magnetic card using the telephone or other terminals
located in the consumer's home.

Use of Credit Cards

A widely used way of paying, although generally unknown by the user as   **16-26**
regards its legal issues, are credit cards. On some ocassions, these are used
as a means of electronic payment.

This means of payment has acquired great importance in the economic
activity of countries around the world and in particular the European Union.
Recommendation 87/598/E.E.C. states that the development of new ways
of payment flows from the financial and monetary integration of the
Community and of the enlargement of Europe's citizenship. The free movement of goods and capital will only be completely achieved if there is
technological support for ways of payment.

Several factors have led to the widespread use of "plastic money". Through
credit and debit cards, this has allowed access to a type of services that had
not existed until now.

No specific legislation in Spain concerns credit cards. They can only be
analysed on the basis of the intention of the contracting parties and on the
general theory of obligations and contracts. They are governed by the general
rules of contracts and obligations, but they have a peculiar characteristic
that must be considered when establishing a contractual relationship.

Conceptually, the credit card can be defined as an electronic and commercial document, by which the owner has access to a credit intrinsically linked to a contract. The owner uses the card to access a credit line with a maximum amount, form, and conditions of use previously agreed.

Through the credit card, the owner may acquire goods or services, and even obtain cash, depending on the previous agreement. The following credit card features can be identified:

- It is a commercial electronic document;
- It is linked to a right of credit depending on a previously reached agreement; and
- Through the credit card and in relation to what has been agreed, access is available to the purchase of goods or services or the obtention of cash.

RIGHTS OF ELECTRONIC INFORMATION

Authors' Rights in Electronic Information

16-27   The Spanish legislature's decision to bring computer programs within the ambit of intellectual property has been dictated by economic and legislative opportunities.

In international legal practice, the evolution of this field is not uniform. Computer programs are protected by way of several formulas, but due to the inadequacy of these formulas, the interested professionals have sought regulation that secures the property in and protection of the works. The Spanish legislature recognises this international issue and has resorted to the protection of computer programs through the application of the author's rights.

Law Number 22/1987 regarding Intellectual Property (Intellectual Property Law) of November 11, 1987, addresses computer programs in article 10 i) together with other objects. It states that all creations that are original, artistic, or scientific expressed through any medium or tangible support, actually known or to be invented in the future, including computer programmes are subjects of intellectual property.

Programs as Intellectual Property

16-28   Article 1 of the Computer Program Law *(Ley de Proteccin de Programas de Ordenador)* of 1993 follows the terms of the European Community Directive of May 14, 1991, and limits itself to a definition of a computer program based on their assimilation to literary works, their expression, and their originality.

16-29   **Assimilation to Literary Works** Computer programmes will be protected through the law of authors' rights as literary works as it is defined in the Berne Convention for the protection of literary and artistic works.

Protection of Expression of Computer Programs The Computer Program **16-30** Law recognises the basic principle that regarding intellectual property the author's rights protect exclusively the form and the expression of an idea and not the idea itself. It is a narrow line between an idea and its form. The establishment of this line where an idea becomes a form constitutes, on its own, a point of friction in the traditional works. The computer program aggravates this friction since, given its peculiar characteristics, the protection tends to extend to non-literary elements.

Requisite Originality Elements The computer program will be protected **16-31** only if it is original, in the sense of being an intellectual creation of its author.

The Computer Program Law of 1993, the Intellectual Property Law of 1987, and the majority of foreign laws regulating this field recognise originality as a fundamental requisite of the protection of computer programs.

Contents of Authors' Rights

Intellectual property is based on rights of a personal character and on rights **16-32** of patrimonial character. These grant to the author the disposition and exclusive right to exploit his works, with no limitations apart from those specified by the Law.[7]

Duration of Exploitation Rights

The time span in which the exploitation rights are protected is not uniform. **16-33** By the application of the specific dispositions of the Intellectual Property Law and the Computer Program Law, the period of protection varies depending on the legal status of the author.

Juridical Person The duration and calculation of the periods established in **16-34** article 97 of the Intellectual Property Law are maintained by express waiver of article 7 of the Computer Program Law where the author is a legal person, providing that:

> "The duration of exploitation rights of a computer program will be fifty years from the first of January of the subsequent year to its publication or creation if it has not been published."

Natural Person Article 97 of the Intellectual Property Law is not applicable **16-35** if the author is a physical person. In this case, the Computer Program Law, in its article 7(1), provides that:

> "The rights recognised in this law will be protected . . . during the life of the author and fifty years after his death or of the last surviving co-author."

---

7 Intellectual Property Law of 1987, article 2.

16-36   **Anonymous and Pseudonymous Works** Article 7(2) of the Computer Program Law states that, when the computer program is anonymous or a pseudonym has been used, the period of protection is 50 years from the moment it was offered to the public. According to the Law, protection starts on January 1 of the year following this act.

Violation of Authors' Rights

16-37   The new Spanish Civil Code, approved by Law Number 10/1995 of May 24, 1995, in its chapter XI on "Offences against property and socio-economic order", deals with intolerable conduct against intellectual property rights.

Article 270 of the Criminal Code conditions the law's application on the fact that all conduct has occurred without the authorisation of the lawful holder of the right. Authorisation must be given by the lawful holder to dispose of the affected right.

Article270 (3) of the Criminal Code is novel by mentioning computer programs. In this manner, the legislator has given the holders of telecommunication and information technology rights such fundamental rights as those of intellectual property.

Protection of Software through Patents Law

16-38   In the Spanish legal system, patents are regulated by Law Number 11/1986 of March 20, 1986, regarding patents (Patent Law). The Patent Law follows the course of action set out in the Agreement on the Concessions of European Patents signed in Munich on October 5, 1973. It establishes a general rule of exclusion subject to certain requirements. There are numerous reasons for adopting this rule of non-patentability of computer programs.[8]

In article 4(2), the Patent Law introduces the interpretation of article 52(2) of the Munich Agreement. In conformity with the Patent Law, computer programs are not inventions (in the sense of new inventions that include an inventive activity and are susceptible to industrial application); thus, they cannot be the object of a patent. According to article 4(2) of the Patent Law, the following are not considered inventions and cannot be the object of a patent:

- Discoveries, scientific theories and mathematic methods;
- Literary or artistic works or any other aesthetic creation, as well as scientific works;
- Plans, rules and methods for the exercise of intellectual activities, for games or economic-commercial activities, as well as computer programs; and
- Ways of presenting information.

8 Patent Co-operation Treaty, concluded in Washington, on June 19, 1970.

Consequently, patentability can be excluded in cases where the object   **16-39**
appearing in the patent application is simply a program.

The exclusion of article 4(2) of the Patent Law is not of an absolute
character. According to article 4(3) of the Patent Law, which provides that
the limitation in the preceding paragraph excludes the patentability of the
mentioned inventions only as far as the object to be patented includes only
one of those.

This formulation must be interpreted according to article 52(3) of the
Munich Agreement, which establishes that the limitation in paragraph 2
excludes the patentability of the elements enumerated in it only when the
application for the European patent refers to one of the elements considered
as such.

There are no obstacles for a computer program to be a part of a patent
as an intrinsic part of a group which, considered as an invention, satisfies
the requirements of patentability considered in article 4(2) of the Patent Law.

The general requirements (novelty, inventive activity and susceptibility
to industrial application) are not unlike those required by foreign patent
legislation.

Novelty

For an invention to be the object of an exclusive right, it must be new. The   **16-40**
kind of novelty required by the Patent Law is a universal novelty. Therefore,
prior utilisation or description in any part of the world would destroy this
condition.

Article 6(1) of the Patent Law considers an invention new when it is not
part of the state of the art. According to article 6(2), the state of the art is
constituted by everything which has been made accessible to the general
public in Spain and abroad by a written or oral description, before the patent
application has been submitted.

Inventive Activity

To merit patent protection, the inventor must have engaged in a minimum   **16-41**
creative activity. An invention implies an inventive activity when it does not
emerge from the state of the art in a manner evident for an expert in the subject.

Susceptible to Industrial Application

The concession of a patent aims to stimulate industrial and technological   **16-42**
development. An invention is considered susceptible to industrial application when its object is a product or procedure susceptible to being produced
in any type of industry, including agriculture.

Effects

If these requisites are fulfilled, the law confers on the holder of the patent   **16-43**
the right to use exclusively the program in the context of the patented
invention.

Since the patent right has an *erga omnes* effect, the holder enjoys within the national territory the right to prevent any third party without his consent from producing, utilising and commercialising the object of the patent for a period of 20 years.

This legal monopoly is limited and the holder of the patent cannot oppose the utilisation of the program in a sphere beyond the object of the patent.

Trade Mark Protection of Software

16-44   Trade marks under Spanish law are regulated by Law Number 32/1988 of November 10, 1988, on trade marks (Trade Marks Law). A trade mark is any sign the object of which is to distinguish in the market products or services of a given person from the products or services of another.

Applied to computer programs, the trade mark does not present any peculiarity. The protection offered by a trade mark to software is peripheral or indirect since, although it has an *erga omnes* character, trade mark protection is reduced to the name with which it is commercialised or to the distinctive sign which accompanies the commercialisation.

The use of a trade mark means that the legal protection of the software is not reduced to an intrinsic value, but it extends to the value represented by its notoriety, to the protection of the form known to the public. The holder of the trade mark enjoys an exclusive right of use. This right includes:

- The identification of the goods (computer programs) or services to be introduced by the holder of the trade mark;
- The commercialisation or introduction to the market of programs or services by the holder to whom the registration has been granted; and
- The utilisation of the trade mark with an advertising end and entrepreneurial identification.

16-45   Therefore, the holder enjoys protection against third parties who infringe his right. However, this right is not absolute. In order for an infringement to exist, a similitude in the sign, in the products and a risk of error or confusion among consumers must exist.

INFORMATION TECHNOLOGY CONDUCT

Regulation of Electronic Communication

National Legislation

16-46   Article 18(3) of the Spanish Constitution guarantees the confidentiality of communications. Organic Law Number 5/1992 on the regulation of automated processing of personal data and Royal Decree Number 1332/1994 of

June 20, 1994, by which certain aspects of the law are developed, constitute the legal framework on legal protection of personal data.

The main objective is to protect all persons against unauthorised manipulation of their personal data in all cases where this data is susceptible to automated processing. Unauthorised manipulation has the following charcteristics: the result of the elaboration of data through information processing must be identified with its holder, or the person must be identified through this data, revealing new characteristics of his personality as a consequence of this process. There must be a handling of data without the holder's permission or for a purpose other than that which was authorised.

Organic Law Number 5/1992 aims at limiting the use of data processing and other techniques of automated processing of data of a personal character to guarantee honour, personal and familiar intimacy of all physical persons and the full exercise of their rights.[9]

The kind of persons protected by Organic Law Number 5/1992, according to article 3e, are exclusively physical persons who are the subjects of the data being treated. Data treatment must be understood as the operations and technical procedures, whether automated or not, that enable the recording, conservation, elaboration, modification, blocking, cancellation, or data concession resulting from communications, consultation, interconnection and transfer.

The exclusion of juridical persons from the scope of protection contrasts with the definition offered by the law on "persons responsible for files". The latter includes physical and legal persons:

"Natural and legal person of a public nature and an administrative organ which decides on the finality, contents and use of the treatment."[10]

Organic Law Number 5/1992 is of general application in the entire Spanish **16-47** territory, but it does not prejudice the possible elaboration of separate data protection laws in Spain's different autonomous regions. These regions are responsible for the regulation of the exercise of the affected rights and their enforcement on the terms and under the limits established in Organic Law Number 5/1992 and in conformity with common administrative procedures.

A certain extraterritoriality may apply in the authorisations of the Director of the Data Protection Agency when international data transfers are involved. The authorisations require a prior analysis of the existence of a level of protection similar to the present law in the countries to which the personal data is transferred.

---

9 Organic Law Number 5/1992, article 1.
10 Organic Law Number 5/1992, article 3d.

International and European Community Legislation

16-48   The contents of Organic Law Number 5/1992 are in accordance with the harmonisation effected by international organisations in the area of data protection. These organisations are the:

- The Organisation for Economic Co-operation and Development (O.E.C.D.);
- The Council of Europe; and
- The European Community.

16-49   **The Recommendations of the Organisation for Economic Co-operation and Development**   The September 23, 1980, O.E.C.D. Recommendations on the protection of international personal data transfers have been adopted. These protective guidelines are focused towards the protection of physical persons and have an effect on the automated and manual indexes of public and private character.

16-50   **Council of Europe**   The Agreement for the Protection of Persons regarding the Automated Processing of Data of a Private Character, adopted in Strasbourg on January 28, 1981, has been effective since October 1, 1985, and forms part of Spanish law since its publication in the *Boletin Oficial del Estado* (*Official Gazette*) on November 15, 1985.

   The Agreement is applied to automated indexes of the private and public sectors that refer to personal data of physical persons.

16-51   **Modified Draft European Community Directive**   European Community activity regarding data protection is expressed in the proposal of the Council Directive of 1990 as modified by the second version in 1992. This proposal responds to the necessity to approximate the laws of the Member States in this area, to comply with the general objectives of the Single European Act.

   The Directive seeks to eliminate the obstacles that emerge in the Member States due to the free circulation of personal data. The achievement of this objective by the draft Directive is essential for the development of the internal market. The legislative comparison would prevent the existence of the denominated "data paradise", which distorts the services of treatment and diffusion of information and which constitutes a bar to the liberties agreed in the Treaty of Rome.

   The proposal removes the distinction between private and public indices and more relevance is given to the informed consent of the affected subjects, who can, at any moment, and for legitimate reasons, oppose the fact that their personal data is the object of treatment.

Sanctioning Regime

16-52   Organic Law Number 5/1992, unlike other European legislation on data protection, does not include any sanction of a criminal character. It distinguishes between the private and public sector. This distinction does not take into account the new legislative tendencies in which the distinction between these sectors tends to disappear.

Computer Offence

General

In the context of computer offences, a number of norms impose administra- 16-53 tive sanctions on those who violate any of the protected rights. The sanctions are administrative and not criminal. For example, article 44 of Organic Law Number 5/1992 refers to the sanctions to be applied against the persons responsible for slight, serious and very serious offences against this law. These sanctions are composed of penalties that range from Pts. 100,000 to Pts. 100-million.

"Computer offence" can be defined as the realisation of an action that fulfils the characteristics of the concept of an offence, and is realised using a data processing element or violating the rights of the holder of a data processing right, whether hardware or software.

The main difficulty regarding computer offences may be defining them.[11] In every "computer offence", one must distinguish between the means and the end. To recognise a damaging act, the medium by which it is committed must be an element, good or service within the context data processing responsibility and the end must pursue some kind of benefit to the subject or author of the offence causing prejudice to another.

The way of committing an offence and the many ways in which data processing can be used make it impossible to classify all the possible offences. There are a number of characteristics common to all the catalogued computer offences. This enables classification in accordance with the function and activities that are used to commit them.

All computer offences centre their activities on the access and/or the manipulation of data or computer programs used in processing. Data processing manipulation can be done in two different ways:

- Access and manipulation of data; and
- Manipulation of programs.

A few determinate actions can be considered within the ambit of computer 16-54 offences and they may be classified if the following are taken into account:

- Handling of data and information of indices or other people's data processing physical support;
- Access and use of data by non-authorised persons;

---

11 Tortras, "The Computer Offence", *Informatics and the Law*, 1989.

- Input of programs or other routines in other computer terminals to destroy information, data or programs;
- Use of the computer terminal and/or programs without authorisation to obtain benefits to the detriment of others;
- Use of a computer with fraudulent aims; and
- Breach of privacy through the use and processing of personal data with an unauthorised aim.

Common Characteristics of Computer Offences

16-55   The method used to commit computer offences and how they are detected make computers peculiar and up to a certain point *sui generis*. The following can be enunciated as the common characteristics of computer offences:

- Speed and distance in relation to the commission of the offence;
- Facility to conceal the act; and
- Facility to erase evidence of the offence.

CHAPTER 17

United States

Ieuan G. Mahony
Sherburne, Powers & Needham, P.C.
Boston, Massachusetts, United States

INTRODUCTION

The United States Telecommunications Act of 1996 defines the Internet as **17-1** "the international computer network of both federal and non-federal interoperable packet switched data networks".[1] With its origins in the 1960s in the "ARPANET" project of the United States Department of Defense Advanced Research Projects Agency,[2] by 1997 the Internet has grown to consist of a "network of networks" including more than 9.4-million "host" computers, with tens of millions of users.[3] The United States Administration views the Internet as the prototype for the United States National Information Infrastructure (NII) — which will provide the digital, interactive services now available on the Internet, as well as services and products contemplated in the future — and as the prototype for the Global Information Infrastructure (GII).[4]

On-line activities are not limited to the Internet. For example, a business may establish a direct link — bypassing the Internet altogether — with an Electronic Data Interchange trading partner; a group of businesses may employ a proprietary Value Added Network, linking just those businesses, independent from the Internet; or a consumer may restrict his or her "surfing"

---

1 47 U.S.C., section 230 (e). "Packet switching" refers to "disassembling" a digital message into smaller "packets" to transmit over a communications network. The technique, developed independently in the mid-1960s by Paul Baran of the RAND Corporation and Donald Davies of the National Physical Laboratory, increases efficiencies. See Hafner and Lyon, *Where Wizards Stay Up Late: The Origins of the Internet*, at pp. 52–67 (1996).

2 Hahn, *The Internet Complete Reference* 2 (2nd edition 1996); Hafner and Lyon, *Where Wizards Stay Up Late: The Origins of the Internet*, at pp. 43–81 (1996).

3 See *A.C.L.U. v. Reno*, 929 F Supp. 824, 830–831 (ED Pa. 1996), juris. noted, *Reno v. A.C.L.U.*, 136 LEd.2d 436 (1996).

4 Intellectual Property and the National Information Infrastructure: The Report of the Working Group on Intellectual Property Rights, Information Infrastructure Task Force (IPNII Report), 2 n.5, at pp. 7–8, 179 (September 5, 1995).

to one of the commercial on-line networks, such as America Online or CompuServe, and refrain from venturing onto the Internet.[5]

The Internet offers the promise of an efficient world-wide market for transacting business and a forum for exchanging ideas.[6] Rapid advances in digital, networking, and communications technologies now allow Internet users — economically and from virtually anywhere in the world — to access vast new markets and resources for information, entertainment, and business.

Yet, the Internet poses challenges to the United States legal system. First, Internet communications — which are paperless and essentially "faceless" — raise concerns over accountability, fraud, and contractual enforceability. Second, the Internet allows the gathering and wide dissemination of personal information, threatening individual privacy. Third, as a low-cost public distribution channel, the Internet may facilitate the broad transmittal of offensive and illegal content. Fourth, the Internet relies on a decentralised, open network, and thus raises concerns over the security and authenticity of transmitted and stored information. Finally, the digital technology that underlies the Internet allows a user to take any work stored in digital form — such as a video, a musical recording, or a novel — and, without the owner's consent, alter the work, effortlessly create exact and undeteriorating copies, and disseminate these copies broadly via the Internet. The Internet, therefore, raises concerns over protecting ownership rights in digital "property".

The United States legal system is adapting to challenges presented by the Internet. The following chapter analyses the current state of United States "on-line" law. It first addresses the regulatory framework, the "players" responsible for regulation, and their jurisdiction. It then discusses the areas of regulation, such as privacy law, taxation, and criminal legislation and next reviews the security and enforceability of on-line transactions and payment mechanisms. It concludes with a discussion of the nature and ownership of rights in on-line information. As shown below, although in a state of change, United States law provides businesses and individuals with a reasoned framework for enjoying and capitalising on the Internet's opportunities, and avoiding its risks.

REGULATION OF ON-LINE ACTIVITY

17-2   On-line activity in the United States takes many forms. These include transferring orders and invoices between businesses through Electronic Data

---

5 For convenience, and unless the context requires greater specificity, the terms "on-line", "electronic", and "Internet" activity will be used interchangeably.

6 As one United States court recently observed, the Internet is "a unique and wholly new medium of world wide human communication", which offers "the most participatory marketplace of mass speech that this country — and indeed the world — has yet seen". *A.C.L.U.* v. *Reno*, 929 F Supp. 824, and 844 (ED Pa. 1996) and at 881 (Dalzell, J., concurring), juris. noted, *Reno* v. *A.C.L.U.*, 136 LEd.2d 436 (1996).

Interchange; "browsing" the World Wide Web for purposes of research, on-line shopping or entertainment; exchanging personal e-mail; participating in newsgroups or "chats"; and uploading and downloading digital files between a host server and a user's computer through File Transfer Protocol (FTP).[7] The United States regulatory framework governing these activities is discussed below.

United States Government Policies Regarding On-line Activity

The United States government has strongly endorsed certain features of the 17-3
Internet, and has stated a policy of promoting the development of the Internet, and fostering this development with minimal governmental intrusion.[8] This endorsement is influenced heavily by the First Amendment, which protects both political and commercial speech.

Legislative and Executive Policy Statements

Specifically, the United States Congress, in the Telecommunications Act of 17-4
1996,[9] declared that it is the policy of the United States to:

- Promote the continued development of the Internet and other interactive computer services and other interactive media;
- Preserve the vibrant and competitive free market that presently exists for the Internet and other interactive computer services, unfettered by federal or state regulation;
- Encourage the development of technologies which maximise user control over what information is received by individuals, families, and schools who use the Internet and other interactive computer services;
- Remove disincentives for the development and utilisation of blocking and filtering technologies that empower parents to restrict their children's access to objectionable or inappropriate on-line material; and
- Ensure vigorous enforcement of federal criminal laws to determine and punish trafficking in obscenity, stalking, and harassment by means of computer.[10]

Underlying this policy statement were various Congressional findings 17-5
with respect to the Internet, including findings that the Internet represents an "extraordinary advance" in the availability of educational and information

---

7 A.C.L.U. v. *Reno*, 929 F Supp. 824, 834 (ED Pa. 1996); Allison, *The Lawyer's Guide to the Internet*, at pp. 59–73 (1995).

8 47 U.S.C., section 230 (b) (1) and (2).

9 Pub. L number 104–104, 110 Stat. 137 (1996).

10 47 U.S.C., section 230 (b).

resources; that the Internet offers a public forum for a "true diversity of political discourse, unique opportunities for cultural development, and myriad avenues for intellectual activities"; and that the Internet must be allowed to "flourish" with a minimum of government regulation.[11]

The United States Administration has similarly endorsed development of the Internet.[12] In its report entitled "Intellectual Property and the National Information Infrastructure" (IPNII Report), for example, the Administration states the goal of encouraging the dissemination of quality works of authorship over the Internet.[13] To achieve this goal, the Report notes, copyright owners and other content provides must be assured a fair return for their efforts. Accordingly, the Report strongly endorses protecting intellectual property rights on the Internet, and preserving individual owners' freedom of contract.[14] The Report thus recommends against:

- Creating additional compulsory licences on the Internet, to allow market forces and owners' freedom of contract to determine pricing and availability of on-line content;[15] and
- "Deregulating" intellectual property rights to allow the free use of on-line, digital information because such deregulation, the Report states, would create a cyberspace "Dodge City", devoid of content.[16]

17-6   Because the Working Group that authored the Report concluded that United States copyright law was fundamentally adequate to address intellectual property issues raised by the Internet, the Report's specific recommendations for changes in United States law were relatively limited. Specifically, the Working Group recommended to Congress, among other points, that the Copyright Act be revised to:

- Provide that transmitting a work over the NII falls, in certain circumstances, within a copyright owner's exclusive distribution right;
- Prohibit the unauthorised deactivation of software or hardware devices designed to protect copyright owners' exclusive rights, such as devices that limit serial copying;
- Grant public performance rights for sound recordings;
- Prohibit tampering with or falsifying copyright management information; and

---

11 47 U.S.C., section 230 (a).
12 IPNII Report (September 1995).
13 IPNII Report, at pp. 7–17 (September 1995).
14 IPNII Report, at pp. 16–17 (September 1995).
15 IPNII Report, at pp. 49–53 (September 1995).
16 IPNII Report, at pp. 14–15 (September 1995).

- Provide criminal sanctions for unauthorised and wilful reproduction or distribution of copies with a retail value of U.S. $5,000 or more.[17]

The Congress has implemented certain of these recommended changes, and it is considering others.[18]

The Administration has also advocated a "duty free" and tax- free trade zone **17-7** for electronic commerce, and recommends a series of international guidelines and accords to insure that the Internet has the means — financial, legal, and technical — to operate securely and efficiently. In particular, the Administration has indicated that governments should not place undue restraints on electronic commerce, should refrain from placing new taxes on electronic commerce, and should recognise the benefits of the Internet's decentralised structure.[19]

Impact of the First Amendment

A central element underlying the United States government's Internet policy **17-8** is the First Amendment to the United States Constitution, protecting freedom of speech. Almost any conduct on the Internet can be viewed as "speech", as the First Amendment protects both political discourse and debate — its central purpose[20] — as well as commercial speech, such as advertising.[21] First Amendment protections are particularly strong where the government attempts to regulate the content of the speech by, for example, forbidding discussion of certain topics.[22] The First Amendment applies only to government action; it does not apply to private individuals or businesses. Accordingly, First Amendment protections do not reach a business, for

---

17 IPNII Report, at pp. 211–235 (September 1995).
18 The Digital Performance Right and Sound Recordings Act of 1995, 17 U.S.C., section 106 (6); see also S 1284; H.R. 2441.
19 Draft Framework for Global Electronic Commerce (November 22, 1996), discussed in Drolte, "Administration Wants Duty-Free Trade Zone For Electronic Commerce, Draft Plan Reveals", 1 *Electronic Information Policy & Law Report* (BNA), at pp. 881 and 882 (December 13, 1996); see also Drolte, "Clinton's Draft Electronic Commerce Policy Undergoes Revisions Based on Comments", 2 *Electronic Information Policy & Law Report* (BNA), at p. 378 (April 4, 1997).
20 *Roth v. United States*, 354 U.S. 476, at p. 484 (1957): the First Amendment is "to assure unfettered interchange of ideas for the bringing about of political and social changes desired by the people".
21 *Virginia State Bd. of Pharmacy v. Virginia Citizens Consumer Council, Inc.*, 425 U.S. 748, at p. 770 (1976).
22 *Sable Communications of California, Inc. v. F.C.C.*, 492 U.S. 115, at p. 126 (1989); see *Turner Broadcasting Sys. v. F.C.C.*, 114 SCt. 2445, at p. 2458 (1994): a law that regulates speech based on its content is "presumptively invalid"; *Police Dep't of Chicago v. Mosley*, 408 U.S. 92, at p. 95 (1972): the First Amendment curtails the government's ability "to restrict expression because of its messages, its ideas, its subject matter, or its content". Cf. *Ward v. Rock Against Racism*, 491 U.S. 781, at p. 791 (1989): the government has greater ability to regulate the place time, place, and manner of expression, as opposed to the content of the expression.

example, that restricts its employees' expression. As the Supreme Court noted in *Turner Broadcasting Sys. v. F.C.C.*:[23]

> "At the heart of the First Amendment lies the principle that each person should decide for him or herself the ideas and beliefs deserving of expression, consideration, and adherence. Our political system and cultural life rest on this ideal. Government action that stifles speech on account of its message, or that requires the utterance of a particular message favoured by the Government, contravenes this essential right."[24]

17-9   Therefore, because the First Amendment curtails the government's ability to regulate speech, and because on-line conduct is a form of speech, any governmental policy concerning the Internet in the United States must accord a strong degree of deference to users and content providers.

Regulators of On-line Activity

17-10   The federal government and the state governments regulate the various aspects of on-line activity.

Federal Government

17-11   In addition to statutory regulation by Congress, electronic commerce in the United States is also regulated by federal administrative agencies. The Federal Communications Commission (F.C.C.), for example, possesses authority to regulate Internet services. The F.C.C. has jurisdiction over telecommunications common carriers, and regulates traditional voice-telephone services.[25] The F.C.C. also has jurisdiction over use of the radio spectrum, including licensing for broadcast facilities,[26] and certain aspects of the cable television industry.[27] As common carriers, providers of traditional voice-telephone services are subject to a number of "public utility" requirements, including requirements that they provide service to all customers at just and reasonable rates;[28] that they refrain from unjustly discriminating among customers; and that they post their rates and tariffs with the F.C.C..[29]

Although the F.C.C. possesses the requisite authority, to date the F.C.C. has declined to regulate Internet services — even though these services rely on the telephone network. Instead, the F.C.C. distinguishes between "basic" transmission services, which are essentially traditional voice-telephone

---

23 114 SCt. 2445 (1994).
24 *Turner Broadcasting Sys. v. F.C.C.*, 114 SCt. 2445, 2458 (1994).
25 47 U.S.C., sections 201–230 and 251–261.
26 47 U.S.C., sections 301, *et seq.*
27 47 U.S.C., sections 521, *et seq.*
28 47 U.S.C., section 201.
29 47 U.S.C., sections 202 and 203.

services[30] and which are regulated as common carrier services, and Internet servi the F.C.C. calls "enhanced services", and which are not regulated as common carrier services.[31] An enhanced service employs "computer processing applications that act on the format, content, code, protocol or similar aspects of the subscriber's transmitted information, or provide the subscriber additional, different, or restructured information, or involve subscriber interaction with stored information".[32] The F.C.C., therefore, has not exercised its authority to regulate Internet service providers as common carriers.

In addition to authority over Internet service providers, federal administrative agencies also have authority over the content of Internet communications. For example, the Federal Trade Commission regulates advertising and protects consumers from unfair business practices,[33] while the Food and Drug Administration regulates advertising and labelling that relate specifically to drugs or food.[34] Federal agencies, as well as Congress, therefore, have regulatory authority over on-line activity.

State Governments

State governments also have authority over on-line activity. A number of **17-12** states, for example, prohibit the dissemination to minors, over the Internet, of sexually explicit and other harmful materials.[35]

In addition, state public utility commissions retain authority to regulate the rates, terms, and conditions of services offered intrastate by telecommunications carriers.[36]

Jurisdictional Issues

The Internet allows a user virtually instantaneous access to "value" stored **17-13** on a server located perhaps continents away. The physical location of this host server is frequently not apparent to the user, and the host is similarly unaware of the physical location of users that access his or her site.

Parties to on-line activity can thus — unknowingly — "cross" geographic borders and "touch" various sovereign states, each with potentially conflicting laws.[37] In the event of a dispute, therefore, on-line conduct raises

---

30 Amendment of section 64.702 of the Commission's Rules and Regulations, 77 F.C.C. 2d 384, 420 (1980).
31 47 C.F.C. section 64.702 (a).
32 Stuckey, *Internet and Online Law,* section 9.02[3] at 9-7 (1996).
33 15 U.S.C., section 45 *et seq.*; 16 C.F.R., section 1-901.
34 21 U.S.C. section 301 *et seq.*; 21 C.F.R., section 1-299.
35 Ga. Code Ann., sections 16-12-100 *et. seq.*; NY Penal Law section 235.21.
36 47 U.S.C., section 152 (b).
37 Johnson and Post, "Law and Borders — The Rise of Law in Cyberspace", 48 *Stan. L Rev.* 1367, at pp. 1370–1371 (1996): on the Internet, "[m]essages can be transmitted from any physical location to any other location without any physical cues or barriers that might otherwise keep certain geographically remote places and people separate from one another".

difficult questions concerning which state's law governs the parties' relationship, and which state possesses jurisdiction over the parties themselves.

Choice of Law in On-line Transactions

17-14   A user in France can access a database maintained on a server in the United States, download information from that database, and store that information on a computer located in Sweden.[38] It is a complex question which country's copyright laws, for example, govern the transaction. Because copyright laws are territorial, and international conventions allow variances in national legislation, the user's conduct might constitute copyright infringement under one country's law, and might constitute fair use of uncopyrightable expression under another country's law.[39]

In a contract case, under choice of law rules — which vary somewhat from state to state within the United States — a court will generally choose the law of the jurisdiction that has the "most significant relationship to the transaction and the parties".[40] In determining which law meets these criteria, a court will examine factors such as the place where the contract was executed; the place where the contract was negotiated; the place of performance; the physical location of the subject matter of the contract; and the domicile of the parties.[41]

To minimise the uncertainty associated with this analysis, parties may select by contract the law they wish to have applied to their relationship. A court in the United States will generally enforce an agreement between the parties that requires application of a particular state's law,[42] and will refuse to enforce such a provision only where either:

- The law the parties have chosen has "no substantial relationship to the parties or the transaction"; or
- Application of the chosen law "would be contrary to fundamental policy of the state which has a materially greater interest" in the dispute, and whose law would control in the absence of the parties' choice of law agreement.[43]

17-15   In tort cases, the law of the state that has the "most significant relationship" to the occurrence and the parties will generally govern.[44]

---

38 This example is given in IPNII Report, at p. 131 (September 1995).
39 In the United States, for example, copyright protection for databases is "thin". *Feist Publications, Inc v. Rural Tel. Serv. Co.*, 499 U.S. 340, at pp. 347 and 349 (1991).
40 *Restatement (Second) of Conflict of Laws*, section 188 (1971).
41 *Restatement (Second) of Conflict of Laws*, section 188.
42 *Restatement (Second) of Conflict of Laws*, section 187(2)(a) and (b); Uniform Laws Annotated, U.C.C. section 1-105 (1989).
43 *Restatement (Second) of Conflict of Laws*, section 187(2)(a) and (b); U.C.C. section 1-105.
44 *Restatement (Second) of Conflict of Laws*, sections 6 and 145 (1971). Preference is generally given to the law of the place of the injury. *Restatement (Second) of Conflict of Laws*, sections 156–166, 172 (1971). See, generally, Scoles and Hay, *Conflict of Laws*, section 17.21 (2nd edition, 1992).

The recent case of *United States* v. *Thomas*[45] highlights certain concerns over the unintended application of another jurisdiction's law. The *Thomas* defendants operated a Bulletin Board System (BBS) from their home in Milpitas, California.[46] After paying a membership fee, subscribers could access this BBS to view and download sexually explicit magazine photographs, which the defendants had converted into digital form by "scanning" the magazines.[47] After paying his membership fee, a Postal Inspector in Tennessee accessed the defendants' BBS and downloaded various images.

The defendants were then prosecuted in the Western District of Tennessee, and were judged by the community standards of "obscenity" in Tennessee, and not California.[48] The defendants argued that they could not select who would receive the BBS materials, and that California's standard for obscenity should control. The court rejected this argument and affirmed the defendants' convictions, finding that the defendants had the ability, through their membership fee procedures, to limit user access in jurisdictions with less tolerant standards for determining obscenity.[49]

In sum, participants in on-line activities cross geographic borders with ease and perhaps unknowingly, thereby subjecting themselves to unfamiliar and perhaps adverse legal standards of conduct.

Personal Jurisdiction on the Internet

Courts have noted that traditional concepts of personal jurisdiction — based **17-16** on borders between sovereign states — should be re-evaluated in light of the economy's increasing globalisation, and recognise that commercial use of the Internet tests these traditional, territorial-based concepts of personal jurisdiction.[50] Under these traditional concepts, a court properly exercises jurisdiction over a defendant either where the defendant is a resident of the "forum state" (the state where the court is located), or where the defendant, through his or her conduct, has submitted to the jurisdiction of courts in the forum state.[51] A defendant generally submits to the jurisdiction of a court where he or she has sufficient "minimum contacts" with the forum state.[52] In gauging whether sufficient minimum contacts exist, a court will examine whether the defendant

---

45 74 F.3d 701 (6 Cir. 1996).
46 A BBS is similar in structure to commercial on-line services, such as CompuServe. With a modem and telephone line, a user can "dial in" to the BBS host computer and, using software running on the host computer, upload files to or download files from the host computer, or participate in discussions maintained on the host computer. A BBS may also provide its users with access, via a "gateway", to the Internet. Allison, *The Lawyer's Guide to the Internet* 47–48 (1995).
47 *United States* v. *Thomas*, 74 F.3d 701, at p. 705 (6 Cir. 1996).
48 *United States* v. *Thomas*, 74 F.3d 701, at pp. 710–712 (6 Cir. 1996).
49 *United States* v. *Thomas*, 74 F.3d 701, at p. 711 (6 Cir. 1996).
50 *CompuServe* v. *Patterson*, 89 F.3d 1257, at p. 1262 (6 Cir. 1996); *Digital Equipment Corp.* v. *Altavista Technology, Inc.*, 960 F Supp. 456, at pp. 462–463 (D Mass. 1997).
51 Wright and Miller, 4 *Federal Practice & Procedure*, sections 1065, 1069 (1987).
52 *International Shoe Co.* v. *Washington*, 326 U.S. 310, at p. 316 (1945).

"should reasonably anticipate being haled into court in the forum state", whether the defendant "purposefully availed" him or herself of the privilege of conducting activities relating to the forum state, and whether the defendant was thus on notice that he or she could be subject to suit in the forum state.[53]

Yet the Internet, courts note, breaks down barriers between physical jurisdictions; when a buyer and seller complete a transaction through a World Wide web site, for example, traditional physical acts — that often determine whether one party will be subject to personal jurisdiction in the courts where the other is located — may not occur.[54] Courts are in the process, therefore, of adapting traditional jurisdictional concepts to on-line activity. Several courts, for example, have found that the sale of goods or the solicitation or conduct of business over the Internet gives rise to jurisdiction in the buyer's home state.[55] Indeed, where a defendant sells goods on-line through a service provider such as CompuServe, the defendant may be subject to personal jurisdiction in the home state of that service provider.[56]

Mere operation of a passive web site — where transactions do not take place — generally will not give rise to jurisdiction in the plaintiff's state, and the fact that the plaintiff is able to access the defendant's site from his or her state is insufficient.[57] Yet, even if no transactions take place "at" a web site,

---

53 *International Shoe Co.* v. *Washington*, 326 U.S. 310, at p. 316 (1945); see *Burger King Corp.* v. *Rudzewicz*, 471 U.S. 462, at p. 474 (1985): a defendant is subject to personal jurisdiction where the defendant enters a contract with a resident of the forum state, and possesses other contacts with the state; *Calder* v. *Jones*, 465 U.S. 783, at pp. 789–790 (1984): a defendant who intentionally injures a plaintiff, such as through defamation, is subject to personal jurisdiction in the state of the plaintiff's domicile.

54 *Digital Equipment Corp.* v. *Altavista Technology, Inc.*, 960 F Supp. 456, at pp. 462–463 (D Mass. 1997) (citation omitted).

55 *CompuServe, Inc.* v. *Patterson*, 89 F.3d 1257, at pp. 1263–1266 (6 Cir. 1996): defendant's repeated sales of allegedly infringing software over plaintiff's Ohio-based computer system constituted purposeful availment of privilege of doing business in Ohio that gave rise to jurisdiction; *Digital Equip. Corp.* v. *AltaVista Technology, Inc.*, 960 F Supp. 456, at pp. 466–467 (D Mass. 1997): finding jurisdiction over company whose allegedly infringing web site solicited sales in every state, including Massachusetts; *Zippo Manufacturing Company* v. *Zippo Dot Com, Inc.*, 952 F Supp. 1119, at pp. 1125–1127 (WD Pa. 1997): finding jurisdiction over company that maintained web site accessible in Pennsylvania that sold passwords to 3,000 subscribers in Pennsylvania, and that had entered into seven contracts with Internet access providers to furnish services to their customers in Pennsylvania.

56 *CompuServe* v. *Patterson*, 89 F.3d 1257, at pp. 1263–1266 (6 Cir. 1996): the defendant's on-line service provider operated, in effect, as a distribution center for the plaintiff; the court, therefore, ruled that "someone like [the defendant] who employs a computer network service like [the plaintiff] to market a product can reasonably expect disputes with that service to yield lawsuits in the service's home state".

57 *McDonough* v. *Fallon McElligott*, 40 U.S.P.Q.2d 1826 (SD Cal. 1996): a California plaintiff sued a Minnesota advertising agency in California for copyright infringement; the plaintiff unsuccessfully attempted to establish jurisdiction based solely on the fact that the defendant's Web page could be accessed in California; *Bensusan Restaurant Corp.* v. *King*, 937 F Supp. 295 (SDNY 1996): a New York jazz club sued a Missouri jazz club in New York for trade mark infringement; the plaintiff unsuccessfully argued that the defendant's web site could be accessed by New York residents; the court found that users of the site could not complete a transaction without calling Missouri and virtually all of the defendant's business was conducted in Missouri.

the web site itself may give rise to jurisdiction, as the web site may infringes a plaintiff's intellectual property rights. Confronted with allegedly infringing web sites, certain courts have ruled that the infringing site amounts to continuous advertising by the defendant that is directed into the forum state, therefore providing a basis for jurisdiction.[58]

Other courts have applied the "effects test" — which focuses on the location where the effects of the defendant's wrongdoing are felt — to assert jurisdiction on the theory that a defendant's allegedly wrongful conduct on its web site caused harm in the state where the injured party was located.[59] Accordingly, the host of an active web site may be subject to jurisdiction where buyers reside, or where competitors who claim infringement from the site reside.

Areas of Regulation

As "a unique and wholly new medium of worldwide human communica- 17-17 tion",[60] the Internet presents wide areas for regulation.

Broadcasting, Telecommunications, and Print Perspective

Approaches to regulating the Internet in the United States often rely, by 17-18 analogy, on regulatory approaches previously adopted with respect to traditional communications media, such as broadcasting, telecommunications, and print media.[61] To introduce the discussion concerning specific areas of regulation, a review of these approaches follows.

"Paradigms" for Internet Regulation United States law treats each commu- 17-19 nications medium differently under the First Amendment,[62] recognising that such media — from television, to newspapers, to handbills — possess

---

58 *Inset Sys., Inc. v. Instruction Set, Inc.*, 937 F Supp. 161, at pp. 164–165 (D Conn. 1996): by maintaining a web site accessible in Connecticut, the defendant had "purposefully directed its advertising activities toward [the] state on a continuing basis" so that the exercise of jurisdiction was appropriate; *Digital Equip. Corp. v. AltaVista Technology, Inc.*, 960 F Supp. 456, at pp. 466–467 (D Mass. 1997): maintaining an allegedly infringing web site accessible in Massachusetts is analogous to broadcasting advertising into the state and supports the exercise of jurisdiction.

59 See *Digital Equip. Corp. v. AltaVista Technology, Inc.*, 960 F Supp. 456, at pp. 469–470, 472 (D Mass. 1997): finding jurisdiction over defendant because its allegedly infringing web site was accessible in Massachusetts and because the plaintiff, which had its headquarters in Massachusetts, would feel the effects most in Massachusetts; *Panavision Int'l LP v. Toeppen*, 938 F Supp. 616, at pp. 621-22 (CD Cal. 1996): defendant whose domain name infringed the plaintiff's trade mark was subject to jurisdiction in the defendant's home state of California because the brunt of the harm was felt there.

60 *A.C.L.U. v. Reno*, 929 F Supp. 824, at p. 844 (ED Pa. 1996), juris. noted, *Reno v. A.C.L.U.*, 136 LEd.2d 436 (1996).

61 *A.C.L.U. v. Reno*, 929 F Supp. 824, at pp. 873–877 (ED Pa. 1996) (Dalzell, J., concurring).

62 *F.C.C. v. Pacifica Foundation*, 438 U.S. 726, at p. 748 (1978): "each medium of expression presents special First Amendment problems".

"differing natures, values, abuses and dangers".[63] The "nature" of on-line communications will determine how these communications are regulated, what regulatory "paradigm" will be employed and how much First Amendment protection they will receive. Permissible regulations vary with the medium; rules for newspapers differ from rules for television and radio, which differ in turn from rules for cable television.[64] A radio station, for example, can be sanctioned for broadcasting speech that would be entirely permissible printed in a newspaper.[65]

Two broad reasons underlie the government's ability to regulate broadcasting media to a greater extent than print media. First, the scarcity of bandwidth for radio and television requires that the government regulate the industry, and actively license use of this "public domain";[66] with the privilege of such a licence comes an obligation on the broadcaster to the public to provide suitable access to "social, political, aesthetic, moral and other ideas and experiences".[67] Indeed, it is the scarcity of bandwidth that distinguishes cable television from broadcast television, and allows cable television greater freedom from government regulation than broadcast television.[68]

Second, broadcast media are a "uniquely pervasive presence", "uniquely accessible to children, even those too young to read".[69] Users of these media — radio and television — are a "captive audience" to whatever content is broadcast, at a minimum, during the period between accessing the station and changing the channel.[70] The nature of broadcast media thus justifies greater government regulation.

In contrast, telephone services, like newspapers, are subject to less restrictive regulation.[71] Telephone services are less intrusive than broadcast services; moreover, via telephone services a content provider may restrict access to potentially objectionable materials with relative ease, in contrast to broadcasting services. Providers of so-called "dial-a-porn services", for

---

63 *Kovacs v. Cooper*, 336 U.S. 77, at p. 97 (1949) (Jackson, J. concurring).
64 *Miami Herald Publishing Co.* v. *Tornillo*, 418 U.S. 241 (1974) (print); *Red Lion Broadcasting Co.* v. *F.C.C.*, 395 U.S. 367 (1969) (broadcast radio and television); *Turner Broadcasting Sys.* v. *F.C.C.*, 114 SCt. 2445 (1994) (cable television).
65 *F.C.C.* v. *Pacifica Foundation*, 438 U.S. 726, at p. 748 (1978); see *Turner Broadcasting Sys.* v. *F.C.C.*, 114 SCt. 2445, at p. 2456 (1994): "[i]t is true that our cases have permitted more intrusive regulation of broadcast speakers than of speakers in other media".
66 *Columbia Broadcasting Sys., Inc.* v. *Democratic Nat'l Comm.*, 412 U.S. 94, at pp. 110–111 (1973).
67 *Red Lion Broadcasting Co.* v. *F.C.C.*, 395 U.S. 367, 390 (1969).
68 See *Turner Broadcasting Sys.* v. *F.C.C.*, 114 SCt. 2445, at p. 2457 (1994). Perhaps in part due to greatly expanding cable television offerings, the Telecommunications Act of 1996 requires that, by February 8, 1998, all television sets with a picture screen 13 inches or larger come equipped with a "V-chip" that will allow viewers to block programmes with objectionable contents. 47 U.S.C., section 303 (x).
69 *F.C.C.* v. *Pacifica Foundation*, 438 U.S. 726, at pp. 748–749 (1978).
70 *F.C.C.* v. *Pacifica Foundation*, 438 U.S. 726, at pp. 748–749 (1978).
71 *Sable Communications of California, Inc.* v. *F.C.C.*, 492 U.S. 115, at pp. 127–128 (1989).

example, can require that a user provide credit card verification to substantiate the user's age, before providing access to content. Accordingly, the government's role in regulating the content of voice communications over telephone lines is limited and, unlike in the broadcasting arena, the government cannot restrict "dial-a-porn" services, for example, to a certain time of day.[72] In further contrast to broadcasting or print media, telephone service providers are regulated as common carriers, and are thus required to provide "universal" access to phone services, and are prohibited from censoring or altering the content of their users' messages.[73]

United States law thus requires a "media-specific" approach to the regulation of mass communication.[74] The precise location of the Internet along this spectrum — from the least restriction, such as for print media, to the greatest restriction, such as for television and radio — is unclear. The Internet appears to be dissimilar to broadcast media. It is not as accessible to children and, due to the ease and extremely low cost of establishing a Web site, for example, Internet communication is an "abundant and growing resource", unlike the essentially fixed capacity and limited number of "speakers" in broadcast media.[75] Accordingly, regulations that are appropriate for broadcasting are not necessarily appropriate for the Internet.

The Internet, with its public newsgroups, is also dissimilar from telephone services, which are essentially private. Also, due to its low entry barriers for both speakers and listeners, the Internet may be "far more speech-enhancing than print".[76] Accordingly, the Internet does not necessarily "fit" well within regulatory frameworks developed for traditional communications media.

Treatment of On-line Services and Telecommunications Services: Access Charges The F.C.C. treatment of so-called "access charges" exemplifies United States governmental policy in distinguishing on-line services from traditional, voice-based telephone services. The F.C.C.'s access charge system sets the prices that users must pay to access local telephone exchange networks for long-distance communications.[77] The F.C.C. distinguishes between on-line service providers (called "enhanced service providers") and long-distance telephone companies (called "interexchange carriers"), and allows on-line service providers to pay flat-rate monthly charges, like residential and business users, rather

17-20

---

72 *Sable Communications of California, Inc.* v. *F.C.C.*, 492 U.S. 115, at pp. 127-28 (1989); Smedinghoff (ed.), *Online Law*, at pp. 310–313 (1996).

73 *F.C.C.* v. *Midwest Video Corp.*, 440 U.S. 689, at p. 701 (1979); 47 U.S.C., sections 201–203.

74 *F.C.C.* v. *Pacifica Foundation*, 438 U.S. 726, at p. 748 (1978).

75 *A.C.L.U.* v. *Reno*, 929 F Supp. 824, at p. 843, (ED Pa. 1996), juris. noted, *Reno* v. *A.C.L.U.*, 136 LEd.2d 436 (1996) at p. 877 (Dalzell, J., concurring.).

76 *A.C.L.U.* v. *Reno*, 929 F Supp. 824, at pp. 843–844 (ED Pa. 1996).

77 47 C.F.R., sections 69.1 *et seq.*

than the higher access charges imposed on the long-distance carriers.[78] As the F.C.C. has noted, allowing on-line service providers to pay local business exchange rates for their interstate access — rather than the higher interexchange rates — helps on-line services providers minimise their costs of operation.[79]

17-21   Convergence of Traditional Communications Media Efforts at distinguishing the Internet from traditional communications media may rapidly be outdated, as these traditional media converge in the Internet and lose their boundaries. Users substitute on-line services for newspapers, records, novels, and videotapes; e-mail messages substitute for private United States mail; and "chat" groups begin to resemble a telephone party line.[80]

Moreover, "players" in the communications industries are expanding their offerings. Broadcasters are converting from an analogue to a digital standard.[81] Telephone companies seek authority to provide video services. Cable television companies seek authority to provide telephone service. So-called "Internet phone" products promise simultaneous voice and video communications using the Internet.[82] As the boundaries between communications media shift, regulatory structures will continue to change.

Privacy

17-22   To perform properly, various entities — such as banks and hospitals — must gather and preserve records concerning an individual's financial, medical, and personal history. To "target" products and marketing campaigns efficiently, businesses also seek information concerning an individual's preferences and purchasing history, for example.

---

78 Amendments of Part 69 of the Commission's Rules Relating to Enhanced Service Providers, 3 F.C.C.R 2631, at p. 2633 (1988); Stuckey, *Internet and Online Law*, section 9.06[2] at pp. 9–23 (1996).
79 Access Charge Reconsideration Order, 97 F.C.C. 2d 682, at p. 715 (1983). The F.C.C.'s Office of Plans and Policy recently released a working paper entitled "Digital Tornado: The Internet and Telecommunications Policy". The working paper discusses the Internet's implications for the F.C.C. and telecommunications policy, and can be found at http://www.fcc.gov/Bureaus/OPP/working_papers/. See "Web-Sources", 2 *Cyberspace Lawyer* at p. 29 (May 1997).
80 *A.C.L.U. v. Reno*, 929 F Supp. 824, at pp. 834–835 (ED Pa. 1996), juris. noted, *Reno* v. *A.C.L.U.*, 136 LEd.2d 436 (1996).
81 See *In the matter of Advanced Television Systems and Their Impact on the Existing Television Broadcast Service*, 61 Fed. Reg. 43209 (August 21, 1996).
82 Scott, *et al.*, *Scott on Multimedia Law*, at p. 24-3 (1997). A trade group for telecommunications carriers, America's Carriers Telecommunication Association (A.C.T.A.), recently requested that the F.C.C. begin to regulate providers of software or hardware that provide "Internet Phone" services. A.C.T.A. Petition for Declaratory Ruling, R.M. number 8775, filed March 4, 1996; Stuckey, *Internet and Online Law* xviii (1996).

The creation and dissemination of records containing this information may provide significant benefits for an individual; the individual, however, may wish to preserve his or her privacy.[83] This privacy interest in practice may require that:

- Record-keepers disclose their data-gathering practices;
- Individuals are provided an opportunity to review the data that is gathered;
- Individuals are given an opportunity to correct or amend the data; and
- Individuals are given the ability to limit further disclosure of the data.[84]

An individual's interest in privacy can be viewed as the right simply "to be let alone by other people";[85] it may also include the right to engage in public debate anonymously.[86]

Privacy Concerns The Internet raises privacy concerns. The Internet allows   17-23
a user to disseminate information to a potentially vast audience, at extremely low cost. Records concerning an individual's off-line activities — such as his medical or financial history — thus may be "shared" easily with others over the Internet. Recent health care reforms, for example, call for the creation of a "universal patient identifier", which would link all of an individual's medical files nationwide. Although swift, nationwide access to all of an individual's medical files may provide significant benefits, this access also raises significant privacy and proper use concerns.[87]

In addition to facilitating the transmittal of records concerning an individual's off-line activity, Internet technology also allows the gathering and transmittal of potentially substantial information concerning an individual's

---

83 The United States Supreme Court has referenced this privacy interest. See *California Bankers Association* v. *Shultz*, 416 U.S. 21, 85 (1974) (Douglas, J., dissenting): "[i]n a sense a person is defined by the checks he writes. By examining them [one] gets to know his doctors, lawyers, creditors, political allies, social connections, religious affiliation, educational interests, the papers and magazines he reads, and so on ad infinitum [T]he banking transactions of an individual give a fairly accurate account of his religion ideology, opinions, and interests.".

84 Advisory Committee on Automated Personal Data Systems, Records, Computers and the Rights of Citizens, Washington, D.C., Dept. of Health, Education and Welfare (1973); see also Directive 95/46/European Community of the European Parliament and of the Counsel, "On the Protection of Individuals with respect to the Processing of Personal Data and on the Free Movement of Such Data", (October 24, 1995).

85 *Katz* v. *United States*, 389 U.S. 347, at p. 350 (1967).

86 *McIntyre* v. *Ohio Elections Commission*, 115 SCt. 1511, at p. 1516 (1995): the First Amendment protects the right to speak anonymously. Through so-called "anonymous remailers", which remove identifying information off an e-mail message before passing it along, an individual may remain essentially anonymous in on-line e-mail communications. See http://www.anonymizer.com (interposes a "layer" between a user and web sites the user visits).

87 "Panel Urges Increased Health Records Privacy", 2 *Cyberspace Lawyer,* at p. 30 (April 1997).

on-line activities. Certain web site hosts collect information on their visitors' personal interests; the host, for example, may record that a particular user was interested in a "Hawaiian vacation", or in "automobile insurance". To properly collate information concerning the user's interests, a so-called "cookies" file may be created on the user's computer, by the information gatherer, to allow this user to be "tracked" during his or her on-line activities.[88]

Technology that tracks users and gathers information concerning their on-line activities similarly raises privacy concerns. Due to these concerns, the Federal Trade Commission recently held open hearings to discuss and gather information on privacy issues surrounding the Internet.[89] The Administration has issued a draft paper for comment detailing the benefits and costs of retaining the current "hodgepodge" structure of United States privacy law.[90]

17-24   **Legal Protection for Privacy Interests On-line**   United States law does not "gather" privacy law into a single statute; instead, privacy law is a loose collection of laws, regulations, and practices that vary from sector to sector.[91] For example, United States law prohibits the interception and disclosure of electronic communications, and thus protects the privacy of this form of communication.[92] Although it protects on-line communications from interception, United States law does not provide a unified framework regulating the gathering and use of personal information on-line; instead, protections for individual privacy reside in discrete federal and state legislation governing particular industries and practices, or in the Common Law.

The Electronic Communications Privacy Act (E.C.P.A.) affords the primary protection for private on-line communications. The E.C.P.A.'s purpose is to address "the growing problem of unauthorised persons deliberately gaining access to, and sometimes tampering with, electronic or wire communications that are not intended to be available to the public".[93] The E.C.P.A. applies to the government as well as to private businesses and individuals, and prohibits a user from:

- Intercepting or disclosing electronic communications; or

---

88 "Privacy Watch: Is Your Computer Spying on You?", *Consumer Reports*, at p. 6 (May 1997).
89 See www.ftc.gov/bcp/privacy2/.
90 Options for Promoting Privacy on the National Information Infrastructure, Information Infrastructure Policy Committee of the National Information Infrastructure Task Force (April 25, 1997), located at http://www.iitf.nist.gov/ipc/ipc-pub.html; see also Privacy and the NII, NTIA Report to the National Information Infrastructure Task Force (October 23, 1995), located at http://www.ntia.doc.gov/ntiahome/privawhitepaper.html.
91 Options for Promoting Privacy on the National Information Infrastructure, Information Infrastructure Policy Committee of the National Information Infrastructure Task Force, http://www.iitf.nist.gov/ipc/ipc-pub.html.
92 18 U.S.C., sections 2510–2522 and 2701–2711.
93 Sen. Rep. Number 541, 99 Cong., 2d Sess. 1 (1986), reprinted in 1986 U.S.C. *Cong. Admin. News*, at pp. 3589 and 3590 (1989).

- Intentionally accessing, without authority, a facility where electronic communications services are provided.[94]

The E.C.P.A. provides for criminal sanctions including fines or imprison-   **17-25** ment of up to five years for violations.[95] In addition, a person whose e-mail, for example, has been intercepted has the right to recover civil damages, including punitive damages and attorney's fees, against the interceptor.[96]

The E.C.P.A. applies to entities which maintain the systems on which an individual's e-mail are stored — such as Internet Service Providers, operators of Bulletin Board Systems and operators of a business's internal computer network — as well as to hackers and others who gain access to such systems without authority. The E.C.P.A. does not prevent an Internet Service Provider's employee, for example, from intercepting or disclosing electronic communications of others, as long as this conduct occurs in the normal course of employment, and is necessarily incident to the rendition of the service or to the protection of the rights or property of the service provider.[97]

In addition to protecting the privacy of electronic communications — irrespective of the content of those communications — United States law also protects privacy interests in particular areas. For example, the Privacy Act of 1974 generally limits the ability of federal agencies to disclose information concerning an individual without notice;[98] the Fair Credit Reporting Act governs credit-reporting agencies' use and collection of personal information;[99] and the Video Privacy Protection Act generally prevents videotape rental stores disclosing data concerning their customers for marketing use.[100]

Individual states also protect privacy interests. Certain states protect financial information from disclosure, and prohibit financial institutions from disclosing certain information without their customers' consent.[101] Other states provide additional protection against wiretapping,[102] and they emphasise the importance of these privacy interests by protecting them in their constitutions.[103]

---

94 18 U.S.C., sections 2511, 2701 and 2702. The statute's protections extend beyond on-line communications to cover transmissions by voice-mail, facsimile and cordless or cellular phone. 18 U.S.C., sections 2510 and 2511 (1).

95 18 U.S.C., section 2511 (4).

96 18 U.S.C., section 2520.

97 18 U.S.C., section 2511 (2) (a).

98 5 U.S.C., section 552a (requiring that federal agencies collect and use personal information properly that the information is current and accurate and that adequate safeguards prevent misuse).

99 15 U.S.C., sections 1681 *et seq.*

100 18 U.S.C., section 2710.

101 Trubow, ed., *Privacy Law and Practices*, section 3.03.

102 Mass. Gen. Law, c272, section 99.

103 *Hill v. National Collegiate Athletic Ass'n*, 865 P.2 633, at pp. 641–644 (Cal. 1994) (California Constitution).

In addition to relying on federal or state legislation, an individual may also rely on the Common Law to protect his or her privacy on-line. Under the Common Law of torts, which varies between the individual states, a person generally has the right to prevent:

- The dissemination of information that places him or her in a false light;
- The appropriation for commercial purposes of his or her "persona", including name and likeness;
- The disclosure of embarrassing information concerning his or her private life; and
- The intrusion on his or her solitude.[104]

17-26   For the conduct to be actionable, it generally must be "highly offensive to a reasonable person".[105] In sum, statutory and Common Law remedies exist to protect the privacy of on-line activities; these remedies, however, are not unified and instead form a patchwork of protection.

17-27   **Employee E-Mail** The E.C.P.A. allows the monitoring of e-mail where one of the parties to the e-mail consents to the monitoring.[106] To obtain authorisation to monitor their employees' e-mail under this provision, employers often institute written e-mail policies, in which employees acknowledge that the e-mail system belongs to their employer, and in which the employees grant consent to their employer to review e-mail on the system for various business purposes.[107]

An employee's consent need not be express. For example, where an employer notifies his or her employees that their telephone conversations with customers will be monitored as part of a program to improve service, the employees' consent to this practice may be implied from the circumstances.[108] The E.C.P.A. allows monitoring — where an employee consents — as a matter of federal law; the laws of the individual states may be more restrictive.[109] Accordingly, an employer who wishes to monitor e-mail for business reasons cannot rely simply on the E.C.P.A., but must also review the law of the various states in which he or she conducts business.

Irrespective of the employer's potential willingness or desire to monitor its employees' e-mail, United State's employers should strongly consider a

---

104 *Restatement (Second) of Torts*, sections 652A–652E.

105 Prosser, *The Law of Torts*, section 117 (5th edition 1984).

106 18 U.S.C., section 2511(2)(d).

107 This monitoring may be extensive. A recently introduced software product, "LittleBrother", for example, allows an employer to track employees' use of the Internet, identify the web sites visited, and record the time spent at each site. See "LittleBrother Is Watching", 2 *Cyberspace Lawyer*, at p. 23 (May 1997).

108 *Watkins* v. *LM Berry & Co.*, 704 F.2d 577, at p. 579 (11 Cir. 1983).

109 Mass. Gen. Laws, c. 272, section 99 (allowing monitoring of communications only where both parties to the communication consent).

written e-mail policy.[110] Commentators urge greater legal protections for employee e-mail,[111] and employers have been exposed to significant lawsuits because of their employees' inappropriate use of e-mail in the office.[112] Employers, therefore, must be mindful of their employees' on-line privacy interests, as well as their potentially detrimental use of on-line communications.

Export Controls

Transactions over the Internet easily cross country borders, with value flowing **17-28** from one country to another. These transactions implicate the export law of the sender's country and the import law of the recipient's country. The Department of Commerce and in some cases the State Department are responsible for regulating exports from the United States.[113] Software and so-called "technical data" are expressly subject to these regulations.[114] Moreover, the threshold for determining when this material has been "exported" is extremely low. An export may occur, for example, merely when a foreign national visually inspects United States-origin equipment or facilities, or where foreign and United States nationals orally discuss software-related information, either inside or outside the United States.[115]

To properly "export" software, for example, a business must export pursuant either to a general licence, which does not require an agency application, or pursuant to a validated licence, which requires an agency application. The applicable entry on the Commerce Control List indicates whether a general licence is available for the particular commodity, and identifies which general licence is appropriate; if no general licence is available, the business must apply for and obtain a specific, validated licence.[116] Generally, where information has become generally available to the public, through periodicals or books, for example, then the information may be freely exported to most countries.[117]

An individual exporter who fails to comply with export regulations faces considerable exposure, including civil penalties of up to U.S. $100,000 per

110 Pochmann, "Intranets and Employee Policy Issues: Can I Control What My Employees Do Online?", 2 *Electronic Information: Policy & Law Report*, at pp. 589–592 (June 6, 1997).
111 Gantt, "An Affront to Human Dignity: Electronic Mail Monitoring in the Private Sector Workplace", 8 *Harv. J L and Tech*. 345, at p. 402 (1995).
112 *Strauss* v. *Microsoft Corp.*, 1995 U.S. Dist. LEXIS 7433 (SDNY June 1, 1995): "jokes" circulated on Microsoft's e-mail system referring to a "spandex queen", and an "amateur gynaecology club" admitted as evidence in female employee's sexual discrimination suit.
113 50 U.S.C. App., sections 2401–2420; 15 C.F.R., parts 700, *et seq.*; 22 U.S.C., sections 2778, *et seq.*; 22 C.F.R., parts 120, *et seq.*
114 15 C.F.R., section 734.
115 15 C.F.R., section 734.2 (b) (3).
116 15 C.F.R., sections 732, 734 and 736. If in doubt, a business may obtain, from the Bureau of Export Administration (BXA), confirmation that it is exporting pursuant to the proper licence. 15 C.F.R., section 748.3.
117 15 C.F.R., sections 732.2 (b) and 734.7.

transaction, and criminal penalties of up to U.S. $250,000 and 10 years in prison for each violation. A corporation that violates export regulations faces even greater exposure, including criminal penalties of the greater of up to five times the value of the exports, or U.S. $1-million, for each violation.[118] The United States government has obtained criminal convictions of individuals who export software in disregard of export regulations.[119]

One area of export regulation with particular relevance to on-line activities is encryption technology.[120] United States export regulations ban the export of software and hardware that incorporate certain types of encryption technology. This ban is based on the concern that the spread of United States encryption technology abroad will hamper United States intelligence gathering and law enforcement.[121] The Administration's policy with respect to encryption issues is changing.[122] The Department of Commerce was recently given responsibility for enforcing export restrictions on encryption technology,[123] and the Administration's current centrepiece for its policy — a so-called "key recovery" system which would allow government officials to "unlock" encrypted information — is facing technical and policy-based challenges.[124]

The Administration has loosened export controls if the exporter employs a "key recovery" system that will allow the government to decrypt messages under proper conditions.[125] The Administration still, however, does not allow the export of so-called "strong" cryptography.[126] Opponents of the Administration's key recovery system argue that allowing government officials to decode messages, even with a court order, raises fear of "Big Brother" on the Internet.[127] In response to this pressure, members of Congress have submitted three new bills which address encryption and which would each liberalise current export restrictions.[128]

---

118 50 U.S.C. App., sections 2410 (a)–(c).
119 *United States* v. *Hoffman*, 1993 U.S. App. LEXIS 30604 (9 Cir. November 12, 1993).
120 The importance of encryption to secure on-line communications and transactions is discussed below.
121 Executive Order 13026, Administration of Export Controls on Encryption Products (November 15, 1996); IPNII Report, at pp. 194–197 (September 5, 1995).
122 See "Crucial Element of United States Encryption Policy Fraught with Technical Snags", 2 *Electronic Information Policy & Law Report* (BNA) at p. 538 (May 23, 1997).
123 61 F.R. 68572 (December 30, 1996).
124 See "Crucial Element of United States Encryption Policy Fraught with Technical Snags", 2 *Electronic Information Policy & Law Report* (BNA) at pp. 538–539 (May 23, 1997); see also Pacheco & Whitney, "Digital Security", *Washington Post Special Report* located at http://www.washingtonpost.com/wp-srv/tech/analysis/encryption/encrypt.htm#TOP.
125 61 F.R. 68572 (December 30, 1996).
126 "E-Law: Rising Awareness Shown in Three New Encryption Bills", 2 *Cyberspace Lawyer*, at p. 13 (April 1997).
127 Key Recovery Draft Legislation, March 12, 1997, "Electronic Data Security Act", section 302 (A) (2), published at http://www.cdt.org/crypto.
128 The Security and Freedom Through Encryption Act (SAFE), H.R. 695; the Encrypted Communications Privacy Act of 1997, section 376; and the Promotion of Commerce Online in the Digital Era ("Pro-CODE"), section 377.

Certain individuals have challenged these export regulations, claiming that the regulations violate their First Amendment rights, among others. In *Karn* v. *Dept. of State*,[129] the court ruled that a computer disk containing a cryptographic algorithm was properly classified as a "defence article" and controlled for export purposes. The court did not regard as relevant the fact that the same source code had been approved for export in a text format. The court assumed that the First Amendment applied to a source code on a disk, but ruled that export controls were a permissible content-neutral regulation of this form of speech.[130]

In contrast, the court in *Bernstein* v. *Department of State*[131] ruled that the First Amendment may prohibit broad export controls on encryption technology, which prevent experts in encryption from communicating with others concerning this subject.[132] Accordingly, United States law regarding the export of encryption technology is in a state of flux.

On-line Gambling

On-line gambling raises numerous implications. A casino may establish an   **17-29** offshore server, for example. A customer in the United States who accesses this server to gamble, is arguably not "gambling" in the United States, but rather is sending a message which is received and interpreted offshore as an instruction to gamble.[133]

Certain states are seeking to extend the jurisdiction of their criminal laws, especially those prohibiting gambling, to cover web site hosts located in other jurisdictions. The Minnesota legislature, for example, has provided in the state's general criminal jurisdiction statute that a person may be convicted and sentenced under the law of Minnesota if that person "being without the state, intentionally causes a result within the state prohibited by the criminal laws of this state".[134]

Minnesota's Attorney General posted a message to Internet Service Providers and to users, warning them of this provision with respect to Internet gambling. The Attorney General took the position that service providers to gambling web sites, for example, risk exposing themselves to criminal liability as accomplices under Minnesota law, particularly if they "continue to provide services to gambling organisations after notice that the activities of the organisations are illegal".[135]

---

129 925 FSupp. 1 (DDC 1996).
130 *Karn* v. *Dept. of State*, 925 FSupp. 1, at pp. 12 and 14 (DDC 1996).
131 922 FSupp. 1426, at pp. 1438–1439 (ND Cal. 1996).
132 *Bernstein* v. *Department of State*, 945 F Supp. 1279, at pp. 1290 and 1292 (ND Cal. 1996): regulation of encryption software is an unconstitutional prior restraint on speech.
133 See "Growth of Internet-Based Gambling Raises Questions for Bank Systems", 2 *Electronic Information Policy & Law Report*, at p. 260 (February 28, 1997).
134 Minn. Stat., section 609.025 (3).
135 Warning to All Internet Users and Providers, Office of the Minnesota Attorney General, published at http://www.state.mn.us/ebranch/ag/memo.txt.

Minnesota's Attorney General then prosecuted a Nevada Internet Service Provider for hosting a web page — available to Minnesota users — which advertised various gambling operations, and the court ruled that the Attorney General indeed had the power to regulate Internet gambling activities originating on a web site outside the State.[136] As other gambling operations turn to the Internet for business,[137] the strength, and reach of local laws prohibiting gambling — such as Minnesota's — will continue to be tested. Moreover, concerns over "virtual casinos" have caused Congress to begin addressing these issues.[138]

Consumer Protection

17-30   The Federal Trade Commission (F.T.C.), which is charged in part with enforcing federal consumer protection law, has been taking an increasingly visible on-line role. For example, the F.T.C. recently co-ordinated an "Internet Pyramid Surf Day", during which possible Internet pyramid schemes were located, and the responsible web site operators notified of possible enforcement. The F.T.C. provides information for identifying possible pyramid schemes on the Internet at its home page.[139]

In addition, the F.T.C. recently obtained a preliminary injunction against two companies that ran "scam" web sites. These web sites surreptitiously disconnected visitors from their Internet Service Provider and reconnected them to a telephone line in Moldova, in Eastern Europe, dramatically increasing the visitors' phone charges. The Moldovian telephone provider then connected the users to the information they sought, located on a server in Canada. The scam web site operators then split the increased telephone charges with the Moldovian telephone provider.[140]

The F.T.C. has also employed the Internet to obtain additional, low-cost comments from the public. For example, the F.T.C. now permits consumers to comment on proposed corporate mergers by means of the F.T.C.'s web site.[141]

Certain states are taking steps to protect consumers in on-line transactions. California, for example, recently enacted a requirement that companies doing business on-line with California residents disclose their legal names and addresses, and provide notice of their return policies; violations of the law are punishable as criminal misdemeanours.[142]

---

136 *State* v. *Granite Gate Resorts, Inc.*, number C6-95-727 (Minn. State Ct. 1996), available at http://www.leepfrog.com/E-Law/Cases/Minn_v_Granite_Gate.html); "State Gets Wide Latitude to Prosecute Online Services", 1 *Cyberspace Lawyer*, at p. 27 (February 1997).
137 Internet Casinos Inc., for example, plans to become the world's largest casino by operating over the Internet. See http://www.casino.org.
138 Section 474 (the Internet Gambling Prohibition Act of 1997).
139 See http://www.ftc.gov/pyramid/index.html.
140 *Federal Trade Commission* v. *Autiotex Connection Inc.*, DC ENY., CV-97-0726 (February 13, 1997).
141 See http://www.ftc.gov.
142 Cal. Business & Professionals Code, section 17538.

Securities Legislation

Financial industries, including the banking, mutual fund, and securities **17-31** industries, are attracted to the Internet, because it allows them to communicate effectively, and at low cost, with the investing public. The Internet also allows issuers of illiquid securities to maintain a common forum — a "virtual market" — for investors to list interest in buying or selling the issuer's securities. Yet this easy access to the investing public can conflict with current United States securities regulation. For example, United States securities laws require that securities be registered before an issuer use any interstate communication media to offer to sell the securities.[143] This requirement, read broadly, may apply to an issuer in the United Kingdom, *e.g.*, which uses its web site to offer to sell its securities. Even if the United Kingdom issuer plans to sell only to United Kingdom investors, the fact that its web site — offering to sell securities — is open to United States investors, may implicate United States securities laws.[144]

In addition, United States securities laws prohibit a company that is about to offer shares to the public from making public statements to "hype" the stock. An Internet-media company was recently forced to terminate plans for a U.S. $272-million initial public offering, when an optimistic e-mail message, which its chief executive officer had sent to the company's 334 employees, was posted to an on-line service, The Well, which has more than 10,000 subscribers.[145]

The United States Securities and Exchange Commission (S.E.C.) and individual states have recently taken measures to facilitate use of the Internet by financial industries, and to police the Internet for securities fraud.

Regulation by the Securities Exchange Commission The S.E.C. has under- **17-32** taken a number of measures to facilitate use of the Internet. For example, the S.E.C. has:

- Provided interpretative guidance to market participants, such as issuers, mutual funds, and broker-dealers, concerning use of the Internet to provide information to investors, such as prospectuses and shareholder reports;
- Provided guidance to issuers and broker-dealers concerning use of the Internet to operate trading systems for securities;
- Established a system (EDGAR) where issuers and mutual funds submit their S.E.C. filings in electronic format, and where the public can access this information through the Internet; and
- Monitored the Internet for fraudulent securities offerings.

---

143 15 U.S.C., section 77e (c).
144 Gavis, "The Offering and Distribution of Securities in Cyberspace: A Review of Regulatory and Industry Initiatives", 52 *The Business Lawyer* 317, at p. 374 (November 1996).
145 Lohse, "Wired Cancels Plan For IPO Amid Talk Of Leaked E-Mail", *The Wall Street Journal*, October 25, 1996.

17-33   *Delivery Requirements*   The S.E.C. has provided interpretative releases addressing whether use of electronic media, such as the Internet, to deliver documents to investors complies with federal securities laws.[146] Federal securities laws require the delivery of certain information to investors and potential investors.[147] In considering the Internet as a means to deliver this information, the S.E.C. has noted that electronic media may enhance the efficiency of the securities markets, by allowing rapid dissemination of information to investors in a more cost-efficient, widespread and equitable manner than traditional paper-based methods.[148]

The S.E.C. has also noted that Internet technology may strongly benefit small investors, by allowing them to communicate quickly and efficiently with corporate issuers as well as with each other.[149] Finally, the S.E.C. has noted that electronic distribution of information provides "numerous benefits", and has recognised that "the use of this type of medium is growing among all participants in the securities industry".[150]

The S.E.C., therefore, has endorsed use of the Internet to deliver information to investors. Electronic media will accordingly be treated equally with paper-based media. As long as the intended recipient effectively consents to use of the electronic medium, it will satisfy securities laws' delivery requirements if certain conditions are met.[151] Market participants should consider three primary factors with respect to electronic delivery:

- The electronic communication should provide timely and adequate notice to investors that information for them is available, comparable to paper-based communications;
- The electronic delivery should provide access to the information which is comparable to that provided by paper-based delivery; and
- The electronic delivery should afford a means of insuring that the investor actually received the information, such as through an electronic

---

146 Use of Electronic Media for Delivery Purposes, S.E.C. Release number 33-7233, 60 F.R. 53457 (October 13, 1995) (interpretation; solicitation of comments); Use of Electronic Media by Broker-Dealers, Transfer Agents, and Investment Advisors for Delivery of Information, S.E.C. Release No. 33-7288, 61 F.R. 24643 (May 15, 1996) (interpretation; solicitation of comments); Use of Electronic Media for Delivery Purposes, S.E.C. Release number 33-7289, 61 F.R. 24652 (May 15, 1996) (final rule).

147 15 U.S.C., sections 77a *et seq.* (the Securities Act of 1933); 15 U.S.C., sections 78a *et seq.* (the Securities Exchange Act of 1934); 15 U.S.C., sections 80a-1 *et seq.* (the Investment Company Act of 1940).

148 Use of Electronic Media for Delivery Purposes, S.E.C. Release number 33-7233, 60 F.R. 53457 (October 13, 1995).

149 Use of Electronic Media for Delivery Purposes, S.E.C. Release number 33-7233, 60 F.R. 53457 (October 13, 1995).

150 Use of Electronic Media by Broker-Dealers, Transfer Agents, and Investment Advisors for Delivery of Information, S.E.C. Release No. 33-7288, 61 F.R. 24643 (May 15, 1996).

151 Use of Electronic Media for Delivery Purposes, S.E.C. Release number 33-7233, 60 F.R. 53457 (October 13, 1995).

mail return receipt or a confirmation.[152] These same basic rules apply as well to broker-dealers, investment advisors, and transfer agents.[153]

The S.E.C. has also addressed privacy concerns, and has indicated that, with **17-34** respect to information that is specific to a person's "personal financial matters" — such as trade confirmation information and account statements — broker-dealers and investment advisors "should take reasonable precautions to ensure the integrity, confidentiality, and security of that information", and should obtain an informed consent from the investor, with either a manual or an electronic signature.[154]

Internet Trading Systems The S.E.C. has also provided guidance, through **17-35** no-action letters, concerning use of the Internet to operate trading systems for securities. In analysing requests from issuers or brokerage firms who seek to establish such systems, the S.E.C. has required compliance with a rigorous set of conditions to obtain no-action relief.[155] For example, an issuer who wished to establish a "passive" bulletin board trading system on the Internet for its publicly traded stock[156] requested, *inter alia*, that the S.E.C. allow it to operate the electronic trading system without:

- Registering as an "investment advisor" under section 203(a) of the Advisors' Act;
- Registering as a "broker" and/or "dealer" under section 15(a) of the Exchange Act;
- Registering the trading system as a "National Securities Exchange" under section 6 of the Exchange Act; and
- Registering offers and sales made through the trading system under the Securities Act.

The S.E.C. granted no action relief if the issuer met certain conditions, **17-36** including that the issuer:

- Receive no compensation for the creation, maintenance or use of the Internet trading system;
- Not become involved in any purchase or sale negotiations arising from the trading system;

152 Use of Electronic Media for Delivery Purposes, S.E.C. Release No. 33-7233, 60 F.R. 53458, 53460–53461 (October 6, 1995).
153 Use of Electronic Media by Broker-Dealers, Transfer Agents, and Investment Advisors for Delivery of Information, S.E.C. Release No. 33-7288, 61 F.R. 24644, 24646 (May 15, 1996).
154 Use of Electronic Media by Broker-Dealers, Transfer Agents, and Investment Advisors for Delivery of Information, S.E.C. Release No. 33-7288, 61 F.R. 24644, 24647 and n. 23 (May 15, 1996).
155 Gavis, "The Offering and Distribution of Securities in Cyberspace: A Review of Regulatory and Industry Initiatives", 52 *The Business Lawyer* 317, at p. 340 (November 1996).
156 Real Goods Trading Corp., S.E.C. No-Action Letter, 1996 W.L. 422670 (S.E.C.) (June 24, 1996).

- Not provide information regarding the advisability of buying or selling securities; and
- Not receive, transfer, or hold funds or securities as an incident of operating the trading system.[157]

17-37   Of the S.E.C.'s requirements for establishing such a trading system, it appears the most important is the general prohibition on the issuer's or brokerage firm's participating actively in the trading system.[158] In large part because of the S.E.C.'s position, certain companies, in competition with traditional venture capitalists, are now offering to assist issuers in raising capital through Internet initial public offerings.[159]

17-38   *Electronic Data Gathering, Analysis and Retrieval System*   As a further encouragement of electronic communications, the S.E.C. mandates electronic filing through its Electronic Data Gathering, Analysis and Retrieval System (EDGAR) of all filings, correspondence, and supplemental information, with certain exceptions, concerning domestic registrants under the Securities Act, the Exchange Act, the Public Utility Holding Company Act, the Trust Indenture Act, and the Investment Company Act.[160]

Any individual with a modem can obtain from EDGAR access to all of this corporate and financial information. He or she can search the EDGAR database concerning a particular public company, view all of this company's filings on his or her computer screen, and download copies of the materials to disk or to a printer.[161] This significantly increased, low cost access to corporate information through EDGAR and the Internet facilitates informed securities markets.

17-39   *Securities Exchange Commission Enforcement*   The S.E.C. has been monitoring the Internet for violations of securities laws.[162] For example, the S.E.C. recently filed suit alleging that a company and others had used the

---

157 *Real Goods Trading Corp.*, S.E.C. no-action letter, 1996 W.L. 422670 (S.E.C..) (June 24, 1996); see http://www.realgoods.com.

158 *Spring Street Brewing Co.*, S.E.C. No-Action Letter, 1996 S.E.C. No-Act. LEXIS 435 (April 17, 1996); IPONET, S.E.C. No-Action Letter, 1996 S.E.C. No-Act. LEXIS 642 (July 26, 1996). Gavis, "The Offering and Distribution of Securities in Cyberspace: A Review of Regulatory and Industry Initiatives", 52 *The Business Lawyer* 317, at p. 374 (November 1996).

159 "Web-based IPOs a Growing Market", 1 *Cyberspace Lawyer*, at p. 38 (September 1996).

160 Securities Act Release No 7122, 59 F.R. 67752 (December 19, 1994); Regulation S-T, 17 C.F.R., sections 232.101, 232.901 and 232.902.

161 See http://www.sec.gov; see also "S.E.C. Chairman Arthur Levit Details Agency Plans to Make Database Widely Available", S.E.C. Press Release 95-175, 1995 W.L. 505904 (August 27, 1995): "One of the main reasons the S.E.C. was created was to act as a library for corporate information and make it available to investors. Technology is so advanced that the cost to the Commission is quite modest. With a personal computer and modem, you'll be able to have the entire S.E.C. Public Reference Room in your living room".

162 The S.E.C. publishes a series of public bulletins at its web site warning investors of various Internet securities fraud schemes. See, *e.g.*, http://www.sec.gov/consumer/cyberfr.htm.

Internet and the telephone to raise over U.S. $3-million by selling securities to approximately 20,000 investors. The defendants had assured investors they would reap enormous profits from a worldwide telephone lottery, with revenues projected at U.S. $300-million. Accepting the S.E.C.'s argument that the defendants failed to disclose the legal and regulatory obstacles to such a lottery, the court enjoined further selling activity and froze the defendants' assets.[163]

The S.E.C. has also successfully enjoined defendants who, for example, use electronic bulletin boards and the Internet to lure investors with misleading statements,[164] and recently obtained a criminal conviction of the chairman of a video teleconferencing company for manipulating the stock of his company by issuing false, favourable information through Internet stock promoters.[165]

State Regulation State securities regulators are also reviewing state securities laws in light of the Internet. A goal is to prevent general postings by issuers on the Internet from triggering state registration and licensing requirements.[166] State securities laws generally require, for example, that a security be registered in that state, or that an exemption be available, before that security is "offered" for sale in the state. Due to the nature of the Internet, an issuer who posts information to its web site concerning its securities, but who has no intention to sell in North Dakota, for example, might be deemed to be offering securities in North Dakota, simply because the web site information is available to North Dakota residents.[167] **17-40**

The North American Securities Administrators Association (NASAA) recently adopted a model interpretative order regarding the general advertising of securities on the Internet.[168] Under this order, securities industry personnel using the Internet to distribute information on available products and services are not subject to state securities jurisdiction if:

- The communication contains a legend stating that the personnel may only transact business in states in which they are registered or otherwise exempt;

---

163 *S.E.C.* v. *Pleasure Time, Inc.*, Litigation Release number 14,825, 1996 S.E.C. No-Act. LEXIS 510 (SD Ohio, February 26, 1996).
164 *S.E.C.* v. *Frye*, Litigation Release number 14,720, 60 S.E.C. docket (CCH) 1787 (SDNY November 15, 1995); *S.E.C.* v. *Octagon Tech. Group*, Litigation Release number 14,942, 62 S.E.C. Docket (CCH) 380 (DDC, June 11, 1996).
165 "Internet Stock Manipulator Sentenced to 46 Months in Prison", 2 *Cyberspace Lawyer*, at p. 18 (May 1997).
166 "Internet Committee Adopts Order on Web Advertising", *NASAA Reports* (CCH) 211 (May 28, 1997).
167 Order of the Pennsylvania Securities Commission, *In Re: Offers Effected Through Internet That Do Not Result in Sales in Pennsylvania*, 1995 W.L. 574678 (Pa. Section Comm., August 31, 1995).
168 "Internet Committee Adopts Order on Web Advertising", *NASAA Reports* (CCH) 211 (May 28, 1997).

- The communication has a mechanism to insure limited subsequent inter-actions with prospective customers residing in states where the person-nel are not registered;
- The communication is limited to information dissemination, and does not effect securities trades or render personalised investment advice for compensation; and
- The personnel clearly disclose their affiliation.[169]

17-41   The NASAA Resolution also has encouraged member jurisdictions to ex-empt Internet offers from state registration provisions if the Internet offer indicates that the securities are not being offered to residents of the particu-lar jurisdiction and if the offer is not specifically directed to any person in a jurisdiction.[170] A number of states have adopted exemptions for Internet offerings, with this framework.[171]

The National Securities Markets Improvement Act of 1996[172] should also help reduce state jurisdictional obstacles in connection with Internet offerings. Among other effects, this Act prevents states from imposing registration requirements on securities issued by investment companies and securities that are listed on a national exchange.[173] Although restricting the states' ability to require registration, the Act does not preclude states from bringing anti-fraud enforcement actions with respect to offerings.[174]

Taxation of Internet Services and Transactions

17-42   To tax an on-line transaction, a state generally must have a sufficient connec-tion, or "nexus" with the transaction. In the United States, a company is protected from income tax or from a sales or use tax in a state, for example, if its only business activity in the state consists of soliciting orders for the sale of tangible goods, and if it accepts and fills these orders by shipment from outside the state.[175]

In *Quill Corp. v. North Dakota*,[176] for example, North Dakota sought to impose a use tax on an out-of-state vendor which sold office products through mail order and over the telephone in North Dakota. The vendor,

---

169 "Internet Committee Adopts Order on Web Advertising", *NASAA Reports* (CCH) 211 (May 28, 1997).
170 Gavis, "The Offering and Distribution of Securities in Cyberspace: A Review of Regulatory and Industry Initiatives", 52 *The Business Lawyer* 324, at p. 357 (November 1996).
171 State Orders Regulating Internet Securities Offerings, http://www.law.ab.umd.edu/marshall/bluesky/table2.htm (listing states with Internet offering exemption).
172 Pub. L No. 104–290, 110 Stat. 3416 (1996).
173 15 U.S.C., section 77r (b).
174 15 U.S.C., section 77r (c).
175 15 U.S.C., section 381 (1976): income tax; sales of tangible personal property; See *Quill Corp. v. North Dakota*, 504 U.S. 298 (1992) (use tax); see also "Multistate Tax Commission Releases March Draft of Nexus Guidelines", *State Tax Review* (CCH), at pp. 1–2 (April 28, 1997).
176 504 U.S. 298 (1992).

which did not have retail outlets or sales representatives in North Dakota, refused to collect the tax on its sales to North Dakota customers, because the vendor claimed it lacked a sufficient nexus with North Dakota. The Supreme Court agreed, and ruled that a state may not require that an out-of-state vendor collect use tax, unless the vendor has a "physical presence" in the state.[177] Some states take the position that the requirement of an in-state "physical presence" does not apply to income tax jurisdiction, but only to sales and use tax jurisdiction.[178] *In Geoffrey, Inc.*, for example, the court ruled that the state had jurisdiction to impose an income tax on an out-of-state licensor of intangible property — consisting in part of the *Toys R' Us* trade mark — used in the state. The court ruled that the licensor's economic presence, its in-state licensing, its in-state accounts receivable, and its in-state franchise created sufficient nexus.[179]

A sufficient "physical presence" for income, sales, or use tax purposes is commonly established where a company has an office, equipment, employees, or independent contractors within the state seeking to impose the tax.[180] For example, employees who "telecommute" by dialling in to a company network, from the state seeking to impose the tax, may establish a sufficient nexus,[181] and the presence of an in-state web server may also be sufficient.[182]

If a state has jurisdiction to impose a tax, issues then arise as to whether the transaction in question gives rise to the tax. Some states do not impose sales tax on custom-designed software, reasoning that such software is essentially an intangible service.[183] Others treat computer software as tangible personal property, subject to sales and use tax, regardless of the form in which possession is transferred to the user, whether electronically or in the form of a disk or CD.[184] The Commissioner of the Alabama Department of Revenue recently ruled that flat-fee or hourly access charges collected by on-line service providers in Alabama relate to "computer exchange services and are subject to the state's tax on utility gross receipts".[185] State tax authorities

---

177 *Quill Corp. v. North Dakota*, 504 U.S. 298, at pp. 314–319 (1992).
178 *Geoffrey, Inc. v. South Carolina Tax Comm'n*, 437 S.E. 2d 13, *cert. denied*, 114 S Ct. 550 (1993).
179 *Geoffrey, Inc. v. South Carolina Tax Comm'n*, 437 S.E. 2d 13, *cert. denied*, 114 S Ct. 550 (1993).
180 *Tyler Pipe Indus., Inc. v. Washington St. Dep't of Rev.*, 483 U.S. 232 (1987): sufficient nexus where independent contractor present in state; *National Geographic Soc'y v. California Bd. of Equalization*, 430 U.S. 551, 556 (1977): sufficient nexus where two offices in state.
181 *Standard Pressed Steel Co. v. Washington Dep't of Rev.*, 419 U.S. 560 (1975).
182 Smedinghoff (ed.), *Online Law*, at pp. 382–383 (1996).
183 Cal. Rev. and Tax Code section 6010.9; *Maccabees Mut. Life Ins. Co. v. State, Dept. of Treasury, Revenue Div.*, 122 Mich. App. 660, 332 NW.2d 561 (1983); 68 Am. Jur. Sales, section 115 (1993 & 1996 Supp.).
184 Idaho Code section 63-3616 (a) (i): "computer software is deemed to be tangible personal property for purposes of [the sales and use tax] regardless of the method by which title, possession, or right to use the software is transferred to the user"; *Comptroller of Treasury v. Equitable Trust Co.*, 296 Md. 459, at p. 464 A.2d 248 (1983).
185 Revenue Ruling 96-003, Alabama Department of Revenue, November 22, 1996; see Blatt, "Is Internet Access Subject to Sales Tax? Current State Practices Discussed", *State Tax Review* (CCH), at pp. 1–4 (March 10, 1997) (listing various state tax practices).

have noted concerns, for example, that the increasing number of electronic transactions may result in a decrease in revenues that were previously available for state and local governments.[186]

On-line transactions may also raise issues concerning possible customs duties on the importation of electronic goods.[187] The Harmonised Tariff Schedules in the United States provide the rates of duty, country of origin, and treaty information for different goods.[188] Because telecommunications are exempt from the tariff schedules,[189] it may be that software delivered on-line to a United States customer from abroad would not be subject to customs duties; in other situations, however, the method of delivery — electronic or physical — may have no impact on whether customs duties are owed.[190]

Taxing authorities in the United States are evaluating whether new approaches will be required to tax on-line commerce,[191] and are considering whether to restrict states' abilities further to tax aspects of electronic commerce.[192] The Treasury Department, in a recent discussion paper, has taken the position that income from on-line commerce will be taxed in the same way as income from traditional commerce.[193] Under this position, the same taxation rules will apply irrespective of the medium in which the product, such as computer software, is transferred. The Treasury Department further recommends that the federal government take a neutral stance in terms of on-line taxation, and that taxation based on residence is preferable to a new national taxation scheme specifically for the Internet.[194]

Criminal Legislation

17-43   United States law provides criminal sanctions for certain on-line conduct, including intercepting electronic communications, obtaining unauthorised access to computer networks, misappropriating proprietary information, and disseminating obscene materials.

17-44   **Interception and Unauthorised Access** In addition to prohibitions on traditional "white collar" criminal conduct, such as mail and wire fraud, federal

---

186 "Boston Conference Wrestles with Issues Triggered by Emergence of Electronic Commerce", *State Tax Review* (CCH) at p. 1, 8–17 (February 18, 1997).
187 19 C.F.R., section 141.4.
188 19 U.S.C., section 1202.
189 Harmonised Tariff Schedules, General Note 16 (b) (1995).
190 Smedinghoff (ed.), *Online Law,* at p. 389 (1996).
191 H.R. 995 (the "Tax-Free Internet Act of 1997"): providing that fees for Internet services are not subject to tax.
192 S 442, H.R. 1054 (the "Internet Tax Freedom Act"): imposing a moratorium on state and local taxes on the Internet; exempting existing taxes from the moratorium.
193 United States Department of the Treasury Office of Tax Policy, "Selected Tax Policy Implications of Global Electronic Commerce" (November 27, 1996), located at http://www.ustreas.gov/treasury/tax/internet.html.
194 United States Department of the Treasury Office of Tax Policy, "Selected Tax Policy Implications of Global Electronic Commerce" (November 27, 1996), located at http://www.ustreas.gov/treasury/tax/internet.html.

law contains two criminal statutes directed specifically at on-line activities: the Computer Fraud and Abuse Act (C.F.A.A.),[195] and the Electronic Communications Privacy Act (E.C.P.A.).[196] The C.F.A.A. prohibits a user from gaining unauthorised access either:

- To a computer containing classified or restricted government information, such as national defence information;[197]
- To a computer belonging to a financial institution to obtain financial information;[198]
- To a computer belonging to a credit-card issuer or a credit reporting agency to obtain credit card or credit information;[199] or
- To a so-called "protected computer",[200] which is either a computer operated by or on behalf of the United States government or a financial institution, or a computer used in interstate or foreign commerce.[201]

The statute provides civil as well as criminal penalties.[202]

17-45

The C.F.A.A. was used successfully to prosecute an individual who created a computer virus which, by relying on a "hole" in the UNIX programming language, obtained access to other Internet computers without the need for a password or log-in, and "reproduced" itself in successive computers to the extent that the computers became overloaded and shut down.[203] The "virus" accessed and shut down computers at leading universities, medical facilities, and defence facilities.[204]

The intent required to violate the C.F.A.A. is merely the intent to access a covered computer. The user need not have the intent to damage files stored on that computer.[205] In *Sablan*, for example, the defendant, a former bank employee, accessed the bank's computer systems by using a bank key and her former password. In the process, certain bank files were changed and deleted. The defendant argued that the government had to prove that she intended to damage the files, to obtain a conviction under the C.F.A.A. The court disagreed, and held that the government need only prove intent to

---

195 18 U.S.C., section 1030.
196 18 U.S.C., sections 2510–2711.
197 18 U.S.C., section 1030 (a) (1).
198 18 U.S.C., section 1030 (a) (2).
199 18 U.S.C., section 1030 (a) (2).
200 18 U.S.C., section 1030 (a) (4).
201 18 U.S.C., section 1030 (e) (2).
202 18 U.S.C., section 1030 (c), (g).
203 *United States* v. *Morris*, 928 F.2d 504 (2d Cir. 1991), *cert. denied*, 502 U.S. 817 (1991). Hafner and Markoff, *Cyberpunk: Outlaws and Hackers on the Computer Frontier*, at pp. 293–310 (1991).
204 *United States* v. *Morris*, 928 F.2d 504 (2d Cir. 1991), *cert. denied*, 502 U.S. 817 (1991). Hafner and Markoff, *Cyberpunk: Outlaws and Hackers on the Computer Frontier*, at pp. 293–310 (1991).
205 *United States* v. *Sablan*, 92 F.3d 865 (9 Cir. 1996).

access, not intent to damage under the C.F.A.A.[206] The government must also generally show that the defendant obtained something "of value" in addition to gaining unauthorised use.[207]

Federal law under the Electronic Communications Privacy Act (E.C.P.A.) also prohibits a user from intercepting or disclosing electronic communications or intentionally accessing, without authority, a facility where electronic communications services are provided.[208] Other likely "hacking" activities are similarly prohibited. For example, it is a federal crime, under the Credit Card Fraud Act, for a user to key multiple combinations of numbers into a credit-card company's computer to discover a valid account,[209] and a federal crime to traffic in computer passwords if the trafficking affects interstate or foreign commerce or if the password is for a United States government computer.[210] States also have passed legislation creating various computer crimes.[211]

17-46   **Electronic Espionage**   The Economic Espionage Act of 1996 makes it a federal crime to misappropriate the trade secrets of another, or to purchase or possess trade secrets with the knowledge that the trade secrets were misappropriated from another.[212] The term "trade secret" is defined broadly to include "all forms and types of financial, business, scientific, technical, economic, or engineering information, whether tangible or intangible, and whether or how stored, compiled or memorialised physically, electronically, graphically, photographically or in writing".[213] In addition, to qualify as a trade secret, the public must not generally know the information, and the owner must have taken reasonable measures to keep the information secret.[214]

The Act is broad enough to cover misappropriation of information by those accessing computers through the Internet,[215] and applies even if the misappropriation takes place from outside the United States.[216] Criminal penalties include fines against organisations of up to U.S. $5-million; the fine is increased up to U.S. $10-million if the misappropriation was intended to benefit a foreign government.[217] Penalties also include imprisonment for up to 10 years, and up to 15 years if the misappropriation was intended to benefit a foreign government.[218]

206 *United States* v. *Sablan*, 92 F.3d 865, at pp. 867–869 (9 Cir. 1996).
207 *United States* v. *Czubinski*, CA 1, number 96-1317 (2/21/1997).
208 18 U.S.C., sections 2511, 2701, 2702. The E.C.P.A. is discussed more fully above.
209 *United States* v. *Taylor*, 945 F.2d 1050, at p. 1051 (8 Cir. 1991): defendant convicted for obtaining access to American Express' computer system by this means; see 18 U.S.C., section 1029 (a) (2).
210 18 U.S.C., section 1030 (a) (6).
211 Mass. Gen. Laws c. 266, sections 30 and 33A.
212 18 U.S.C., sections 1831–1839.
213 18 U.S.C., section 1839 (3).
214 18 U.S.C., section 1839 (3).
215 18 U.S.C., section 1839 (3).
216 18 U.S.C., section 1837.
217 18 U.S.C., sections 1831 and 1832.
218 18 U.S.C., sections 1831 and 1832.

Pornography Federal law prohibits the dissemination of obscene materials **17-47**
and child pornography.[219] The First Amendment does not protect obscenity
and child pornography.[220] Because these forms of speech have little social
value, the minimal benefits they provide are outweighed by society's
interest in order and morality.[221] A work is "obscene", and thus without
First Amendment protection, if the "average person, applying contemporary
community standards" would find that the work, taken as a whole, appeals
to "the prurient interest"; if the work depicts or describes, in a "patently
offensive" way, sexual conduct that is specifically defined by the applicable
law; and if the work, taken as a whole, "lacks serious literary, artistic, political
or scientific value".[222]

Materials that do not rise to the level of "obscenity" are considered
merely "indecent"; the dissemination of indecent speech may be regulated,
but not completely banned.[223] Indecent materials are typically regulated by
prohibiting their distribution to minors,[224] although federal law, under the
Communications Decency Act of 1996, provides criminal sanctions for
using the Internet to disseminate indecent materials, or allowing a computer
network to be used to disseminate indecent materials, to a person under age
18,[225] these provisions have been enjoined by the courts as unconstitutional.[226] State statutes also prohibit distribution of harmful materials and
advertisements to minors through a computer or computer network.[227] In
enjoining the "indecency" provisions of the Communications Decency Act,
the *A.C.L.U.* v. *Reno* court reasoned that content providers on the Internet,
for technical reasons, are unable effectively to determine the identity and age
of users accessing their material. Accordingly, the court noted, the possibility
of criminal prosecution for communications to minors would "chill" speech
generally on the Internet, and effectively restrict constitutionally protected
speech targeted at adults.[228]

---

219 47 U.S.C., section 223 (a) (obscene telephone calls); 18 U.S.C., section 1464 (obscene radio
broadcasts); section 1465: transporting obscene materials; 18 U.S.C., sections 2251–2252:
child pornography.
220 *New York* v. *Ferber*, 458 U.S. 747, at p. 764 (1982).
221 *Sable Communications of California, Inc.* v. *F.C.C.* , 492 U.S. 115, at p. 126 (1989).
222 *Miller* v. *California*, 413 U.S. 15, at p. 24 (1973).
223 *Butler* v. *Michigan*, 352 U.S. 380, at p. 383 (1957); *Sable Communications of California,
Inc.* v. *F.C.C.* , 492 U.S. 115, at p. 126 (1989).
224 Ginsberg v. *NY*, 390 U.S. 629, at p. 636 (1968).
225 47 U.S.C., sections 223(a)(1)(B), 223(a)(2), 223(d)(1), 223(d)(2).
226 *A.C.L.U.* v. *Reno*, 929 F Supp. 824 (ED Pa. 1996), juris. noted, *Reno* v. *A.C.L.U.*, 136
LEd.2d 436 (1996); *Sheaex rel. American Reporter* v. *Reno*, 930 F Supp. 916 (1996).
227 Ga. Code Ann., Sections 12-16-100 et. seq.
228 929 F Supp. 824, at pp. 849 and 855 (ED Pa. 1996), juris. noted, *Reno* v. *A.C.L.U.*, 136
LEd.2d 436 (1996).

With respect to telecommunications transmissions, the F.C.C. provides a defence for providers that implement certain procedures, such as:

- Requiring credit card payment before transmission of the indecent message;
- Requiring an authorised access or identification code before transmission of the message; or
- Scrambling a message so that it is incomprehensible to callers without a descrambling device.[229]

17-48   Digital technology allows a user to "morph" images and exchange, for example, the image of a child's head for an adult head. A publisher thus may produce "child pornography" using the bodies of young-looking adults digitally "attached" to the faces of children.[230] States have reacted to this possibility, by prohibiting child pornography produced through composite images.[231]

17-49   **Hate Literature**   The First Amendment generally protects the dissemination of "hate" literature, unless the literature creates a clear and present danger of imminent lawless action.[232] In addition, there must be evidence of an intent to produce, and a likelihood of producing, imminent disorder, to overcome First Amendment protections.[233]

The First Amendment, however, reaches only government, and not private action. Accordingly, certain Internet Service Providers have self-regulated "hate" literature, and have refused to host anti-gay web sites, for example.[234]

On-line Advertising

17-50   As a form of speech, advertising is entitled to First Amendment protection; this protection, however, is greatly reduced due to the commercial nature of advertising.[235] Accordingly, a wide array of federal statutes and regulations govern both the content of and the permissible channels for advertising in the United States, including the Lanham Act,[236] the Federal Trade Commission Act[237] and the Federal Food, Drug and Cosmetics Act.[238]

---

229 47 C.F.R., section 64.201.
230 *New York* v. *Ferber*, 458 U.S. 747, at p. 763 (1982): using young-looking adults to portray children may be permissible; see also 18 U.S.C., sections 2251 *et seq.*
231 Ariz. Rev. Stat. Ann., section 13-3554 (1995): depicting adults as minors; Va. Code Ann., section 18.2-374.3 (1995).
232 *Shenck* v. *United States*, 249 U.S. 47, at p. 52 (1919).
233 *Hess* v. *Indiana*, 414 U.S. 105, at p. 109 (1973).
234 "Site with Anti-Gay Domain Name Unplugged (Again)", 2 *Cyberspace Lawyer*, at pp. 34–35 (May 1996).
235 *Virginia State Bd. of Pharmacy* v. *Virginia Citizens Consumer Council, Inc.*, 425 U.S. 748, at p. 770 (1976); *Bates* v. *State Bar of Arizona*, 433 U.S. 350, at p. 381 (1977).
236 15 U.S.C., section 1125 (a).
237 15 U.S.C., sections 45 *et seq.*; 16 C.F.R., section 1-901.
238 21 U.S.C., sections 301 *et seq.* 21 C.F.R., section 1-299.

The Federal Trade Commission Act, for example, makes it unlawful to "disseminate, or cause to be disseminated, any false advertisement in commerce by any means".[239] States have similar legislation that proscribes false advertising.[240] Under federal false advertising law, Virgin Atlantic Airways was recently assessed a civil fine for advertising on the Internet a fare that was no longer available; the airline had neglected to update its Web page after the particular fare had expired.[241]

SECURITY

Information security is a fundamental concern in electronic commerce.   **17-51**

Need for On-line Security

Businesses increasingly depend on networks to expedite communications   **17-52**
and transactions among their own employees, and with customers and suppliers. To enjoy these advantages, a business must interconnect its computers — to its own private network, to private networks of other companies, and to the Internet. Insuring proper security is crucial to such a business.

Interconnected computers are vulnerable to break-ins. In the on-line world, an unscrupulous business need not physically "pick the lock" of its competitor's safe to access trade secrets; instead, the wrongdoer may access these secrets electronically — with no physical "break-in" — if the competitor's on-line security procedures are lax. Of course, a wrongdoer, instead of seeking proprietary company information, could simply want cash. In 1994, for example, a group of Russian hackers accessed Citibank's computer network, and effected illegal transfers of U.S. $10-million.[242]

To compound the concern, a company whose computer network has been broken into often will not know where the "hackers" went, or whether they copied and misappropriated data. In addition, the hackers may use that company's network as a "springboard" from which to break into other connected networks, causing additional damage and potentially exposing the original company to liability to the networks damaged "downstream" by its lax security system.[243]

---

239 15 U.S.C., section 52.
240 Mass. Gen. Laws, c. 93A, section 2.
241 "Virgin Atlantic Internet Penalty", *New York Times* (November 21, 1995).
242 Behar, "Who's Reading Your E-Mail?" *Fortune* 57, 64 (February 3, 1997). A list of risks for electronic banking generally can be found in FDIC, Division of Supervision, "Electronic Banking: Safety and Soundness Procedures", located at http://www.fdic.gov/publish/elecbank.pdf.
243 Behar, "Who's Reading Your E-Mail?" *Fortune* 57, at pp. 58–61 (February 3, 1997).

Apart from concerns over the security of information stored on its own network, a business may also be concerned over the security of information it transmits, or receives over the Internet. The Internet is a decentralised, open "network of networks", which no single organisation can control or monitor.[244] E-mail transmitted over the Internet, for example, is usually routed to numerous intermediate servers before reaching its intended recipient, and could perhaps be viewed or intercepted at each of these servers.[245]

In addition, hackers using so-called "sniffer" technology may attempt to intercept passwords transmitted by visitors to a particular server, and then later seek to use those passwords to obtain unauthorised access.[246] A hacker, moreover, may penetrate a company's web site, if it is not properly secured, and replace corporate information with material of his or her own choosing for all visitors to view.[247] Insuring the security of information in the on-line environment, therefore, is a central concern.

Legal Solutions to Security Issues

17-53   United States law provides criminal sanctions for all of the conduct described above. The hackers, for example, would potentially be subject to federal criminal prosecution for illegally using passwords,[248] for unlawful interception of electronic communications,[249] for destructive activity in connection with computers[250] and for computer espionage.[251] United States law, therefore, provides significant deterrence to conduct which threatens on-line security.

Technical Solutions to Security Issues

17-54   Businesses and individuals also have available a number of technical solutions to on-line security issues.

System Access Controls: Passwords and Firewalls

17-55   Passwords are designed to insure that only authorised users have access to a network; the network associates the network name of a particular user with a particular secret password; if the name provided by a user and the

---

244 A.C.L.U. v. Reno, 929 F Supp. 824, at pp. 830, 832 and 838 (ED Pa. 1996).
245 A.C.L.U. v. Reno, 929 F Supp. 824, at p. 834 (ED Pa. 1996).
246 Allison, The Lawyer's Guide to the Internet, at p. 132 (1995); Behar, "Who's Reading Your E-Mail?", Fortune 57, at p. 66 (February 3, 1997).
247 For example, hackers recently replaced the home page of the National Collegiate Athletic Association with racial slurs and materials stating "Badminton Rules!" and "Stop commercialisation of the Internet". See "Racial Slurs Replace Sports Site", 2 Cyberspace Lawyer, at p. 33 (April 1997).
248 18 U.S.C., section 1029.
249 18 U.S.C., section 2511.
250 18 U.S.C., section 1030.
251 These criminal sanctions are discussed in greater detail above.

secret password do not match, the network denies the user access. Companies should insure that their network users select sufficiently complex passwords, and that they do not disclose these passwords to others. Hackers can simply guess common passwords, such as "guest"; use software that is freely available over the Internet — such as "Crack" — to decode simple passwords; and employ so-called "social engineering skills" to trick employees into revealing passwords by posing, for example, as outside vendors.[252] Certain companies are developing so-called "biometric" devices to verify a user's identity — and grant access to a computer network — not through passwords but through unique personal characteristics of the user.[253]

In addition to insuring good password procedures, companies interested in maintaining an Internet presence also set up so-called "firewalls". With a firewall, a company configures its internal network so that only one computer, the "gateway", connects to the external network — such as the Internet — and this gateway strictly controls the link between the internal network, which contains the company's information, and the external network, which may harbour potential intruders.[254]

It may be necessary for a company to control system access to enjoy the protections, for example, of the Economic Espionage Act of 1996. In order successfully to prosecute a wrongdoer under this statute, it must be demonstrated that the wrongdoer's target took reasonable measures to maintain secrecy, which measures, in the on-line environment, would certainly include the use of secure passwords and firewalls.[255]

Authenticity and Confidentiality Controls: Encryption and Digital Signatures

To further insure the security and authenticity of electronic information, businesses can employ encryption technology, digital signatures, or both. Encryption technology employs mathematical principles to allow a user to "scramble" an electronic message, such as a word-processing document; in scrambled form the message is indecipherable, and cannot be manipulated in the way it could when it was simply a word-processing document. It is only a reader with the proper "key" who can decode the scrambled message, transform it back into the word-processing document, and view or change its contents. The requirement that a "key" be transferred to the intended reader causes problems,

17-56

252 Behar, "Who's Reading Your E-Mail?", *Fortune* 57, at p. 66 (February 3, 1997); Hafner and Markoff, *Cyberpunk: Outlaws and Hackers on the Computer Frontier*, at pp. 60–61, 151–152 and 300–301 (1991).
253 McGarvey, "Keeping Networks Safe Gets a Personal Touch", *Inter@ctive Week*, at p. 41 (June 2, 1997). Biometric devices that control access to computer networks include fingertip readers, palm readers, eye (iris and retina) scanners, voice-response systems, signature readers, and face-recognition systems.
254 IPNII Report, at pp. 183–185 (September 5, 1995); Allison, *The Lawyer's Guide to the Internet*, at pp. 133–134 (1995).
255 18 U.S.C., section 1839 (3).

however, because during or after its transfer, the key may be disclosed or intercepted, allowing unauthorised readers access to the message.[256]

A popular form of encryption used for secure electronic communication, which avoids the need to transfer a "key" to authorised readers, is so-called "public key" encryption. A user has a pair of keys: a "public key", which is made publicly available; and a private key, which the user keeps secret. The two keys are related in that a message encrypted with the user's public key can only be decrypted with the user's private key, and *vice versa*.

Accordingly, if A wishes to send B a secure electronic message, A would use B's openly available public key to encrypt the message. Because B is the only holder of the private key that can decrypt messages encrypted with B's public key, A is assured that only B will have access to the contents of the message. On receipt of A's message, B is also assured that the message has not been modified or changed since A encrypted the message with B's public key.[257] Commentators note that robust electronic commerce relies on constant improvement in advanced encryption technology.[258]

Businesses may also employ digital signatures. Like a manual signature, a digital signature is designed to prove a message's authenticity — that the message did in fact originate from "Josephine Smith". Unlike a manual signature, however, a digital signature also provides assurances as to the integrity of the message. If A wishes to digitally sign a message, A first runs the message through standard software to create a unique, so-called "message digest"; no two messages should have the same message digest. A encrypts the message digest using A's private key to obtain the desired "digital signature", and then attaches this digital signature to the message to B.[259]

When B receives the message, B uses A's public key to decrypt the digital signature. B is assured that A sent the message, because A's public key will decrypt only those messages that have been encrypted with A's private key. B can also generate B's own "message digest" for the message using standard software; if B's message digest matches the message digest A forwarded as

---

256 IPNII Report, at pp. 185–187 (September 5, 1995).
257 Information Security Committee, Electronic Commerce and Information Technology Division, section of Science and Technology, American Bar Association, Digital Signature Guidelines (Draft October 5, 1995); IPNII Report, at pp. 185–187 (September 5, 1995).
258 Roger, "Experts: Crypto Export Bills Vague", *Inter@ctive Week,* at p. 33 (June 9, 1997); ABA Electronic Messaging Services Task Force, The Commercial Use of Electronic Data Interchange — A Report and Model Trading Agreement, 45 *Business Lawyer* 1645, at p. 1729, Comment 1 (June, 1990): "adequate security procedures are recognised by general industry practice as critical to the efficacy of electronic communication and [the reliability of] resulting business records".
259 A description of digital signature software can be found at http://www.verisign.com. A need not encrypt the text of the message, and can sign an unencrypted message with a digital signature.

the basis for the digital signature, B is assured, in addition, that the message has not been altered since A digitally signed it.[260]

To provide and obtain assurance that the public key listed openly as "A's public key" really is A's public key, and therefore that digital signatures which can be decrypted using this public key really are A's digital signatures, parties can employ so-called "certification authorities". A certification authority is responsible for ascertaining, and certifying that a particular public key, of a public-private key pair, belongs to a particular individual or business.[261]

Digital signatures are beginning to be used more frequently in mass-market transactions. Certain software companies, for example, are using digital signatures to assure that applications users download over the Internet are authentic and have not been tampered with.[262] Indeed, the National Conference of Commissioners on Uniform State Laws (N.C.C.U.S.L) recently met to discuss a uniform law regarding digital signatures.[263]

Record-Keeping

As part of its security measures for electronic information, a business will 17-57 also generally implement record-keeping and backup procedures for electronic records.

Just as with traditional records, electronic records serve ongoing business needs, as well as tax, regulatory, contractual and evidentiary purposes.[264] Electronic records, therefore, should be subject to similar retention periods, and appropriate procedures.

Use of Outside Vendors

Given the potential complexities involved in insuring on-line security, some 17-58 businesses committed to transacting business electronically through a web site are "outsourcing" these tasks to large vendors.[265] IBM, for example, hosts a web site for companies in the petroleum industry.

---

260 Information Security Committee, Electronic Commerce and Information Technology Division, section of Science and Technology, American Bar Association, Digital Signature Guidelines, section 1.12. Draft October 5, 1995; IPNII Report, at pp. 187–188 (September 5, 1995).

261 Utah Code Ann., sections 46-3-301 to 46-3-310; Information Security Committee, Electronic Commerce and Information Technology Division, section of Science and Technology, American Bar Association, Digital Signature Guidelines section 1.5 (Draft October 5, 1995). The United States Postal Service will offer services to facilitate electronic commerce, including acting as a certification authority. See http://www.usps.gov.

262 "Microsoft, Netscape Squabble over New Security Measure", Inter@ctive Week, at p. 5 (June 9, 1997) (to prevent users from downloading wayward Java applets, a digital signature verifies the source of the applet and its integrity).

263 Draft Uniform Electronic Communication in Contractual Transactions Act, http://www.law.upenn.edu/library/ulc/uecicta/ecomm.htm.

264 Armstrong v. Executive Office of the President, 810 F Supp. 335 (DDC), aff'd in part, rev'd and remanded in part, 1 F.3d 1274 (DC Cir. 1993). See generally Smedinghoff (ed.), Online Law, at p. 67 (1996).

265 Barrett, "Super-Hosting for Super Bucks", Inter@ctive Week, at p. 43 (June 2, 1997).

Companies that provide petroleum-related information, such as seismic maps, reach their customers through IBM's web site, with IBM insuring that transactions between the content providers and their customers are secure.[266]

ELECTRONIC TRANSACTIONS

17-59   Electronic commerce offers companies the potential for significantly increased efficiencies. By contracting on-line, a company can reduce paper transaction costs and redirect staff.[267] Moreover, a company with an on-line presence can offer more than simply products for sale on its web site; it can offer technical assistance to users, tools for tracking customers' orders, and general reference and marketing materials.[268]

The concerns of a party wishing to engage in electronic transactions include insuring that its on-line contract is enforceable and insuring that on-line payment mechanisms are trustworthy.

Creating Enforceable On-line Contracts

17-60   Electronic transactions can be divided between those that take place pursuant to a negotiated master trading partner agreement — which are business-to-business transactions — and those that do not, which are predominantly consumer transactions.[269]

Before discussing these two areas of electronic contracting, however, it is helpful to discuss briefly the ways in which electronic contracting is constrained by the concepts of traditional contract law.

266 Jones, "IBM Goes to the Net with Broad Service Plan", *Inter@ctive Week*, at p. 40 (June 9, 1997).
267 Jones, "Cisco Buys Ariba Purchasing System", *Inter@ctive Week*, at p. 53 (June 2, 1997): Cisco Systems Inc. (Cisco) purchases U.S. $450-million annually in general office and industrial supplies; Cisco is automating these purchases through electronic commerce technology to reduce the average paper transaction costs, and realise savings.
268 Haar, "Dell Tailors Web for Business", *Inter@ctive Week*, at p. 19 (June 9, 1997). Dell Computer Corp. ("Dell"), for example, provides on its web site (http://www.dell.com) 35,000 pages of technical assistance information to users, and order tracking information. After selling its personal computers to the general public on-line for approximately a year, Dell is now launching custom password-protected web sites for major customers, featuring products pre-selected by the customer, to be purchased by employees at volume discount prices. Dell reports on-line sales of U.S. $1-million daily.
269 Consumer transactions over the Internet in 1996 totaled only between U.S. $500- to U.S. $600-million, and only approximately 15 per cent of World Wide Web users report making purchases on-line. However, major on-line players, such as IBM, Microsoft, Netscape Communications Corp., and Oracle, all struggle to lead this market, anticipating explosive growth. See Vernadakis, "Window Shopping on the Web", *Inter@ctive Week*, at p. 42 (June 9, 1997); Jones, "IBM Goes to the Net with Broad Service Plan", *Inter@ctive Week*, at p. 41 (June 9, 1997).

Traditional Contract Law: Requirement of a Signed Writing

Traditional contract law in the United States — which is based on signed   **17-61**
writings — presents challenges for electronic contracting, where traditional
"writings" do not change hands between the parties. The traditional requirement of a signed writing appears in the so-called Statute of Frauds, a version of
which most states have adopted.[270] The Statute of Frauds is designed to protect
parties from fraud and deceit in contractual relationships.[271] On-line transactions
perhaps present a greater risk of fraud and deceit than traditional paper-based
transactions, given the ease with which a wrongdoer can create or alter a
purported contract which is in digital form. Accordingly, the purpose of the
Statute of Frauds — the prevention of fraud and deceit in contractual dealings —
applies as strongly in the on-line world as in the traditional paper-based world.

To achieve the purpose of the Statute of Frauds in paper-based transactions,
a court generally will refuse to enforce certain contracts unless a writing,
signed by the party to be held to the contract evidences them.[272] Among these
types of unenforceable contracts are those for the sale of goods valued at over
U.S. $500.[273] Consequently, any on-line transaction involving goods valued
at more than U.S. $500 implicates the Statute of Frauds, and its requirement
for a signed writing.

Transactions Pursuant to Trading Partner Agreements: Electronic Data Interchange

One method to insure that a court will enforce electronic contracts — despite   **17-62**
the absence of traditional, signed writings — is for the parties to enter into
an offline, signed contract, typically called a "trading partner agreement",
that establishes the conditions for enforceable, subsequent on-line contracts
and the exchange of data.[274] These types of transactions are referred to as
Electronic Data Interchange (EDI).

---

270 These state Statutes of Fraud may be immaterial in international transactions. Under the
   United Nations Convention on Contracts for the International Sale of Goods (C.I.S.G.), no
   writing or signature is required in international sales of goods. C.I.S.G., article 11. The
   C.I.S.G. governs where the seller and buyer are located in different countries; both countries
   are parties to the C.I.S.G.; the contract calls for the sale of goods; and the parties have not
   expressly agreed to exclude the provisions of the C.I.S.G. (C.I.S.G., article 6).
271 Calamari and Perillo, *The Law of Contracts*, section 19-1 (3rd edition, 1987).
272 Restatement (Second) of Contracts section 110.
273 U.C.C., section 2-201 (1); see also section 1-206 (1): "[a] contract for the sale of property
   is not enforceable by way of action or defense beyond U.S. $5,000 in amount or value of
   remedy unless there is some writing which indicates that a contract for sale has been made
   between the parties at a defined or stated price, reasonably identifies the subject matter, and
   is signed by the party against whom enforcement is sought or by his authorized agent".
274 ABA Electronic Messaging Services Task Force, The Commercial Use of Electronic Data
   Interchange — A Report and Model Trading Agreement, 45 *Business Lawyer* 1645, at p.
   1722, Comment 3 (June, 1990): "the execution and delivery of [a trading partner
   agreement] and the performance of [subsequent electronic transactions], together with the
   conduct of the parties in accordance with its terms, should be considered sufficient to show
   the existence of contracts for the sale of goods".

With EDI technology and legal arrangements, parties can structure their relationship so that their computer networks will "talk" directly to each other, exchange information, and create enforceable contracts, all with minimal human intervention. Businesses typically use EDI transactions to exchange purchase orders, invoices, and other pre-negotiated, standard forms. EDI techniques can significantly reduce costs and streamline operations.[275]

To insure that a court fully enforces their subsequent EDI transactions, parties will memorialise their intentions expressly; pursuant to model trading partner agreements, for example, the parties' express purpose is "to facilitate purchase and sale transactions by electronically transmitting and receiving data in agreed formats in substitution for conventional paper-based documents and to assure that such transactions are not legally invalid or unenforceable as a result of the use of available electronic technologies".[276]

To satisfy the "signature" requirement of the Statute of Frauds, parties to a trading partner agreement may settle on a particular "electronic identification", consisting of symbols or code. The parties agree that the presence of party A's proper "electronic identification" — its adopted signature — on an electronic document verifies that the document originated from party A. Given the weight attached to these adopted signatures, parties generally agree to restrict access to the signatures.[277]

Businesses interested in EDI transactions can assign the various responsibilities associated with these transactions to a third party, who will provide these services for a fee.[278] In sum, through trading partner agreements, businesses can create enforceable electronic contracts.

Contracting On-line Absent a Trading Partner Agreement

17-63   In a trading partner agreement, parties define in advance — through traditional, offline negotiation processes — the precise on-line conduct to which they wish to be contractually bound. In the absence of a trading partner agreement, parties must rely on other means to create enforceable on-line

---

275 EDI transactions typically take place between parties over direct telephone links, based on agreed-on data formats and protocols, and do not take place over the Internet, using its protocols. However, commentators, referring to EDI as the "big daddy" of electronic commerce generally, note that businesses are exploring ways of conducting EDI transactions on the Internet. Vernadakis, "Window Shopping on the Web", *Inter@ctive Week,* at p. 42 (June 9, 1997).

276 ABA Electronic Messaging Services Task Force, Model Electronic Data Interchange Trading Partner Agreement, 45 *Business Lawyer* 1717, at p. 1721 (June, 1990).

277 ABA Electronic Messaging Services Task Force, Model Electronic Data Interchange Trading Partner Agreement, 45 *Business Lawyer* 1717, at p. 1731, sections 1.5, 3.3 (June, 1990): "[t]he parties agree not to contest the validity or enforceability of Signed Documents under the provisions of any applicable law relating to whether certain agreements are to be in writing or signed by the party to be bound thereby".

278 ABA Electronic Messaging Services Task Force, Model Electronic Data Interchange Trading Partner Agreement, 45 *Business Lawyer* 1717, at pp. 1726–1728, sections 1.2 (June, 1990); see also *Inter@ctive Week,* at p. 33 (June 2, 1997): healthcare organisation to use a third party's EDI service to improve the exchange of electronic business documents between trading partners in the organisation's industry.

contracts. Parties are presented with three issues generally: formation of a contract, attribution, and enforcement.

Traditional contract law will be sufficiently broad under many circumstances to provide a basis for an enforceable on-line contract, particularly where the parties' offline conduct recognises the existence of such a contract. Under traditional state contract law governing the sale of goods, contract formation can occur by any manner sufficient to show agreement between the parties, whether this agreement is through an offer and an acceptance, or through conduct that recognises the existence of a contract.[279] Indeed, a party may accept an offer "in any manner and by any medium reasonable in the circumstances".[280] Traditional contract law also supplies terms the parties may not have expressly addressed, including:

- Terms implied by the parties' conduct;[281]
- Terms implied by the customs and practices of the industry;[282] and
- Terms implied by law, such as certain warranties.[283]

Finally, traditional contract law recognises that a formal handwritten signature is not necessarily needed to satisfy the "signed writing" requirement of the Statute of Frauds, and provides that a "signature" can be "any symbol executed or adopted by a party with present intention to authenticate a writing".[284] Therefore, parties may rely on traditional contract law to create enforceable on-line contracts, under certain circumstances.   17-64

Traditional contract law, however, is not well tailored to the on-line environment. Accordingly, there are a number of legislative initiatives in the United States designed to adapt current contract law to the on-line environment. For example, the National Conference of Commissioners on Uniform State Laws is currently drafting a uniform statute, Uniform Commercial Code, article 2B, for enactment by individual states that will govern licensing and on-line transactions in software and other materials in digital form, such as information from on-line databases.[285] Draft article 2B treats electronic records as the equivalent of traditional paper records, and allows parties to use a "digital identifier" to authenticate documents, in substitution

---

279 1 Uniform Laws Annotated, U.C.C., section 2-204 (1989).
280 1 Uniform Laws Annotated, U.C.C., section 2-206 (1) (a) (1989).
281 1 Uniform Laws Annotated, U.C.C., sections 1-205, 2-208 (1989).
282 1 Uniform Laws Annotated, U.C.C., section 1-205 (1989).
283 1A Uniform Laws Annotated, U.C.C., sections 2-314: implied warranty of merchantability; section 2-315: implied warranty of fitness for a particular purpose (1989).
284 1 Uniform Laws Annotated, U.C.C., section 1-201 (39) (1989).
285 National Conference of Commissioners on Uniform State Laws, Uniform Commercial Code, article 2B, Licenses (Draft March 21, 1997). Concerns have been raised as to whether the Draft is sufficiently fair to consumers. See "U.C.C. 2B: The Longer It Goes, the More Complicated It Gets", *Information Law Alert*, at p. 4 (January 24, 1997). The draft article can be located at http://www.law.upenn.edu/library/ulc/ucc2/ ucc2b397.htm.

for a traditional signature.[286] The Draft also provides that, if parties agree to a commercially reasonable method of attributing a document to a party, compliance with that methodology conclusively constitutes a signature.[287]

Other initiatives also address the use of digital signatures. The Utah Digital Signature Act, for example, provides that parties may satisfy the requirement of a "signed writing" through use of a digital signature, and creates a legal presumption that digitally signed documents are authentic and unaltered.[288] Many states are pursuing legislation to facilitate electronic commerce, such as the enactment of digital signature laws similar to Utah's law.[289] Indeed, the number of these initiatives has caused federal lawmakers to consider a uniform federal law to preempt these varying state laws.[290] In sum, contract law in the United States is adapting to the on-line environment.

Shrink-Wrap Licences

17-65   So-called "shrink-wrap licences" are one paper-based method parties in the computer industry employ for controlling use of their products and for establishing for the terms of their relationships with customers. The term "shrink-wrap" licence comes from the fact that these licenses traditionally were printed on software packaging under a shrink-wrap, and state that once the buyer opened the packaging, he or she became bound by the licensee's terms. Although United States courts initially did not favour these types of contracts, and held that such contracts are unenforceable,[291] the Seventh Circuit Court of Appeals has recently held that shrink-wrap licences are enforceable.[292]

---

286 National Conference of Commissioners on Uniform State Laws, Uniform Commercial Code, article 2B, Licenses, sections 2B-102 (30): definition of "record"; 2B-102(1): definition of "authenticate" (Draft March 21, 1997).

287 National Conference of Commissioners on Uniform State Laws, Uniform Commercial Code, article 2B, Licenses, section 2B-110 (Draft, March 21, 1997).

288 Utah Code Ann., sections 46-3101 to 46-3-504. California has digital signature legislation, which applies to contracts with the State of California. Cal. Gov't Code section 16.5. See generally Information Security Committee, Electronic Commerce and Information Technology Division, section of Science and Technology, American Bar Association, Digital Signature Guidelines (Draft October 5, 1995).

289 Ariz. Rev. Stat., section 41-121; Iowa Code, section 48A.13. A list of proposed and enacted state laws governing digital signatures can be found at, — http://nii.nist.gov/pubs/enstsign.html.

290 "House Panel to Mull Role for Preemption in Easing Growth of Electronic Commerce", 2 *Electronic Information Policy & Law Report* (BNA), at p. 258 (February 28, 1997).

291 *ProCD, Inc.* v. *Zeidenberg*, 908 F Supp. 640, at p. 644 (WD Wis., 1996); *Step Saver Data Systems, Inc.* v. *Wyse Technology*, 939 F.2d 91 (3 Cir. 1991); *Vault Corp.* v. *Quaid Software Ltd.*, 847 F.2d 255, at pp. 268–270 (5 Cir. 1988); *Arizona Retail Systems, Inc.* v. *Software Link* 831 F Supp. 759, at p. 766 (D Ariz. 1993).

292 *Hill* v. *Gateway 2000*, 105 F.3d 1147, at pp. 1149–1150 (7 Cir. 1997); *ProCD, Inc.* v. *Zeidenberg*, 86 F.3d 1447, at pp. 1452–1453 (7 Cir. 1996). *Compare Morgan Laboratories, Inc.* v. *Mirco Data Base Systems, Inc.*, 41 U.S.P.Q. 2d 1850 (ND Cal. 1997): written licence containing an integration clause, and a clause that disallowed modifications without a signed writing, controlled a subsequent shrinkwrap licence.

U.C.C. Draft, article 2B, endorses the use of shrink-wrap licences and contracts in on-line transactions. These types of contracts, under the current Draft, are legally binding if the buyer or licensee first had an opportunity to reject the transaction and obtain a refund, and if the shrink-wrap terms could be reasonably anticipated, and are conscionable.[293]

Mistakes and Impostors in On-line Contracts

Due to the nature of digital technology, alterations or mistakes in digital   **17-66**
records are not readily apparent. On-line contracts, therefore, may be more subject to mistakes and impostors than traditional paper-based contracts. Under traditional, paper-based contract law, a majority of courts rule that the risk of a mistake is on the sender, unless the recipient had reason to know of the error.[294] Under Draft U.C.C., article 2B, the sender similarly bears the risk of error, unless the recipient either should reasonably have discovered the error; or failed to use an agreed-on authentication system.[295]

The laws governing forgery and unauthorised signatures may change dramatically in the on-line environment. Traditional paper-based contract law generally provides that a person is not legally responsible for forgeries or other unauthorised signatures.[296]

In on-line transactions, in contrast, a person will generally be responsible for documents signed with his or her digital signature, even if the "signer" acted without authority.[297] A premium is placed, therefore, on maintaining the security of a digital signature or other digital identifier.

Payment Mechanics for Electronic Transactions

Secure and efficient payment mechanisms are crucial for electronic com-   **17-67**
merce. Indeed, to encourage development, the United States government is

---

293 National Conference of Commissioners on Uniform State Laws, Uniform Commercial Code, article 2B, Licenses, sections 2B-307, 2B-308, 2B-112 (c), 2B-114, 2B-109 (Draft March 21, 1997).

294 Calamari and Perillo, *The Law of Contracts*, section 2-26 (2nd edition 1977); 1 *Williston on Contracts* section 94 (3rd edition, 1957).

295 National Conference of Commissioners on Uniform State Laws, Uniform Commercial Code, article 2B, Licenses, sections 2B-322, 2-213 (Draft, March 21, 1997).

296 U.C.C. section 3-404.

297 See Utah Code Ann., section 46-3-406; National Conference of Commissioners on Uniform State Laws, Uniform Commercial Code, article 2B, Licenses, sections 2B-114 (Draft, March 21, 1997) (electronic document's recipient may attribute the document to the party shown as the sender if the recipient followed an agreed-on security procedure, and concluded that the message came from the person shown as the sender); Compare 2B Uniform Laws Annotated, U.C.C., section 4A-202 and 4A-203 (similar rule for non-consumer electronic funds transfers) (1991).

mandating that certain businesses adopt electronic payment techniques.[298] On-line payment models generally fall into two categories:

- Models where representations of actual assets, such as credit card information — and not the assets themselves — move in the system; and
- Models where the assets themselves — such as so-called "digital cash" — move in the system.[299]

17-68   Before discussing on-line use of credit cards and digital cash, it is helpful briefly to review current law governing electronic funds transfers between businesses, and electronic funds transfers involving consumers.

Electronic Funds Transfers

17-69   The term "electronic funds transfer" (EFT) refers to the movement of funds from one bank account to another by payment instructions that are communicated electronically. Credit transfers — whereby the buyer instructs its bank to transfer funds for credit to the seller's account — are governed by Uniform Commercial Code article 4A,[300] while consumer credit and debit transfers are covered by the Electronic Fund Transfer Act of 1978,[301] and Regulation E.[302]

Under article 4A, an electronic instruction to a bank to transfer funds to a payee is valid, and the bank is authorised to transfer the funds in accordance with the instruction either if the bank's customer actually authorised the order or if the order is "verified" pursuant to a "commercially reasonable" security procedure, such as a digital signature, on which the parties have agreed, irrespective of whether the customer actually authorised the order.[303]

The Electronic Fund Transfer Act, as implemented by Regulation E, governs the relationship between banks and consumers regarding electronic transactions in consumer accounts, such as Automated Teller Machine (ATM) card transactions. Unlike U.C.C., article 4A, a consumer will not be bound where his or her electronic "signature" is used without authority, and the consumer's liability for unauthorised electronic funds transfers is limited as long as the unauthorised transfer is reported diligently.[304]

---

298 For example, under the Electronic Federal Tax Payment System, certain businesses must make their federal tax deposits electronically, 26 U.S.C., section 6302 (h), and electronic funds transfers are now the mandatory method of federal payment on most new government contracts. "Payment by Electronic Funds Transfer", F.A.C. 90–42, F.A.R. Case 91-118; see "Electronic Funds Transfer to Become Mandatory Method of Payment for Government Contracts", 1 *Cyberspace Lawyer*, at p. 18 (December 1996).
299 IPNII Report, at pp. 192–194 (September 5, 1995).
300 2B Uniform Laws Annotated, U.C.C., article 4A (1991). Debit transfers between businesses are not covered by article 4A.
301 15 U.S.C., section 1693 *et seq.*
302 12 C.F.R., section 205.
303 2B Uniform Laws Annotated, U.C.C., section 4A-202 (1991).
304 12 C.F.R., section 205.6.

On-line Credit Card Payments

Credit card transactions are relatively expensive due to the number of parties   **17-70**
involved.[305] A number of companies nonetheless are working on facilitating
credit card transactions over the Internet. For example, certain credit card
companies have been developing the so-called Secure Electronic Transactions (SET) standard, to provide a common framework for secure on-line credit
card transactions. The goal of SET is a universal technical standard for
conducting trusted, electronic commerce over the Internet and other open
networks.[306] The establishment of such a standard will allow vendors to
develop products compliant with SET's communications protocols.[307]

   To avoid security issues on the Internet, a consumer may encrypt his or
her credit card information at the consumer's computer, using certain encryption software, before sending the information over the Internet to a seller.
The seller then forwards this encrypted credit card information to a central
location, where it is decrypted, processed as a standard credit card transaction, and the seller receives a confirming electronic receipt verifying the
buyer's transaction.[308] In the alternative, a consumer may use a "substitute"
for his or her credit card number over the Internet. A central company then
verifies to a prospective seller that the "substitute" is authentic.[309]

Digital Cash

An alternative to transmitting credit card information over the Internet is to   **17-71**
transmit actual assets, in the form of "digital cash", over the Internet. Digital
cash can be stored on various devices, including so-called "smart cards", or
"stored-value cards". These devices contain either magnetic strips or micro-
chips to allow them to hold the digital equivalent of money. Commentators
estimate that 30 per cent of all payments will be made with smart cards by
the year 2005, and that the electronic cash market will account for approximately 250-billion transactions by that time.[310] Certain companies are also
seeking to develop "electronic checks", which would function in a manner
similar to paper checks.[311]

---

305 IPNII Report, at pp. 192–194 (September 5, 1995); *A.C.L.U.* v. *Reno*, 929 F Supp. 824, at
   p. 846 (ED Pa. 1996).
306 The standard has been developed by MasterCard International and Visa International, and
   is published at http://www.mastercard.com and at http://visa.com. See Haar, "E-Commerce
   Spec Ready", *Inter@ctive Week,* at p. 9 (June 2, 1997).
307 Select employees of Chase Manhattan Bank and Wal-Mart Stores are using a pilot of the
   Secure Electronic Transaction standard to purchase goods from Wal-Mart Online using a
   SET-enabled Wal-Mart Chase MasterCard. *Inter@ctive Week,* at p. 19 (June 9,1997).
308 See http://www.cybercash.com (CyberCash system).
309 See http://www.fv.com (First Virtual Holdings, Inc. system).
310 *Inter@ctive Week,* at p. 73 (June 2, 1997); "Online Purchasing to Blossom by 2000 with
   New Micromarket, Researcher Says", 2 *Electronic Information Policy & Law Report,* at
   pp. 158–159 (February 7, 1997).
311 Financial Services Technology Consortium, "Electronic Check Project".

A number of companies have been demonstrating smart card technology; "closed" systems, such as stadiums, college campuses and resorts are popular venues for such systems.[312] Federal bank regulators have also given certain United States banks permission to operate and service the Mondex stored-value system in the United States.[313]

Digital cash and smart cards present certain advantages over credit-card payments. First, in a credit card system, a buyer may purchase only from sellers who have registered with the buyer's credit card company; digital cash allows a buyer to purchase from any seller. Second, due to the relatively high cost of transactions, credit card payments are not practical for "micropayments".[314]

With its advantages, digital cash also raises a number of new issues. For example, there are questions as to whether Regulation E, with its pro-consumer stance and its relatively high costs, will be applied to smart cards.[315] Another issue is whether the funds underlying stored-value cards or other similar electronic payment systems qualify for federal deposit insurance.[316] Finally, the ability to send anonymous digital cash efficiently over the Internet may facilitate money laundering and other crimes, and may, as some commentators note, make taxation "voluntary".[317] To assist law enforcement efforts, the Department of Justice has urged developers of smart cards to structure the systems so that transactions over a certain dollar amount generate and store a record of the transaction, to allow later tracing.[318]

---

312 *Inter@ctive Week*, at p. 25 (June 9, 1997). California State University, for example, recently awarded AT&T Corp. a contract to provide the University with a smart card system. Cardholders will use the cards to enter campus facilities, buy meals, purchase books, use vending machines, vote in school elections, and access library and health-care services on campus. *Inter@ctive Week*, at pp. 33 and 49 (June 2, 1997).

313 "OCC Approves National Bank Role in United States Operations of Mondex System", 1 *Electronic Information Policy & Law Report,* at pp. 844–845 (December 6, 1996).

314 Smedinghoff (ed.), *Online Law,* at p. 114 (1996).

315 Drolte, "Electronic Communications Should Satisfy 'Writings' Requirements for Reg E Purposes", 1 *Electronic Information Policy & Law Report* (BNA), at p. 493 (August 30, 1996).

316 The F.D.I.C. recently issued a General Counsel's Opinion concluding that the funds underlying stored-value cards do not give rise to a deposit liability and are not deposits under the Federal Deposit Insurance Act. The F.D.I.C. noted in its opinion that depository institutions could design cards in such a way as to carry deposit insurance. 61 F.R. 40490 (August 2, 1996).

317 Johnson-Laird, "Legislating the Internet: Is It Already Too Late?", 1 *Cyberspace Lawyer,* at p. 19 (September 1996); "Boston Conference Wrestles with Issues Triggered by Emergence of Electronic Commerce", *State Tax Review* (CCH), at p. 9 (February 18, 1997): the United States Department of the Treasury noted that "tax administration issues includ[e] the potential for tax evasion due to the use of electronic money, which can be stored on a computer hard drive and securely transported in a manner comparable to cash".

318 "Smart Cards Should Generate a Record over a Certain Dollar Amount, Official Says", 1 *Electronic Information Policy & Law Report* (BNA), at p. 712 (November 1, 1996).

ON-LINE INTELLECTUAL PROPERTY RIGHTS

A central purpose of intellectual property law in the United States is to **17-72** encourage innovation. United States intellectual property law provides this encouragement by assuring an innovator a fair return on his or her investment in creating the "property" to which these laws attach — whether that property is a distinctive and easily recognisable trade mark, a new formula for rocket fuel, or a short story.

Digital technology and the Internet present challenges to United States intellectual property law. Digital technology offers significant benefits: it allows information captured in diverse incompatible media — such as films, vinyl records and newspapers — to be communicated and stored in a uniform, easily accessible manner: as a collection of 0s and 1s. In digital form, the information can be copied, modified, and shared with relative dispatch.

Despite its significant benefits, digital technology also entails potentially high risks, as it facilitates the misappropriation of intellectual property. For example, it may be far easier to add a counterfeit trade mark to a digital product than to a tangible product. In addition, it is certainly far easier and more efficient to produce counterfeit copies of a short story by using digital technology than by using non-digital technology, such as photocopying.[319]

The Internet offers an efficient, and potentially lucrative method for distributing intellectual property in digital form. Yet, because of its size, its extremely low entry barriers, and the difficulties in monitoring on-line conduct, counterfeiters and others who misappropriate intellectual property may select the Internet as their preferred distribution channel. Accordingly, digital technology and the Internet present significant benefits and risks to intellectual property owners.

Owners in the United States prevent misappropriation and distribution of their intellectual property by relying on copyright law, trade mark law, patent law, and trade secret law. The on-line environment impacts each of these areas of law differently.

Copyright Law

The most important intellectual property rights in the United States on-line **17-73** environment are those protected under copyright law.

Applicability of Copyright Law to On-line Communications

On-line activity almost always raises copyright issues. Copyright law in the **17-74** United States grants an author the exclusive right, among others, to make copies of his or her work; to adapt that work and recast it in another form;

---

319 IPNII Report, at pp. 10–12 and 168–172 (September 1995).

to display the work publicly; to perform the work; and to distribute the work.[320] Copyright law protects a wide variety of works,[321] and this protection arises automatically — without the need for any formalities — once the author "fixes" the work in tangible form, such as by, for example, writing his or her thoughts down on paper.

To access a web page over the Internet, a copy of the page must be loaded into the random access memory (RAM) of the user's computer. Loading a copyrighted work into RAM constitutes making a copy of that work and, if done without authority, infringes the owner's exclusive reproduction right.[322] Moreover, whenever a user "browses" through copies of works on a web site, for example, a "display" occurs, further implicating an exclusive right of copyright owners.[323]

In sum, because many on-line materials are protected by copyright, and because even commonplace on-line activity, such as browsing, implicates copyright owners' exclusive rights, copyright issues will almost always be present in the United States on-line environment.

Limitations on Exclusive Rights

17-75   Copyright law contains a number of limitations. First, copyright protection attaches only to the specific expression of an idea, but not to the underlying idea itself.[324] Second, copyright protection does not extend to factual material, regardless of the effort the author expended in collecting this material.[325] Copyright protection for a database compilation of facts, therefore, extends only to the "original" elements of the database, such as its selection and arrangement of the data.[326] Consequently, an on-line user may copy the ideas and facts contained in a protected work; copyright law, however, prohibits the user from copying the precise expression of those ideas, or the selection and arrangement of the factual data.[327]

---

320 17 U.S.C., section 106.
321 17 U.S.C., section 102 (a): copyright protection includes (1) literary works; (2) musical works; (3) dramatic works; (4) pantomimes and choreographic works; (5) motion pictures and other audiovisual works; (6) pictorial, graphic, and sculptural works; (7) sound recordings; and (8) architectural works.
322 *MAI Systems Corp. v. Peak Computer, Inc.*, 991 F.2d 511, at p. 519 (9 Cir. 1993), *cert. denied*, 114 SCt. 671 (1994); *Vault Corp. v. Quaid Software Ltd.*, 847 F.2d 255, at p. 260 (5 Cir. 1988).
323 *Playboy Enterprises, Inc. v. Frena*, 839 F Supp. 1552, 1559 (MD Fla. 1993); 17 U.S.C., section 101 (definition of "display").
324 17 U.S.C., section 102 (b): "[i]n no case does copyright protection for an original work of authorship extend to any idea, procedure, process, system, method of operation, concept, principle, or discovery, regardless of the form in which it is described, explained, illustrated, or embodied in such a work".
325 *Feist Publications, Inc. v. Rural Telephone Service Co.*, 499 U.S. 340, 365 (1991).
326 *Feist Publications, Inc. v. Rural Telephone Service Co.*, 499 U.S. 340, 349 (1991).
327 See *CCC Information Services, Inc. v. Maclean Hunter Market Reports, Inc.*, 44 F.3d 61, at p. 67 (2d Cir., 1994), *cert. denied*, 116 S Ct. 72 (1995).

Even if an on-line user has copied protected expression, various defences to an infringement claim may be applicable. For example, the user may successfully assert that his or her copying amounted to "fair use". Under the "fair use" doctrine, a person may copy portions of a protected work, without liability for infringement, for purposes such as criticism, comment, news reporting, teaching, scholarship, or research, for example.[328] In assessing a fair use defence, courts generally examine:

- The purpose and character of the use, including whether such use is of a commercial nature or is for non-profit educational purposes;
- The nature of the copyrighted work;
- The amount and substantiality of the portion used in relation to the copyrighted work as a whole; and
- The effect of the use on the potential market for, or value of, the copyrighted work.[329] Copying for a commercial purpose, by itself, will not preclude a fair use defence.[330]

In addition to raising a fair use defence, an on-line copier may also claim   **17-76** that the copyright owner granted an "implied licence" to use the work. A court would likely rule that a copyright owner had granted such an implied licence, for example, if the owner posted the work to an automatic e-mail distribution list.[331]

Infringement by Web site "Framing"

New Internet technology may be creating new types of infringement. In *The*   **17-77** *Washington Post Co.* v. *Total News, Inc.*,[332] for example, the plaintiffs, a group of news services that provide on-line news, sued the defendant, Total News, on the basis of its "framed" links to the plaintiffs' copyrighted web sites. Framing technology allows the host of the initial web site to "wrap" its web site's content, including its advertising, around the content of a linked page, in a "frame". This frame remains with the user as he or she "surfs" subsequent linked sites.

The defendant in *Total News* had created framed links to the plaintiffs' new services, and while a user viewed the plaintiffs' copyrighted news stories, advertisements by Total News framed these stories. The plaintiffs argued that the defendant's use of framing technology "pirated" the plaintiffs' copyrighted materials, and also infringed their trade marks.[333] No court decision has yet been reached.

---

328 17 U.S.C., section 107.
329 17 U.S.C., section 107.
330 *Campbell* v. *Acuff-Rose Music*, 114 S Ct. 1164, at p. 1171 (1994).
331 IPNII Report, at p. 130 (September 5, 1995).
332 SDNY., 97 Civ. 1190.
333 *The Washington Post Co.* v. *Total News, Inc.*, SDNY., 97 Civ. 1190, *Electronic Information: Policy & Law Report* (BNA), at p. 262 (February 28, 1997).

Technical Protections

17-78   Once a user posts content on the Internet, he or she cannot prevent that content from potentially reaching a worldwide audience.[334] Companies are in the process of developing technical solutions to restrict the audience of protected works. For example, digital watermarking, or "steganography", embeds identifying information within digitised audio or visual data, such as the licensed user's, and the copyright owner's name and address. The embedded information cannot be removed and thus, if unauthorised copies of the work are made, they can be traced to the originally licensed user.[335]

In addition, certain companies are experimenting with so-called secure "envelopes", which contain terms for use on the "outside", and the protected work on the inside.[336] Finally, companies are beginning to specialise in "policing" the Internet for copyright violations, using digital scanning technology.[337]

Trade Secrets

17-79   Trade secrets are protected under state law. Trade secrets are generally defined as any information that is secret and that has economic value by virtue of its secrecy.[338] The Uniform Trade Secrets Act, for example, which most states have adopted, broadly defines a trade secret as "information, including a formula, pattern, compilation, program, device, method, technique or process, that: (i) derives independent economic value, actual or potential, from not being generally known to, and not being readily ascertainable by a proper means by other persons who can obtain economic value from its disclosure, and (ii) is the subject of efforts that are reasonable under the circumstances to maintain its secrecy".[339] Accordingly, to claim trade secret protection for information, a business must take steps to preserve the secrecy of that information. A competitor nevertheless can properly acquire trade secret information through reverse engineering, for example.[340]

The Internet poses problems for trade secret owners, due to its wide audience. Once a trade secret is publicly disclosed, trade secret protection

---

334 *A.C.L.U. v. Reno*, 929 F Supp. 824, at p. 846 (ED Pa. 1996), juris. noted, *Reno v. A.C.L.U.*, 136 LEd.2d 436 (1996).
335 IPNII Report, at pp. 188–189 (September 5, 1995).
336 See http://www.cryptolope.ibm.com (IBM's Cryptolope); http://www.intertrust.com (DigiBox product).
337 *Inter@ctive Week*, at p. 19 (June 9, 1997) (company searches for unauthorised publication of copyrighted audio and video works by scanning the Internet for MPEG, Audio Layer 3, RealAudio, and other new-media file formats.
338 Uniform Trade Secrets Act, 14 Uniform Laws Annotated, section 1 (3); *Restatement (Third) of Unfair Competition*, section 39 (1995).
339 Uniform Trade Secrets Act, 14 Uniform Laws Annotated, section 1 (4).
340 *Restatement (Third) of Unfair Competition*, section 43 (1995): "independent discovery and analysis of publicly available products or information are not improper means of acquisition".

for the information is lost. Therefore, a trade secret owner may be particularly vulnerable to disclosure by a judgment-proof defendant over the Internet.[341]

Trade Marks

A trade mark is a symbol that identifies the source of particular goods or services, assists the public in distinguishing one product or service from another, and assures the public of the quality of the products or services sold under the particular mark.[342] The primary policy of trade mark law, therefore, is the protection of consumers.   **17-80**

Generally, under United States trade mark law, the more distinctive and "strong" a mark is, the greater protection from infringement and unfair competition it will receive. A business, therefore, can obtain strong trade mark protection by adopting an arbitrary or fanciful name or symbol, previously not associated with that industry or type of good.

Acquiring and Protecting Trade Mark Rights On-line

A person need not register his or her mark under United States trade mark law to be able to prohibit others from using the same or a similar mark in a manner likely to confuse consumers.[343] Indeed, the first business that properly uses a mark to distinguish its services from others will have priority over all businesses who later seek to use that mark in the same markets.[344] Therefore, by simply using a sufficiently distinctive mark on-line, in connection with services or goods, a business can obtain trade mark rights. A business may also file for registration of its mark with the Patent and Trade Mark Office, either based on previous use, or based on an intent to use.[345] In such a registration, the business must specify the particular goods and services with which the mark is used.   **17-81**

Although for most marks protection does not extend beyond the particular goods and services to which the mark is attached, certain well-known marks receive broad protection from "dilution" generally.[346] "Dilution" occurs when a business uses the well-known mark of another and when, even though the goods of the two businesses are not competing and there is

---

341 *Religious Technology Center* v. *Netcom Online Communications Services, Inc.*, 923 F Supp. 1231, at p. 1256 (ND Cal. 1995): "One of the Internet's virtues that it gives even the poorest individuals the power to publish to millions of readers, can also be a detriment to the value of intellectual property rights. The anonymous (or judgment proof) defendant can permanently destroy valuable trade secrets, leaving no one to hold liable for the misappropriation. Although a work posted to an Internet news group remains accessible to the public for only a limited amount of time, once that trade secret has been released into the public domain there is no retrieving it".
342 15 U.S.C., sections 1051, *et seq.*
343 15 U.S.C., section 1125.
344 McCarthy, 3 *McCarthy on Trademarks and Unfair Competition*, section 16.02.
345 15 U.S.C., sections 1051 (a), (b).
346 15 U.S.C., section 1125 (c).

no likelihood of customer confusion, the use nevertheless will reduce the "capacity of [the] famous mark to identify and distinguish goods or services". Owners of famous marks, therefore, receive protection even in the absence of traditional infringement.[347]

The Internet's lack of geographic boundaries presents challenges to trade mark law in the United States. Trade mark protection is based on geographic boundaries, and boundaries between markets and advertising channels. Because the Internet blurs these boundaries, similar trade marks, which previously could co-exist in their separate markets, may now come into conflict on the Internet.

Infringement

17-82   Trade mark law protects against unfair competition and infringement on-line. For example, in *Sega Enterprises, Inc.* v. *MAPHIA*,[348] the court held that a bulletin board operator who engaged in the on-line distribution of unauthorised copies of Sega games had infringed Sega's trade marks. The court reasoned that the defendant's conduct created a likelihood that on-line consumers would be confused, and would believe that the games were authorised by Sega.[349]

Trade mark owners may also obtain injunctive relief that is tailored to the on-line environment. The recent case of *Playboy Enterprises, Inc.* v. *Chuckleberry Publishing, Inc.*,[350] for example, involved an Italian web site, which displayed a trade mark that had previously been found to infringe on the United States plaintiff's "Playboy" mark. After finding that use of the mark on the Italian web site similarly infringed the plaintiff's mark in the United States, the court ordered, among other points, the Italian web site host to shut down its web site completely or to refrain from accepting any subscriptions from United States customers; to invalidate passwords previously given to United States customers; and to revise its web site to prohibit access by United States customers.[351]

The standard Internet practice of "linking" a web page to other web pages located at different sites may give rise to trade mark claims. In *Ticketmaster Corp.* v. *Microsoft Corp.*,[352] the plaintiff, Ticketmaster, claimed that Microsoft had misappropriated Ticketmaster's name and trade marks by including unauthorised links to Ticketmaster's site at one of Microsoft's sites. To avoid these types of disputes, certain web site hosts are

---

347 15 U.S.C., section 1125 (c); see *Clinique Laboratories, Inc.* v. *Dep Corp.*, 945 F Supp. 547, at pp. 561–563 (SDNY 1996).
348 857 F Supp. 679 (ND Cal. 1994).
349 *Sega Enterprises, Inc.* v. *MAPHIA*, 857 F Supp. 679, at p. 688 (ND Cal. 1994); see *Playboy Enterprises, Inc.* v. *Frena*, 839 F Supp. 1552, at p. 1561 (ND Fla. 1993).
350 939 F Supp. 1032 (SDNY 1996).
351 *Playboy Enterprises, Inc.* v. *Chuckleberry Publishing*, Inc., 939 F Supp. 1032, at p. 1041 (SDNY 1996).
352 Number 97-3055 (CD Cal., complaint filed April 28, 1997).

beginning to offer commissions to other web site hosts that direct users to their sites through web links.[353]

Right of Publicity

A celebrity may possess a so-called "right of publicity", which protects his or her "persona" — including name, likeness, and other attributes by which the celebrity is recognised — from commercial use by others.   **17-83**

Courts have compared this publicity right loosely to trade mark rights.[354] On-line conduct referencing a celebrity might well implicate publicity rights.

Domain Names

A "domain name" is an Internet address, such as "acme.com." A party can obtain a domain name by applying to various registrars, such as Network Solutions, Inc. (NSI) in the United States. NSI assigns domain names on a first-come, first-served basis. An easily remembered domain name that is closely connected with the company's name or trade mark is valuable in that users can readily locate, and thus visit, the site. A domain name, therefore, can function as a trade mark in that it may identify a particular source and quality of goods or services on the Internet.   **17-84**

This connection between domain names and trade marks has led to a number of disputes between trade mark and domain name owners. The current NSI dispute resolution policy favours trade mark owners,[355] and courts have consistently ruled that registration of another person's trademark as a domain name constitutes trade mark infringement.[356] There are proposals pending for reforming the domain name system.[357]

353 Haar, "NECX Offers Commissions to Referral Sites", *Inter@ctive Week*, at p. 24 (June 2, 1997).

354 *White* v. *Samsung Electronics America, Inc.*, 971 F.2d 1395, at p. 1400 (9 Cir. 1992), *cert. denied*, 113 SCt. 2443 (1993).

355 See rs.internic.net/domain-info/internic-domain-6.html.

356 *Cardservice International* v. *McGee*, 950 F Supp. 737, at p. 742 (ED Va. 1997); *Toys 'R Us, Inc.* v. *Mohama Ahmad Akkaoui*, 1996 U.S. Dist. LEXIS 17090 (ND Cal. October 29, 1996); *Comp Examiner Agency, Inc.* v. *Juris Inc.*, 1996 U.S. Dist. LEXIS 20259 (CD Cal. April 26, 1996); *Hasbro, Inc.* v. *Internet Entertainment Group*, 1996 U.S. Dist. LEXIS 11626 (WD Wash. February 9, 1996).

357 Final Report of the International Ad Hoc Committee: Recommendations for Administration and Management of gTLDs [generic Top Level Domains]", http://www.iahc.org/draft-iahc-recommend-00.html. Not all agree with this plan; the Internet Service Providers Consortium, for example, does not endorse it. See http://www.ispc.org. See generally International Trademark Association White Paper, The Intersection of Trademarks and Domain Names (April 1, 1997), a copy can be found at http://www.inta.org.

library, in that it did not exercise editorial control over its users' discussions, and did not know or have reason to know about the defamatory comments posted by a subscriber, and injurious to the plaintiff. Accordingly, the court dismissed the plaintiff's defamation claim.[370]

In contrast, the court in *Stratton Oakmont, Inc.* v. *Prodigy Services Co.*[371] held Prodigy liable for defamatory statements by one of its subscribers. The court reasoned that Prodigy exercised "sufficient control over its computer bulletin boards to render it a publisher with the same responsibilities as a newspaper". Prodigy had a policy of systematically monitoring messages submitted to the particular forum at issue, and had pledged to be a family-oriented computer network that would bar or remove objectionable messages. The court, therefore, held that Prodigy was responsible for defamatory postings.[372]

The *Stratton Oakmont, Inc.* v. *Prodigy Services Co.* decision was legislatively overruled, and Internet service providers were provided with broad protection from such defamation claims, by the Communications Decency Act of 1996. Under the Act's "Good Samaritan" provisions, "no provider or user of an interactive computer service shall be treated as the publisher or speaker of any information" provided by another user.[373] The court, in *Zeran* v. *America Online, Inc.*,[374] recently interpreted this "Good Samaritan" provision, section 230, to preempt a state law negligence claim against an Internet service provider for distributing allegedly defamatory material through its system.

The plaintiff in *Zeran* was the target of anonymous postings linking the plaintiff's name and telephone number to T-shirts and other materials glorifying the bombing of the federal building in Oklahoma City. Although America Online took steps to delete the materials, the plaintiff claimed that America Online was negligent in not acting faster and in not taking further steps. The court held that the plaintiff's claims were barred by the Communication Decency Act's Good Samaritan provision, and granted judgment in favour of America Online.[375] Consequently, an Internet service provider enjoys extensive protection from claims for defamation based on its role as conduit for the wrongful statements.

Intellectual Property Infringement

17-91   As a rule, under the doctrine of "contributory infringement", liability attaches to any person who knowingly provides facilities that allow another to infringe a trade mark or copyright.[376] The protection the Communications

---

370   *Cubby, Inc.* v. *CompuServe, Inc.*, 776 F Supp. 135, at p. 140 (SDNY 1991).
371   1995 W.L. 323710 (NY Sup. Ct., May 24, 1995).
372   *Stratton Oakmont, Inc.* v. *Prodigy Services Co.*, 1995 W.L. 323710 (NY Sup. Ct., May 24, 1995).
373   47 U.S.C., section 230 (c) (1).
374   958 F Supp. 1124 (ED Va. 1997).
375   *Zeran* v. *America Online, Inc.*, 958 F Supp. 1124, at p. 1137 (ED Va. 1997).
376   *Getty Petroleum Corp.* v. *Aris Getty, Inc.*, 55 F.3d 718, at p. 719 (1 Cir. 1995) (trade mark); *Lewis Galoob Toys, Inc* v. *Nintendo of Am. Inc.*, 964 F.2d 965, at p. 970 (9 Cir. 1992) (copyright).

Decency Act of 1996 provides to Internet service providers for defamation claims does not apply to claims for infringement of intellectual property.[377] Accordingly, an Internet service provider may be liable for contributory infringement.

Recently, the court in *Religious Technology Center* v. *Netcom On-Line Communication Services, Inc.*[378] ruled that Netcom, one of the largest Internet providers, could be liable for contributory copyright infringement if it ignored warnings from copyright owners that postings by users at its site were infringing. The plaintiff in *Religious Technology Center* v. *Netcom On-Line Communication Services, Inc.*[379] was the exclusive licensee of certain unpublished copyrighted works relating to the Church of Scientology. These works had been posted by others on a bulletin board, and the defendant Netcom provided this bulletin board with access to the Internet. Netcom had failed to remove the works from its server when the plaintiff objected to the posting.[380]

Reasoning that Netcom provided facilities for the allegedly infringing activity, and that Netcom had allowed the direct infringers to continue using these facilities despite objection by the copyright owner, the court ruled that Netcom could be liable for contributory infringement.[381] Accordingly, an Internet service provider may be liable for contributory infringement where it has notice that infringing materials reside on its server, and it takes no action.[382]

Right to Exclude or Restrict Users

For various reasons, an Internet service provider may wish to restrict the   **17-92** activities of certain users, and foreclose access to its services for others. The Communications Decency Act of 1996 protects Internet service providers when they restrict their users' access to certain objectionable materials.[383]

---

377 47 U.S.C., section 230 (d): "[n]othing in this section shall be construed to limit or expand any law pertaining to intellectual property".

378 907 FSupp. 1361 (NDCal. 1995).

379 907 FSupp. 1361 (NDCal. 1995).

380 Netcom has subsequently established a protocol for addressing claims of intellectual property infringement. "Procedures for Postings Challenged as Improper", http://www.netcom.com/about/protectcopy.html.

381 *Religious Technology Center* v. *Netcom On-Line Communication Services*, Inc., 907 FSupp. 1361, at p. 1375 (NDCal. 1995). *Compare Playboy Enterprises, Inc* v. *Frena*, 839 FSupp. 1552, at p. 1554 (MD Fla. 1993): operator of electronic bulletin board service which contained digital versions of 170 of plaintiff's copyrighted photographs directly liable for infringement of plaintiff's distribution and display rights; *Sega Enterprises Ltd* v. *MAPHIA*, 948 F Supp. 923, at p. 933 (ND Cal. 1996): operator of electronic bulletin board service who encouraged users to upload and download unauthorised copies of plaintiff's work held liable for infringement.

382 The Software Publishers Association (the SPA) has requested Internet Service Providers (ISPs) to sign an "ISP Code of Conduct" to detect and deter copyright infringement occurring on their systems. See http://www.spa.org.

383 47 U.S.C., section 230 (c) (2).

Specifically, the Act provides that an Internet service provider will not be liable "on account of any action voluntarily taken in good faith to restrict access to or availability of material that the provider considers to be obscene, lewd, lascivious, filthy, excessively violent, harassing, or otherwise objectionable, whether or not such material is constitutionally protected; or any action taken to enable or make available to information content providers or others the technical means to restrict access" to such material.[384] Accordingly, an Internet service provider has the right to "police" its server and its offerings for certain objectionable content.

The right of an Internet service provider to restrict or foreclose access was recently the central issue in the so-called "spamming" cases. The on-line term "spamming" refers to the practice of sending multiple copies of unsolicited e-mail advertisements to Internet users.[385] In *CompuServe, Inc.* v. *Cyber Promotions, Inc.*, the plaintiff, CompuServe, successfully blocked the defendants from sending unsolicited advertisements to any e-mail addresses maintained by CompuServe for its subscribers.

The court reasoned that the defendants' conduct amounted to a "trespass" on the plaintiff's personal property.[386] America Online was similarly successful in blocking unsolicited e-mail advertisements, even in the face of claims that its conduct foreclosed the advertiser's access to "essential facilities" under antitrust laws.[387]

CONCLUSION

17-93   A United States judge, quoting expert testimony, recently noted that "the strength of the Internet is [its] chaos".[388] The Internet can be chaotic, and presents novel legal issues. United States law, nevertheless, provides a sound framework for utilising this new medium.

---

384 47 U.S.C., section 230 (c) (2).
385 The term is based on a comedy skit by Monte Python, during which the term "spam" is recited repeatedly. See *CompuServe, Inc.* v. *Cyber Promotions, Inc.*, 962 FSupp. 1015, at p. 1018, n.1 (SD Ohio 1997).
386 *CompuServe, Inc.* v. *Cyber Promotions, Inc.*, 962 F Supp. 1015, at p. 1027 (SD Ohio 1997).
387 *Cyber Promotions Inc.* v. *America Online*, 948 F Supp. 456, at pp. 461–463 (ED Pa. 1996). Congress is currently considering proposed legislation to restrict or prohibit "spam". H.R. 1748 (the "Netizens Protection Act of 1997"); S771 (the "Unsolicited Commercial Electronic Mail Choice Act of 1997"). See generally "Congress Mulls Bill to Can Spam", *Inter@ctive Week*, at p. 7 (May 26, 1997). Several states are also considering banning or regulating spam. See http://www.jmls.edu/cyber/statutes/e-mail/.
388 *A.C.L.U.* v. *Reno*, 929 F Supp. 824, at p. 883 (ED Pa. 1996) (Dalzell, J., concurring), juris. noted, *Reno* v. *A.C.L.U.*, 136 LEd.2d 436 (1996).

Glossary

ADSL (Asymmetric Digital Subscriber Line) — A method for moving data over regular phone lines. An ADSL circuit is much faster than a normal telephone connection.

Applet — A small Java program that can be embedded in an HTML page. Applets differ from full-fledged Java applications in that they are not allowed to access certain resources on the local computer, such as files and serial devices (*e.g.*, modems and printers) and are prohibited from communicating with most other computers across a network.

Archie — A tool for finding files stored on anonymous FTP sites.

ARPANet (Advanced Research Projects Agency Network) — The precursor to the Internet.

ASCII (American Standard Code for Information Interchange) — The *de facto* worldwide standard for the code numbers used by computers to represent all the upper and lower case Latin letters, numbers, and punctuation. There are 128 standard ASCII codes, each of which can be represented by a seven-digit binary number.

Asymmetric Cryptography — See Public-Key Cryptography.

Audio-visual Works — Audio-visual works are copyrightable works that consist of a series of related images that are intrinsically intended to be shown by the use of machines or devices such as projectors, viewers, or electronic equipment, together with accompanying sounds.

Authenticity, Authentication — Authenticity refers to the business and legal requirement that a recipient of an electronic communication be able to ascertain or establish that the communication comes from the purported source and is what it purports to be.

Backbone — A high-speed line or series of connections that forms a major pathway within a network.

Bandwidth — The amount of data that can be sent through a connection and usually measured in bits per second. A full page of English text is approximately 16,000 bits — the transmission capacity of the lines that carry the Internet's electronic traffic.

Binhex (BINary HEXadecimal) — A method for converting non-text files (non-ASCII) into ASCII.

Bps (Bits per Second) — A measurement of how fast data is moved from one place to another. A 28.8 modem can move 28,800 bits per second.

Browser — A client program (software) that is used to look at various kinds of Internet resources.

Brute-force Attack — A brute-force attack is a cryptanalytic attack in which all possible keys are employed until one decrypts the ciphertext.

Byte — A set of bits that represent a single character. Usually, there are eight bits in a byte, depending on how the measurement is made.

CA — See Certification Authority.

CD-ROM — Acronym for Compact Disc Read-Only Memory.

Certificate — A certificate is a computer-based record that documents that a particular public key belongs to an identified person. A certificate is issued by a certification authority after that authority has ascertained the identity of the person, called a subscriber. The certificate usually includes the name of the certification authority issuing it, the name of the subscriber, the subscriber's public key, and the digital signature of the certification authority.

Certificate Authority — An issuer of security certificates used in SSL connections.

Certificate Revocation List — A certificate revocation list (CRL) is a list of certificates that had been revoked by the issuing certification authority. A CRL is maintained by the certification authority and lists only certificates issued by that certification authority.

Certification Authority — A certification authority (CA) is a person or entity that ascertains the identity of a person and issues a computer-based record known as a certificate that associates that person with a public-private key pair used to create digital signatures.

CGI (Common Gateway Interface) — A set of rules that describe how a Web Server communicates with another piece of software on the same machine, and how the other piece of software (the CGI program) talks to the web server.

Checksum — See Hash Value.

Ciphertext — Ciphertext is the encrypted version of a communication.

Client — A software program that is used to contact and obtain data from a server software program on another computer, often across a great distance.

Client/Server — Computer technology that separates computers and their users into two categories, clients and servers. The party seeking information from a computer on the Internet is the client. The computer that delivers the information is the server. A server both stores information and makes it available to any authorised client who requests the information.

Commerce Server — Sophisticated, multipart software program that turns a high-performance workstation into a World Wide Web site capable of handling on-line transactions and related functions including database and inventory management, order taking, billing, security, and customer service.

Commission on New Technological Uses of Copyrighted Works — The commission was established by the United States Congress on December 31, 1974 to analyse the impact of the computer on copyrighted works. The Commission issued its final report in 1978.

Compact Disc Read-Only Memory — Compact disc read-only memory (or CD-ROM) is a laser-encoded optical memory storage medium similar in appearance to compact audio discs. CD-ROMs can hold approximately 550 megabytes of data.

Compilation — A compilation is a copyrightable work formed by the collection and assembling of pre-existing materials or of data that is selected, co-ordinated, or arranged in such a way that the resulting work as a whole constitutes an original work of authorship.

Computer Program — A computer program is defined as a set of statements or instructions to be used directly or indirectly in a computer in order to bring about a certain result.

Content — Content is used to refer to the various types of data that can be displayed by a computer, such as text, sound, images, photographs, and motion pictures.

Conventional Cryptography — Conventional cryptography, also known as symmetric cryptography, refers to a type of cryptography in which the same key is used both to encrypt and to decrypt communications.

Cookie — Information sent by a Web server to a Web browser that the browser software is expected to save and to send back to the server whenever the browser makes additional requests from the server.

Creation — A copyrightable work is created when it is fixed in a copy of phonorecord for the first time; where a work is prepared over a period of time, the portion of it that has been fixed at any particular time constitutes the work as of that time, and where the work has been prepared in different versions, each version constitutes a separate work.

CRL — See Certificate Revocation List.

Cryptanalysis — Cryptanalysis is the art and science of defeating encrypted communications.

Cryptography — Cryptography is the art and science of defeating encrypted communications.

Cyberspace — Cyberspace is currently used to refer to the world of electronic communications over computer networks.

Data Encryption Standard (DES) — See DES.

Date/Time Stamp — To date/stamp means to append or attach to a communication, digital signature, or certificate a digitally signed notation indicating at least the date, time, and identity of the person appending or attaching the notation.

Decryption — Decryption is a process of converting ciphertext back to its original, readable form.

DES — DES, also known as Data Encryption Standard, is a conventional encryption algorithm.

Digital Certificates — Software used to authenticate identity of shoppers and merchants in on-line financial transactions.

Digital Content — Digital content is used to refer to any information that is published or distributed in a digital form, including text, data, sound recordings, photographs and images, motion pictures, and software.

Digital Signature — A digital signature is a transformation of a communication using a public-key cryptosystem such that a person having the communication and the signer's public key can accurately determine whether the transformation was created using the private key that corresponds to the signer's public key and whether the communication has been altered since the transformation was made.

Digital Signature Algorithm (DSA) — See DSA.

Digital Signature Guidelines — Digital Signature Guidelines refers to a publication of the Information Security Committee, Electronic Commerce and Information Technology Division, Section of Science and Technology of the American Bar Association, which sets forth a set of general, abstract statements of principle intended to serve as long-term, unifying foundations for the development of sound law and practice regarding digital signatures.

Digital Signature Verification — Digital signature verification is the process of checking a digital signature by reference to the original communication and a public key, thereby determining whether the digital signature was created for that same communication using the private key that corresponds to the referenced public key.

Display — To display a copyright work means to show an original work or a copy of it, either directly or by means of a film, slide, television image, or any other device or process or, in the case of a motion picture or audio-visual work, to show individual images non-sequentially.

Distribution Right — The term distribution right refers to the exclusive right granted to the owner of a copyright to distribute copies of his or her copyrighted work publicly by sale, rental, lease, or lending.

Domain Name — A domain name is mnemonic, corresponding to a numeric Internet network address that uniquely identifies a host computer on the Internet and is the unique name that identifies an Internet site. Domain names always have two or more parts, separated by dots.

DSA — DSA, also known as the Digital Signature Algorithm, is an algorithm approved as a United States government standard for use in generating and verifying digital signatures using public-key cryptography.

EDI — See Electronic Data Interchange.

EDI (Electronic Data Interchange) — Private, proprietary electronic networks first used in the 1960s and 1970s to connect large corporations and their primary trading partners, now moving to the Internet and corporate intranets.

EFT — See Electronic Funds Transfer.

Electronic Commerce — Electronic commerce refers to the end-to-end, all-electronic performance of business activities. Electronic commerce includes EDI, as well as the use of electronic mail, electronic transfer of digital content, electronic purchasing and payments, and the business process re-engineering necessary to implement the broad capabilities of on-line technology. Trade of goods and services through computer networks such as the Internet, as well as related pre- and post-sale activities.

Electronic Data Interchange (EDI) — Electronic data interchange (or EDI) refers to the on-line exchange of routine business transactions in a computer-processable format, covering such traditional applications as inquiries, purchasing, acknowledgments, pricing, order status, scheduling, test results, shipping and receiving, invoices, payments, and financial reporting. The data is exchanged directly between computers, utilising standardised formats, so that the data can be implemented directly by the receiving computer.

Electronic Funds Transfer (EFT) — An electronic funds transfer refers to the series of electronically communicated transactions, beginning with the payment order of the originator (such as a buyer making payment to a seller), made for the purpose of making payment to the beneficiary of the payment order (such as the seller).

Electronic Mail — Electronic mail (e-mail) is the computer-to-computer exchange of messages, usually written in free text, rather than a structured format.

Electronic Mail Policy — An electronic mail policy is a policy statement issued by an employer to its employees outlining the business purpose of the company electronic mail system, the scope of the employer's right to monitor e-mail messages, and guidelines for proper usage.

E-Mail — See Electronic Mail.

Encryption — Encryption refers to the process of disguising a readable communication into an unintelligible scramble of characters according to some code or cipher.

FAQs (Frequently Asked Questions) — Files that commonly are maintained at Internet sites to answer frequently asked questions.

FDDI (Fibre Distributed Data Interface) — A standard for transmitting data on optical fibre cables at a rate of approximately 100,000,000 bits per second.

Finger — An Internet function that enables one user to query (finger) the location of another Internet user. Finger can be applied to any computer on the Internet, if set up properly.

Firewall — A combination of hardware and software that protects a local area network (LAN) from Internet hackers. It separates the network into two or more parts and restricts outsiders to the area "outside" the firewall. Private or sensitive information is kept "inside" the firewall.

Fixed — A copyrightable work is fixed in a tangible medium of expression when its embodiment in a copy or phonorecord, by or under the authority of the author, is sufficiently permanent or stable to permit it to be perceived, reproduced, or otherwise communicated for a period of more than transitory duration. A work consisting of sounds, images, or both, that are being transmitted, is fixed if a fixation of the work is being made simultaneously with its transmission.

Flames — Insulting, enraged Internet messages.

Flame War — When an on-line discussion degenerates into a series of personal attacks against the debaters, rather than discussion of their positions.

FQDN (Fully Qualified Domain Name) — The "official" name assigned to a computer. Organisations register names, such as ford.com or cils.org or fplc.edu.

FTP (File Transfer Protocol) — A common method of moving files between two Internet sites. FTP is a special way to log in to another Internet site for the purposes of retrieving and/or sending files.

Gateway — A host computer that connects networks that communicate in different languages.

GIF (Graphics Interchange Format) — A graphics file format that is commonly used on the Internet to provide graphics images in Web pages.

Gigabyte — 1,000 Megabytes.

Gopher — A searching tool that was the primary tool for finding Internet resources before the World Wide Web became popular.

Hash Function — A hash function is an algorithm mapping or translating one sequence of bits into another, such that a communication yields the same hash result every time the algorithm is executed using the same communication as input; it is computationally infeasible that a communication can be derived or reconstituted from the hash result produced by the algorithm, and it is computationally infeasible that two communications can be found that produce the same hash result using the algorithm.

Hash Value — A hash value is the output produced by a hash function upon processing a communication. A hash value may also be referred to as a hash result, message digest, manipulation detection code, integrity check value, or checksum.

Hit — As used in reference to the World Wide Web, "hit" means a single request from a Web browser for a single item from a Web server.

Home Page — Originally, the Web page that one's browser is set to use when it starts. The more common meaning refers to the main Web page for a business, organisation, or person.

Host — A computer that hosts outside computer users by providing files and services or by sharing its resources.

Hosting — Electronic transaction services provided by third-party service bureaux.

HTML — See Hypertext Markup Language.

HTTP (Hypertext Transfer Protocol) — The protocol (rules) computers used to transfer hypertext documents.

Hypertext — Text that contains links to other documents, words, or phrases in the document that can be chosen by a reader and which cause another document to be retrieved and displayed.

Hypertext Markup Language — Hypertext markup language (often referred to as HTML) is the coding language used to create hypertext documents for use on the World Wide Web.

IDEA — IDEA, also known as the International Data Encryption Algorithm, is a conventional encryption algorithm in card readers.

Information Security — Information security refers to measures that a business can take to protect information itself while it is passing through an outside network or while it resides on a computer system beyond the business's control.

Integrity — Integrity refers to the business and legal requirement that a party be able to verify that a communication or record has not been changed while in transit or storage.

Integrity Check Value — See Hash Value.

International Data Encryption Algorithms — See IDEA.

Internet — The Internet is a worldwide network of networks, made up of more than seven-million computers interconnected through more than 60,000 networks, all sharing a common communications technology.

Intranets — Internal company computer networks built on Internet standards such as TCP/IP and HTML and connected through security firewalls to the global computer network.

IP (Internet Protocol) — The rules that provide basic Internet functions (see TCP/IP).

IP Number — An Internet address that is a unique number consisting of four parts separated by dots, sometimes called a "dotted quad". Every Internet computer has an IP number and most computers also have one or more domain names that are plain language substitutes for the dotted quad.

IRC (Internet Relay Chat) — A huge multi-user live chat facility. There are a number of major IRC servers around the world which are linked to each other. Anyone can create a channel and anything that anyone types in a given channel is seen by all others in the channel. Private channels are created for multi-person conference calls. An Internet tool with a limited use that lets users join a chat channel and exchange typed, text messages.

ISDN (Integrated Services Digital Network) — A set of communications standards that enables a single telephone line or optical cable to carry voice, digital network services, and video.

ISP (Internet Service Provider) — An institution that provides access to the Internet in some form, usually for money.

Java — A network-oriented programming language invented by Sun Microsystems that is specifically designed for writing programs that can be safely downloaded through the Internet and immediately run without fear of viruses or other harm.

JDK (Java Development Kit) — A software development package from Sun Microsystems that implements the basic set of tools needed to write, test, and debug Java applications and applets.

JPEG (Joint Photographic Experts Group) — The name of the committee that designed the photographic image compression standard. JPEG is optimised for compressing full colour or grayscale photographic.

kbps (kilobits per second) — A speed rating for computer modems that measures (in units of 1,024 bits) the maximum number of bits the device can transfer in one second under ideal conditions.

kBps (kilobytes per second) — One byte is equal to eight bits.

Key — A key is a secret value used in an encryption algorithm. A key may consist of letters and numbers, alphanumeric characters, printable characters, or ASCII characters. The key may be known by one or both of the communicating parties. It is analogous to a combination number for a safe.

Key Management — Key management is the process by which the keys are generated, distributed, used, stored, updated, and destroyed. Key management is a significant vulnerability of cryptography.

Key Pair — In public-key cryptography, a key pair is a private key and its corresponding public key, having the property that the public key can decrypt ciphertext that was encrypted using the private key and "vice versa".

Kilobyte — 1,024 bytes.

LAN (Local Area Network) — A computer network limited to the immediate area, usually the same building or floor of a building.

Leased Line — A leased phone line that provides a full line.

Listserv — An Internet application that automatically serves mailing lists by sending electronic newsletters to a stored database of Internet user addresses.

Manipulation Detection Code — See Hash Value.

Megabyte — 1 million bytes, or 1,000 kilobytes.

Message Digest — A message digest is a condensation or summary of a communication in the form of a fixed-length, unintelligible string of characters that results from applying a hash function to a variable-length communication. A message digest is unique to the communication on which it is based. Because the message digest is derived from the variable-length communication, a change in that communication will result in a change to the resulting message digest.

MIDI Files — Musical instrument digital interface files, or MIDI files, are computer files that contain instructions controlling how and when devices such as digital synthesisers produce sound. They can be stored in a digital form on computer-readable media such as disks and CD-ROMs and later recalled to play back the music work that is the subject of the MIDI recording.

MIME (Multipurpose Internet Mail Extensions) — A set of Internet functions that extends normal e-mail capabilities and enables computer files to be attached to e-mail. Files sent by MIME arrive at their destination as exact copies of the original so that you can send fully formatted word processing files, spreadsheets, graphics images, and software applications to other users via e-mail.

Mirror — To mirror is to maintain an exact copy of something. The most common use of the term on the Internet refers to mirror sites, which are web sites or FTP sites that maintain exact copies of material originated at another location, usually in order to provide more widespread access to the resource.

Modem — An electronic device that lets computers communicate electronically. The name is derived from "modulator/demodulator" because of their function in processing data over analogue telephone lines.

Morphine — Morphine (short for metamorphosis) is a process that involves a transition of two documents (such as pictures) into a third; a dynamic blending of two still images creating a sequence of in-between images that, when played back rapidly, metamorphose the first image into the last.

Mosaic — The first browser available for the Macintosh, Windows, and UNIX all with the same interface. Mosaic really started the popularity of the Web.

Netiquette — The etiquette on the Internet.

Netscape — A WWW Browser and the name of a company.

NIC (Networked Information Centre) — Generally, any office that handles information for a network. The most famous of these on the Internet is the InterNIC, which is where new domain names are registered.

NNTP (Network News Transport ProtocolY9Y) — The protocol used by client and server software to carry USENET postings back and forth over a TCP/IP network.

NODE — A single computer connected to a network.

One-way Function — See Hash Function.

Password — A code used to gain access to a locked system. Good passwords contain letters and non-letters.

Plaintext — Plaintext is the readable form of a communication.

PoP (Point of Presence) — A site that has an array of telecommunications equipment, *i.e.*, modems, digital, leased lines, and Internet routers. An Internet access provider may operate several regional PoPs to provide Internet connections within local phone service areas. An alternative is for access providers to employ virtual PoPs (virtual Points of Presence) in conjunction with a third-party provider.

POP (Post Office Protocol) — An Internet protocol that enables a single user to read e-mail from a mail server.

Posting — A single message entered into a network communications system.

Private Key — In public-key cryptography, a private key is the key of a key pair kept secret by its holder and used to create a digital signature.

Protocols — Computer rules that provide uniform specifications so that computer hardware and operating systems can communicate.

Public Key — In public-key cryptography, a public key is the key of a key pair publicly disclosed by the holder of the corresponding private key and used by the recipient of a digitally signed message from that person to verify the digital signature.

Public-Key Cryptography — Public-key cryptography is a form of cryptography in which two keys are used: one to encrypt a message and the other to decrypt the message. One key is kept secret, and the other is made available to recipients of encrypted communications.

Public-Private Key Pair — See Key Pair.

Repository — A repository is a system for storing and retrieving certificates or other information relevant to digital signatures.

Router — A network device that enables the network to reroute messages it receives that are intended for other networks. The network with the router receives the message and sends it on exactly as received.

RSA — RSA is a public-key encryption algorithm named after its inventors — Rivest, Shamir, and Adelman.

Sampling — Sampling is the conversion of analogue sound waves into a digital code. The digital code that describes the sampled music can then be reused, manipulated, or combined with other digitised or recorded sounds using a machine with digital data processing capabilities, such as a computerised synthesiser.

Scan — Scanning is the process by which an image (such as a photograph, drawing, or text) is digitised — that is, converted into a digital form. The resulting digital image is also called a scan second and can be used with almost any kind of computer.

SET (Secured Electronic Transaction) — Standard protocols providing for secure credit card transactions created by a consortium led by MasterCard and Visa and implemented in on-line transactions in 1997.

Shrink-wrap Licence — Technically, a shrink-wrap licence is a software licence agreement that appears on the outside of a software package, visible through the clear plastic shrink-wrap covering the package, that states that the user is deemed to accept the terms of the licence by opening the package or using the software.

Signature File — An ASCII text file, maintained within e-mail programs, that contains a few lines of text for the sender's signature.

SLIP (Serial Line Internet Protocol) — A standard for using a regular telephone line (a serial line) and a modem to connect a computer as a real Internet site. SLIP is gradually being replaced by PPP.

SLIP/PPP (Serial Line Internet Protocol/Point Point Protocol) — The basic rules that enable personal computers to connect, usually by dial-up modem, directly to other computers that provide Internet services.

Smart Card — A smart card is a plastic laminated card, similar in appearance to a credit card, that contains a computer chip. Smart cards can be used to generate and/or store passwords and encryption keys. Plastic card similar to a credit card with embedded electronics that store cash in encrypted form to be used with personal computers, telephones, ATMs, and other devices.

SMDS (Switched Multimegabit Data Service) — A new standard for very high speed data transfer.

SMTP (Simple Mail Transport Protocol) — The main protocol used to send electronic mail on the Internet.

SNMP (Simple Network Management Protocol) — A set of standards for communication with devices connected to a TCP/IP network.

Software — See Computer Program.

Spam — The term applies primarily to commercial messages posted across a large number of Internet newsgroups.

SSL (Secure Sockets Layer) — A protocol designed by Netscape Communications to enable encrypted, authenticated communications across the Internet. SSL is used mostly in communications between Web browsers and Web servers. URLs that begin with "https" indicate that an SSL connection will be used. SSL provides privacy, authentication, and message integrity.

Subscriber — A subscriber is a person who is identified in a certificate and who holds a private key that corresponds to a public key listed in the certificate.

Symmetric Cryptography — See Conventional Cryptography.

System Security — System security refers to the measures that a business can take to protect its computer systems and the records and other information they contain from attack from outside and inside.

T1 — An Internet backbone line that carries up to 1.536 million bits per second (1.536 Mbps).

T3 — An Internet line that carries up to 45 million bits per second (45 Mbps).

TA — See Terminal Adapter.

TCP/IP (Transmission Control Protocol/Internet Protocol) — The basic programming foundation that carries computer messages around the globe via the Internet.

Telnet — An Internet protocol that allows connection of a personal computer as a remote workstation to a host computer anywhere in the world and to use that computer as if logged on locally.

Terabyte — 1,000 gigabytes.

Terminal Adapter — An electronic device that interfaces a personal computer with an Internet host computer via an ISDN telephone line.

Time Stamp — See Date/Time Stamp.

Transaction Set — Each set of formatted data exchanged via electronic data interchange, such as requests for quotation, purchase orders, and invoices, is referred to as a transaction set.

Transborder Data Flow — Transborder data flow refers to the electronic communication of data across national borders.

Trusted Third Party — A trusted third party is a disinterested person who has no vested interest and no allegiance to either of the primary parties involved in a communication and who is trusted by both of the primary parties to perform some act honestly and correctly.

UNIX — The computer operating system that was used to write most of the programs and protocols that built the Internet.

URL (*Uniform Resource Locator*) — The standard way to give the address of any resource on the Internet that is part of the World Wide Web (WWW).

Usenet — Another name for Internet newsgroups.

UUENCODE (*Unix to Unix Encoding*) — A method for converting files from binary to ASCII (text) so that they can be sent across the Internet via e-mail.

Value-Added Network — A value-added network, or VAN, is an intermediary computer network that provides a variety of services to its customers, including translation services for EDI documents in incompatible formats, a secure network over which information can be sent, and record-keeping and audit functions.

VAN — See Value-Added Network.

Verify Digital Signature — To verify a digital signature, with respect to a given digital signature, message, and public key, means to determine accurately that the digital signature was created by the private key corresponding to the public key, and the message has not been altered since its digital signature was created.

Virtual Wallet — Software stored on a consumer's computer hard drive that contains encrypted payment and billing information used to order goods on-line.

WAIS (Wide Area Information Servers) — A distributed information retrieval system that is sponsored by Apple Computer, Thinking Machines, and Dow Jones, Inc. Users can locate documents using keyword searches that return a list of documents, ranked according to the frequency of occurrence of the search criteria.

WinVN — The most widely used stand-alone Windows-based Internet Usenet newsgroup reader application.

World Wide Web — The World Wide Web is the name for a collection of information resources (commercial and non-commercial) available on the Internet using a protocol known as "http". These resources (or Web sites) contain text, graphic, audio, and video files organised using a set of instructions called hypertext markup language (HTML). An Internet client server-distributed information and retrieval system based on the hypertext transfer protocol that transfers hypertext documents across a varied array of computer systems.

INDEX